THE POORCRAFT COOKBOOK

WRITTEN & DRAWN BY
NERO VILLAGALLOS O'REILLY

CHARACTERS CREATED BY
C. SPIKE TROTMAN

IRON CIRCUS COMICS

strange and amazing

inquiry@ironcircus.com   www.ironcircus.com

Writer & Artist: Nero Villagallos O'Reilly
Poorcraft Characters Created by C. Spike Trotman

Publisher: C. Spike Trotman
Editor: Andrea Purcell
Art Director: Matt Sheridan
Print Technician & Book Design: Beth Scorzato
Proofreader: Abby Lerkhe

Published by
Iron Circus Comics
329 West 18th Street, Suite 604
Chicago, IL 60616
ironcircus.com

First Edition: March 2022

ISBN: 978-1-945820-93-9

10 9 8 7 6 5 4 3 2 1

Printed in United States

The Poorcraft Cookbook

Publisher's Cataloging-In-Publication Data
(Prepared by The Donohue Group, Inc.)

Names: O'Reilly, Nero Villagallos, author, illustrator. | Spike, 1978- author.
Title: The poorcraft cookbook / written & drawn by Nero Villagallos O'Reilly ; characters created by C. Spike Trotman.
Description: First edition. | Chicago, IL : Iron Circus Comics, 2022. | Series: Poorcraft ; [3]
Identifiers: ISBN 9781945820939 (trade paperback)
Subjects: LCSH: Low budget cooking--Comic books, strips, etc. | Vegetarian cooking--Comic books, strips, etc. | Grocery shopping--Comic books, strips, etc. | LCGFT: Graphic novels. | Cookbooks. | Didactic fiction.
Classification: LCC PN6727.O732 P66 2022 TX652 | DDC 741.5973 641.552--dc23

TABLE OF CONTENTS

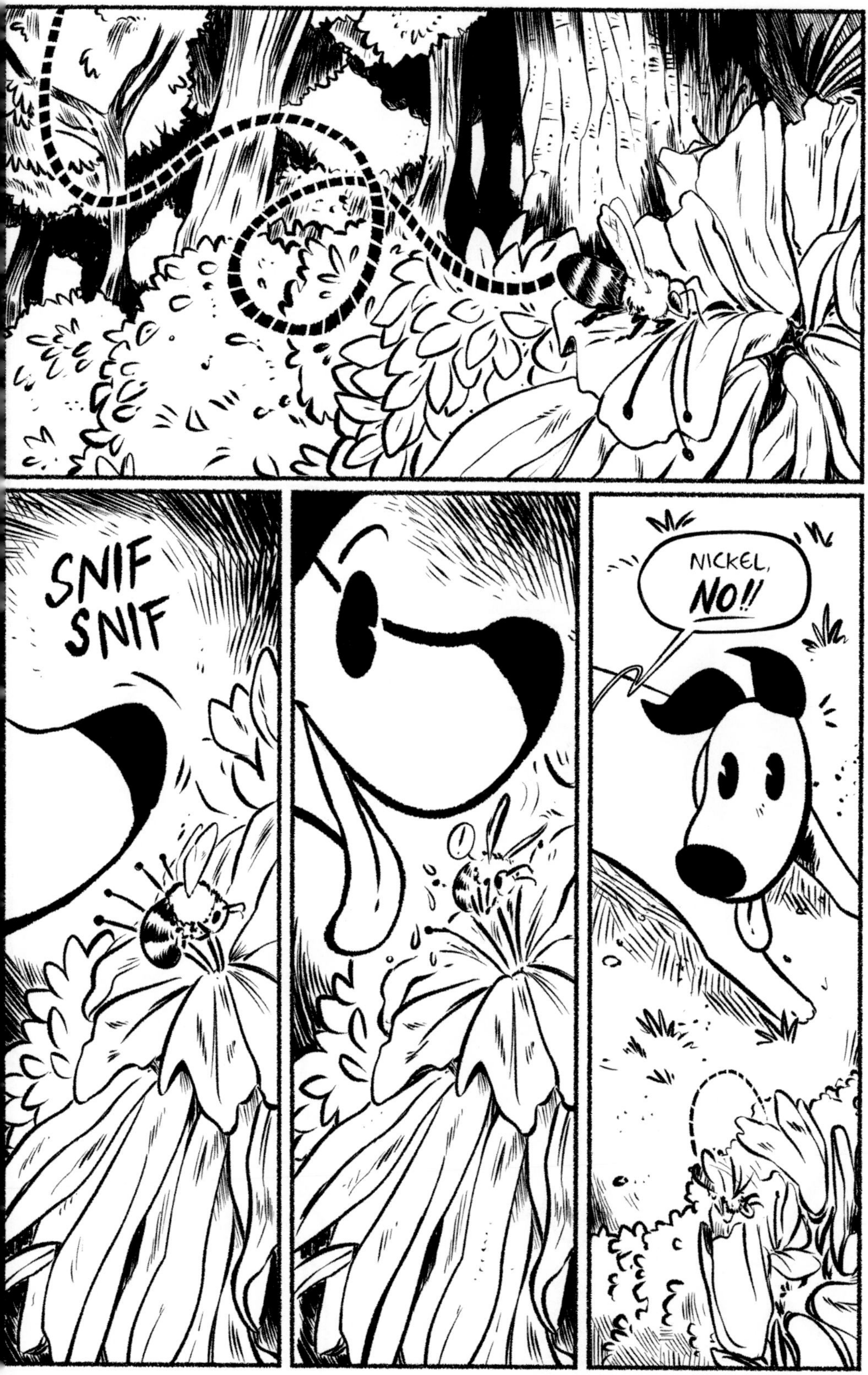
SNIF
SNIF
NICKEL,
NO!!

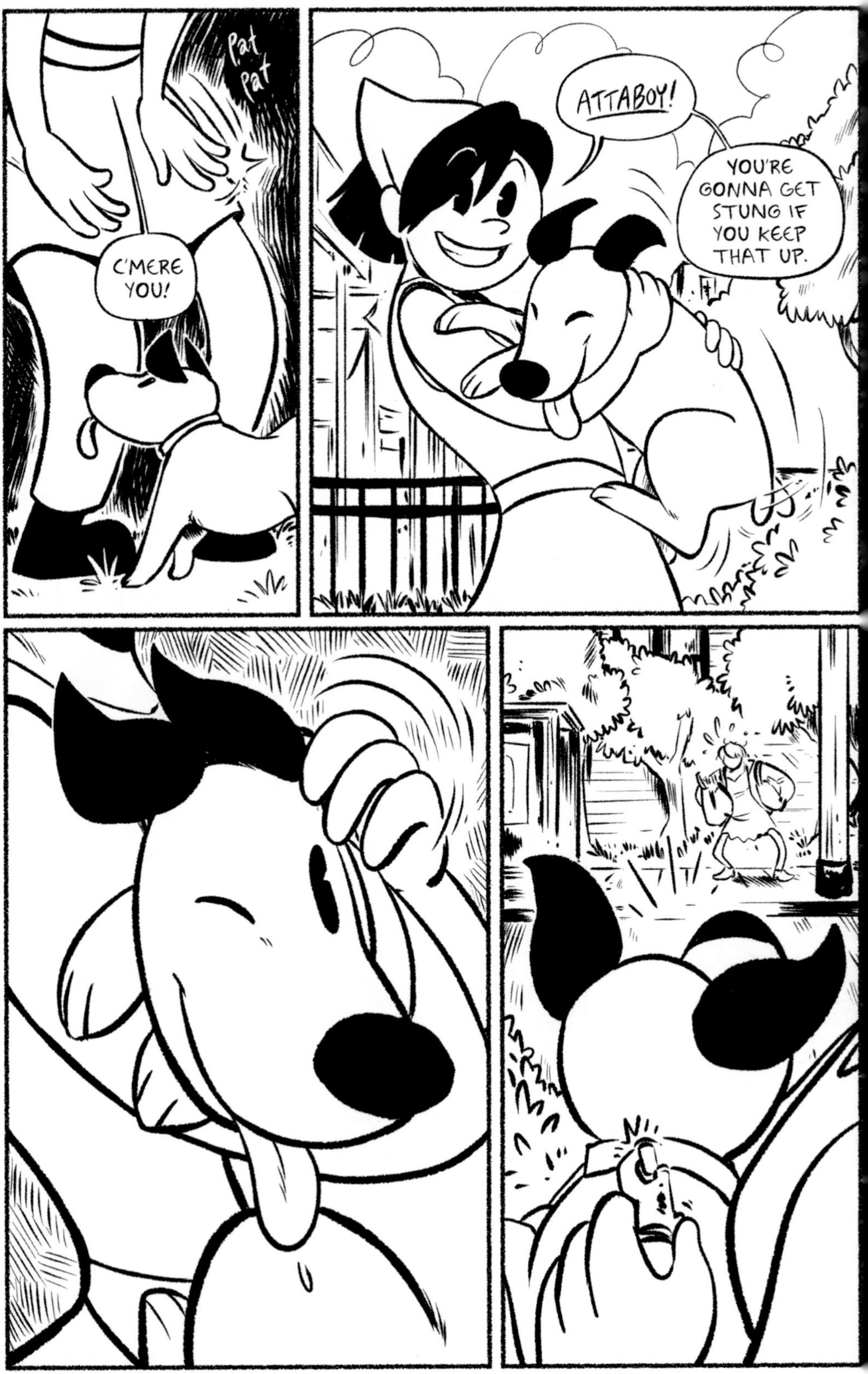
pat pat
C'MERE YOU!
ATTABOY!
YOU'RE GONNA GET STUNG IF YOU KEEP THAT UP.

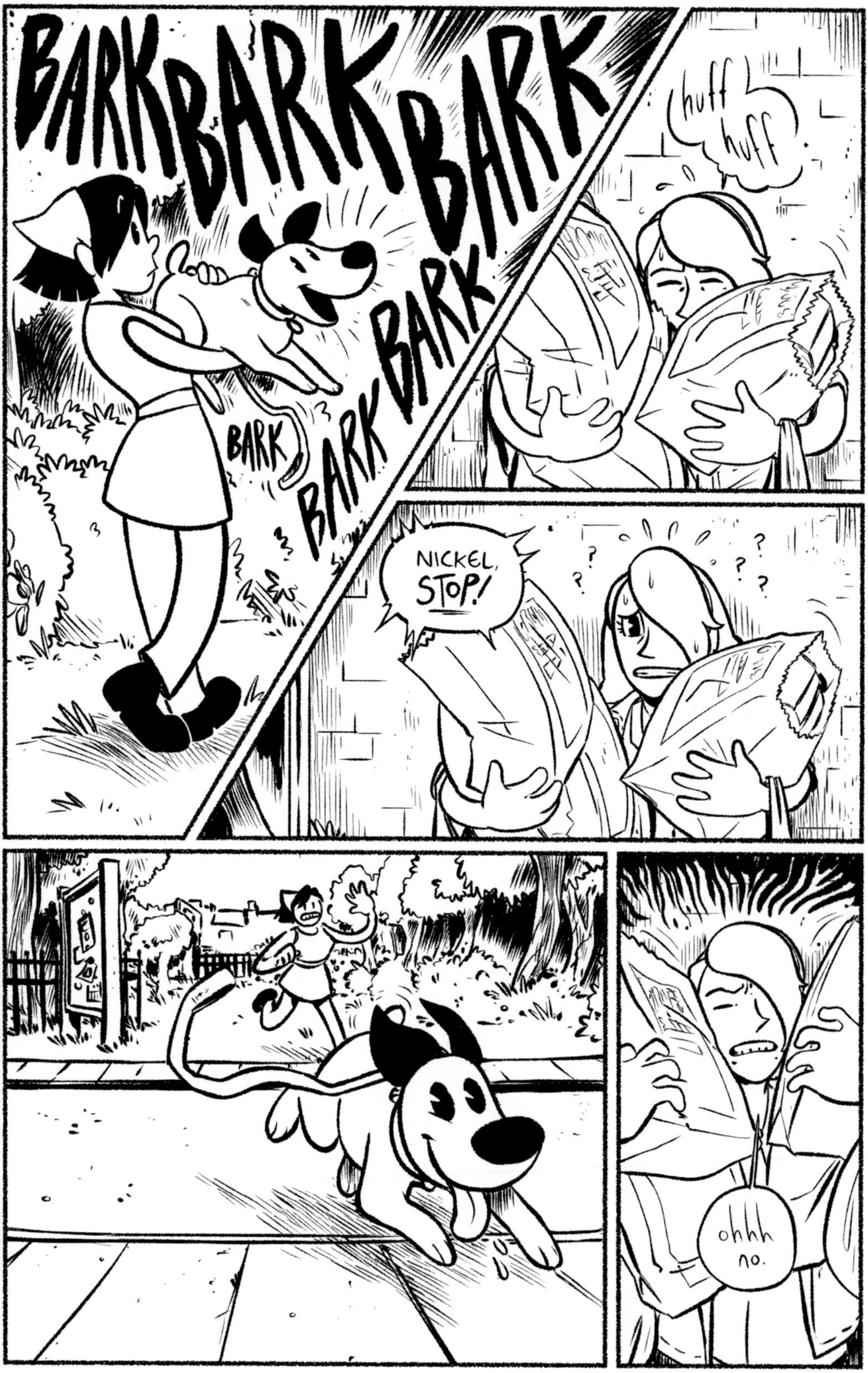
BARK BARK BARK
BARK
BARK
BARK
BARK
huff huff
NICKEL, STOP!
ohhh no.

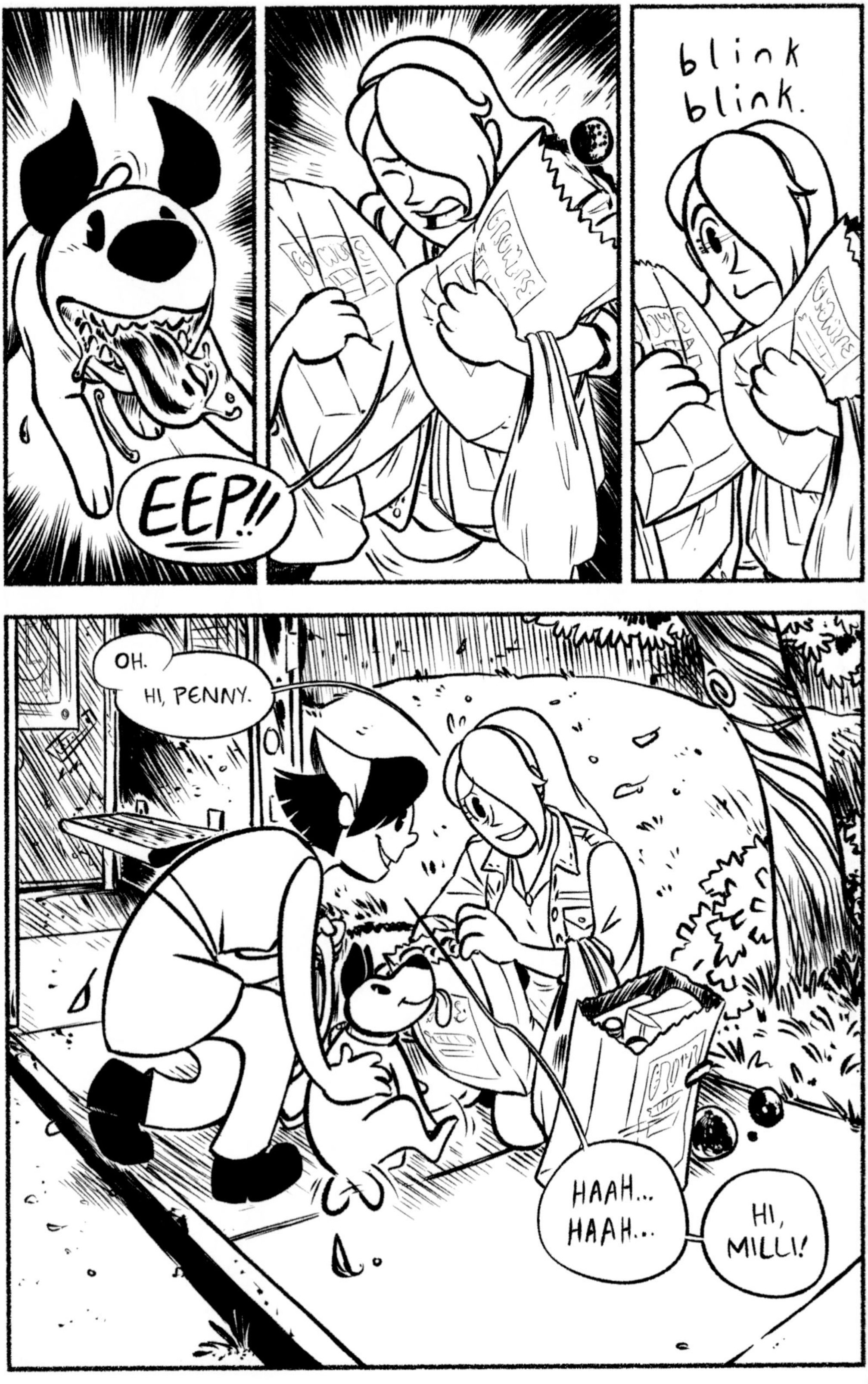
EEP!!
blink
blink.
OH.
HI, PENNY.
HAAH...
HAAH...
HI,
MILLI!

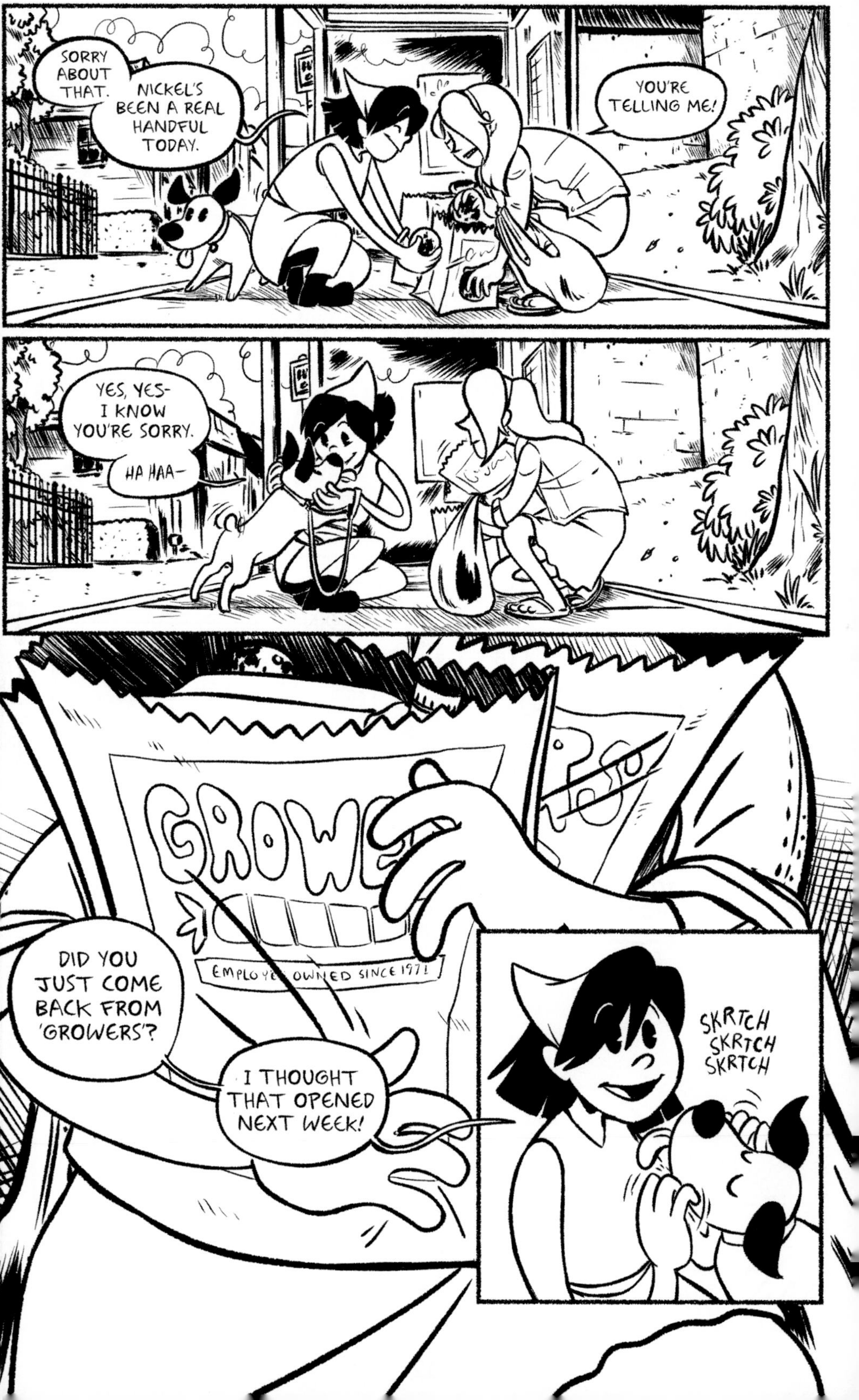

SORRY ABOUT THAT.
NICKEL'S BEEN A REAL HANDFUL TODAY.
YOU'RE TELLING ME!
YES, YES- I KNOW YOU'RE SORRY.
HA HAA-
GROWE
EMPLOYEE OWNED SINCE 1971
DID YOU JUST COME BACK FROM 'GROWERS'?
I THOUGHT THAT OPENED NEXT WEEK!
SKRTCH SKRTCH SKRTCH

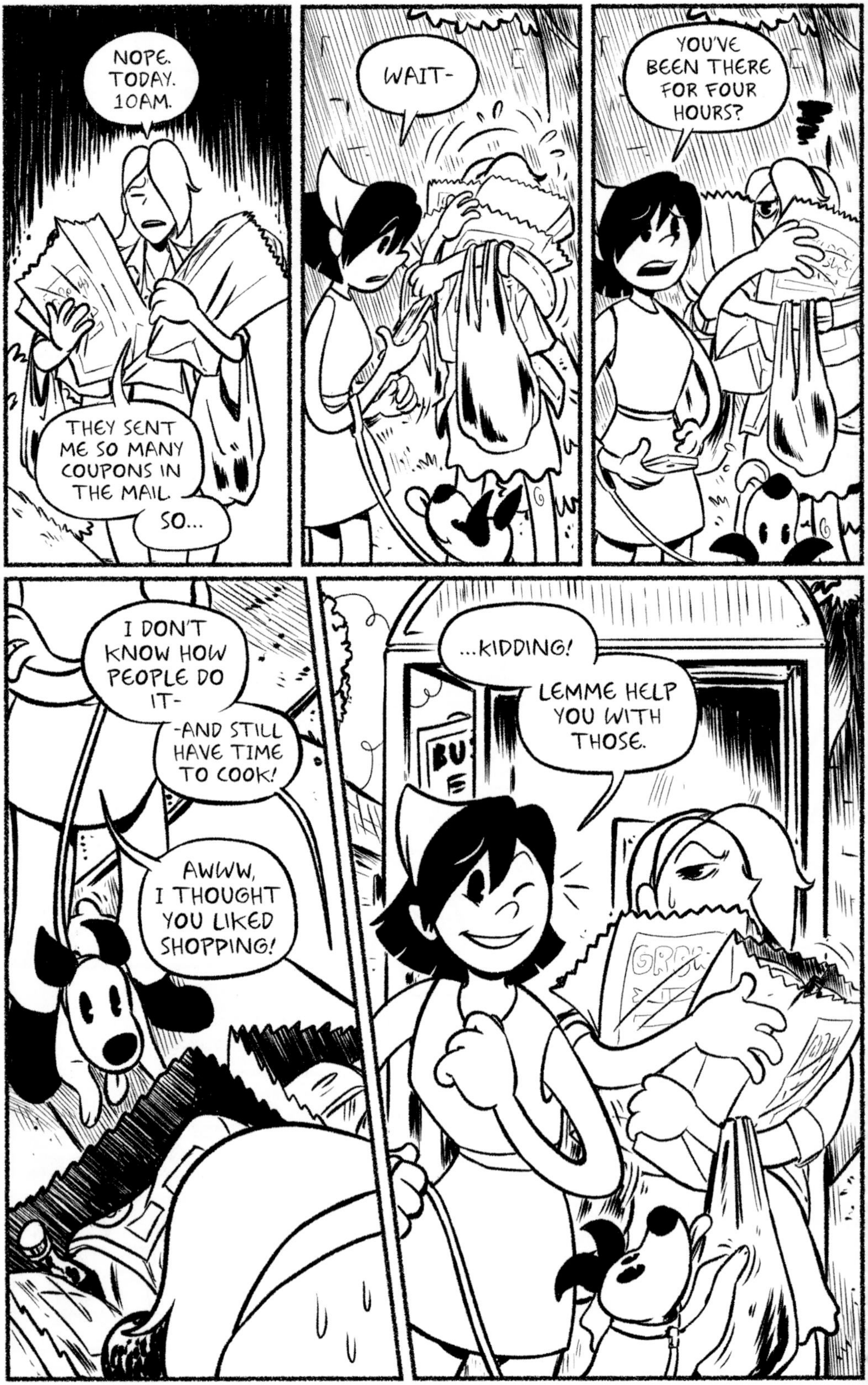
NOPE. TODAY. 10AM.
THEY SENT ME SO MANY COUPONS IN THE MAIL.
SO...
WAIT-
YOU'VE BEEN THERE FOR FOUR HOURS?
I DON'T KNOW HOW PEOPLE DO IT-
-AND STILL HAVE TIME TO COOK!
AWWW, I THOUGHT YOU LIKED SHOPPING!
...KIDDING!
LEMME HELP YOU WITH THOSE.

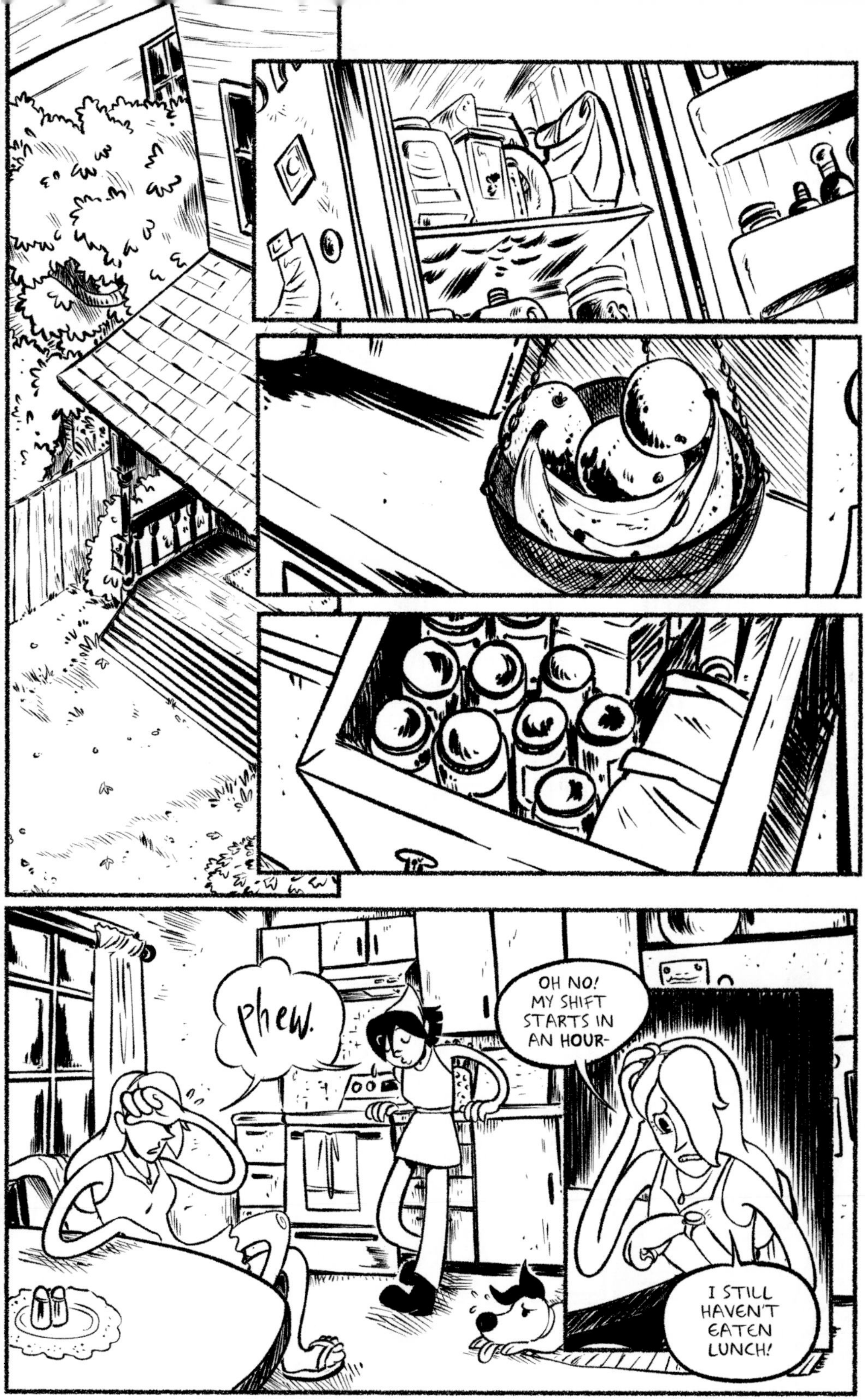
phew.
OH NO! MY SHIFT STARTS IN AN HOUR-
I STILL HAVEN'T EATEN LUNCH!

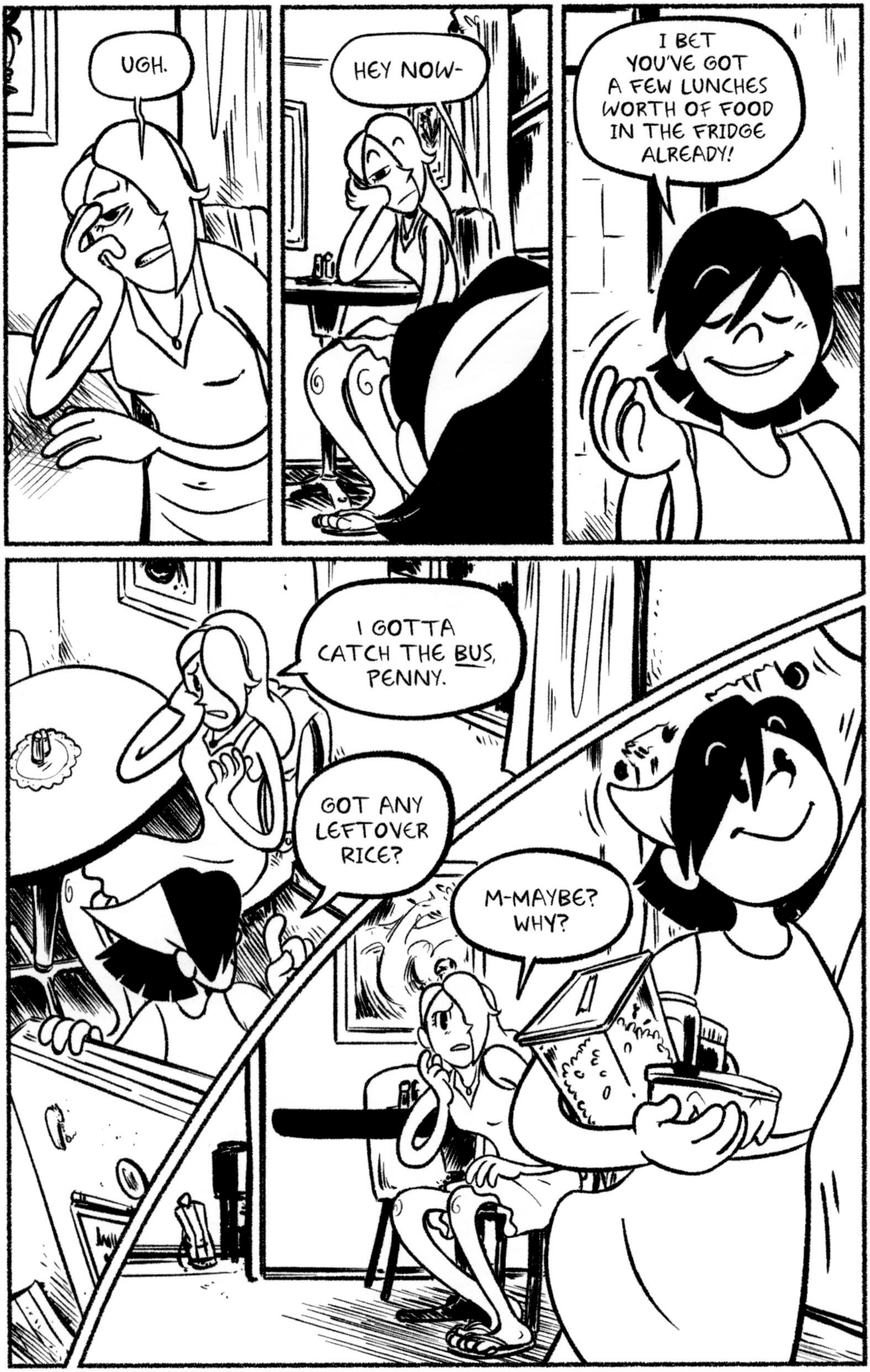
UGH.
HEY NOW-
I BET YOU'VE GOT A FEW LUNCHES WORTH OF FOOD IN THE FRIDGE ALREADY!
I GOTTA CATCH THE BUS, PENNY.
GOT ANY LEFTOVER RICE?
M-MAYBE? WHY?

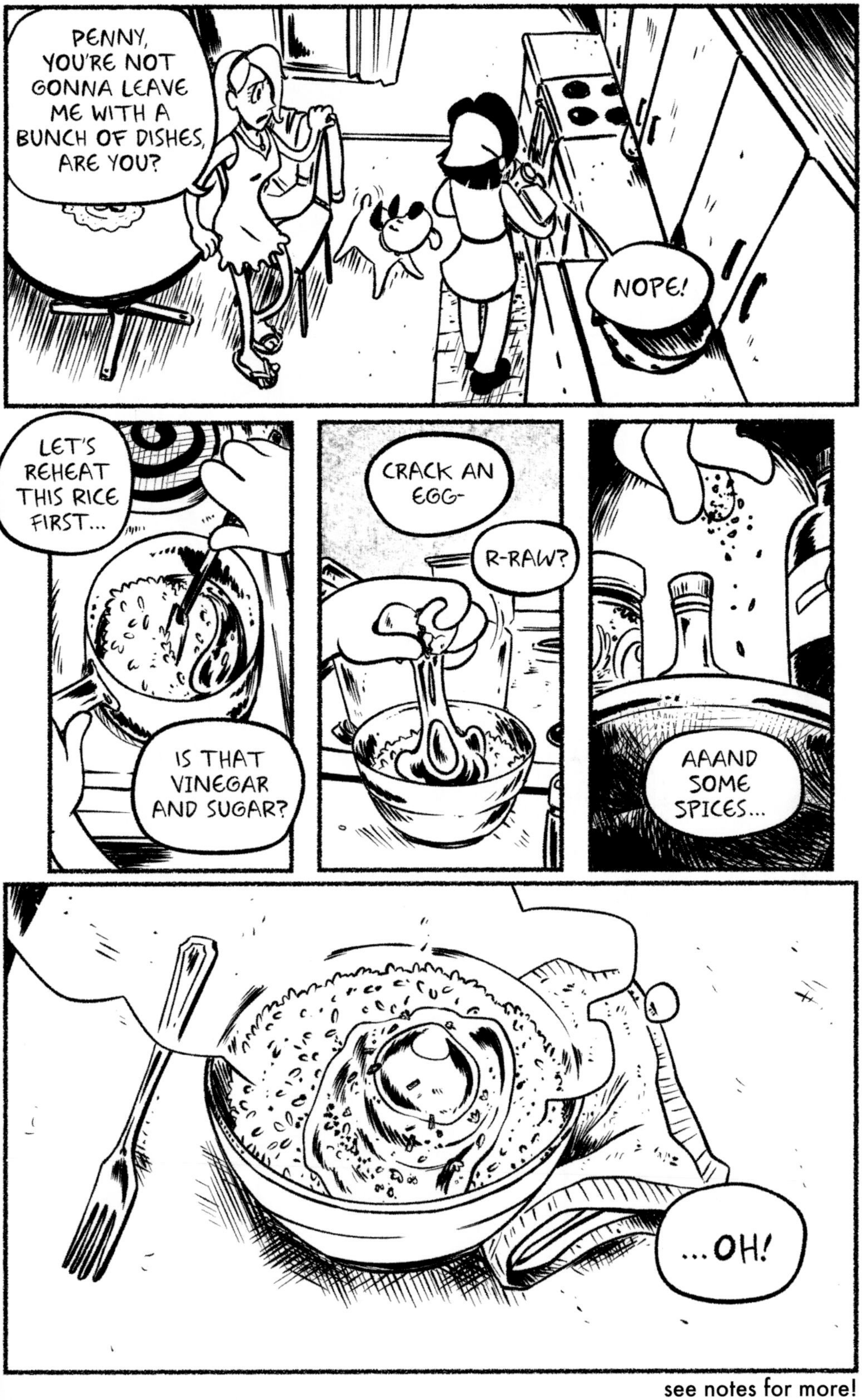
PENNY, YOU'RE NOT GONNA LEAVE ME WITH A BUNCH OF DISHES, ARE YOU?
NOPE!
LET'S REHEAT THIS RICE FIRST...
IS THAT VINEGAR AND SUGAR?
CRACK AN EGG-
R-RAW?
AAAND SOME SPICES...
...OH!

see notes for more!

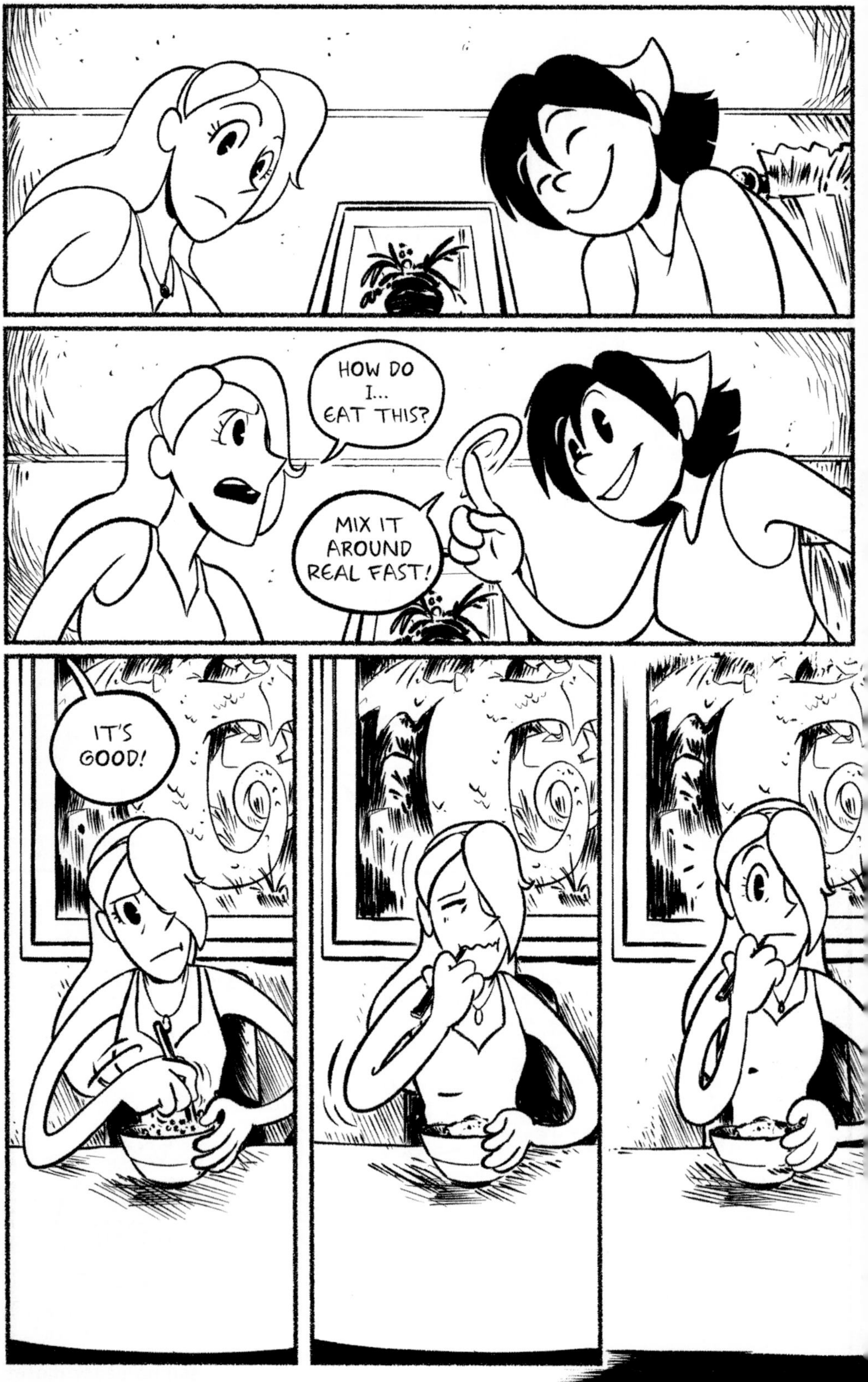
HOW DO I... EAT THIS?
MIX IT AROUND REAL FAST!
IT'S GOOD!

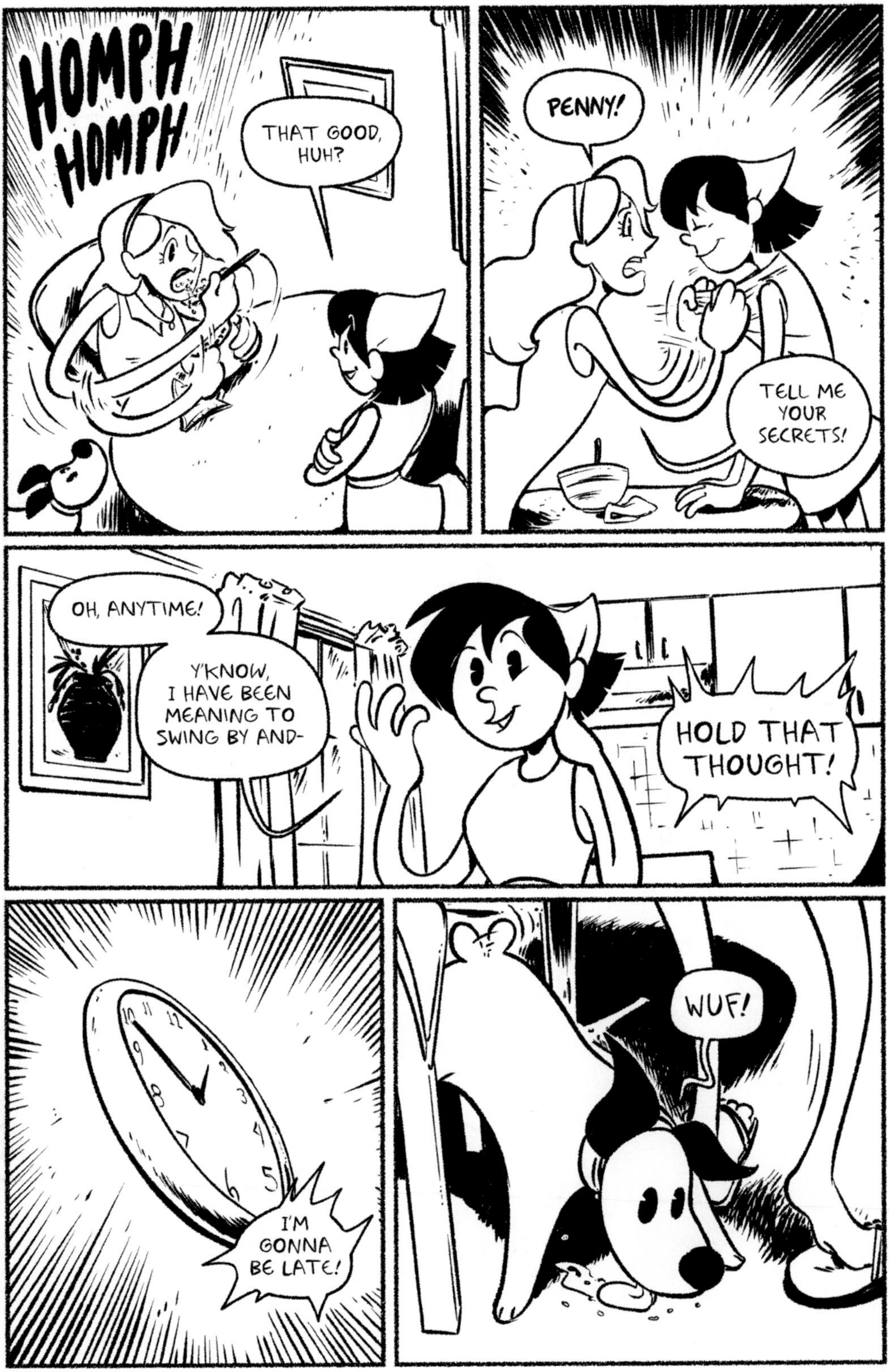
HOMPH HOMPH
THAT GOOD, HUH?
PENNY!
TELL ME YOUR SECRETS!
OH, ANYTIME!
Y'KNOW, I HAVE BEEN MEANING TO SWING BY AND-
HOLD THAT THOUGHT!
I'M GONNA BE LATE!
WUF!

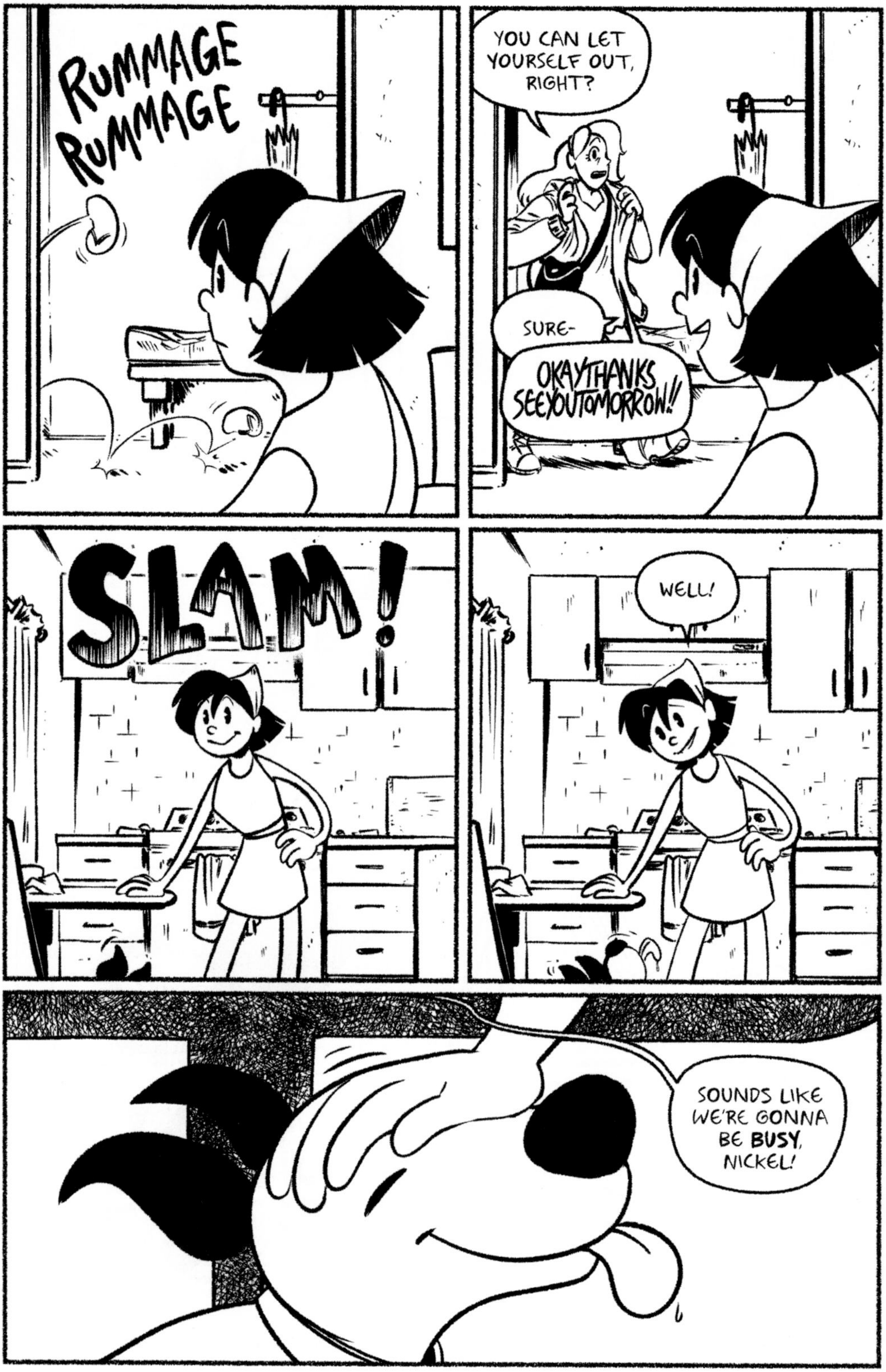
RUMMAGE RUMMAGE
YOU CAN LET YOURSELF OUT, RIGHT?
SURE-
OKAYTHANKS SEEYOUTOMORROW!!
SLAM!
WELL!
SOUNDS LIKE WE'RE GONNA BE **BUSY**, NICKEL!

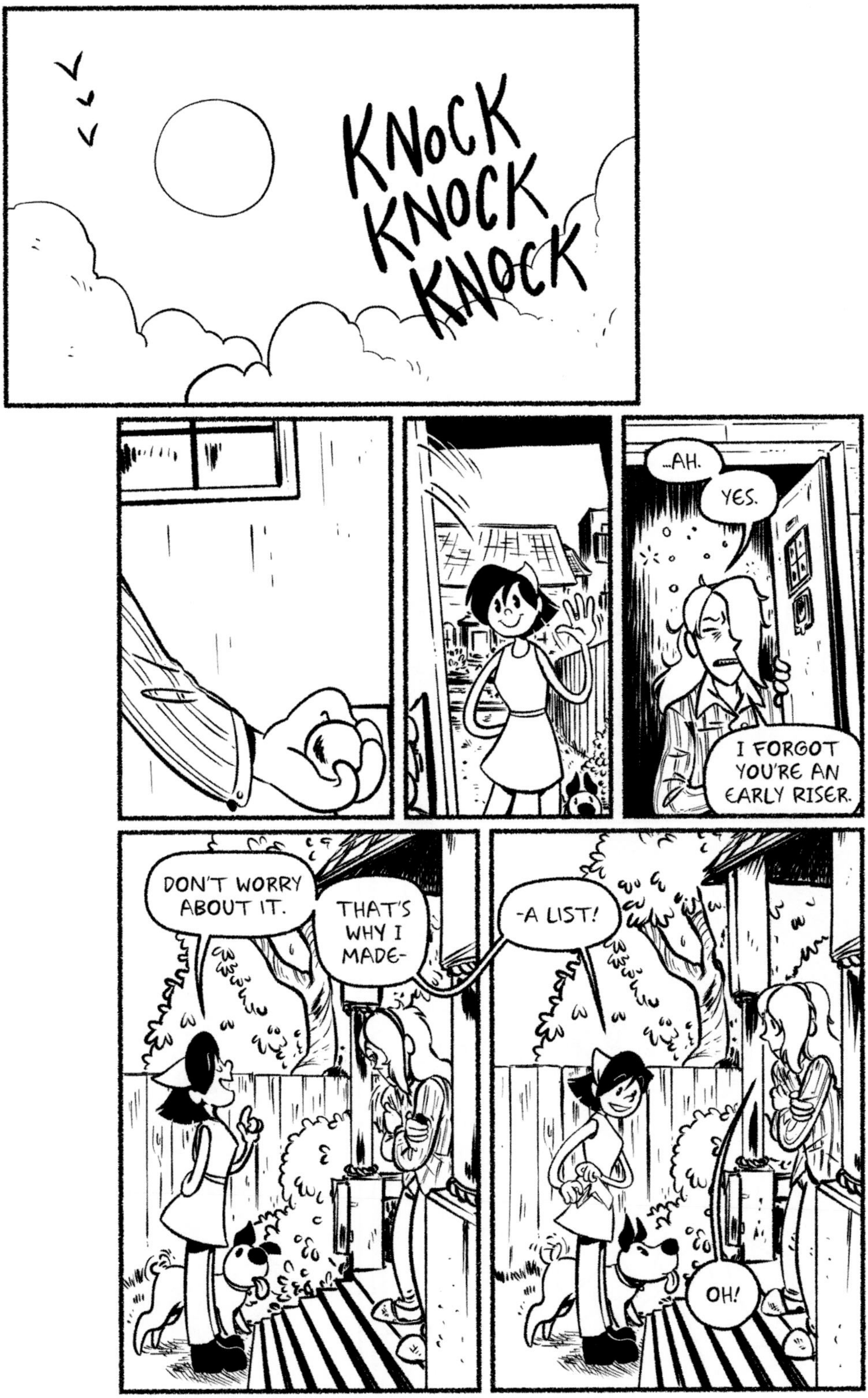
KNOCK KNOCK KNOCK
...AH.
YES.
I FORGOT YOU'RE AN EARLY RISER.
DON'T WORRY ABOUT IT.
THAT'S WHY I MADE-
-A LIST!
OH!

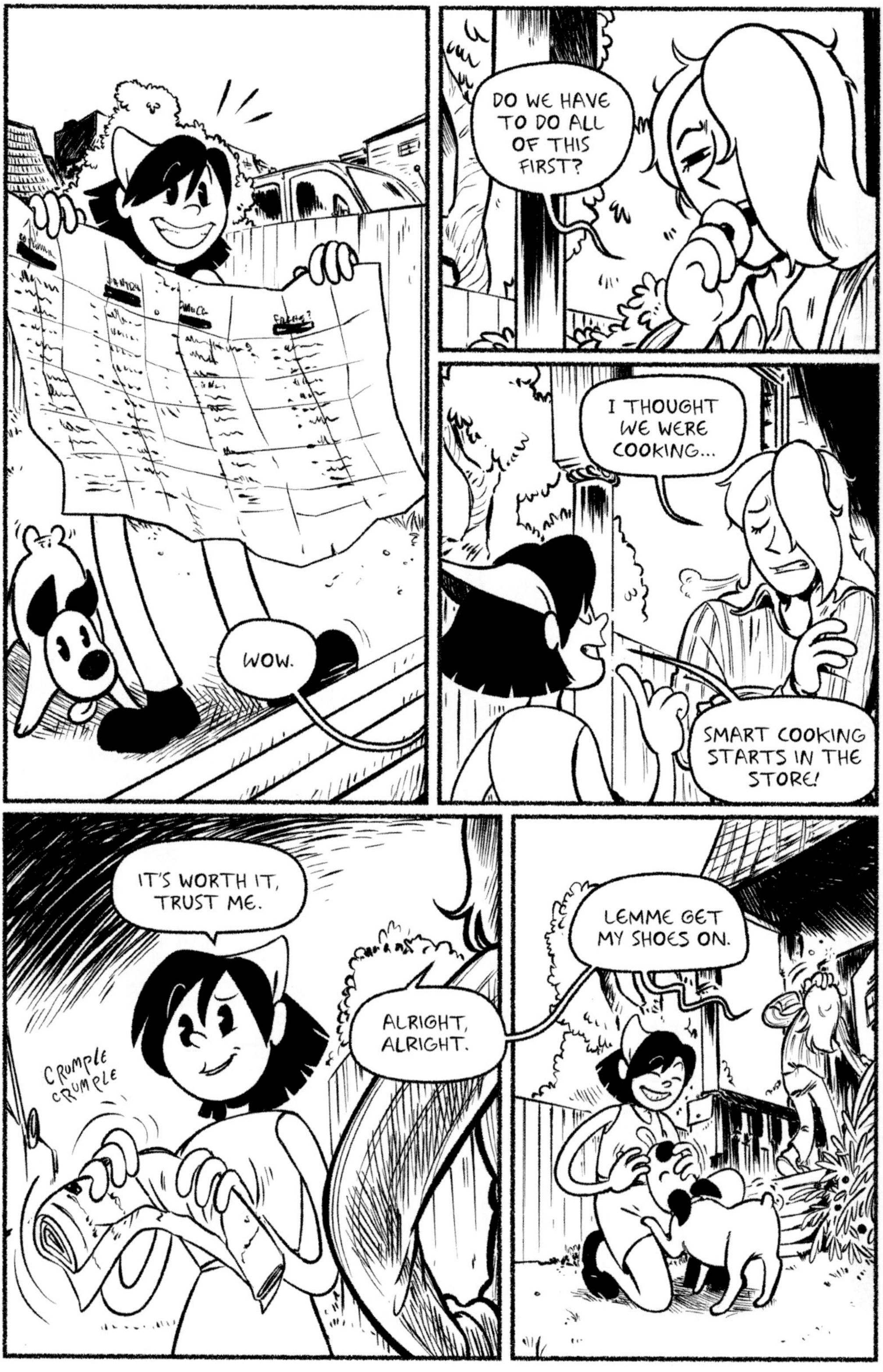
WOW.
DO WE HAVE TO DO ALL OF THIS FIRST?
I THOUGHT WE WERE COOKING...
SMART COOKING STARTS IN THE STORE!
IT'S WORTH IT, TRUST ME.
CRUMPLE CRUMPLE
ALRIGHT, ALRIGHT.
LEMME GET MY SHOES ON.

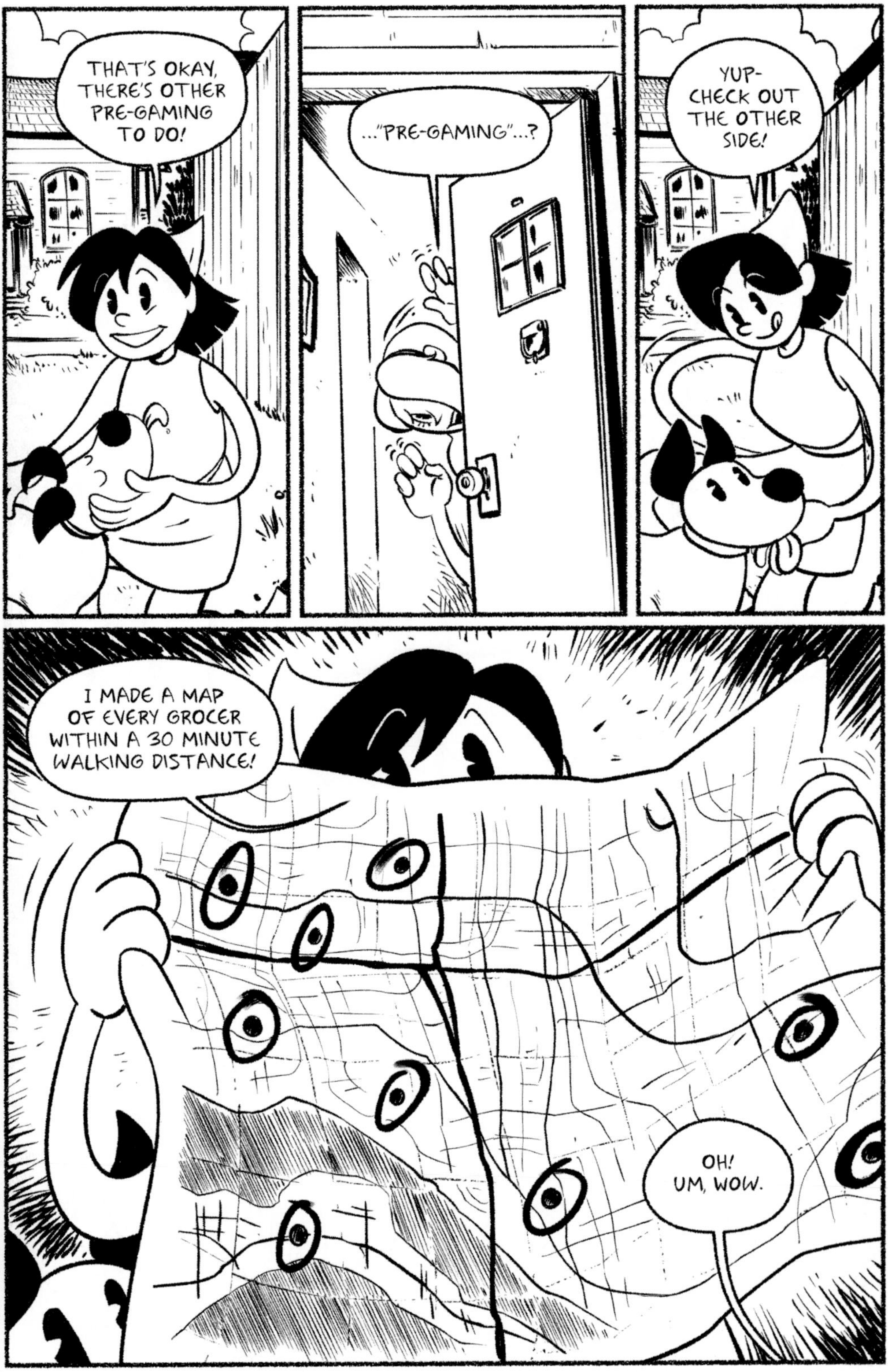
THAT'S OKAY, THERE'S OTHER PRE-GAMING TO DO!
..."PRE-GAMING"...?
YUP- CHECK OUT THE OTHER SIDE!
I MADE A MAP OF EVERY GROCER WITHIN A 30 MINUTE WALKING DISTANCE!
OH! UM, WOW.

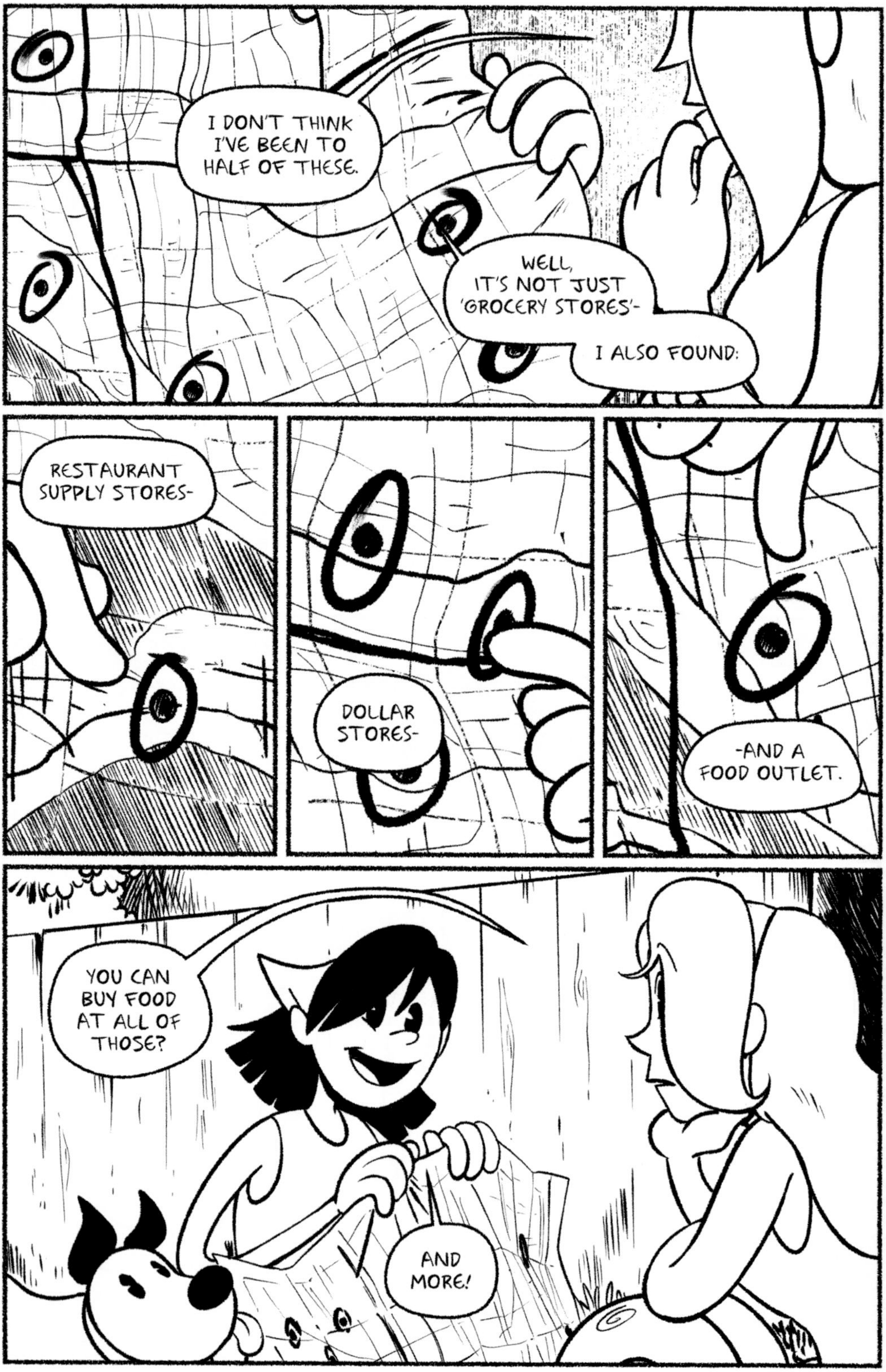
I DON'T THINK I'VE BEEN TO HALF OF THESE.
WELL, IT'S NOT JUST 'GROCERY STORES'-
I ALSO FOUND:
RESTAURANT SUPPLY STORES-
DOLLAR STORES-
-AND A FOOD OUTLET.
YOU CAN BUY FOOD AT ALL OF THOSE?
AND MORE!

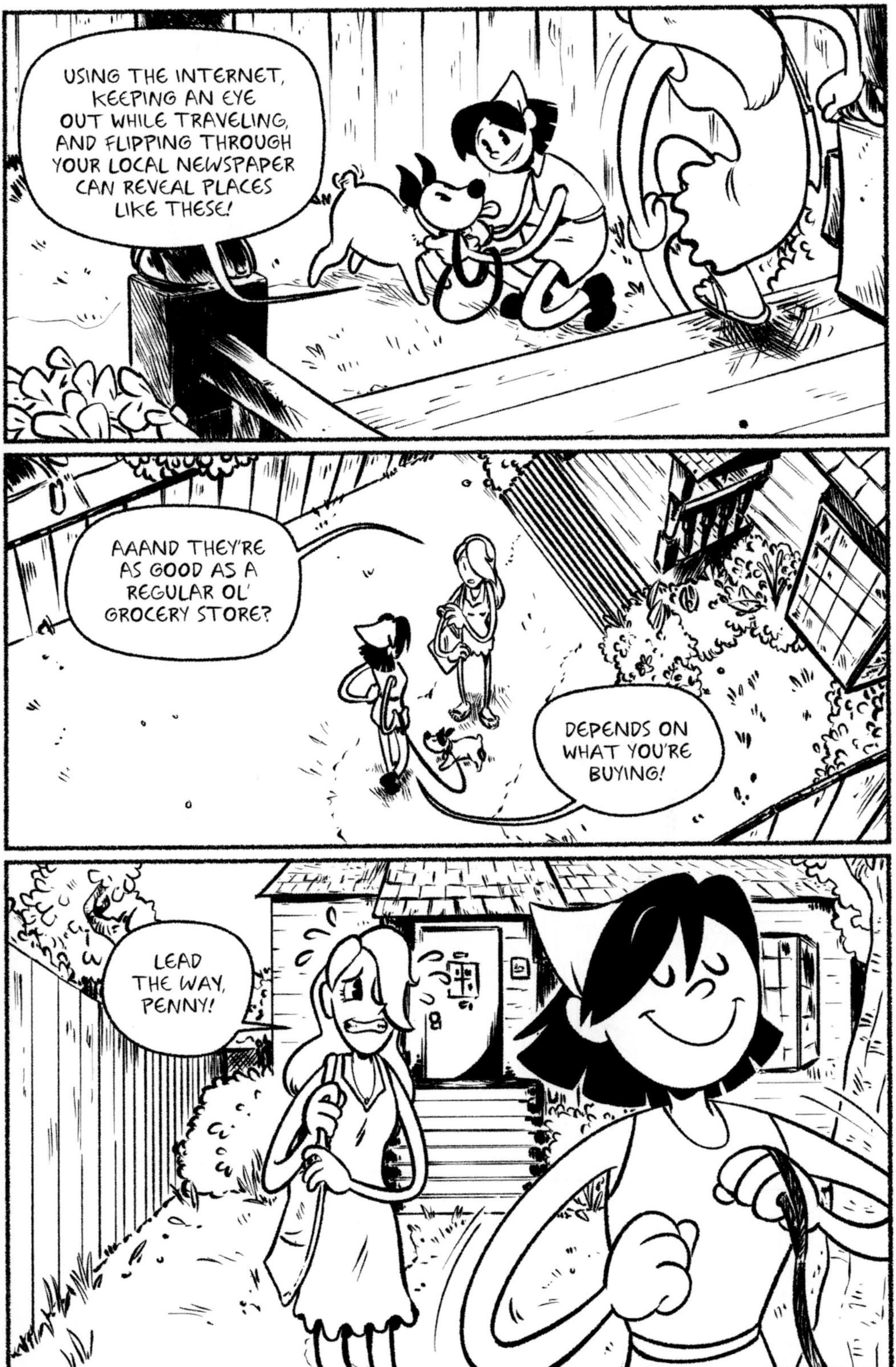
USING THE INTERNET, KEEPING AN EYE OUT WHILE TRAVELING, AND FLIPPING THROUGH YOUR LOCAL NEWSPAPER CAN REVEAL PLACES LIKE THESE!
AAAND THEY'RE AS GOOD AS A REGULAR OL' GROCERY STORE?
DEPENDS ON WHAT YOU'RE BUYING!
LEAD THE WAY, PENNY!

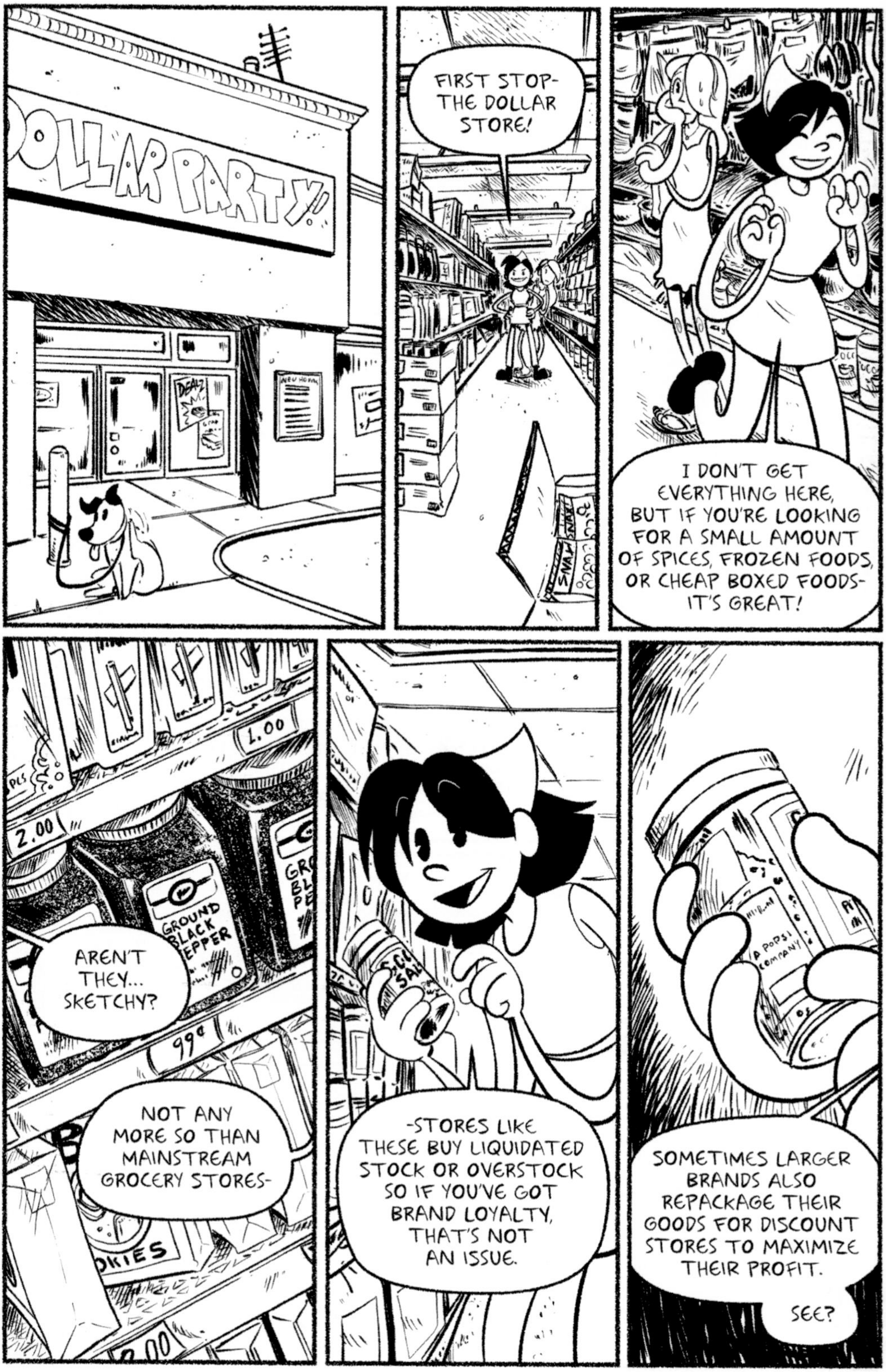
DOLLAR PARTY!
FIRST STOP- THE DOLLAR STORE!
I DON'T GET EVERYTHING HERE, BUT IF YOU'RE LOOKING FOR A SMALL AMOUNT OF SPICES, FROZEN FOODS, OR CHEAP BOXED FOODS- IT'S GREAT!
1.00
2.00
GROUND BLACK PEPPER
AREN'T THEY... SKETCHY?
99¢
NOT ANY MORE SO THAN MAINSTREAM GROCERY STORES-
-STORES LIKE THESE BUY LIQUIDATED STOCK OR OVERSTOCK SO IF YOU'VE GOT BRAND LOYALTY, THAT'S NOT AN ISSUE.
A POPSI COMPANY
SOMETIMES LARGER BRANDS ALSO REPACKAGE THEIR GOODS FOR DISCOUNT STORES TO MAXIMIZE THEIR PROFIT.
SEE?

see notes for more!

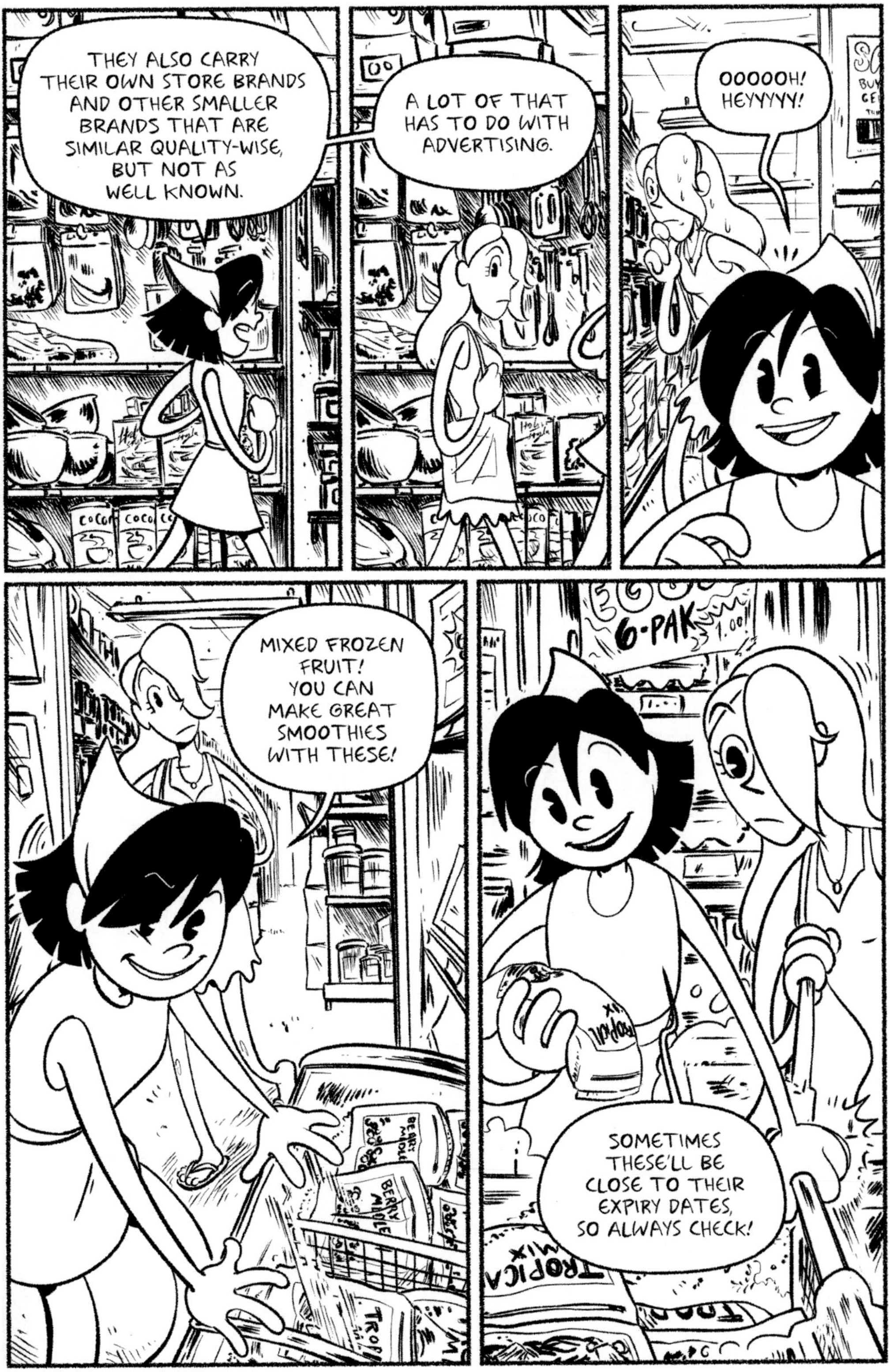
THEY ALSO CARRY THEIR OWN STORE BRANDS AND OTHER SMALLER BRANDS THAT ARE SIMILAR QUALITY-WISE, BUT NOT AS WELL KNOWN.
A LOT OF THAT HAS TO DO WITH ADVERTISING.
OOOOOH! HEYYYYY!
MIXED FROZEN FRUIT! YOU CAN MAKE GREAT SMOOTHIES WITH THESE!
6-PAK 1.00!
SOMETIMES THESE'LL BE CLOSE TO THEIR EXPIRY DATES, SO ALWAYS CHECK!
TROPICAL MIX

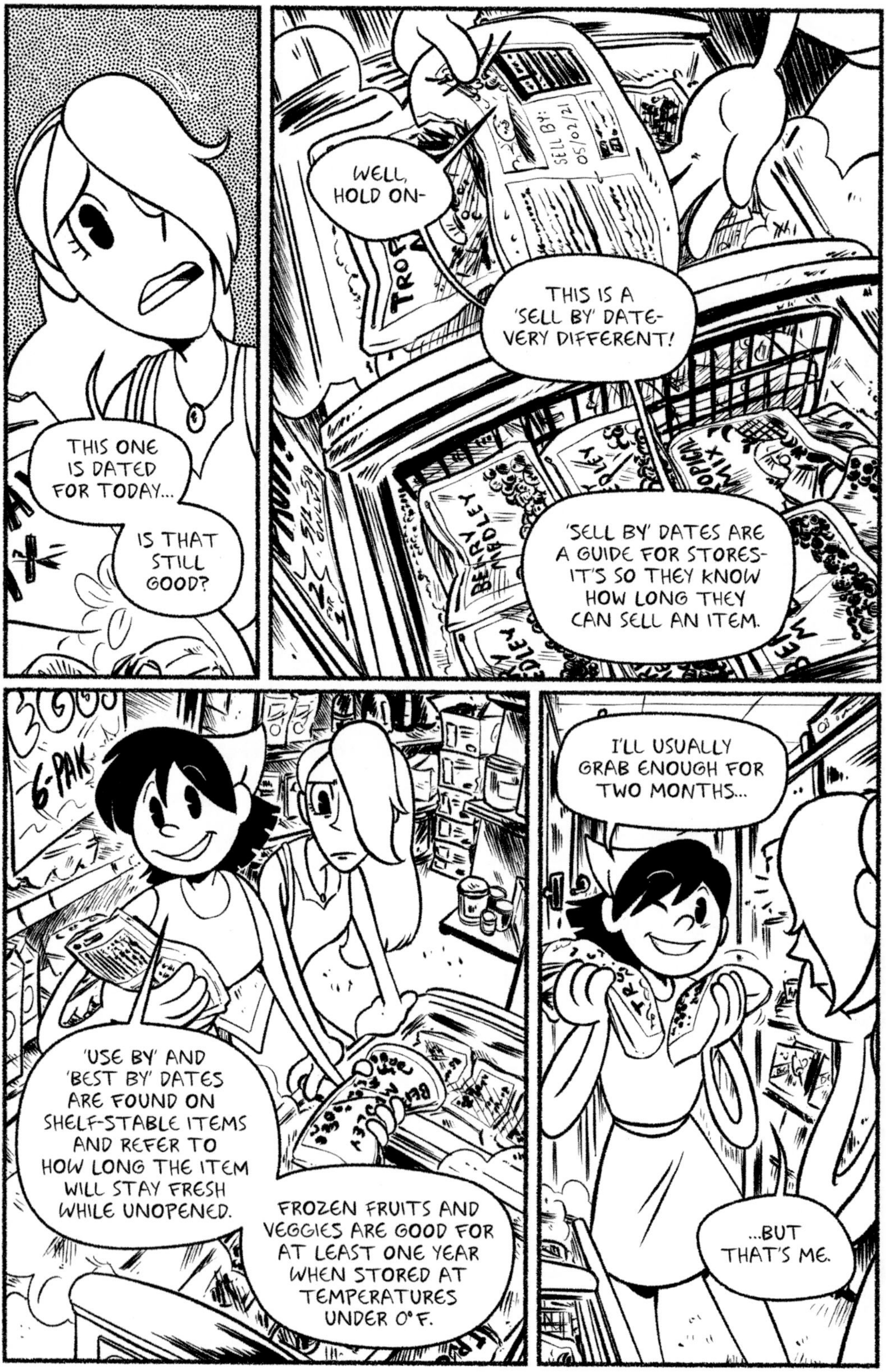
THIS ONE IS DATED FOR TODAY...
IS THAT STILL GOOD?
WELL, HOLD ON-
SELL BY: 05/02/21
THIS IS A 'SELL BY' DATE- VERY DIFFERENT!
BERRY MEDLEY
'SELL BY' DATES ARE A GUIDE FOR STORES- IT'S SO THEY KNOW HOW LONG THEY CAN SELL AN ITEM.
6-PAK
'USE BY' AND 'BEST BY' DATES ARE FOUND ON SHELF-STABLE ITEMS AND REFER TO HOW LONG THE ITEM WILL STAY FRESH WHILE UNOPENED.
FROZEN FRUITS AND VEGGIES ARE GOOD FOR AT LEAST ONE YEAR WHEN STORED AT TEMPERATURES UNDER 0°F.
I'LL USUALLY GRAB ENOUGH FOR TWO MONTHS...
...BUT THAT'S ME.

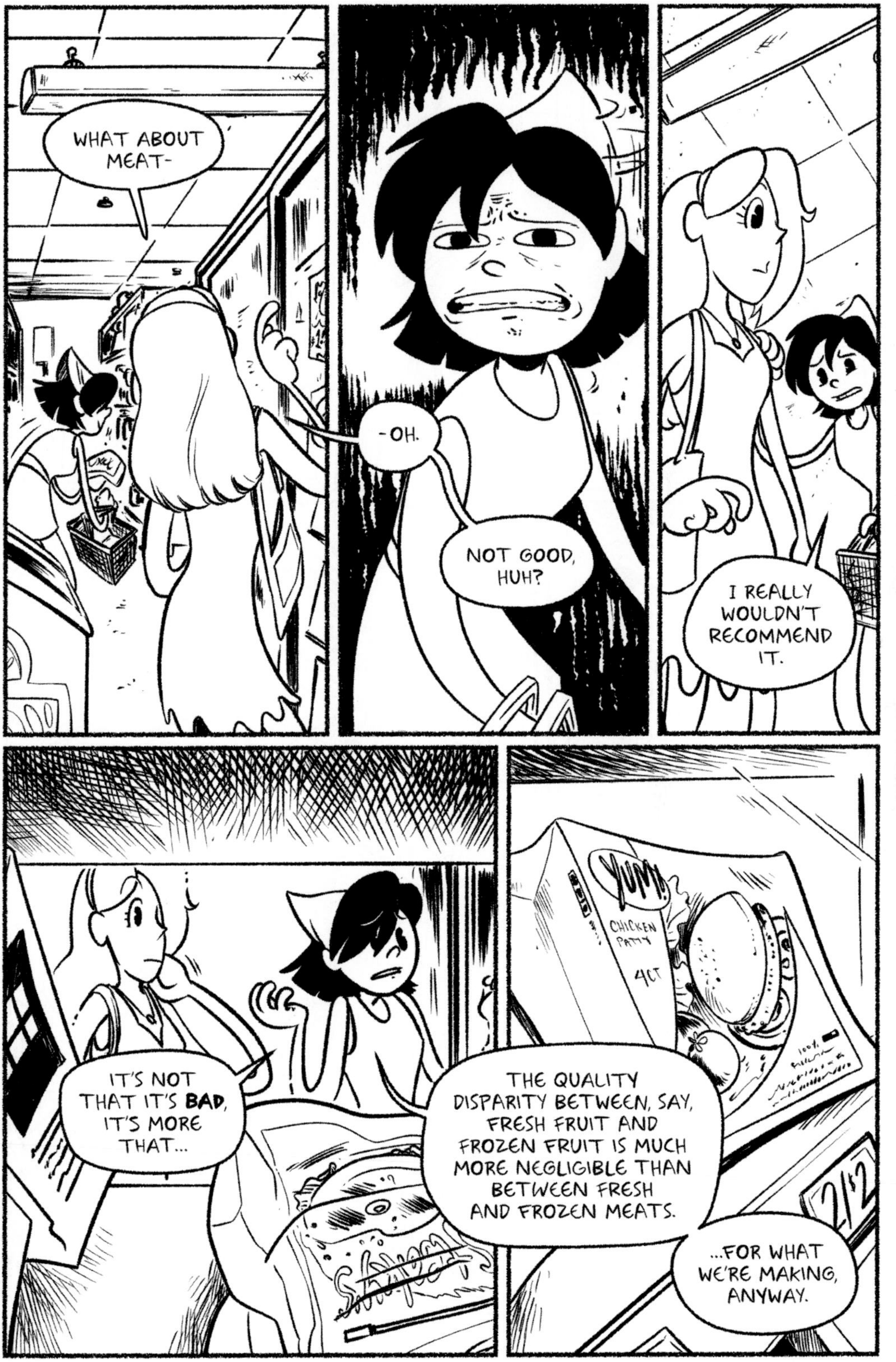
WHAT ABOUT MEAT-
-OH.
NOT GOOD, HUH?
I REALLY WOULDN'T RECOMMEND IT.
IT'S NOT THAT IT'S **BAD**, IT'S MORE THAT...
THE QUALITY DISPARITY BETWEEN, SAY, FRESH FRUIT AND FROZEN FRUIT IS MUCH MORE NEGLIGIBLE THAN BETWEEN FRESH AND FROZEN MEATS.
CHICKEN PATTY
4CT
...FOR WHAT WE'RE MAKING, ANYWAY.

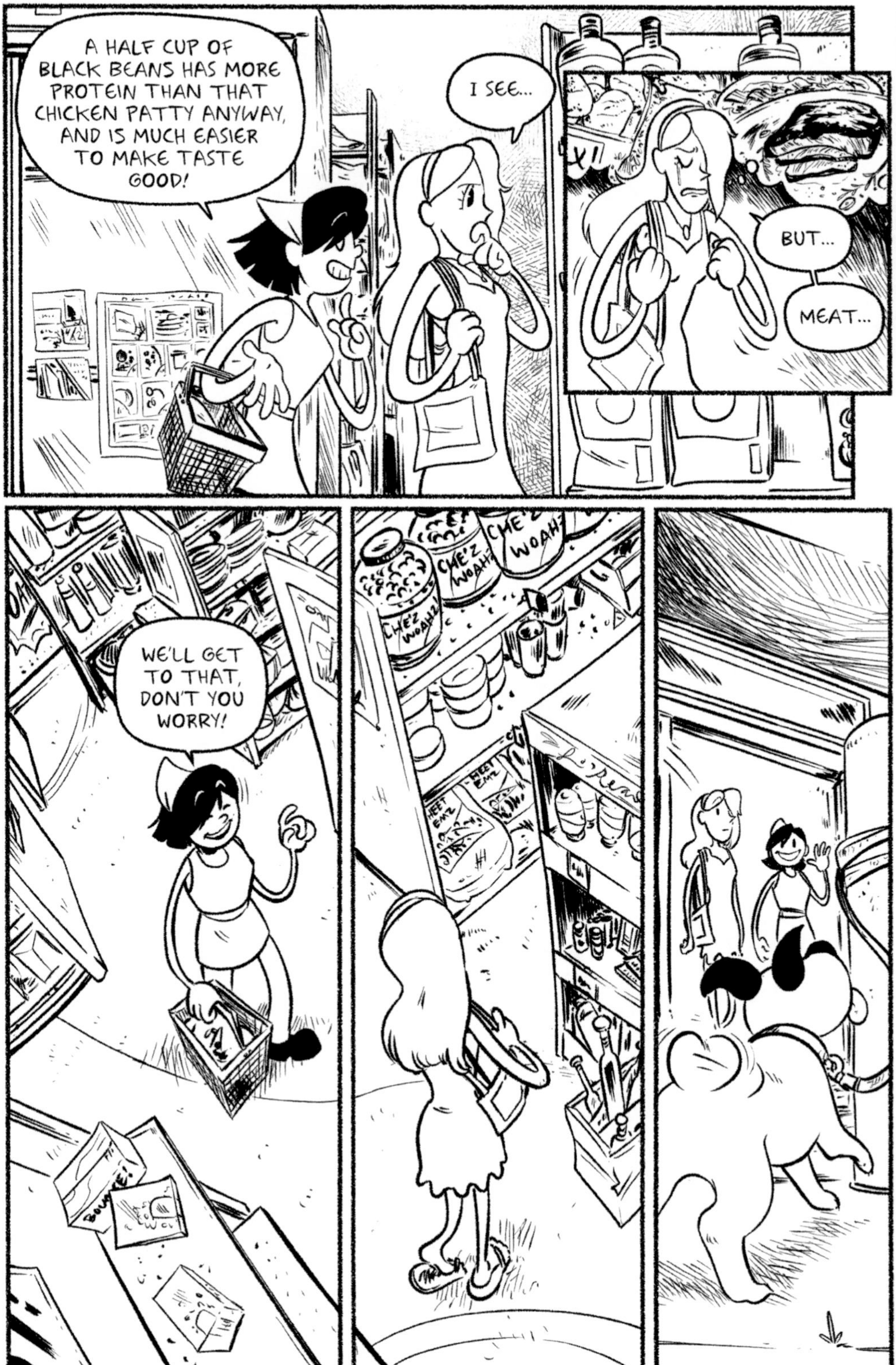
A HALF CUP OF BLACK BEANS HAS MORE PROTEIN THAN THAT CHICKEN PATTY ANYWAY, AND IS MUCH EASIER TO MAKE TASTE GOOD!
I SEE...
BUT...
MEAT...
WE'LL GET TO THAT, DON'T YOU WORRY!
CHE'Z WOAHZ

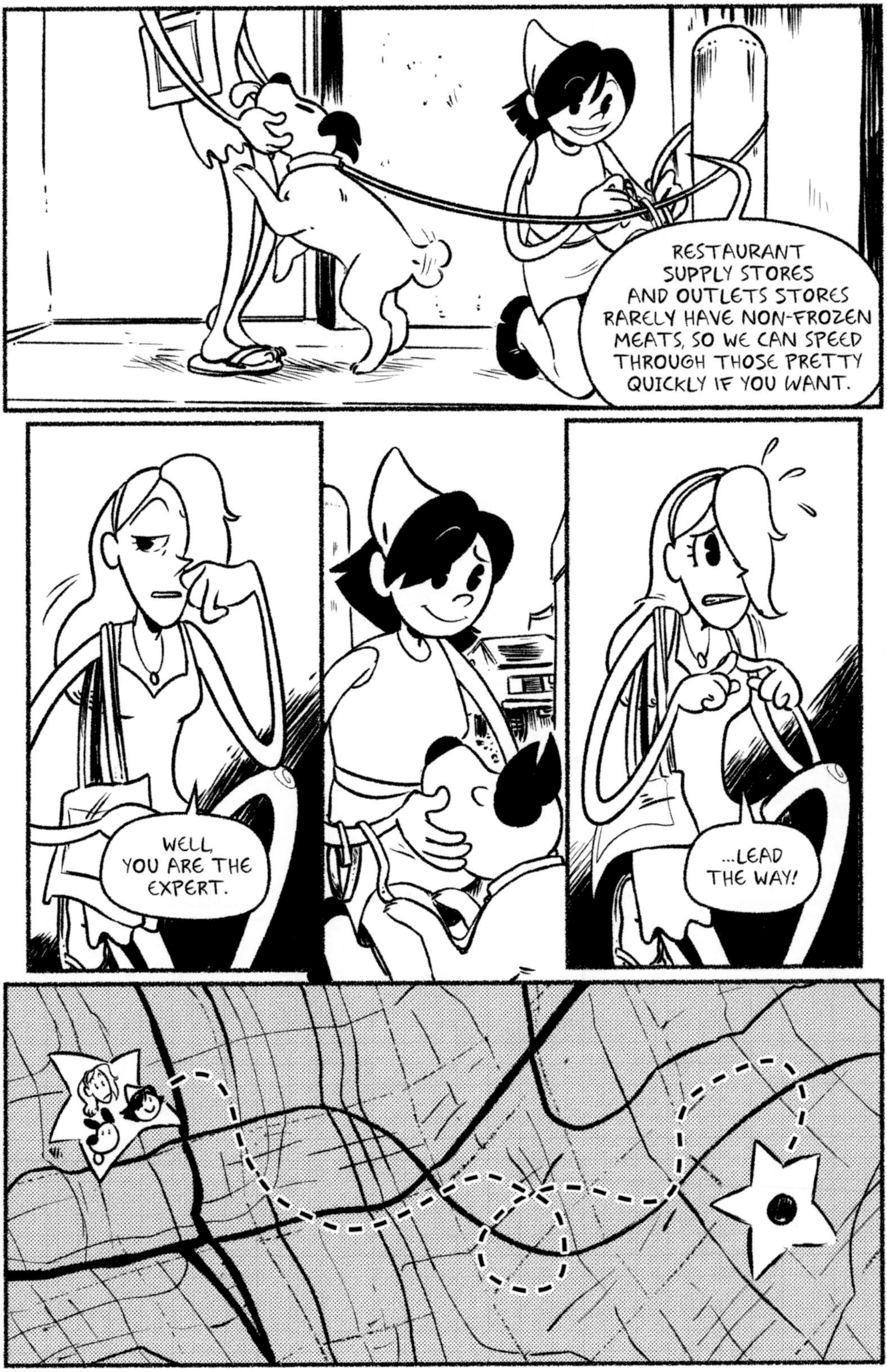
RESTAURANT SUPPLY STORES AND OUTLETS STORES RARELY HAVE NON-FROZEN MEATS, SO WE CAN SPEED THROUGH THOSE PRETTY QUICKLY IF YOU WANT.
WELL, YOU ARE THE EXPERT.
...LEAD THE WAY!

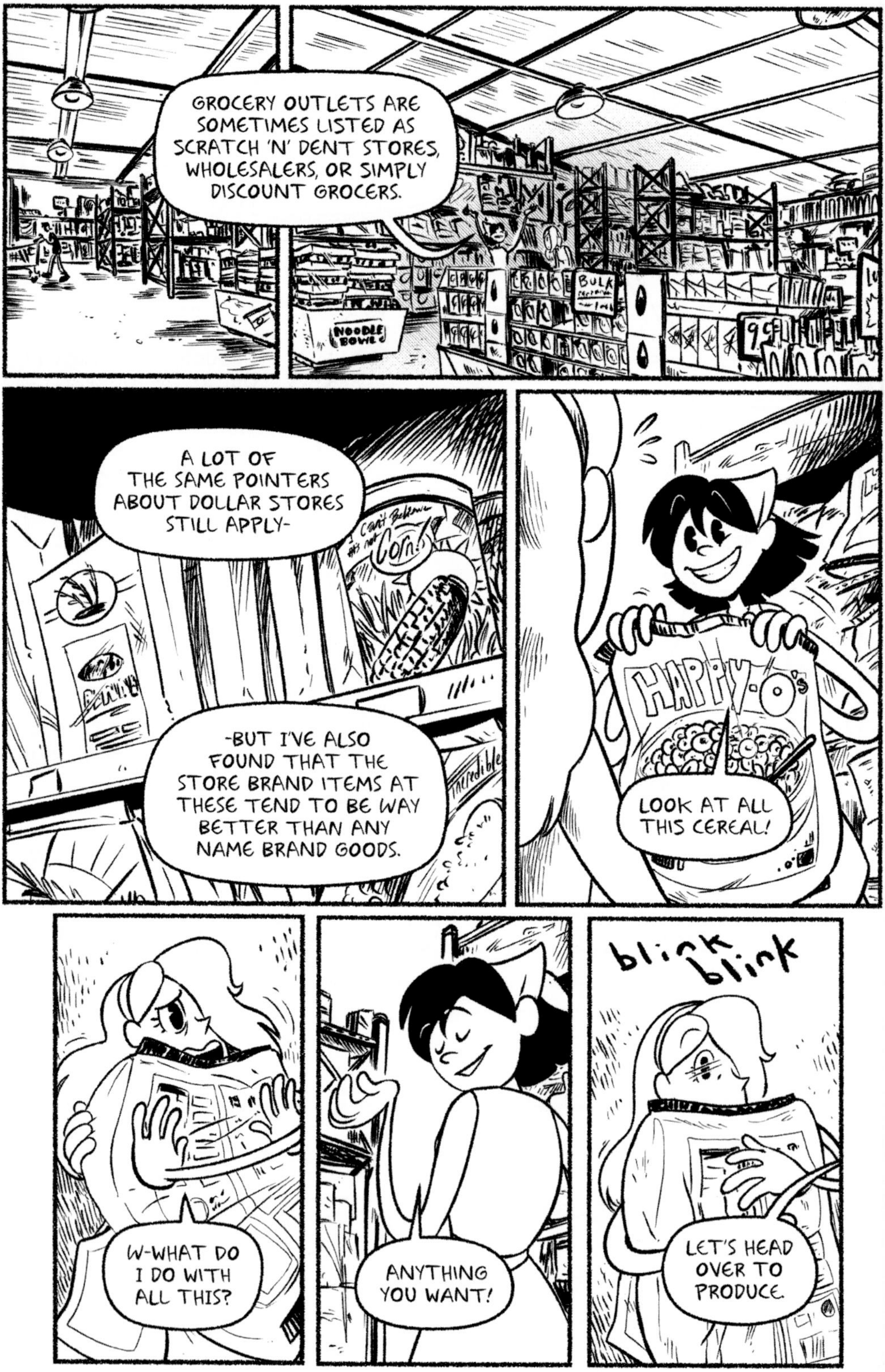
GROCERY OUTLETS ARE SOMETIMES LISTED AS SCRATCH 'N' DENT STORES, WHOLESALERS, OR SIMPLY DISCOUNT GROCERS.
NOODLE BOWL
BULK
A LOT OF THE SAME POINTERS ABOUT DOLLAR STORES STILL APPLY-
Corn!
-BUT I'VE ALSO FOUND THAT THE STORE BRAND ITEMS AT THESE TEND TO BE WAY BETTER THAN ANY NAME BRAND GOODS.
Incredible
HAPPY-O's
LOOK AT ALL THIS CEREAL!
W-WHAT DO I DO WITH ALL THIS?
ANYTHING YOU WANT!
blink blink
LET'S HEAD OVER TO PRODUCE.

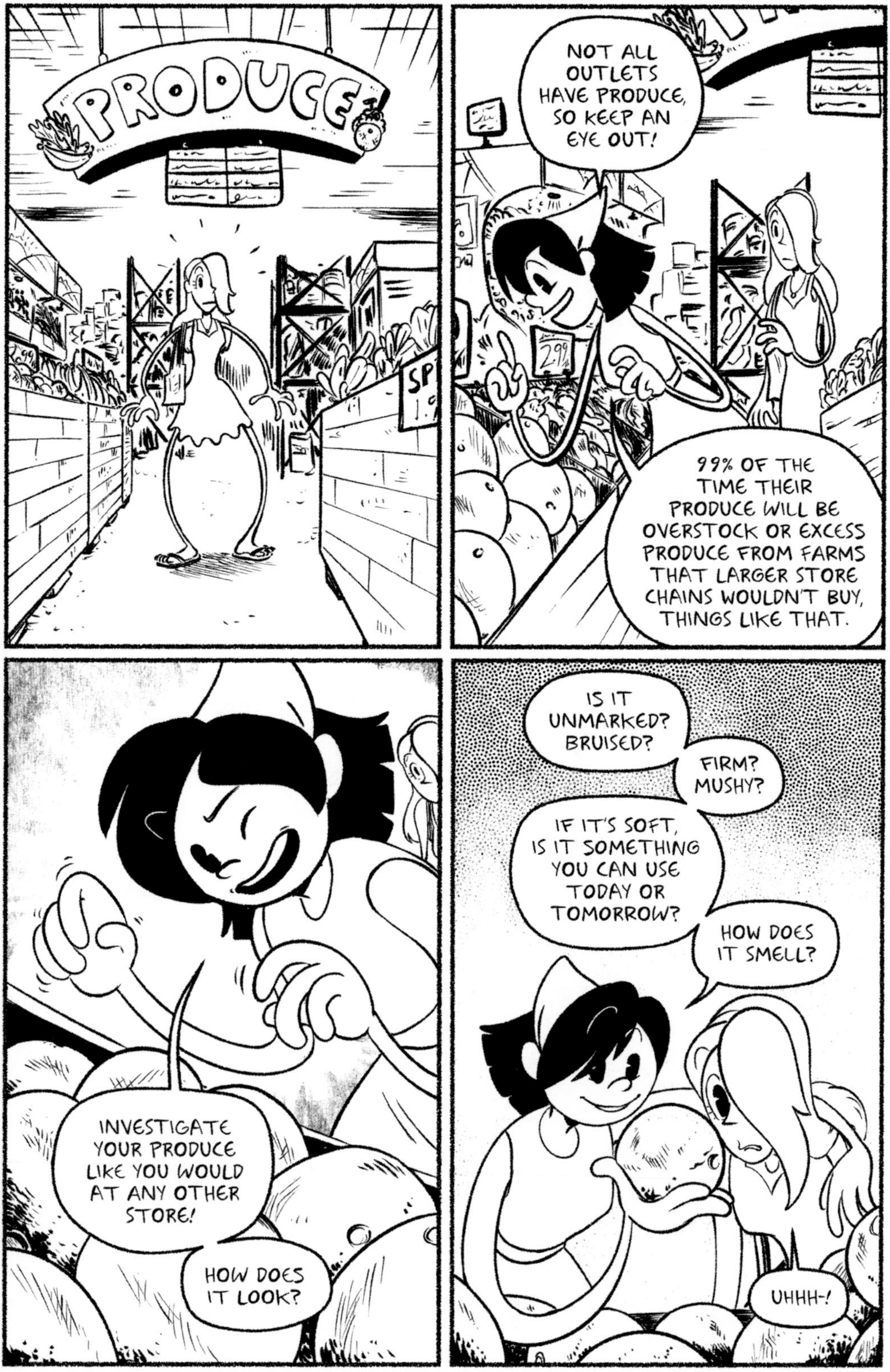
PRODUCE
NOT ALL OUTLETS HAVE PRODUCE, SO KEEP AN EYE OUT!
2.99
99% OF THE TIME THEIR PRODUCE WILL BE OVERSTOCK OR EXCESS PRODUCE FROM FARMS THAT LARGER STORE CHAINS WOULDN'T BUY, THINGS LIKE THAT.
INVESTIGATE YOUR PRODUCE LIKE YOU WOULD AT ANY OTHER STORE!
HOW DOES IT LOOK?
IS IT UNMARKED? BRUISED?
FIRM? MUSHY?
IF IT'S SOFT, IS IT SOMETHING YOU CAN USE TODAY OR TOMORROW?
HOW DOES IT SMELL?
UHHH-!

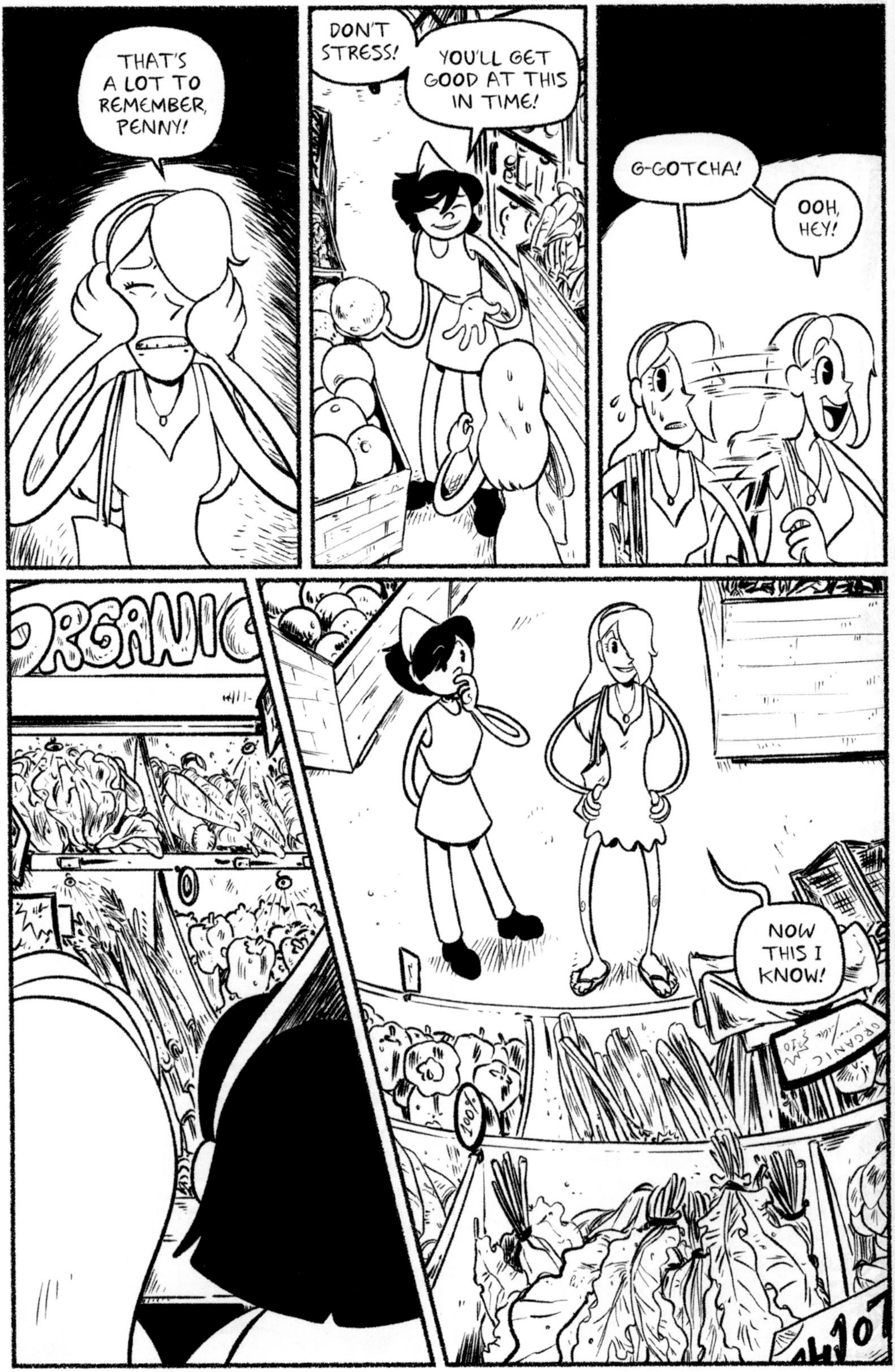
THAT'S A LOT TO REMEMBER, PENNY!
DON'T STRESS!
YOU'LL GET GOOD AT THIS IN TIME!
G-GOTCHA!
OOH, HEY!
NOW THIS I KNOW!

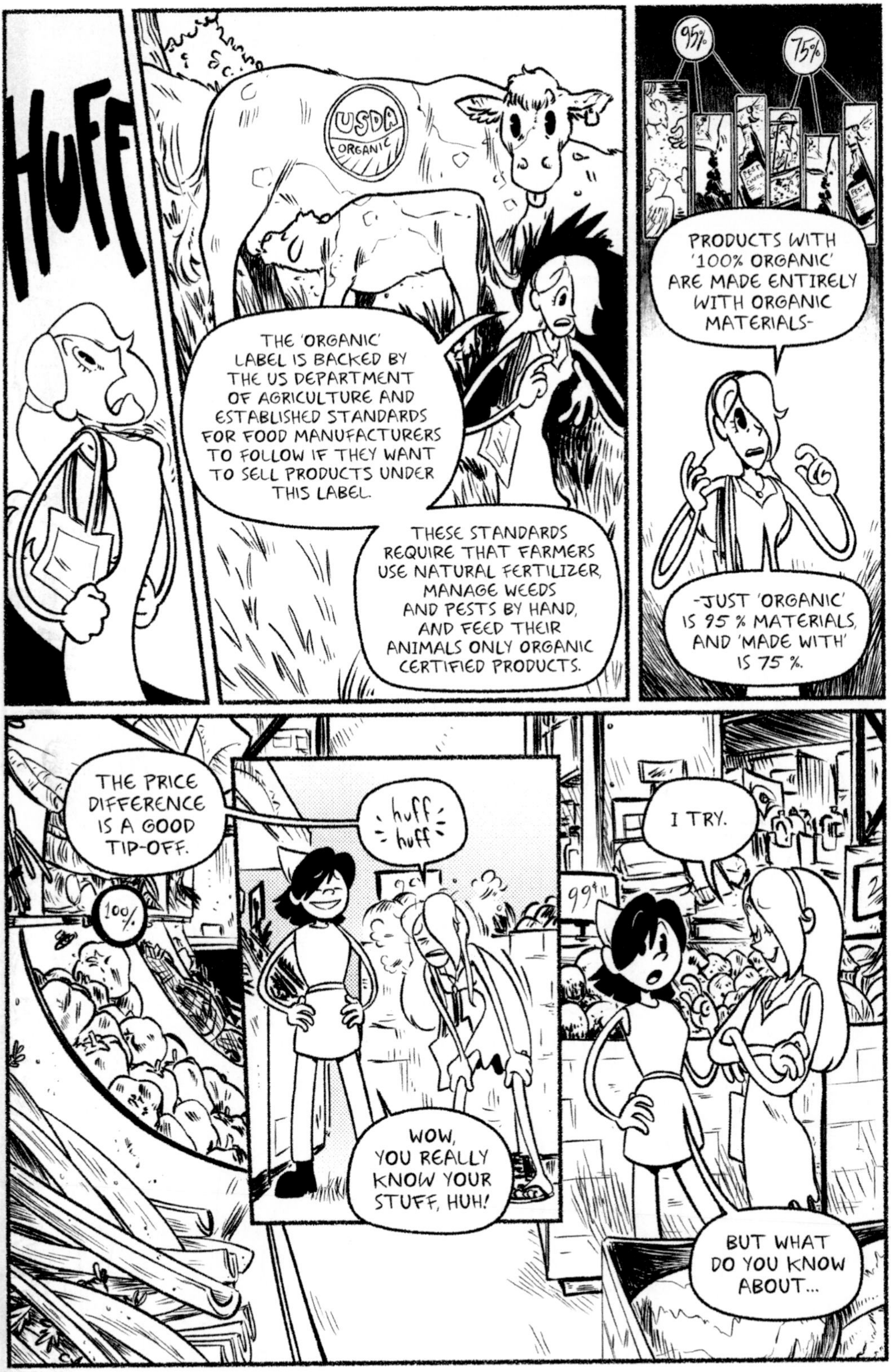
HUFF
USDA ORGANIC
THE 'ORGANIC' LABEL IS BACKED BY THE US DEPARTMENT OF AGRICULTURE AND ESTABLISHED STANDARDS FOR FOOD MANUFACTURERS TO FOLLOW IF THEY WANT TO SELL PRODUCTS UNDER THIS LABEL.
THESE STANDARDS REQUIRE THAT FARMERS USE NATURAL FERTILIZER, MANAGE WEEDS AND PESTS BY HAND, AND FEED THEIR ANIMALS ONLY ORGANIC CERTIFIED PRODUCTS.
95%
75%
PRODUCTS WITH '100% ORGANIC' ARE MADE ENTIRELY WITH ORGANIC MATERIALS-
-JUST 'ORGANIC' IS 95 % MATERIALS, AND 'MADE WITH' IS 75 %.
THE PRICE DIFFERENCE IS A GOOD TIP-OFF.
100%
huff huff
WOW, YOU REALLY KNOW YOUR STUFF, HUH!
99¢
I TRY.
BUT WHAT DO YOU KNOW ABOUT...

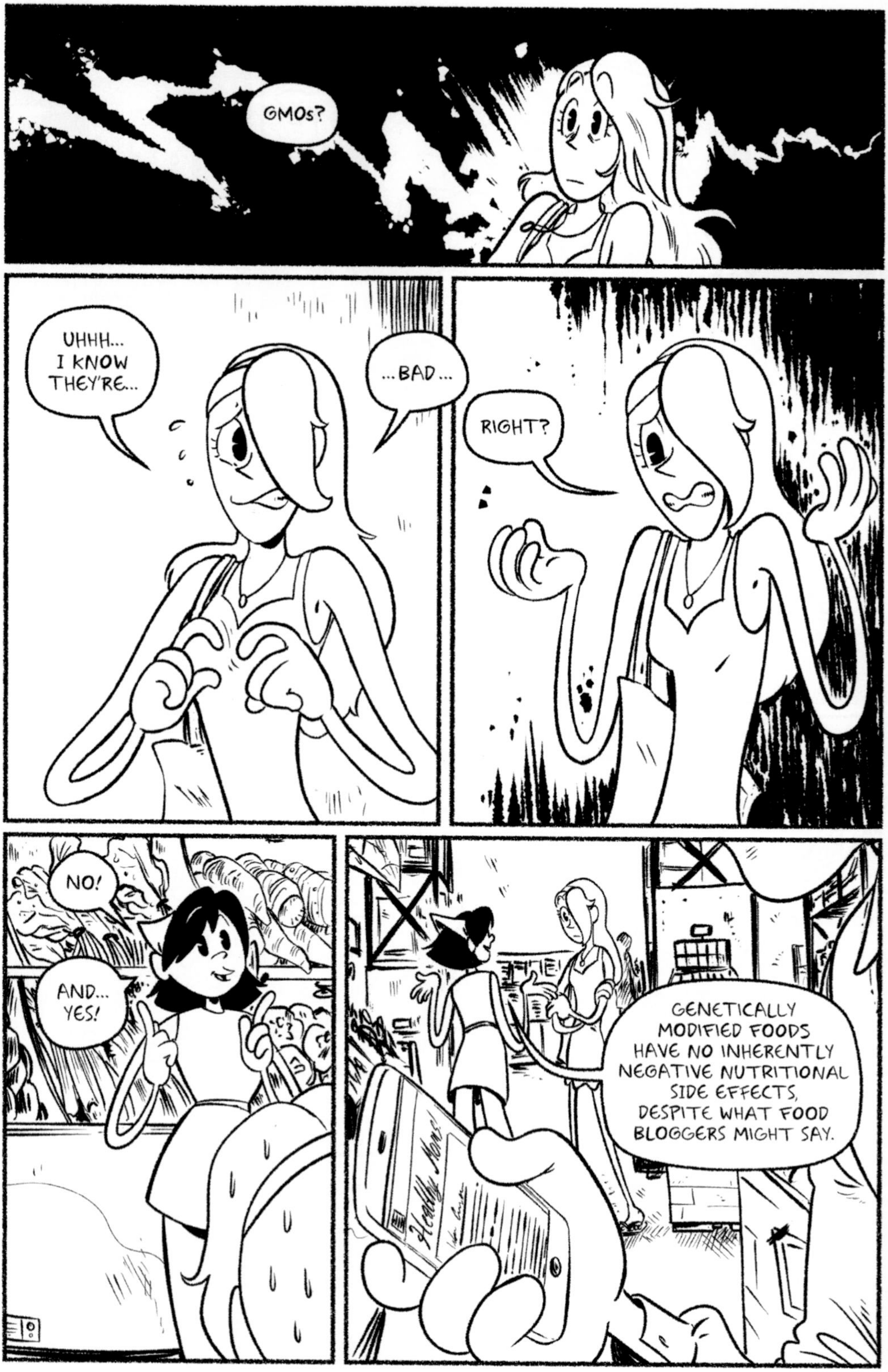
GMOs?
UHHH... I KNOW THEY'RE...
...BAD...
RIGHT?
NO!
AND... YES!
GENETICALLY MODIFIED FOODS HAVE NO INHERENTLY NEGATIVE NUTRITIONAL SIDE EFFECTS, DESPITE WHAT FOOD BLOGGERS MIGHT SAY.

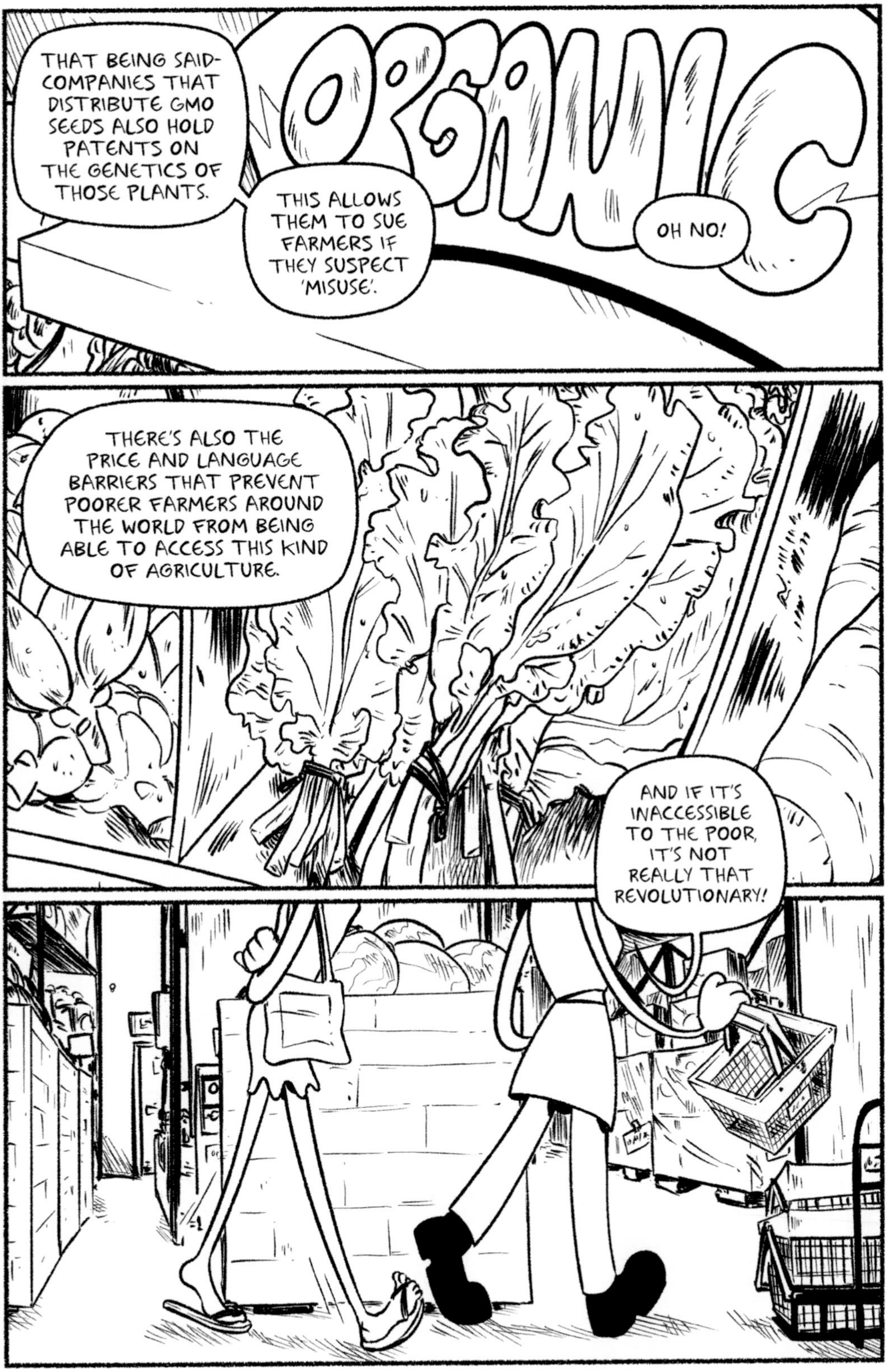
THAT BEING SAID- COMPANIES THAT DISTRIBUTE GMO SEEDS ALSO HOLD PATENTS ON THE GENETICS OF THOSE PLANTS.
THIS ALLOWS THEM TO SUE FARMERS IF THEY SUSPECT 'MISUSE'.
ORGANIC
OH NO!
THERE'S ALSO THE PRICE AND LANGUAGE BARRIERS THAT PREVENT POORER FARMERS AROUND THE WORLD FROM BEING ABLE TO ACCESS THIS KIND OF AGRICULTURE.
AND IF IT'S INACCESSIBLE TO THE POOR, IT'S NOT REALLY THAT REVOLUTIONARY!

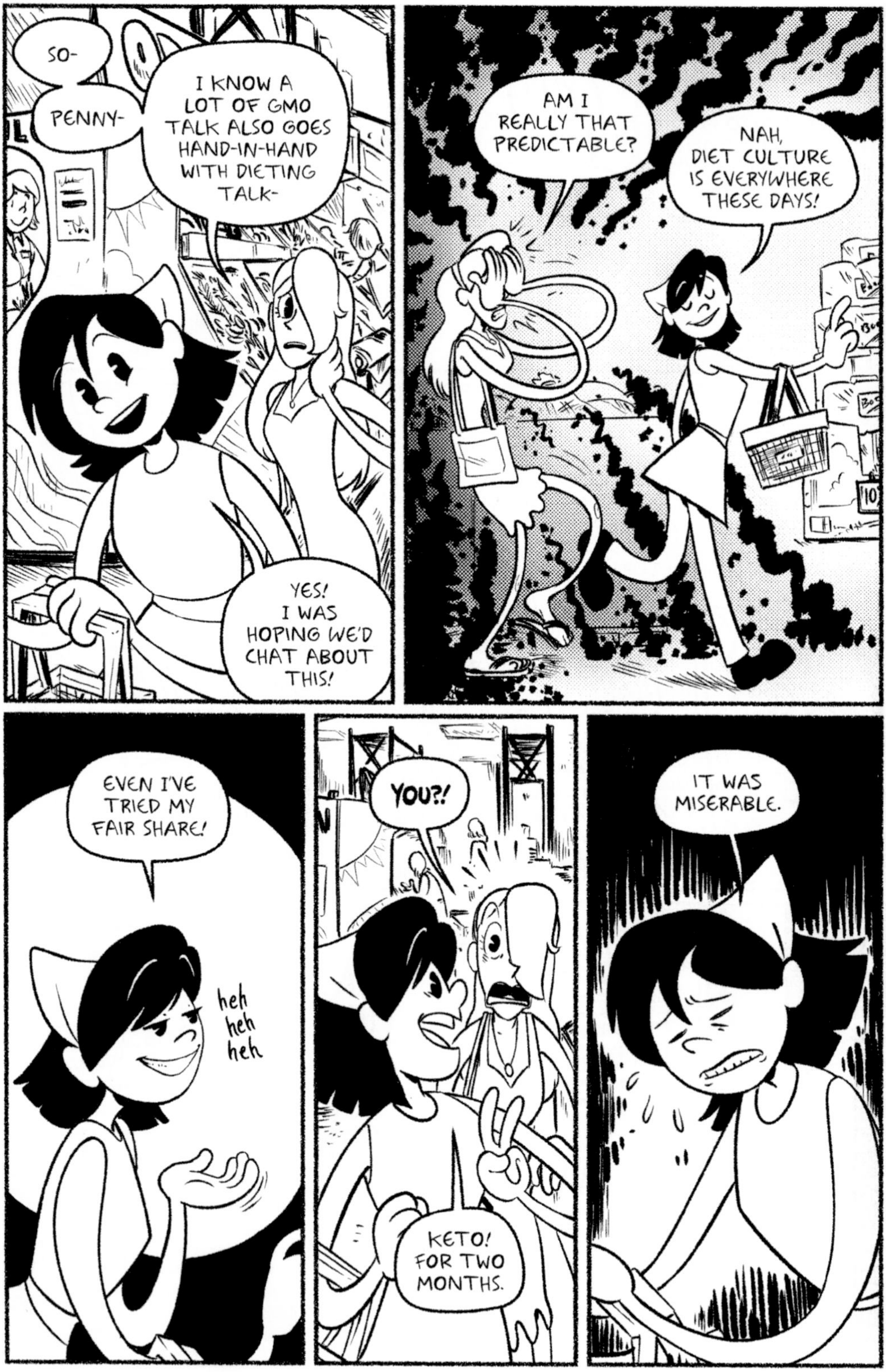
SO-
PENNY-
I KNOW A LOT OF GMO TALK ALSO GOES HAND-IN-HAND WITH DIETING TALK-
YES! I WAS HOPING WE'D CHAT ABOUT THIS!
AM I REALLY THAT PREDICTABLE?
NAH, DIET CULTURE IS EVERYWHERE THESE DAYS!
EVEN I'VE TRIED MY FAIR SHARE!
heh heh heh
YOU?!
KETO! FOR TWO MONTHS.
IT WAS MISERABLE.

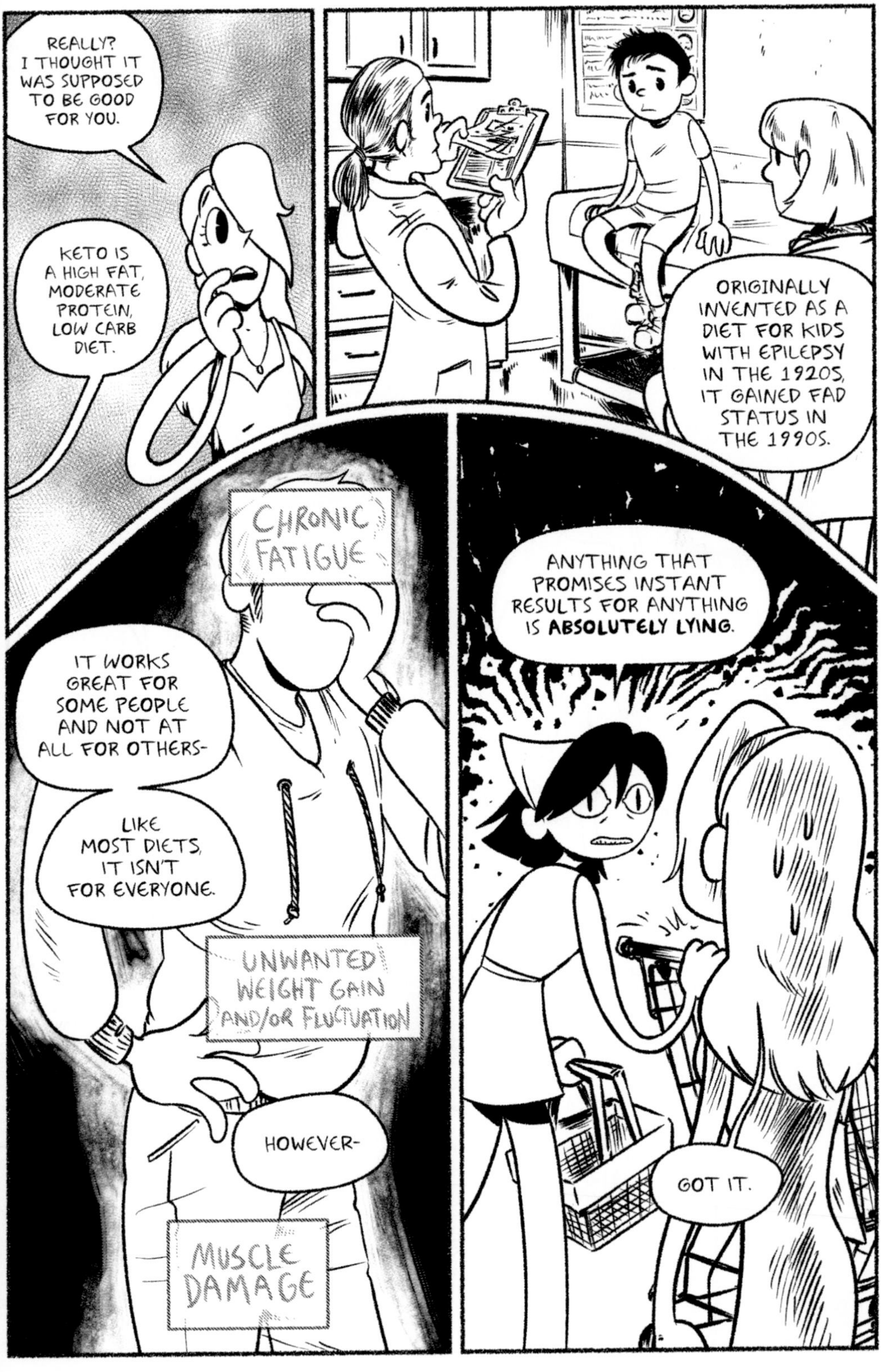
REALLY? I THOUGHT IT WAS SUPPOSED TO BE GOOD FOR YOU.
KETO IS A HIGH FAT, MODERATE PROTEIN, LOW CARB DIET.
ORIGINALLY INVENTED AS A DIET FOR KIDS WITH EPILEPSY IN THE 1920S, IT GAINED FAD STATUS IN THE 1990S.
CHRONIC FATIGUE
IT WORKS GREAT FOR SOME PEOPLE AND NOT AT ALL FOR OTHERS-
LIKE MOST DIETS, IT ISN'T FOR EVERYONE.
UNWANTED WEIGHT GAIN AND/OR FLUCTUATION
HOWEVER-
MUSCLE DAMAGE
ANYTHING THAT PROMISES INSTANT RESULTS FOR ANYTHING IS **ABSOLUTELY LYING**.
GOT IT.

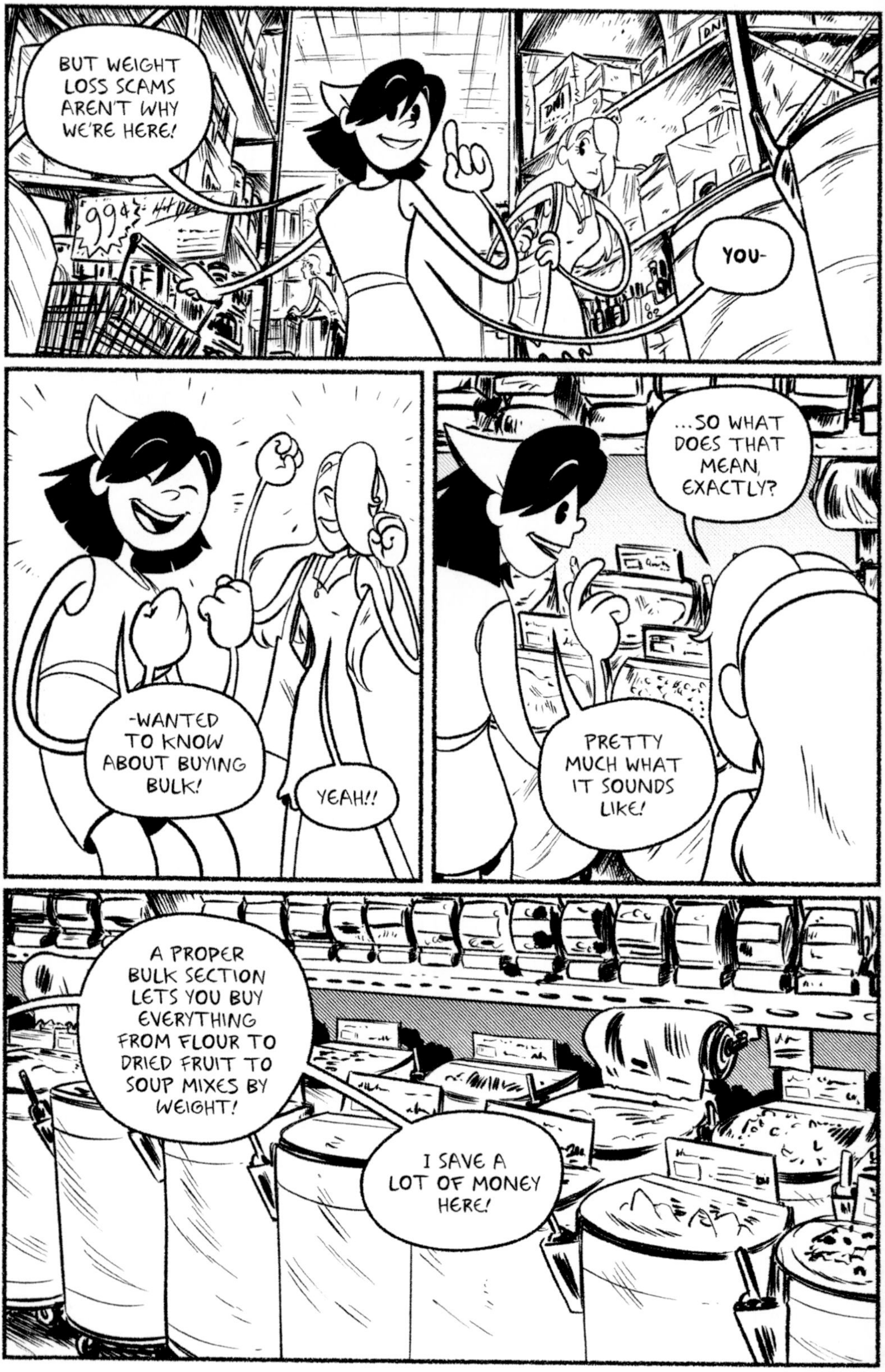
BUT WEIGHT LOSS SCAMS AREN'T WHY WE'RE HERE!
99¢
YOU-
-WANTED TO KNOW ABOUT BUYING BULK!
YEAH!!
...SO WHAT DOES THAT MEAN, EXACTLY?
PRETTY MUCH WHAT IT SOUNDS LIKE!
A PROPER BULK SECTION LETS YOU BUY EVERYTHING FROM FLOUR TO DRIED FRUIT TO SOUP MIXES BY WEIGHT!
I SAVE A LOT OF MONEY HERE!

see notes for more!

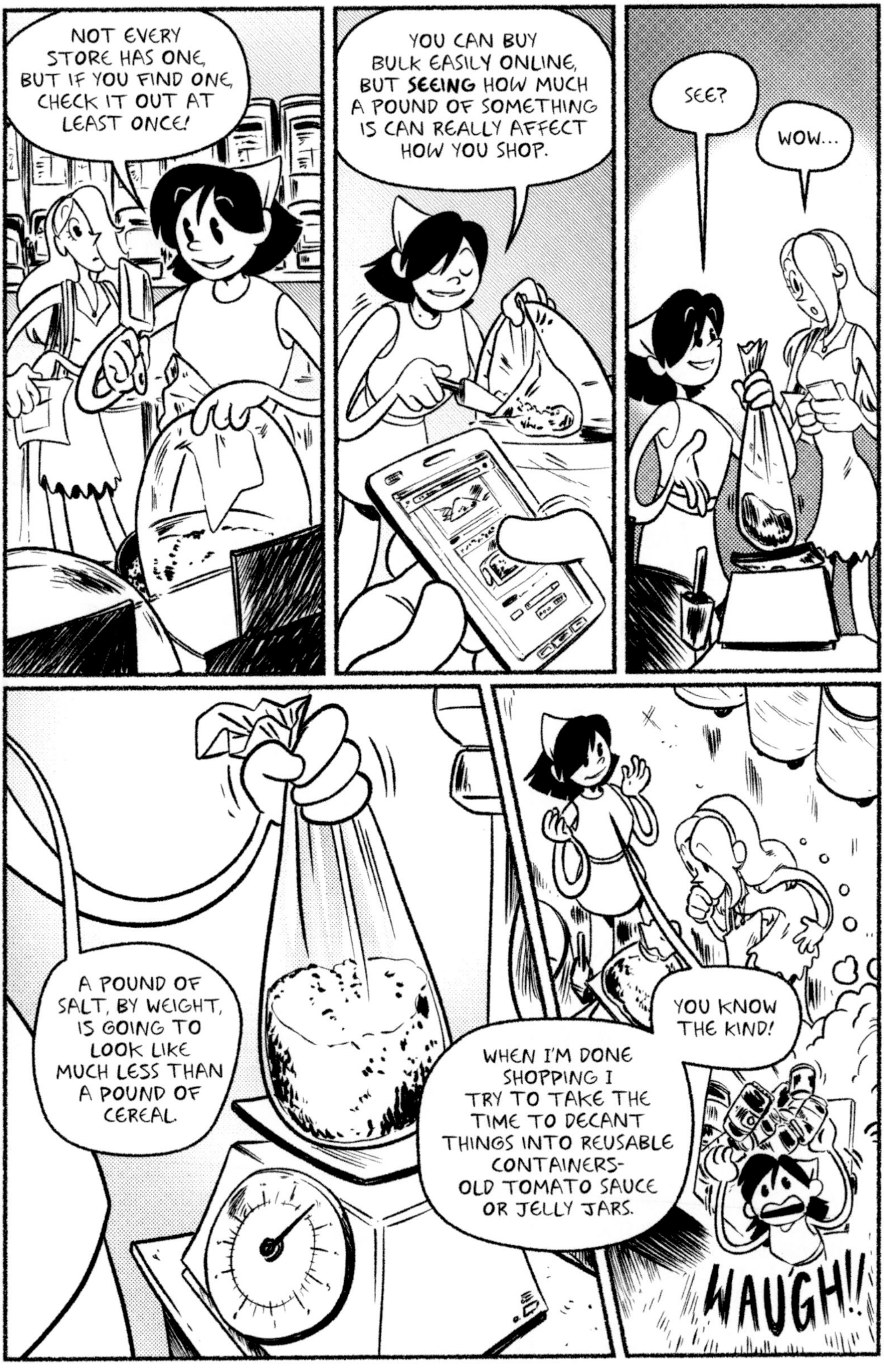
NOT EVERY STORE HAS ONE, BUT IF YOU FIND ONE, CHECK IT OUT AT LEAST ONCE!
YOU CAN BUY BULK EASILY ONLINE, BUT **SEEING** HOW MUCH A POUND OF SOMETHING IS CAN REALLY AFFECT HOW YOU SHOP.
SEE?
WOW...
A POUND OF SALT, BY WEIGHT, IS GOING TO LOOK LIKE MUCH LESS THAN A POUND OF CEREAL.
WHEN I'M DONE SHOPPING I TRY TO TAKE THE TIME TO DECANT THINGS INTO REUSABLE CONTAINERS- OLD TOMATO SAUCE OR JELLY JARS.
YOU KNOW THE KIND!
WAUGH!!

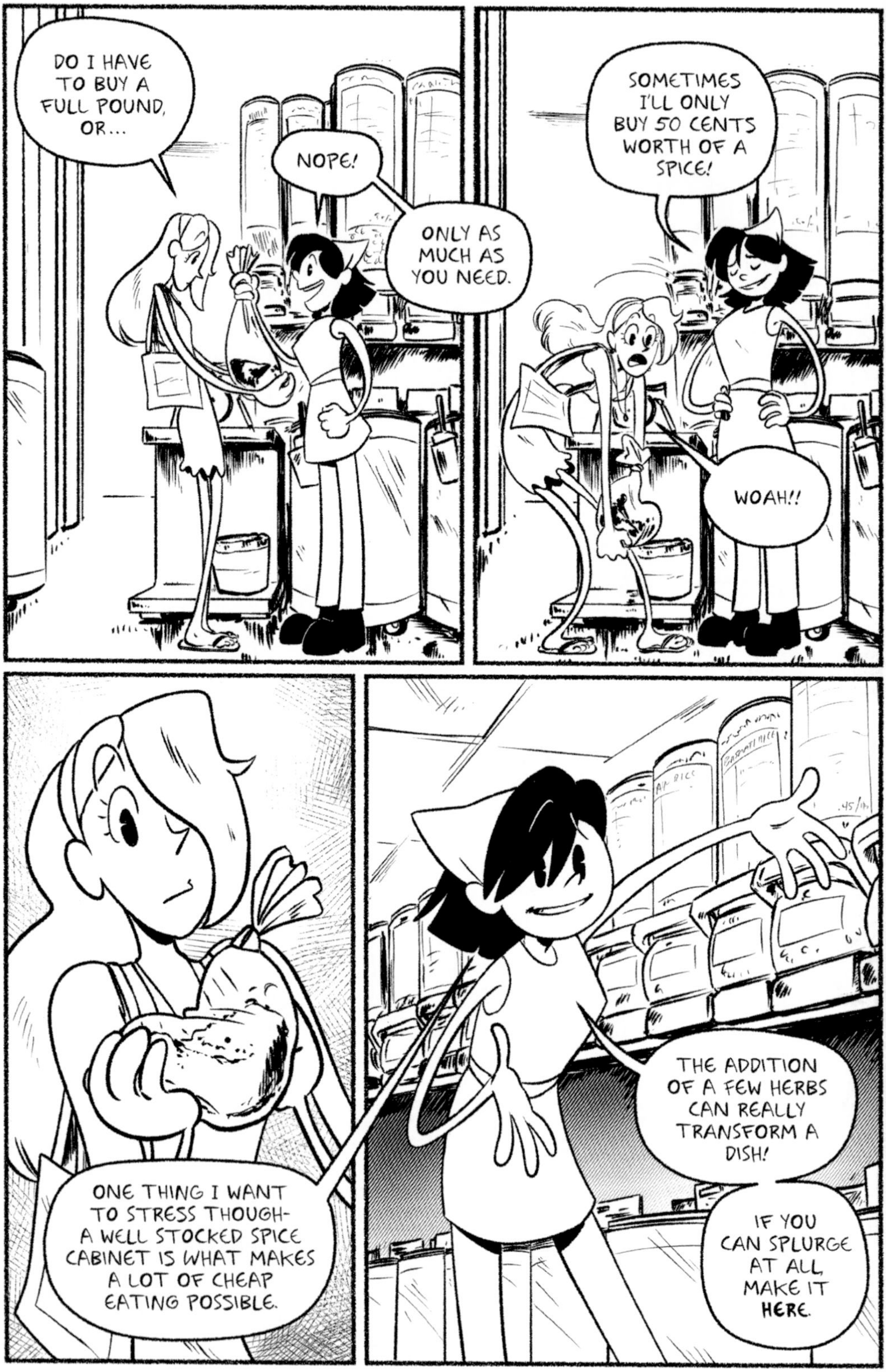
DO I HAVE TO BUY A FULL POUND, OR...
NOPE!
ONLY AS MUCH AS YOU NEED.
SOMETIMES I'LL ONLY BUY 50 CENTS WORTH OF A SPICE!
WOAH!!
ONE THING I WANT TO STRESS THOUGH- A WELL STOCKED SPICE CABINET IS WHAT MAKES A LOT OF CHEAP EATING POSSIBLE.
THE ADDITION OF A FEW HERBS CAN REALLY TRANSFORM A DISH!
IF YOU CAN SPLURGE AT ALL, MAKE IT **HERE**.

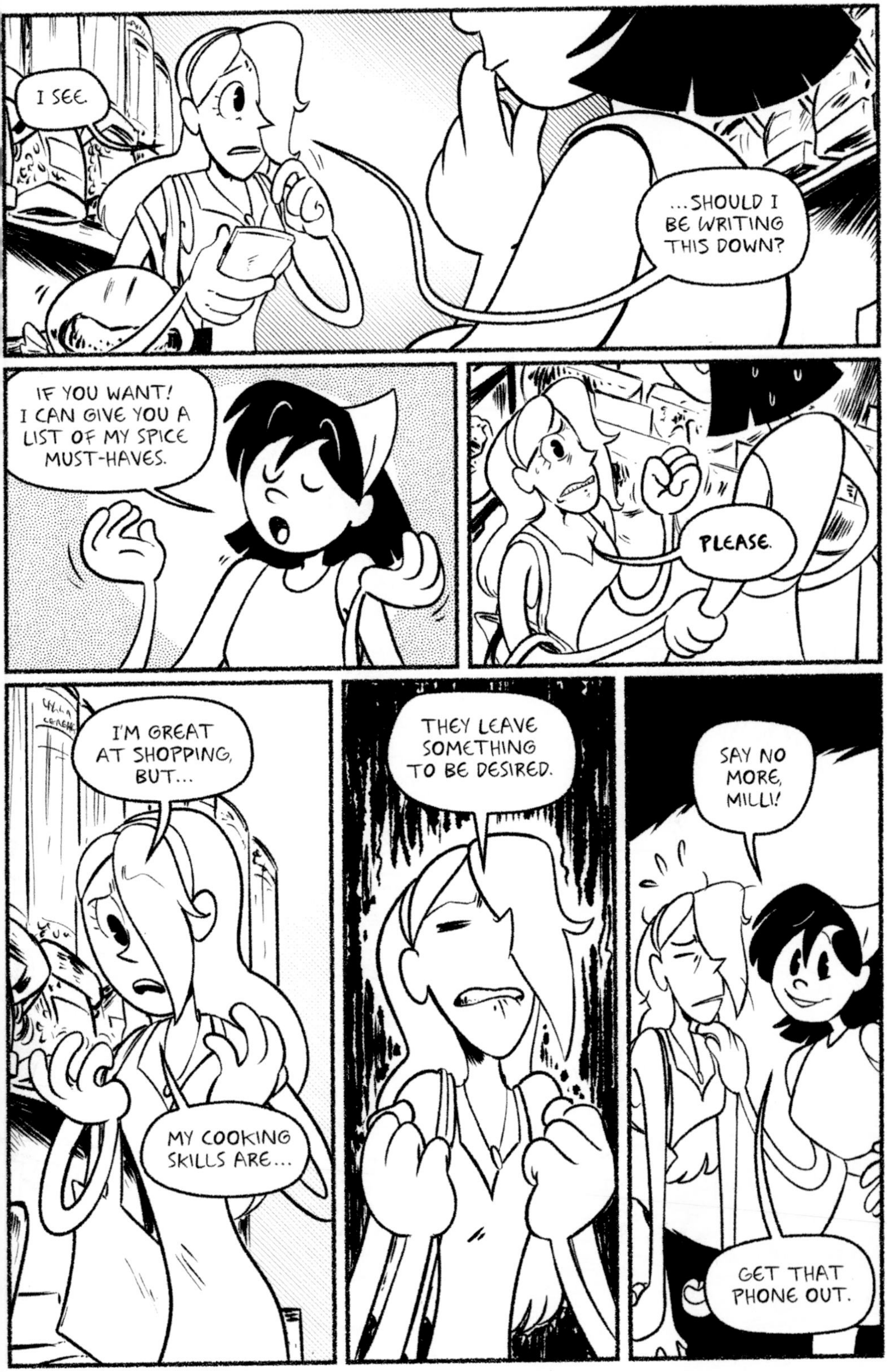
I SEE.
...SHOULD I BE WRITING THIS DOWN?
IF YOU WANT! I CAN GIVE YOU A LIST OF MY SPICE MUST-HAVES.
PLEASE.
I'M GREAT AT SHOPPING, BUT...
MY COOKING SKILLS ARE...
THEY LEAVE SOMETHING TO BE DESIRED.
SAY NO MORE, MILLI!
GET THAT PHONE OUT.

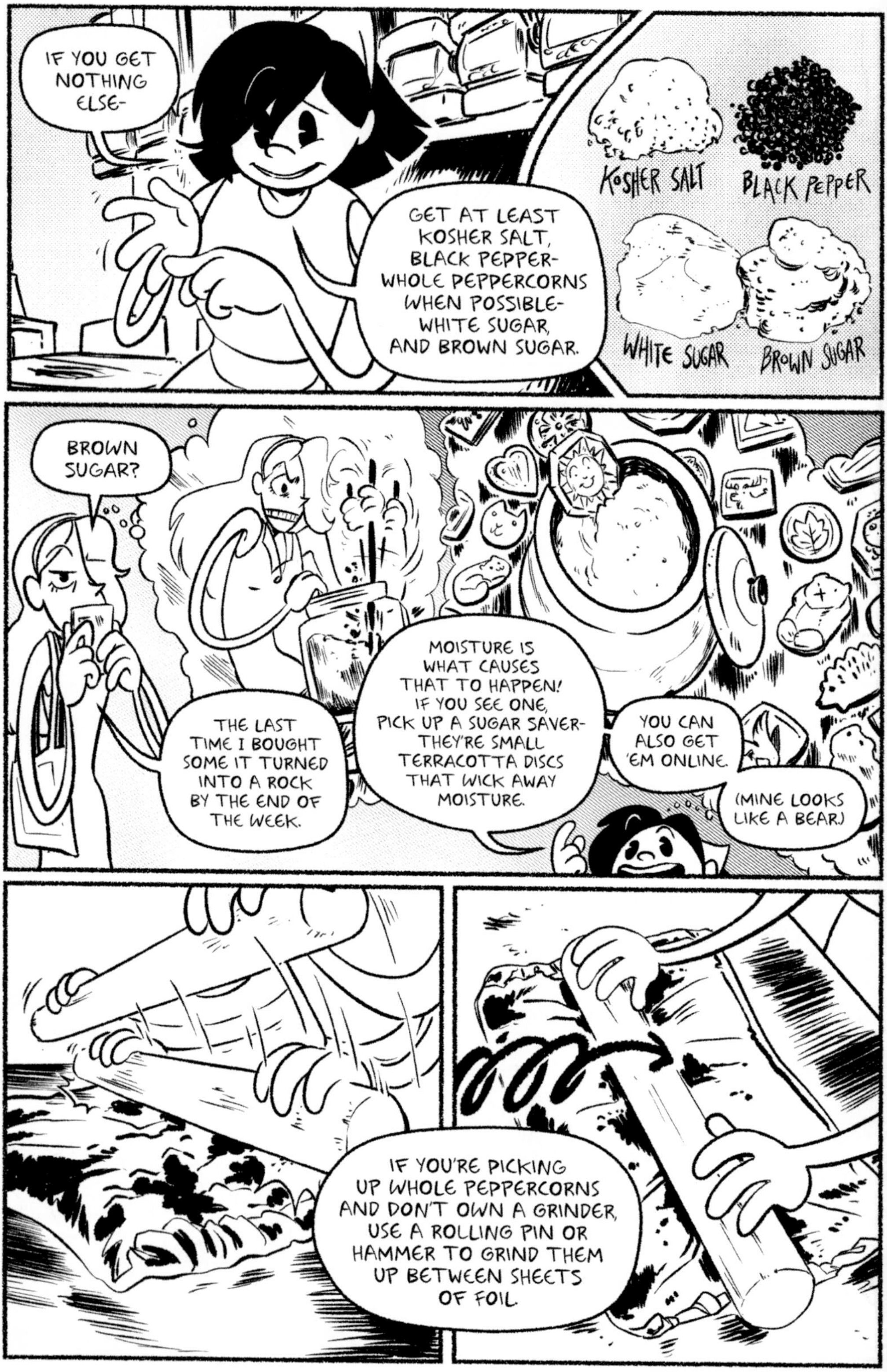
IF YOU GET NOTHING ELSE-
GET AT LEAST KOSHER SALT, BLACK PEPPER- WHOLE PEPPERCORNS WHEN POSSIBLE- WHITE SUGAR, AND BROWN SUGAR.
KOSHER SALT
BLACK PEPPER
WHITE SUGAR
BROWN SUGAR
BROWN SUGAR?
THE LAST TIME I BOUGHT SOME IT TURNED INTO A ROCK BY THE END OF THE WEEK.
MOISTURE IS WHAT CAUSES THAT TO HAPPEN! IF YOU SEE ONE, PICK UP A SUGAR SAVER- THEY'RE SMALL TERRACOTTA DISCS THAT WICK AWAY MOISTURE.
YOU CAN ALSO GET 'EM ONLINE.
(MINE LOOKS LIKE A BEAR.)
IF YOU'RE PICKING UP WHOLE PEPPERCORNS AND DON'T OWN A GRINDER, USE A ROLLING PIN OR HAMMER TO GRIND THEM UP BETWEEN SHEETS OF FOIL.

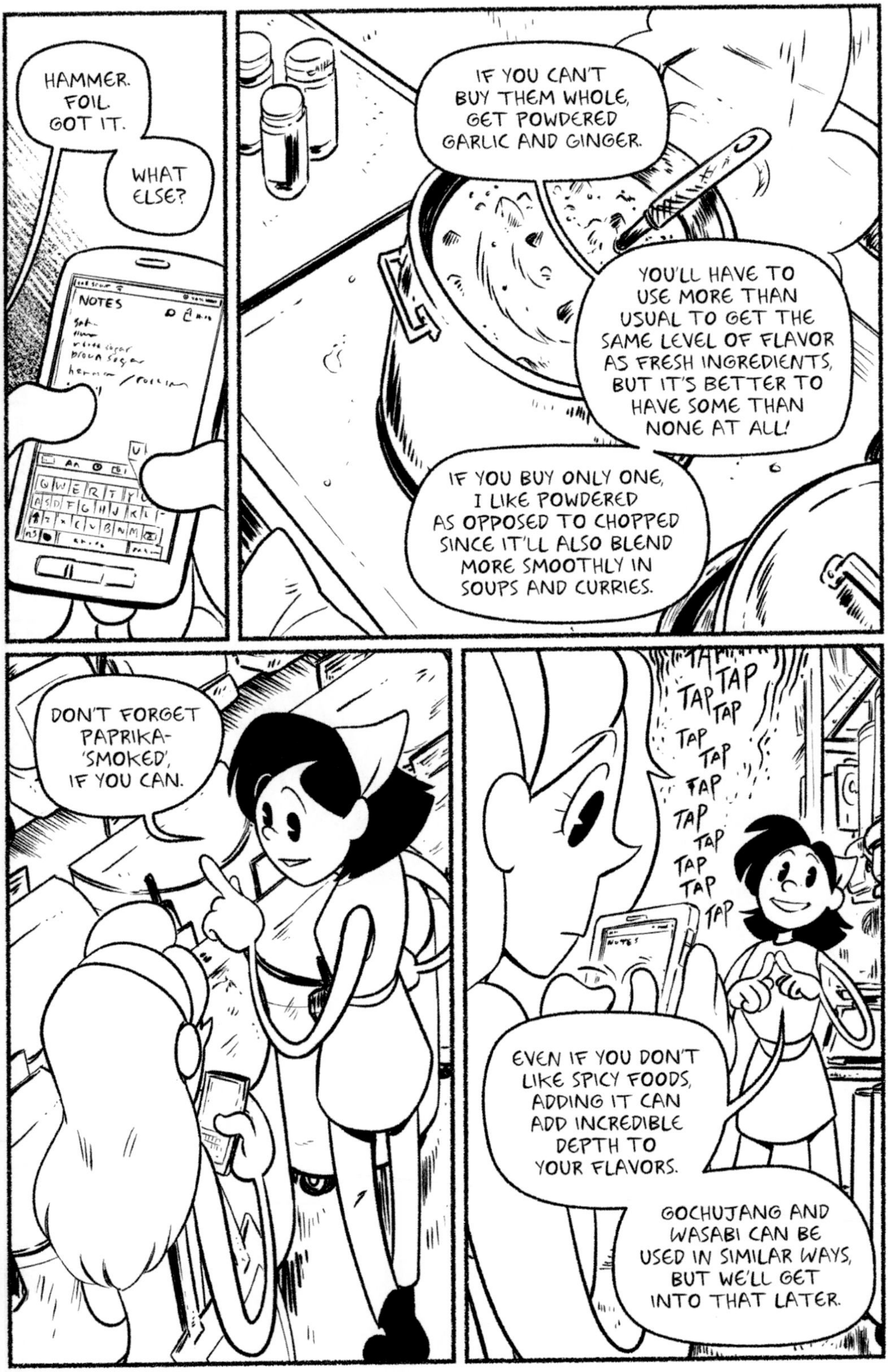
HAMMER. FOIL. GOT IT.
WHAT ELSE?
NOTES
IF YOU CAN'T BUY THEM WHOLE, GET POWDERED GARLIC AND GINGER.
YOU'LL HAVE TO USE MORE THAN USUAL TO GET THE SAME LEVEL OF FLAVOR AS FRESH INGREDIENTS, BUT IT'S BETTER TO HAVE SOME THAN NONE AT ALL!
IF YOU BUY ONLY ONE, I LIKE POWDERED AS OPPOSED TO CHOPPED SINCE IT'LL ALSO BLEND MORE SMOOTHLY IN SOUPS AND CURRIES.
DON'T FORGET PAPRIKA- 'SMOKED', IF YOU CAN.
TAP TAP TAP TAP TAP TAP TAP TAP TAP TAP TAP TAP
EVEN IF YOU DON'T LIKE SPICY FOODS, ADDING IT CAN ADD INCREDIBLE DEPTH TO YOUR FLAVORS.
GOCHUJANG AND WASABI CAN BE USED IN SIMILAR WAYS, BUT WE'LL GET INTO THAT LATER.

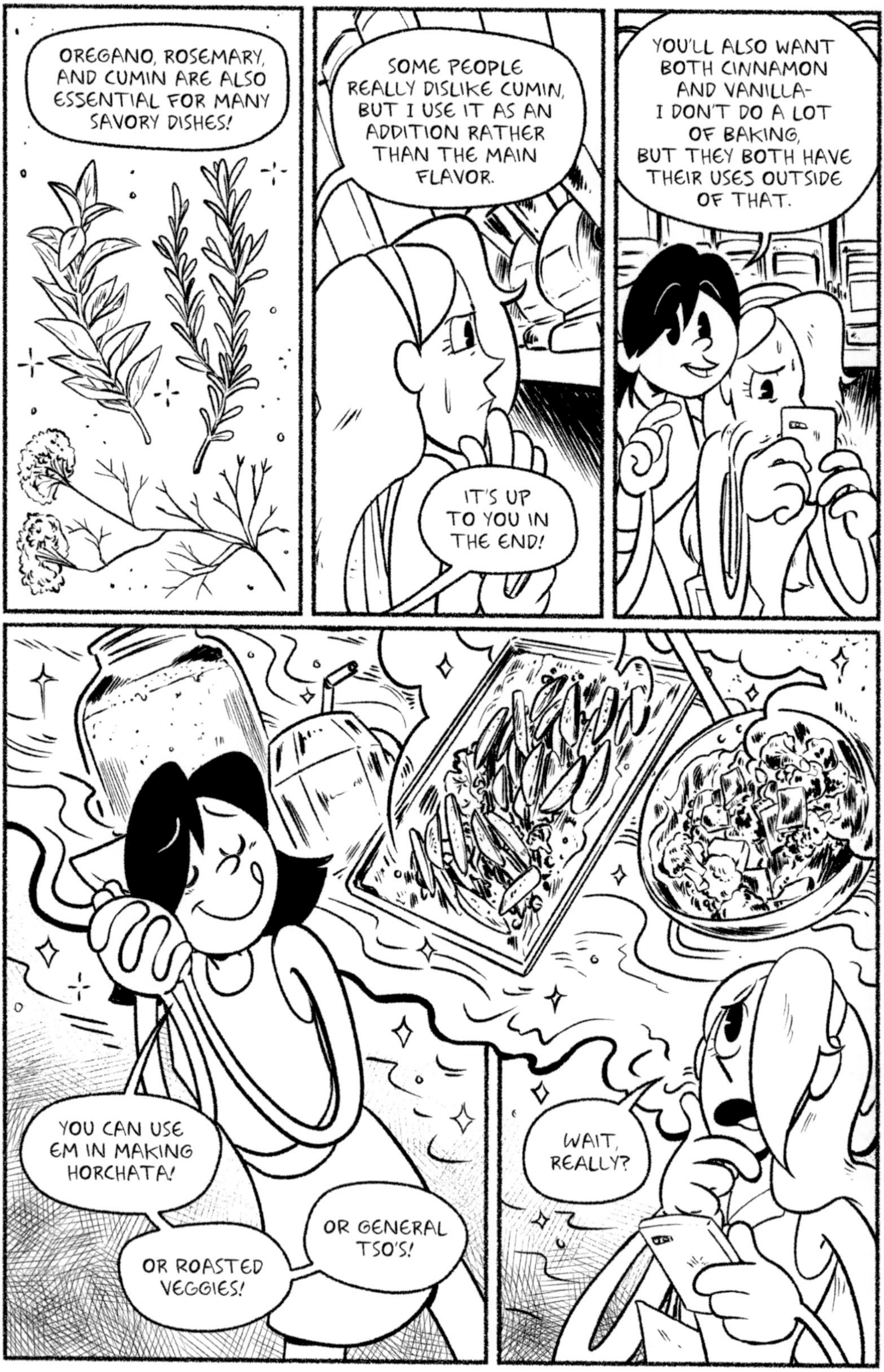
OREGANO, ROSEMARY, AND CUMIN ARE ALSO ESSENTIAL FOR MANY SAVORY DISHES!
SOME PEOPLE REALLY DISLIKE CUMIN, BUT I USE IT AS AN ADDITION RATHER THAN THE MAIN FLAVOR.
IT'S UP TO YOU IN THE END!
YOU'LL ALSO WANT BOTH CINNAMON AND VANILLA- I DON'T DO A LOT OF BAKING, BUT THEY BOTH HAVE THEIR USES OUTSIDE OF THAT.
YOU CAN USE EM IN MAKING HORCHATA!
OR ROASTED VEGGIES!
OR GENERAL TSO'S!
WAIT, REALLY?

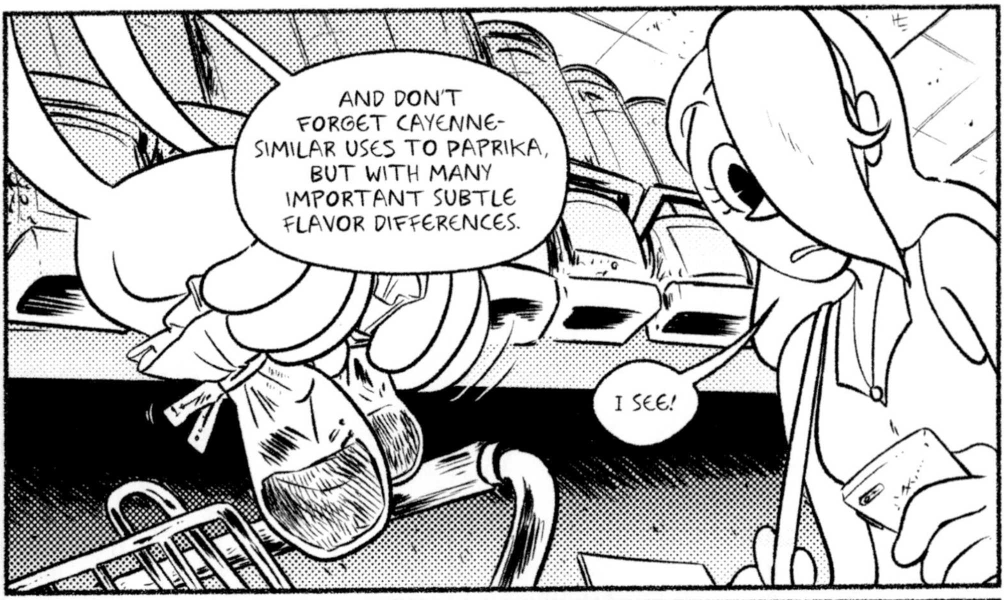
AND DON'T FORGET CAYENNE- SIMILAR USES TO PAPRIKA, BUT WITH MANY IMPORTANT SUBTLE FLAVOR DIFFERENCES.
I SEE!

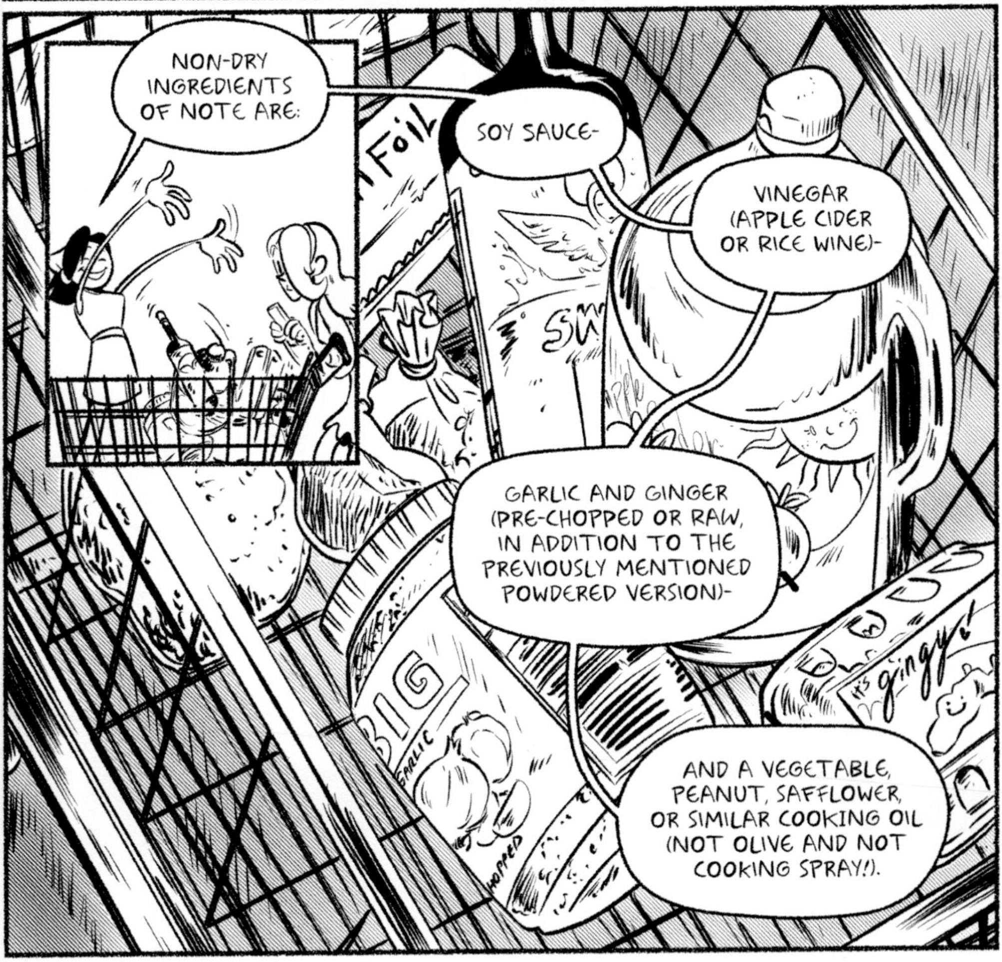
NON-DRY INGREDIENTS OF NOTE ARE:
SOY SAUCE-
VINEGAR (APPLE CIDER OR RICE WINE)-
GARLIC AND GINGER (PRE-CHOPPED OR RAW, IN ADDITION TO THE PREVIOUSLY MENTIONED POWDERED VERSION)-
AND A VEGETABLE, PEANUT, SAFFLOWER, OR SIMILAR COOKING OIL (NOT OLIVE AND NOT COOKING SPRAY!).
FOIL
BIG
GARLIC
CHOPPED
IT'S gingy!

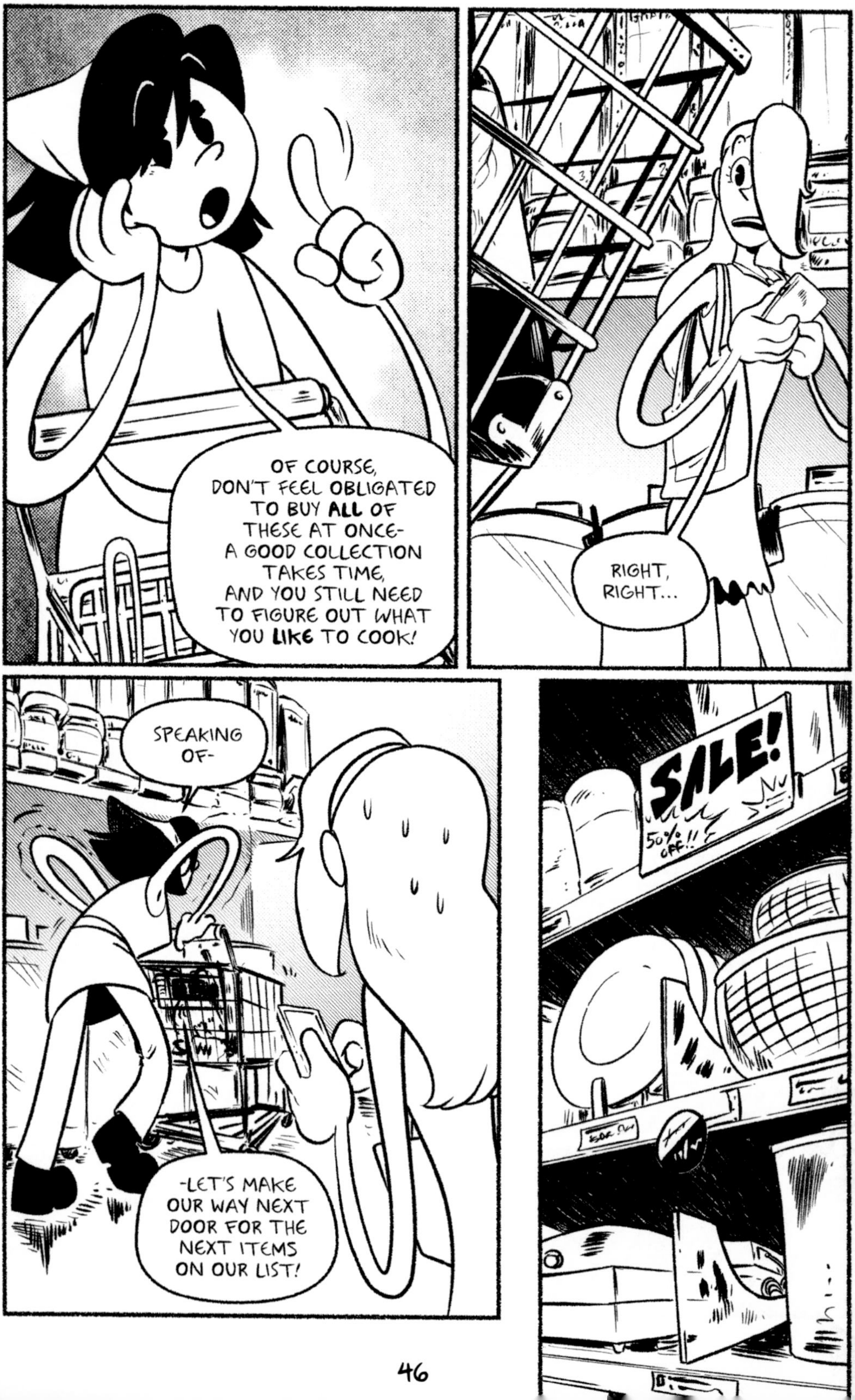
OF COURSE, DON'T FEEL OBLIGATED TO BUY **ALL** OF THESE AT ONCE- A GOOD COLLECTION TAKES TIME, AND YOU STILL NEED TO FIGURE OUT WHAT YOU **LIKE** TO COOK!
RIGHT, RIGHT...
SPEAKING OF-
-LET'S MAKE OUR WAY NEXT DOOR FOR THE NEXT ITEMS ON OUR LIST!
SALE!
50% OFF!!

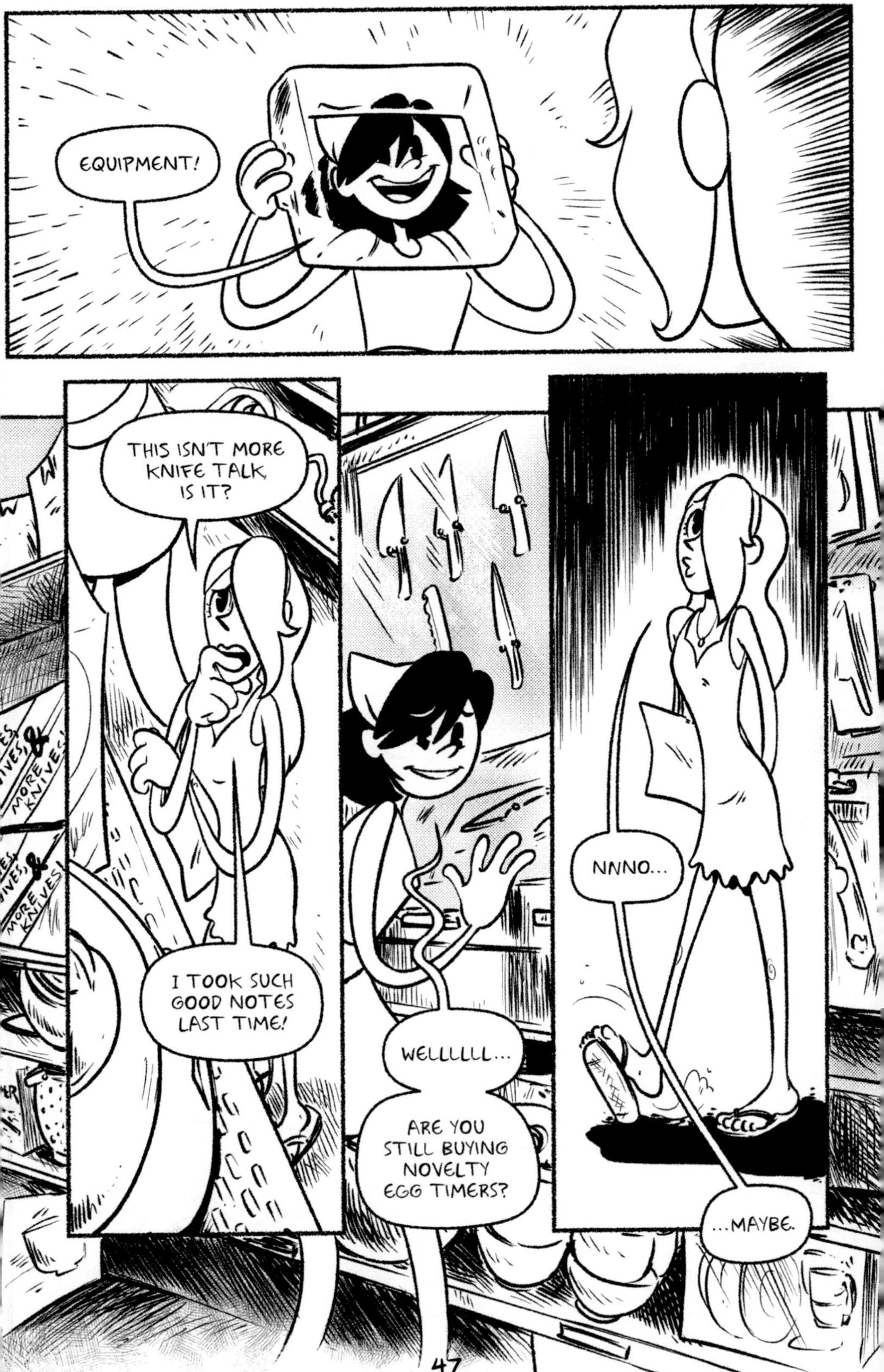
EQUIPMENT!
THIS ISN'T MORE KNIFE TALK, IS IT?
I TOOK SUCH GOOD NOTES LAST TIME!
WELLLLLL...
ARE YOU STILL BUYING NOVELTY EGG TIMERS?
NNNO...
...MAYBE.

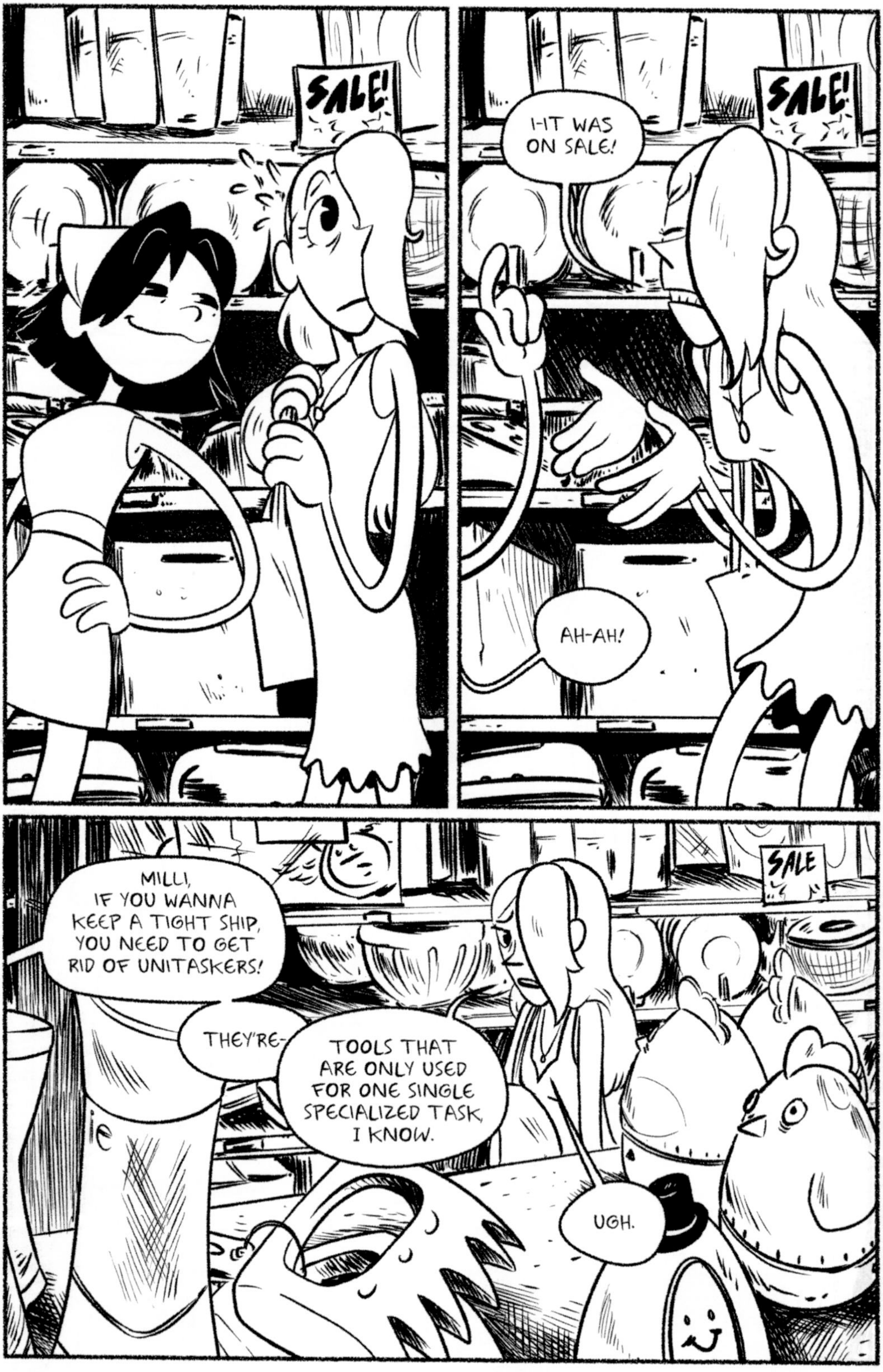
SALE!
SALE!
I-IT WAS ON SALE!
AH-AH!
MILLI, IF YOU WANNA KEEP A TIGHT SHIP, YOU NEED TO GET RID OF UNITASKERS!
THEY'RE-
TOOLS THAT ARE ONLY USED FOR ONE SINGLE SPECIALIZED TASK, I KNOW.
SALE
UGH.

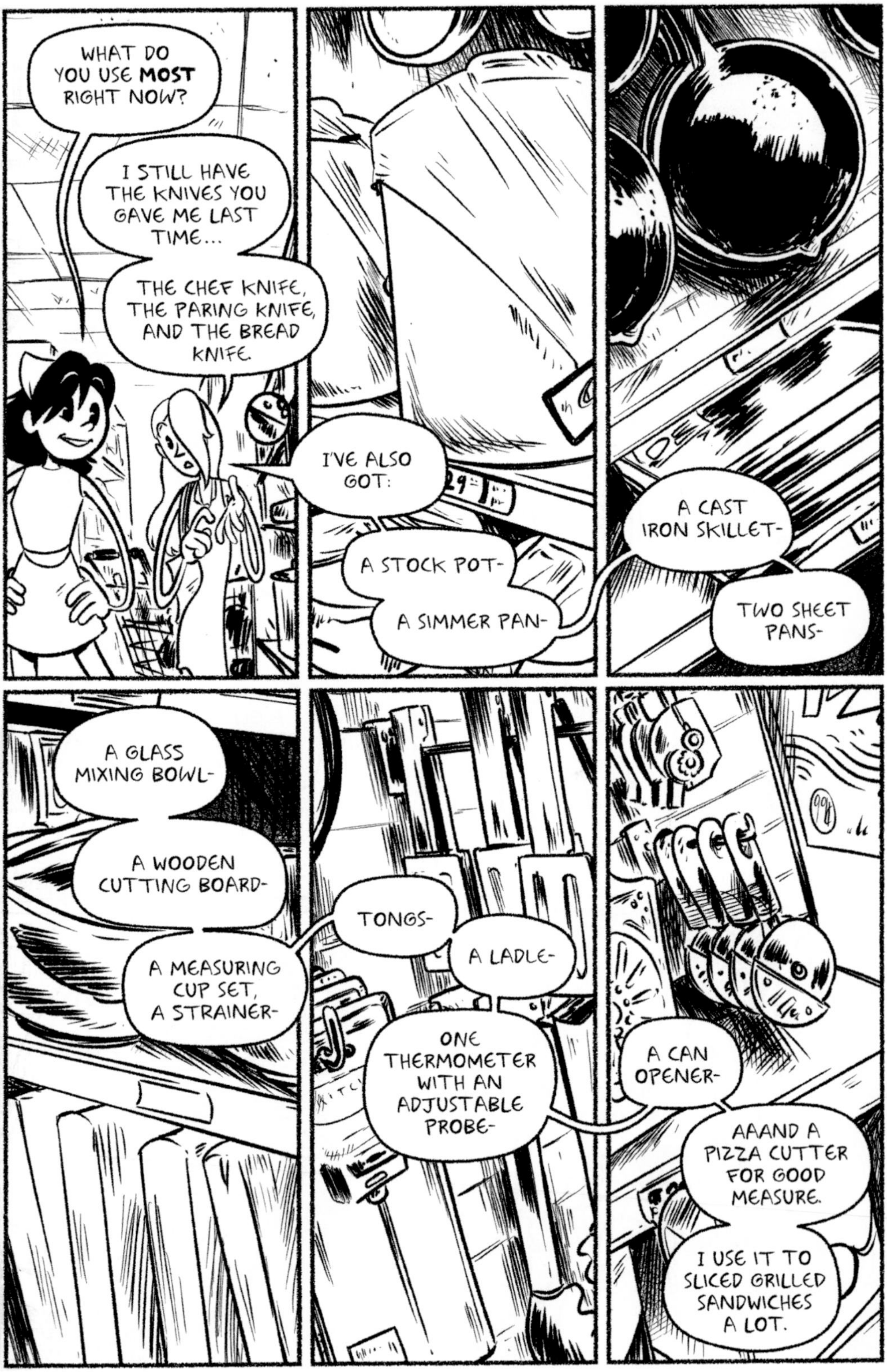
WHAT DO YOU USE **MOST** RIGHT NOW?
I STILL HAVE THE KNIVES YOU GAVE ME LAST TIME...
THE CHEF KNIFE, THE PARING KNIFE, AND THE BREAD KNIFE.
I'VE ALSO GOT:
A STOCK POT-
A SIMMER PAN-
A CAST IRON SKILLET-
TWO SHEET PANS-
A GLASS MIXING BOWL-
A WOODEN CUTTING BOARD-
A MEASURING CUP SET, A STRAINER-
TONGS-
A LADLE-
ONE THERMOMETER WITH AN ADJUSTABLE PROBE-
A CAN OPENER-
AAAND A PIZZA CUTTER FOR GOOD MEASURE.
I USE IT TO SLICED GRILLED SANDWICHES A LOT.

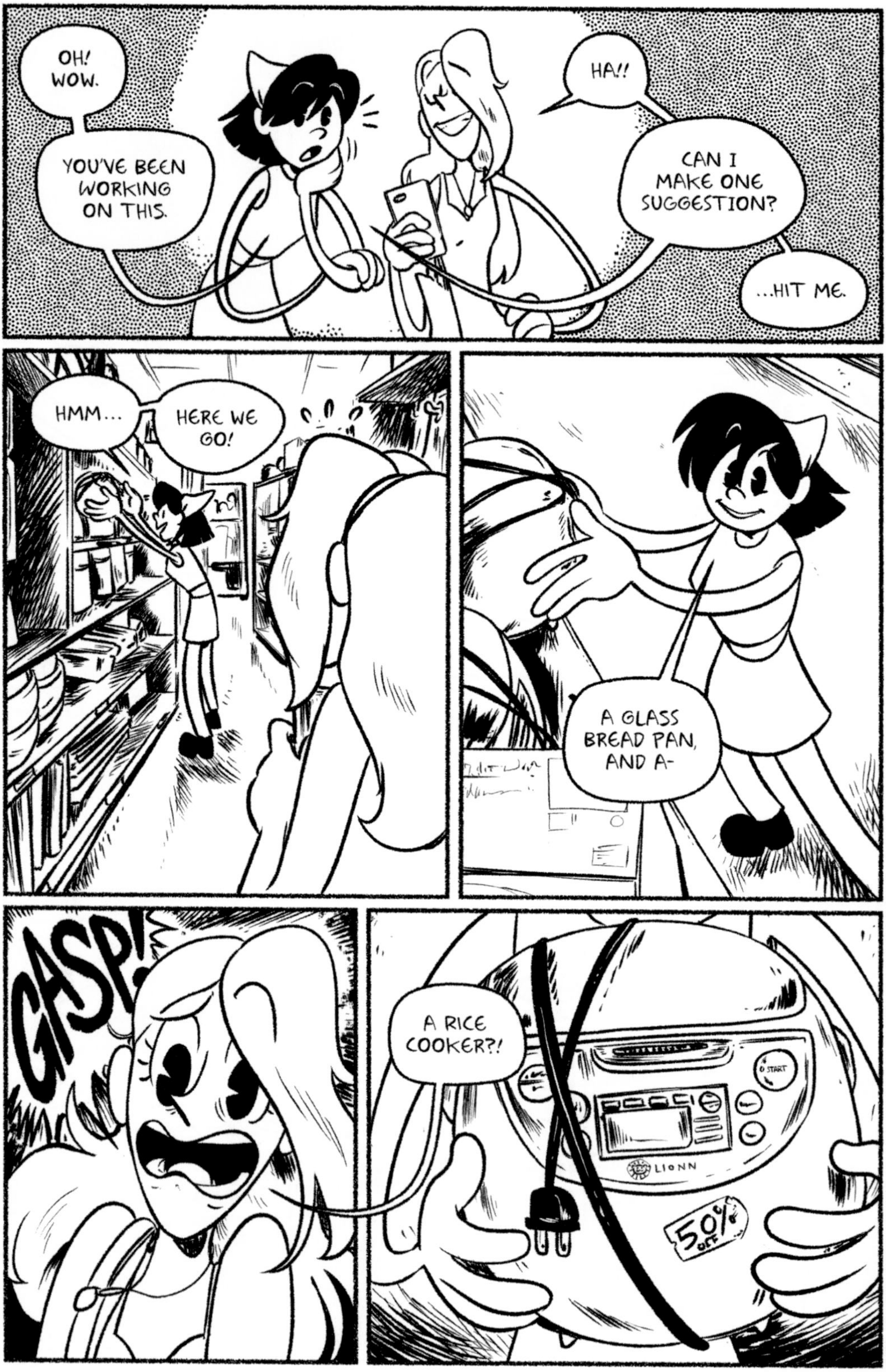
OH! WOW.
YOU'VE BEEN WORKING ON THIS.
HA!!
CAN I MAKE ONE SUGGESTION?
...HIT ME.
HMM...
HERE WE GO!
A GLASS BREAD PAN, AND A-
GASP!
A RICE COOKER?!
START
LIONN
50% OFF

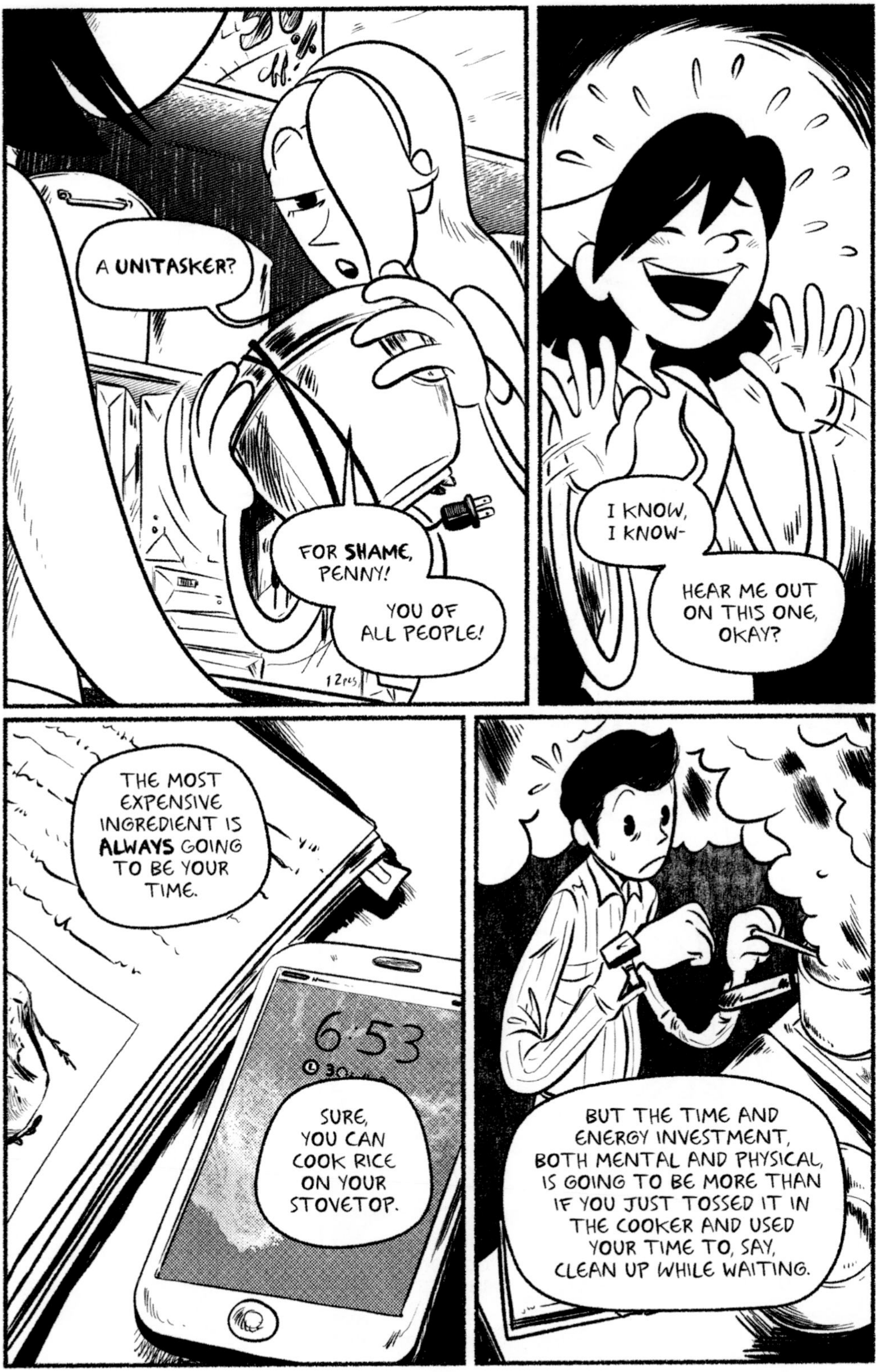
A UNITASKER?
FOR SHAME, PENNY!
YOU OF ALL PEOPLE!
I KNOW, I KNOW-
HEAR ME OUT ON THIS ONE, OKAY?
THE MOST EXPENSIVE INGREDIENT IS ALWAYS GOING TO BE YOUR TIME.
6:53
SURE, YOU CAN COOK RICE ON YOUR STOVETOP.
BUT THE TIME AND ENERGY INVESTMENT, BOTH MENTAL AND PHYSICAL, IS GOING TO BE MORE THAN IF YOU JUST TOSSED IT IN THE COOKER AND USED YOUR TIME TO, SAY, CLEAN UP WHILE WAITING.

see notes for more!

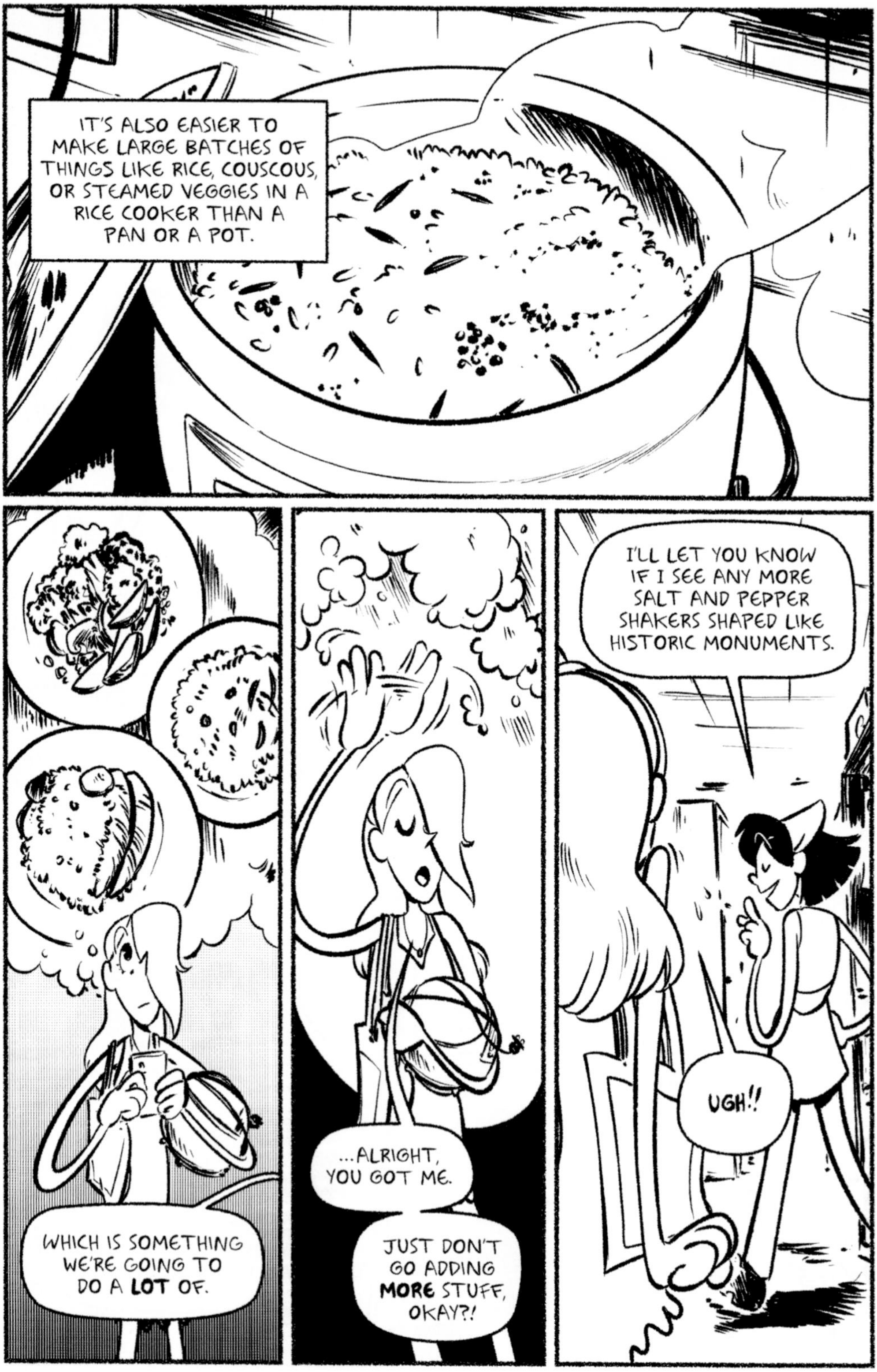

IT'S ALSO EASIER TO MAKE LARGE BATCHES OF THINGS LIKE RICE, COUSCOUS, OR STEAMED VEGGIES IN A RICE COOKER THAN A PAN OR A POT.
WHICH IS SOMETHING WE'RE GOING TO DO A **LOT** OF.
...ALRIGHT, YOU GOT ME.
JUST DON'T GO ADDING **MORE** STUFF, OKAY?!
I'LL LET YOU KNOW IF I SEE ANY MORE SALT AND PEPPER SHAKERS SHAPED LIKE HISTORIC MONUMENTS.
UGH!!

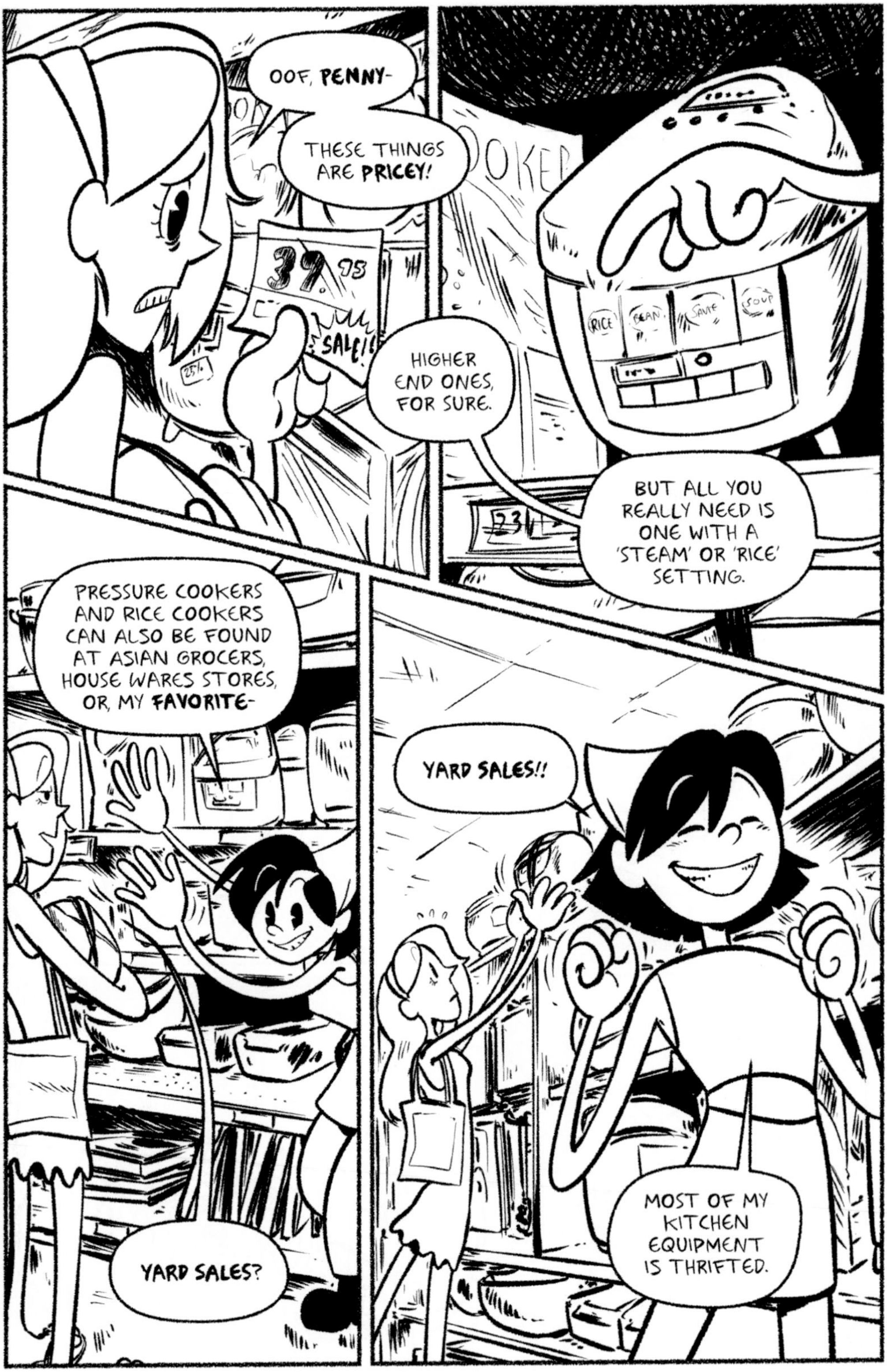
OOF, PENNY-
THESE THINGS ARE PRICEY!
SALE!!
HIGHER END ONES, FOR SURE.
BUT ALL YOU REALLY NEED IS ONE WITH A 'STEAM' OR 'RICE' SETTING.
PRESSURE COOKERS AND RICE COOKERS CAN ALSO BE FOUND AT ASIAN GROCERS, HOUSE WARES STORES, OR, MY FAVORITE-
YARD SALES!!
YARD SALES?
MOST OF MY KITCHEN EQUIPMENT IS THRIFTED.

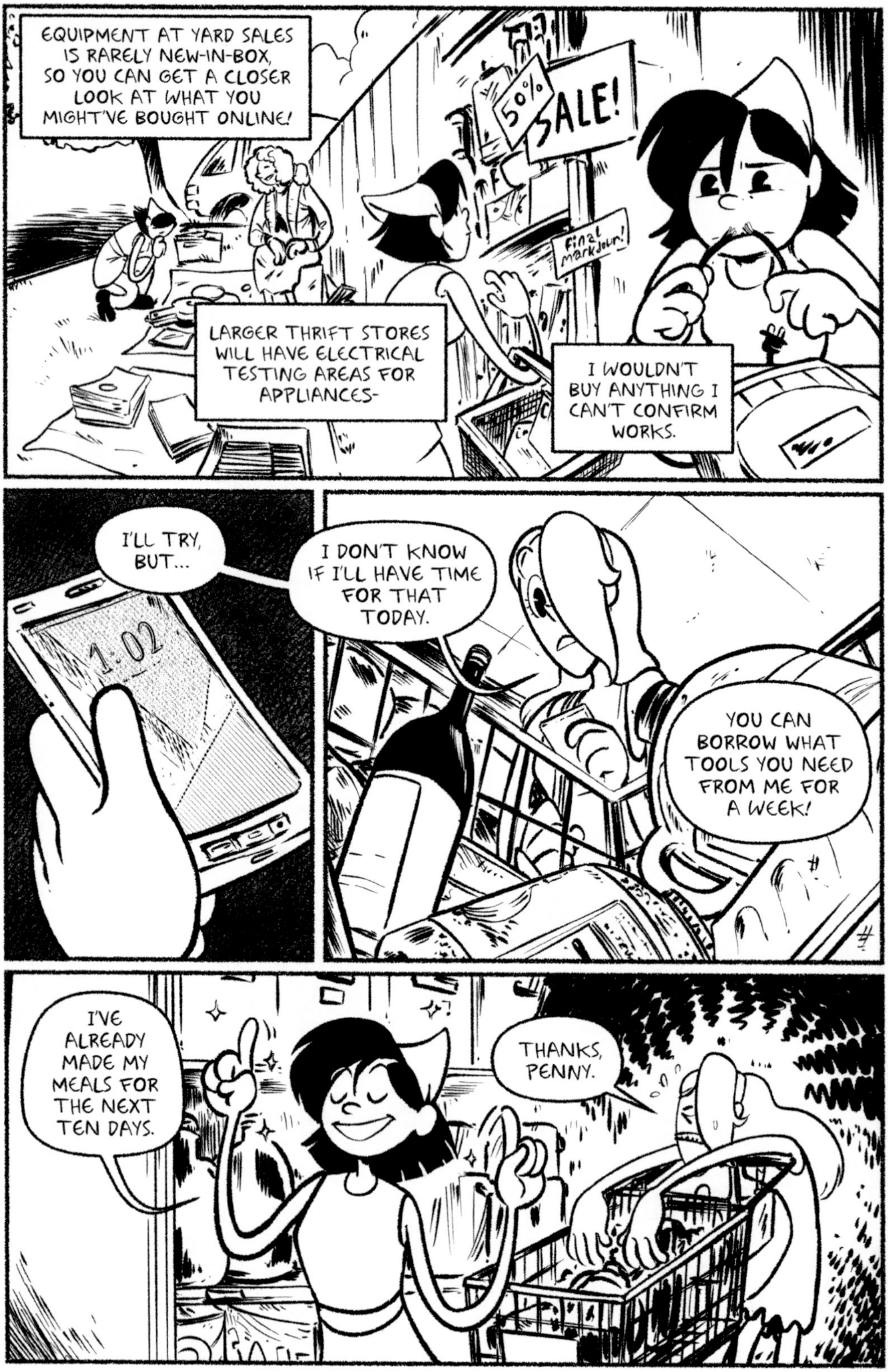
EQUIPMENT AT YARD SALES IS RARELY NEW-IN-BOX, SO YOU CAN GET A CLOSER LOOK AT WHAT YOU MIGHT'VE BOUGHT ONLINE!
50%
SALE!
Final markdown!
LARGER THRIFT STORES WILL HAVE ELECTRICAL TESTING AREAS FOR APPLIANCES-
I WOULDN'T BUY ANYTHING I CAN'T CONFIRM WORKS.
I'LL TRY, BUT...
1:02
I DON'T KNOW IF I'LL HAVE TIME FOR THAT TODAY.
YOU CAN BORROW WHAT TOOLS YOU NEED FROM ME FOR A WEEK!
I'VE ALREADY MADE MY MEALS FOR THE NEXT TEN DAYS.
THANKS, PENNY.

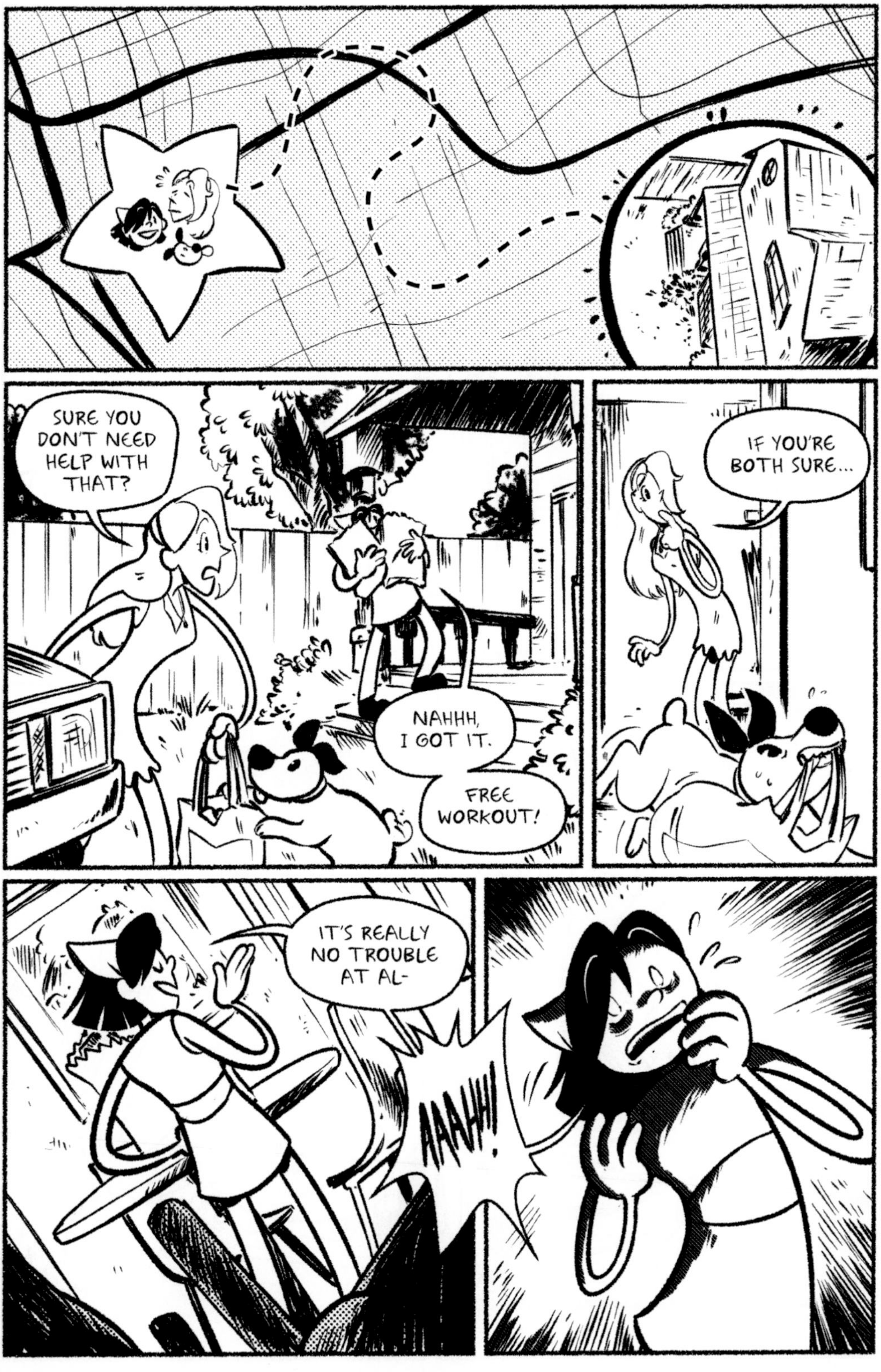
SURE YOU DON'T NEED HELP WITH THAT?
NAHHH, I GOT IT.
FREE WORKOUT!
IF YOU'RE BOTH SURE...
IT'S REALLY NO TROUBLE AT AL-
AAAHH!

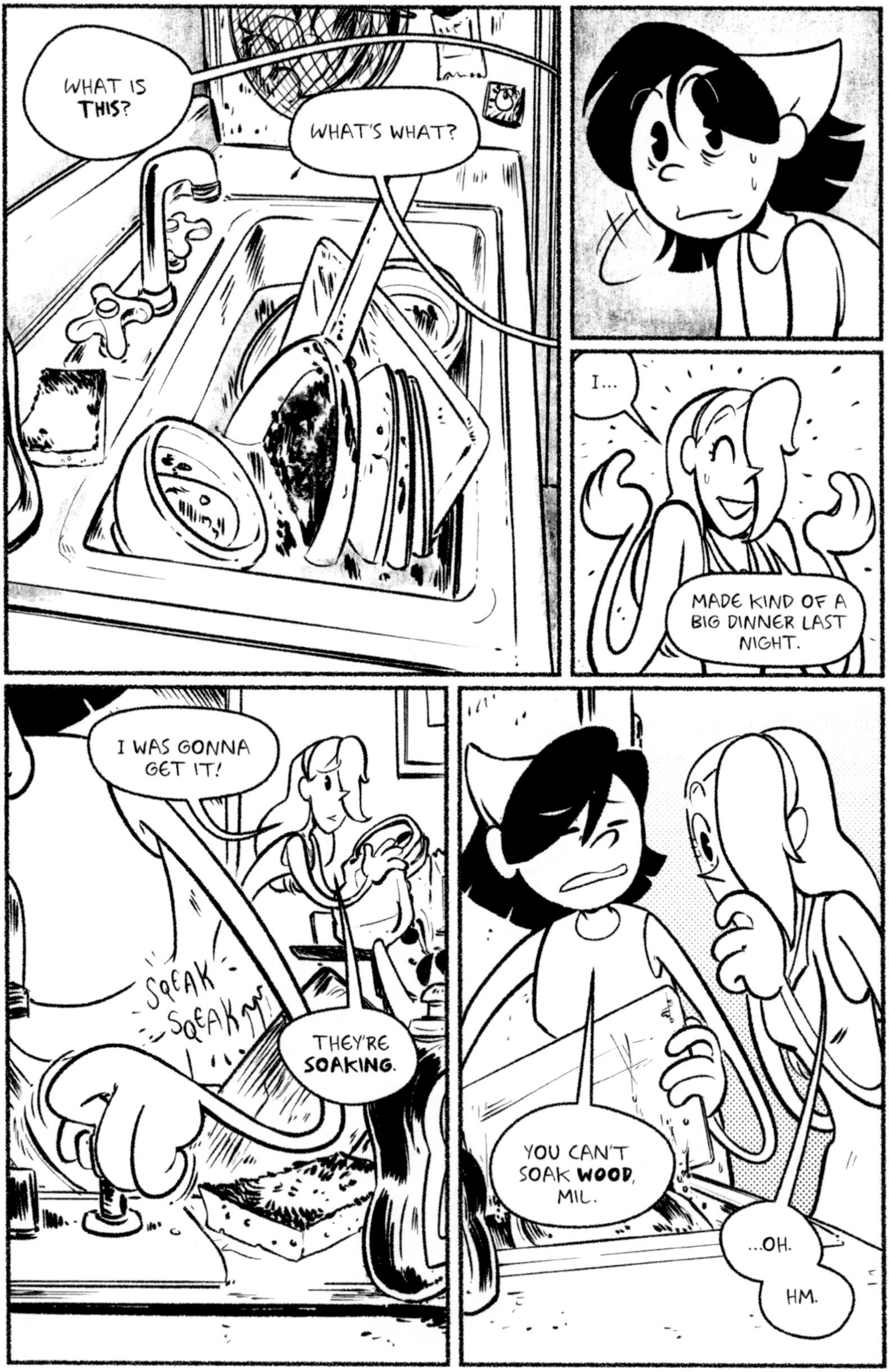
WHAT IS THIS?
WHAT'S WHAT?
I...
MADE KIND OF A BIG DINNER LAST NIGHT.
I WAS GONNA GET IT!
SQEAK SQEAK
THEY'RE SOAKING.
YOU CAN'T SOAK WOOD, MIL.
...OH.
HM.

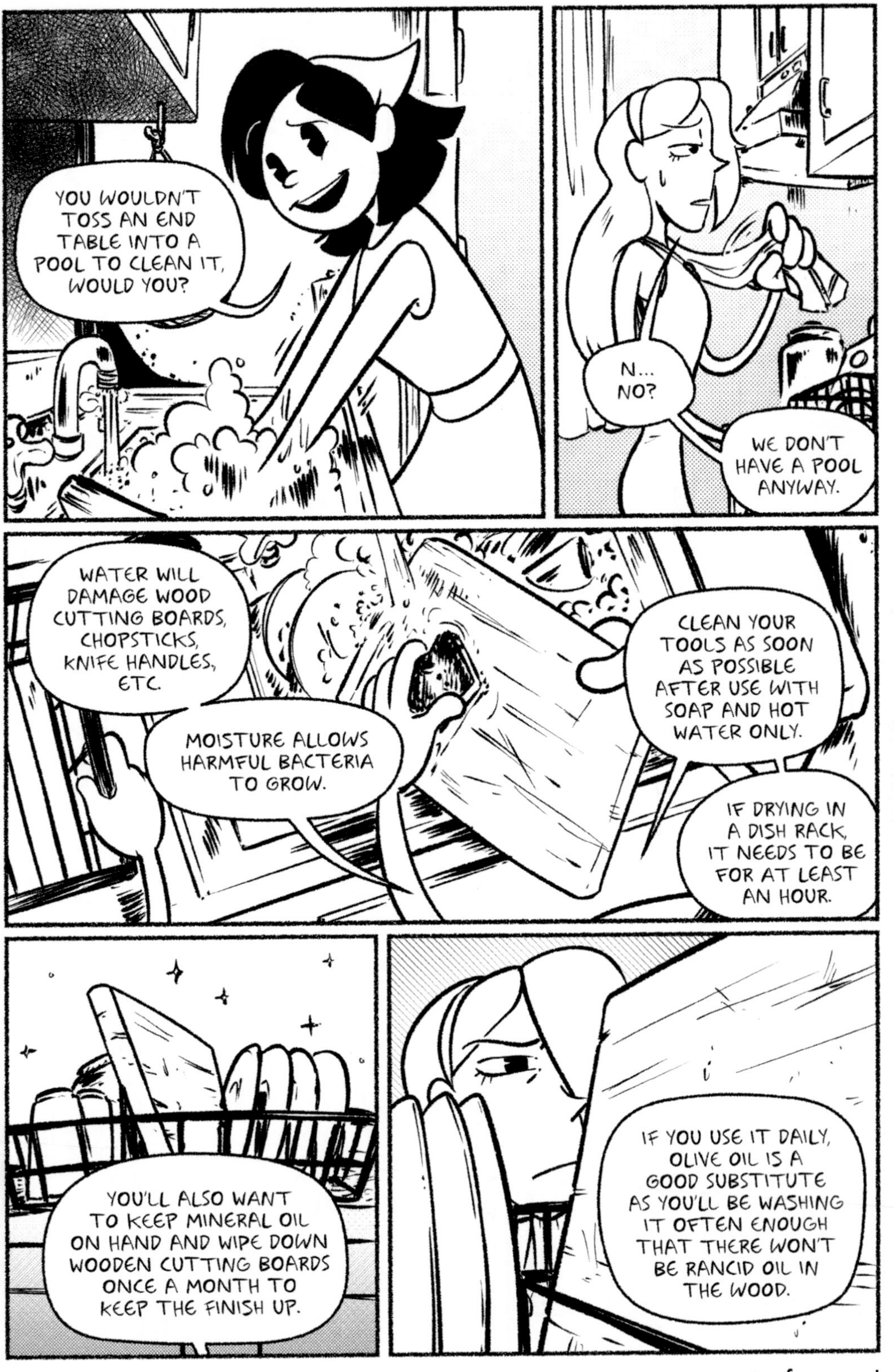
YOU WOULDN'T TOSS AN END TABLE INTO A POOL TO CLEAN IT, WOULD YOU?
N... NO?
WE DON'T HAVE A POOL ANYWAY.
WATER WILL DAMAGE WOOD CUTTING BOARDS, CHOPSTICKS, KNIFE HANDLES, ETC.
MOISTURE ALLOWS HARMFUL BACTERIA TO GROW.
CLEAN YOUR TOOLS AS SOON AS POSSIBLE AFTER USE WITH SOAP AND HOT WATER ONLY.
IF DRYING IN A DISH RACK, IT NEEDS TO BE FOR AT LEAST AN HOUR.
YOU'LL ALSO WANT TO KEEP MINERAL OIL ON HAND AND WIPE DOWN WOODEN CUTTING BOARDS ONCE A MONTH TO KEEP THE FINISH UP.
IF YOU USE IT DAILY, OLIVE OIL IS A GOOD SUBSTITUTE AS YOU'LL BE WASHING IT OFTEN ENOUGH THAT THERE WON'T BE RANCID OIL IN THE WOOD.

see notes for more!

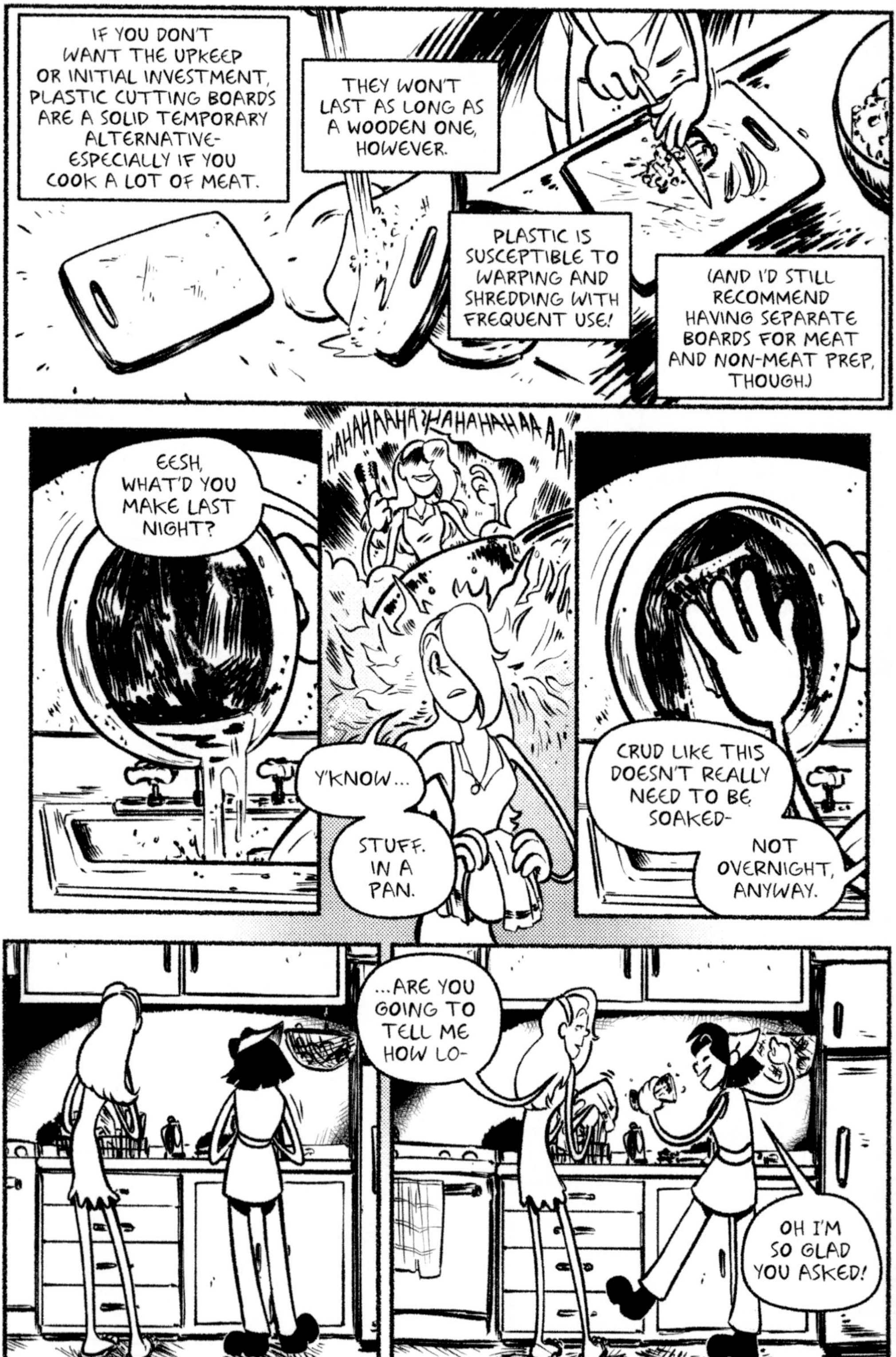
IF YOU DON'T WANT THE UPKEEP OR INITIAL INVESTMENT, PLASTIC CUTTING BOARDS ARE A SOLID TEMPORARY ALTERNATIVE- ESPECIALLY IF YOU COOK A LOT OF MEAT.
THEY WON'T LAST AS LONG AS A WOODEN ONE, HOWEVER.
PLASTIC IS SUSCEPTIBLE TO WARPING AND SHREDDING WITH FREQUENT USE!
(AND I'D STILL RECOMMEND HAVING SEPARATE BOARDS FOR MEAT AND NON-MEAT PREP, THOUGH.)
EESH, WHAT'D YOU MAKE LAST NIGHT?
HAHAHAAHAHAHAHAHAHAAAA
Y'KNOW...
STUFF. IN A PAN.
CRUD LIKE THIS DOESN'T REALLY NEED TO BE SOAKED-
NOT OVERNIGHT, ANYWAY.
...ARE YOU GOING TO TELL ME HOW LO-
OH I'M SO GLAD YOU ASKED!

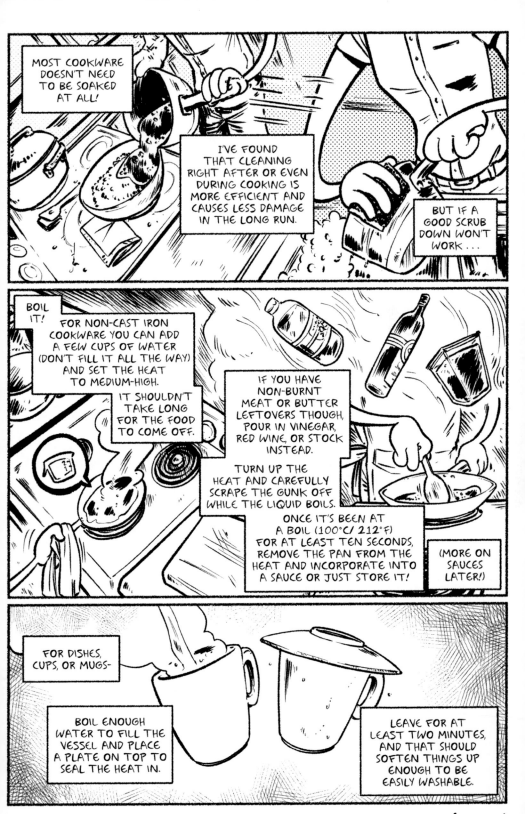

MOST COOKWARE DOESN'T NEED TO BE SOAKED AT ALL!

I'VE FOUND THAT CLEANING RIGHT AFTER OR EVEN DURING COOKING IS MORE EFFICIENT AND CAUSES LESS DAMAGE IN THE LONG RUN.

BUT IF A GOOD SCRUB DOWN WON'T WORK . . .

BOIL IT! FOR NON-CAST IRON COOKWARE YOU CAN ADD A FEW CUPS OF WATER (DON'T FILL IT ALL THE WAY) AND SET THE HEAT TO MEDIUM-HIGH.

IT SHOULDN'T TAKE LONG FOR THE FOOD TO COME OFF.

IF YOU HAVE NON-BURNT MEAT OR BUTTER LEFTOVERS THOUGH, POUR IN VINEGAR, RED WINE, OR STOCK INSTEAD.

TURN UP THE HEAT AND CAREFULLY SCRAPE THE GUNK OFF WHILE THE LIQUID BOILS.

ONCE IT'S BEEN AT A BOIL (100°C/ 212°F) FOR AT LEAST TEN SECONDS, REMOVE THE PAN FROM THE HEAT AND INCORPORATE INTO A SAUCE OR JUST STORE IT!

(MORE ON SAUCES LATER!)

FOR DISHES, CUPS, OR MUGS—

BOIL ENOUGH WATER TO FILL THE VESSEL AND PLACE A PLATE ON TOP TO SEAL THE HEAT IN.

LEAVE FOR AT LEAST TWO MINUTES, AND THAT SHOULD SOFTEN THINGS UP ENOUGH TO BE EASILY WASHABLE.

see notes for more!

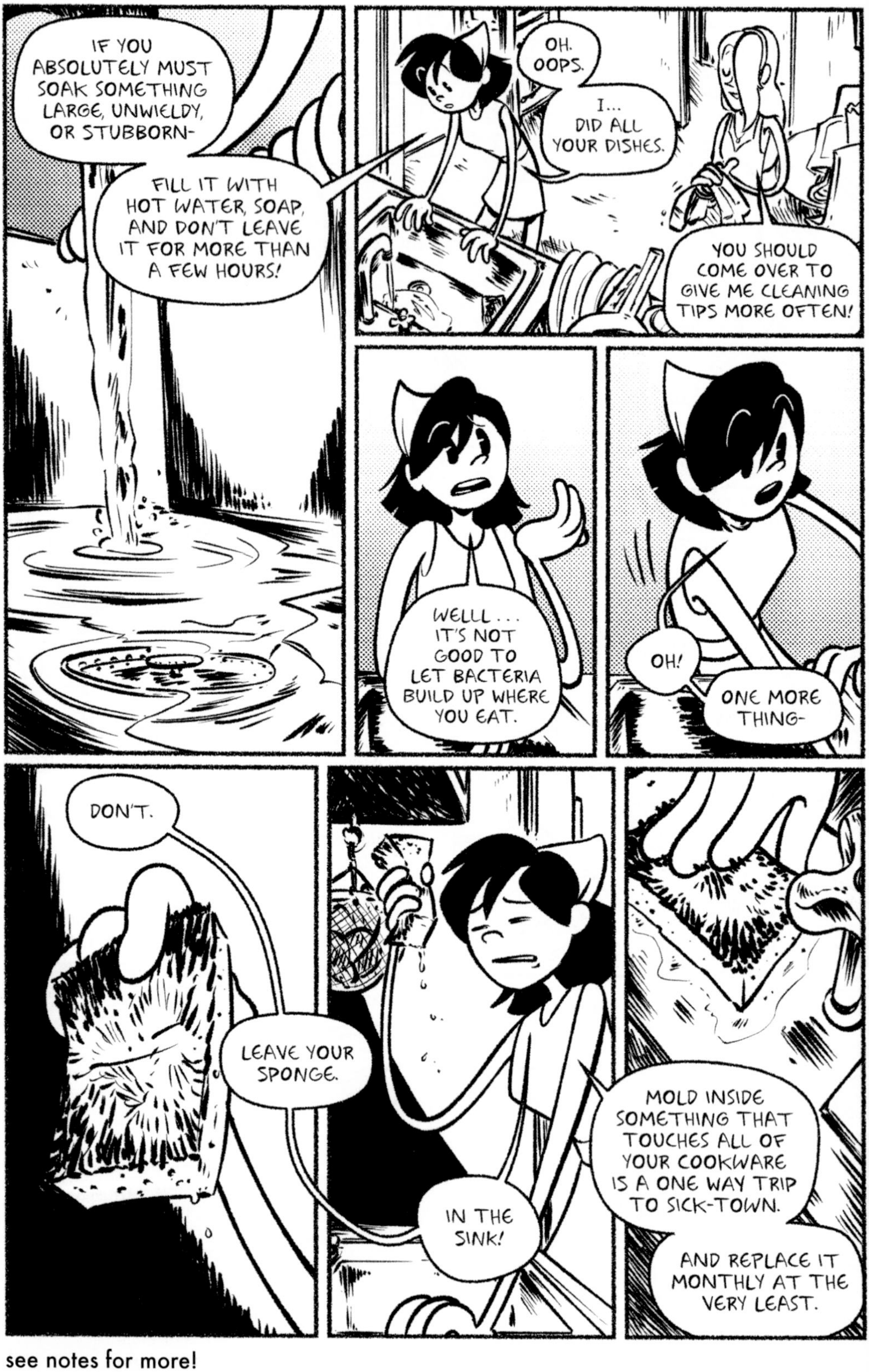
IF YOU ABSOLUTELY MUST SOAK SOMETHING LARGE, UNWIELDY, OR STUBBORN-
FILL IT WITH HOT WATER, SOAP, AND DON'T LEAVE IT FOR MORE THAN A FEW HOURS!
OH. OOPS.
I... DID ALL YOUR DISHES.
YOU SHOULD COME OVER TO GIVE ME CLEANING TIPS MORE OFTEN!
WELLL . . . IT'S NOT GOOD TO LET BACTERIA BUILD UP WHERE YOU EAT.
OH!
ONE MORE THING-
DON'T.
LEAVE YOUR SPONGE.
IN THE SINK!
MOLD INSIDE SOMETHING THAT TOUCHES ALL OF YOUR COOKWARE IS A ONE WAY TRIP TO SICK-TOWN.
AND REPLACE IT MONTHLY AT THE VERY LEAST.

see notes for more!

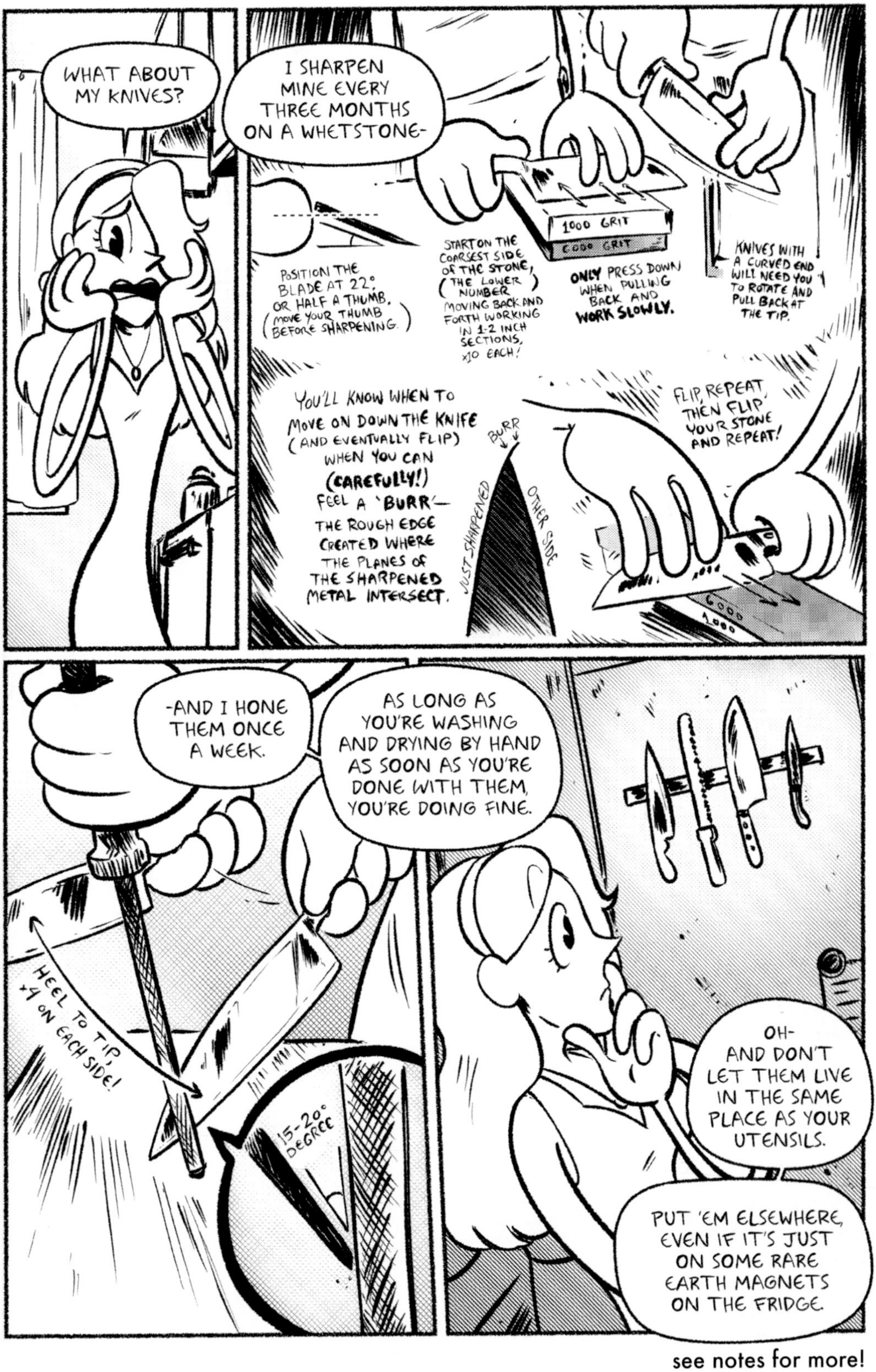
WHAT ABOUT MY KNIVES?
I SHARPEN MINE EVERY THREE MONTHS ON A WHETSTONE-
1000 GRIT
6000 GRIT
POSITION THE BLADE AT 22°, OR HALF A THUMB. (MOVE YOUR THUMB BEFORE SHARPENING.)
START ON THE COARSEST SIDE OF THE STONE, (THE LOWER NUMBER) MOVING BACK AND FORTH WORKING IN 1-2 INCH SECTIONS, x10 EACH!
ONLY PRESS DOWN WHEN PULLING BACK AND WORK SLOWLY.
KNIVES WITH A CURVED END WILL NEED YOU TO ROTATE AND PULL BACK AT THE TIP.
YOU'LL KNOW WHEN TO MOVE ON DOWN THE KNIFE (AND EVENTUALLY FLIP) WHEN YOU CAN (CAREFULLY!) FEEL A 'BURR'— THE ROUGH EDGE CREATED WHERE THE PLANES OF THE SHARPENED METAL INTERSECT.
BURR
JUST SHARPENED
OTHER SIDE
FLIP, REPEAT, THEN FLIP YOUR STONE AND REPEAT!
6000
1000
-AND I HONE THEM ONCE A WEEK.
AS LONG AS YOU'RE WASHING AND DRYING BY HAND AS SOON AS YOU'RE DONE WITH THEM, YOU'RE DOING FINE.
HEEL TO TIP, x4 ON EACH SIDE!
15-20° DEGREE
OH- AND DON'T LET THEM LIVE IN THE SAME PLACE AS YOUR UTENSILS.
PUT 'EM ELSEWHERE, EVEN IF IT'S JUST ON SOME RARE EARTH MAGNETS ON THE FRIDGE.

see notes for more!

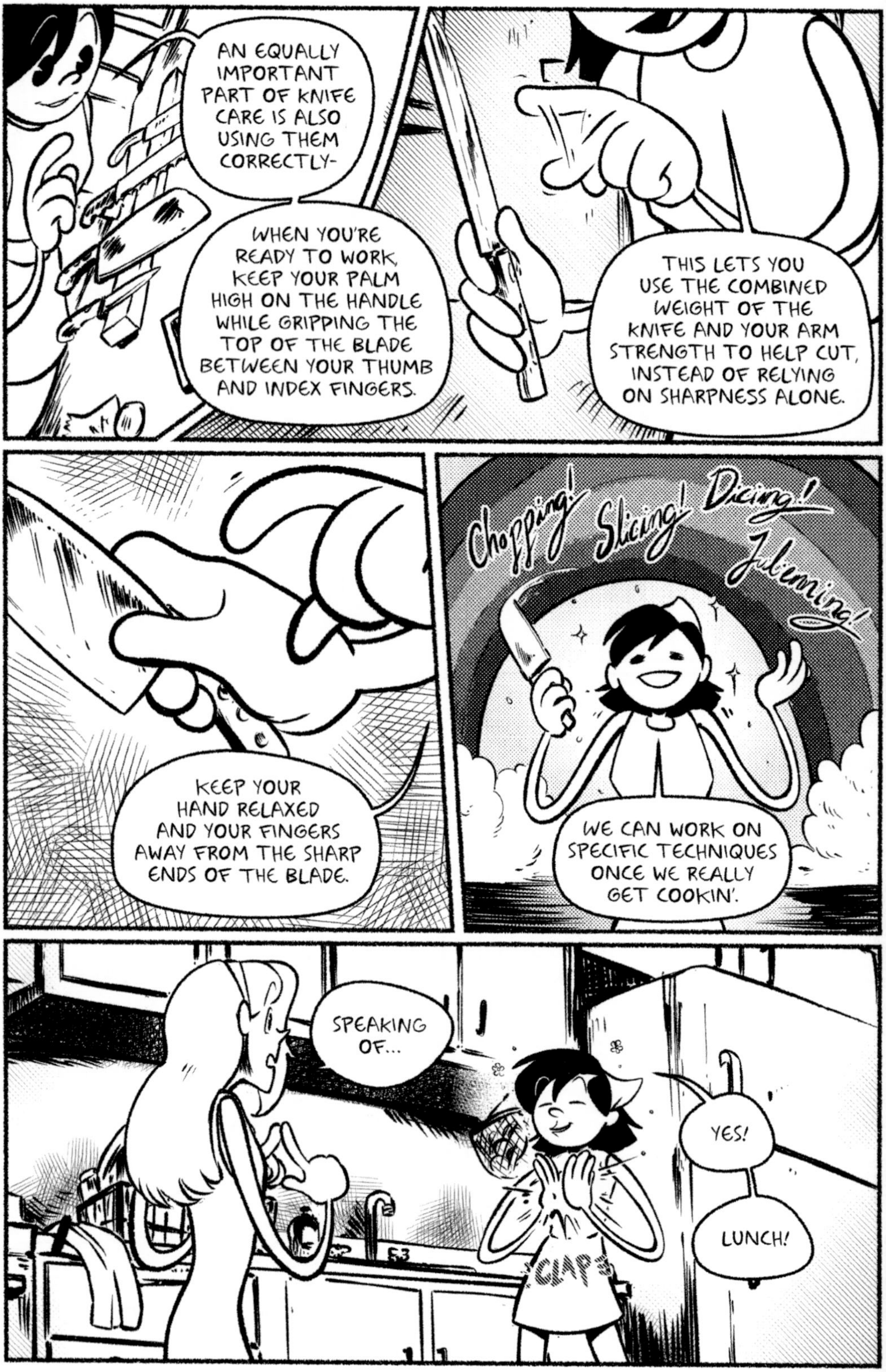
AN EQUALLY IMPORTANT PART OF KNIFE CARE IS ALSO USING THEM CORRECTLY-
WHEN YOU'RE READY TO WORK, KEEP YOUR PALM HIGH ON THE HANDLE WHILE GRIPPING THE TOP OF THE BLADE BETWEEN YOUR THUMB AND INDEX FINGERS.
THIS LETS YOU USE THE COMBINED WEIGHT OF THE KNIFE AND YOUR ARM STRENGTH TO HELP CUT, INSTEAD OF RELYING ON SHARPNESS ALONE.
KEEP YOUR HAND RELAXED AND YOUR FINGERS AWAY FROM THE SHARP ENDS OF THE BLADE.
Chopping! Slicing! Dicing! Julienning!
WE CAN WORK ON SPECIFIC TECHNIQUES ONCE WE REALLY GET COOKIN'.
SPEAKING OF...
YES!
LUNCH!
CLAP

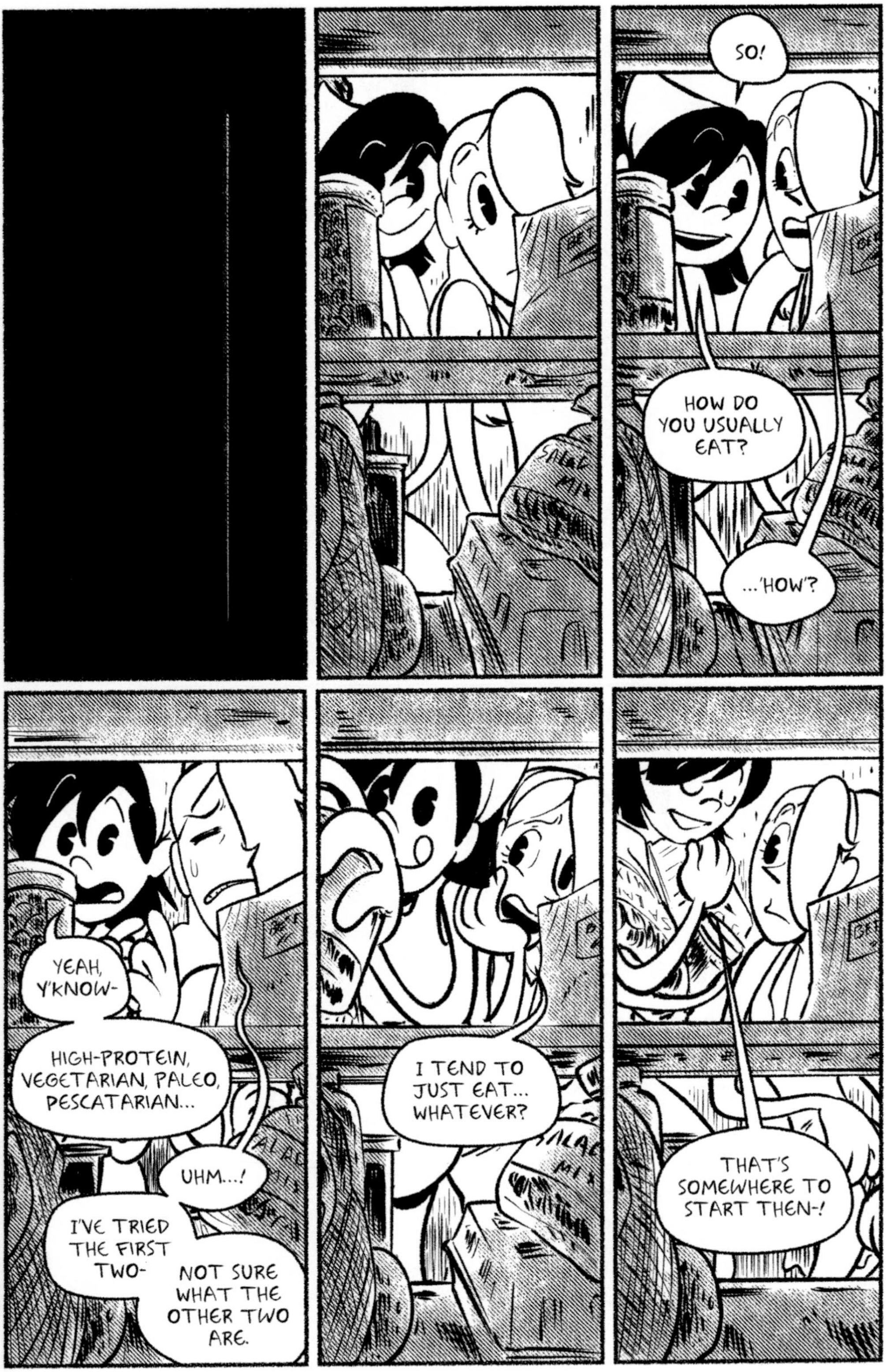
SO!
HOW DO YOU USUALLY EAT?
...'HOW'?
YEAH, Y'KNOW-
HIGH-PROTEIN, VEGETARIAN, PALEO, PESCATARIAN...
UHM...!
I'VE TRIED THE FIRST TWO-
NOT SURE WHAT THE OTHER TWO ARE.
I TEND TO JUST EAT... WHATEVER?
THAT'S SOMEWHERE TO START THEN-!

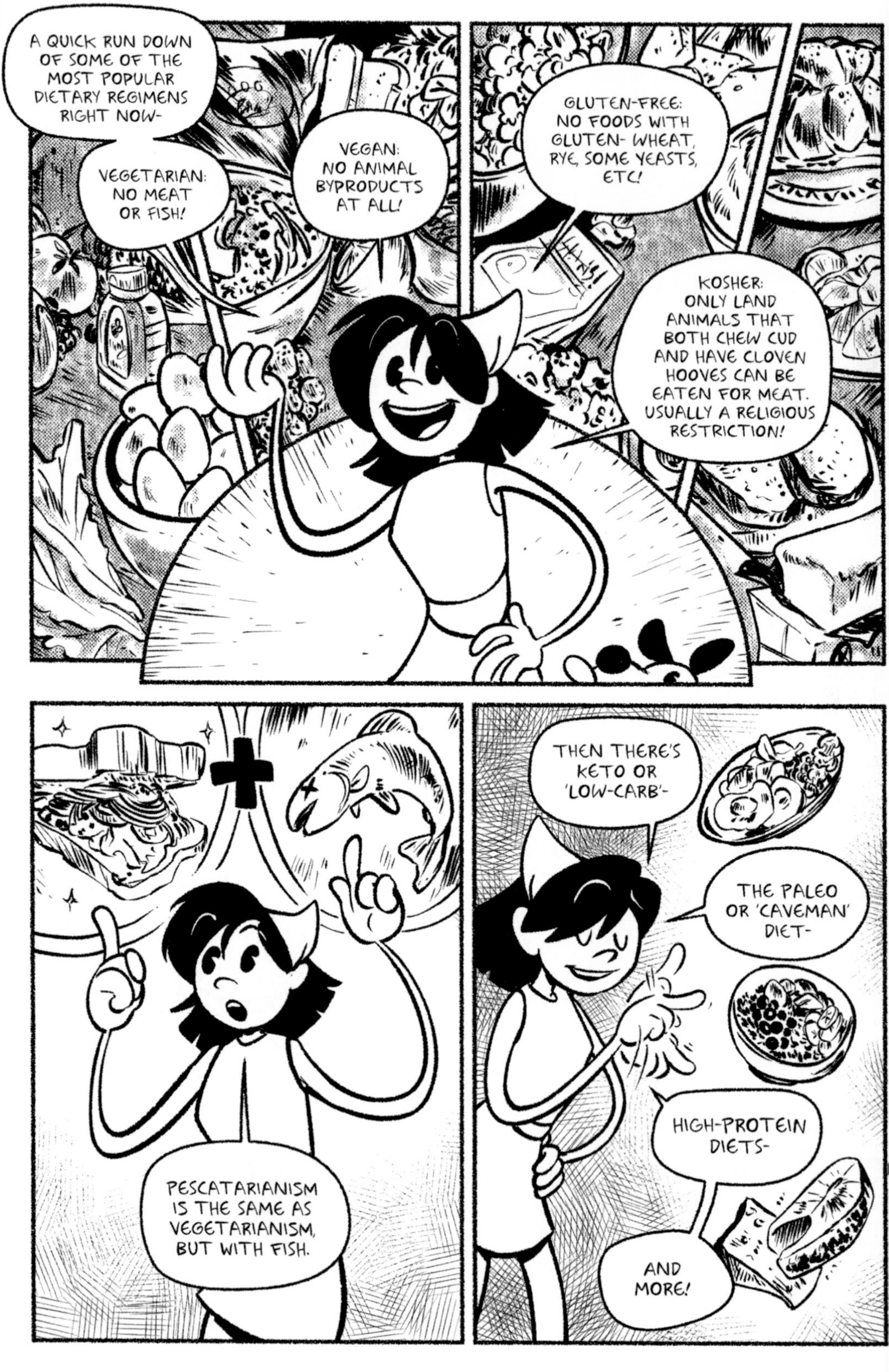
A QUICK RUN DOWN OF SOME OF THE MOST POPULAR DIETARY REGIMENS RIGHT NOW-
VEGETARIAN: NO MEAT OR FISH!
VEGAN: NO ANIMAL BYPRODUCTS AT ALL!
GLUTEN-FREE: NO FOODS WITH GLUTEN- WHEAT, RYE, SOME YEASTS, ETC!
KOSHER: ONLY LAND ANIMALS THAT BOTH CHEW CUD AND HAVE CLOVEN HOOVES CAN BE EATEN FOR MEAT. USUALLY A RELIGIOUS RESTRICTION!
PESCATARIANISM IS THE SAME AS VEGETARIANISM, BUT WITH FISH.
THEN THERE'S KETO OR 'LOW-CARB'-
THE PALEO OR 'CAVEMAN' DIET-
HIGH-PROTEIN DIETS-
AND MORE!

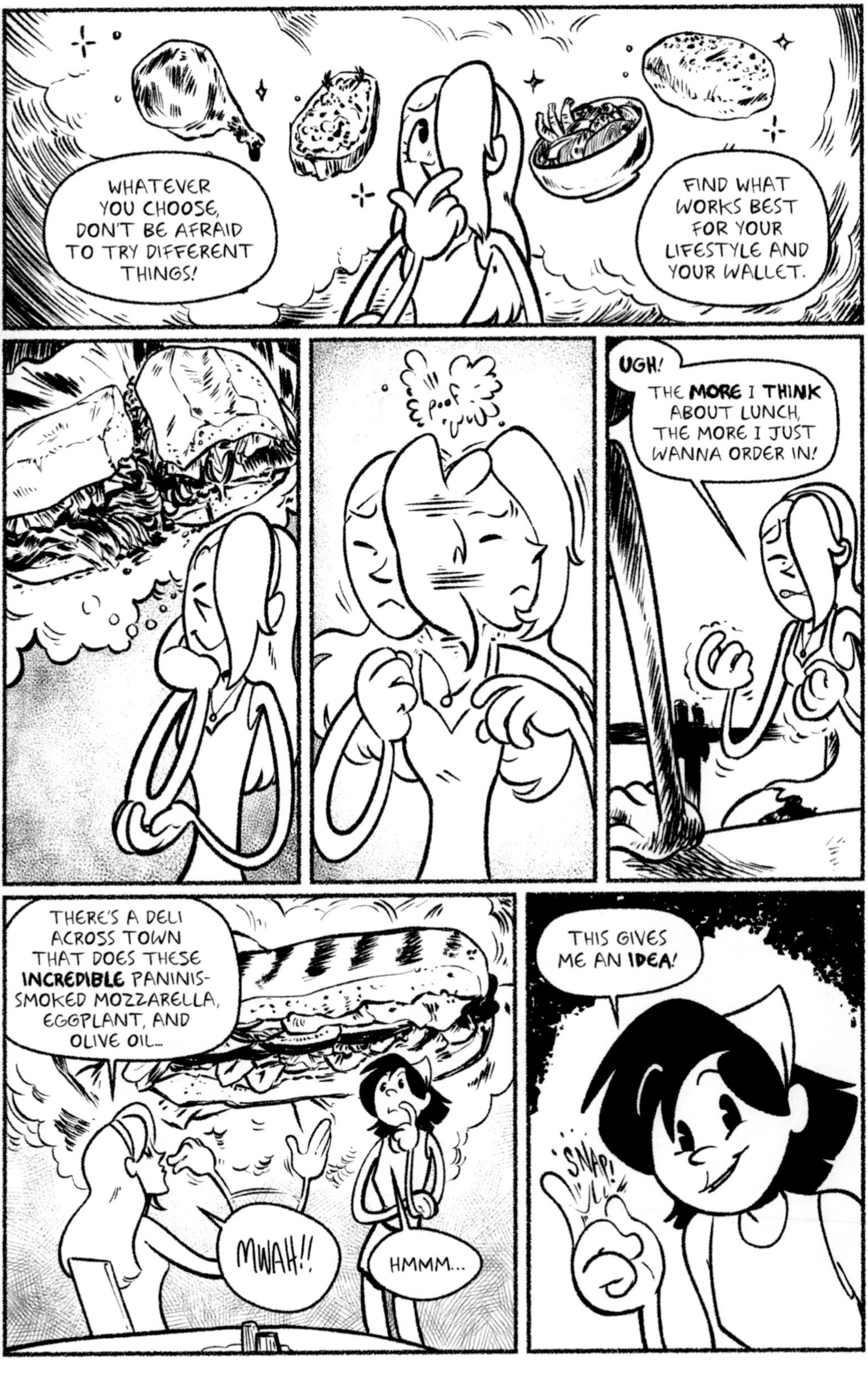
WHATEVER YOU CHOOSE, DON'T BE AFRAID TO TRY DIFFERENT THINGS!
FIND WHAT WORKS BEST FOR YOUR LIFESTYLE AND YOUR WALLET.
poof
UGH!
THE MORE I THINK ABOUT LUNCH, THE MORE I JUST WANNA ORDER IN!
THERE'S A DELI ACROSS TOWN THAT DOES THESE INCREDIBLE PANINIS-SMOKED MOZZARELLA, EGGPLANT, AND OLIVE OIL...
MWAH!!
HMMM...
THIS GIVES ME AN IDEA!
SNAP!

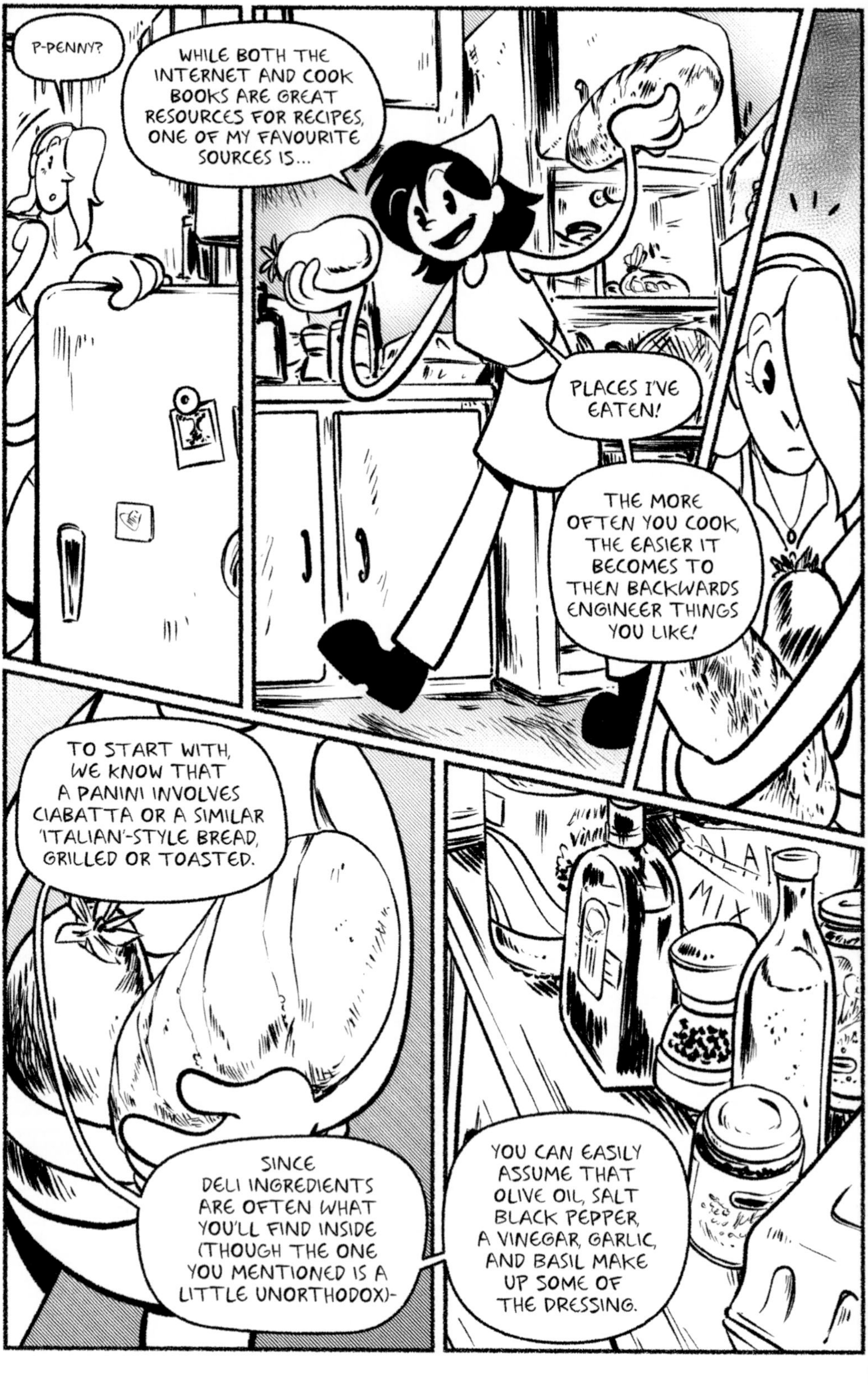
P-PENNY?
WHILE BOTH THE INTERNET AND COOK BOOKS ARE GREAT RESOURCES FOR RECIPES, ONE OF MY FAVOURITE SOURCES IS...
PLACES I'VE EATEN!
THE MORE OFTEN YOU COOK, THE EASIER IT BECOMES TO THEN BACKWARDS ENGINEER THINGS YOU LIKE!
TO START WITH, WE KNOW THAT A PANINI INVOLVES CIABATTA OR A SIMILAR 'ITALIAN'-STYLE BREAD, GRILLED OR TOASTED.
SALAD MIX
SINCE DELI INGREDIENTS ARE OFTEN WHAT YOU'LL FIND INSIDE (THOUGH THE ONE YOU MENTIONED IS A LITTLE UNORTHODOX)-
YOU CAN EASILY ASSUME THAT OLIVE OIL, SALT BLACK PEPPER, A VINEGAR, GARLIC, AND BASIL MAKE UP SOME OF THE DRESSING.

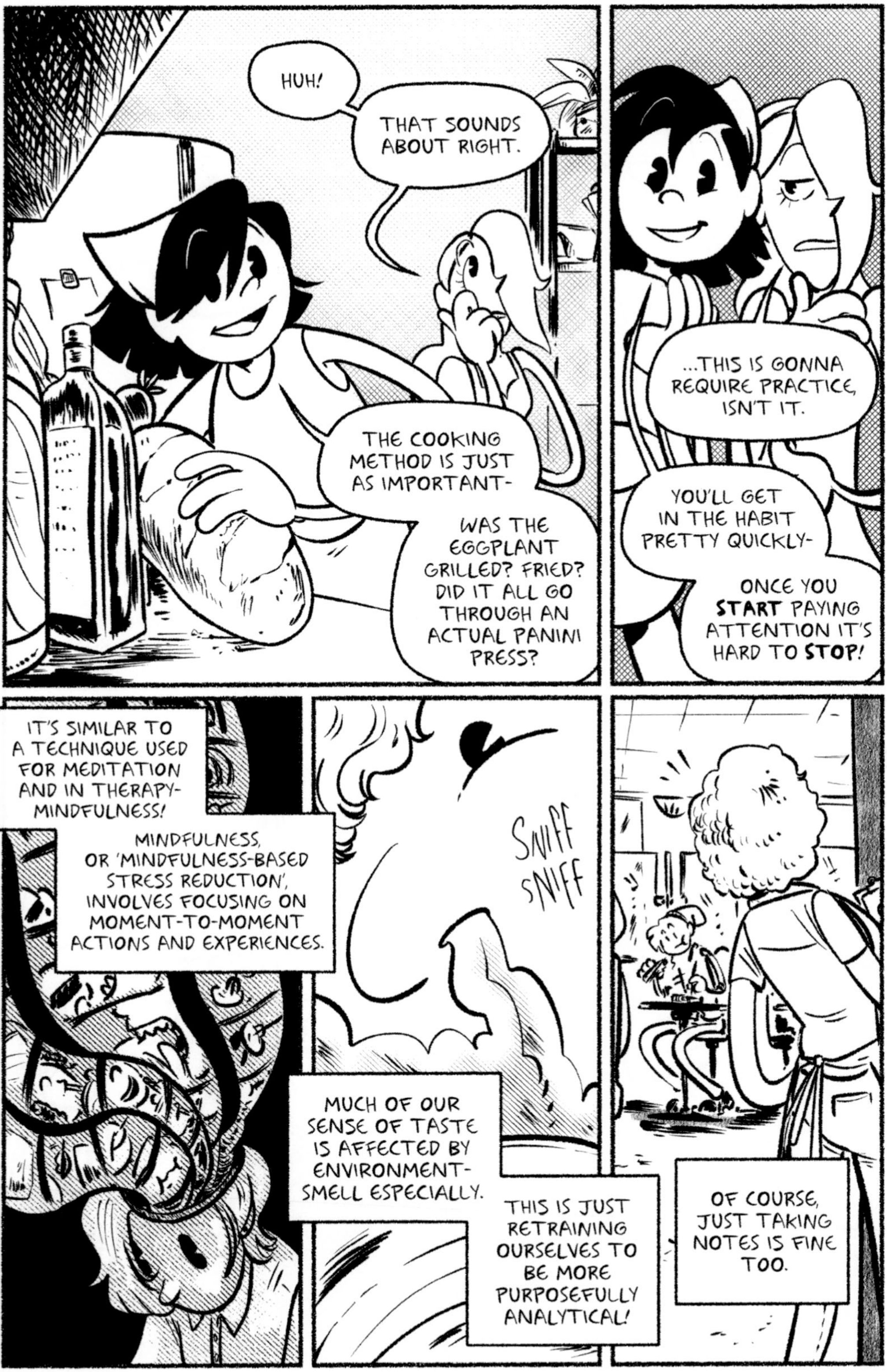
HUH!
THAT SOUNDS ABOUT RIGHT.
THE COOKING METHOD IS JUST AS IMPORTANT-
WAS THE EGGPLANT GRILLED? FRIED? DID IT ALL GO THROUGH AN ACTUAL PANINI PRESS?
...THIS IS GONNA REQUIRE PRACTICE, ISN'T IT.
YOU'LL GET IN THE HABIT PRETTY QUICKLY-
ONCE YOU **START** PAYING ATTENTION IT'S HARD TO **STOP**!
IT'S SIMILAR TO A TECHNIQUE USED FOR MEDITATION AND IN THERAPY- MINDFULNESS!
MINDFULNESS, OR 'MINDFULNESS-BASED STRESS REDUCTION', INVOLVES FOCUSING ON MOMENT-TO-MOMENT ACTIONS AND EXPERIENCES.
SNIFF SNIFF
MUCH OF OUR SENSE OF TASTE IS AFFECTED BY ENVIRONMENT- SMELL ESPECIALLY.
THIS IS JUST RETRAINING OURSELVES TO BE MORE PURPOSEFULLY ANALYTICAL!
OF COURSE, JUST TAKING NOTES IS FINE TOO.

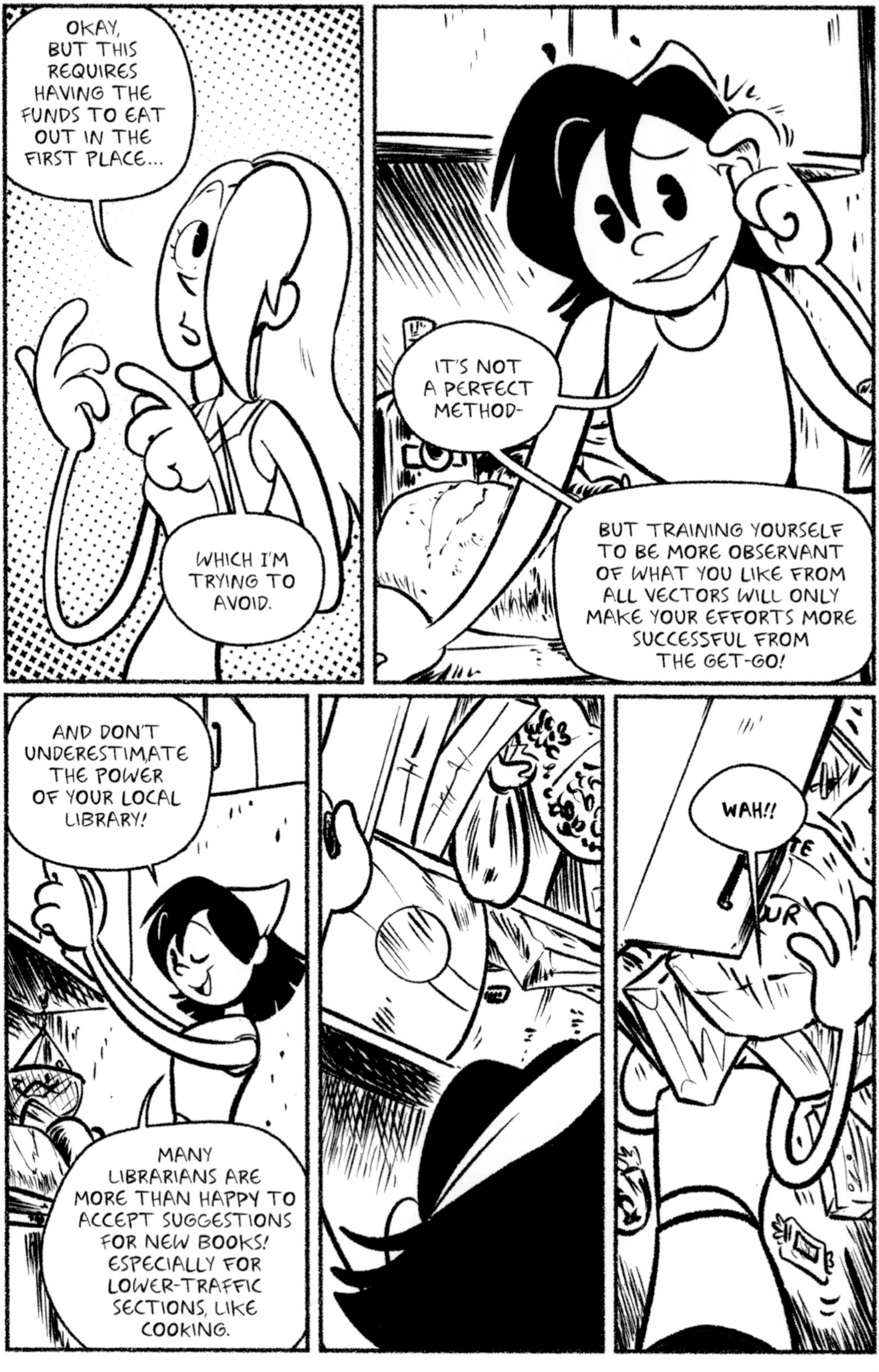
OKAY, BUT THIS REQUIRES HAVING THE FUNDS TO EAT OUT IN THE FIRST PLACE...
WHICH I'M TRYING TO AVOID.
IT'S NOT A PERFECT METHOD-
BUT TRAINING YOURSELF TO BE MORE OBSERVANT OF WHAT YOU LIKE FROM ALL VECTORS WILL ONLY MAKE YOUR EFFORTS MORE SUCCESSFUL FROM THE GET-GO!
AND DON'T UNDERESTIMATE THE POWER OF YOUR LOCAL LIBRARY!
MANY LIBRARIANS ARE MORE THAN HAPPY TO ACCEPT SUGGESTIONS FOR NEW BOOKS! ESPECIALLY FOR LOWER-TRAFFIC SECTIONS, LIKE COOKING.
WAH!!

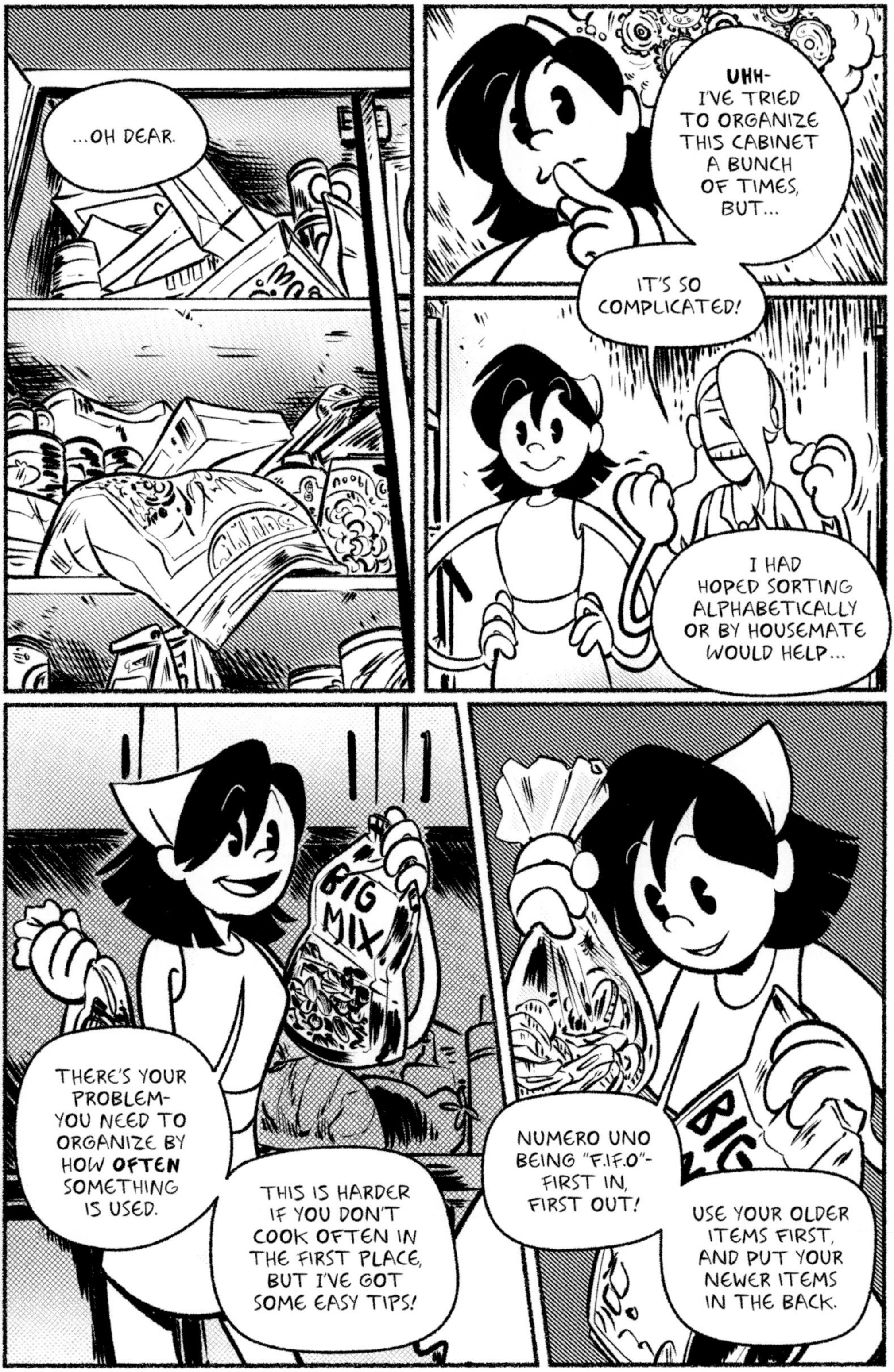
...OH DEAR.
UHH- I'VE TRIED TO ORGANIZE THIS CABINET A BUNCH OF TIMES, BUT...
IT'S SO COMPLICATED!
I HAD HOPED SORTING ALPHABETICALLY OR BY HOUSEMATE WOULD HELP...
BIG MIX
THERE'S YOUR PROBLEM- YOU NEED TO ORGANIZE BY HOW **OFTEN** SOMETHING IS USED.
THIS IS HARDER IF YOU DON'T COOK OFTEN IN THE FIRST PLACE, BUT I'VE GOT SOME EASY TIPS!
NUMERO UNO BEING "F.I.F.O"- FIRST IN, FIRST OUT!
USE YOUR OLDER ITEMS FIRST, AND PUT YOUR NEWER ITEMS IN THE BACK.

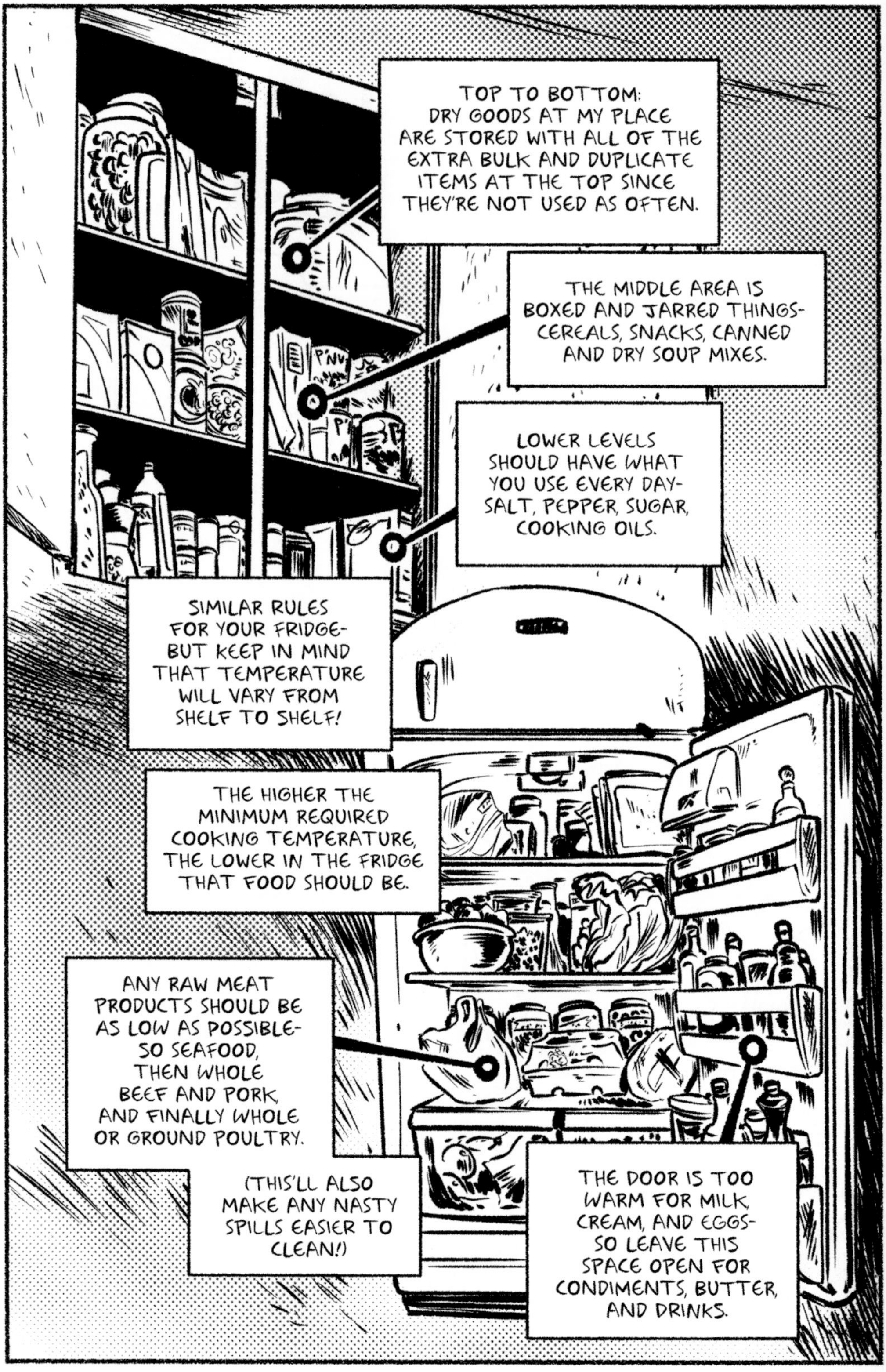
TOP TO BOTTOM: DRY GOODS AT MY PLACE ARE STORED WITH ALL OF THE EXTRA BULK AND DUPLICATE ITEMS AT THE TOP SINCE THEY'RE NOT USED AS OFTEN.
THE MIDDLE AREA IS BOXED AND JARRED THINGS- CEREALS, SNACKS, CANNED AND DRY SOUP MIXES.
LOWER LEVELS SHOULD HAVE WHAT YOU USE EVERY DAY- SALT, PEPPER, SUGAR, COOKING OILS.
SIMILAR RULES FOR YOUR FRIDGE- BUT KEEP IN MIND THAT TEMPERATURE WILL VARY FROM SHELF TO SHELF!
THE HIGHER THE MINIMUM REQUIRED COOKING TEMPERATURE, THE LOWER IN THE FRIDGE THAT FOOD SHOULD BE.
ANY RAW MEAT PRODUCTS SHOULD BE AS LOW AS POSSIBLE- SO SEAFOOD, THEN WHOLE BEEF AND PORK, AND FINALLY WHOLE OR GROUND POULTRY.
(THIS'LL ALSO MAKE ANY NASTY SPILLS EASIER TO CLEAN!)
THE DOOR IS TOO WARM FOR MILK, CREAM, AND EGGS- SO LEAVE THIS SPACE OPEN FOR CONDIMENTS, BUTTER, AND DRINKS.

see notes for more!

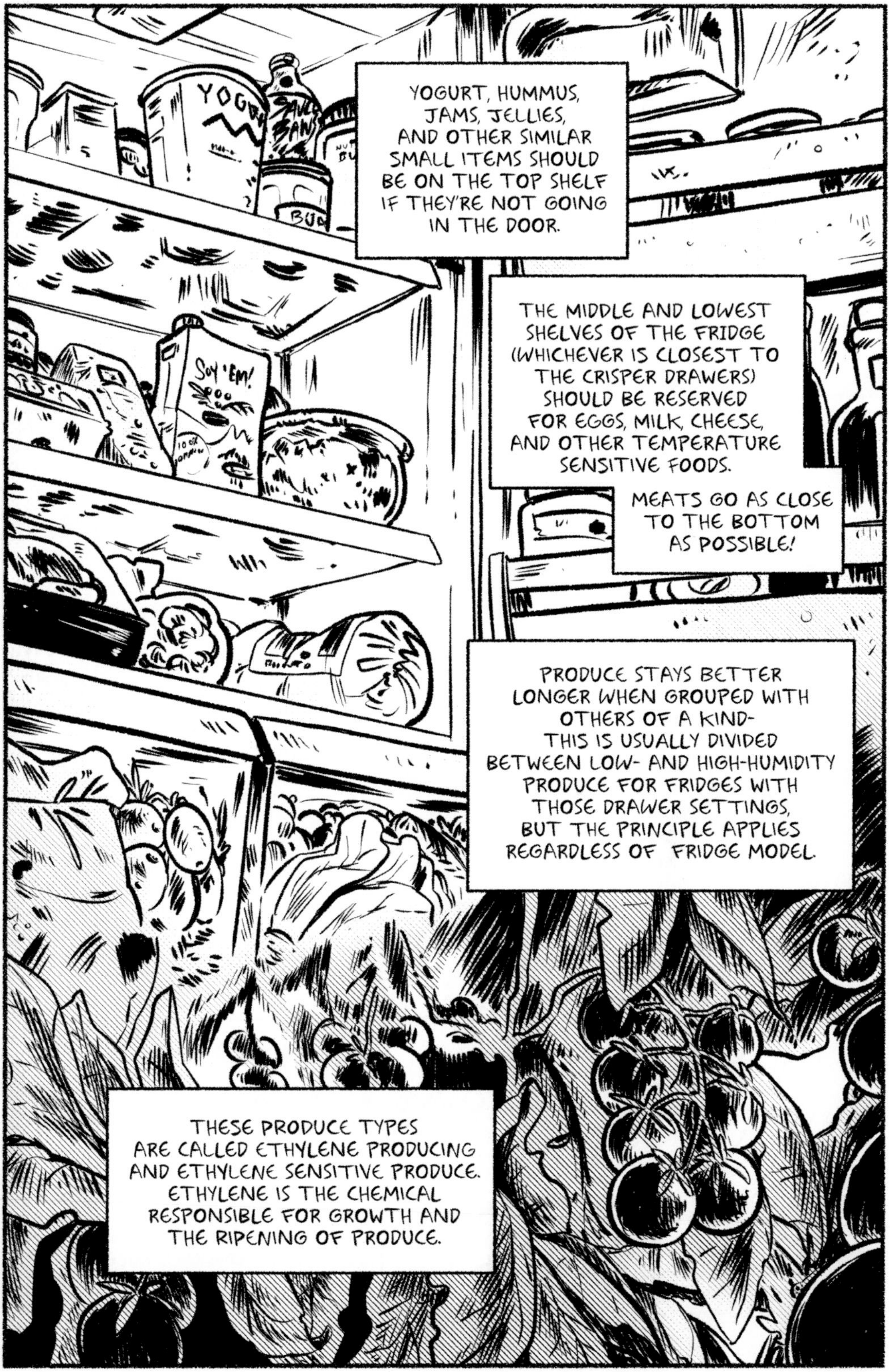
YOGURT, HUMMUS, JAMS, JELLIES, AND OTHER SIMILAR SMALL ITEMS SHOULD BE ON THE TOP SHELF IF THEY'RE NOT GOING IN THE DOOR.
Soy 'Em!
THE MIDDLE AND LOWEST SHELVES OF THE FRIDGE (WHICHEVER IS CLOSEST TO THE CRISPER DRAWERS) SHOULD BE RESERVED FOR EGGS, MILK, CHEESE, AND OTHER TEMPERATURE SENSITIVE FOODS.
MEATS GO AS CLOSE TO THE BOTTOM AS POSSIBLE!
PRODUCE STAYS BETTER LONGER WHEN GROUPED WITH OTHERS OF A KIND- THIS IS USUALLY DIVIDED BETWEEN LOW- AND HIGH-HUMIDITY PRODUCE FOR FRIDGES WITH THOSE DRAWER SETTINGS, BUT THE PRINCIPLE APPLIES REGARDLESS OF FRIDGE MODEL.
THESE PRODUCE TYPES ARE CALLED ETHYLENE PRODUCING AND ETHYLENE SENSITIVE PRODUCE. ETHYLENE IS THE CHEMICAL RESPONSIBLE FOR GROWTH AND THE RIPENING OF PRODUCE.

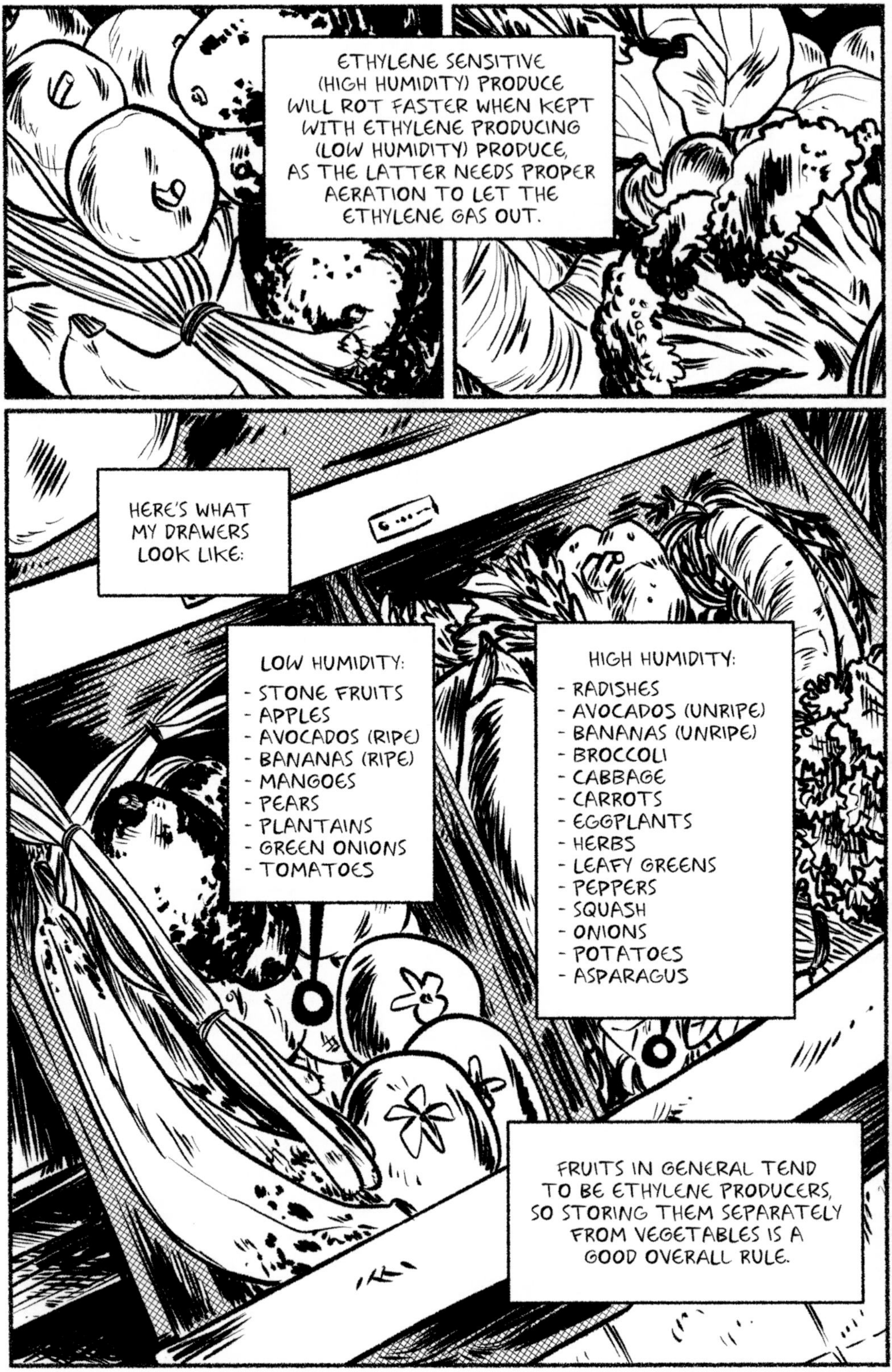
ETHYLENE SENSITIVE (HIGH HUMIDITY) PRODUCE WILL ROT FASTER WHEN KEPT WITH ETHYLENE PRODUCING (LOW HUMIDITY) PRODUCE, AS THE LATTER NEEDS PROPER AERATION TO LET THE ETHYLENE GAS OUT.
HERE'S WHAT MY DRAWERS LOOK LIKE:
LOW HUMIDITY:
- STONE FRUITS
- APPLES
- AVOCADOS (RIPE)
- BANANAS (RIPE)
- MANGOES
- PEARS
- PLANTAINS
- GREEN ONIONS
- TOMATOES
HIGH HUMIDITY:
- RADISHES
- AVOCADOS (UNRIPE)
- BANANAS (UNRIPE)
- BROCCOLI
- CABBAGE
- CARROTS
- EGGPLANTS
- HERBS
- LEAFY GREENS
- PEPPERS
- SQUASH
- ONIONS
- POTATOES
- ASPARAGUS
FRUITS IN GENERAL TEND TO BE ETHYLENE PRODUCERS, SO STORING THEM SEPARATELY FROM VEGETABLES IS A GOOD OVERALL RULE.

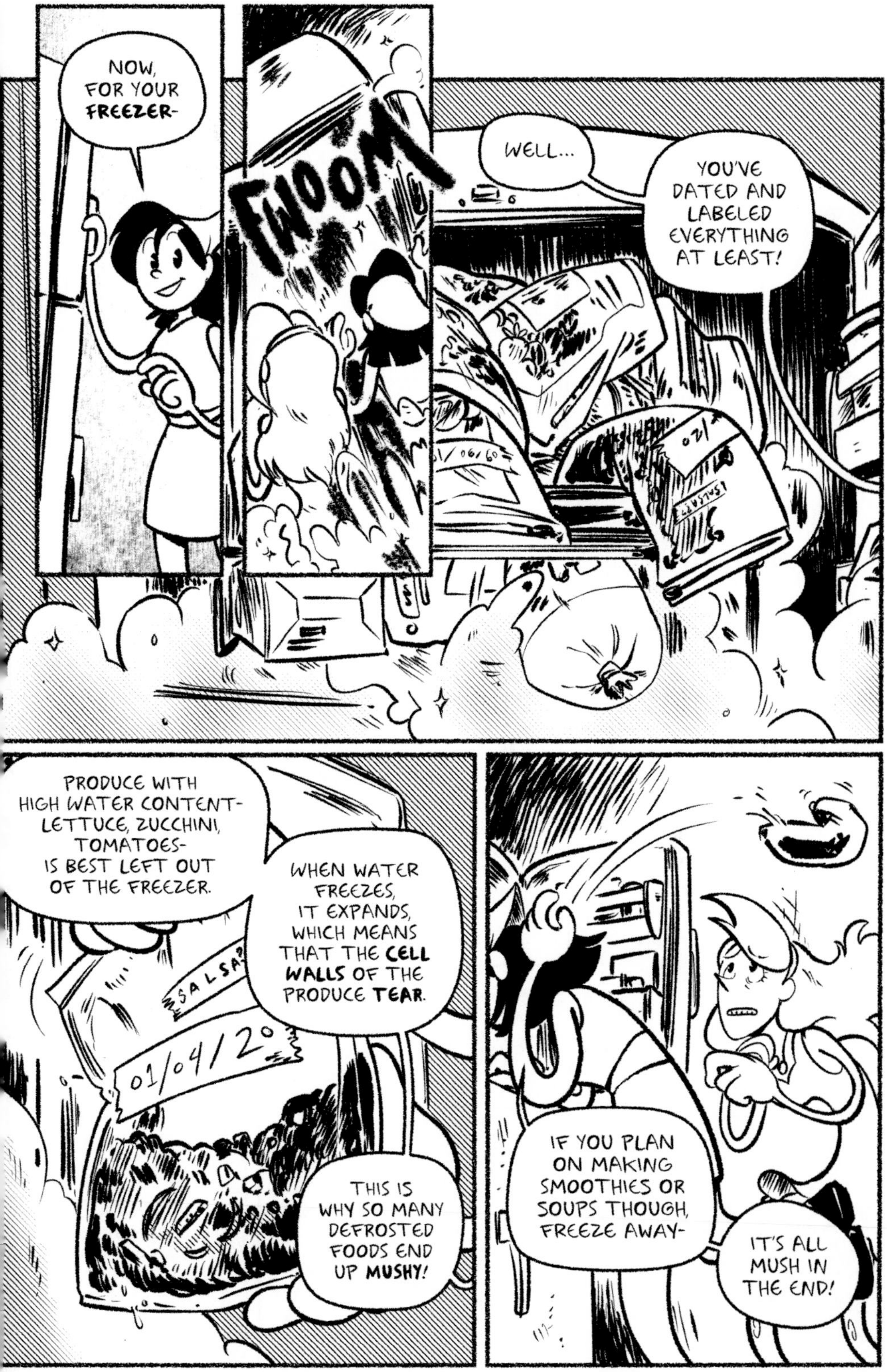
NOW, FOR YOUR **FREEZER**-
FWOOM
WELL...
YOU'VE DATED AND LABELED EVERYTHING AT LEAST!
PRODUCE WITH HIGH WATER CONTENT- LETTUCE, ZUCCHINI, TOMATOES- IS BEST LEFT OUT OF THE FREEZER.
WHEN WATER FREEZES, IT EXPANDS, WHICH MEANS THAT THE **CELL WALLS** OF THE PRODUCE **TEAR**.
SALSA?
01/04/20
THIS IS WHY SO MANY DEFROSTED FOODS END UP **MUSHY**!
IF YOU PLAN ON MAKING SMOOTHIES OR SOUPS THOUGH, FREEZE AWAY-
IT'S ALL MUSH IN THE END!

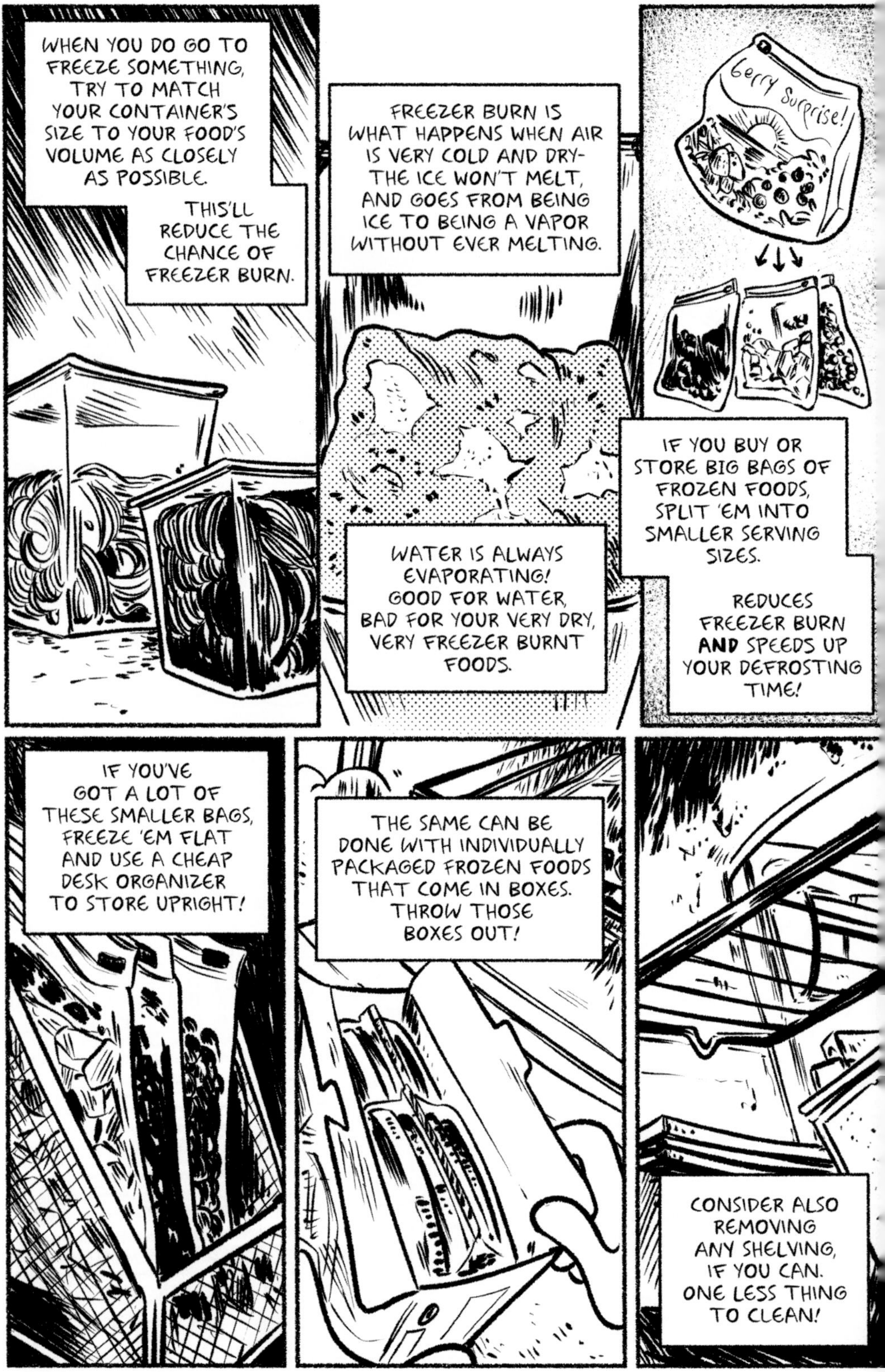
WHEN YOU DO GO TO FREEZE SOMETHING, TRY TO MATCH YOUR CONTAINER'S SIZE TO YOUR FOOD'S VOLUME AS CLOSELY AS POSSIBLE.
THIS'LL REDUCE THE CHANCE OF FREEZER BURN.
FREEZER BURN IS WHAT HAPPENS WHEN AIR IS VERY COLD AND DRY- THE ICE WON'T MELT, AND GOES FROM BEING ICE TO BEING A VAPOR WITHOUT EVER MELTING.
WATER IS ALWAYS EVAPORATING! GOOD FOR WATER, BAD FOR YOUR VERY DRY, VERY FREEZER BURNT FOODS.
Berry Surprise!
IF YOU BUY OR STORE BIG BAGS OF FROZEN FOODS, SPLIT 'EM INTO SMALLER SERVING SIZES.
REDUCES FREEZER BURN **AND** SPEEDS UP YOUR DEFROSTING TIME!
IF YOU'VE GOT A LOT OF THESE SMALLER BAGS, FREEZE 'EM FLAT AND USE A CHEAP DESK ORGANIZER TO STORE UPRIGHT!
THE SAME CAN BE DONE WITH INDIVIDUALLY PACKAGED FROZEN FOODS THAT COME IN BOXES. THROW THOSE BOXES OUT!
CONSIDER ALSO REMOVING ANY SHELVING, IF YOU CAN. ONE LESS THING TO CLEAN!

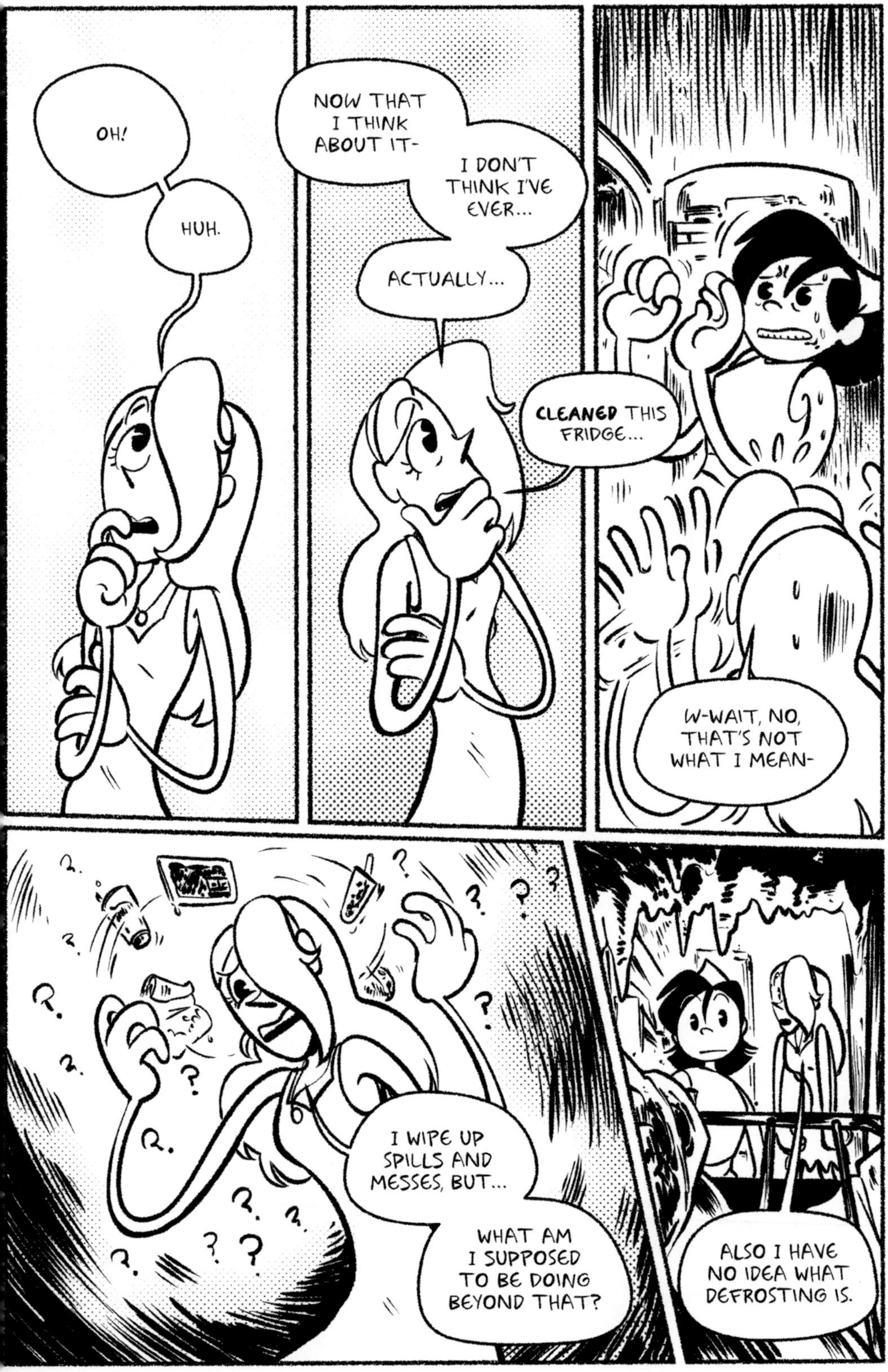
OH!
HUH.
NOW THAT I THINK ABOUT IT-
I DON'T THINK I'VE EVER...
ACTUALLY...
CLEANED THIS FRIDGE...
W-WAIT, NO, THAT'S NOT WHAT I MEAN-
I WIPE UP SPILLS AND MESSES, BUT...
WHAT AM I SUPPOSED TO BE DOING BEYOND THAT?
ALSO I HAVE NO IDEA WHAT DEFROSTING IS.

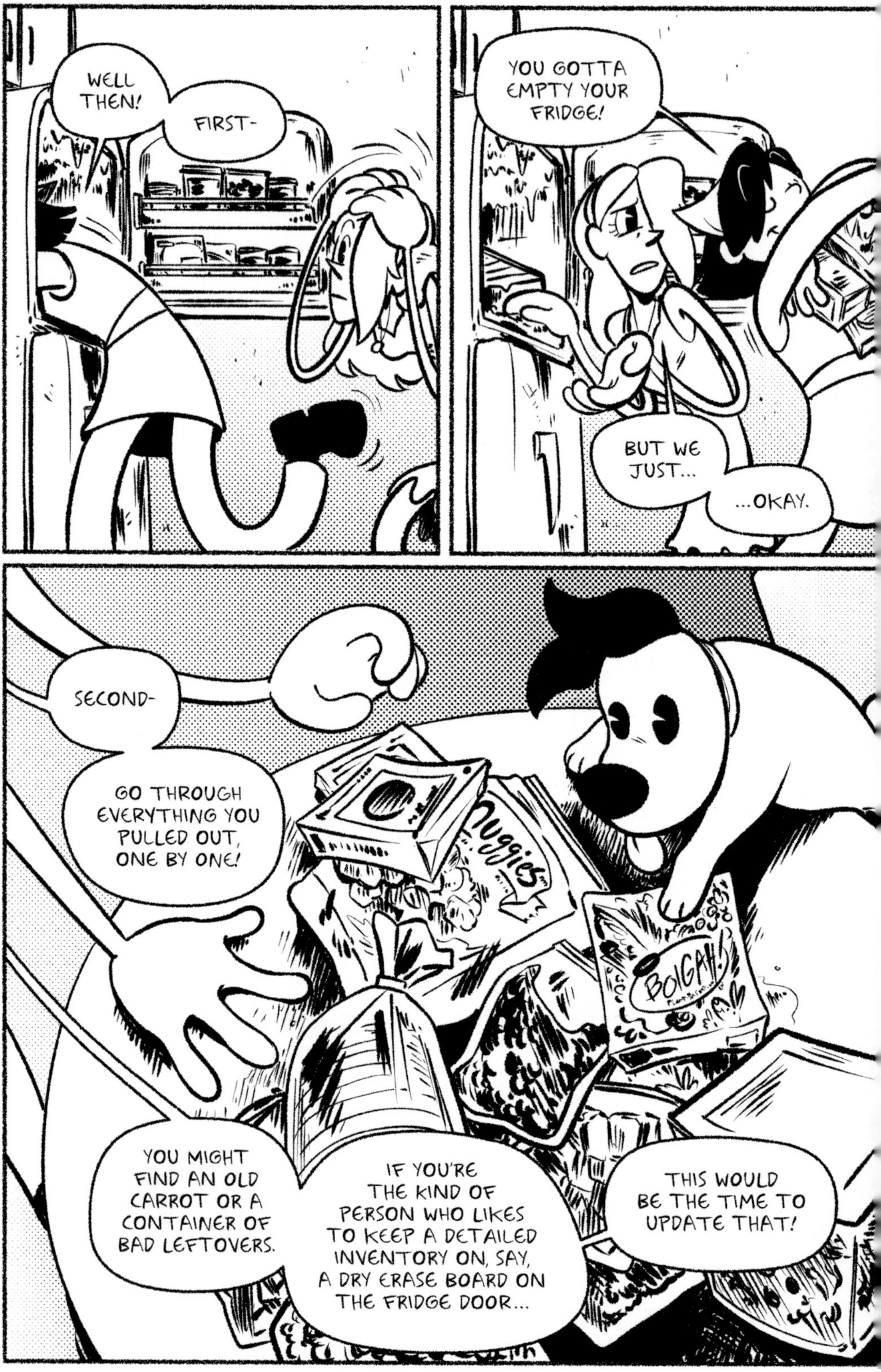
WELL THEN!
FIRST-
YOU GOTTA EMPTY YOUR FRIDGE!
BUT WE JUST...
...OKAY.
SECOND-
GO THROUGH EVERYTHING YOU PULLED OUT, ONE BY ONE!
nuggies
BOIGAH!
YOU MIGHT FIND AN OLD CARROT OR A CONTAINER OF BAD LEFTOVERS.
IF YOU'RE THE KIND OF PERSON WHO LIKES TO KEEP A DETAILED INVENTORY ON, SAY, A DRY ERASE BOARD ON THE FRIDGE DOOR...
THIS WOULD BE THE TIME TO UPDATE THAT!

ONCE YOU'VE SWEPT OUT THE CRUMBS AND DUST WITH A MOIST PAPER OR HAND TOWEL, WE CAN GET INTO THE **GOOD STUFF!**

THE DEEP CLEAN!

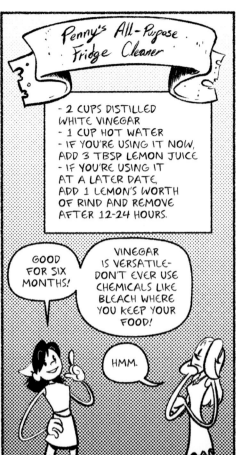

Penny's All-Purpose Fridge Cleaner

- 2 CUPS DISTILLED WHITE VINEGAR
- 1 CUP HOT WATER
- IF YOU'RE USING IT NOW, ADD 3 TBSP LEMON JUICE
- IF YOU'RE USING IT AT A LATER DATE, ADD 1 LEMON'S WORTH OF RIND AND REMOVE AFTER 12-24 HOURS.

GOOD FOR SIX MONTHS!

VINEGAR IS VERSATILE- DON'T EVER USE CHEMICALS LIKE BLEACH WHERE YOU KEEP YOUR FOOD!

HMM.

IF I'M OUT OF LEMONS, CAN I USE ESSENTIAL OILS INSTEAD?

IT'S JUST FOR THE SCENT, RIGHT?

NO!!

THE VAST MAJORITY OF ESSENTIAL OILS ARE NOT FOOD-GRADE- DON'T USE THEM ON ANY SURFACE WHERE THEY COULD BE INGESTED.

ANYTHING THAT COMES IN CONTACT WITH FOOD IS OFF-LIMITS!

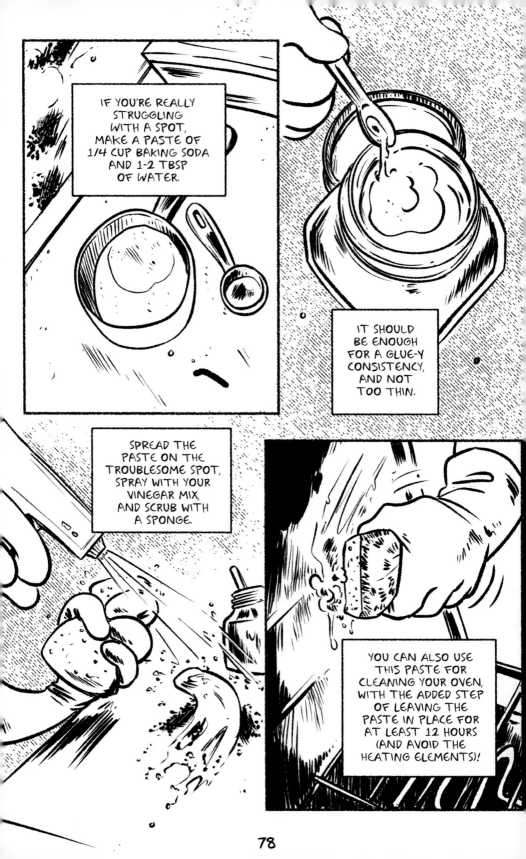

IF YOU'RE REALLY STRUGGLING WITH A SPOT, MAKE A PASTE OF 1/4 CUP BAKING SODA AND 1-2 TBSP OF WATER.

IT SHOULD BE ENOUGH FOR A GLUE-Y CONSISTENCY, AND NOT TOO THIN.

SPREAD THE PASTE ON THE TROUBLESOME SPOT, SPRAY WITH YOUR VINEGAR MIX, AND SCRUB WITH A SPONGE.

YOU CAN ALSO USE THIS PASTE FOR CLEANING YOUR OVEN, WITH THE ADDED STEP OF LEAVING THE PASTE IN PLACE FOR AT LEAST 12 HOURS (AND AVOID THE HEATING ELEMENTS)!

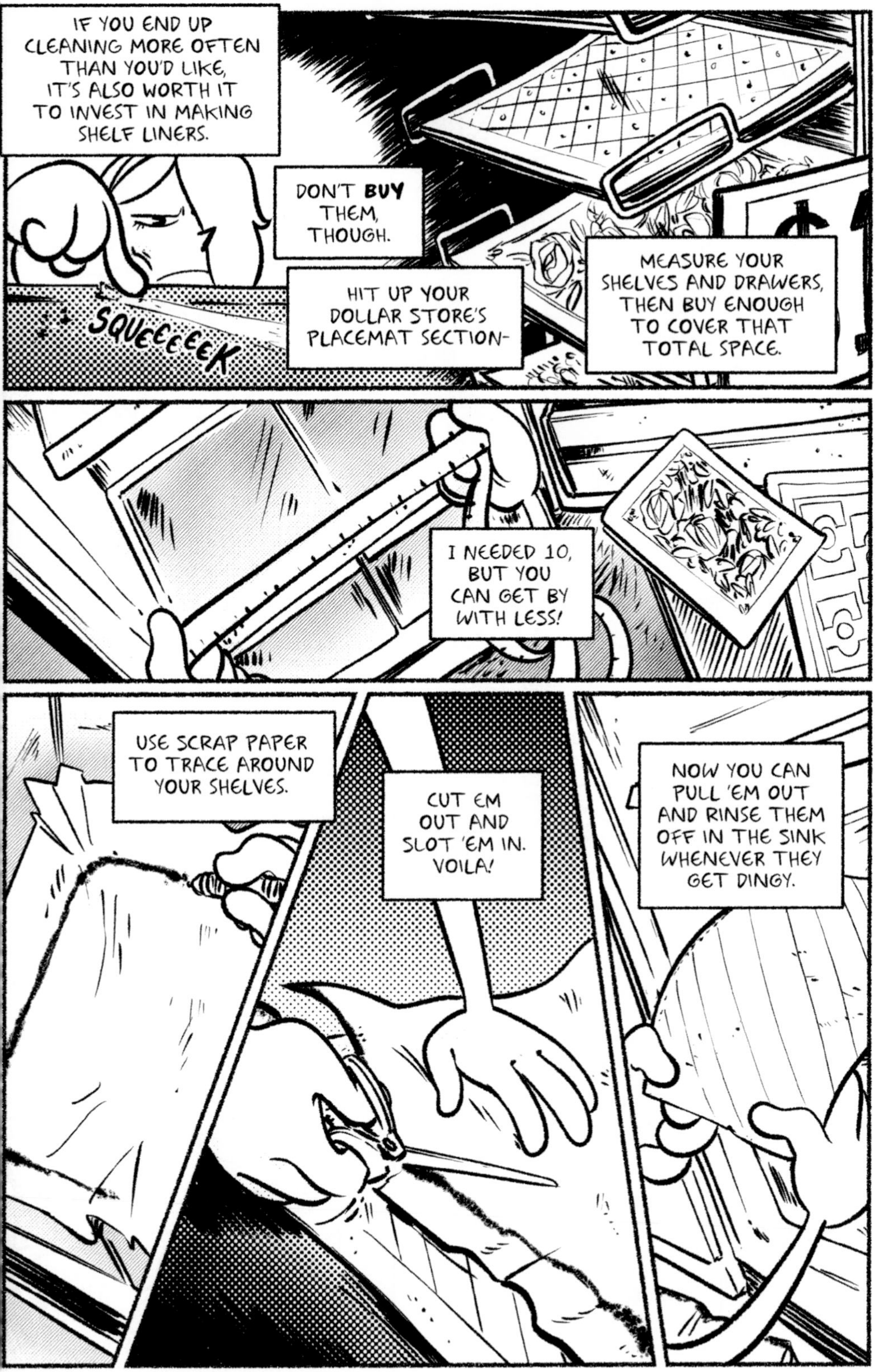
IF YOU END UP CLEANING MORE OFTEN THAN YOU'D LIKE, IT'S ALSO WORTH IT TO INVEST IN MAKING SHELF LINERS.
DON'T **BUY** THEM, THOUGH.
SQUEEEEEEK
HIT UP YOUR DOLLAR STORE'S PLACEMAT SECTION-
MEASURE YOUR SHELVES AND DRAWERS, THEN BUY ENOUGH TO COVER THAT TOTAL SPACE.
I NEEDED 10, BUT YOU CAN GET BY WITH LESS!
USE SCRAP PAPER TO TRACE AROUND YOUR SHELVES.
CUT EM OUT AND SLOT 'EM IN. VOILA!
NOW YOU CAN PULL 'EM OUT AND RINSE THEM OFF IN THE SINK WHENEVER THEY GET DINGY.

I'D ADVISE AGAINST DOING THIS FOR YOUR FREEZER, THOUGH- DON'T WANNA HAVE TO DEFROST EVERY TIME YOU WIPE IT DOWN.
PENNY!!
WHAT **IS** DEFROSTING?!
IT'S NOT REALLY A **SECRET** OR ANYTHING-
FIND THE CORD FOR YOUR FRIDGE-
UNPLUG-
LEAVE ONLY THE FREEZER DOOR OPEN, AND WAIT.
YOU'RE GONNA NEED TO GRAB SOME TOWELS TOO.
...THAT'S IT?
JUST... LET ALL THE ICE MELT?
THAT'S IT!

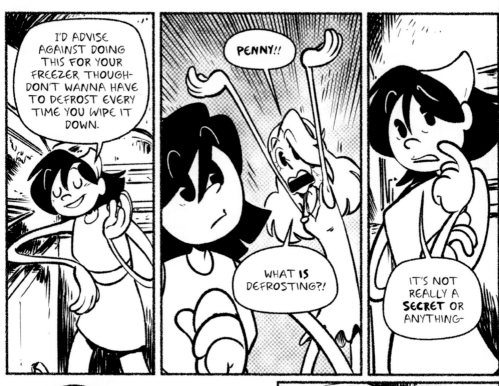

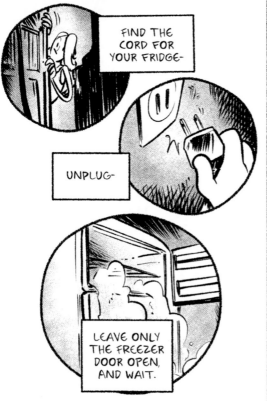

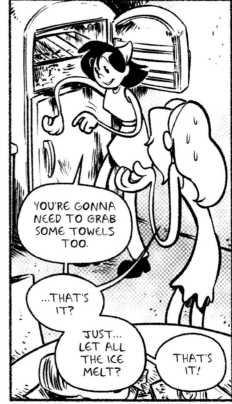

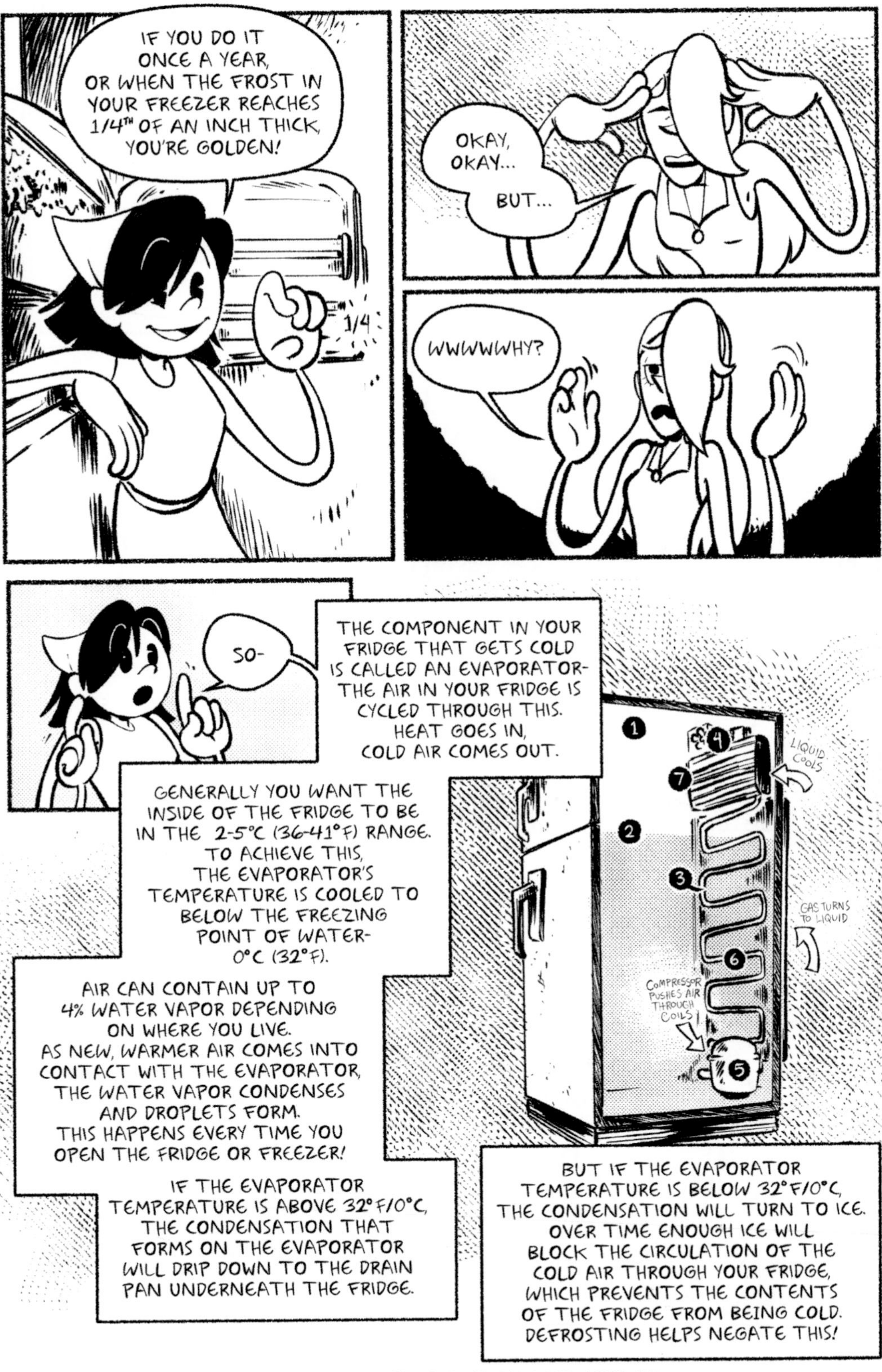
IF YOU DO IT ONCE A YEAR, OR WHEN THE FROST IN YOUR FREEZER REACHES 1/4TH OF AN INCH THICK, YOU'RE GOLDEN!
1/4
OKAY, OKAY...
BUT...
WWWWWHY?
SO-
THE COMPONENT IN YOUR FRIDGE THAT GETS COLD IS CALLED AN EVAPORATOR- THE AIR IN YOUR FRIDGE IS CYCLED THROUGH THIS. HEAT GOES IN, COLD AIR COMES OUT.
GENERALLY YOU WANT THE INSIDE OF THE FRIDGE TO BE IN THE 2-5°C (36-41°F) RANGE. TO ACHIEVE THIS, THE EVAPORATOR'S TEMPERATURE IS COOLED TO BELOW THE FREEZING POINT OF WATER- 0°C (32°F).
LIQUID COOLS
GAS TURNS TO LIQUID
COMPRESSOR PUSHES AIR THROUGH COILS
AIR CAN CONTAIN UP TO 4% WATER VAPOR DEPENDING ON WHERE YOU LIVE. AS NEW, WARMER AIR COMES INTO CONTACT WITH THE EVAPORATOR, THE WATER VAPOR CONDENSES AND DROPLETS FORM. THIS HAPPENS EVERY TIME YOU OPEN THE FRIDGE OR FREEZER!
IF THE EVAPORATOR TEMPERATURE IS ABOVE 32°F/0°C, THE CONDENSATION THAT FORMS ON THE EVAPORATOR WILL DRIP DOWN TO THE DRAIN PAN UNDERNEATH THE FRIDGE.
BUT IF THE EVAPORATOR TEMPERATURE IS BELOW 32°F/0°C, THE CONDENSATION WILL TURN TO ICE. OVER TIME ENOUGH ICE WILL BLOCK THE CIRCULATION OF THE COLD AIR THROUGH YOUR FRIDGE, WHICH PREVENTS THE CONTENTS OF THE FRIDGE FROM BEING COLD. DEFROSTING HELPS NEGATE THIS!

1. FREEZER CABINET 2. REFRIGERATOR CABINET 3. CONDENSER COILS 4. EVAPORATOR 5. COMPRESSOR 6. COMPRESSOR COILS 7. COOLANT COILS

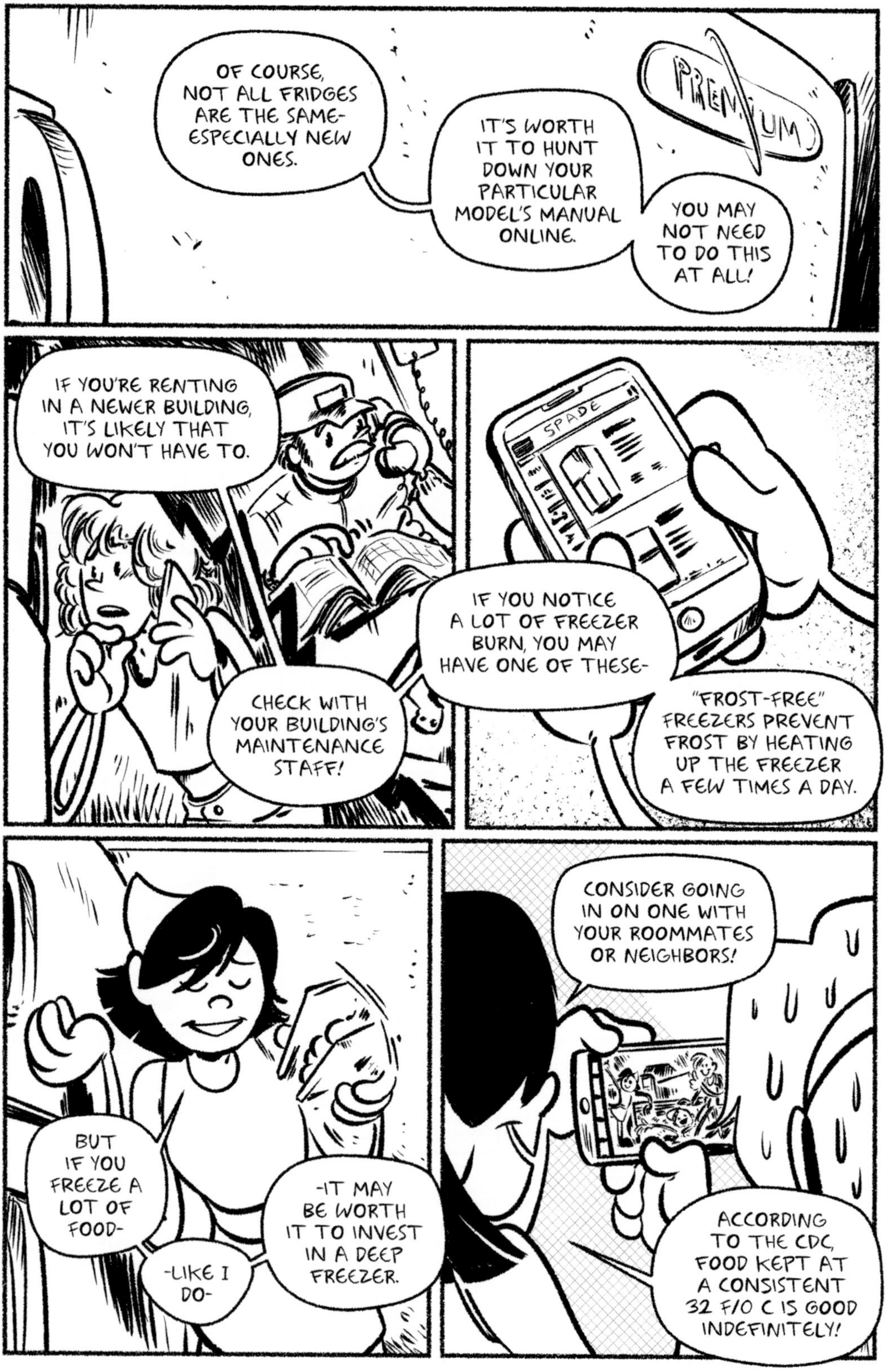
OF COURSE, NOT ALL FRIDGES ARE THE SAME- ESPECIALLY NEW ONES.
IT'S WORTH IT TO HUNT DOWN YOUR PARTICULAR MODEL'S MANUAL ONLINE.
PREMIUM
YOU MAY NOT NEED TO DO THIS AT ALL!
IF YOU'RE RENTING IN A NEWER BUILDING, IT'S LIKELY THAT YOU WON'T HAVE TO.
CHECK WITH YOUR BUILDING'S MAINTENANCE STAFF!
SPADE
IF YOU NOTICE A LOT OF FREEZER BURN, YOU MAY HAVE ONE OF THESE-
"FROST-FREE" FREEZERS PREVENT FROST BY HEATING UP THE FREEZER A FEW TIMES A DAY.
BUT IF YOU FREEZE A LOT OF FOOD-
-LIKE I DO-
-IT MAY BE WORTH IT TO INVEST IN A DEEP FREEZER.
CONSIDER GOING IN ON ONE WITH YOUR ROOMMATES OR NEIGHBORS!
ACCORDING TO THE CDC, FOOD KEPT AT A CONSISTENT 32 F/0 C IS GOOD INDEFINITELY!

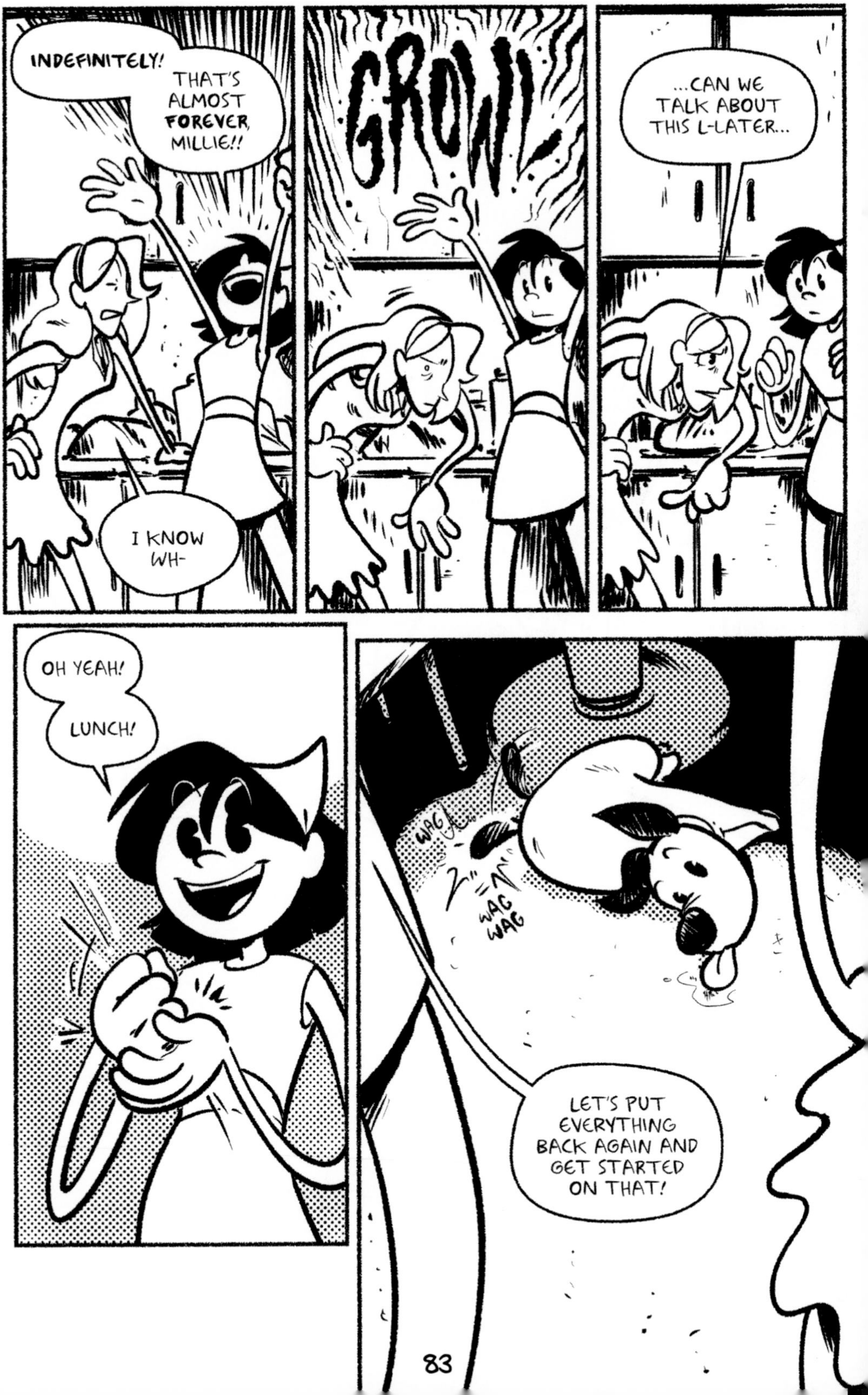
INDEFINITELY!
THAT'S ALMOST FOREVER, MILLIE!!
I KNOW WH-
GROWL!
...CAN WE TALK ABOUT THIS L-LATER...
OH YEAH!
LUNCH!
WAG
WAG WAG
LET'S PUT EVERYTHING BACK AGAIN AND GET STARTED ON THAT!

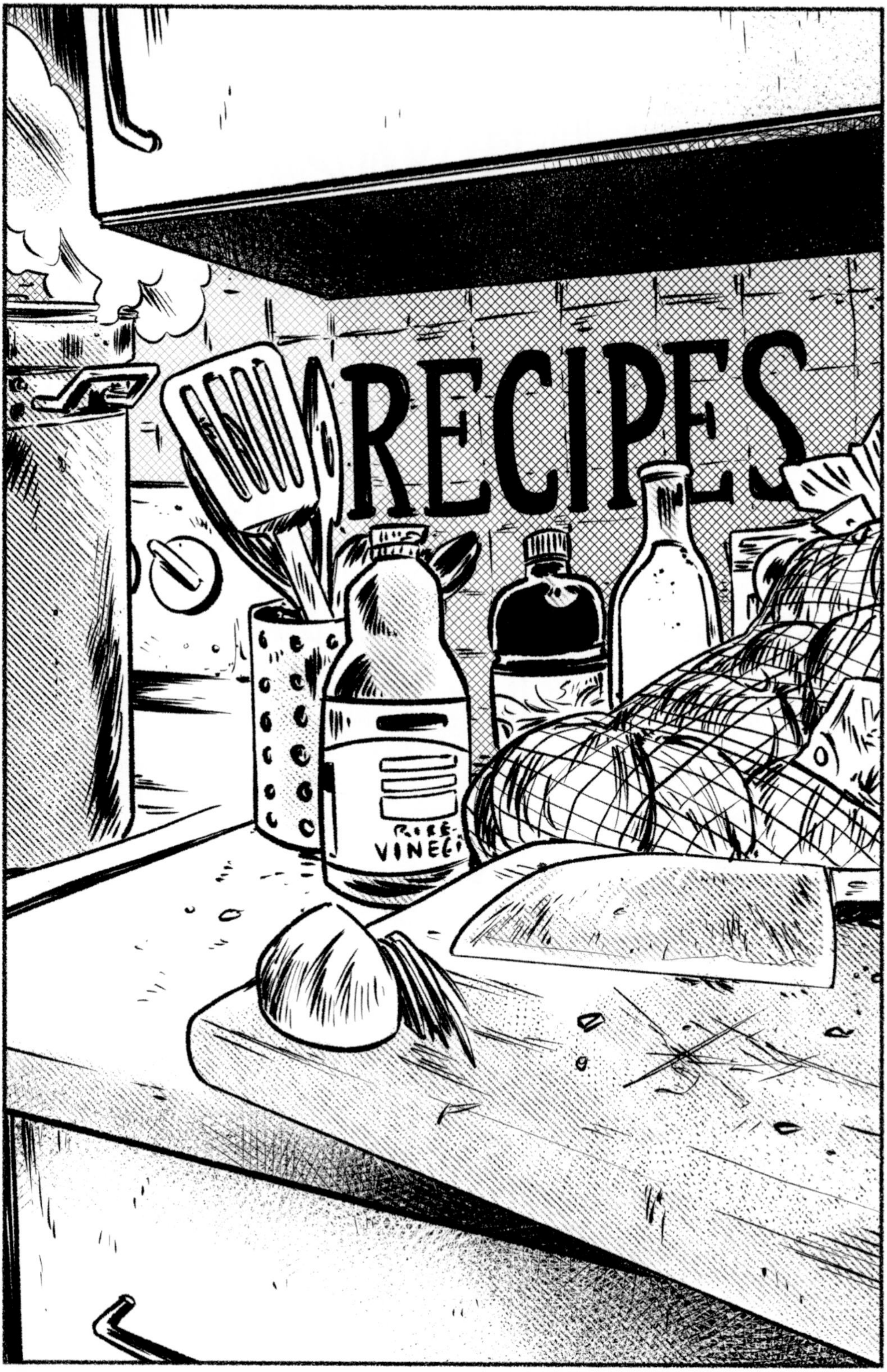
RECIPES

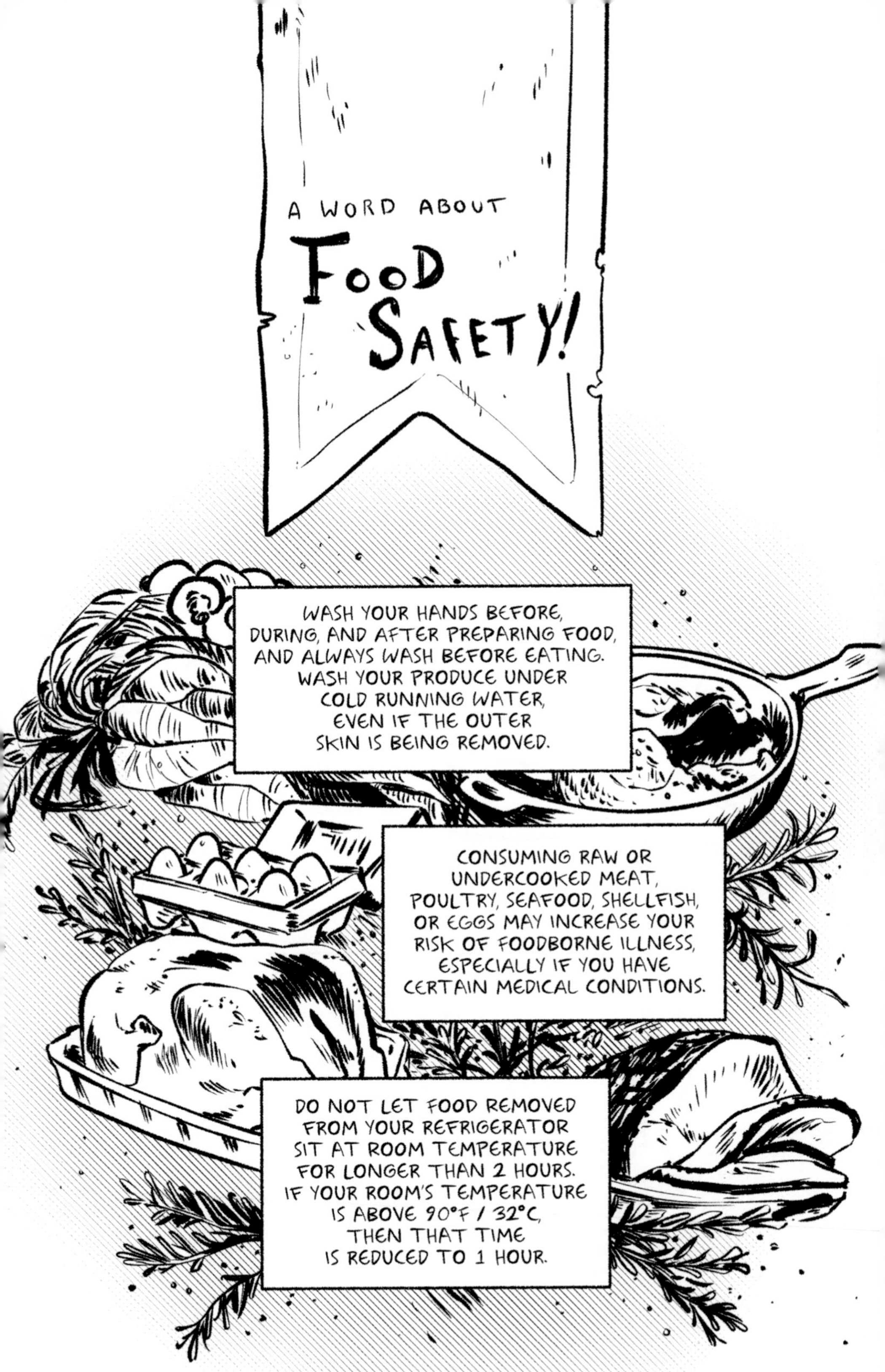
A WORD ABOUT
FOOD SAFETY!
WASH YOUR HANDS BEFORE, DURING, AND AFTER PREPARING FOOD, AND ALWAYS WASH BEFORE EATING. WASH YOUR PRODUCE UNDER COLD RUNNING WATER, EVEN IF THE OUTER SKIN IS BEING REMOVED.
CONSUMING RAW OR UNDERCOOKED MEAT, POULTRY, SEAFOOD, SHELLFISH, OR EGGS MAY INCREASE YOUR RISK OF FOODBORNE ILLNESS, ESPECIALLY IF YOU HAVE CERTAIN MEDICAL CONDITIONS.
DO NOT LET FOOD REMOVED FROM YOUR REFRIGERATOR SIT AT ROOM TEMPERATURE FOR LONGER THAN 2 HOURS. IF YOUR ROOM'S TEMPERATURE IS ABOVE 90°F / 32°C, THEN THAT TIME IS REDUCED TO 1 HOUR.

BASIC BREAD

HANDS ON: 30 MIN
HANDS OFF: 2 HR

-1 CUP WATER
-2 1/2 TSP ACTIVE DRY YEAST
-2 TSP GRANULATED WHITE SUGAR
-1 TSP SALT
-3 CUPS ALL-PURPOSE FLOUR
-1 TBSP OLIVE OIL (OPTIONAL)

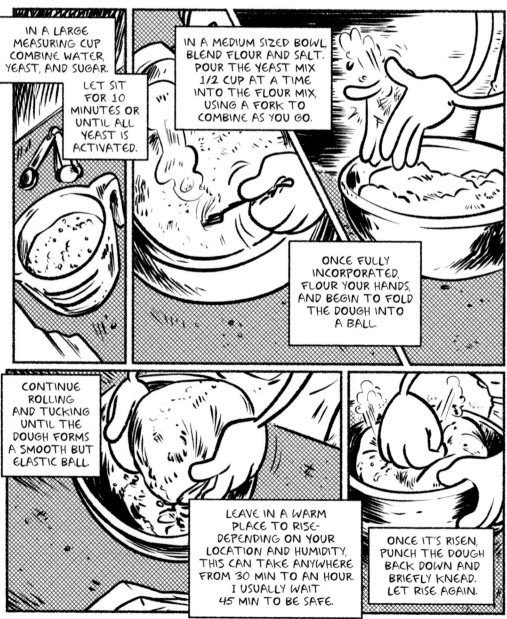

IN A LARGE MEASURING CUP COMBINE WATER, YEAST, AND SUGAR.

LET SIT FOR 10 MINUTES OR UNTIL ALL YEAST IS ACTIVATED.

IN A MEDIUM SIZED BOWL, BLEND FLOUR AND SALT. POUR THE YEAST MIX 1/2 CUP AT A TIME INTO THE FLOUR MIX, USING A FORK TO COMBINE AS YOU GO.

ONCE FULLY INCORPORATED, FLOUR YOUR HANDS, AND BEGIN TO FOLD THE DOUGH INTO A BALL.

CONTINUE ROLLING AND TUCKING UNTIL THE DOUGH FORMS A SMOOTH BUT ELASTIC BALL

LEAVE IN A WARM PLACE TO RISE- DEPENDING ON YOUR LOCATION AND HUMIDITY, THIS CAN TAKE ANYWHERE FROM 30 MIN TO AN HOUR. I USUALLY WAIT 45 MIN TO BE SAFE.

ONCE IT'S RISEN, PUNCH THE DOUGH BACK DOWN AND BRIEFLY KNEAD. LET RISE AGAIN.

see notes for more!

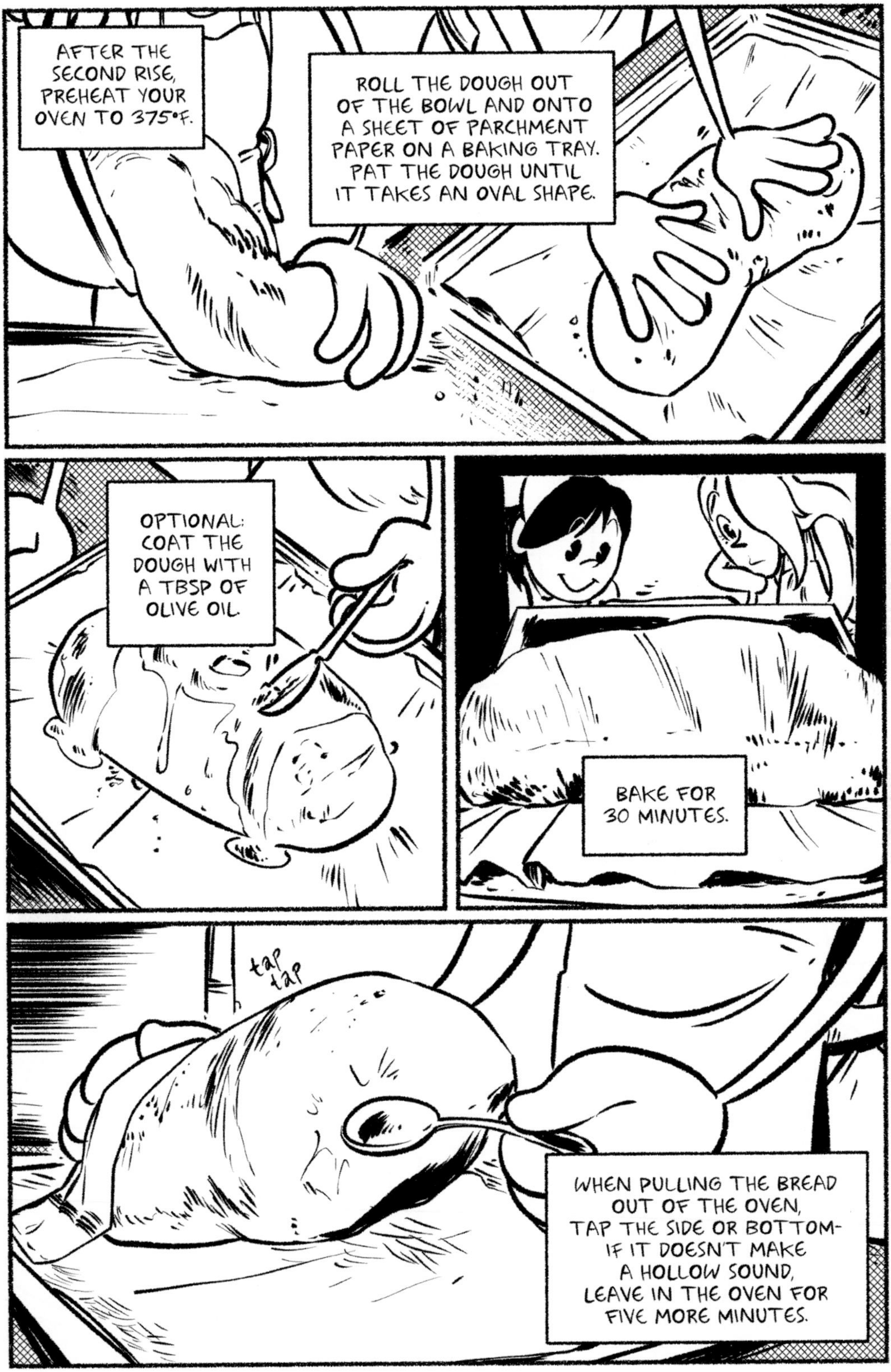
AFTER THE SECOND RISE, PREHEAT YOUR OVEN TO 375°F.
ROLL THE DOUGH OUT OF THE BOWL AND ONTO A SHEET OF PARCHMENT PAPER ON A BAKING TRAY. PAT THE DOUGH UNTIL IT TAKES AN OVAL SHAPE.
OPTIONAL: COAT THE DOUGH WITH A TBSP OF OLIVE OIL.
BAKE FOR 30 MINUTES.
tap tap
WHEN PULLING THE BREAD OUT OF THE OVEN, TAP THE SIDE OR BOTTOM- IF IT DOESN'T MAKE A HOLLOW SOUND, LEAVE IN THE OVEN FOR FIVE MORE MINUTES.

SOURDOUGH STARTER

HANDS ON: 15 MIN
HANDS OFF: 4-5 DAYS

- 1/2 TBSP ACTIVE DRY YEAST
- 2 CUPS ALL-PURPOSE FLOUR
- 2 CUPS WARM WATER

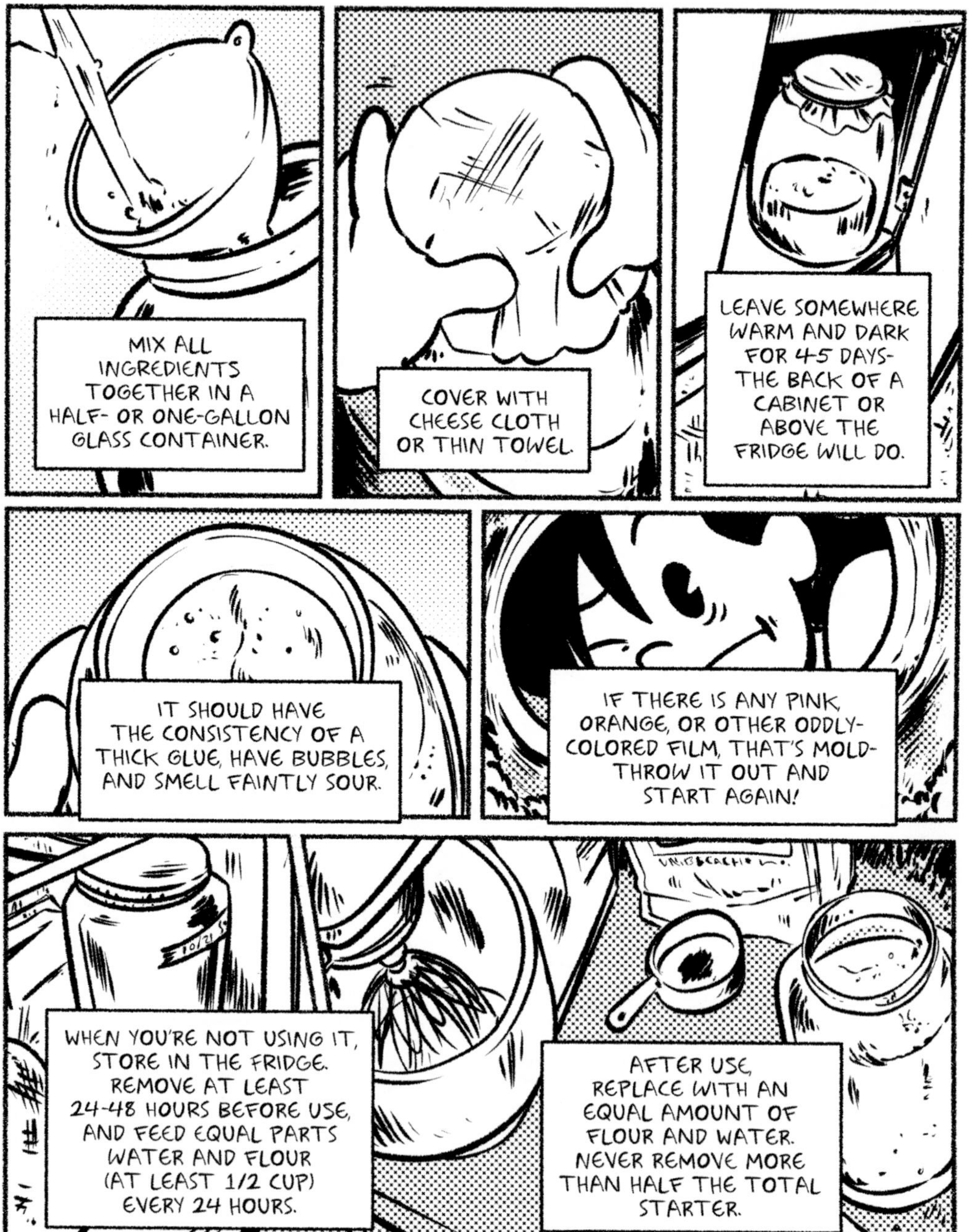
MIX ALL INGREDIENTS TOGETHER IN A HALF- OR ONE-GALLON GLASS CONTAINER.
COVER WITH CHEESE CLOTH OR THIN TOWEL.
LEAVE SOMEWHERE WARM AND DARK FOR 4-5 DAYS- THE BACK OF A CABINET OR ABOVE THE FRIDGE WILL DO.
IT SHOULD HAVE THE CONSISTENCY OF A THICK GLUE, HAVE BUBBLES, AND SMELL FAINTLY SOUR.
IF THERE IS ANY PINK, ORANGE, OR OTHER ODDLY-COLORED FILM, THAT'S MOLD- THROW IT OUT AND START AGAIN!
10/21
WHEN YOU'RE NOT USING IT, STORE IN THE FRIDGE. REMOVE AT LEAST 24-48 HOURS BEFORE USE, AND FEED EQUAL PARTS WATER AND FLOUR (AT LEAST 1/2 CUP) EVERY 24 HOURS.
AFTER USE, REPLACE WITH AN EQUAL AMOUNT OF FLOUR AND WATER. NEVER REMOVE MORE THAN HALF THE TOTAL STARTER.

see notes for more!

SOURDOUGH BREAD

HANDS ON: 25 MIN
HANDS OFF: 50 MIN

- 1 1/2 TSP YEAST
- 1 1/2 TSP SALT
- 1 1/2 TSP GRANULATED WHITE SUGAR
- 2 1/2 CUPS ALL-PURPOSE FLOUR
- 2 CUPS JUST-FED STARTER
- 1/2 CUP LUKEWARM WATER
- 3 TBSP OIL (EXTRA VIRGIN OLIVE PREFERRED)

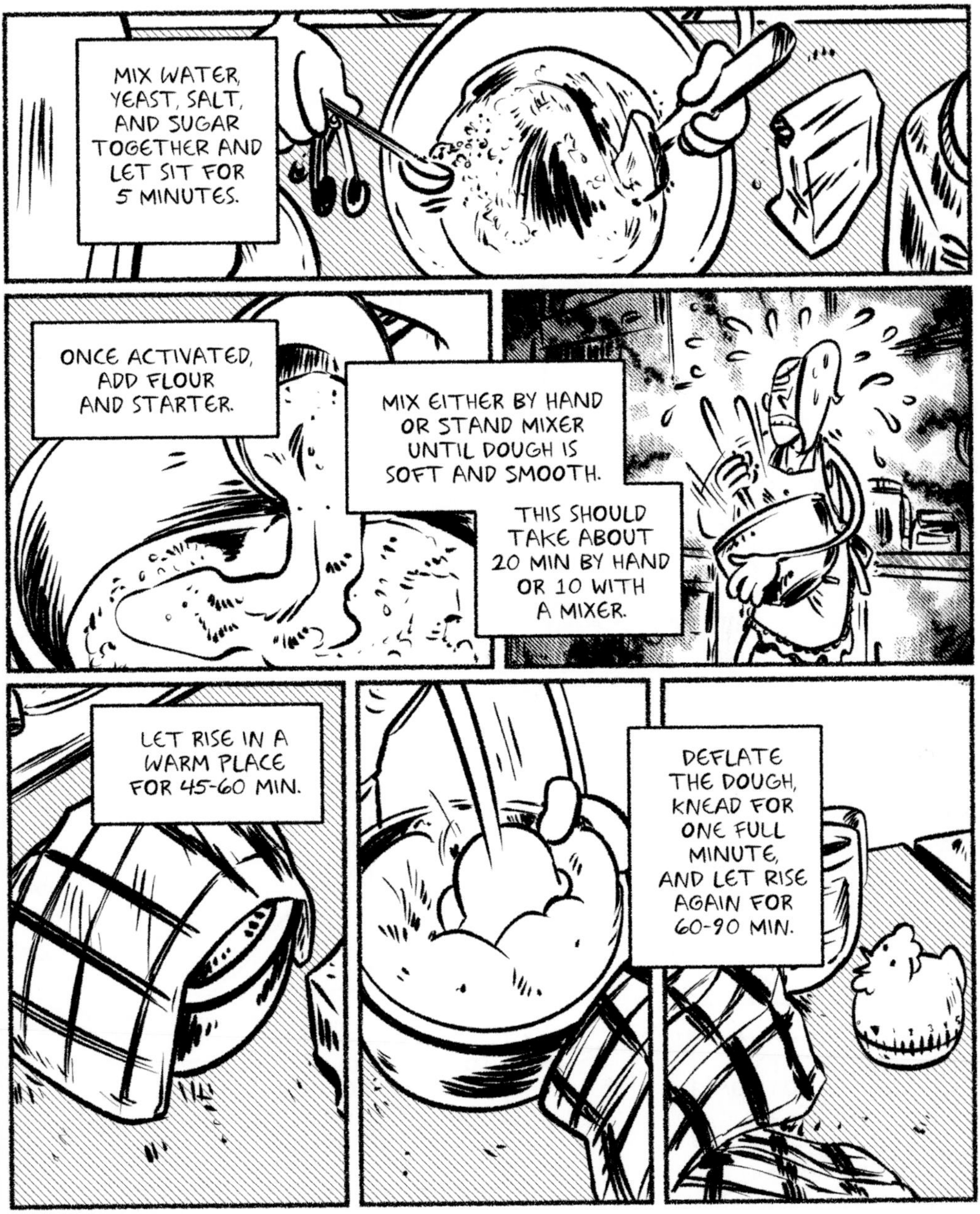

MIX WATER, YEAST, SALT, AND SUGAR TOGETHER AND LET SIT FOR 5 MINUTES.
ONCE ACTIVATED, ADD FLOUR AND STARTER.
MIX EITHER BY HAND OR STAND MIXER UNTIL DOUGH IS SOFT AND SMOOTH.
THIS SHOULD TAKE ABOUT 20 MIN BY HAND OR 10 WITH A MIXER.
LET RISE IN A WARM PLACE FOR 45-60 MIN.
DEFLATE THE DOUGH, KNEAD FOR ONE FULL MINUTE, AND LET RISE AGAIN FOR 60-90 MIN.

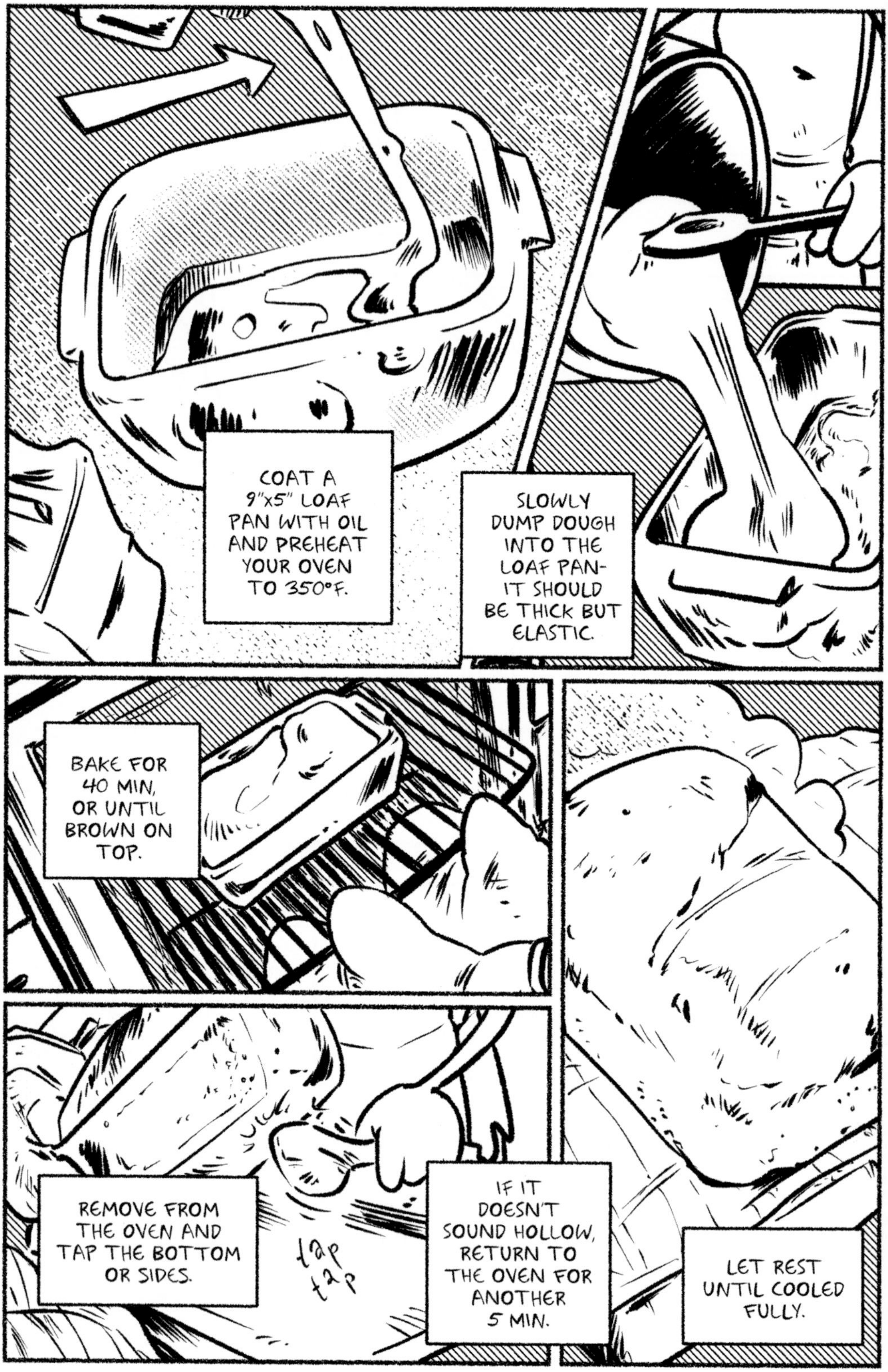
COAT A 9"x5" LOAF PAN WITH OIL AND PREHEAT YOUR OVEN TO 350°F.
SLOWLY DUMP DOUGH INTO THE LOAF PAN- IT SHOULD BE THICK BUT ELASTIC.
BAKE FOR 40 MIN, OR UNTIL BROWN ON TOP.
REMOVE FROM THE OVEN AND TAP THE BOTTOM OR SIDES.
tap tap
IF IT DOESN'T SOUND HOLLOW, RETURN TO THE OVEN FOR ANOTHER 5 MIN.
LET REST UNTIL COOLED FULLY.

FLATBREAD

HANDS ON: 30 MIN

-2 CUPS WHOLE FAT GREEK YOGURT
-2 1/4 CUPS ALL-PURPOSE FLOUR
-1 TBSP BAKING POWDER
-1/2 TSP SALT
-2 TSP COOKING OIL OF CHOICE (OPTIONAL)
-2 TSP SPICES OF CHOICE (OPTIONAL)

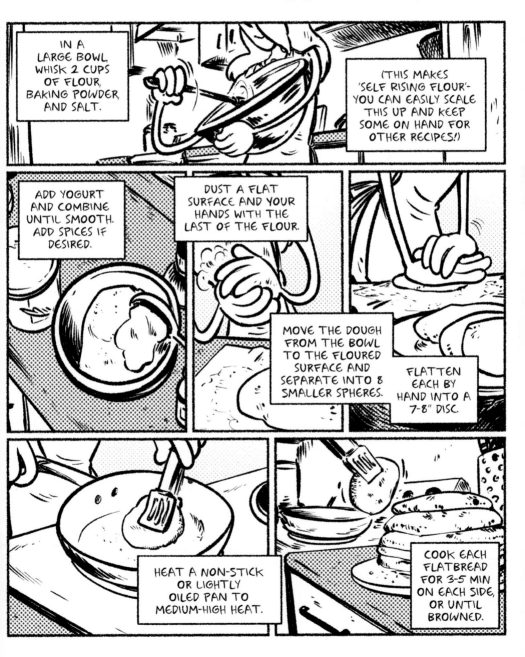

IN A LARGE BOWL, WHISK 2 CUPS OF FLOUR, BAKING POWDER, AND SALT.

(THIS MAKES 'SELF RISING FLOUR'- YOU CAN EASILY SCALE THIS UP AND KEEP SOME ON HAND FOR OTHER RECIPES!)

ADD YOGURT AND COMBINE UNTIL SMOOTH. ADD SPICES IF DESIRED.

DUST A FLAT SURFACE AND YOUR HANDS WITH THE LAST OF THE FLOUR.

MOVE THE DOUGH FROM THE BOWL TO THE FLOURED SURFACE AND SEPARATE INTO 8 SMALLER SPHERES.

FLATTEN EACH BY HAND INTO A 7-8" DISC.

HEAT A NON-STICK OR LIGHTLY OILED PAN TO MEDIUM-HIGH HEAT.

COOK EACH FLATBREAD FOR 3-5 MIN ON EACH SIDE, OR UNTIL BROWNED.

BAGUETTES

HANDS ON: 45 MIN
HANDS OFF: 2 HOURS

- -4 CUPS ALL-PURPOSE FLOUR
- -1 TSP SALT
- -1 TSP SUGAR
- -1 TSP DISTILLED WHITE VINEGAR
- -2 TSP ACTIVE DRY YEAST
- -1 2/3 CUPS WARM WATER
- -1 TBSP OLIVE OIL

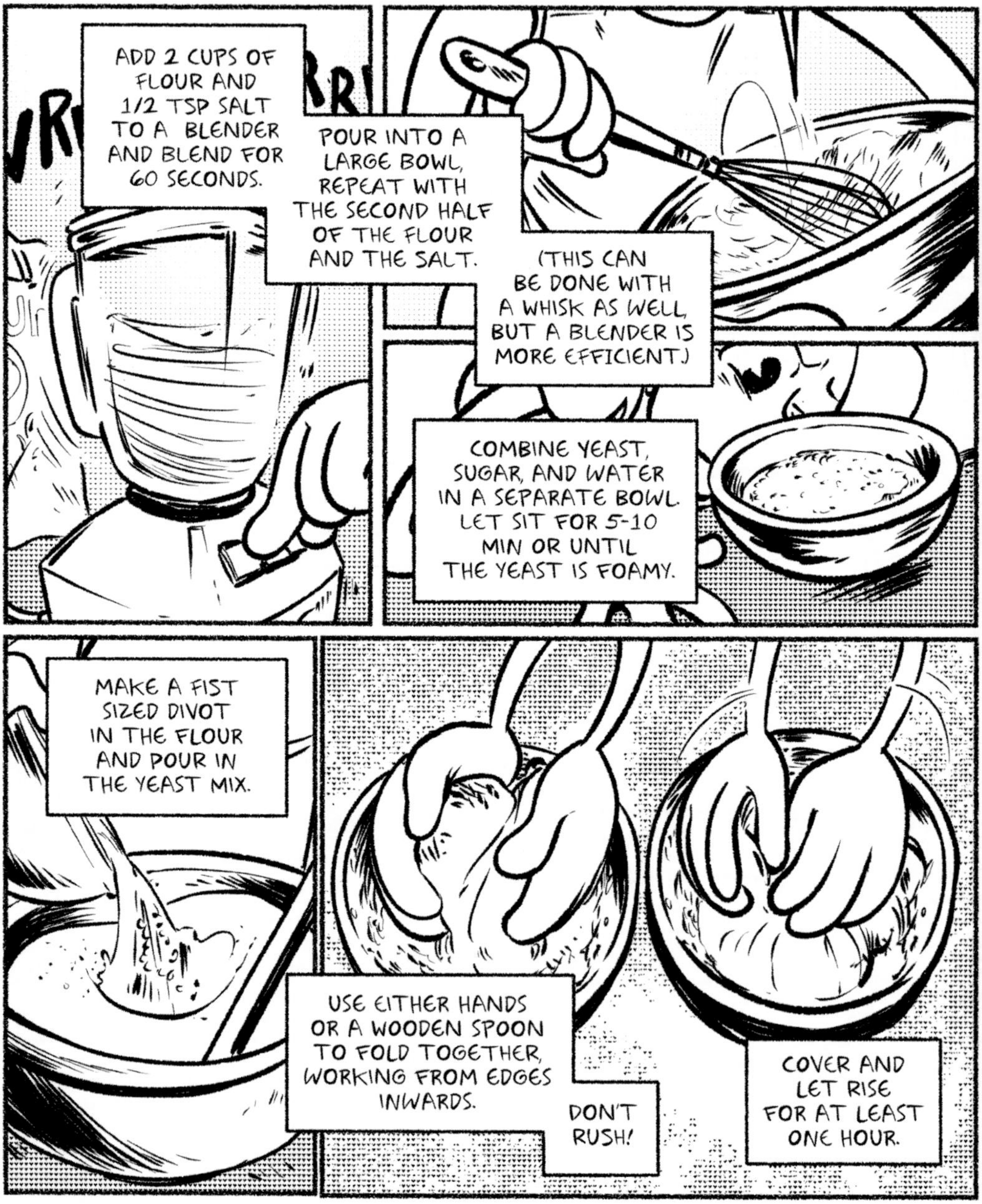

ADD 2 CUPS OF FLOUR AND 1/2 TSP SALT TO A BLENDER AND BLEND FOR 60 SECONDS.
POUR INTO A LARGE BOWL, REPEAT WITH THE SECOND HALF OF THE FLOUR AND THE SALT.
(THIS CAN BE DONE WITH A WHISK AS WELL, BUT A BLENDER IS MORE EFFICIENT.)
COMBINE YEAST, SUGAR, AND WATER IN A SEPARATE BOWL. LET SIT FOR 5-10 MIN OR UNTIL THE YEAST IS FOAMY.
MAKE A FIST SIZED DIVOT IN THE FLOUR AND POUR IN THE YEAST MIX.
USE EITHER HANDS OR A WOODEN SPOON TO FOLD TOGETHER, WORKING FROM EDGES INWARDS.
DON'T RUSH!
COVER AND LET RISE FOR AT LEAST ONE HOUR.

see notes for more!

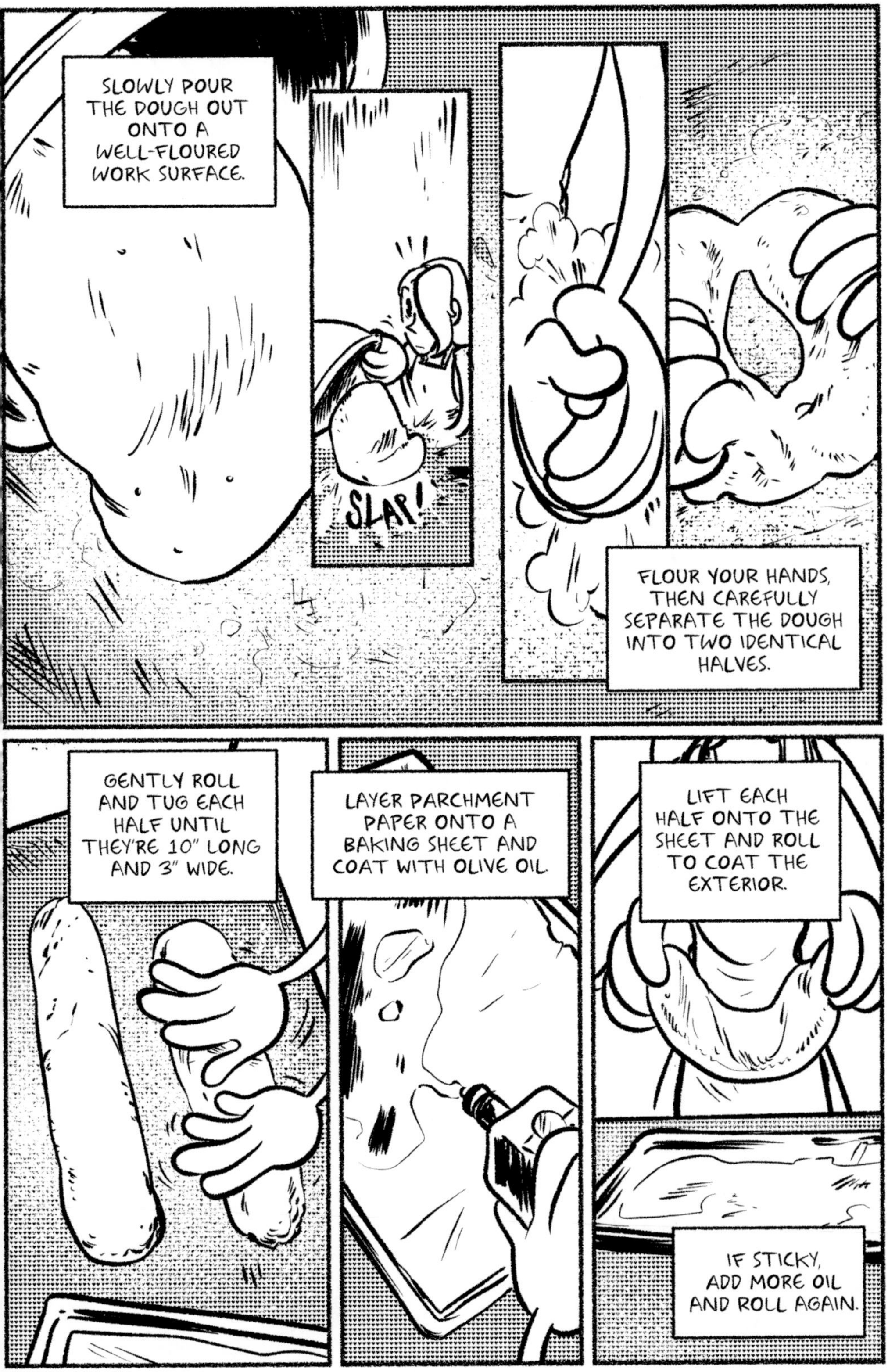
SLOWLY POUR THE DOUGH OUT ONTO A WELL-FLOURED WORK SURFACE.
SLAP!
FLOUR YOUR HANDS, THEN CAREFULLY SEPARATE THE DOUGH INTO TWO IDENTICAL HALVES.
GENTLY ROLL AND TUG EACH HALF UNTIL THEY'RE 10" LONG AND 3" WIDE.
LAYER PARCHMENT PAPER ONTO A BAKING SHEET AND COAT WITH OLIVE OIL.
LIFT EACH HALF ONTO THE SHEET AND ROLL TO COAT THE EXTERIOR.
IF STICKY, ADD MORE OIL AND ROLL AGAIN.

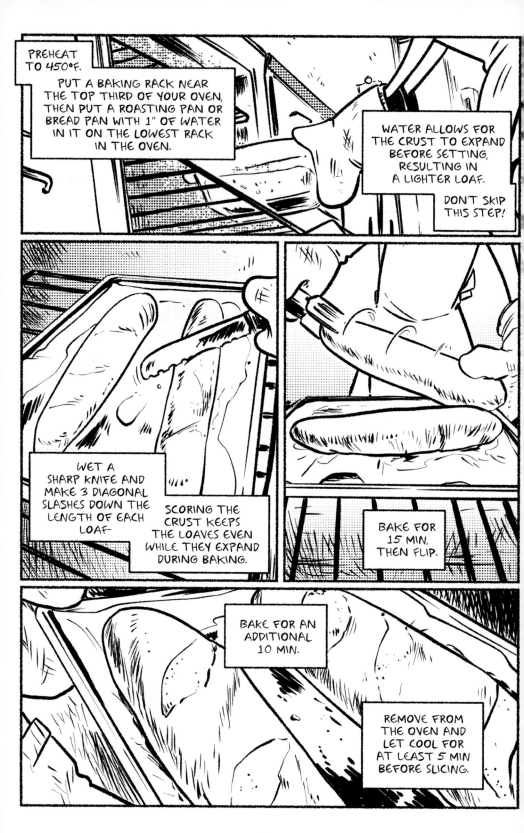

PREHEAT TO 450°F.

PUT A BAKING RACK NEAR THE TOP THIRD OF YOUR OVEN, THEN PUT A ROASTING PAN OR BREAD PAN WITH 1" OF WATER IN IT ON THE LOWEST RACK IN THE OVEN.

WATER ALLOWS FOR THE CRUST TO EXPAND BEFORE SETTING, RESULTING IN A LIGHTER LOAF.

DON'T SKIP THIS STEP!

WET A SHARP KNIFE AND MAKE 3 DIAGONAL SLASHES DOWN THE LENGTH OF EACH LOAF.

SCORING THE CRUST KEEPS THE LOAVES EVEN WHILE THEY EXPAND DURING BAKING.

BAKE FOR 15 MIN, THEN FLIP.

BAKE FOR AN ADDITIONAL 10 MIN.

REMOVE FROM THE OVEN AND LET COOL FOR AT LEAST 5 MIN BEFORE SLICING.

BISCUITS

HANDS ON: 5 MIN
HANDS OFF: 15 MIN

- 2 CUPS ALL-PURPOSE FLOUR
- 1 TBSP BAKING POWDER
- 1/2 TSP SALT
- 2/3 CUP NON-DAIRY MILK + 1/3 CUP VEGETABLE OIL OR 1 1/4 CUPS HEAVY CREAM
- 2 TBSP SUGAR (OPTIONAL)

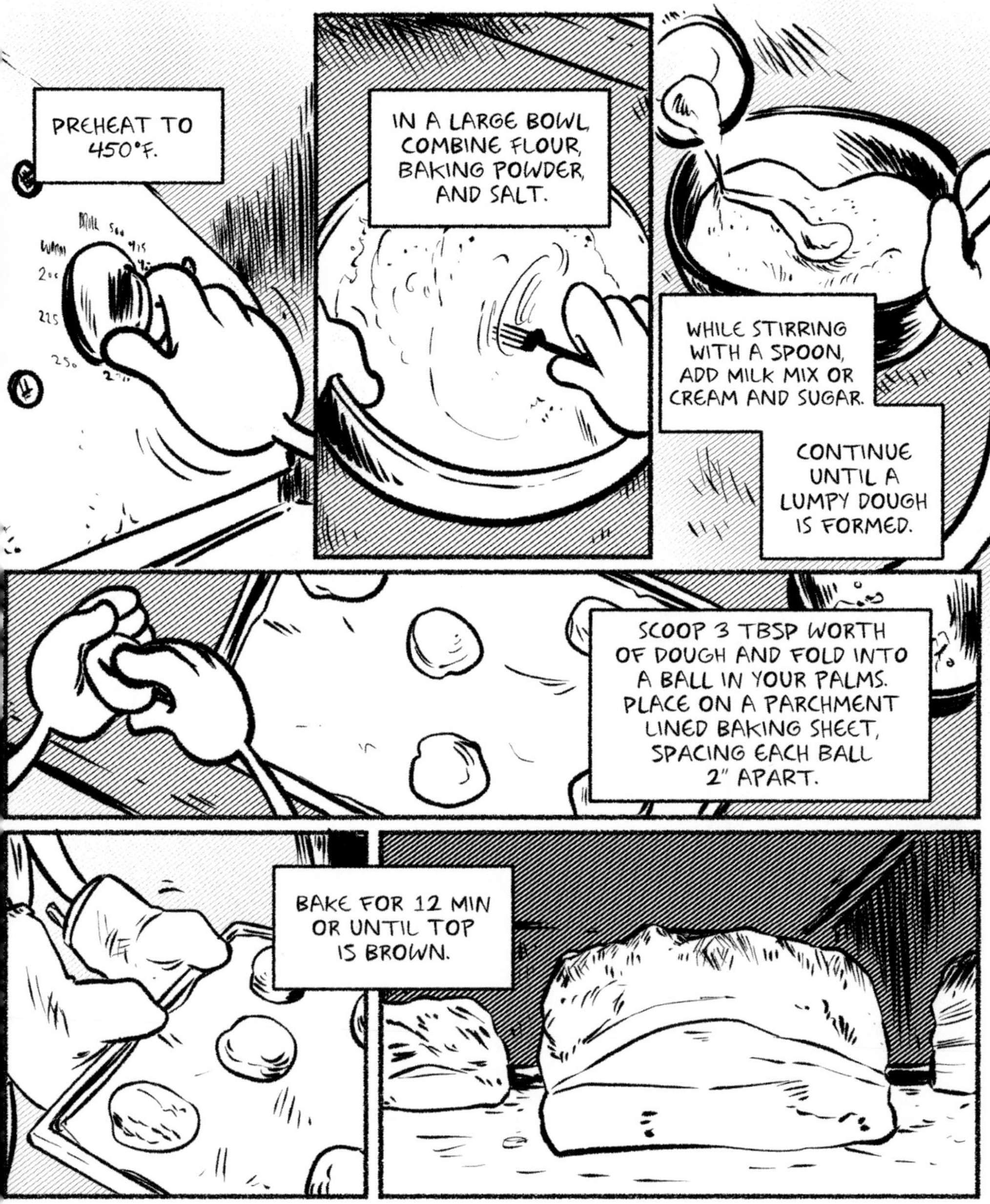
PREHEAT TO 450°F.
IN A LARGE BOWL, COMBINE FLOUR, BAKING POWDER, AND SALT.
WHILE STIRRING WITH A SPOON, ADD MILK MIX OR CREAM AND SUGAR.
CONTINUE UNTIL A LUMPY DOUGH IS FORMED.
SCOOP 3 TBSP WORTH OF DOUGH AND FOLD INTO A BALL IN YOUR PALMS. PLACE ON A PARCHMENT LINED BAKING SHEET, SPACING EACH BALL 2" APART.
BAKE FOR 12 MIN OR UNTIL TOP IS BROWN.

see notes for more!

TORTILLAS

HANDS ON: 30 MIN

- 2 CUPS MASA HARINA
- 1/2 TSP SALT
- 1 1/2 CUPS WARM WATER

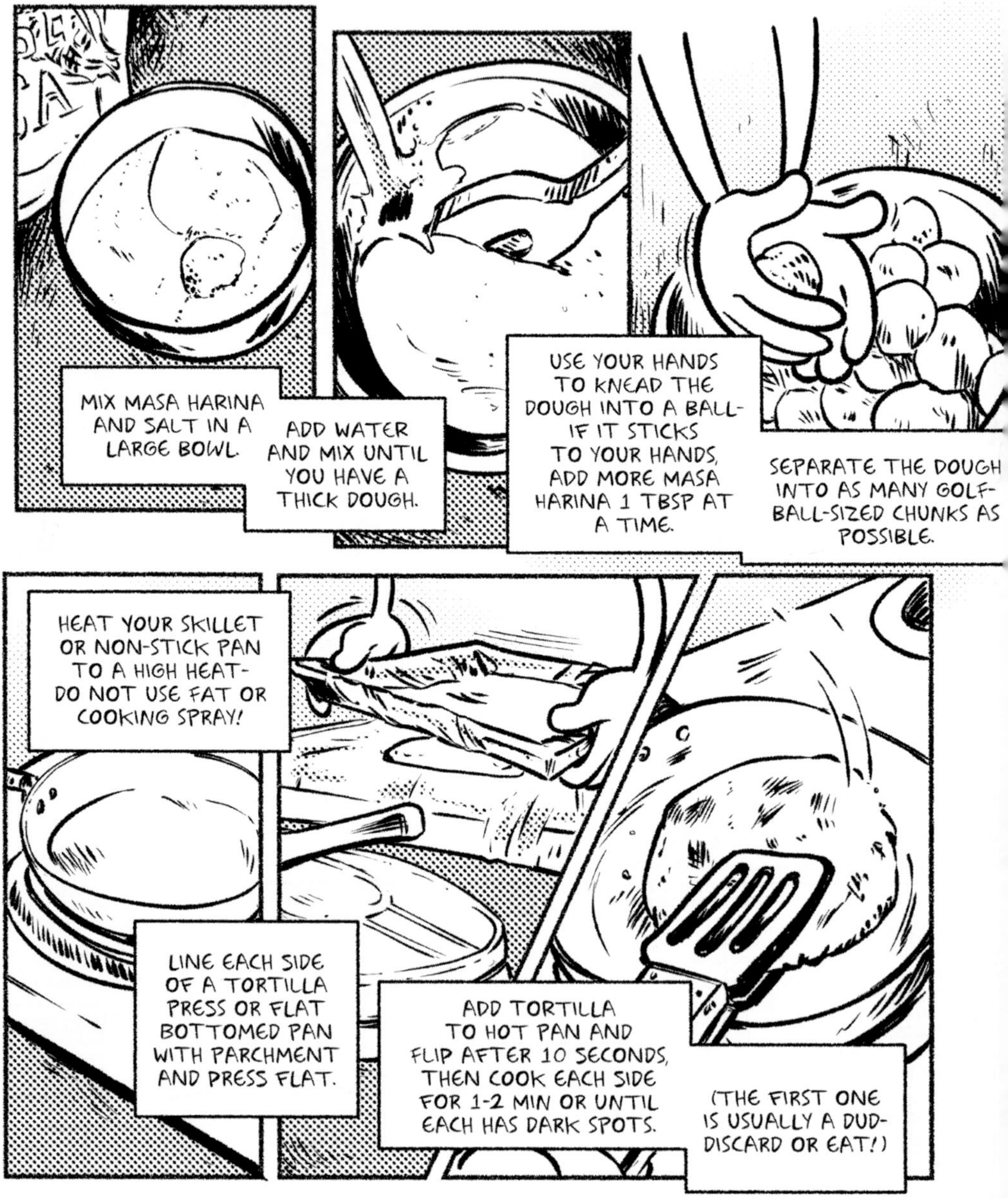
MIX MASA HARINA AND SALT IN A LARGE BOWL.
ADD WATER AND MIX UNTIL YOU HAVE A THICK DOUGH.
USE YOUR HANDS TO KNEAD THE DOUGH INTO A BALL- IF IT STICKS TO YOUR HANDS, ADD MORE MASA HARINA 1 TBSP AT A TIME.
SEPARATE THE DOUGH INTO AS MANY GOLF-BALL-SIZED CHUNKS AS POSSIBLE.
HEAT YOUR SKILLET OR NON-STICK PAN TO A HIGH HEAT- DO NOT USE FAT OR COOKING SPRAY!
LINE EACH SIDE OF A TORTILLA PRESS OR FLAT BOTTOMED PAN WITH PARCHMENT AND PRESS FLAT.
ADD TORTILLA TO HOT PAN AND FLIP AFTER 10 SECONDS, THEN COOK EACH SIDE FOR 1-2 MIN OR UNTIL EACH HAS DARK SPOTS.
(THE FIRST ONE IS USUALLY A DUD- DISCARD OR EAT!)

see notes for more!

PIZZA DOUGH

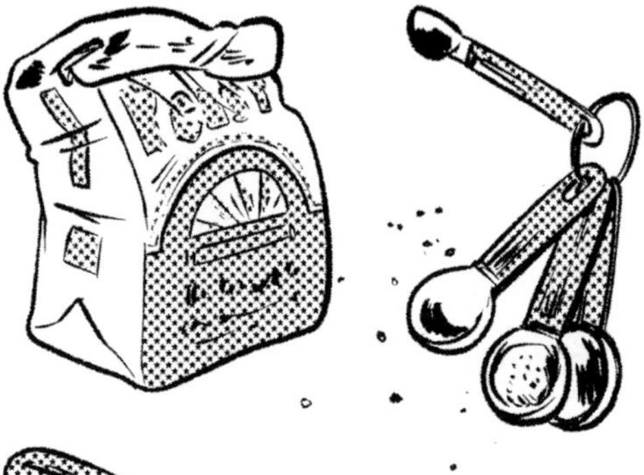

HANDS ON: 15 MIN
HANDS OFF: 35 MIN

- 1/2 TBSP INSTANT YEAST
- 1 TSP GRANULATED WHITE SUGAR
- 1 CUP WARM WATER
- 1 TSP SALT
- 2 1/2 CUPS ALL-PURPOSE FLOUR
- 1/4 CUP EXTRA VIRGIN OLIVE OIL (CAN BE SUBSTITUTED FOR SAFFLOWER, VEGETABLE, OR AVOCADO IN A PINCH, BUT EVO TASTES BEST!)

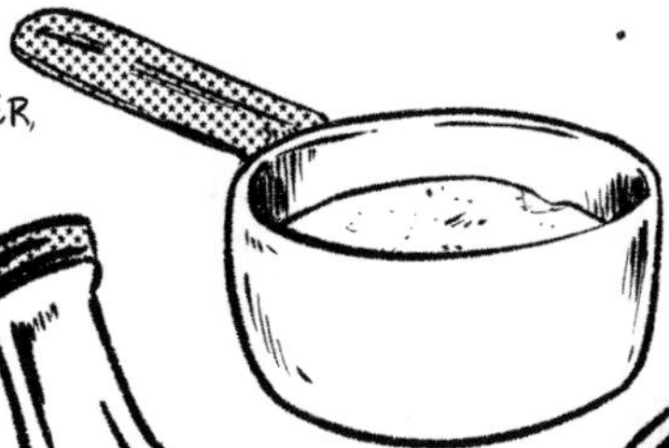

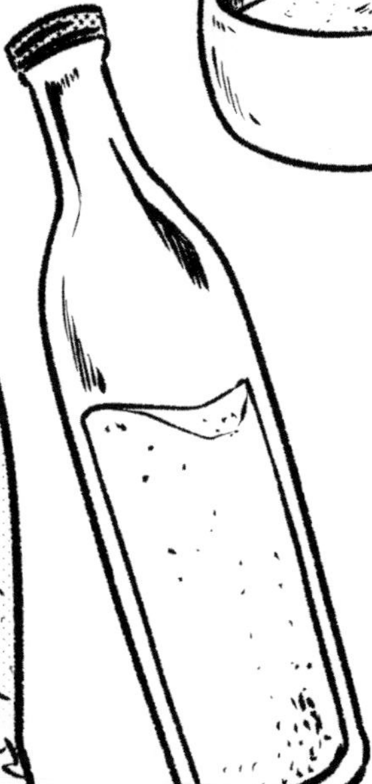

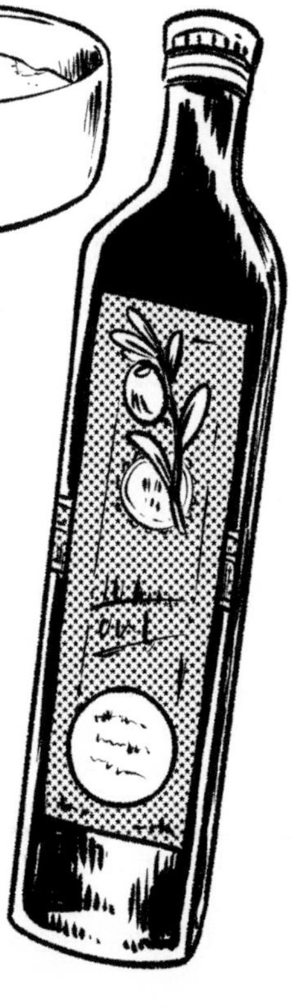

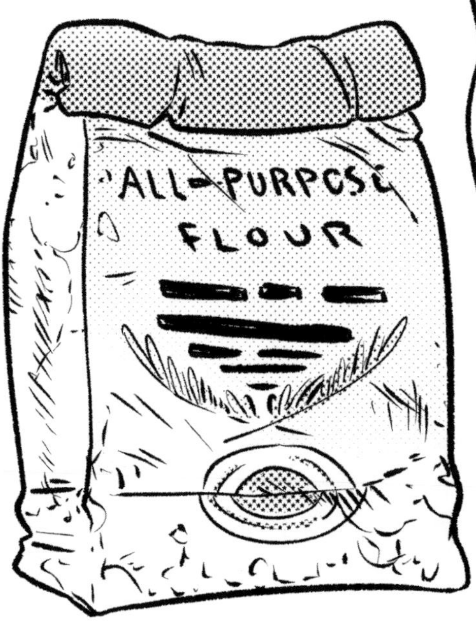
ALL-PURPOSE
FLOUR

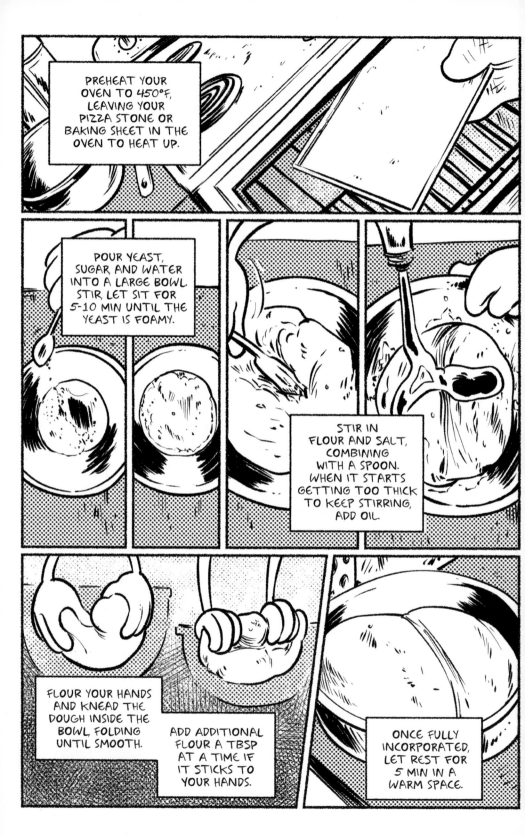

PREHEAT YOUR OVEN TO 450°F, LEAVING YOUR PIZZA STONE OR BAKING SHEET IN THE OVEN TO HEAT UP.

POUR YEAST, SUGAR, AND WATER INTO A LARGE BOWL. STIR, LET SIT FOR 5-10 MIN UNTIL THE YEAST IS FOAMY.

STIR IN FLOUR AND SALT, COMBINING WITH A SPOON. WHEN IT STARTS GETTING TOO THICK TO KEEP STIRRING, ADD OIL.

FLOUR YOUR HANDS AND KNEAD THE DOUGH INSIDE THE BOWL, FOLDING UNTIL SMOOTH.

ADD ADDITIONAL FLOUR A TBSP AT A TIME IF IT STICKS TO YOUR HANDS.

ONCE FULLY INCORPORATED, LET REST FOR 5 MIN IN A WARM SPACE.

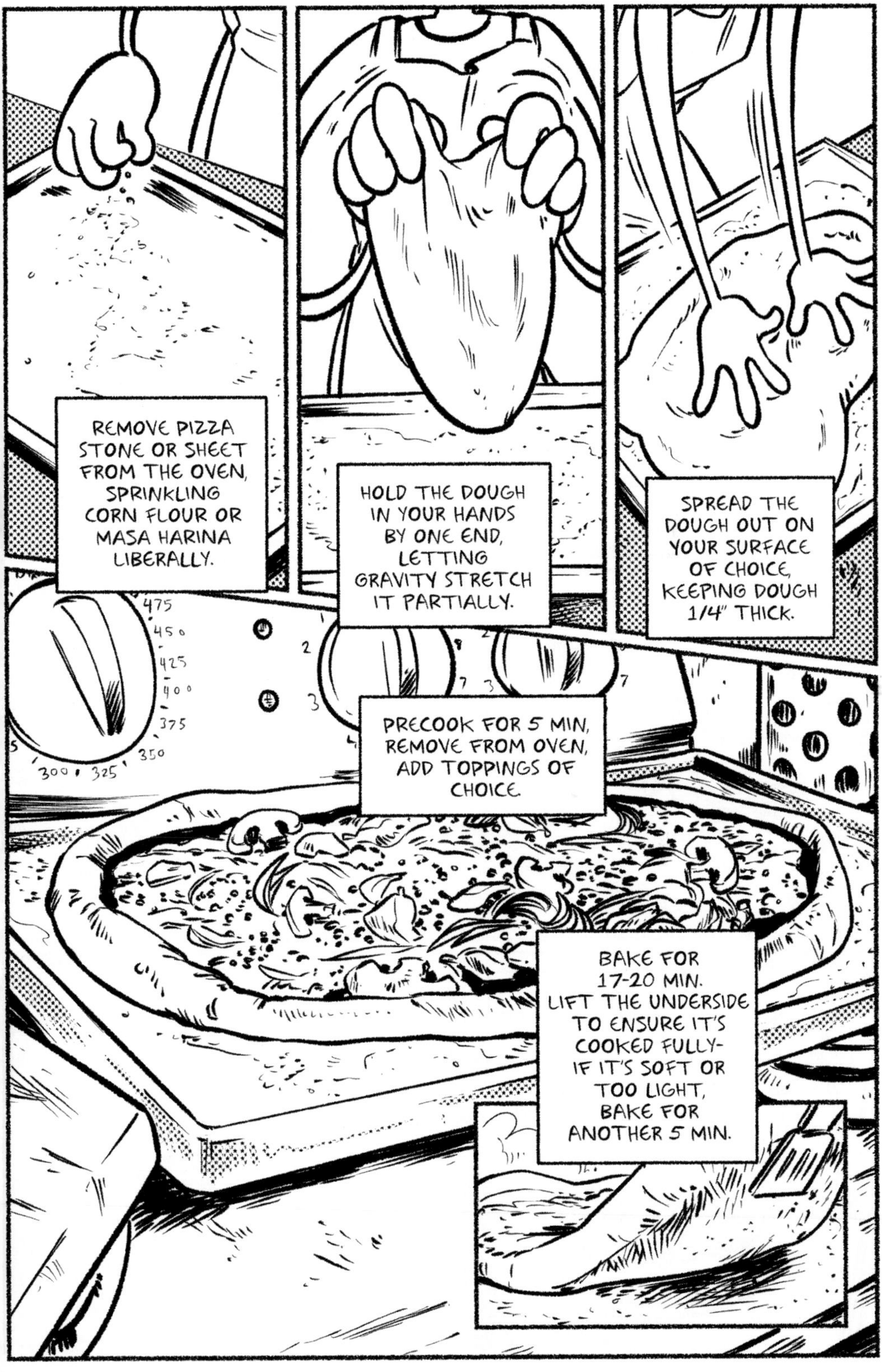

REMOVE PIZZA STONE OR SHEET FROM THE OVEN, SPRINKLING CORN FLOUR OR MASA HARINA LIBERALLY.
HOLD THE DOUGH IN YOUR HANDS BY ONE END, LETTING GRAVITY STRETCH IT PARTIALLY.
SPREAD THE DOUGH OUT ON YOUR SURFACE OF CHOICE, KEEPING DOUGH 1/4" THICK.
475
450
425
400
375
350
325
300
PRECOOK FOR 5 MIN, REMOVE FROM OVEN, ADD TOPPINGS OF CHOICE.
BAKE FOR 17-20 MIN. LIFT THE UNDERSIDE TO ENSURE IT'S COOKED FULLY- IF IT'S SOFT OR TOO LIGHT, BAKE FOR ANOTHER 5 MIN.

HASHBROWNS

HANDS ON: 15 MIN

-2 LARGE POTATOES (RUSSET OR RED)
-ENOUGH VEGETABLE OR COCONUT OIL TO COVER THE BOTTOM OF YOUR PAN OF CHOICE
-PINCH OF SALT
-PINCH OF BLACK PEPPER

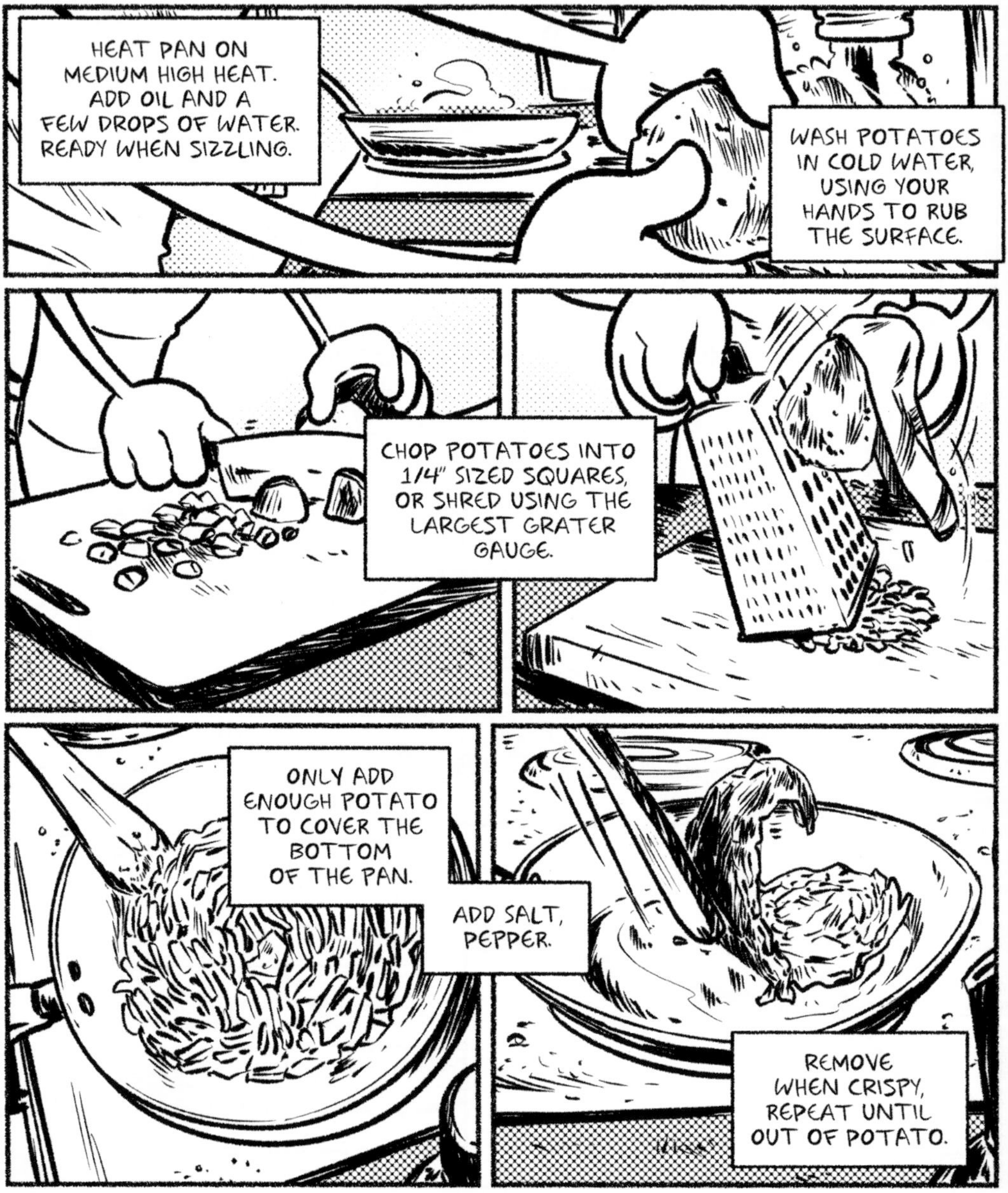
HEAT PAN ON MEDIUM HIGH HEAT. ADD OIL AND A FEW DROPS OF WATER. READY WHEN SIZZLING.
WASH POTATOES IN COLD WATER, USING YOUR HANDS TO RUB THE SURFACE.
CHOP POTATOES INTO 1/4" SIZED SQUARES, OR SHRED USING THE LARGEST GRATER GAUGE.
ONLY ADD ENOUGH POTATO TO COVER THE BOTTOM OF THE PAN.
ADD SALT, PEPPER.
REMOVE WHEN CRISPY, REPEAT UNTIL OUT OF POTATO.

PANCAKES

HANDS ON: 25 MIN

- -1 1/2 CUPS ALL-PURPOSE FLOUR
- -3 1/2 TSP BAKING POWDER
- -1 TSP SALT
- -1 TSP GRANULATED WHITE SUGAR
- -1 1/4 CUPS MILK, ROOM TEMP
- -1 EGG (LARGE)
- -1 TBSP BUTTER, MELTED
- -ENOUGH VEGETABLE OR COCONUT OIL TO COVER THE BOTTOM OF YOUR PAN OF CHOICE OR 1 ADDTL TBSP BUTTER (USE OIL FOR CRISPY PANCAKES, AND BUTTER FOR SOFTER ONES.)

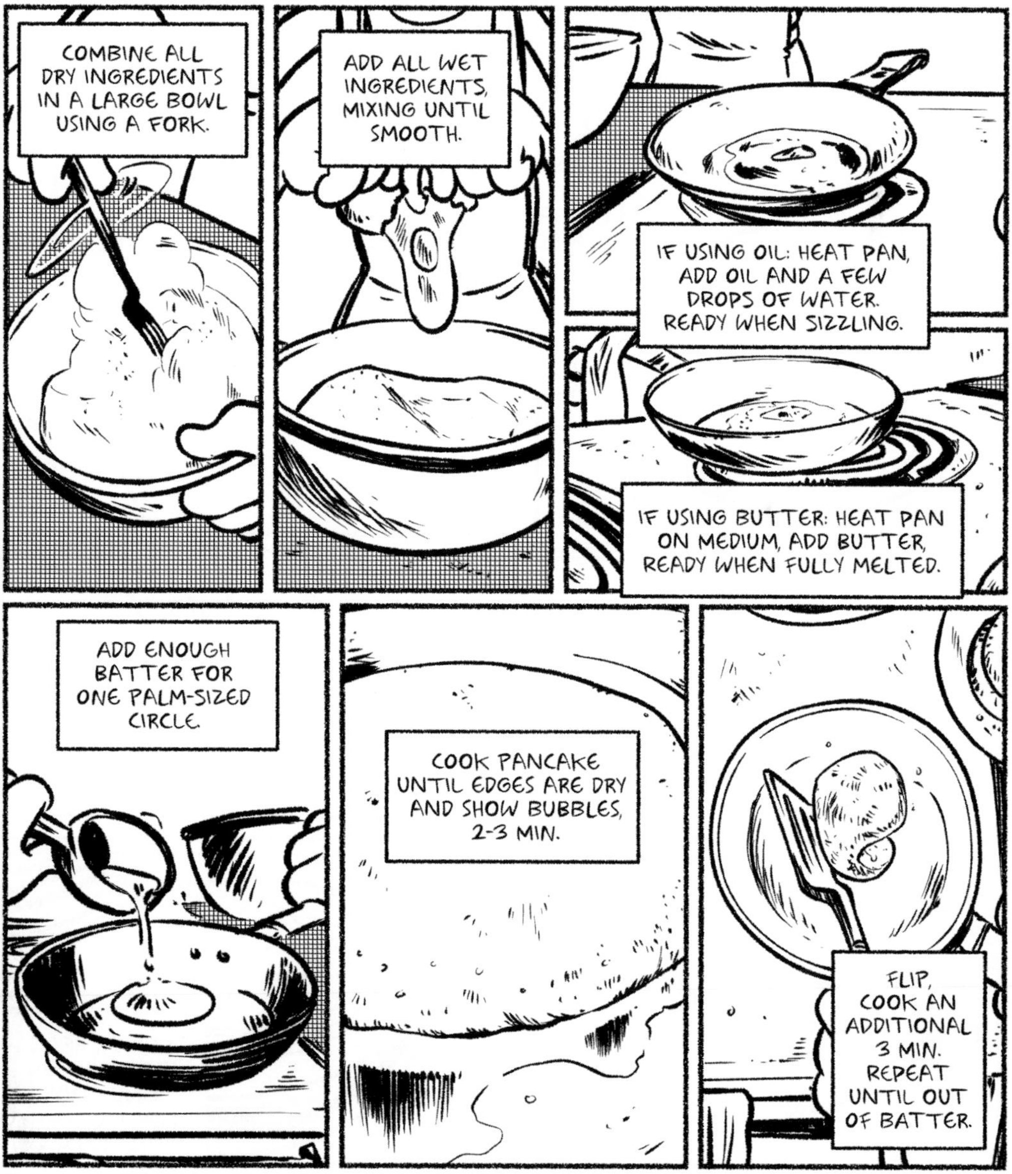
COMBINE ALL DRY INGREDIENTS IN A LARGE BOWL USING A FORK.
ADD ALL WET INGREDIENTS, MIXING UNTIL SMOOTH.
IF USING OIL: HEAT PAN, ADD OIL AND A FEW DROPS OF WATER. READY WHEN SIZZLING.
IF USING BUTTER: HEAT PAN ON MEDIUM, ADD BUTTER, READY WHEN FULLY MELTED.
ADD ENOUGH BATTER FOR ONE PALM-SIZED CIRCLE.
COOK PANCAKE UNTIL EDGES ARE DRY AND SHOW BUBBLES, 2-3 MIN.
FLIP, COOK AN ADDITIONAL 3 MIN. REPEAT UNTIL OUT OF BATTER.

VERY BASIC OMELETTE

HANDS ON: 15 MIN

-2 EGGS, LARGE
-1 TSP UNSALTED BUTTER
-PINCH OF SALT
-SPICES OF CHOICE

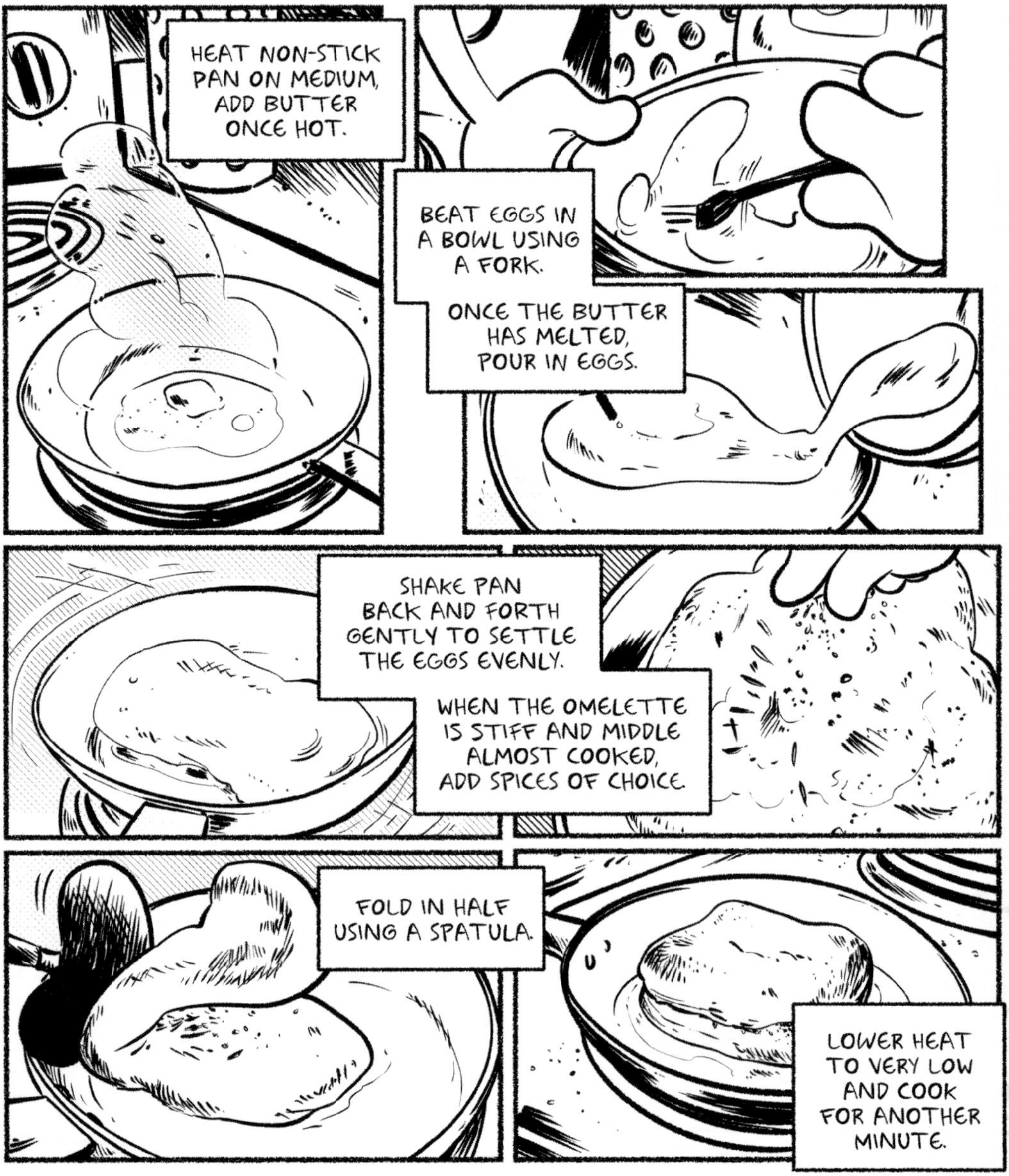

HEAT NON-STICK PAN ON MEDIUM, ADD BUTTER ONCE HOT.
BEAT EGGS IN A BOWL USING A FORK.
ONCE THE BUTTER HAS MELTED, POUR IN EGGS.
SHAKE PAN BACK AND FORTH GENTLY TO SETTLE THE EGGS EVENLY.
WHEN THE OMELETTE IS STIFF AND MIDDLE ALMOST COOKED, ADD SPICES OF CHOICE.
FOLD IN HALF USING A SPATULA.
LOWER HEAT TO VERY LOW AND COOK FOR ANOTHER MINUTE.

SCRAMBLED EGGS

HANDS ON: 15 MIN

-3 EGGS
-1/4 CUP MILK, DAIRY OR NON, OR WATER
-1 TSP UNSALTED BUTTER
-PINCH OF SALT

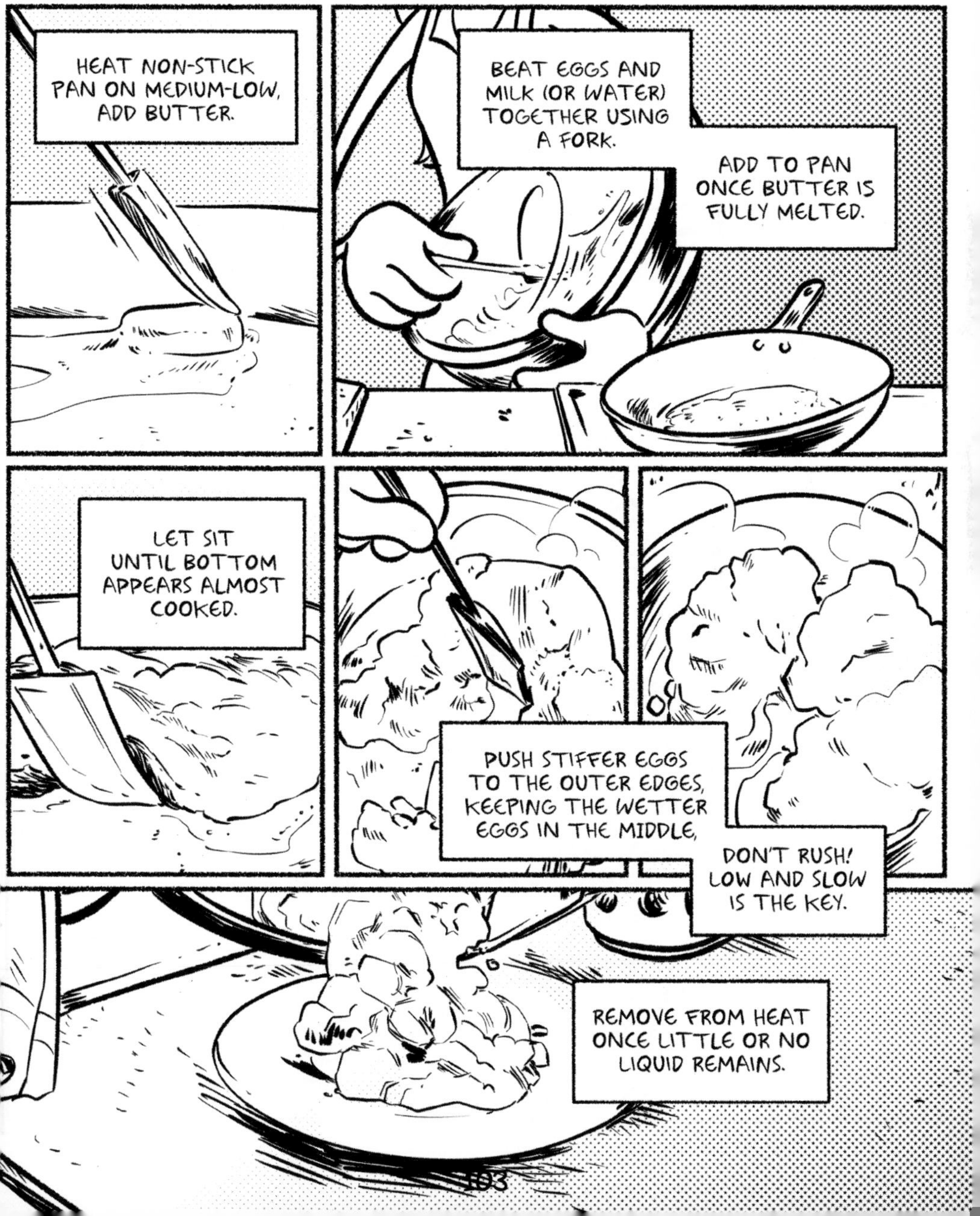
HEAT NON-STICK PAN ON MEDIUM-LOW, ADD BUTTER.
BEAT EGGS AND MILK (OR WATER) TOGETHER USING A FORK.
ADD TO PAN ONCE BUTTER IS FULLY MELTED.
LET SIT UNTIL BOTTOM APPEARS ALMOST COOKED.
PUSH STIFFER EGGS TO THE OUTER EDGES, KEEPING THE WETTER EGGS IN THE MIDDLE.
DON'T RUSH! LOW AND SLOW IS THE KEY.
REMOVE FROM HEAT ONCE LITTLE OR NO LIQUID REMAINS.

TAMAGO KAKE GOHAN
(EGG ON RICE)

HANDS ON: 15 MIN
HANDS OFF: 15 MIN
(IF COOKING RICE FRESH)

- 1 CUP UNCOOKED RICE OR 1 1/2 CUPS PRECOOKED RICE
- 1 EGG, LARGE
- 1 TBSP SOY SAUCE
- 2 GREEN ONIONS
- 1/2 CUP WATER OR BROTH FOR REHEATING PRECOOKED RICE

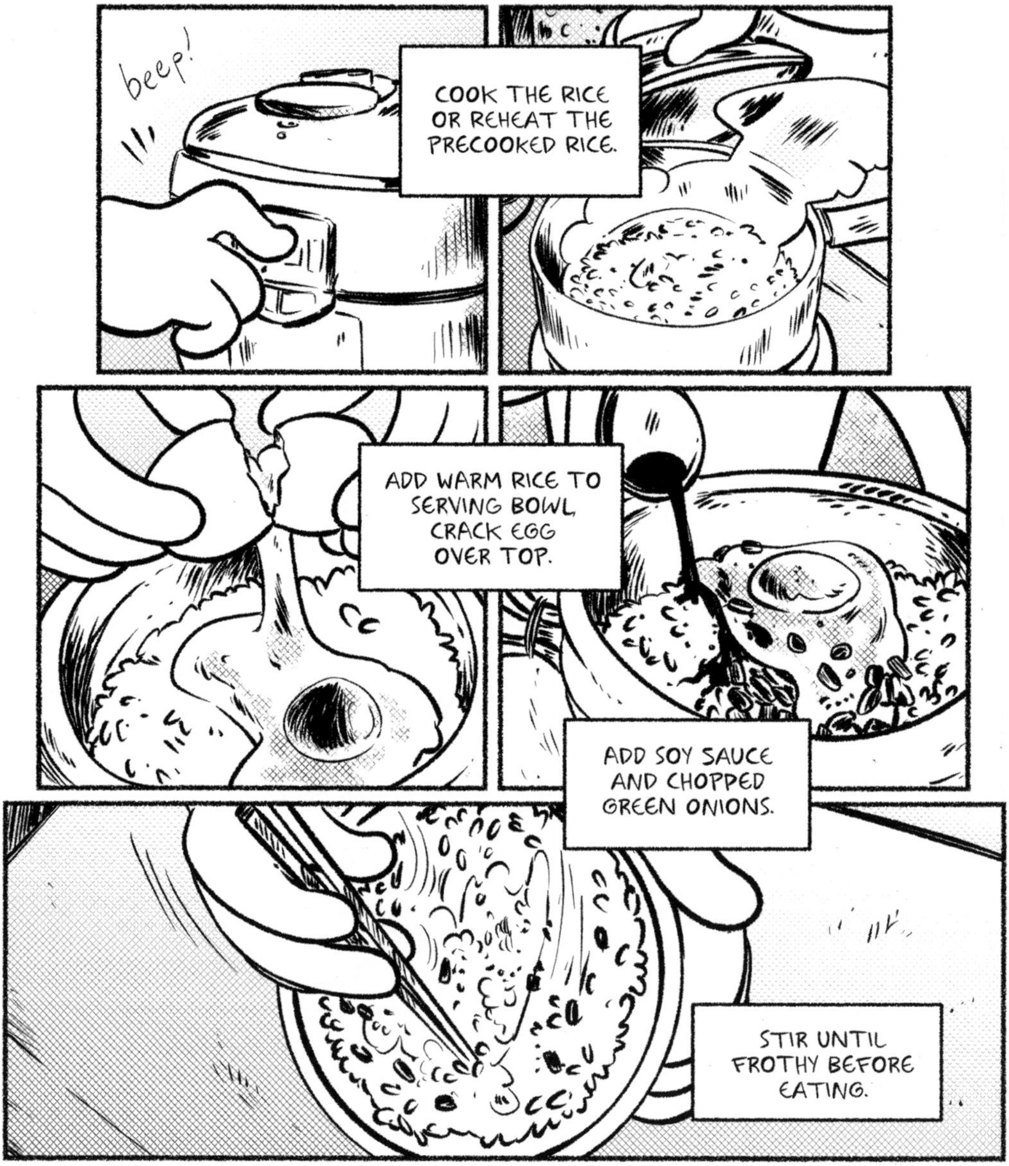

beep!
COOK THE RICE OR REHEAT THE PRECOOKED RICE.
ADD WARM RICE TO SERVING BOWL, CRACK EGG OVER TOP.
ADD SOY SAUCE AND CHOPPED GREEN ONIONS.
STIR UNTIL FROTHY BEFORE EATING.

HUEVOS RANCHEROS

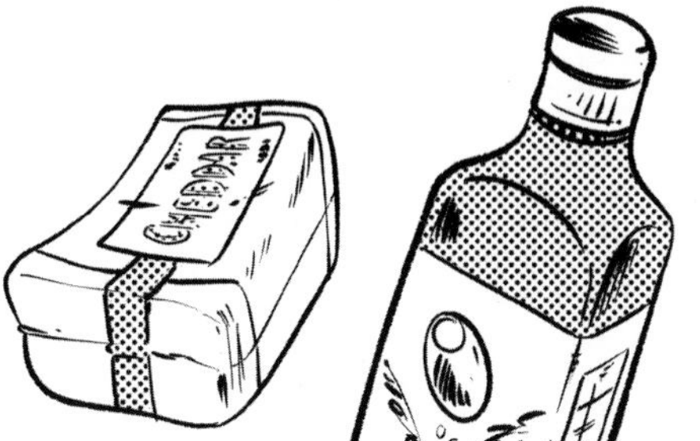
CHEDDAR

HANDS ON: 35 MIN

- -2 TBSP OLIVE OIL
- -1/2 CUP CHEDDAR OR MONTEREY JACK CHEESE
- -1 EGG, LARGE
- -1 CUP BLACK BEANS
- -1/2 CUP BELL PEPPER
- -1/2 CUP YELLOW ONION
- -1/3 CUP ROMA TOMATO
- -1 TORTILLA, FLOUR OR CORN
- -1/3 CUP AVOCADO
- -2 CLOVES OF GARLIC

- -1 TBSP LIME JUICE
- -1 TBSP SALT
- -1 TBSP BLACK PEPPER
- -2 TSP PAPRIKA
- -2 TSP CAYENNE
- -1 TSP CUMIN
- -1 TBSP CILANTRO
- -CHILI SAUCE OR TABASCO (OPTIONAL)

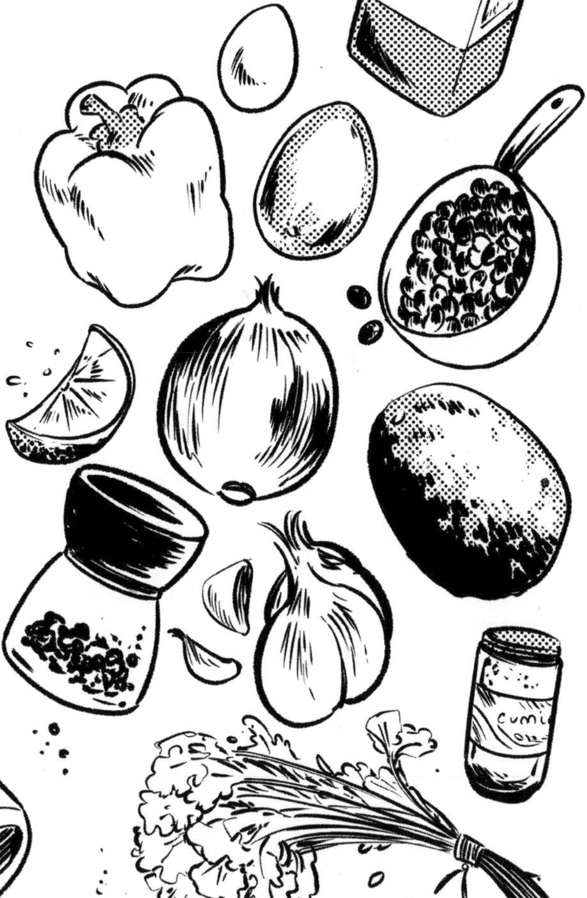

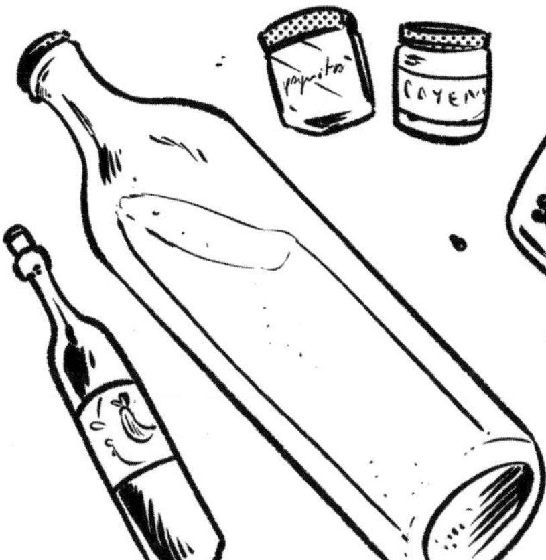

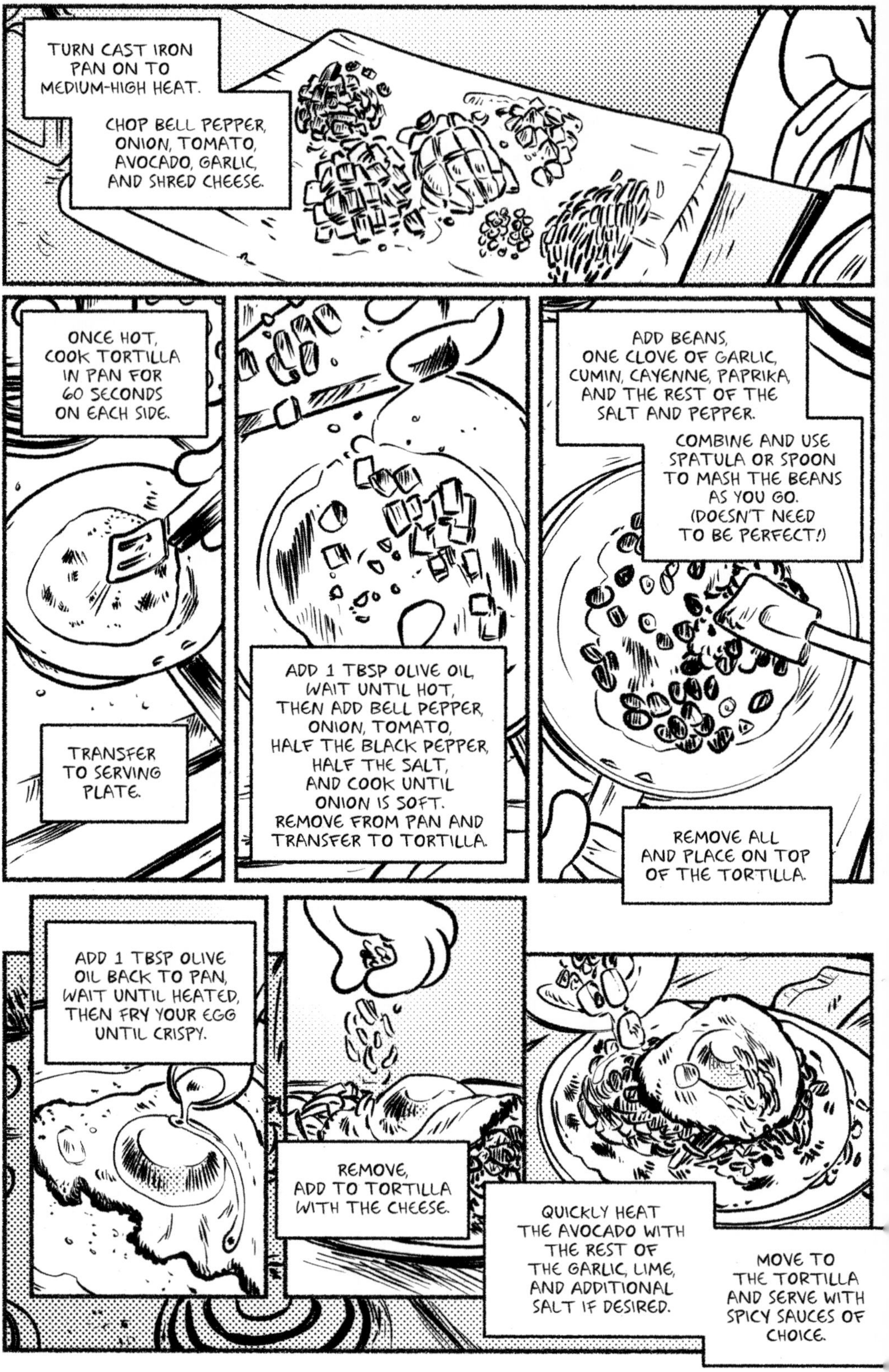
TURN CAST IRON PAN ON TO MEDIUM-HIGH HEAT.
CHOP BELL PEPPER, ONION, TOMATO, AVOCADO, GARLIC, AND SHRED CHEESE.
ONCE HOT, COOK TORTILLA IN PAN FOR 60 SECONDS ON EACH SIDE.
TRANSFER TO SERVING PLATE.
ADD 1 TBSP OLIVE OIL, WAIT UNTIL HOT, THEN ADD BELL PEPPER, ONION, TOMATO, HALF THE BLACK PEPPER, HALF THE SALT, AND COOK UNTIL ONION IS SOFT. REMOVE FROM PAN AND TRANSFER TO TORTILLA.
ADD BEANS, ONE CLOVE OF GARLIC, CUMIN, CAYENNE, PAPRIKA, AND THE REST OF THE SALT AND PEPPER.
COMBINE AND USE SPATULA OR SPOON TO MASH THE BEANS AS YOU GO. (DOESN'T NEED TO BE PERFECT!)
REMOVE ALL AND PLACE ON TOP OF THE TORTILLA.
ADD 1 TBSP OLIVE OIL BACK TO PAN, WAIT UNTIL HEATED, THEN FRY YOUR EGG UNTIL CRISPY.
REMOVE, ADD TO TORTILLA WITH THE CHEESE.
QUICKLY HEAT THE AVOCADO WITH THE REST OF THE GARLIC, LIME, AND ADDITIONAL SALT IF DESIRED.
MOVE TO THE TORTILLA AND SERVE WITH SPICY SAUCES OF CHOICE.

DUTCH BABY

HANDS ON: 5 MIN
HANDS OFF: 30 MIN

- 2 EGGS
- 1/2 CUP UNBLEACHED FLOUR
- 1/2 CUP MILK, DAIRY OR NON
- 1 TBSP SUGAR
- 1 TSP NUTMEG
- 4 TBSP UNSALTED BUTTER
- SYRUP, PRESERVES, OR OTHER
  TOPPING OF CHOICE.

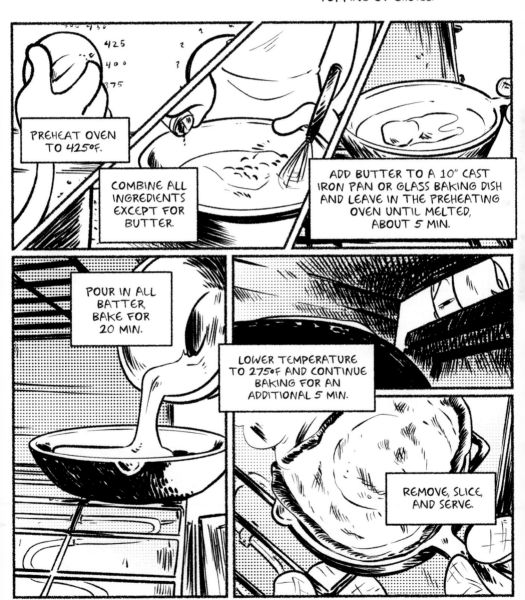

PREHEAT OVEN TO 425°F.

COMBINE ALL INGREDIENTS EXCEPT FOR BUTTER.

ADD BUTTER TO A 10" CAST IRON PAN OR GLASS BAKING DISH AND LEAVE IN THE PREHEATING OVEN UNTIL MELTED, ABOUT 5 MIN.

POUR IN ALL BATTER, BAKE FOR 20 MIN.

LOWER TEMPERATURE TO 275°F AND CONTINUE BAKING FOR AN ADDITIONAL 5 MIN.

REMOVE, SLICE, AND SERVE.

TOFU BACON

HANDS ON: 10 MIN
HANDS OFF: 12 HR 30 MIN TO 24 HR

- 8OZ PACKAGE OF FIRM TOFU
- 4 TBSP SMOKED PAPRIKA
- 4 TBSP CAYENNE
- 3 TBSP APPLE CIDER VINEGAR
- 2 TBSP NUTRITIONAL YEAST
- 1/2 TBSP BLACK PEPPER
- 1/2 CUP SOY SAUCE
- 1/4 CUP MAPLE SYRUP

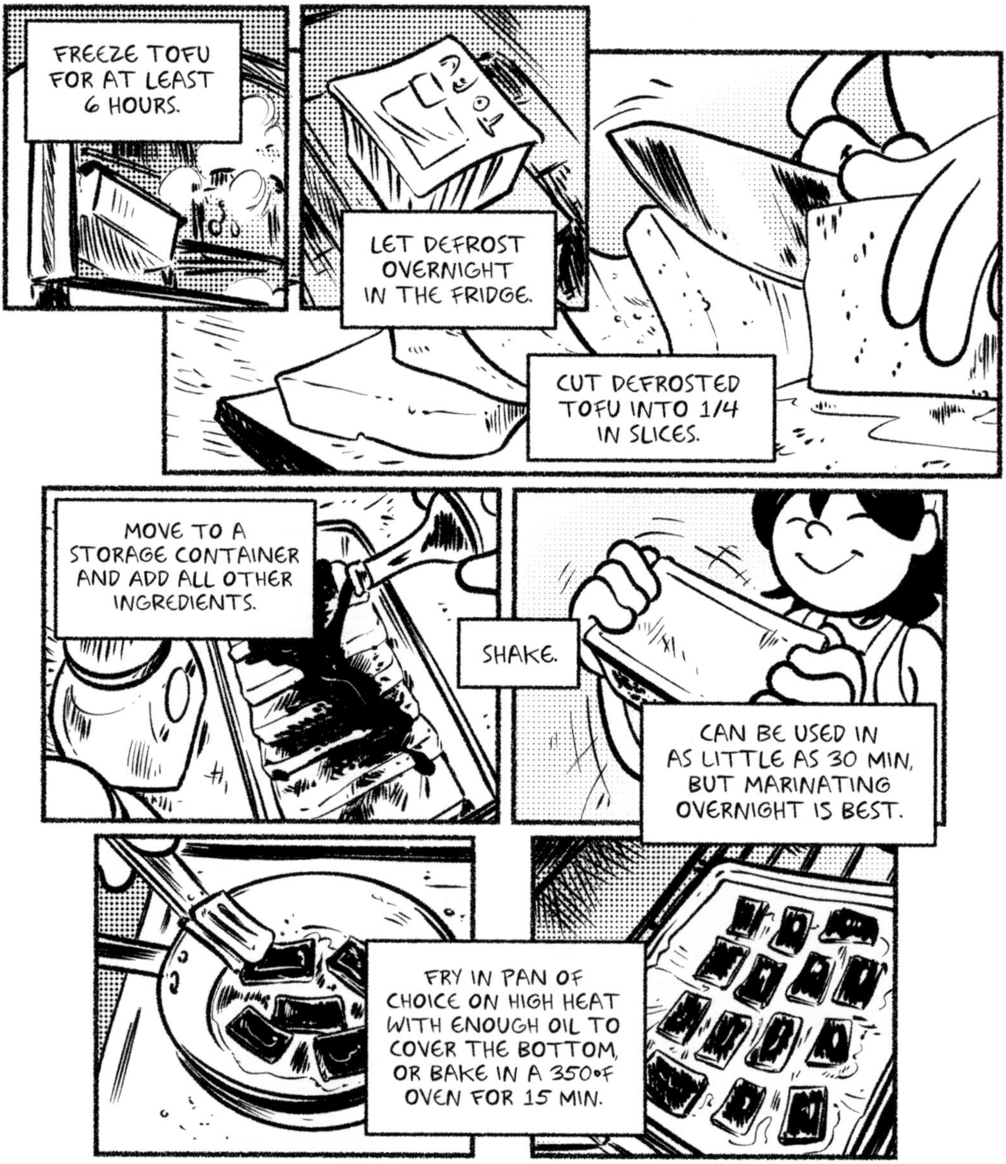
FREEZE TOFU FOR AT LEAST 6 HOURS.
LET DEFROST OVERNIGHT IN THE FRIDGE.
CUT DEFROSTED TOFU INTO 1/4 IN SLICES.
MOVE TO A STORAGE CONTAINER AND ADD ALL OTHER INGREDIENTS.
SHAKE.
CAN BE USED IN AS LITTLE AS 30 MIN, BUT MARINATING OVERNIGHT IS BEST.
FRY IN PAN OF CHOICE ON HIGH HEAT WITH ENOUGH OIL TO COVER THE BOTTOM, OR BAKE IN A 350°F OVEN FOR 15 MIN.

CHILAQUILES

HANDS ON: 15 MIN
HANDS OFF: 10 MIN

- 3 LARGE FLOUR TORTILLAS, SLICED, OR 6 SMALL CORN TORTILLAS, SLICED, OR 2-3 CUPS OF TORTILLA CHIPS.
- 2 TBSP OLIVE OIL (1 TBSP IF USING CHIPS)
- 1 CUP SALSA OR PICO DE GALLO
- 1/3 CUP WHITE ONION (IF USING SALSA)
- 1 TBSP CORIANDER OR 1 SPRIG EPAZOTE
- 2 TBSP CILANTRO
- PINCH OF SALT
- 1/4 CUP CHEDDAR OR QUESO FRESCO (OPTIONAL)
- 1 EGG, FRIED (OPTIONAL)

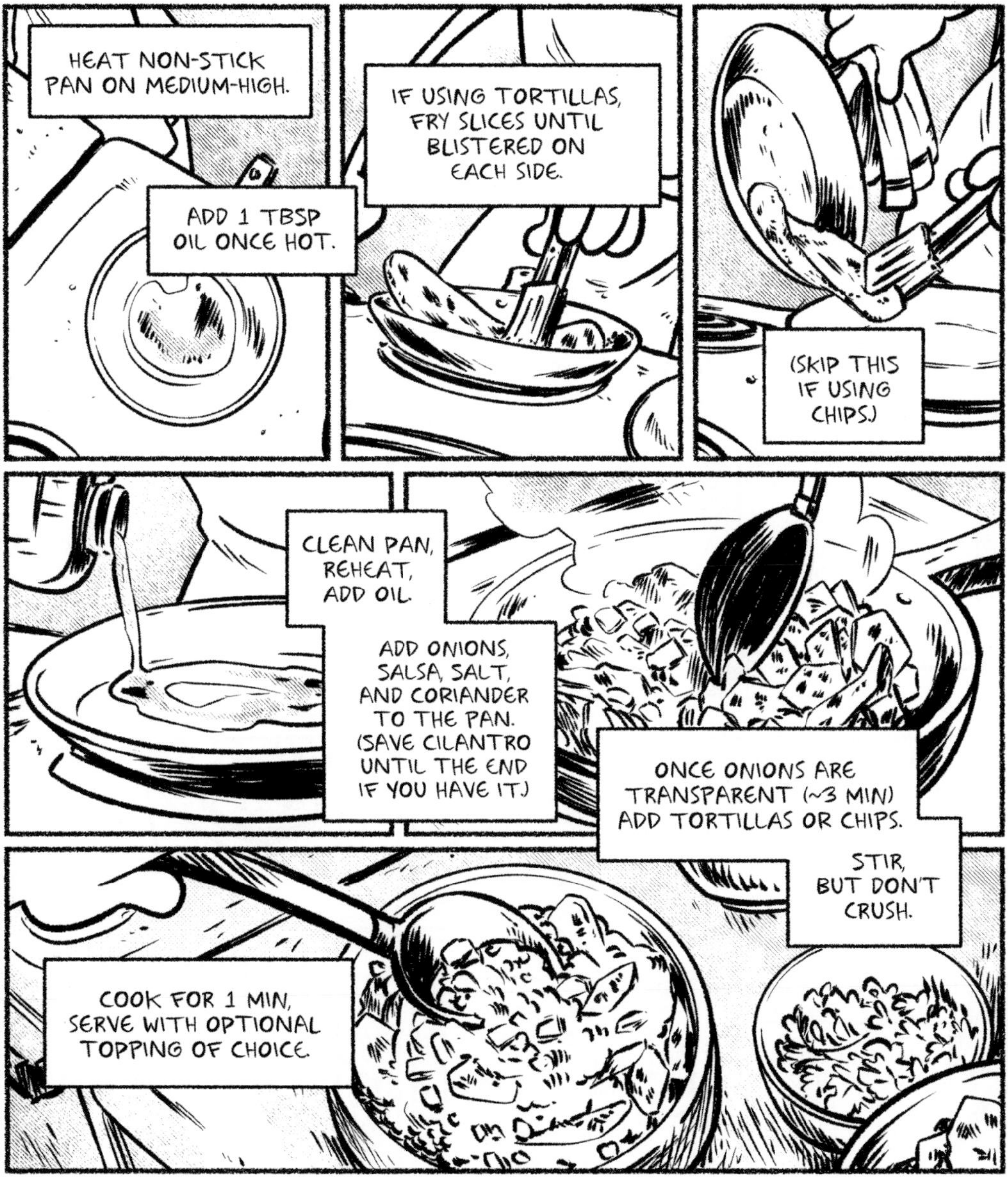
HEAT NON-STICK PAN ON MEDIUM-HIGH.
ADD 1 TBSP OIL ONCE HOT.
IF USING TORTILLAS, FRY SLICES UNTIL BLISTERED ON EACH SIDE.
(SKIP THIS IF USING CHIPS.)
CLEAN PAN, REHEAT, ADD OIL.
ADD ONIONS, SALSA, SALT, AND CORIANDER TO THE PAN. (SAVE CILANTRO UNTIL THE END IF YOU HAVE IT.)
ONCE ONIONS ARE TRANSPARENT (~3 MIN) ADD TORTILLAS OR CHIPS.
STIR, BUT DON'T CRUSH.
COOK FOR 1 MIN, SERVE WITH OPTIONAL TOPPING OF CHOICE.

SHAKSHUKA

HANDS ON: 15 MIN
HANDS OFF: 15 MIN

-2 TBSP OLIVE OR VEGETABLE OIL
-3 CLOVES OF GARLIC
-1/2 WHITE TO YELLOW ONION
-1 28OZ CAN DICED TOMATOES
-2 TSP SALT
-2 TSP BLACK PEPPER
-1 TSP CUMIN
-2 TSP SMOKED PAPRIKA
-1 TSP CAYENNE
-1 TSP ROSEMARY
-1/2 CUP FETA
-4 EGGS
-1 TBSP CILANTRO (OPTIONAL)

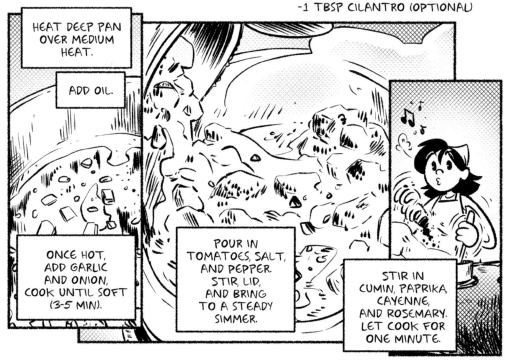

HEAT DEEP PAN OVER MEDIUM HEAT.

ADD OIL.

ONCE HOT, ADD GARLIC AND ONION, COOK UNTIL SOFT (3-5 MIN).

POUR IN TOMATOES, SALT, AND PEPPER. STIR, LID, AND BRING TO A STEADY SIMMER.

STIR IN CUMIN, PAPRIKA CAYENNE, AND ROSEMARY. LET COOK FOR ONE MINUTE.

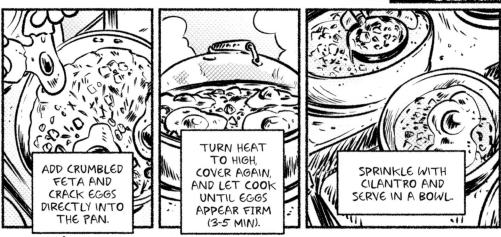

ADD CRUMBLED FETA AND CRACK EGGS DIRECTLY INTO THE PAN.

TURN HEAT TO HIGH, COVER AGAIN, AND LET COOK UNTIL EGGS APPEAR FIRM (3-5 MIN).

SPRINKLE WITH CILANTRO AND SERVE IN A BOWL.

see notes for more!

SCONES

HANDS ON 15 MIN
HANDS OFF: 45 MIN

- 2 CUPS ALL-PURPOSE FLOUR
  + EXTRA FOR WORKSPACE
- 2 TBSP GRANULATED WHITE SUGAR
- 4 TSP BAKING POWDER
- 1/2 TSP SALT
- 3 TBSP UNSALTED BUTTER
- 2/3 CUP MILK
- 1 EGG YOLK
- FRUIT JAM OR COMPOTE (OPTIONAL)

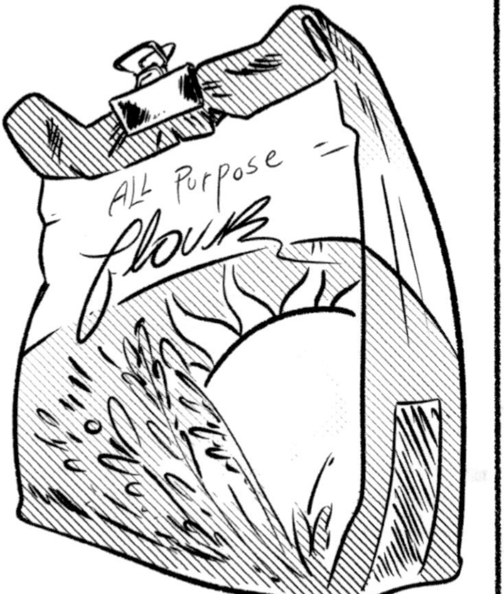
All Purpose
flour

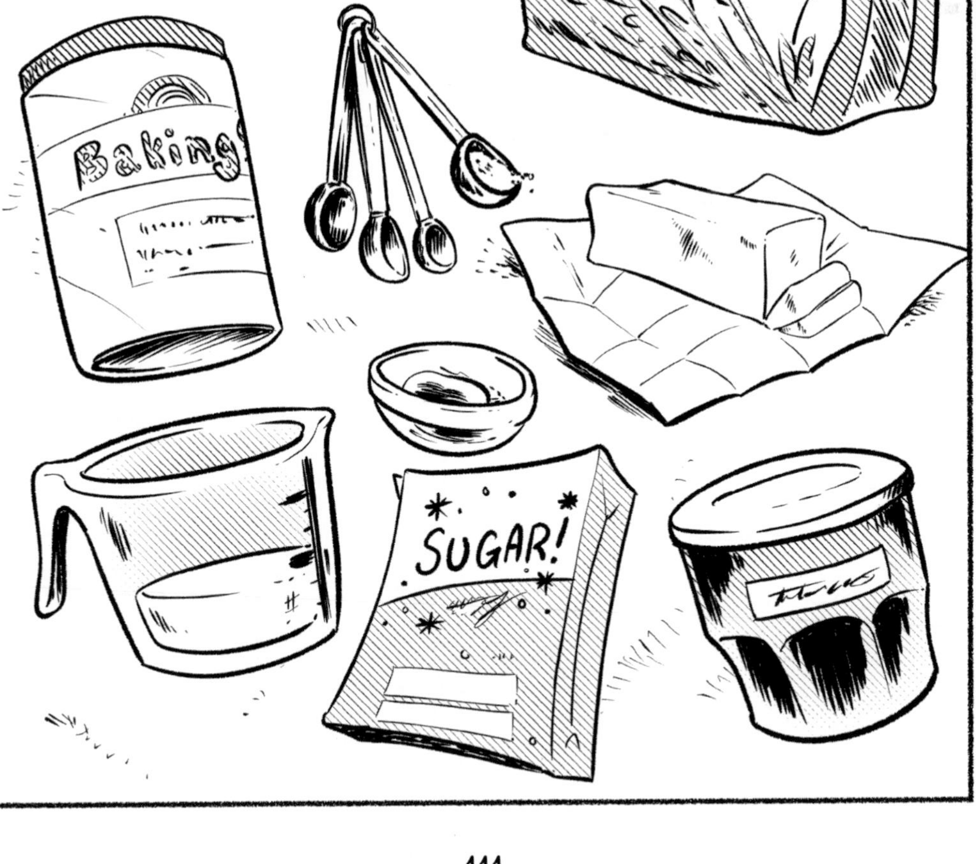
Baking
SUGAR!

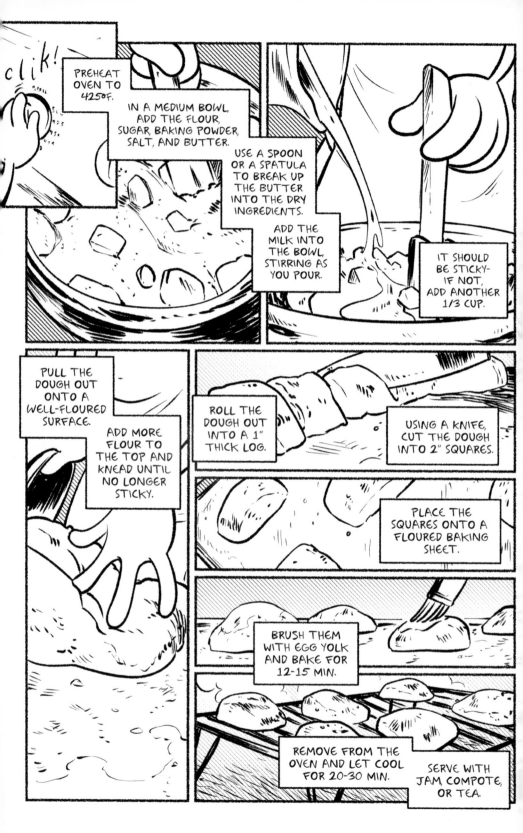

clik!

PREHEAT OVEN TO 425ºF.

IN A MEDIUM BOWL, ADD THE FLOUR, SUGAR, BAKING POWDER, SALT, AND BUTTER.

USE A SPOON OR A SPATULA TO BREAK UP THE BUTTER INTO THE DRY INGREDIENTS.

ADD THE MILK INTO THE BOWL, STIRRING AS YOU POUR.

IT SHOULD BE STICKY-IF NOT, ADD ANOTHER 1/3 CUP.

PULL THE DOUGH OUT ONTO A WELL-FLOURED SURFACE.

ADD MORE FLOUR TO THE TOP AND KNEAD UNTIL NO LONGER STICKY.

ROLL THE DOUGH OUT INTO A 1" THICK LOG.

USING A KNIFE, CUT THE DOUGH INTO 2" SQUARES.

PLACE THE SQUARES ONTO A FLOURED BAKING SHEET.

BRUSH THEM WITH EGG YOLK AND BAKE FOR 12-15 MIN.

REMOVE FROM THE OVEN AND LET COOL FOR 20-30 MIN.

SERVE WITH JAM, COMPOTE, OR TEA.

MIGAS

HANDS ON: 15 MIN
HANDS OFF: 5 MIN

- -2 EGGS, BEATEN
- -2 CUPS CRUSHED TORTILLA CHIPS (THE MORE THE BETTER)
- -1/2 CUP SALSA OR PICO DE GALLO
- -1/2 CUP QUESO FRESCO OR CHEDDAR
- -1 TBSP CILANTRO
- -1 TBSP GARLIC, CHOPPED
- -1 TSP SALT
- -1 TSP BLACK PEPPER
- -1 TBSP VEGETABLE OIL
- -1 CUP BLACK OR REFRIED BEANS (OPTIONAL)

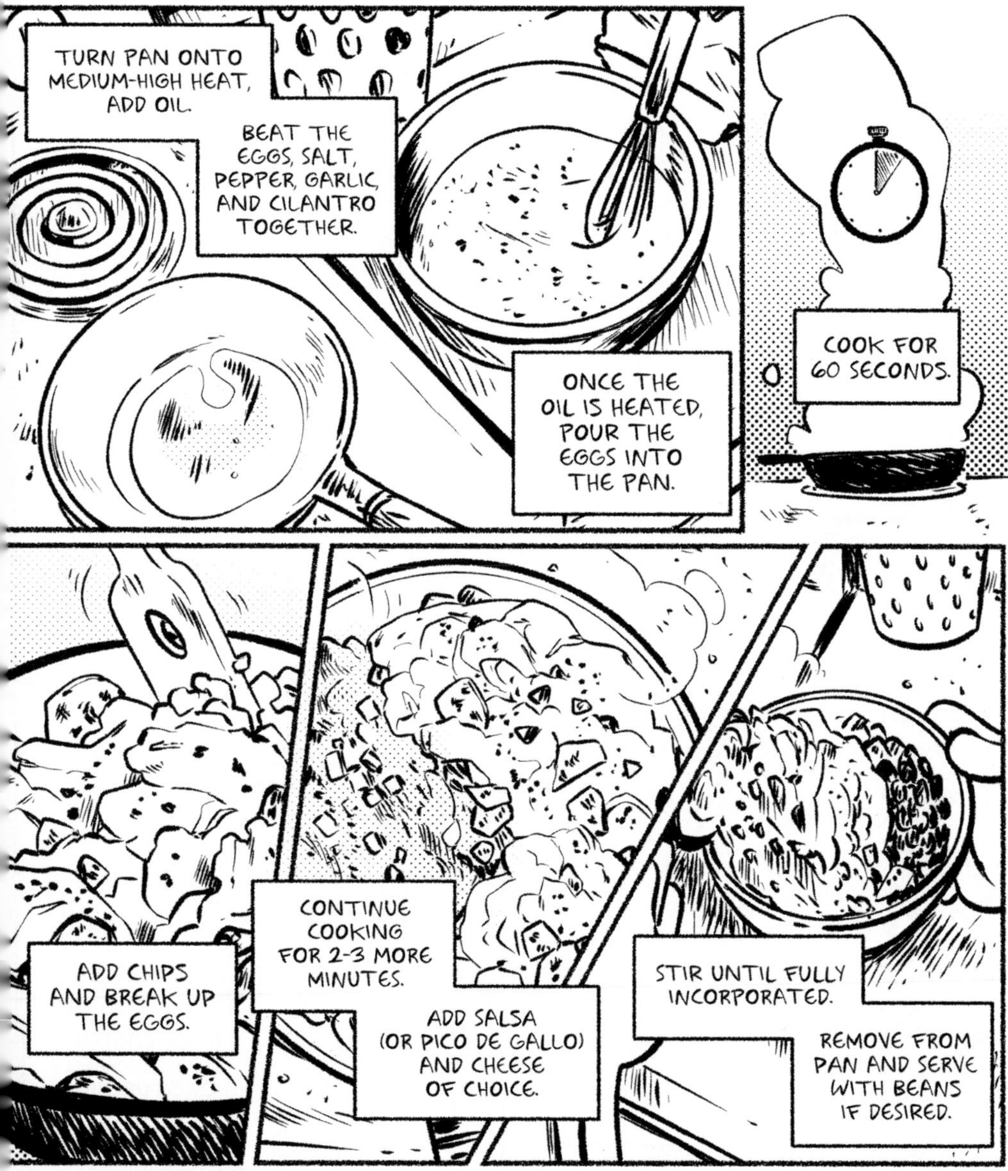

TURN PAN ONTO MEDIUM-HIGH HEAT, ADD OIL.
BEAT THE EGGS, SALT, PEPPER, GARLIC, AND CILANTRO TOGETHER.
ONCE THE OIL IS HEATED, POUR THE EGGS INTO THE PAN.
COOK FOR 60 SECONDS.
ADD CHIPS AND BREAK UP THE EGGS.
CONTINUE COOKING FOR 2-3 MORE MINUTES.
ADD SALSA (OR PICO DE GALLO) AND CHEESE OF CHOICE.
STIR UNTIL FULLY INCORPORATED.
REMOVE FROM PAN AND SERVE WITH BEANS IF DESIRED.

GRANOLA

HANDS ON: 10 MIN
HANDS OFF: 30 MIN

- 2 CUPS ROLLED OATS (NOT INSTANT)
- 1/3 CUP MELTED BUTTER
- 1/3 CUP MAPLE SYRUP OR BROWN SUGAR
- 1 TSP VANILLA EXTRACT
- 1/2 TSP SALT
- 1 TBSP CINNAMON
- 1/2 CUP PUMPKIN OR SUNFLOWER SEEDS
- 1/2 CUP SLIVERED OR CHOPPED ALMONDS
- 1/2 CUP WALNUTS
- 1/2 CUP COCONUT FLAKES OR MACADAMIA NUTS
- 1/3 CUP DRIED FRUITS OF CHOICE

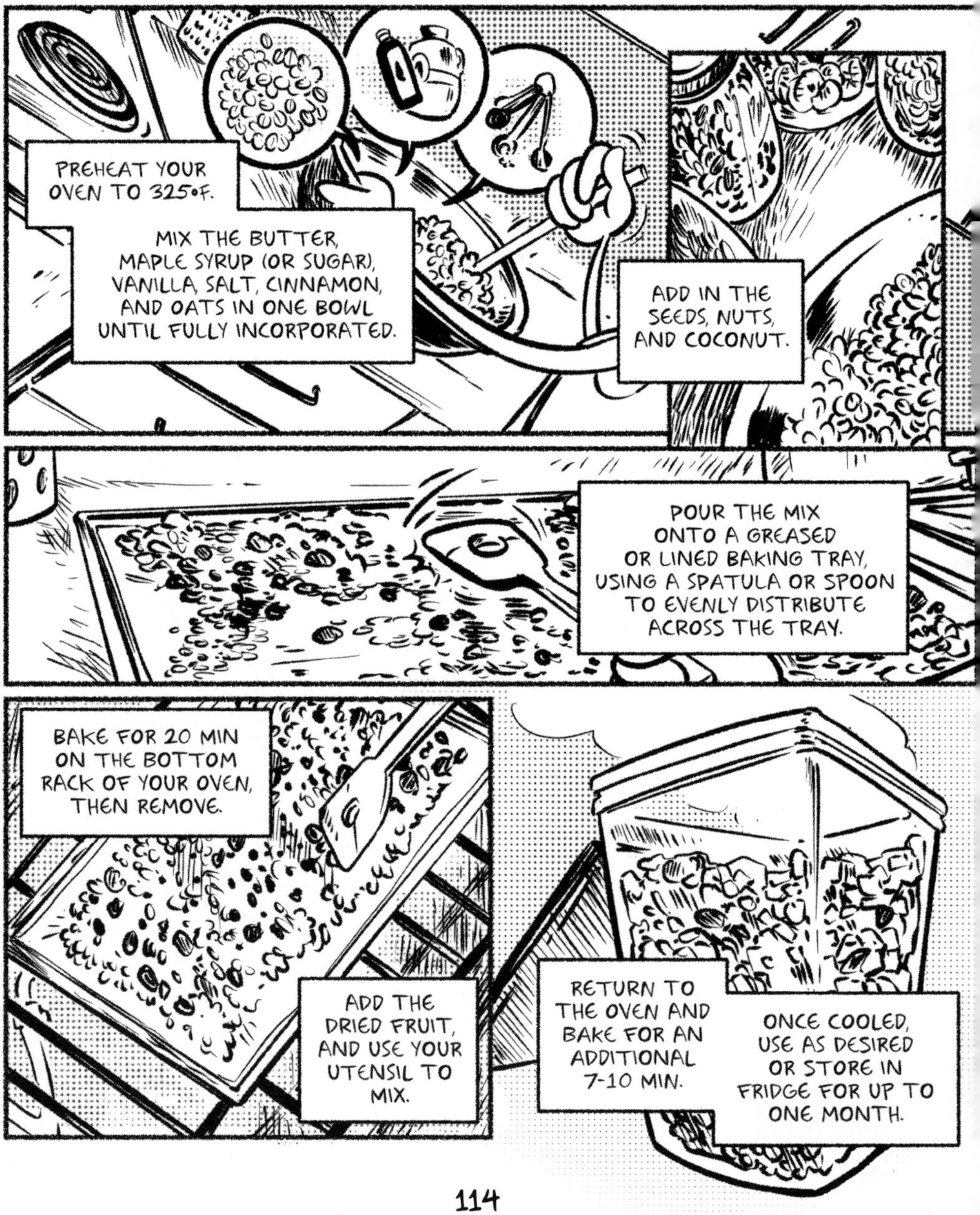
PREHEAT YOUR OVEN TO 325°F.
MIX THE BUTTER, MAPLE SYRUP (OR SUGAR), VANILLA, SALT, CINNAMON, AND OATS IN ONE BOWL UNTIL FULLY INCORPORATED.
ADD IN THE SEEDS, NUTS, AND COCONUT.
POUR THE MIX ONTO A GREASED OR LINED BAKING TRAY, USING A SPATULA OR SPOON TO EVENLY DISTRIBUTE ACROSS THE TRAY.
BAKE FOR 20 MIN ON THE BOTTOM RACK OF YOUR OVEN, THEN REMOVE.
ADD THE DRIED FRUIT, AND USE YOUR UTENSIL TO MIX.
RETURN TO THE OVEN AND BAKE FOR AN ADDITIONAL 7-10 MIN.
ONCE COOLED, USE AS DESIRED OR STORE IN FRIDGE FOR UP TO ONE MONTH.

CHICKPEA SALAD

-1 CAN CHICKPEAS, (12 OZ) DRAINED,
  OR 2 CUPS SOAKED CHICKPEAS
-1 TBSP LEMON JUICE
-1 TBSP GARLIC, CHOPPED
-1 TSP SALT
-1 TSP BLACK PEPPER
-1 TSP CUMIN
-1 TBSP RED PEPPER FLAKES
-1/4 CUP WHITE OR YELLOW ONION
-1 CUP ROMA TOMATO
-1/2 CUP GREEN BELL PEPPER
-1/4 CUP OLIVE OIL
-2 TBSP RED OR RICE WINE VINEGAR

HANDS ON: 30 MIN
HANDS OFF: 9 HOURS

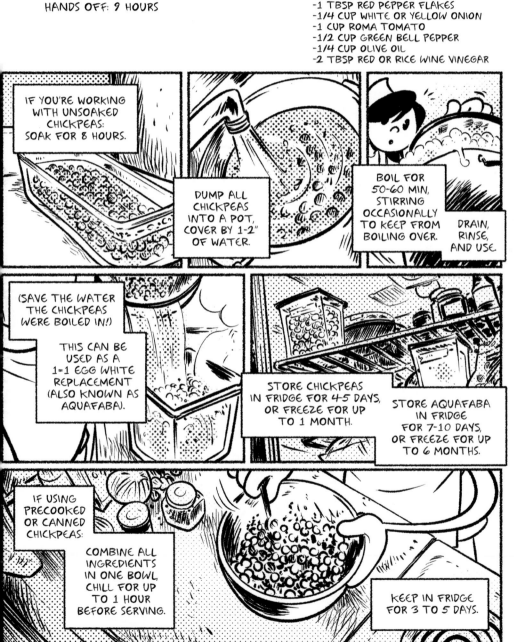

IF YOU'RE WORKING WITH UNSOAKED CHICKPEAS: SOAK FOR 8 HOURS.

DUMP ALL CHICKPEAS INTO A POT, COVER BY 1-2" OF WATER.

BOIL FOR 50-60 MIN, STIRRING OCCASIONALLY TO KEEP FROM BOILING OVER.

DRAIN, RINSE, AND USE.

(SAVE THE WATER THE CHICKPEAS WERE BOILED IN!)

THIS CAN BE USED AS A 1=1 EGG WHITE REPLACEMENT (ALSO KNOWN AS AQUAFABA).

STORE CHICKPEAS IN FRIDGE FOR 4-5 DAYS, OR FREEZE FOR UP TO 1 MONTH.

STORE AQUAFABA IN FRIDGE FOR 7-10 DAYS, OR FREEZE FOR UP TO 6 MONTHS.

IF USING PRECOOKED OR CANNED CHICKPEAS:

COMBINE ALL INGREDIENTS IN ONE BOWL, CHILL FOR UP TO 1 HOUR BEFORE SERVING.

KEEP IN FRIDGE FOR 3 TO 5 DAYS.

TUNA SALAD

HANDS ON: 20 MIN
HANDS OFF: 1 HOUR

- 1 12OZ CAN OF TUNA OR 2 CUPS FRESH
- 1/3 CUP OLIVE OIL OR 3 TBSP JAPANESE MAYO
- 1 TBSP SOY SAUCE
- 1 TBSP RICE WINE OR APPLE CIDER VINEGAR
- 1 TSP SALT
- 1 TSP BLACK PEPPER
- 1 TBSP PAPRIKA
- 1 TBSP CAYENNE
- 1 TBSP LEMON JUICE
- 1/2 CUP GREEN OR WHITE ONION, CHOPPED
- 1 CUP SPINACH OR KALE, CHOPPED

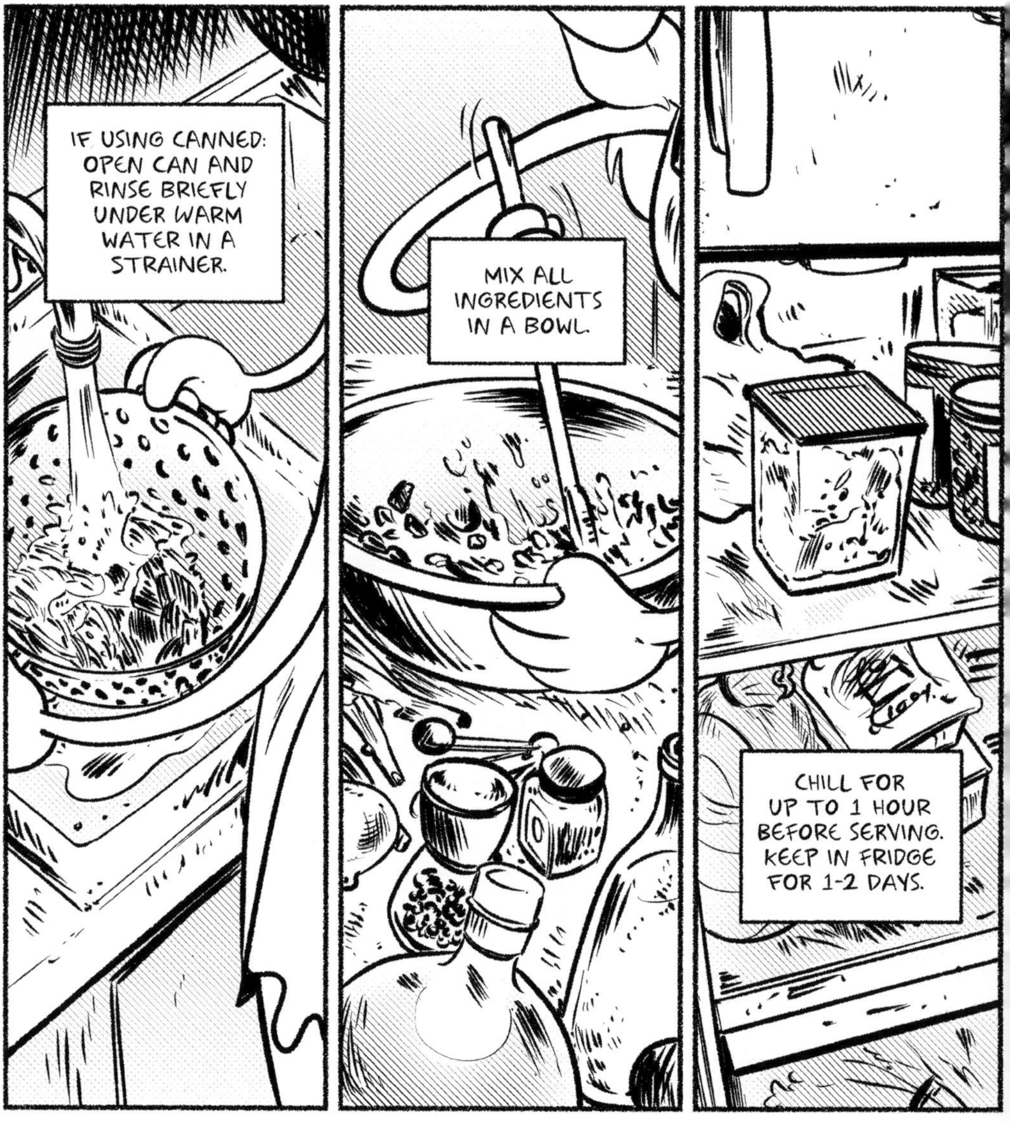
IF USING CANNED: OPEN CAN AND RINSE BRIEFLY UNDER WARM WATER IN A STRAINER.
MIX ALL INGREDIENTS IN A BOWL.
CHILL FOR UP TO 1 HOUR BEFORE SERVING. KEEP IN FRIDGE FOR 1-2 DAYS.

see notes for more!

POKÉ

HANDS ON: 10 MIN
HANDS OFF: 10 MIN

- 1 1/2 CUP TUNA STEAKS, FILETS, OR TIPS, CHOPPED
- 1/2 CUP GREEN ONION, CHOPPED
- 4 TBSP SOY SAUCE
- 1 TSP SESAME OIL
- 1 TSP CHILI OIL
- 1 TBSP GARLIC, CHOPPED
- 1 TBSP GINGER, CHOPPED
- 1 TBSP SESAME SEEDS (TOASTED IS PREFERRED BUT OPTIONAL)
- 1/2 CUP SHALLOT OR WHITE ONION, CHOPPED (OPTIONAL)
- 1 CUP PRECOOKED RICE (OPTIONAL)

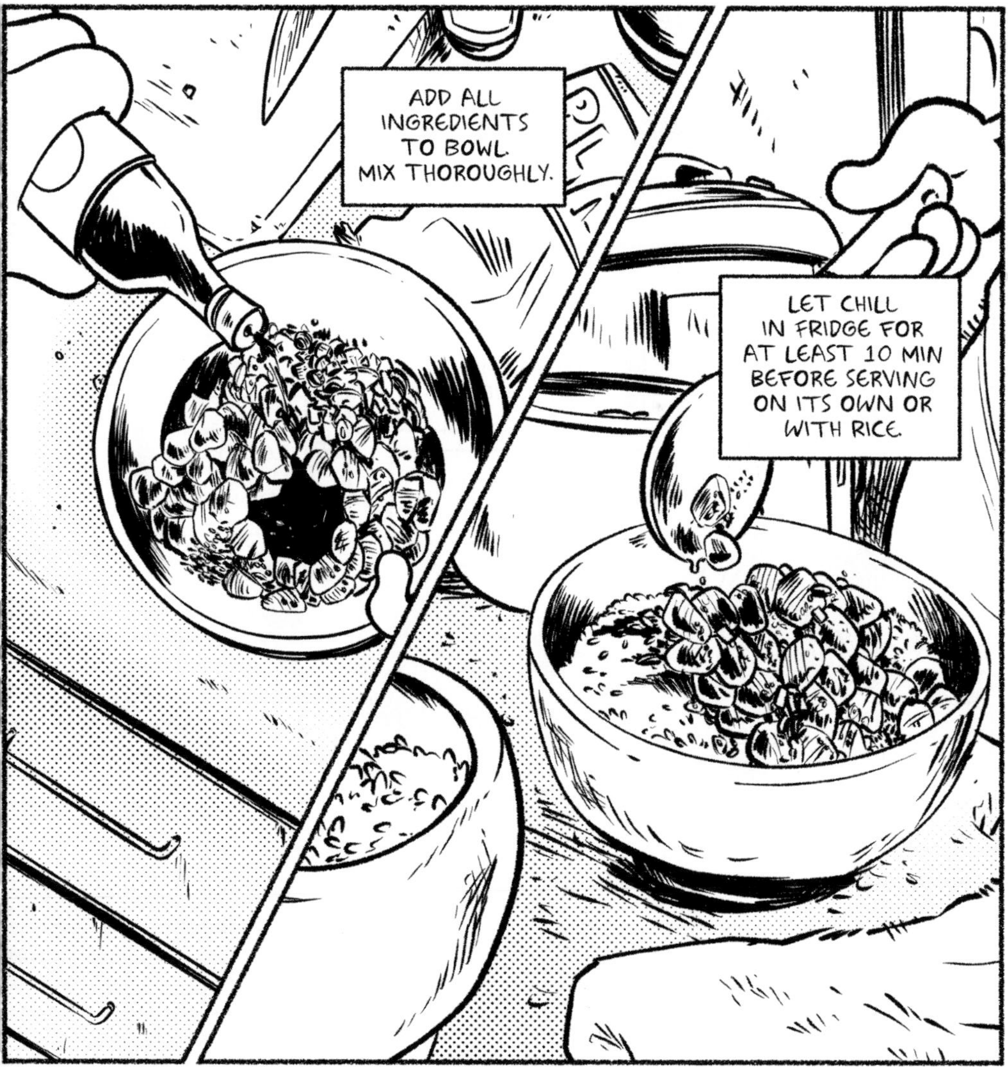
ADD ALL INGREDIENTS TO BOWL. MIX THOROUGHLY.
LET CHILL IN FRIDGE FOR AT LEAST 10 MIN BEFORE SERVING ON ITS OWN OR WITH RICE.

BOWLS

ANYTHING CAN BE A BOWL! BUT THEY ALL HAVE A STRUCTURE:

STARCH (RICE, QUINOA, BEANS, PASTA, POTATOES)

PROTEIN (MEAT, BEANS, TOFU, OR SIMILAR)

VEGETABLE (MORE THAN ONE!)

A 'DRESSING' TO HELP UNITE THE FLAVORS (I USE THIS PHRASE LOOSELY!)

THESE CAN BE ORGANIZED INTO:

3 COMPLEMENTARY FLAVORS

2 CONTRASTING FLAVORS

SOME QUICK 'N' DIRTY EXAMPLES:

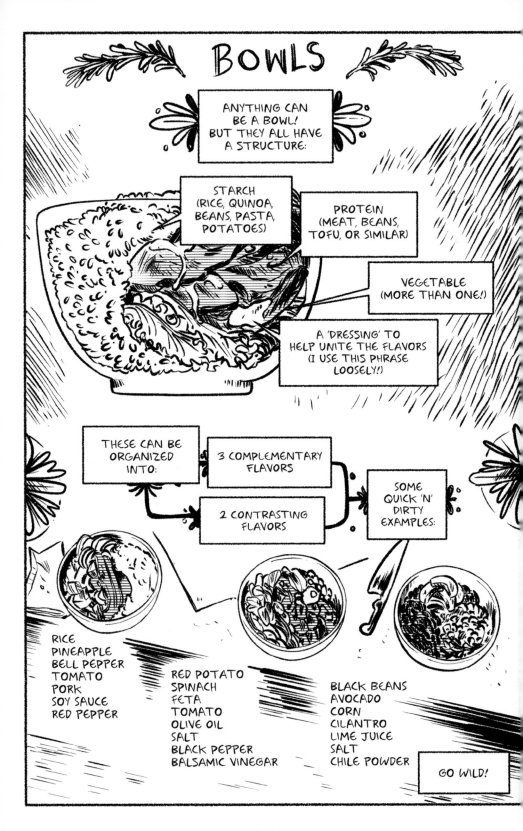

RICE
PINEAPPLE
BELL PEPPER
TOMATO
PORK
SOY SAUCE
RED PEPPER

RED POTATO
SPINACH
FETA
TOMATO
OLIVE OIL
SALT
BLACK PEPPER
BALSAMIC VINEGAR

BLACK BEANS
AVOCADO
CORN
CILANTRO
LIME JUICE
SALT
CHILE POWDER

GO WILD!

CONGEE

- 1 CUP WHITE RICE
- 1 TBSP VEGETABLE OR SESAME OIL
- 8 CUPS BROTH OF CHOICE OR WATER

OPTIONAL TOPPINGS:

- SALT
- BLACK OR WHITE PEPPER
- CHILI OIL
- EGGS
- GREEN ONION, CHOPPED
- SHREDDED NORI
- SMALL FISH, LIKE ANCHOVIES OR SARDINES
- KIMCHI

HANDS ON: 10 MIN
HANDS OFF: 1.5 HR

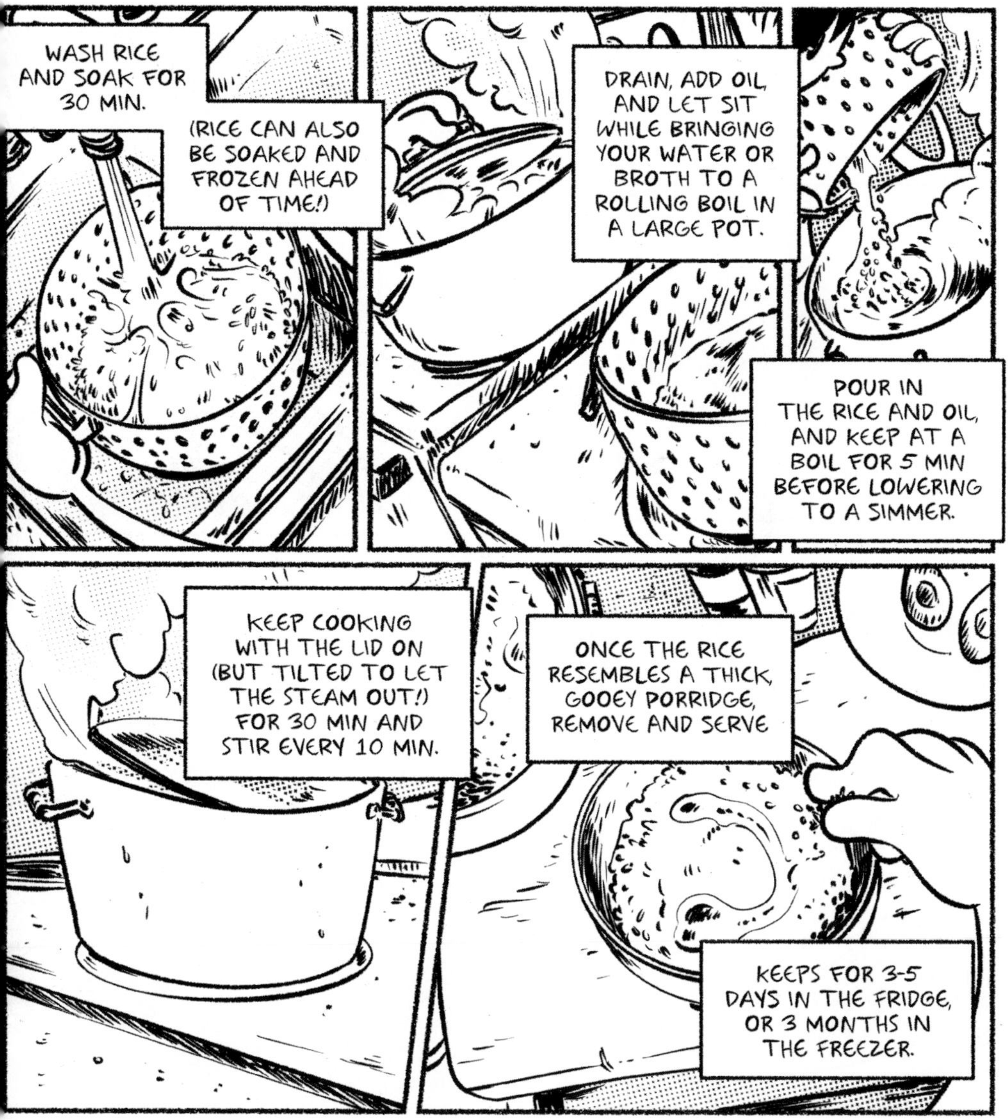
WASH RICE AND SOAK FOR 30 MIN.
(RICE CAN ALSO BE SOAKED AND FROZEN AHEAD OF TIME!)
DRAIN, ADD OIL, AND LET SIT WHILE BRINGING YOUR WATER OR BROTH TO A ROLLING BOIL IN A LARGE POT.
POUR IN THE RICE AND OIL, AND KEEP AT A BOIL FOR 5 MIN BEFORE LOWERING TO A SIMMER.
KEEP COOKING WITH THE LID ON (BUT TILTED TO LET THE STEAM OUT!) FOR 30 MIN AND STIR EVERY 10 MIN.
ONCE THE RICE RESEMBLES A THICK, GOOEY PORRIDGE, REMOVE AND SERVE
KEEPS FOR 3-5 DAYS IN THE FRIDGE, OR 3 MONTHS IN THE FREEZER.

TERIYAKI

('TERIYAKI' IS A COOKING TECHNIQUE RATHER THAN ONE SPECIFIC FOOD OR SAUCE, BUT THIS SHOULD GET YOU STARTED!)

HANDS ON: 20 MIN

- 1/2 CUP SOY SAUCE
- 1/2 CUP MIRIN (SUBSTITUTIONS INCLUDE DRY SHERRY, DRY WHITE WINE, OR RICE WINE / APPLE CIDER VINEGAR + 4 TSP SUGAR)
- 1/2 CUP SAKE (OR 1/2 CUP WATER- ONLY SUB SAKE IF YOU AREN'T SUBBING MIRIN!)
- 1/4 CUP WHITE SUGAR
- 1 TSP GARLIC, CHOPPED (OPTIONAL)
- 1 TSP GINGER, CHOPPED (OPTIONAL)

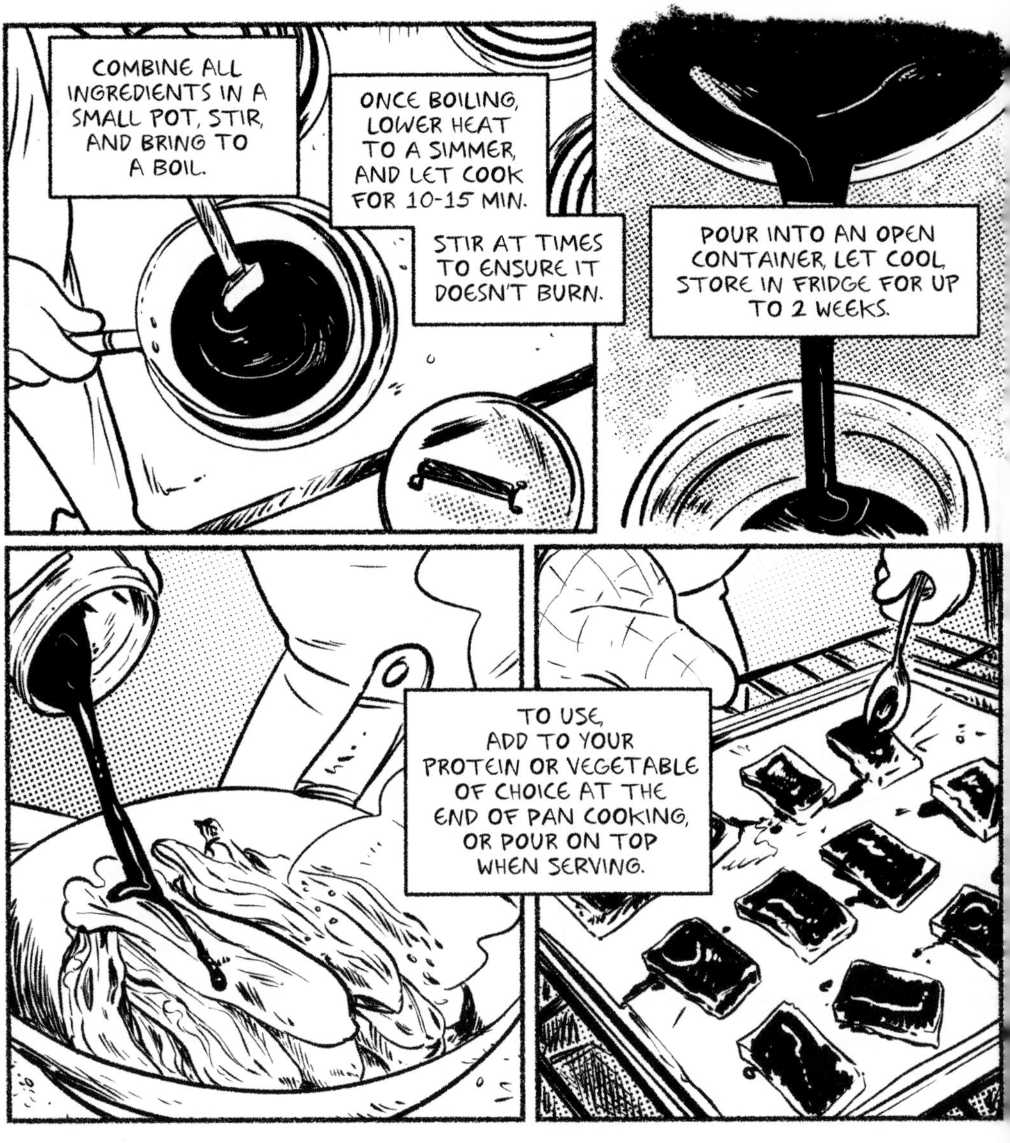
COMBINE ALL INGREDIENTS IN A SMALL POT, STIR, AND BRING TO A BOIL.
ONCE BOILING, LOWER HEAT TO A SIMMER, AND LET COOK FOR 10-15 MIN.
STIR AT TIMES TO ENSURE IT DOESN'T BURN.
POUR INTO AN OPEN CONTAINER, LET COOL, STORE IN FRIDGE FOR UP TO 2 WEEKS.
TO USE, ADD TO YOUR PROTEIN OR VEGETABLE OF CHOICE AT THE END OF PAN COOKING, OR POUR ON TOP WHEN SERVING.

ONIGIRI

HANDS ON: 20 MIN
HANDS OFF: 10 MIN

-2 CUPS UNCOOKED SHORT GRAIN RICE OR
3 CUPS PRECOOKED SHORT GRAIN RICE
-2 1/2 CUPS WATER OR BROTH (FOR UNCOOKED RICE)
-1 CUP WATER (FOR YOUR HANDS)
-3 TBSP SALT
-4 SHEETS NORI

FILLINGS:
-SALMON (CHOPPED JERKY IS GOOD FOR THIS!)
-TUNA MAYO (1/2 CUP DRAINED CANNED TUNA
+ 1 TBSP SOY SAUCE + 1 TBSP JAPANESE MAYO)
-SHRIMP MAYO (1/2 CUP CHOPPED SHRIMP
+ 1/2 TBSP SOY SAUCE + 1 TBSP JAPANESE MAYO)
-UMEBOSHI (PICKLED PLUMS)
-SALT (JUST SALT!)
-EGGS (SCRAMBLED OR HARDBOILED)

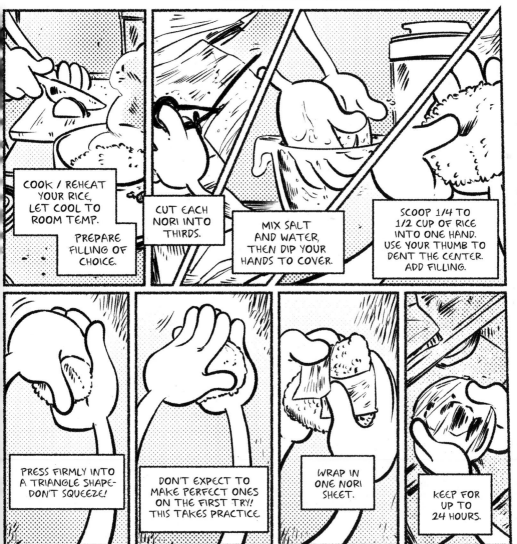

COOK / REHEAT YOUR RICE, LET COOL TO ROOM TEMP. PREPARE FILLING OF CHOICE.

CUT EACH NORI INTO THIRDS.

MIX SALT AND WATER, THEN DIP YOUR HANDS TO COVER.

SCOOP 1/4 TO 1/2 CUP OF RICE INTO ONE HAND. USE YOUR THUMB TO DENT THE CENTER. ADD FILLING.

PRESS FIRMLY INTO A TRIANGLE SHAPE- DON'T SQUEEZE!

DON'T EXPECT TO MAKE PERFECT ONES ON THE FIRST TRY! THIS TAKES PRACTICE.

WRAP IN ONE NORI SHEET.

KEEP FOR UP TO 24 HOURS.

EMPANADAS

HANDS ON: 1 HOUR
HANDS OFF: 2 HR 20 MIN

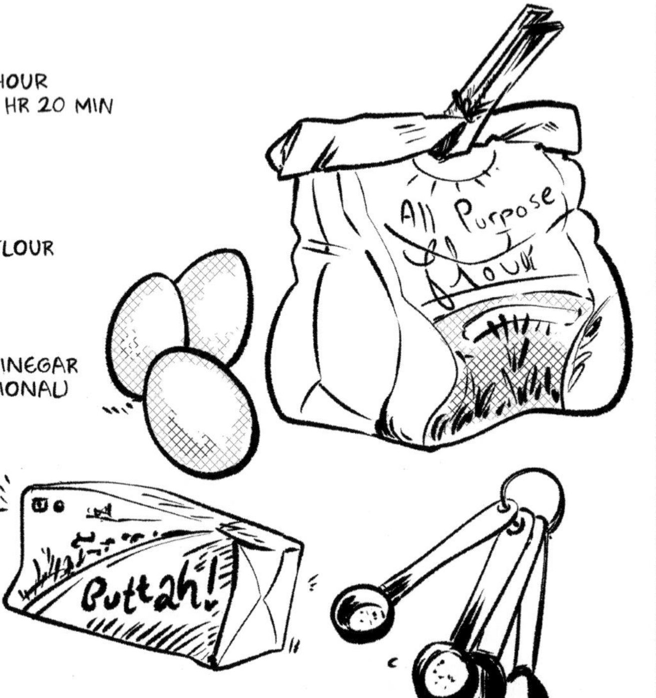
All Purpose flour
Buttah!

DOUGH:
- 3 1/4 CUPS ALL PURPOSE FLOUR
- 12 TBSP BUTTER, COLD
- 1 1/2 TSP SALT
- 3 EGGS
- 1/2 CUP (COLD) WATER
- 1 1/2 TBSP APPLE CIDER VINEGAR
- 1 CUP QUESO FRESCO (OPTIONAL)

FILLING:
- 1 TBSP BUTTER
- 1/2 TSP SALT
- 1/2 TSP BLACK PEPPER
- 1 TBSP BROTH OF CHOICE
- 1/2 TSP CUMIN
- 1 TSP OREGANO
- 2 TSP SMOKED PAPRIKA
- 2 TSP CAYENNE
- 1/2 CUP WHITE ONION
- 2 TBSP GARLIC, CHOPPED
- 1 TSP APPLE CIDER VINEGAR
- 1 TSP TOMATO PASTE
- 2 CUPS POTATO, CHOPPED
- 1 CUP MUSHROOMS

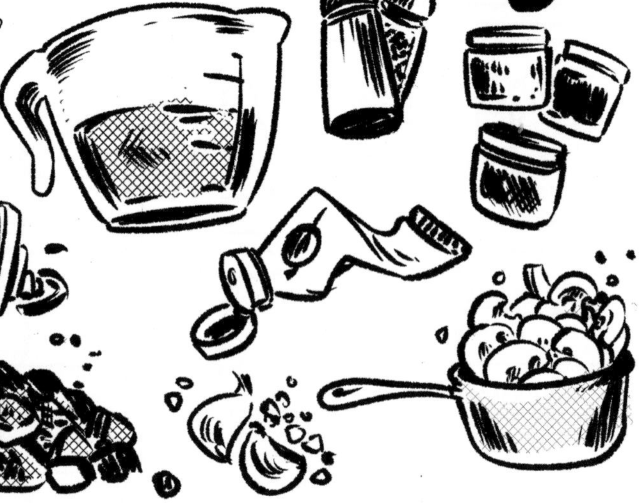

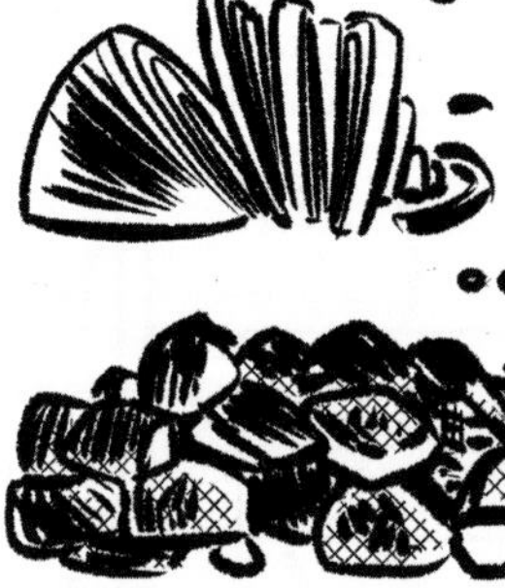

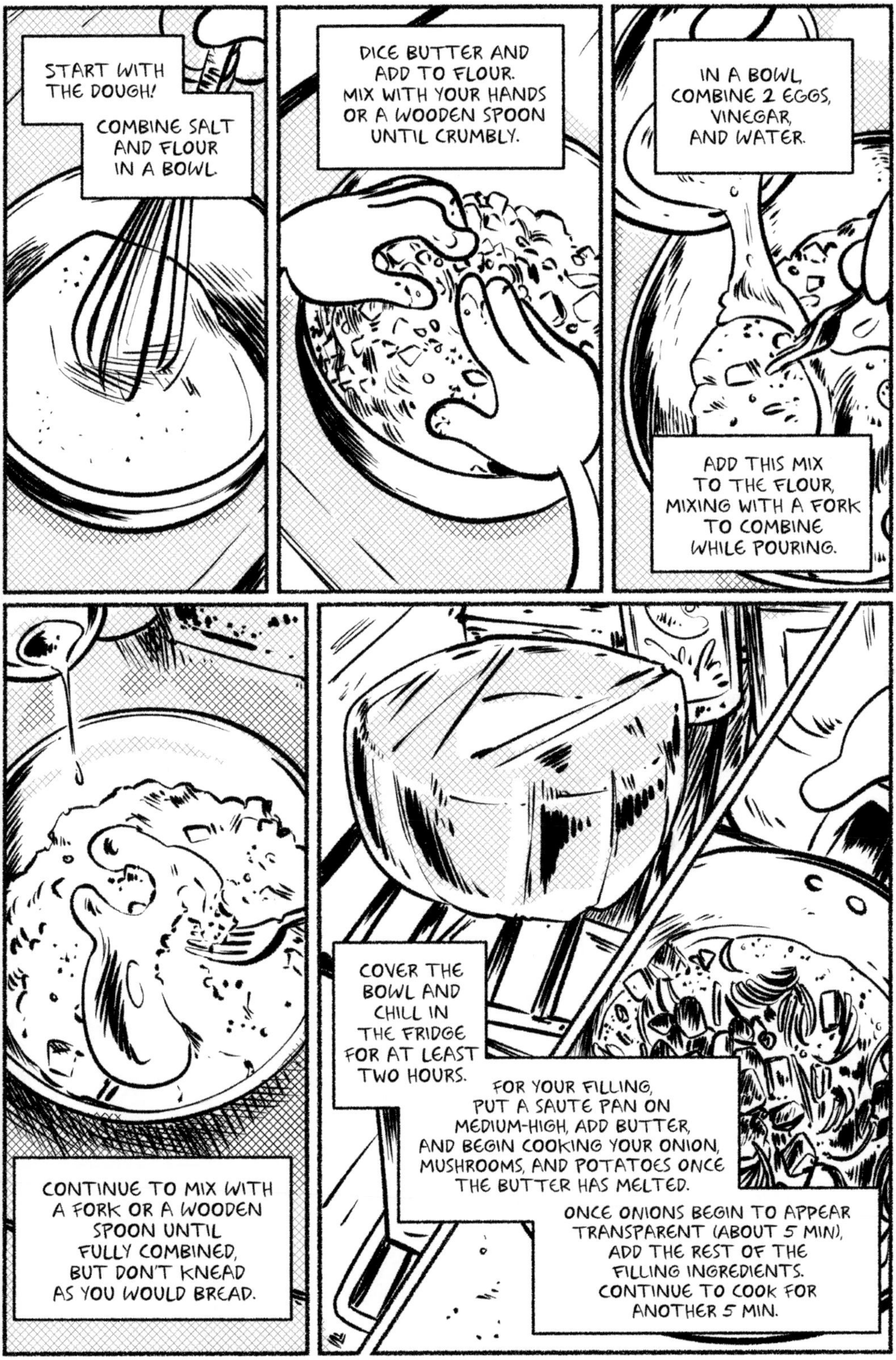
START WITH THE DOUGH!
COMBINE SALT AND FLOUR IN A BOWL.
DICE BUTTER AND ADD TO FLOUR. MIX WITH YOUR HANDS OR A WOODEN SPOON UNTIL CRUMBLY.
IN A BOWL, COMBINE 2 EGGS, VINEGAR, AND WATER.
ADD THIS MIX TO THE FLOUR, MIXING WITH A FORK TO COMBINE WHILE POURING.
CONTINUE TO MIX WITH A FORK OR A WOODEN SPOON UNTIL FULLY COMBINED, BUT DON'T KNEAD AS YOU WOULD BREAD.
COVER THE BOWL AND CHILL IN THE FRIDGE FOR AT LEAST TWO HOURS.
FOR YOUR FILLING, PUT A SAUTE PAN ON MEDIUM-HIGH, ADD BUTTER, AND BEGIN COOKING YOUR ONION, MUSHROOMS, AND POTATOES ONCE THE BUTTER HAS MELTED.
ONCE ONIONS BEGIN TO APPEAR TRANSPARENT (ABOUT 5 MIN), ADD THE REST OF THE FILLING INGREDIENTS. CONTINUE TO COOK FOR ANOTHER 5 MIN.

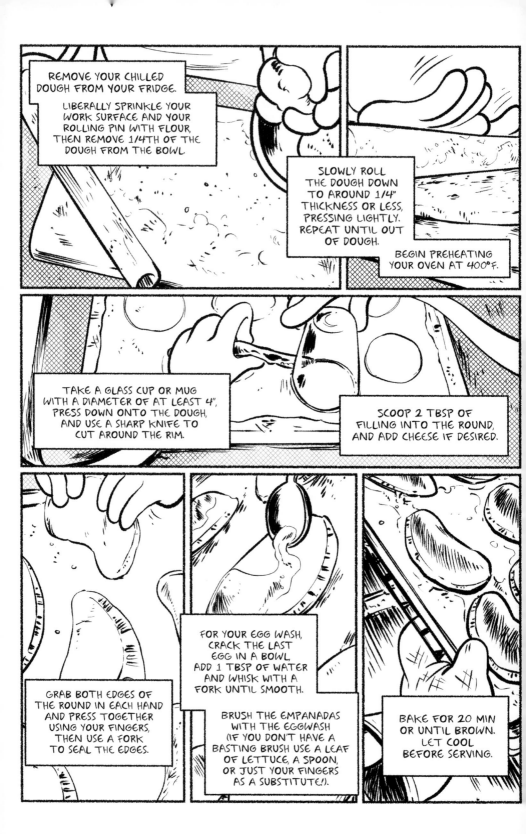

REMOVE YOUR CHILLED DOUGH FROM YOUR FRIDGE.

LIBERALLY SPRINKLE YOUR WORK SURFACE AND YOUR ROLLING PIN WITH FLOUR, THEN REMOVE 1/4TH OF THE DOUGH FROM THE BOWL.

SLOWLY ROLL THE DOUGH DOWN TO AROUND 1/4" THICKNESS OR LESS, PRESSING LIGHTLY. REPEAT UNTIL OUT OF DOUGH.

BEGIN PREHEATING YOUR OVEN AT 400°F.

TAKE A GLASS CUP OR MUG WITH A DIAMETER OF AT LEAST 4", PRESS DOWN ONTO THE DOUGH, AND USE A SHARP KNIFE TO CUT AROUND THE RIM.

SCOOP 2 TBSP OF FILLING INTO THE ROUND, AND ADD CHEESE IF DESIRED.

GRAB BOTH EDGES OF THE ROUND IN EACH HAND AND PRESS TOGETHER USING YOUR FINGERS, THEN USE A FORK TO SEAL THE EDGES.

FOR YOUR EGG WASH, CRACK THE LAST EGG IN A BOWL, ADD 1 TBSP OF WATER AND WHISK WITH A FORK UNTIL SMOOTH.

BRUSH THE EMPANADAS WITH THE EGGWASH (IF YOU DON'T HAVE A BASTING BRUSH USE A LEAF OF LETTUCE, A SPOON, OR JUST YOUR FINGERS AS A SUBSTITUTE!).

BAKE FOR 20 MIN OR UNTIL BROWN. LET COOL BEFORE SERVING.

GRILLED CHEESE

HANDS ON: 10 MIN

- 2 TBSP OF UNSALTED BUTTER (FOR COOKING)
- 1/2 TSP SALT
- 1/2 TSP BLACK PEPPER

TWO SLICES OF BREAD OF CHOICE, RECOMMENDED CHOICES INCLUDE:
- SOURDOUGH
- RYE
- CIABATTA
- WHEAT
- BRIOCHE

TWO DIFFERENT CHEESES OF CHOICE, ENOUGH TO COVER YOUR BREAD SLICES. RECOMMENDED COMBINATIONS INCLUDE:
- EXTRA SHARP CHEDDAR & FETA
- BLUE CHEESE & MOZZARELLA
- COLBY CHEESE & MONTEREY JACK
- REGULAR CHEDDAR & BRIE
- EXTRA SHARP CHEDDAR & MANCHEGO
- GRUYERE & EXTRA SHARP CHEDDAR

OPTIONAL:
- CHOPPED JALAPENO
- CHOPPED GARLIC
- SLICED TOMATO
- CHOPPED GREEN ONION

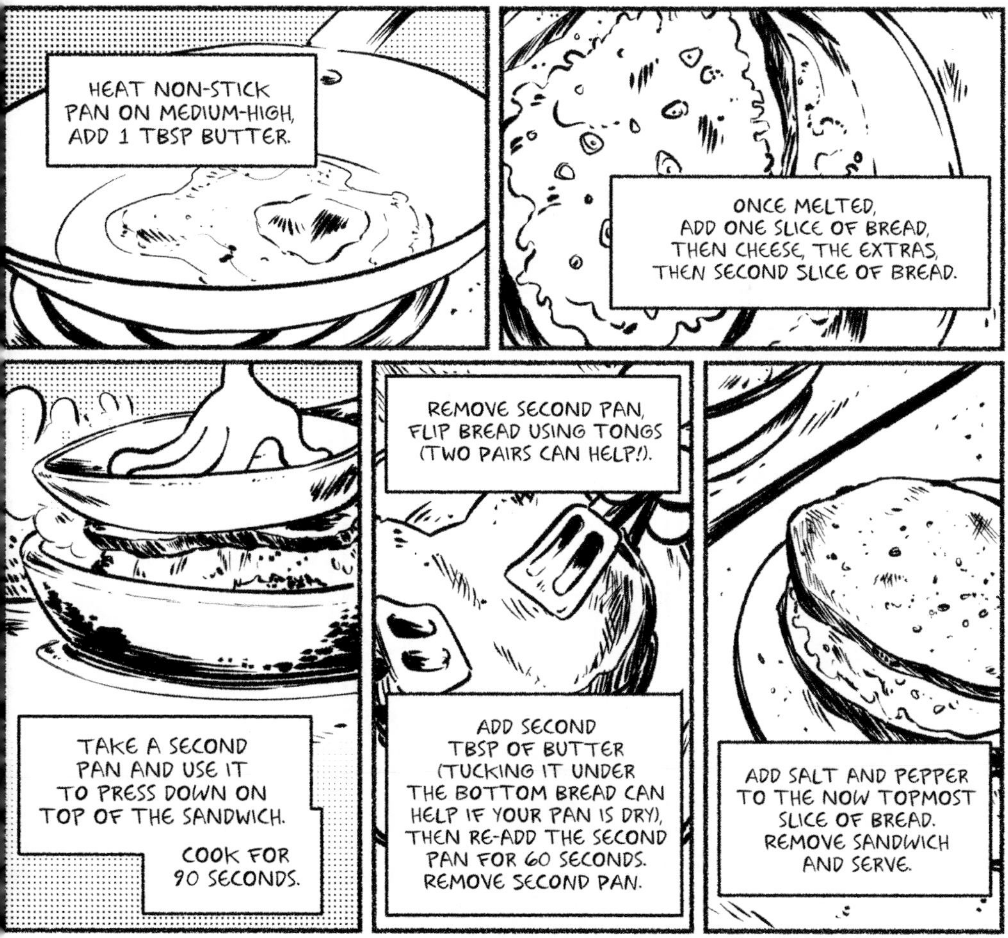
HEAT NON-STICK PAN ON MEDIUM-HIGH, ADD 1 TBSP BUTTER.
ONCE MELTED, ADD ONE SLICE OF BREAD, THEN CHEESE, THE EXTRAS, THEN SECOND SLICE OF BREAD.
TAKE A SECOND PAN AND USE IT TO PRESS DOWN ON TOP OF THE SANDWICH.
COOK FOR 90 SECONDS.
REMOVE SECOND PAN, FLIP BREAD USING TONGS (TWO PAIRS CAN HELP!).
ADD SECOND TBSP OF BUTTER (TUCKING IT UNDER THE BOTTOM BREAD CAN HELP IF YOUR PAN IS DRY), THEN RE-ADD THE SECOND PAN FOR 60 SECONDS. REMOVE SECOND PAN.
ADD SALT AND PEPPER TO THE NOW TOPMOST SLICE OF BREAD. REMOVE SANDWICH AND SERVE.

VEGETARIAN FRENCH DIP

HANDS ON: 20 MIN

- -1 CUP WHITE ONION, SLICED
- -2 PORTOBELLO MUSHROOM CAPS, SLICED
- -2 CUPS GREEN BELL PEPPER, SLICED
- -2 TBSP BUTTER
- -1 TBSP SALT
- -1 TBSP BLACK PEPPER
- -1/2 TBSP BROWN SUGAR
- -1/4 TSP THYME (DOUBLE IF DRIED)
- -1/4 TSP OREGANO (DOUBLE IF DRIED)
- -2 CUPS VEGETABLE BROTH
- -1 TBSP SOY SAUCE
- -1/2 TBSP CHOPPED GARLIC (DOUBLE IF USING POWDER)
- -2 CRUSTY ROLLS

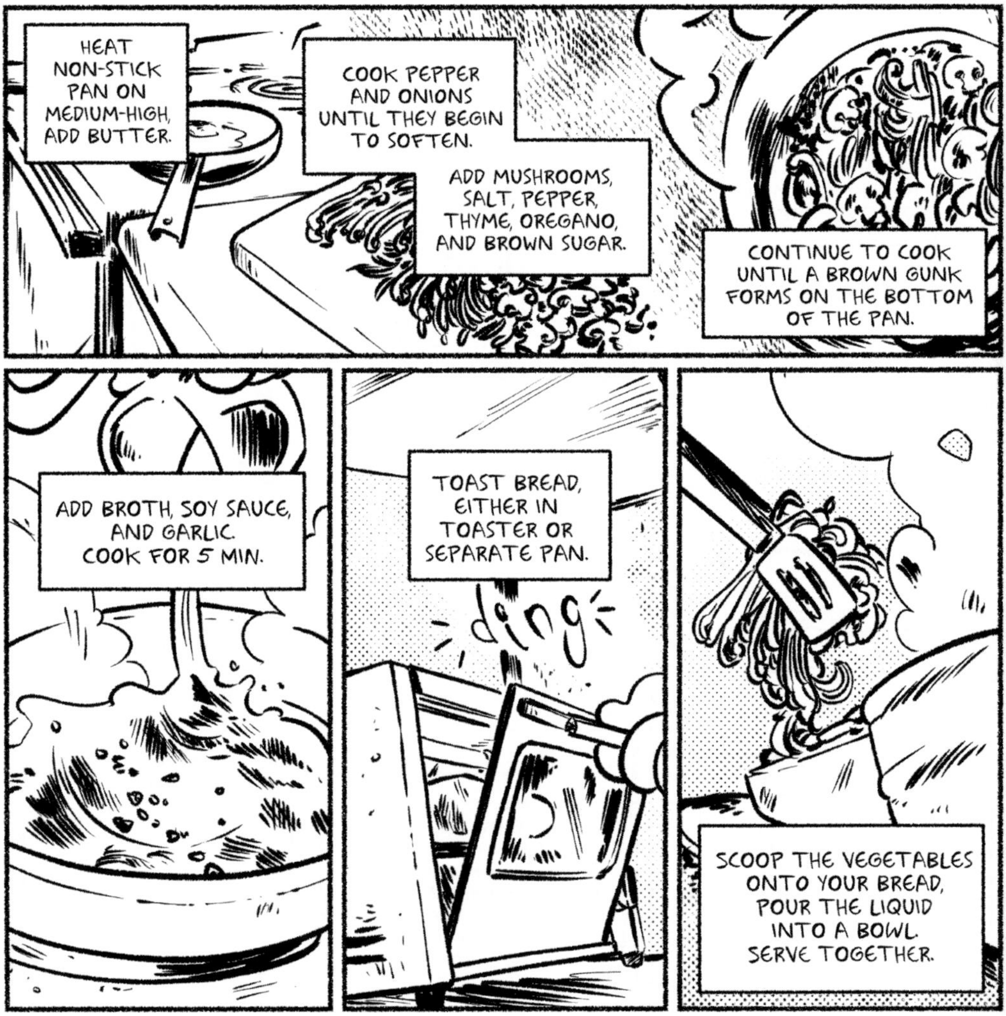
HEAT NON-STICK PAN ON MEDIUM-HIGH, ADD BUTTER.
COOK PEPPER AND ONIONS UNTIL THEY BEGIN TO SOFTEN.
ADD MUSHROOMS, SALT, PEPPER, THYME, OREGANO, AND BROWN SUGAR.
CONTINUE TO COOK UNTIL A BROWN GUNK FORMS ON THE BOTTOM OF THE PAN.
ADD BROTH, SOY SAUCE, AND GARLIC. COOK FOR 5 MIN.
TOAST BREAD, EITHER IN TOASTER OR SEPARATE PAN.
ding
SCOOP THE VEGETABLES ONTO YOUR BREAD, POUR THE LIQUID INTO A BOWL. SERVE TOGETHER.

BÁNH MÌ

HANDS ON: 10 MIN

- -1 PREMADE OR HOMEMADE BAGUETTE ROLL, SLICED IN TWO
- -1 TSP SOY SAUCE
- -1 TBSP MAYO (KEWPIE OR 'LIGHT'/VEGAN PREFERRED, HALF IF USING REGULAR MAYO)
- -1 TSP CILANTRO (DOUBLE IF DRIED, FRESH RECOMMENDED)
- -1 TSP SALT
- -1 TSP SUGAR
- -1 TBSP WHITE VINEGAR
- -1/3 CUP WATER
- -1/4 CUP JALAPENO, SLICED INTO MEDALLIONS
- -1 CUP CUCUMBER, CUT INTO MATCHSTICKS
- -1 CUP PEELED CARROT, CUT INTO MATCHSTICKS
- -1 CUP PEELED DAIKON, CUT INTO MATCHSTICKS
- -MARINATED OR PLAIN TOFU OF CHOICE, DRAINED AND SLICED

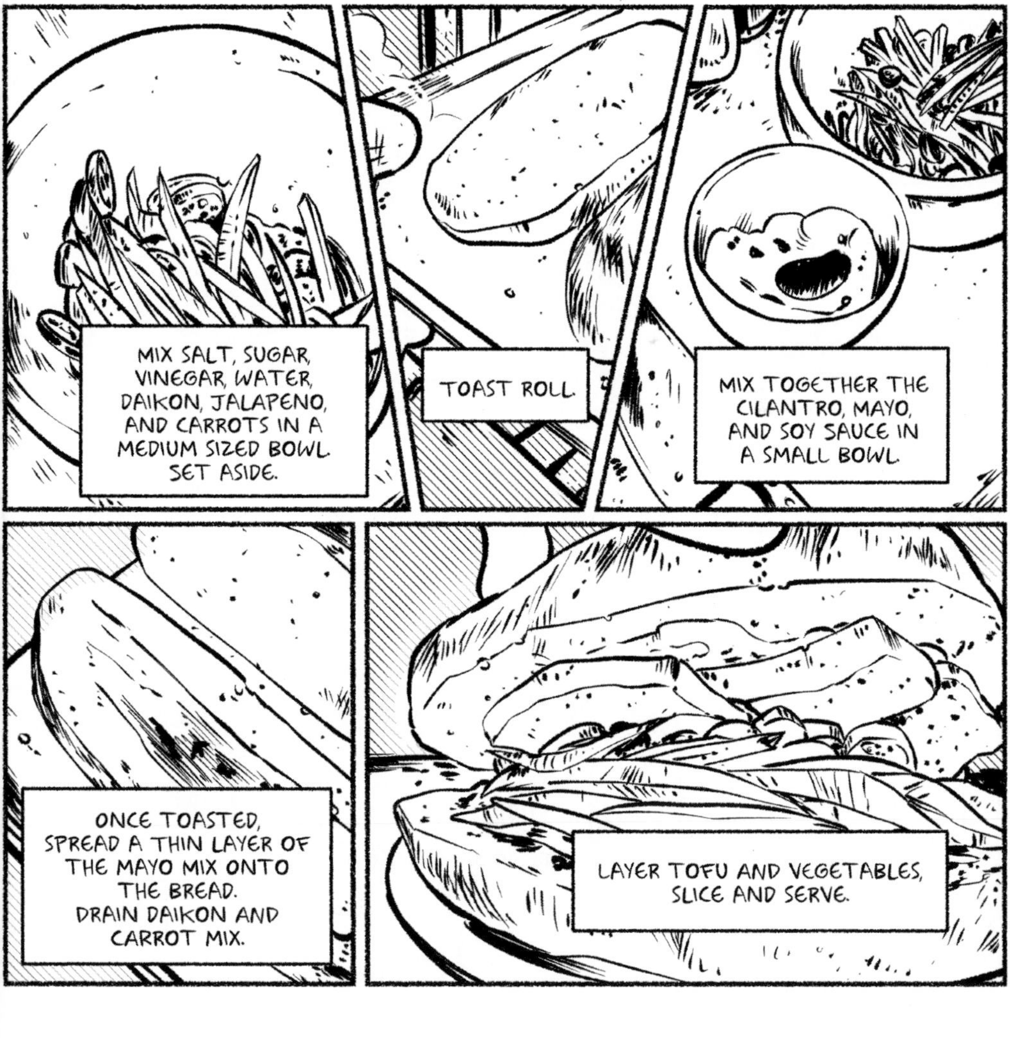
MIX SALT, SUGAR, VINEGAR, WATER, DAIKON, JALAPENO, AND CARROTS IN A MEDIUM SIZED BOWL. SET ASIDE.
TOAST ROLL.
MIX TOGETHER THE CILANTRO, MAYO, AND SOY SAUCE IN A SMALL BOWL.
ONCE TOASTED, SPREAD A THIN LAYER OF THE MAYO MIX ONTO THE BREAD. DRAIN DAIKON AND CARROT MIX.
LAYER TOFU AND VEGETABLES, SLICE AND SERVE.

BLT

HANDS ON: 10 MIN

- 2 SLICES OF SOURDOUGH OR RYE BREAD
- ENOUGH SPINACH TO COVER YOUR BREAD
- 1 ROMA TOMATO, SLICED
- 2 TBSP PESTO, BASIL PREFERRED
- 4 SLICES OF TOFU BACON (SEE PREVIOUS RECIPE)
- 1 TSP OLIVE OIL

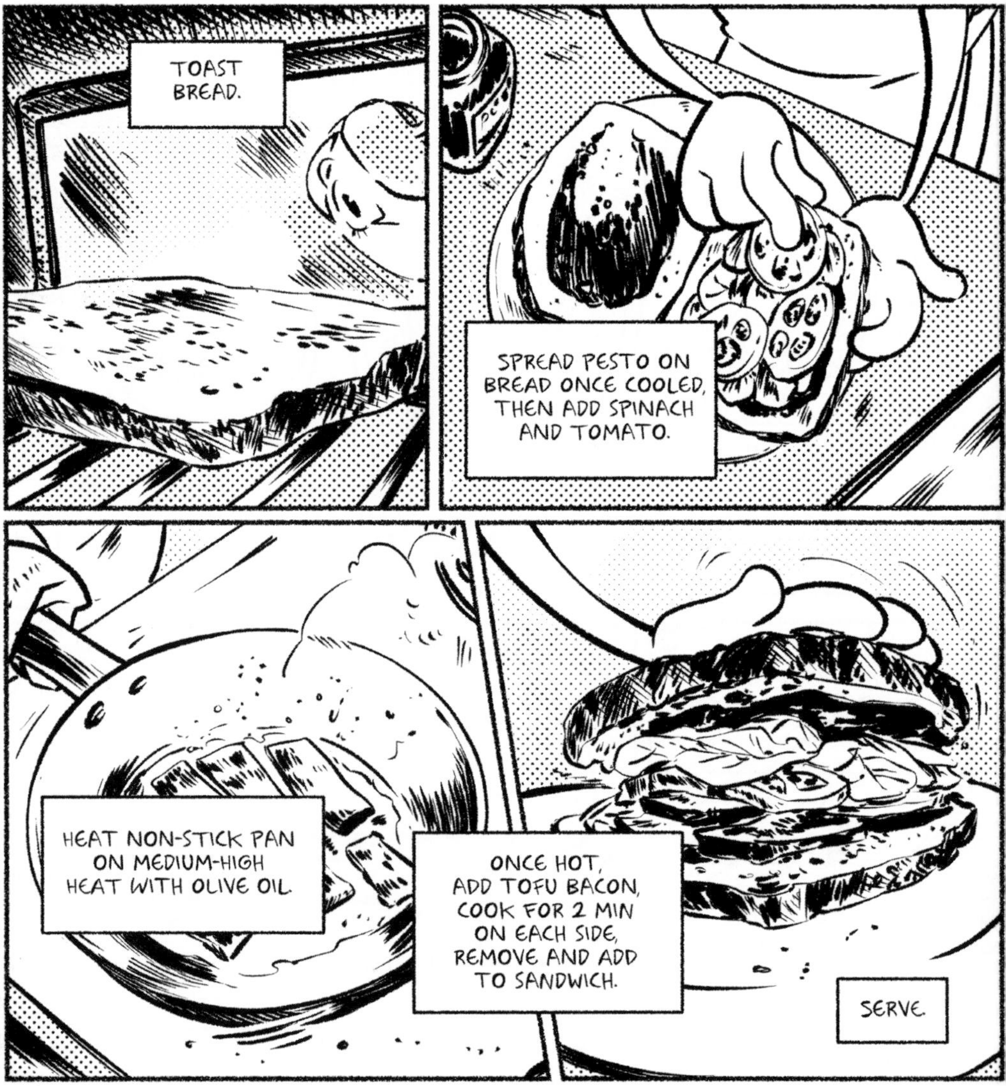
TOAST BREAD.
SPREAD PESTO ON BREAD ONCE COOLED, THEN ADD SPINACH AND TOMATO.
HEAT NON-STICK PAN ON MEDIUM-HIGH HEAT WITH OLIVE OIL.
ONCE HOT, ADD TOFU BACON, COOK FOR 2 MIN ON EACH SIDE, REMOVE AND ADD TO SANDWICH.
SERVE.

FALAFEL

-1 CUPS DRIED CHICKPEAS
-1 TSP BAKING POWDER
-1/2 CUP FRESH PARSLEY LEAVES (DOUBLE IF DRIED)
-1/4 CUP FRESH CILANTRO LEAVES (DOUBLE IF DRIED)
-1/4 CUP FRESH DILL (DOUBLE IF DRIED)
-1 TBSP SESAME SEEDS
-2 TSP KOSHER SALT
-1 TBSP GROUND BLACK PEPPER
-1 TBSP GROUND CUMIN
-1 TBSP GROUND CORIANDER
-1 TSP CAYENNE PEPPER
-1/2 CUP WHITE ONION
-8 GARLIC CLOVES OR 3 TBSP CHOPPED GARLIC
-VEGETABLE OIL (FOR BAKING SHEET)

HANDS ON: 20 MIN
HANDS OFF: 13 HR

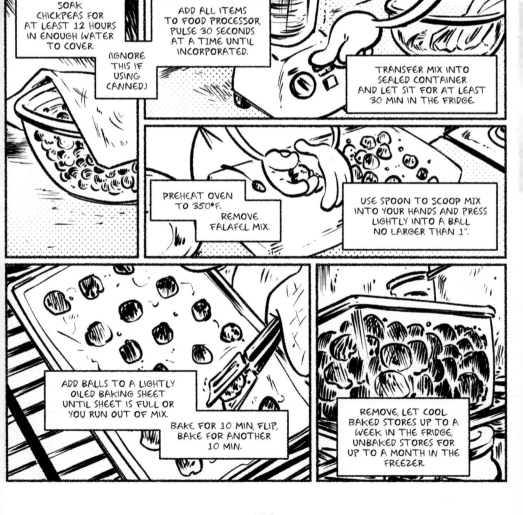

SOAK CHICKPEAS FOR AT LEAST 12 HOURS IN ENOUGH WATER TO COVER.

(IGNORE THIS IF USING CANNED.)

ADD ALL ITEMS TO FOOD PROCESSOR, PULSE 30 SECONDS AT A TIME UNTIL INCORPORATED.

TRANSFER MIX INTO SEALED CONTAINER AND LET SIT FOR AT LEAST 30 MIN IN THE FRIDGE.

PREHEAT OVEN TO 350°F. REMOVE FALAFEL MIX.

USE SPOON TO SCOOP MIX INTO YOUR HANDS AND PRESS LIGHTLY INTO A BALL NO LARGER THAN 1".

ADD BALLS TO A LIGHTLY OILED BAKING SHEET UNTIL SHEET IS FULL OR YOU RUN OUT OF MIX.

BAKE FOR 10 MIN, FLIP, BAKE FOR ANOTHER 10 MIN.

REMOVE, LET COOL BAKED STORES UP TO A WEEK IN THE FRIDGE, UNBAKED STORES FOR UP TO A MONTH IN THE FREEZER.

ONE POT SPAGHETTI

HANDS ON: 40 MIN

- 2 TBSP OLIVE OIL
- 1 TSP KOSHER SALT
- 1/2 ONION, CHOPPED
- 1 CUP MUSHROOMS, CHOPPED
- 3 TBSP GARLIC
- 1 TBSP RED PEPPER FLAKES
- 1 TBSP BLACK PEPPER
- 2 TBSP NUTRITIONAL YEAST
- 1 CUP ROMA TOMATO, CHOPPED
- 14 OZ (1 3/4 CUPS) CANNED TOMATOES OR 2 ADDITIONAL CUPS OF ROMA TOMATO
- 4 CUPS VEGETABLE BROTH OR WATER
- 16 OZ (2 CUPS) OF DRY SPAGHETTI NOODLE
- 1 TBSP SOY SAUCE
- 1 TBSP SHIRO MISO OR 1/2 TBSP FISH SAUCE
- 2 TBSP BASIL (DOUBLE IF DRIED)
- 1/3 CUP PARMESAN, SHREDDED OR POWDERED

OPTIONAL VEGETABLES:

- 1/2 CUP CARROTS
- 3 CUPS SPINACH
- 1 CUP GREEN PEPPERS
- 1/2 CUP ZUCCHINI
- 1/2 CUP BROCCOLI

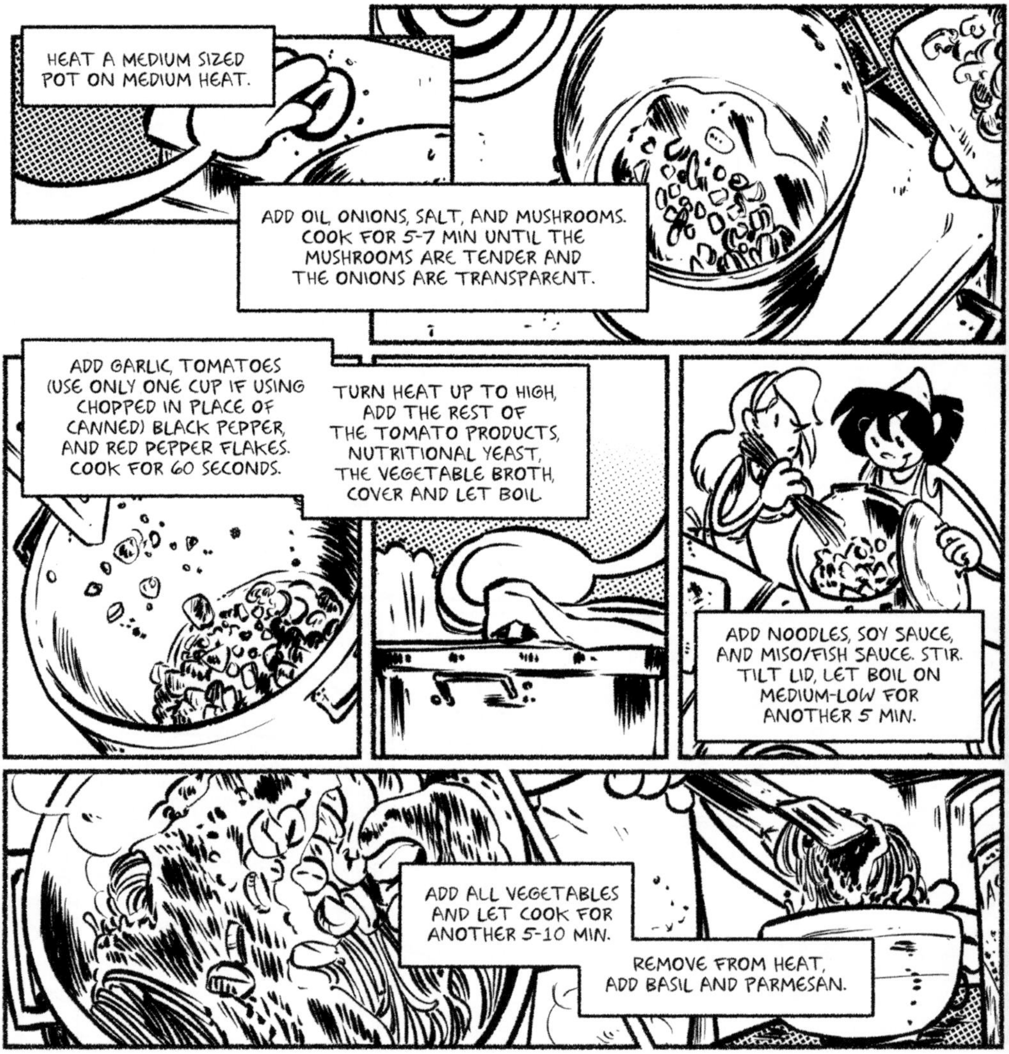
HEAT A MEDIUM SIZED POT ON MEDIUM HEAT.
ADD OIL, ONIONS, SALT, AND MUSHROOMS. COOK FOR 5-7 MIN UNTIL THE MUSHROOMS ARE TENDER AND THE ONIONS ARE TRANSPARENT.
ADD GARLIC, TOMATOES (USE ONLY ONE CUP IF USING CHOPPED IN PLACE OF CANNED) BLACK PEPPER, AND RED PEPPER FLAKES. COOK FOR 60 SECONDS.
TURN HEAT UP TO HIGH, ADD THE REST OF THE TOMATO PRODUCTS, NUTRITIONAL YEAST, THE VEGETABLE BROTH, COVER AND LET BOIL.
ADD NOODLES, SOY SAUCE, AND MISO/FISH SAUCE. STIR. TILT LID, LET BOIL ON MEDIUM-LOW FOR ANOTHER 5 MIN.
ADD ALL VEGETABLES AND LET COOK FOR ANOTHER 5-10 MIN.
REMOVE FROM HEAT, ADD BASIL AND PARMESAN.

MAC & CHEESE

HANDS ON: 30 MIN

- -3 CUPS NOODLES (ELBOW, RIGATONI, ZITI, OR PENNE)
- -2 TBSP BUTTER
- -2 TBSP FLOUR
- -1 TSP SALT
- -1 TSP BLACK PEPPER
- -1 CUP MILK
- -1 CUP CHEESE OF CHOICE, SHREDDED (EXTRA SHARP CHEDDAR CHEESE)

- -OPTIONAL TOPPINGS:
- -1 TSP SMOKED PAPRIKA
- -GREEN ONIONS, CHOPPED
- -OTHER CHEESE (BLUE OR FETA ARE GREAT!)
- -TOMATOES, CHOPPED
- -SPINACH, CHOPPED
- -PANKO BREADCRUMBS

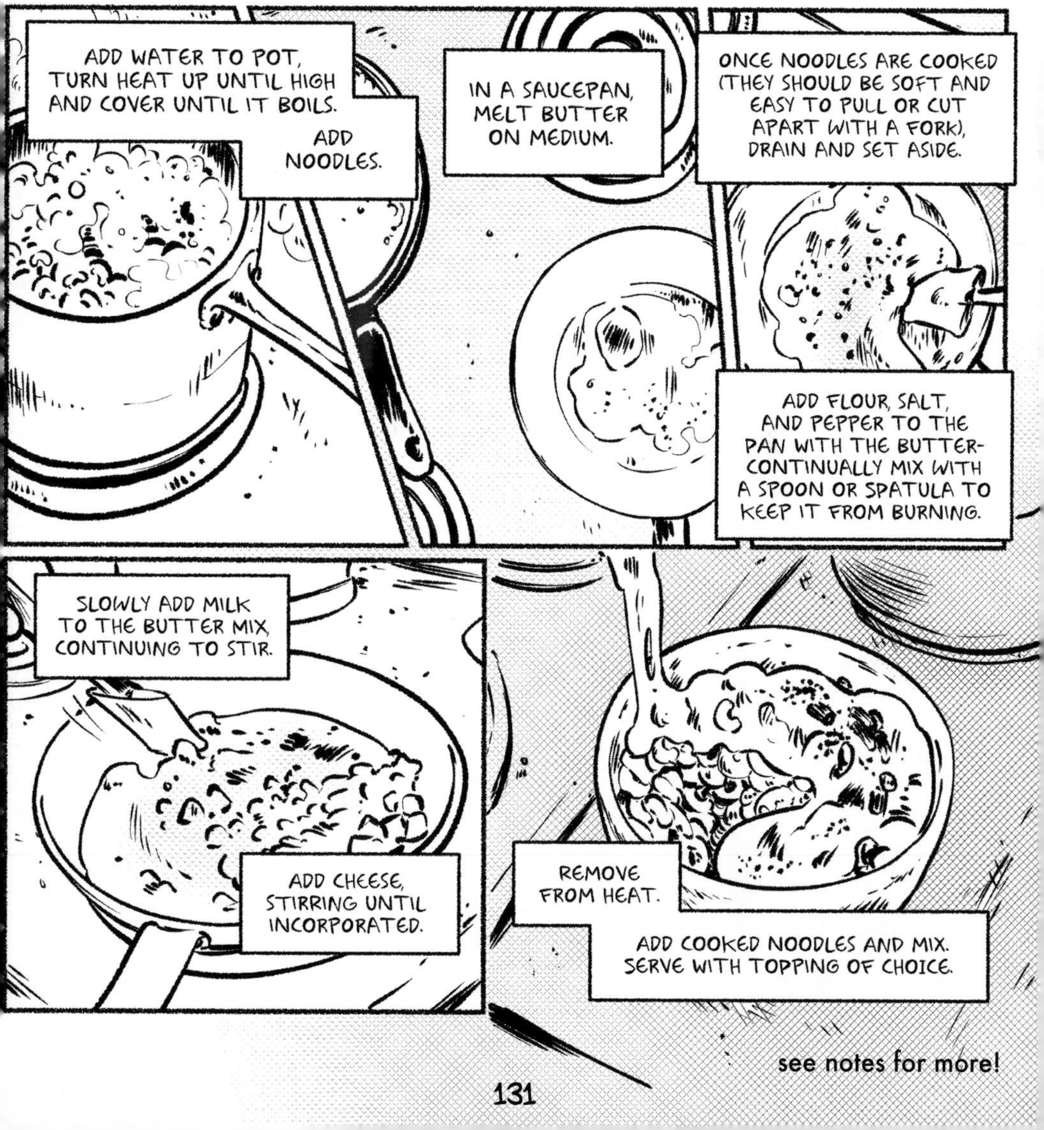
ADD WATER TO POT, TURN HEAT UP UNTIL HIGH AND COVER UNTIL IT BOILS.
ADD NOODLES.
IN A SAUCEPAN, MELT BUTTER ON MEDIUM.
ONCE NOODLES ARE COOKED (THEY SHOULD BE SOFT AND EASY TO PULL OR CUT APART WITH A FORK), DRAIN AND SET ASIDE.
ADD FLOUR, SALT, AND PEPPER TO THE PAN WITH THE BUTTER- CONTINUALLY MIX WITH A SPOON OR SPATULA TO KEEP IT FROM BURNING.
SLOWLY ADD MILK TO THE BUTTER MIX, CONTINUING TO STIR.
ADD CHEESE, STIRRING UNTIL INCORPORATED.
REMOVE FROM HEAT.
ADD COOKED NOODLES AND MIX. SERVE WITH TOPPING OF CHOICE.

see notes for more!

GENERAL TSO'S TOFU

- -3 TBSP VEGETABLE OIL
- -1 CUP (6OZ) TOFU, DRAINED AND SLICED
- -1/2 CUP SOY SAUCE
- -2 TBSP CHILI OIL
- -2 TBSP SESAME OIL
- -4 TBSP MAPLE SYRUP OR 1 TBSP VANILLA EXTRACT
- -1 TBSP GARLIC, MINCED
- -1 TBSP GINGER, MINCED
- -1 TBSP RICE VINEGAR
- -2 TBSP CORN STARCH
- -1 CUP WHITE ONION, SLICED
- -1/3 CUP GREEN ONION, CHOPPED
- -2 CUP BROCCOLI, ROUGHLY CHOPPED

HANDS ON: 35 MIN

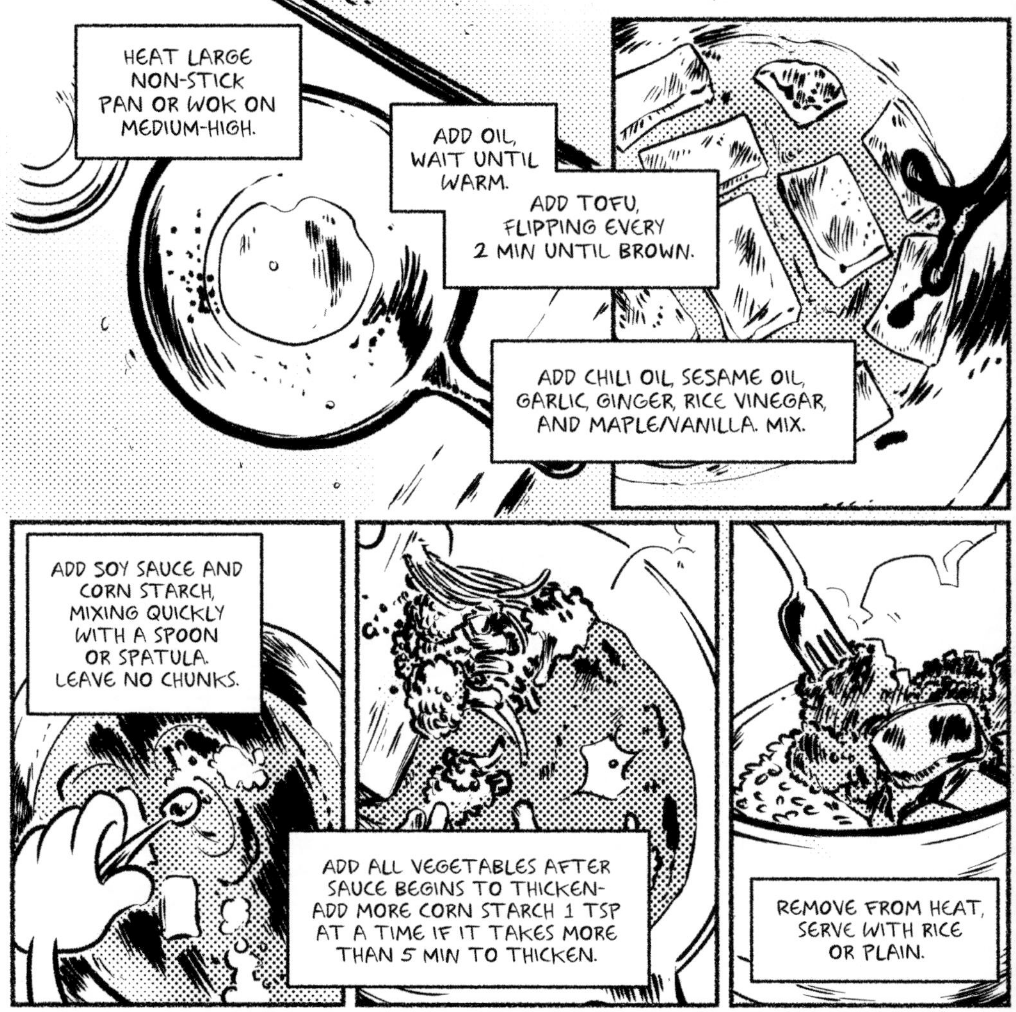
HEAT LARGE NON-STICK PAN OR WOK ON MEDIUM-HIGH.
ADD OIL, WAIT UNTIL WARM.
ADD TOFU, FLIPPING EVERY 2 MIN UNTIL BROWN.
ADD CHILI OIL, SESAME OIL, GARLIC, GINGER, RICE VINEGAR, AND MAPLE/VANILLA. MIX.
ADD SOY SAUCE AND CORN STARCH, MIXING QUICKLY WITH A SPOON OR SPATULA. LEAVE NO CHUNKS.
ADD ALL VEGETABLES AFTER SAUCE BEGINS TO THICKEN- ADD MORE CORN STARCH 1 TSP AT A TIME IF IT TAKES MORE THAN 5 MIN TO THICKEN.
REMOVE FROM HEAT, SERVE WITH RICE OR PLAIN.

VEGETABLE TIAN

HANDS ON: 20 MIN
HANDS OFF: 45 MIN

- 1 TBSP OLIVE OIL
- 1 TBSP GARLIC, CHOPPED
- 1 CUP WHITE ONION, CHOPPED
- 2 CUPS POTATOES, SLICED
- 2 CUPS TOMATOES, SLICED
- 2 CUPS ZUCCHINI SLICED
- 1 CUP MOZZARELLA, SHREDDED
- 1/3 PARMESAN, SHREDDED OR POWDERED
- 2 TSP SALT
- 2 TSP PEPPER
- 1/2 TBSP OREGANO (DOUBLE IF DRIED)
- 1/2 TBSP BASIL (DOUBLE IF DRIED)
- 1/2 TBSP ROSEMARY (DOUBLE IF DRIED)
- 1/2 TBSP PARSLEY (DOUBLE IF DRIED)
- 1 TBSP RED PEPPER FLAKES

SUGGESTED, BUT SWAPPABLE:
- 2 CUPS YELLOW SQUASH, SLICED
- 1 CUP EGGPLANT, SLICED
- 1/2 CUP CARROT, SLICED

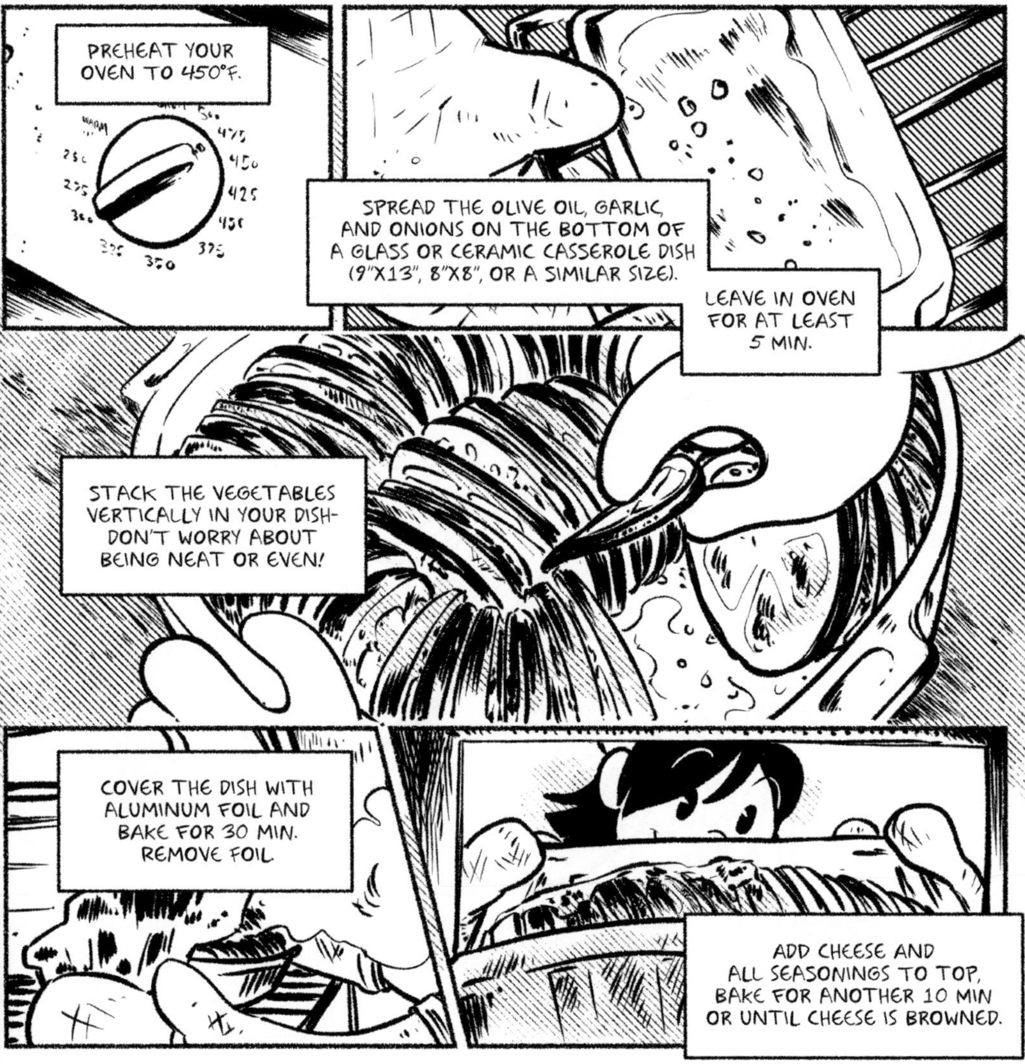

PREHEAT YOUR OVEN TO 450°F.
WARM
250
275
300
325
350
375
400
425
450
475
500
SPREAD THE OLIVE OIL, GARLIC, AND ONIONS ON THE BOTTOM OF A GLASS OR CERAMIC CASSEROLE DISH (9"X13", 8"X8", OR A SIMILAR SIZE).
LEAVE IN OVEN FOR AT LEAST 5 MIN.
STACK THE VEGETABLES VERTICALLY IN YOUR DISH- DON'T WORRY ABOUT BEING NEAT OR EVEN!
COVER THE DISH WITH ALUMINUM FOIL AND BAKE FOR 30 MIN. REMOVE FOIL.
ADD CHEESE AND ALL SEASONINGS TO TOP, BAKE FOR ANOTHER 10 MIN OR UNTIL CHEESE IS BROWNED.

BEAN BURGERS

HANDS ON: 25 MIN

-2 TBSP VEGETABLE OIL
-9 OZ (1 1/2 CUPS) BLACK BEANS
-1 EGG
-2 TSP SALT
-2 TSP BLACK PEPPER
-2 TSP SMOKED PAPRIKA
-1/2 CUP FLOUR

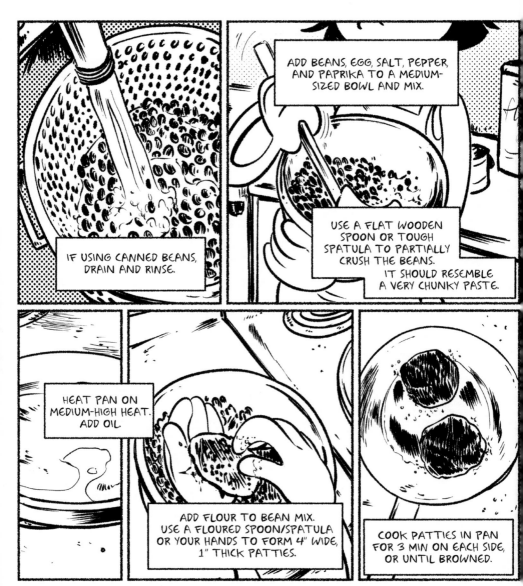

IF USING CANNED BEANS, DRAIN AND RINSE.

ADD BEANS, EGG, SALT, PEPPER, AND PAPRIKA TO A MEDIUM-SIZED BOWL AND MIX.

USE A FLAT WOODEN SPOON OR TOUGH SPATULA TO PARTIALLY CRUSH THE BEANS. IT SHOULD RESEMBLE A VERY CHUNKY PASTE.

HEAT PAN ON MEDIUM-HIGH HEAT. ADD OIL.

ADD FLOUR TO BEAN MIX. USE A FLOURED SPOON/SPATULA OR YOUR HANDS TO FORM 4" WIDE, 1" THICK PATTIES.

COOK PATTIES IN PAN FOR 3 MIN ON EACH SIDE, OR UNTIL BROWNED.

TACOS

-TORTILLAS (SEE PREVIOUS RECIPE)

HANDS ON: 45 MIN
(INCLUDING TORTILLAS)

SUGGESTED FILLING MIX:
- 1/2 CUP WHITE ONION, CHOPPED
- 1/2 CUP TOMATO, CHOPPED
- 1/2 CUP SERRANO OR JALAPENO, CHOPPED
- 2 TSP CILANTRO (DOUBLE IF DRIED)
- 1 TSP GARLIC
- 1 TSP SALT
- 1 TSP BLACK PEPPER
- 1 CUP PRECOOKED CHICKEN OR PRECOOKED TVP (TEXTURED VEGETABLE PROTEIN)
- LEAFY GREEN OF CHOICE (OPTIONAL)
- CHEESE OF CHOICE (OPTIONAL)

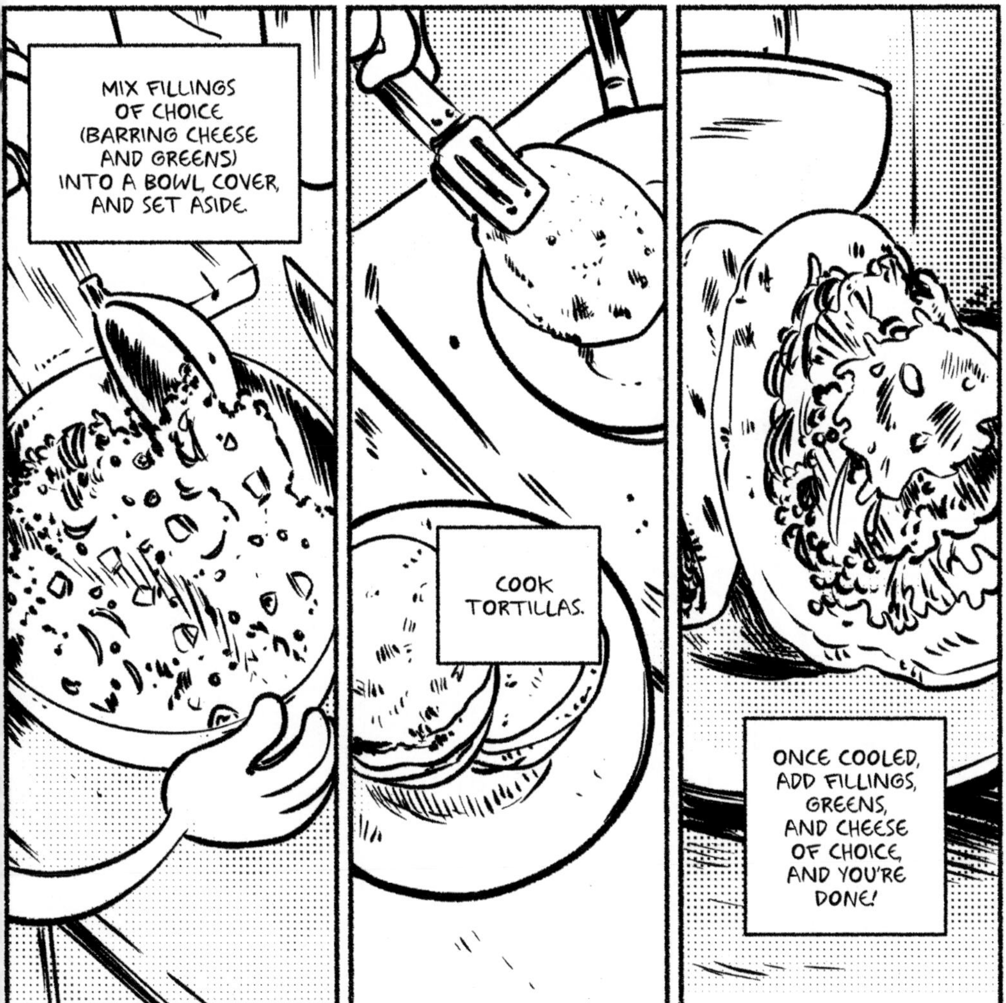
MIX FILLINGS OF CHOICE (BARRING CHEESE AND GREENS) INTO A BOWL, COVER, AND SET ASIDE.
COOK TORTILLAS.
ONCE COOLED, ADD FILLINGS, GREENS, AND CHEESE OF CHOICE, AND YOU'RE DONE!

CEVICHE

HANDS ON: 15 MIN
HANDS OFF: 6 HRS

- 1 LB FISH FILLETS (CATFISH, TILAPIA OR TUNA)
- 1/2 CUP GRAPEFRUIT JUICE
- 1/2 CUP LIME JUICE
- 1/3 CUP LEMON JUICE
- 1 CUP ROMA TOMATO, CHOPPED
- 1/2 CUP WHITE ONION, CHOPPED
- 1 TSP GARLIC, MINCED
- 1/2 CUP JALAPENO, CHOPPED OR 1 TBSP RED PEPPER FLAKES
- 1 TBSP CILANTRO (DOUBLE IF DRIED)
- 1 TBSP KOSHER SALT
- 2 TBSP OLIVE OIL
- 1 AVOCADO, PITTED AND DICED
- TORTILLA CHIPS (OPTIONAL)

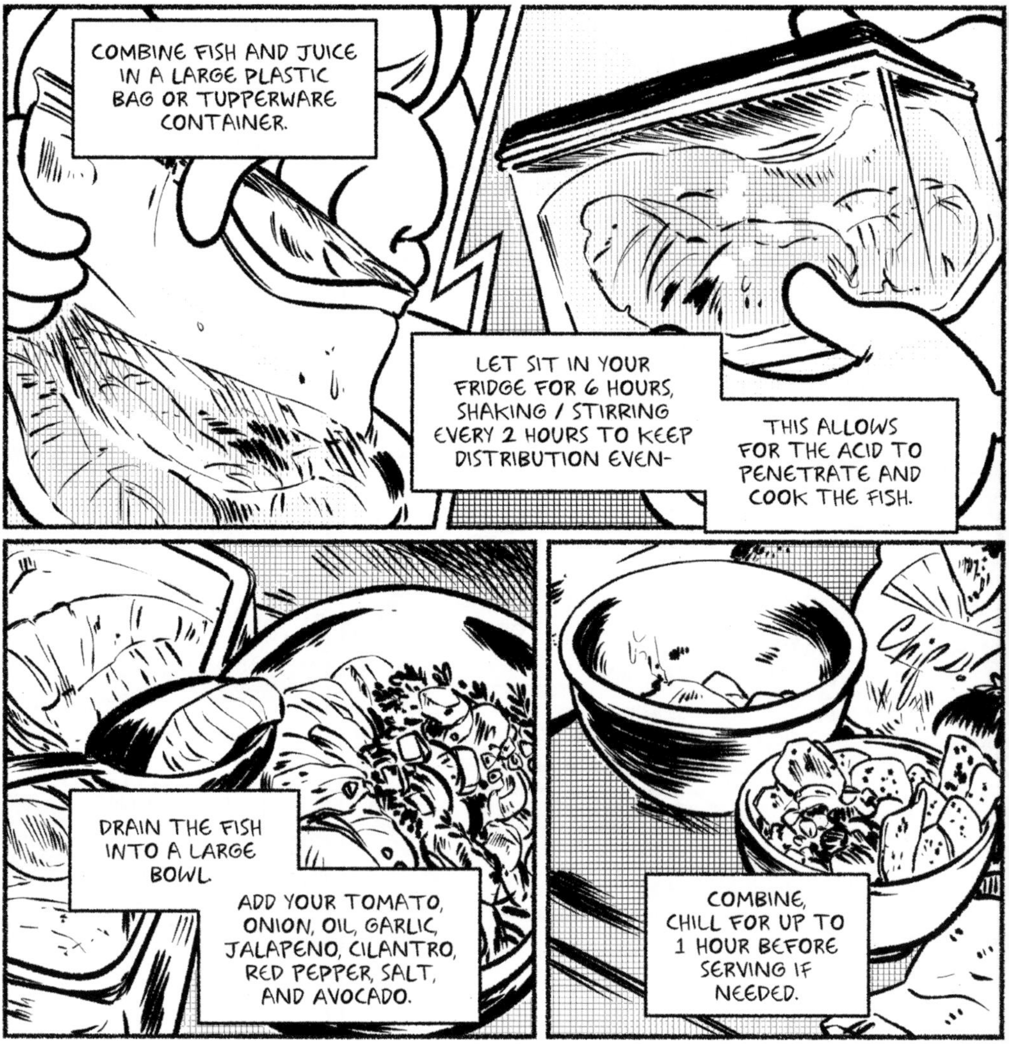
COMBINE FISH AND JUICE IN A LARGE PLASTIC BAG OR TUPPERWARE CONTAINER.
LET SIT IN YOUR FRIDGE FOR 6 HOURS, SHAKING / STIRRING EVERY 2 HOURS TO KEEP DISTRIBUTION EVEN-
THIS ALLOWS FOR THE ACID TO PENETRATE AND COOK THE FISH.
DRAIN THE FISH INTO A LARGE BOWL.
ADD YOUR TOMATO, ONION, OIL, GARLIC, JALAPENO, CILANTRO, RED PEPPER, SALT, AND AVOCADO.
COMBINE, CHILL FOR UP TO 1 HOUR BEFORE SERVING IF NEEDED.

OKONOMIYAKI
(CABBAGE PANCAKES)

HANDS ON: 1 HOUR
HANDS OFF: 30 MIN

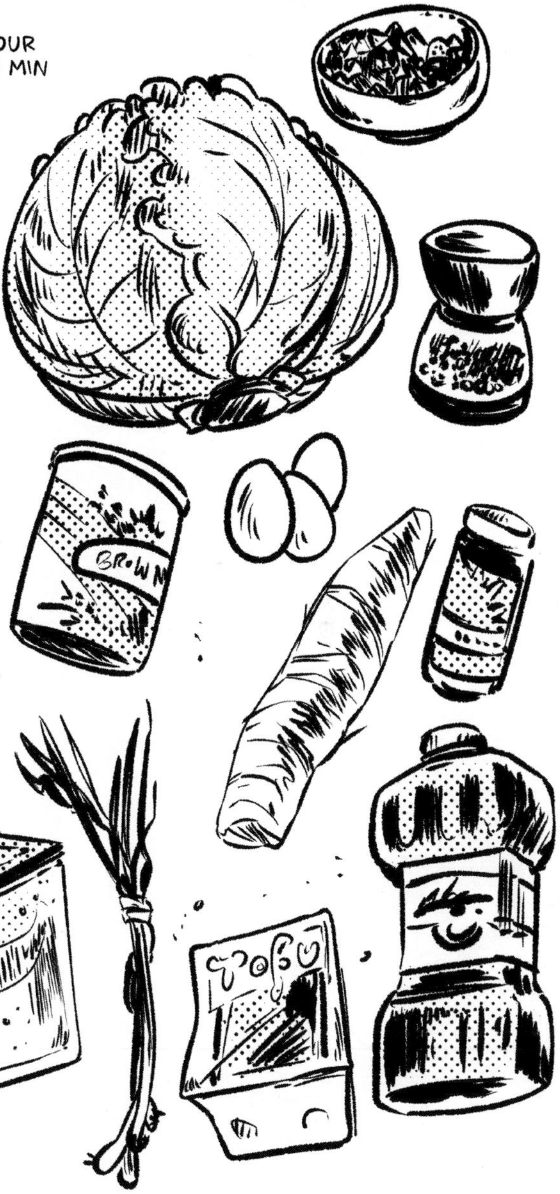
TOFU

- 1 CUP ALL PURPOSE FLOUR
- 1/2 TSP SALT
- 1/2 TSP SUGAR
- 1/2 TSP BAKING POWDER
- 1/2 CUP CHINESE YAM (NAGAIMO), GRATED (DON'T SUB!)
- 5 CUPS CABBAGE SHREDDED OR CHOPPED INTO 1/2" PIECES
- 3 EGGS
- 1/2 CUP TENKASU/AGEDAMA OR TOASTED AND CHOPPED BREAD OF CHOICE
- 3/4 CUP DASHI OR BROTH OF CHOICE (IF SUBBING, ADD 2 TSP SALT AND 1 TSP BLACK PEPPER)
- 3 TBSP VEGETABLE OIL
- 3 TBSP GREEN ONIONS, CHOPPED (OPTIONAL)
- SLICED PORK BELLY, CHOPPED SHRIMP, OR TOFU (OPTIONAL)

OPTIONAL SAUCE:
- 4 TBSP KETCHUP
- 4 TBSP WORCHESTERSHIRE SAUCE
- 2 TBSP SOY SAUCE
- 1 TBSP SUGAR

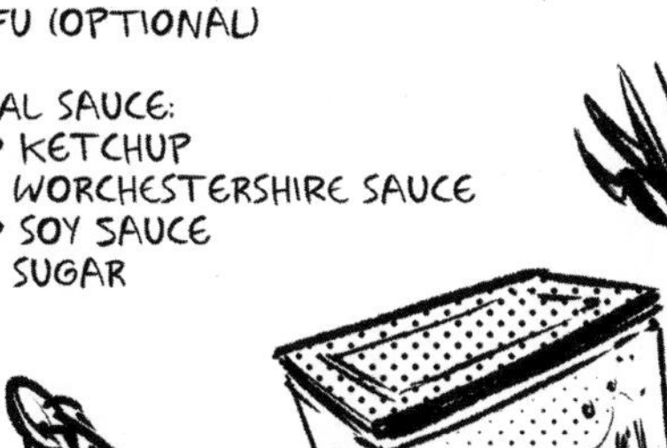

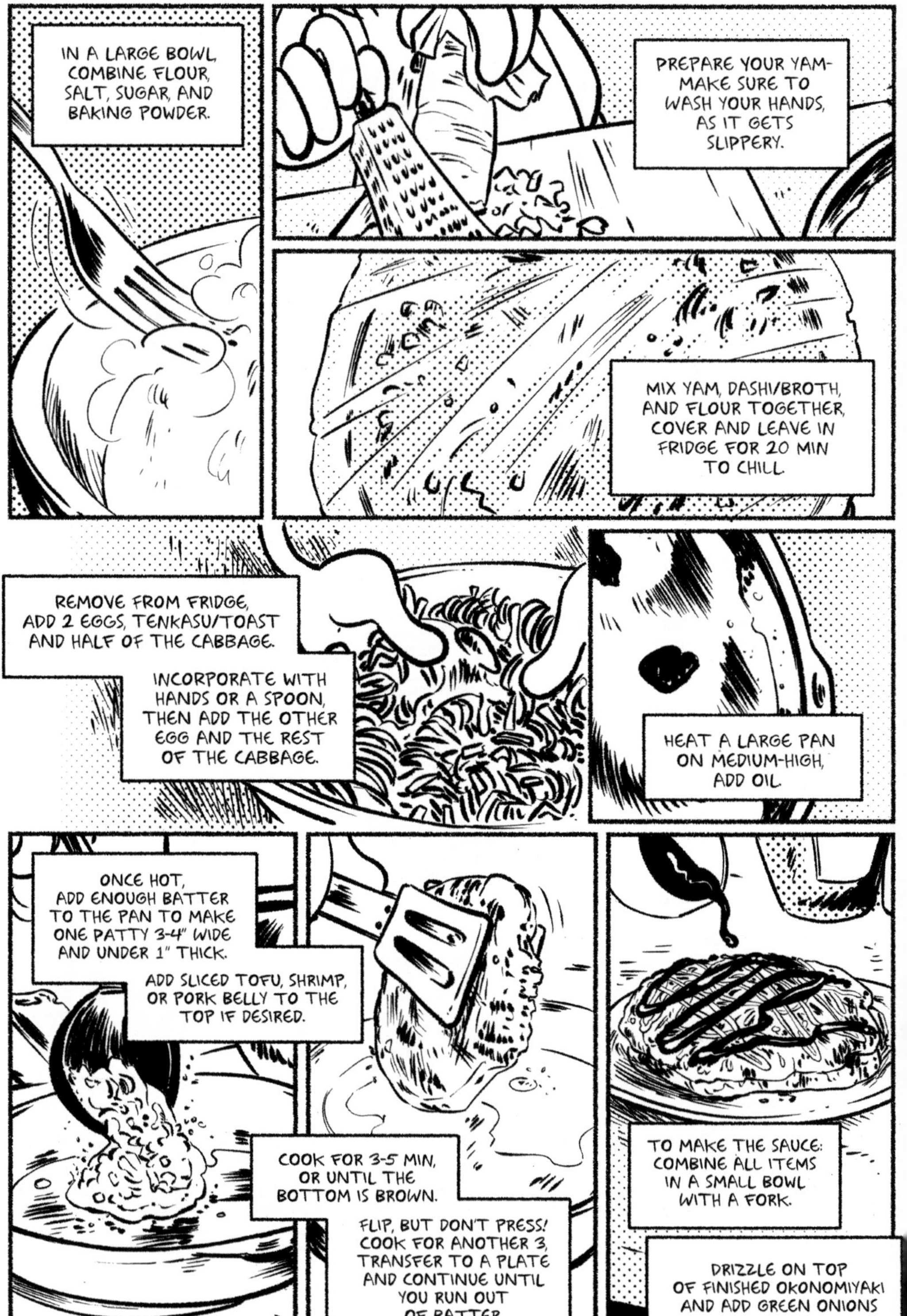
IN A LARGE BOWL, COMBINE FLOUR, SALT, SUGAR, AND BAKING POWDER.
PREPARE YOUR YAM-MAKE SURE TO WASH YOUR HANDS, AS IT GETS SLIPPERY.
MIX YAM, DASHI/BROTH, AND FLOUR TOGETHER, COVER AND LEAVE IN FRIDGE FOR 20 MIN TO CHILL.
REMOVE FROM FRIDGE, ADD 2 EGGS, TENKASU/TOAST AND HALF OF THE CABBAGE.
INCORPORATE WITH HANDS OR A SPOON, THEN ADD THE OTHER EGG AND THE REST OF THE CABBAGE.
HEAT A LARGE PAN ON MEDIUM-HIGH, ADD OIL.
ONCE HOT, ADD ENOUGH BATTER TO THE PAN TO MAKE ONE PATTY 3-4" WIDE AND UNDER 1" THICK.
ADD SLICED TOFU, SHRIMP, OR PORK BELLY TO THE TOP IF DESIRED.
COOK FOR 3-5 MIN, OR UNTIL THE BOTTOM IS BROWN.
FLIP, BUT DON'T PRESS! COOK FOR ANOTHER 3, TRANSFER TO A PLATE AND CONTINUE UNTIL YOU RUN OUT OF BATTER.
TO MAKE THE SAUCE: COMBINE ALL ITEMS IN A SMALL BOWL WITH A FORK.
DRIZZLE ON TOP OF FINISHED OKONOMIYAKI AND ADD GREEN ONIONS AND MAYO.

MISO SOUP

HANDS ON: 15 MIN

- -4 CUPS OF BROTH OR WATER
- -4 TBSP MISO
- -1 TBSP GREEN ONION, CHOPPED
- -1/3 CUP TOFU, CHOPPED

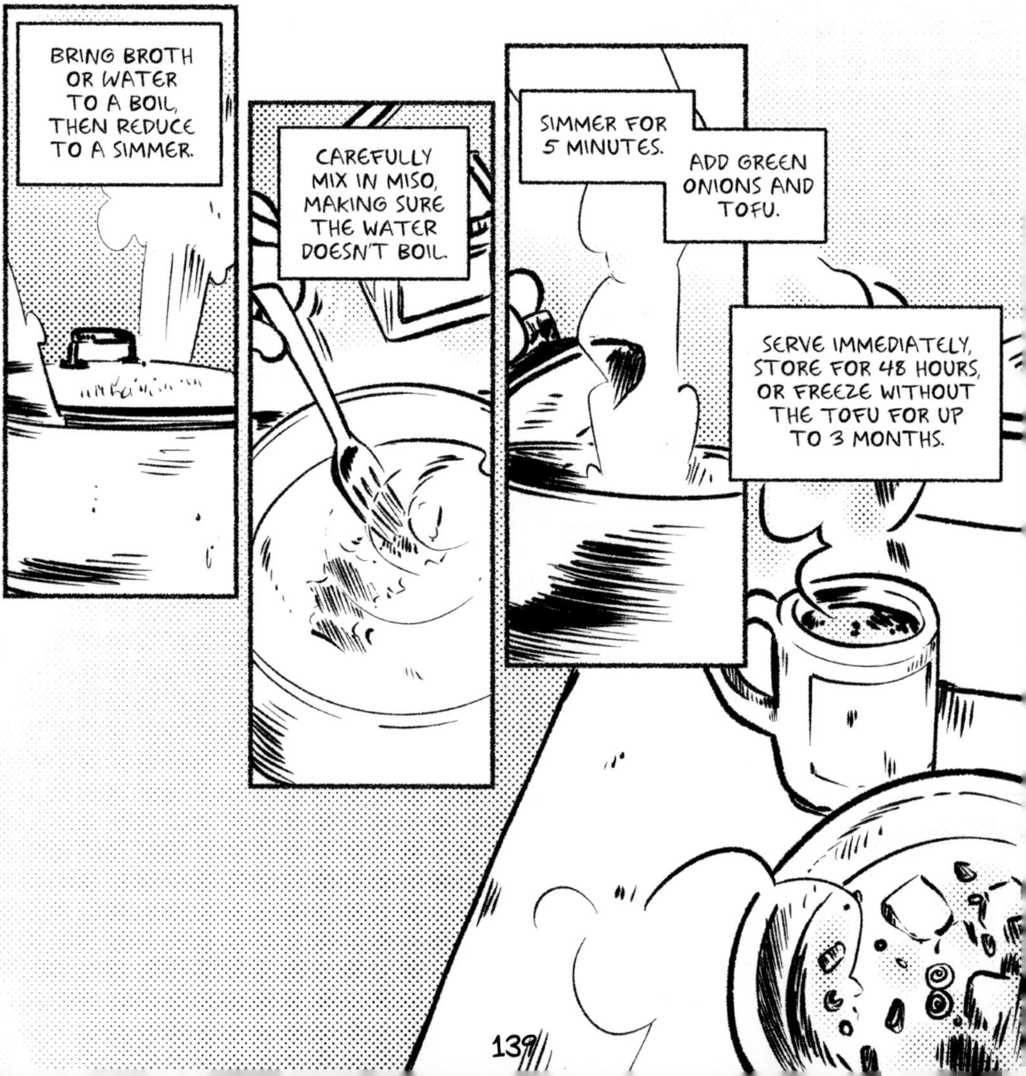
BRING BROTH OR WATER TO A BOIL, THEN REDUCE TO A SIMMER.
CAREFULLY MIX IN MISO, MAKING SURE THE WATER DOESN'T BOIL.
SIMMER FOR 5 MINUTES.
ADD GREEN ONIONS AND TOFU.
SERVE IMMEDIATELY, STORE FOR 48 HOURS, OR FREEZE WITHOUT THE TOFU FOR UP TO 3 MONTHS.

TOMATO BASIL SOUP

HANDS ON: 10 MIN
HANDS OFF: 20 MIN

- 1/2 CUP BUTTER
- 1 CUP WHITE ONION, CHOPPED
- 2 TBSP GARLIC, MINCED
- 4 CUPS TOMATOES, DICED
- 1 CUP BROTH OF CHOICE, VEGETABLE RECOMMENDED
- 2 TSP KOSHER SALT
- 1 TSP BLACK PEPPER
- 1/4 CUP FRESH BASIL, CHOPPED
- 2 TSP BALSAMIC VINEGAR OR 2 TSP APPLE CIDER VINEGAR + 1 TSP BROWN SUGAR

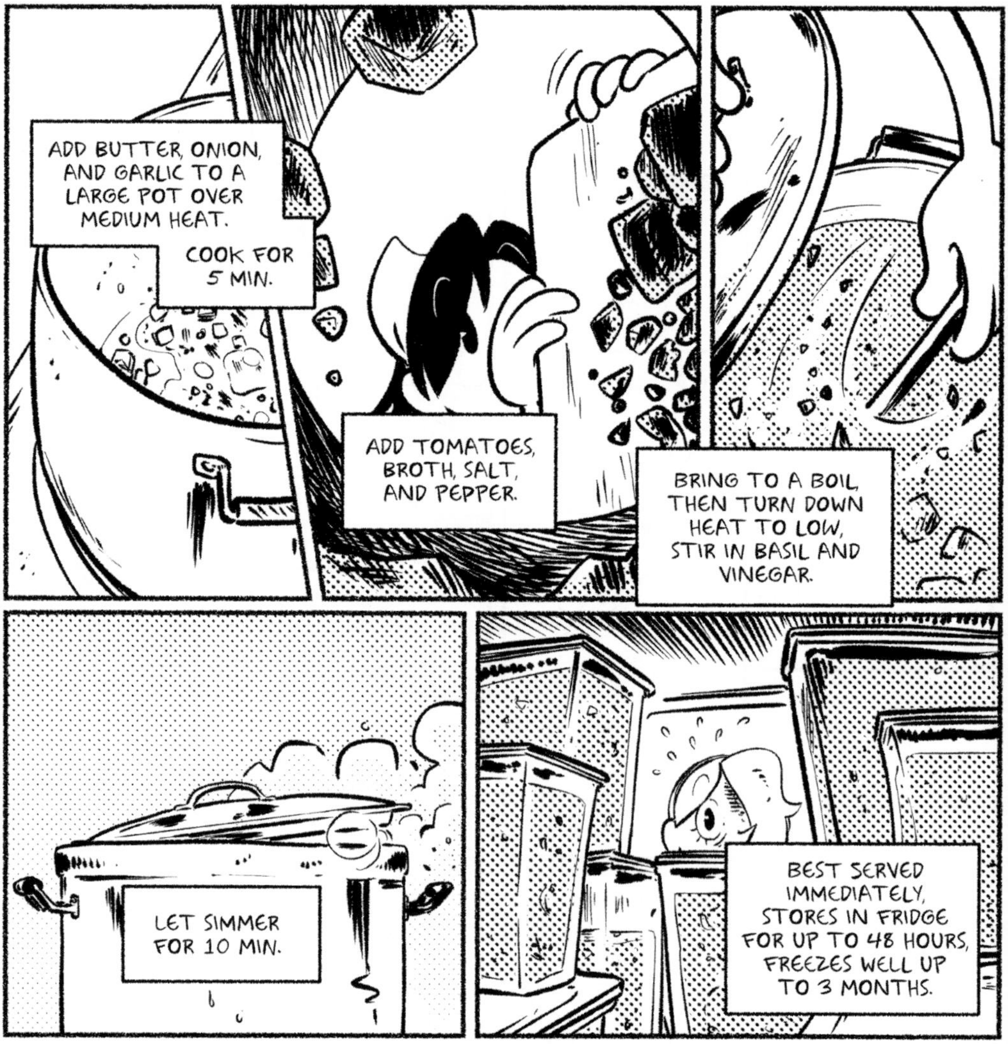
ADD BUTTER, ONION, AND GARLIC TO A LARGE POT OVER MEDIUM HEAT.
COOK FOR 5 MIN.
ADD TOMATOES, BROTH, SALT, AND PEPPER.
BRING TO A BOIL, THEN TURN DOWN HEAT TO LOW, STIR IN BASIL AND VINEGAR.
LET SIMMER FOR 10 MIN.
BEST SERVED IMMEDIATELY, STORES IN FRIDGE FOR UP TO 48 HOURS, FREEZES WELL UP TO 3 MONTHS.

 # 5 VEGETABLE SOUP

HANDS ON: 20 MIN
HANDS OFF: 30 MIN

-3 TBSP OLIVE OIL
-4 TBSP GARLIC, MINCED
-1 1/2 CUPS YELLOW ONION, CHOPPED
-2 CUPS PEELED AND CHOPPED CARROTS
-2 CUPS GREEN BELL PEPPER, SLICED
-2 CUPS CORN
-1 CUP GREEN PEAS
-3 CUPS POTATOES, DICED
-8 CUPS BROTH OF CHOICE
-4 CUPS DICED OR CANNED TOMATOES

-2 BAY LEAVES
-1 TBSP OREGANO (DOUBLE IF DRIED)
-1 TBSP BASIL (DOUBLE IF DRIED)
-1 TBSP THYME (DOUBLE IF DRIED)
-1 TBSP KOSHER SALT
-1 TBSP BLACK PEPPER
-1 TSP CUMIN
-1 TSP RED PEPPER FLAKES
-ANY OTHER VEGETABLES YOU MIGHT
HAVE SITTING AROUND!

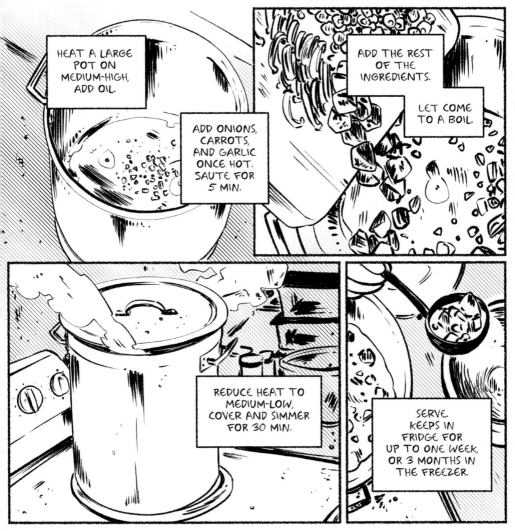

HEAT A LARGE POT ON MEDIUM-HIGH, ADD OIL.

ADD ONIONS, CARROTS, AND GARLIC ONCE HOT. SAUTE FOR 5 MIN.

ADD THE REST OF THE INGREDIENTS.

LET COME TO A BOIL.

REDUCE HEAT TO MEDIUM-LOW, COVER AND SIMMER FOR 30 MIN.

SERVE. KEEPS IN FRIDGE FOR UP TO ONE WEEK, OR 3 MONTHS IN THE FREEZER.

see notes for more!

POTATO & LEEK SOUP

HANDS ON: 15 MIN
HANDS OFF: 40 MIN

- 5 TBSP BUTTER
- 2 TBSP GARLIC, CHOPPED
- 6 CUPS LEEK, CHOPPED
- 7 CUPS BROWN OR YELLOW POTATOES, CHOPPED
- 8 CUPS BROTH OF CHOICE
- 1 TSP SALT
- 1 TBSP BLACK PEPPER
- 3 TBSP NUTRITIONAL YEAST
- 1 TSP DILL

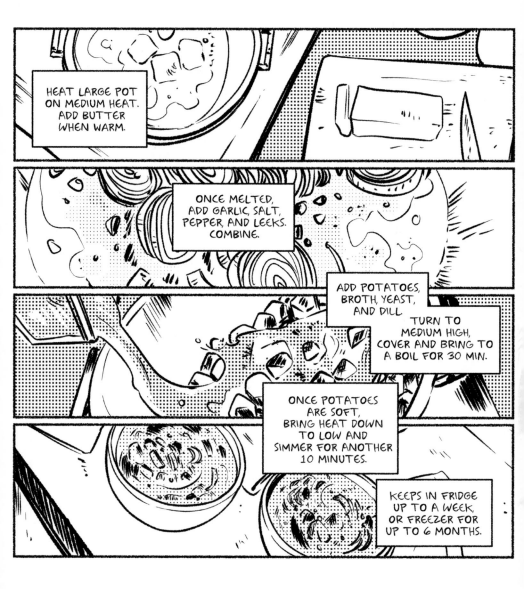

HEAT LARGE POT ON MEDIUM HEAT. ADD BUTTER WHEN WARM.

ONCE MELTED, ADD GARLIC, SALT, PEPPER, AND LEEKS. COMBINE.

ADD POTATOES, BROTH, YEAST, AND DILL. TURN TO MEDIUM HIGH, COVER AND BRING TO A BOIL FOR 30 MIN.

ONCE POTATOES ARE SOFT, BRING HEAT DOWN TO LOW AND SIMMER FOR ANOTHER 10 MINUTES.

KEEPS IN FRIDGE UP TO A WEEK, OR FREEZER FOR UP TO 6 MONTHS.

KIMCHI SOUP

HANDS ON: 10 MIN
HANDS OFF: 40 MIN

- 2 CUPS KIMCHI
- 2 TBSP SOY SAUCE
- 3 TBSP GOCHUJANG OR 2 TBSP RED PEPPER FLAKES (ONLY IF GOCHUJANG IS UNAVAILABLE)
- 1 TSP WHITE SUGAR
- 4 CUPS WATER OR BROTH OF CHOICE
- 1/3 CUP GREEN ONIONS, CHOPPED
- 2 CUPS FIRM TOFU, DRAINED AND CHOPPED

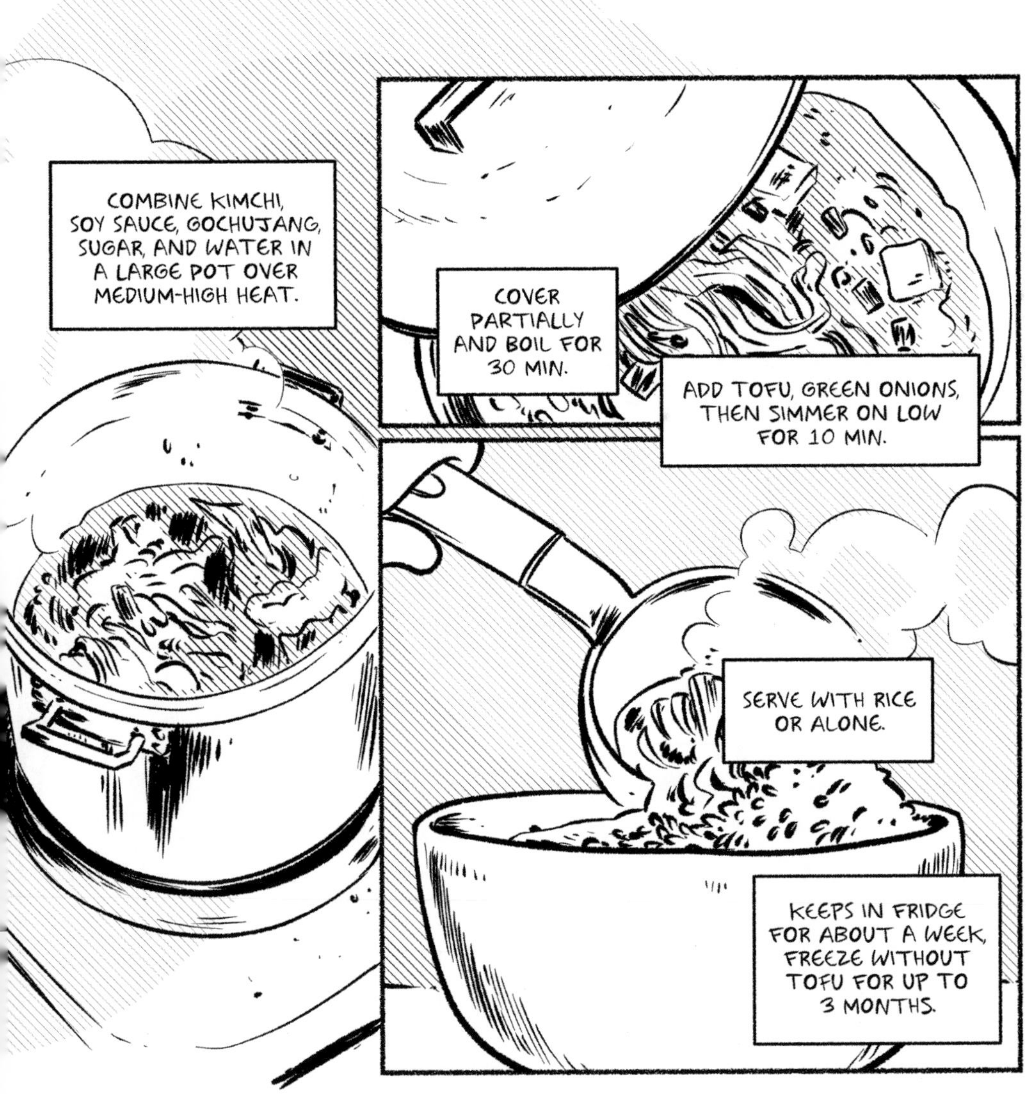
COMBINE KIMCHI, SOY SAUCE, GOCHUJANG, SUGAR, AND WATER IN A LARGE POT OVER MEDIUM-HIGH HEAT.
COVER PARTIALLY AND BOIL FOR 30 MIN.
ADD TOFU, GREEN ONIONS, THEN SIMMER ON LOW FOR 10 MIN.
SERVE WITH RICE OR ALONE.
KEEPS IN FRIDGE FOR ABOUT A WEEK, FREEZE WITHOUT TOFU FOR UP TO 3 MONTHS.

SANCOCHO

HANDS ON: 30 MIN
HANDS OFF: 1 HR

-1 TSP OLIVE OIL
-4 TBSP GARLIC, CHOPPED
-2 CUPS WHITE ONION, CHOPPED
-1 TOMATO, CHOPPED
-1/2 LB OF SKINLESS CHICKEN BREAST
 OR 2 CUPS SEITAN
-1 TSP KOSHER SALT
-1 TSP OREGANO
-1/4 CUP CILANTRO (DOUBLE IF DRIED)
-1 TBSP CORIANDER, POWDERED

-1 TBSP CUMIN
-1/2 CUP GREEN BELL PEPPER
-1/2 CUP RED BELL PEPPER
-4 CUPS BROWN POTATOES, PEELED AND CHOPPED
-3 CUPS SWEET POTATOES, PEELED AND CHOPPED
-2 CUPS CORN, OR 3 EARS CHOPPED INTO THIRDS
-2 CUPS GREEN PLANTAIN, PEELED AND CHOPPED,
 OR 1 ADDITIONAL CUP OF SWEET POTATO
-6 CUPS WATER, OR BROTH OF CHOICE

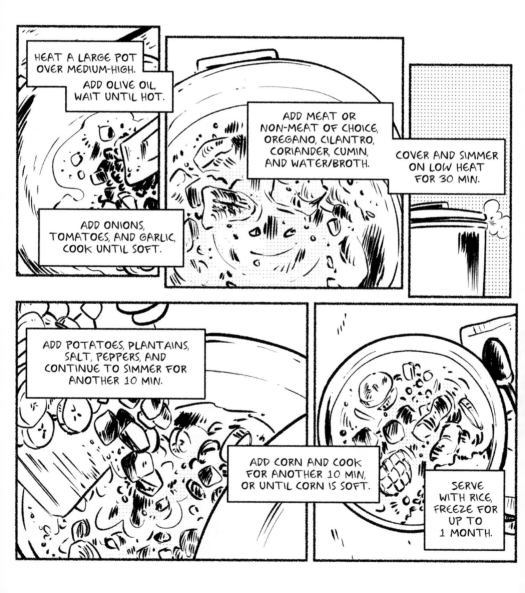

HEAT A LARGE POT OVER MEDIUM-HIGH. ADD OLIVE OIL, WAIT UNTIL HOT.

ADD ONIONS, TOMATOES, AND GARLIC, COOK UNTIL SOFT.

ADD MEAT OR NON-MEAT OF CHOICE, OREGANO, CILANTRO, CORIANDER, CUMIN, AND WATER/BROTH.

COVER AND SIMMER ON LOW HEAT FOR 30 MIN.

ADD POTATOES, PLANTAINS, SALT, PEPPERS, AND CONTINUE TO SIMMER FOR ANOTHER 10 MIN.

ADD CORN AND COOK FOR ANOTHER 10 MIN, OR UNTIL CORN IS SOFT.

SERVE WITH RICE, FREEZE FOR UP TO 1 MONTH.

RAMEN

HANDS ON: 30 MIN
HANDS OFF: 30 MIN

(SUBSTITUTIONS NOT RECOMMENDED FOR THIS RECIPE! I USUALLY MAKE THIS IN LARGE BATCHES SPLIT WITH FRIENDS TO SAVE COST ON THE MORE EXPENSIVE INGREDIENTS. THIS CAN BE EASILY DOUBLED OR TRIPLED FOR THIS REASON.)

-1 TBSP SESAME OIL
-4 CUPS WATER OR BROTH OF CHOICE
 (CHICKEN OR VEGETABLE RECOMMENDED)
-1/4 LB GROUND PORK OR 1/4 LB CHICKEN
 OR 1 CUP MUSHROOMS (BUTTON, CRIMINI,
 PORTOBELLO, OR SHIITAKE)
-1/2 CUP YELLOW ONION, CHOPPED, OR
 1/4 CUP SHALLOT, CHOPPED
-2 TSP GARLIC, MINCED
-1 TSP GINGER MINCED
-1 TBSP SUGAR
-1 TBSP SESAME SEEDS, CRUSHED
-1 TSP SALT
-1 TSP WHITE PEPPER POWDER
-3 TBSP BROWN MISO
-3 TBSP RED PEPPER FLAKES
-1 TBSP SAKE OR RICE WINE VINEGAR
-2 SERVINGS RAMEN NOODLES
(IF YOU CAN'T FIND THESE PLAIN,
BUY INSTANT RAMEN AND USE THE
NOODLES FROM THERE!)

OPTIONAL TOPPINGS
(THESE ARE SUGGESTED COMPLEMENTS,
DON'T GO OVERBOARD AND USE ALL AT ONCE!):
-2 EGGS, HARDBOILED AND MARINATED IN
 2 TBSP SOY SAUCE AND
 2 TBSP MIRIN OVERNIGHT
-1 EGG, FRIED
-NORI, SLICED THIN
-GREEN ONION, CHOPPED
-ADDITIONAL WHITE
 PEPPER POWDER
-CHINESE BROCCOLI
-SPINACH, SLICED
-GREEN PEPPERS, CHOPPED
-BEAN SPROUTS
-GYOZA, PRE-COOKED
-PICKLED GINGER
-CORN
-BUTTER

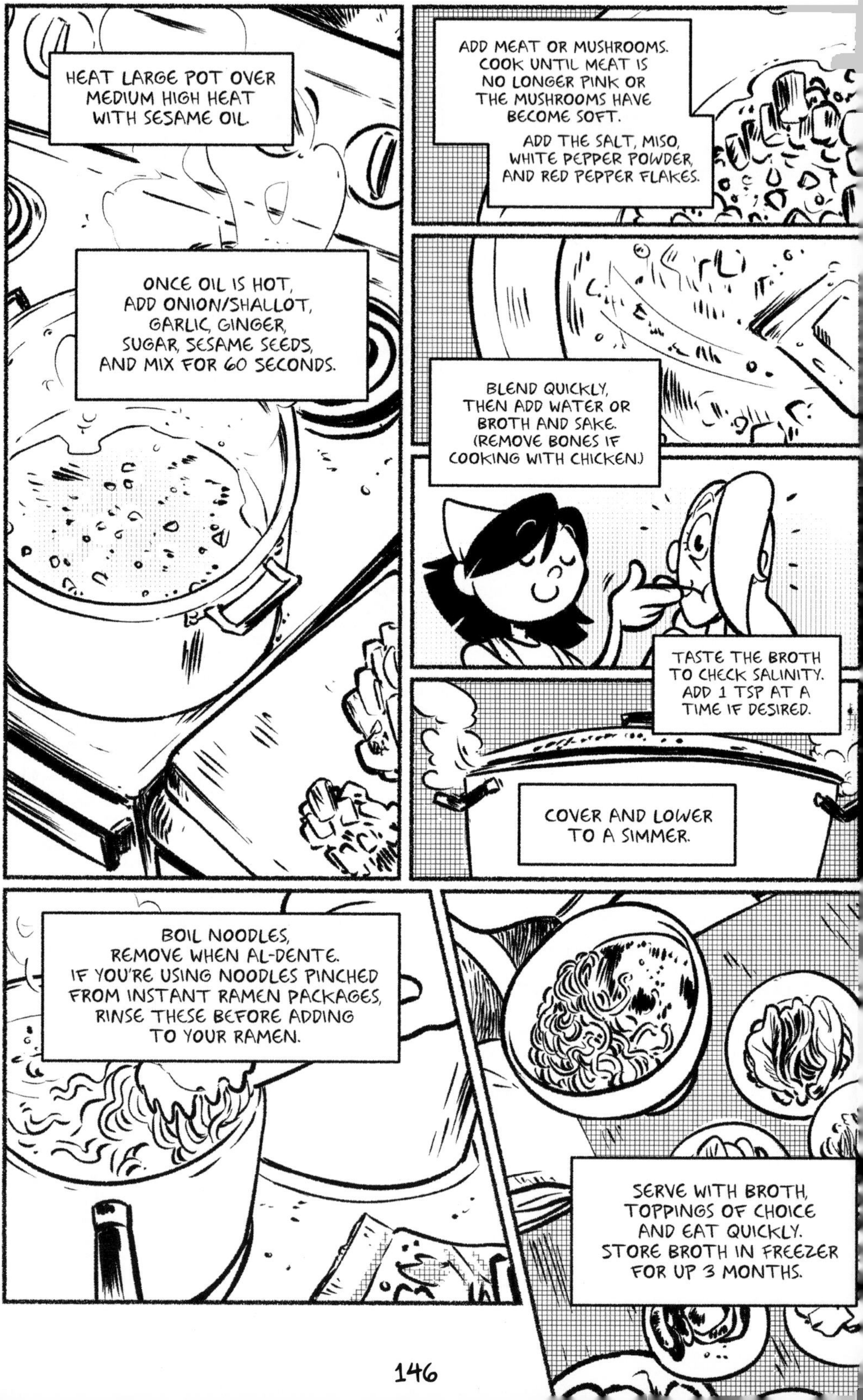
HEAT LARGE POT OVER MEDIUM HIGH HEAT WITH SESAME OIL.
ONCE OIL IS HOT, ADD ONION/SHALLOT, GARLIC, GINGER, SUGAR, SESAME SEEDS, AND MIX FOR 60 SECONDS.
ADD MEAT OR MUSHROOMS. COOK UNTIL MEAT IS NO LONGER PINK OR THE MUSHROOMS HAVE BECOME SOFT.
ADD THE SALT, MISO, WHITE PEPPER POWDER, AND RED PEPPER FLAKES.
BLEND QUICKLY, THEN ADD WATER OR BROTH AND SAKE. (REMOVE BONES IF COOKING WITH CHICKEN.)
TASTE THE BROTH TO CHECK SALINITY. ADD 1 TSP AT A TIME IF DESIRED.
COVER AND LOWER TO A SIMMER.
BOIL NOODLES, REMOVE WHEN AL-DENTE. IF YOU'RE USING NOODLES PINCHED FROM INSTANT RAMEN PACKAGES, RINSE THESE BEFORE ADDING TO YOUR RAMEN.
SERVE WITH BROTH, TOPPINGS OF CHOICE AND EAT QUICKLY. STORE BROTH IN FREEZER FOR UP 3 MONTHS.

GREEN CURRY PASTE

HANDS ON: 30 MIN

- 1 TBSP CORIANDER (WHOLE)
- 1/2 TBSP CUMIN
- 1/2 TSP PEPPERCORNS (WHOLE)
- 1 1/2 TBSP GALANGAL (DRIED/POWDERED IS EASIEST TO GET), CHOPPED, OR 1 TBSP GINGER + 1 TBSP LEMONGRASS, BOTH CHOPPED
- 4 TSP KOSHER SALT
- 3 TBSP LEMONGRASS, CHOPPED
- 1 TBSP CILANTRO ROOTS, CHOPPED, OR 1 TBSP CILANTRO STEMS, CHOPPED, OR 1 1/2 TBSP DRIED CILANTRO
- 3 TBSP GARLIC, CHOPPED
- 1 TBSP LIME ZEST
- 15 GREEN BIRD'S EYE/THAI CHILI PEPPERS, CHOPPED
- 1 TSP SHRIMP PASTE, OR 2 TBSP FISH SAUCE, OR 1 TSP KOSHER SALT
- 1/2 CUP SHALLOTS, CHOPPED, OR 1/3 CUP RED ONION, MINCED

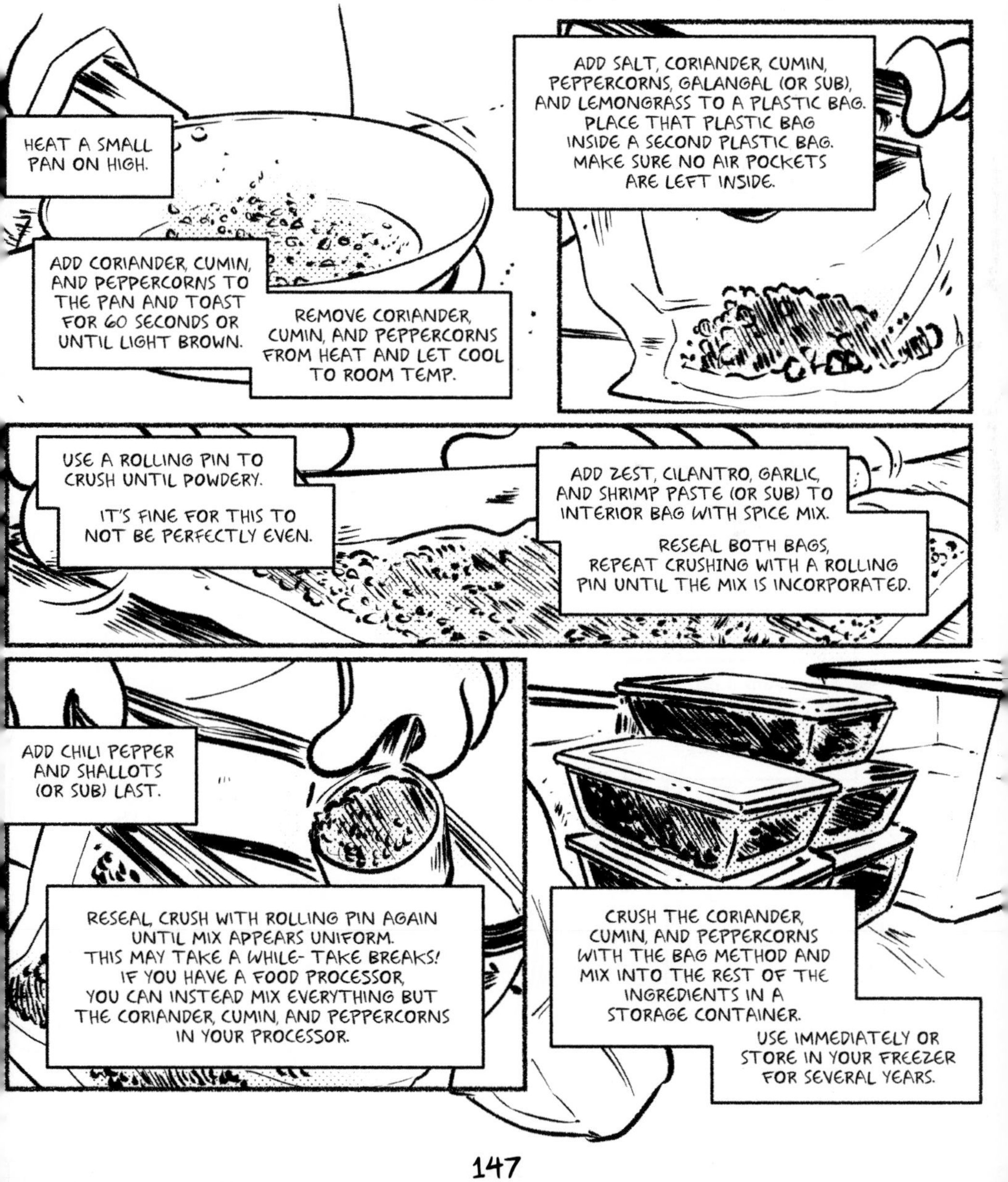
HEAT A SMALL PAN ON HIGH.
ADD CORIANDER, CUMIN, AND PEPPERCORNS TO THE PAN AND TOAST FOR 60 SECONDS OR UNTIL LIGHT BROWN.
REMOVE CORIANDER, CUMIN, AND PEPPERCORNS FROM HEAT AND LET COOL TO ROOM TEMP.
ADD SALT, CORIANDER, CUMIN, PEPPERCORNS, GALANGAL (OR SUB), AND LEMONGRASS TO A PLASTIC BAG. PLACE THAT PLASTIC BAG INSIDE A SECOND PLASTIC BAG. MAKE SURE NO AIR POCKETS ARE LEFT INSIDE.
USE A ROLLING PIN TO CRUSH UNTIL POWDERY.
IT'S FINE FOR THIS TO NOT BE PERFECTLY EVEN.
ADD ZEST, CILANTRO, GARLIC, AND SHRIMP PASTE (OR SUB) TO INTERIOR BAG WITH SPICE MIX.
RESEAL BOTH BAGS, REPEAT CRUSHING WITH A ROLLING PIN UNTIL THE MIX IS INCORPORATED.
ADD CHILI PEPPER AND SHALLOTS (OR SUB) LAST.
RESEAL, CRUSH WITH ROLLING PIN AGAIN UNTIL MIX APPEARS UNIFORM. THIS MAY TAKE A WHILE- TAKE BREAKS! IF YOU HAVE A FOOD PROCESSOR, YOU CAN INSTEAD MIX EVERYTHING BUT THE CORIANDER, CUMIN, AND PEPPERCORNS IN YOUR PROCESSOR.
CRUSH THE CORIANDER, CUMIN, AND PEPPERCORNS WITH THE BAG METHOD AND MIX INTO THE REST OF THE INGREDIENTS IN A STORAGE CONTAINER.
USE IMMEDIATELY OR STORE IN YOUR FREEZER FOR SEVERAL YEARS.

GREEN CURRY

HANDS ON: 25 MIN
HANDS OFF: 20 MIN

-2 TBSP GREEN CURRY PASTE (HOMEMADE OR STOREBOUGHT)
-1 GREEN BIRD'S EYE/THAI CHILI PEPPER, SLICED, OR 1/3 CUP RED BELL PEPPER, MINCED
-1 CUP COCONUT MILK
-4 CUPS EGGPLANT, PEELED AND CHOPPED
-2 TBSP FISH SAUCE
-5 LIME LEAVES (ALSO KNOWN AS MAKRUT LIME LEAVES), OR 2 TBSP LIME ZEST + 3 TSP LEMON ZEST
-1 TBSP SUGAR
-1 TBSP THAI BASIL, CHOPPED OR 2 TSP ANISE (POWDERED OR LIQUID), OR 3 TBSP FENNEL, POWDERED
-1 CUP WATER, OR VEGETABLE BROTH

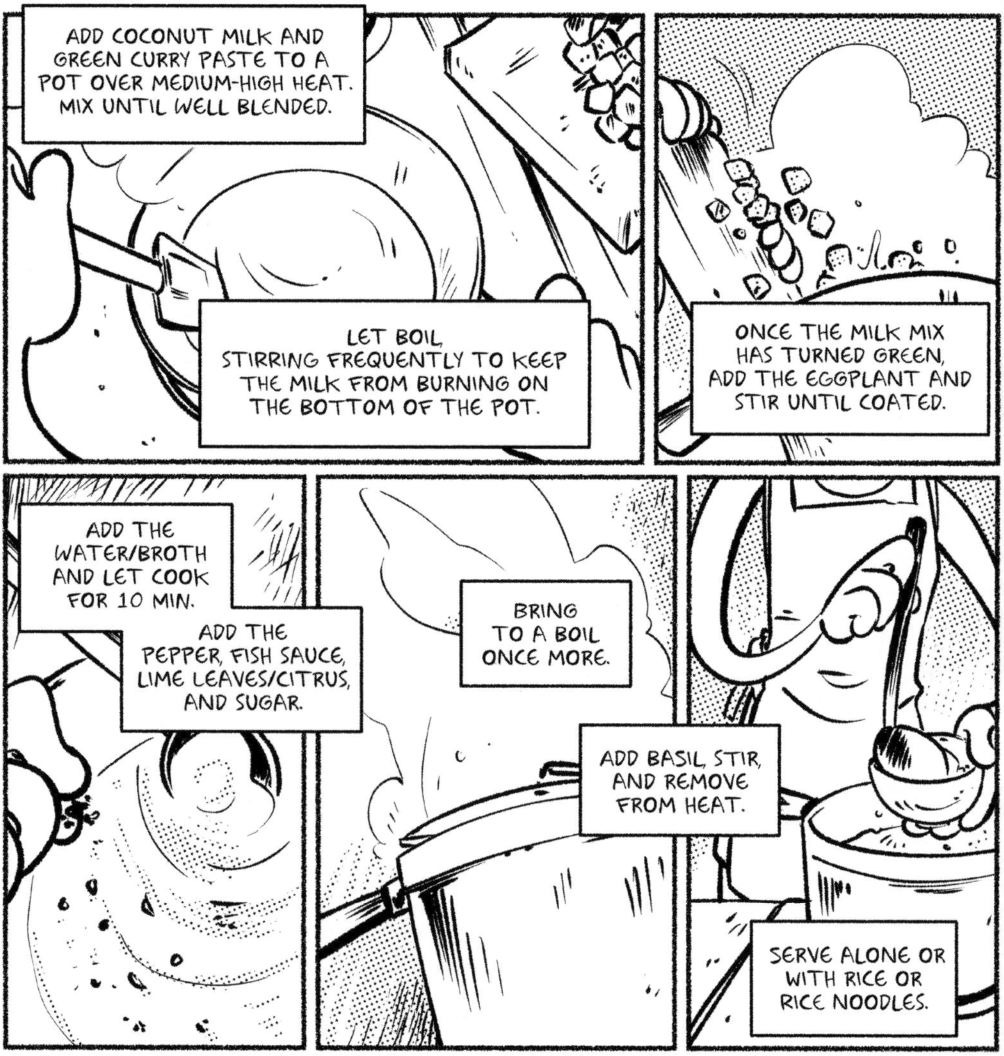
ADD COCONUT MILK AND GREEN CURRY PASTE TO A POT OVER MEDIUM-HIGH HEAT. MIX UNTIL WELL BLENDED.
LET BOIL, STIRRING FREQUENTLY TO KEEP THE MILK FROM BURNING ON THE BOTTOM OF THE POT.
ONCE THE MILK MIX HAS TURNED GREEN, ADD THE EGGPLANT AND STIR UNTIL COATED.
ADD THE WATER/BROTH AND LET COOK FOR 10 MIN.
ADD THE PEPPER, FISH SAUCE, LIME LEAVES/CITRUS, AND SUGAR.
BRING TO A BOIL ONCE MORE.
ADD BASIL, STIR, AND REMOVE FROM HEAT.
SERVE ALONE OR WITH RICE OR RICE NOODLES.

 # RED CURRY PASTE

-1 TBSP CORIANDER (WHOLE)
-1/2 TBSP CUMIN
-2 TSP PEPPERCORNS (WHOLE)
-1 1/2 TBSP GALANGAL
 (DRIED/POWDERED IS EASIEST TO GET),
 CHOPPED, OR 1 TBSP GINGER + 1 TBSP LEMONGRASS,
 BOTH CHOPPED
-2 TSP SALT
-4 TBSP LEMONGRASS, CHOPPED
-4 TBSP GARLIC, CHOPPED
-1 TBSP LIME ZEST
-5 RED BIRD'S EYE/THAI CHILI PEPPER, DRIED
-1/2 CUP SHALLOTS, CHOPPED,
 OR 1/3 CUP RED ONION, MINCED

HANDS ON: 50 MIN

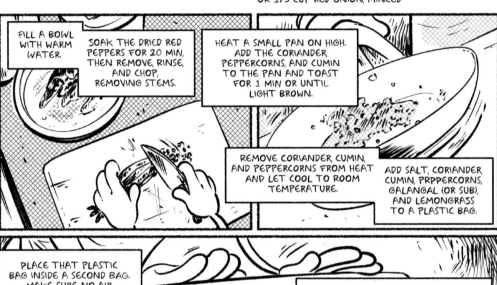

FILL A BOWL WITH WARM WATER.

SOAK THE DRIED RED PEPPERS FOR 20 MIN, THEN REMOVE, RINSE, AND CHOP, REMOVING STEMS.

HEAT A SMALL PAN ON HIGH. ADD THE CORIANDER, PEPPERCORNS, AND CUMIN TO THE PAN AND TOAST FOR 1 MIN OR UNTIL LIGHT BROWN.

REMOVE CORIANDER, CUMIN, AND PEPPERCORNS FROM HEAT AND LET COOL TO ROOM TEMPERATURE.

ADD SALT, CORIANDER, CUMIN, PRPPERCORNS, GALANGAL (OR SUB), AND LEMONGRASS TO A PLASTIC BAG.

PLACE THAT PLASTIC BAG INSIDE A SECOND BAG. MAKE SURE NO AIR POCKETS ARE LEFT INSIDE.

USE A ROLLING PIN TO CRUSH THE SPICES UNTIL POWDERY. IT'S FINE FOR THIS TO NOT BE PERFECTLY EVEN.

ADD ZEST AND GARLIC TO INTERIOR BAG WITH YOUR SPICE MIX. RESEAL BOTH BAGS, REPEAT CRUSHING WITH A ROLLING PIN UNTIL THE MIX IS MOSTLY INCORPORATED.

ADD CHILI PEPPERS AND SHALLOTS (OR SUB) TO YOUR MIX LAST.

RESEAL, CRUSH WITH ROLLING PIN AGAIN UNTIL MIX APPEARS UNIFORM. THIS MAY TAKE A WHILE- TAKE BREAKS! IF YOU HAVE A FOOD PROCESSOR, YOU CAN JUST MIX EVERYTHING BUT THE CORIANDER, CUMIN, AND PEPPERCORNS IN YOUR PROCESSOR.

CRUSH THE CORIANDER, CUMIN, AND PEPPERCORNS WITH THE BAG METHOD AND MIX INTO THE REST OF YOUR INGREDIENTS IN A STORAGE CONTAINER.

USE IMMEDIATELY OR STORE IN YOUR FREEZE FOR SEVERAL YEARS.

RED CURRY

HANDS ON: 25 MIN
HANDS OFF: 20 MIN

-3 TBSP RED CURRY PASTE
 (HOMEMADE OR STOREBOUGHT)
-1 CUP COCONUT MILK
-1 CUP FIRM TOFU, DRAINED AND CUBED
-2 TBSP FISH SAUCE
-1 TBSP SUGAR
-1 TBSP THAI BASIL, CHOPPED OR
 2 TSP ANISE, POWDERED OR LIQUID OR
 3 TBSP FENNEL, POWDERED
-1 CUP WATER, OR VEGETABLE BROTH

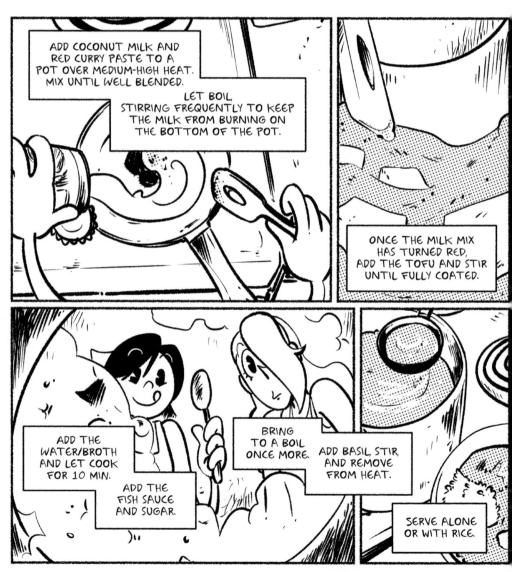

FISH CURRY

HANDS ON: 25 MIN
HANDS OFF: 10 MIN

- 1 LB FISH OF CHOICE
- 2 TSP GINGER, MINCED
- 2 TSP GARLIC, MINCED
- 1 TBSP TURMERIC
- 1 TBSP CAYENNE POWDER
- 1 TBSP SMOKED PAPRIKA
- 2 TSP SALT
- 1 TSP CUMIN
- 2 TBSP OLIVE OIL
- 1 TSP FENNEL SEEDS
- 1 BAY LEAF
- 1 CUP WHITE ONIONS, SLICED
- 2 CUPS TOMATOES, CHOPPED
- 2 TSP GARAM MASALA
- 1 1/2 CUP WATER OR BROTH OF CHOICE (VEGETABLE RECOMMENDED)
- 2 CUPS COCONUT MILK

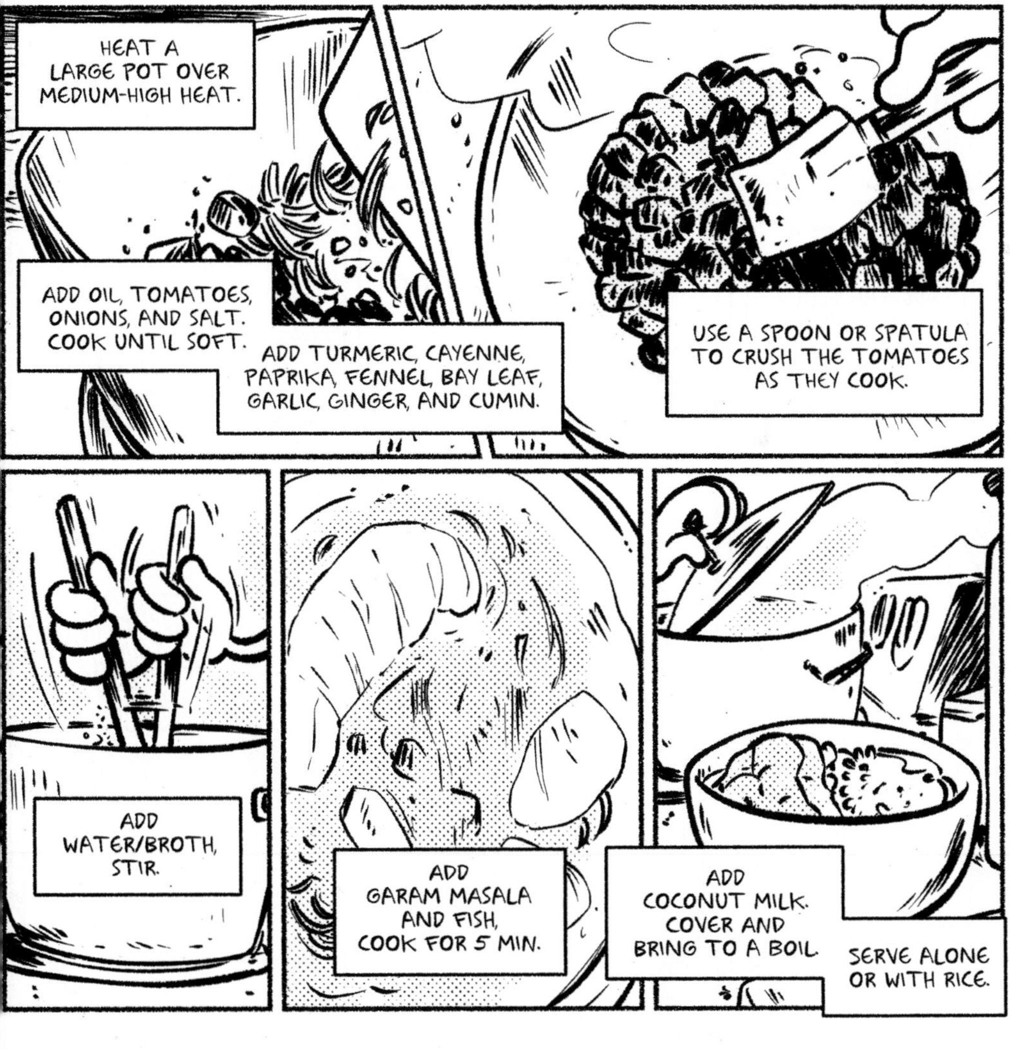
HEAT A LARGE POT OVER MEDIUM-HIGH HEAT.
ADD OIL, TOMATOES, ONIONS, AND SALT. COOK UNTIL SOFT.
ADD TURMERIC, CAYENNE, PAPRIKA, FENNEL, BAY LEAF, GARLIC, GINGER, AND CUMIN.
USE A SPOON OR SPATULA TO CRUSH THE TOMATOES AS THEY COOK.
ADD WATER/BROTH, STIR.
ADD GARAM MASALA AND FISH, COOK FOR 5 MIN.
ADD COCONUT MILK. COVER AND BRING TO A BOIL.
SERVE ALONE OR WITH RICE.

JAPANESE CURRY ROUX

HANDS ON: 30 MIN

-8 TBSP UNSALTED BUTTER
-12 TBSP ALL-PURPOSE FLOUR
-3 TBSP GARAM MASALA
-3 TBSP CURRY POWDER
-3 TSP CAYENNE POWDER

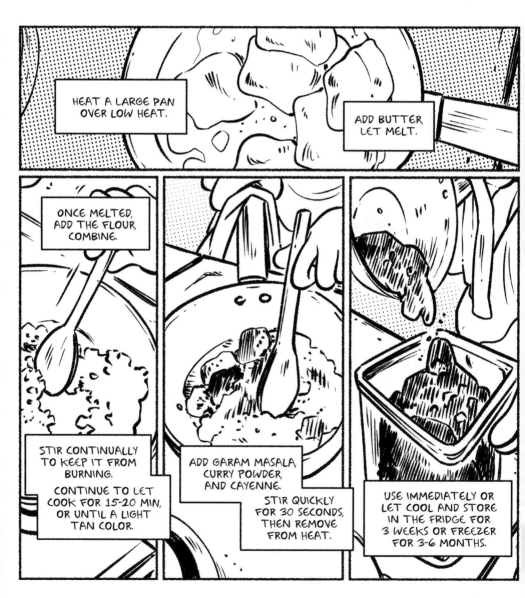

HEAT A LARGE PAN OVER LOW HEAT.

ADD BUTTER, LET MELT.

ONCE MELTED, ADD THE FLOUR, COMBINE.

STIR CONTINUALLY TO KEEP IT FROM BURNING.

CONTINUE TO LET COOK FOR 15-20 MIN, OR UNTIL A LIGHT TAN COLOR.

ADD GARAM MASALA, CURRY POWDER, AND CAYENNE.

STIR QUICKLY FOR 30 SECONDS, THEN REMOVE FROM HEAT.

USE IMMEDIATELY OR LET COOL AND STORE IN THE FRIDGE FOR 3 WEEKS OR FREEZER FOR 3-6 MONTHS.

JAPANESE CURRY

HANDS ON: 20 MIN
HANDS OFF: 30 MIN

-1 CUP WHITE ONION, CHOPPED
-1/2 CUP CARROTS, CHOPPED
-2 CUPS BROWN POTATOES, CHOPPED
-2 TBSP OLIVE OIL
-2 TSP GARLIC, CHOPPED
-4 CUPS WATER, OR BROTH OF CHOICE
-3 TBSP CURRY ROUX
  (HOMEMADE OR STOREBOUGHT)

OPTIONAL:
-1/2 LB BEEF, CUT INTO CUBES,
  OR 1/2 LB CHICKEN, CUT INTO THUMB SIZED PIECES,
  OR 1 CUP FIRM TOFU, DRAINED AND CUBED
-1/3 CUP GREEN ONIONS, CHOPPED
-1 TBSP KETCHUP
-1 TBSP WORCESTER SAUCE
-1 TBSP SOY SAUCE
-1/4 CUP APPLE, GRATED
  (FUJI RECOMMENDED, NEVER RED DELICIOUS)
-1 TBSP HONEY

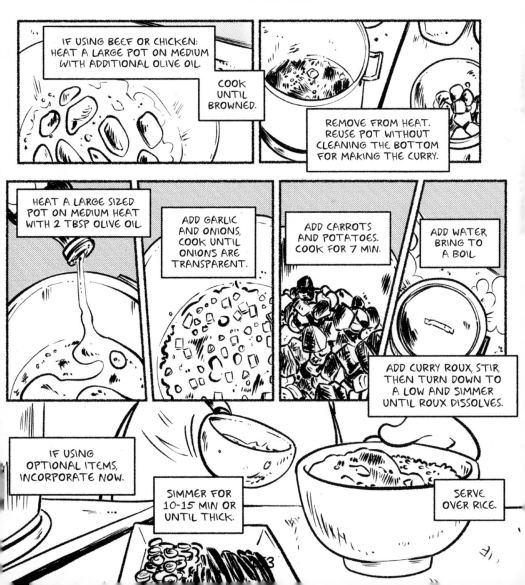

IF USING BEEF OR CHICKEN: HEAT A LARGE POT ON MEDIUM WITH ADDITIONAL OLIVE OIL.

COOK UNTIL BROWNED.

REMOVE FROM HEAT. REUSE POT WITHOUT CLEANING THE BOTTOM FOR MAKING THE CURRY.

HEAT A LARGE SIZED POT ON MEDIUM HEAT WITH 2 TBSP OLIVE OIL

ADD GARLIC AND ONIONS, COOK UNTIL ONIONS ARE TRANSPARENT.

ADD CARROTS AND POTATOES. COOK FOR 7 MIN.

ADD WATER, BRING TO A BOIL.

ADD CURRY ROUX, STIR, THEN TURN DOWN TO A LOW AND SIMMER UNTIL ROUX DISSOLVES.

IF USING OPTIONAL ITEMS, INCORPORATE NOW.

SIMMER FOR 10-15 MIN OR UNTIL THICK.

SERVE OVER RICE.

3

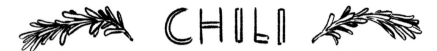

CHILI

HANDS ON: 10 MIN
HANDS OFF: 45 MIN

- -2 TBSP OLIVE OIL
- -1 CUP YELLOW ONION, CHOPPED
- -1 CUP GREEN BELL PEPPER, CHOPPED
- -2 JALAPENO PEPPERS, CHOPPED
- -3 TBSP GARLIC, CHOPPED
- -4 CUPS (2 15OZ CANS) TOMATOES, DICED
- -4 CUPS (2 15OZ CANS) BLACK BEANS, RINSED
- -2 CUPS (1 15OZ CAN) PINTO BEANS, RINSED
- -2 CUPS (1 15OZ CAN) KIDNEY BEANS, RINSED
- -2 CUPS MISC VEGGIES (POTATO, ZUCCHINI, ETC)
- -1 TBSP RED PEPPER FLAKES
- -1 TBSP CAYENNE PEPPER
- -1 TSP ROSEMARY
- -1 TBSP SMOKED PAPRIKA
- -1/2 CUP SOY SAUCE
- -1/2 CUP KETCHUP
- -2 TBSP APPLE CIDER VINEGAR
- -1 TSP OREGANO (DOUBLE IF DRIED)
- -1 TBSP KOSHER SALT
- -1 TBSP BLACK PEPPER

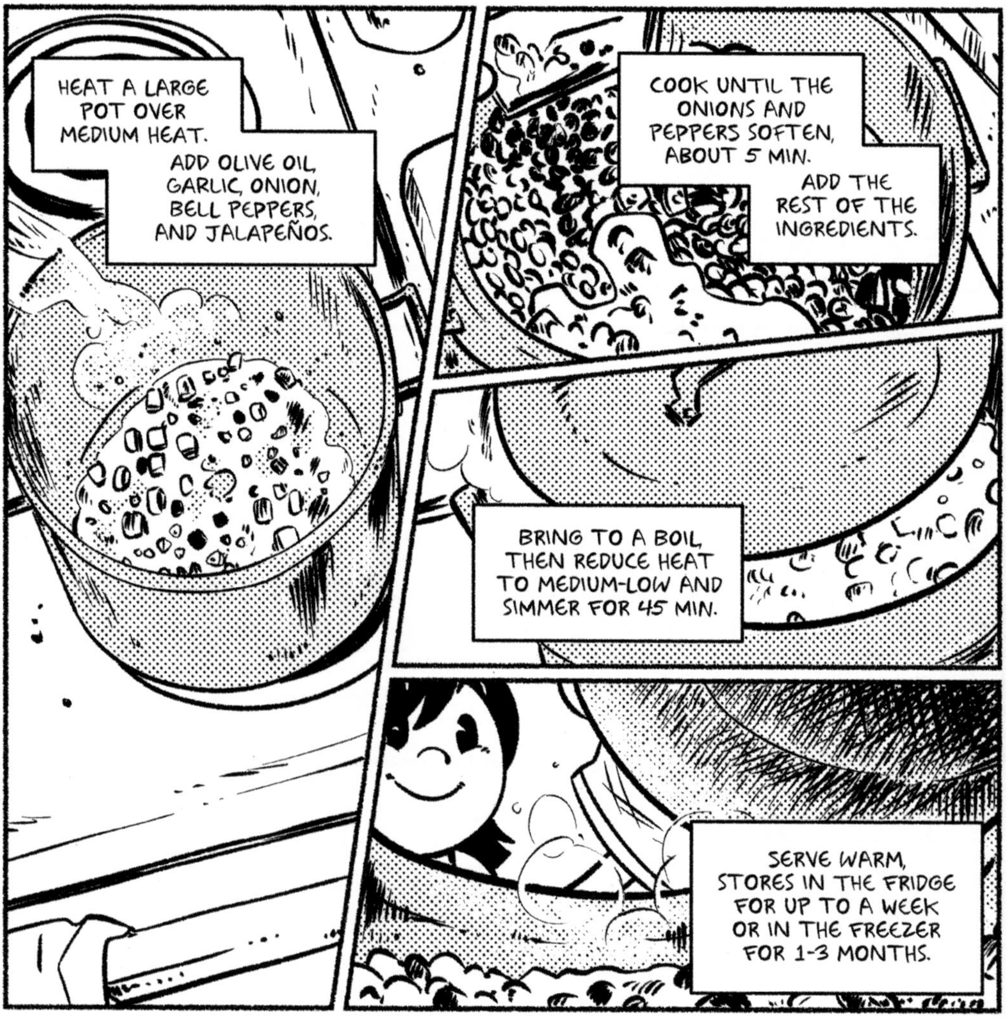
HEAT A LARGE POT OVER MEDIUM HEAT.
ADD OLIVE OIL, GARLIC, ONION, BELL PEPPERS, AND JALAPEÑOS.
COOK UNTIL THE ONIONS AND PEPPERS SOFTEN, ABOUT 5 MIN.
ADD THE REST OF THE INGREDIENTS.
BRING TO A BOIL, THEN REDUCE HEAT TO MEDIUM-LOW AND SIMMER FOR 45 MIN.
SERVE WARM, STORES IN THE FRIDGE FOR UP TO A WEEK OR IN THE FREEZER FOR 1-3 MONTHS.

QUICHE

HANDS ON: 20 MIN
HANDS OFF: 20 MIN

-1/2 CUP TOMATO, CHOPPED
-1/2 CUP SPINACH, CHOPPED
-1/4 CUP STALE CRUSTY BREAD OR CROUTONS
-1 TSP OREGANO
-1 TSP BASIL
-1 TSP ROSEMARY
-1 TSP THYME
-1 TBSP OLIVE OIL
-4 LARGE EGGS
-1/4 CUP WATER OR BROTH OF CHOICE
 (VEGETABLE PREFERRED)
-1/4 TSP KOSHER SALT

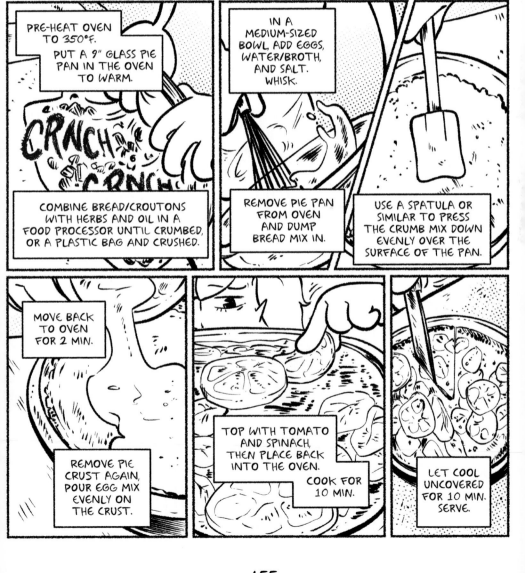

PRE-HEAT OVEN TO 350°F.
PUT A 9" GLASS PIE PAN IN THE OVEN TO WARM.

CRNCH
CRNCH

COMBINE BREAD/CROUTONS WITH HERBS AND OIL IN A FOOD PROCESSOR UNTIL CRUMBED, OR A PLASTIC BAG AND CRUSHED.

IN A MEDIUM-SIZED BOWL, ADD EGGS, WATER/BROTH, AND SALT. WHISK.

REMOVE PIE PAN FROM OVEN AND DUMP BREAD MIX IN.

USE A SPATULA OR SIMILAR TO PRESS THE CRUMB MIX DOWN EVENLY OVER THE SURFACE OF THE PAN.

MOVE BACK TO OVEN FOR 2 MIN.

REMOVE PIE CRUST AGAIN, POUR EGG MIX EVENLY ON THE CRUST.

TOP WITH TOMATO AND SPINACH, THEN PLACE BACK INTO THE OVEN.
COOK FOR 10 MIN.

LET COOL UNCOVERED FOR 10 MIN. SERVE.

ROASTED VEGETABLES

HANDS ON: 20 MIN
HANDS OFF: 40 MIN

- 1 CUP SWEET POTATO, SKIN ON, SLICED INTO 1/4 IN ROUNDS OR CHUNKS
- 1 CUP BEET, SKIN ON, SLICED INTO 1/4" ROUNDS
- 1 CUP CARROTS, CHOPPED OR SLICED
- 2 TBSP GARLIC, CHOPPED OR WHOLE
- 1 CUP RED OR WHITE ONION, SLICED THIN
- 2 CUPS BROCCOLI, ROUGHLY CHOPPED
- 2 CUPS OF ANY OTHER EXTRA OR SEASONAL VEGETABLES YOU MIGHT HAVE AROUND
- 2 TBSP VEGETABLE, CANOLA, OR SUNFLOWER OIL (IF YOU DON'T WANT TO USE OIL, STEAM STARCHY VEGETABLES UNTIL TENDER BEFOREHAND)
- 2 TSP KOSHER SALT
- 1 TBSP OF ANY OTHER SPICES OF CHOICE (OPTIONAL)

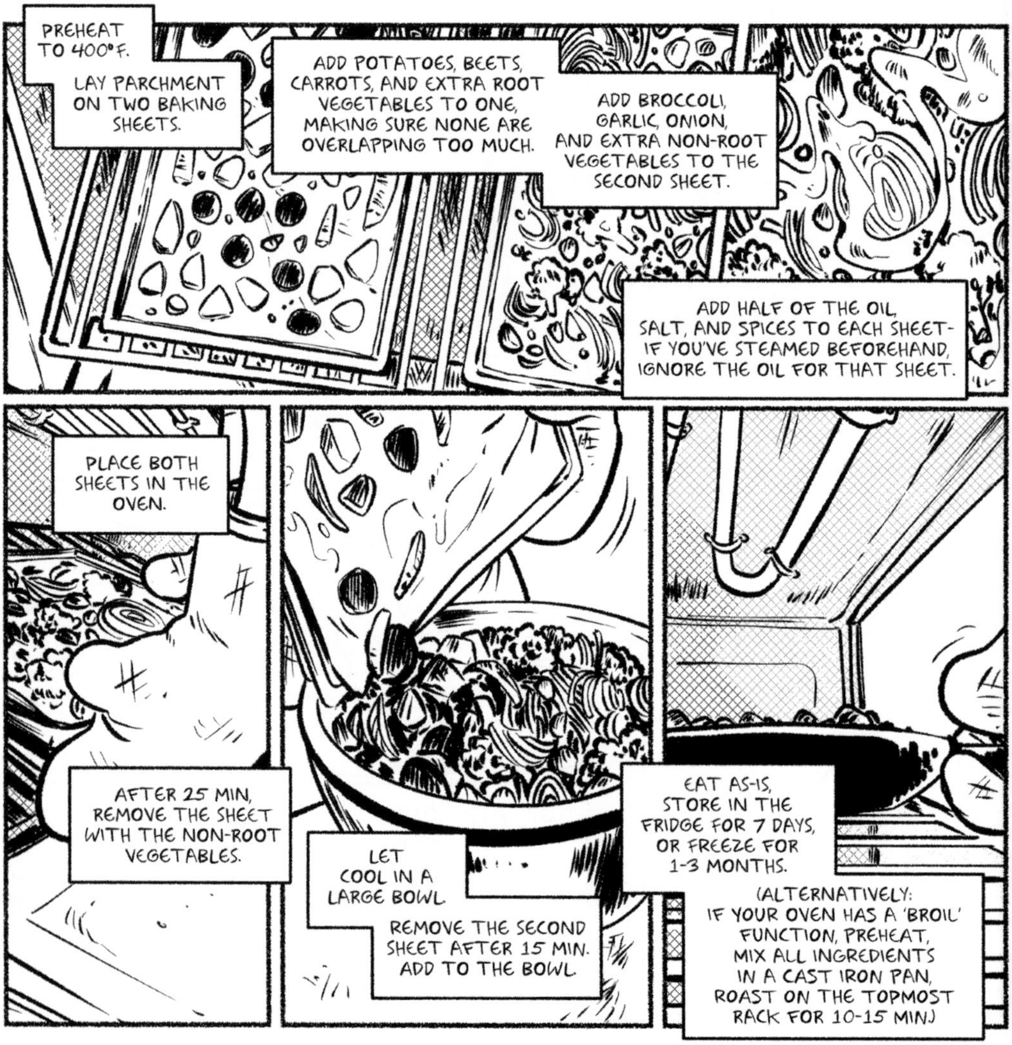
PREHEAT TO 400°F.
LAY PARCHMENT ON TWO BAKING SHEETS.
ADD POTATOES, BEETS, CARROTS, AND EXTRA ROOT VEGETABLES TO ONE, MAKING SURE NONE ARE OVERLAPPING TOO MUCH.
ADD BROCCOLI, GARLIC, ONION, AND EXTRA NON-ROOT VEGETABLES TO THE SECOND SHEET.
ADD HALF OF THE OIL, SALT, AND SPICES TO EACH SHEET- IF YOU'VE STEAMED BEFOREHAND, IGNORE THE OIL FOR THAT SHEET.
PLACE BOTH SHEETS IN THE OVEN.
AFTER 25 MIN, REMOVE THE SHEET WITH THE NON-ROOT VEGETABLES.
LET COOL IN A LARGE BOWL.
REMOVE THE SECOND SHEET AFTER 15 MIN. ADD TO THE BOWL.
EAT AS-IS, STORE IN THE FRIDGE FOR 7 DAYS, OR FREEZE FOR 1-3 MONTHS.
(ALTERNATIVELY: IF YOUR OVEN HAS A 'BROIL' FUNCTION, PREHEAT, MIX ALL INGREDIENTS IN A CAST IRON PAN, ROAST ON THE TOPMOST RACK FOR 10-15 MIN.)

see notes for more!

BAKED MAC & CHEESE

HANDS ON: 10 MIN
HANDS OFF: 40 MIN

-PRE-MADE MAC & CHEESE
(PREFERABLY LEFTOVERS FROM THE PREVIOUS DAY-
THE PREVIOUS MAC & CHEESE RECIPE IS GREAT FOR THIS!)
-1 TBSP UNSALTED BUTTER
-1 TSP KOSHER SALT
-1 TSP BLACK PEPPER
-1 TSP GROUND MUSTARD (OPTIONAL)
-1/3 CUP ANY EXTRA CHEESE OF CHOICE (OPTIONAL)
-ANY LEFTOVER VEGETABLES (OPTIONAL)

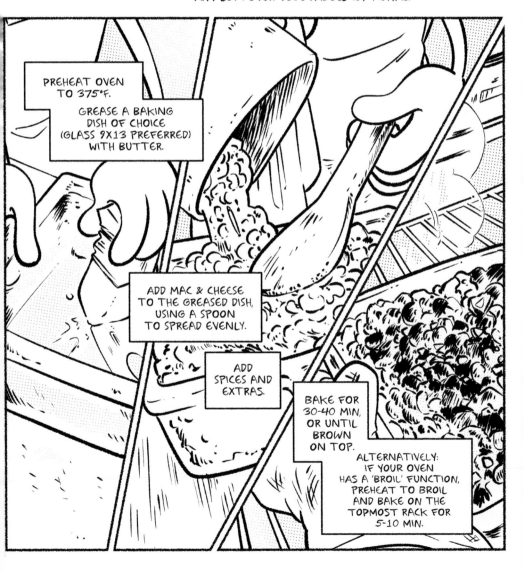

PREHEAT OVEN TO 375°F.

GREASE A BAKING DISH OF CHOICE (GLASS 9X13 PREFERRED) WITH BUTTER.

ADD MAC & CHEESE TO THE GREASED DISH, USING A SPOON TO SPREAD EVENLY.

ADD SPICES AND EXTRAS.

BAKE FOR 30-40 MIN, OR UNTIL BROWN ON TOP.

ALTERNATIVELY: IF YOUR OVEN HAS A 'BROIL' FUNCTION, PREHEAT TO BROIL AND BAKE ON THE TOPMOST RACK FOR 5-10 MIN.

BAKED ZITI

HANDS ON: 30 MIN
HANDS OFF: 30 MIN

- 2 CUPS DRY ZITI PASTA
- 3 CUPS SPAGHETTI SAUCE
- 1 LARGE EGG
- 1 CUP MOZZARELLA CHEESE, SHREDDED
- 1 CUP RICOTTA CHEESE
- 1/3 CUP SOUR CREAM
- 1/3 CUP YELLOW ONION, CHOPPED
- 1 TSP KOSHER SALT
- 1 TSP BLACK PEPPER
- 1 TBSP OLIVE OIL
- 1 CUP PROVOLONE CHEESE, SLICED THINLY
- 3 TBSP PARMESAN CHEESE
- 1/2 TSP OREGANO (DOUBLE IF DRIED)

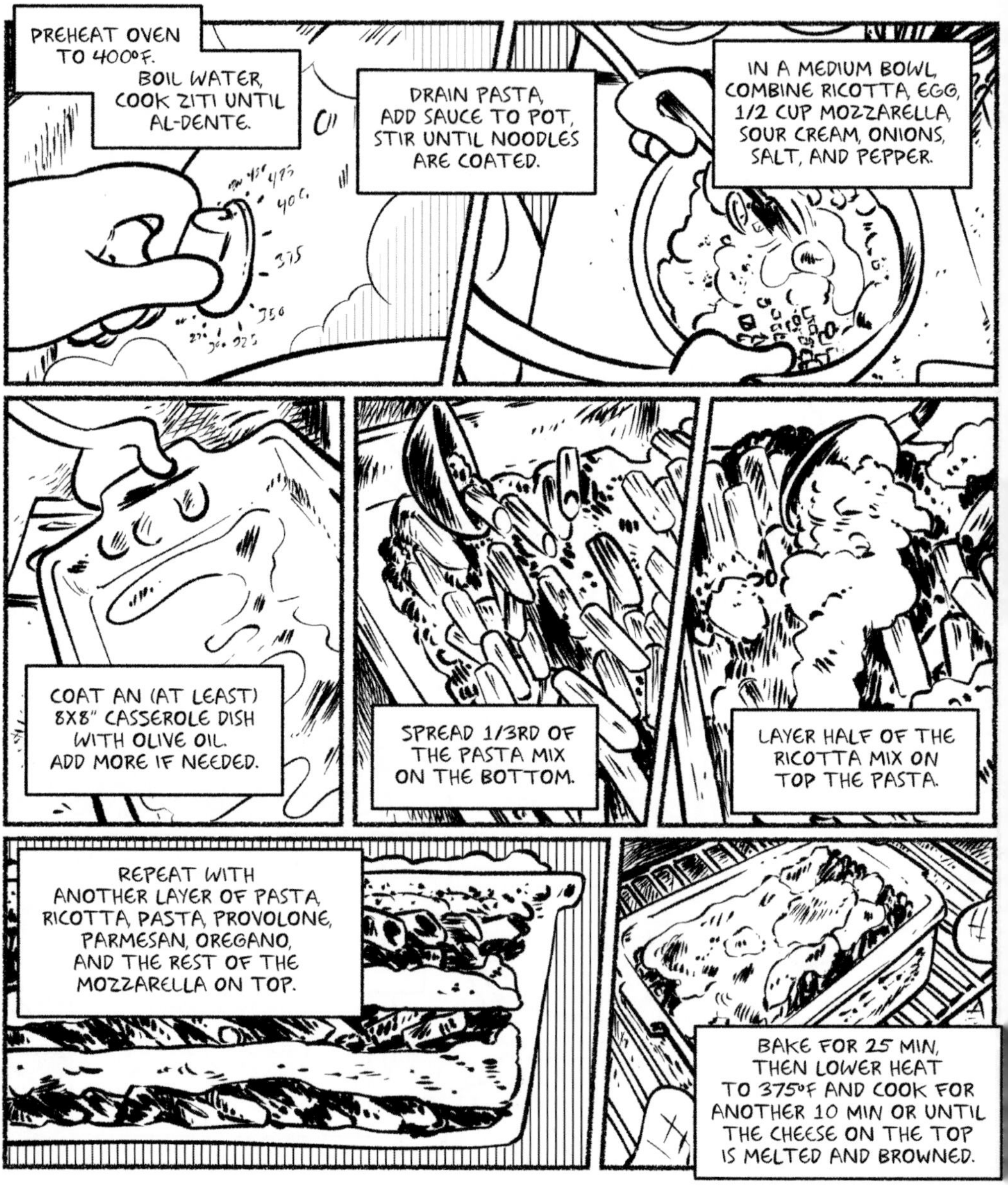
PREHEAT OVEN TO 400°F.
BOIL WATER, COOK ZITI UNTIL AL-DENTE.
DRAIN PASTA, ADD SAUCE TO POT, STIR UNTIL NOODLES ARE COATED.
IN A MEDIUM BOWL, COMBINE RICOTTA, EGG, 1/2 CUP MOZZARELLA, SOUR CREAM, ONIONS, SALT, AND PEPPER.
COAT AN (AT LEAST) 8X8" CASSEROLE DISH WITH OLIVE OIL. ADD MORE IF NEEDED.
SPREAD 1/3RD OF THE PASTA MIX ON THE BOTTOM.
LAYER HALF OF THE RICOTTA MIX ON TOP THE PASTA.
REPEAT WITH ANOTHER LAYER OF PASTA, RICOTTA, PASTA, PROVOLONE, PARMESAN, OREGANO, AND THE REST OF THE MOZZARELLA ON TOP.
BAKE FOR 25 MIN, THEN LOWER HEAT TO 375°F AND COOK FOR ANOTHER 10 MIN OR UNTIL THE CHEESE ON THE TOP IS MELTED AND BROWNED.

HUMMUS

HANDS ON: 15 MIN
HANDS OFF: 10 MIN - 1 HOUR

- 1 CUP CHICKPEAS, UNCOOKED OR PRECOOKED/CANNED
- 1/4 TSP BAKING SODA (OPTIONAL)
- 2 TBSP GARLIC, CHOPPED
- 1/3 CUP TAHINI
- 2 TBSP LEMON JUICE
- 3/4 TSP KOSHER SALT
- 1 TBSP OLIVE OIL (IF YOU'RE AVOIDING OIL, USE WATER)

OPTIONAL INGREDIENTS
(AMOUNTS UP TO PERSONAL TASTE, NOT MEANT TO BE USED ALL AT ONCE. CHOP EM FINELY AND MAKE SURE YOU BALANCE YOUR WET/DRY INGREDIENTS. GET CREATIVE!):

SMOKED PAPRIKA
CILANTRO
EXTRA GARLIC
CUMIN
AVOCADO
BLACK PEPPER
LIME JUICE
BASIL
SALTED/ROASTED PEANUTS
CARROTS
EDAMAME

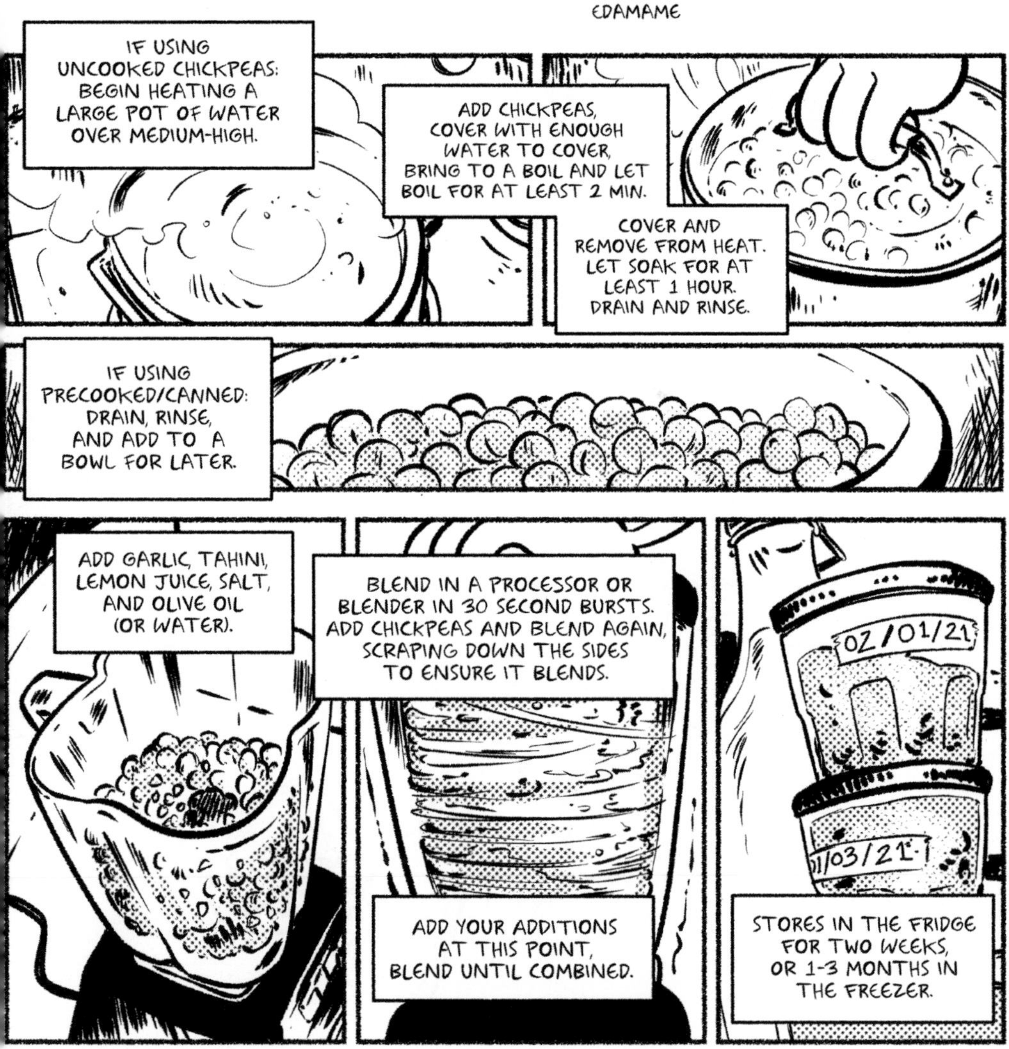

IF USING UNCOOKED CHICKPEAS: BEGIN HEATING A LARGE POT OF WATER OVER MEDIUM-HIGH.
ADD CHICKPEAS, COVER WITH ENOUGH WATER TO COVER, BRING TO A BOIL AND LET BOIL FOR AT LEAST 2 MIN.
COVER AND REMOVE FROM HEAT. LET SOAK FOR AT LEAST 1 HOUR. DRAIN AND RINSE.
IF USING PRECOOKED/CANNED: DRAIN, RINSE, AND ADD TO A BOWL FOR LATER.
ADD GARLIC, TAHINI, LEMON JUICE, SALT, AND OLIVE OIL (OR WATER).
BLEND IN A PROCESSOR OR BLENDER IN 30 SECOND BURSTS. ADD CHICKPEAS AND BLEND AGAIN, SCRAPING DOWN THE SIDES TO ENSURE IT BLENDS.
ADD YOUR ADDITIONS AT THIS POINT, BLEND UNTIL COMBINED.
02/01/21
1/03/21
STORES IN THE FRIDGE FOR TWO WEEKS, OR 1-3 MONTHS IN THE FREEZER.

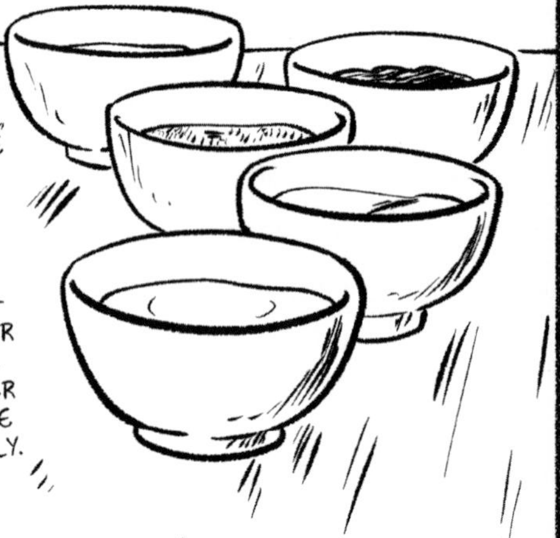

BECHAMEL, VELOUTE, ESPAGNOLE, HOLLANDAISE, AND TOMATO ARE THE FIVE 'MOTHER SAUCES' USED IN FRENCH COOKING.

THESE AREN'T MEANT TO BE USED ON FOOD DIRECTLY USUALLY- THEY'RE THE STARTING POINT FOR MANY OTHER 'DAUGHTER' SAUCES. MAKING THE FOLLOWING IN LARGER BATCHES ALLOWS YOU TO UPGRADE MEALS PRETTY QUICKLY ON THE FLY.

BECHAMEL

HANDS ON: 30 MIN

-4 TBSP UNSALTED BUTTER
-1/4 ALL-PURPOSE FLOUR
-4 1/2 CUPS WHOLE MILK
-1 SMALL, GOLF BALL SIZED WHITE ONION, PEELED
-1 BAY LEAF
-1 TSP SALT
-1 TSP BLACK PEPPER

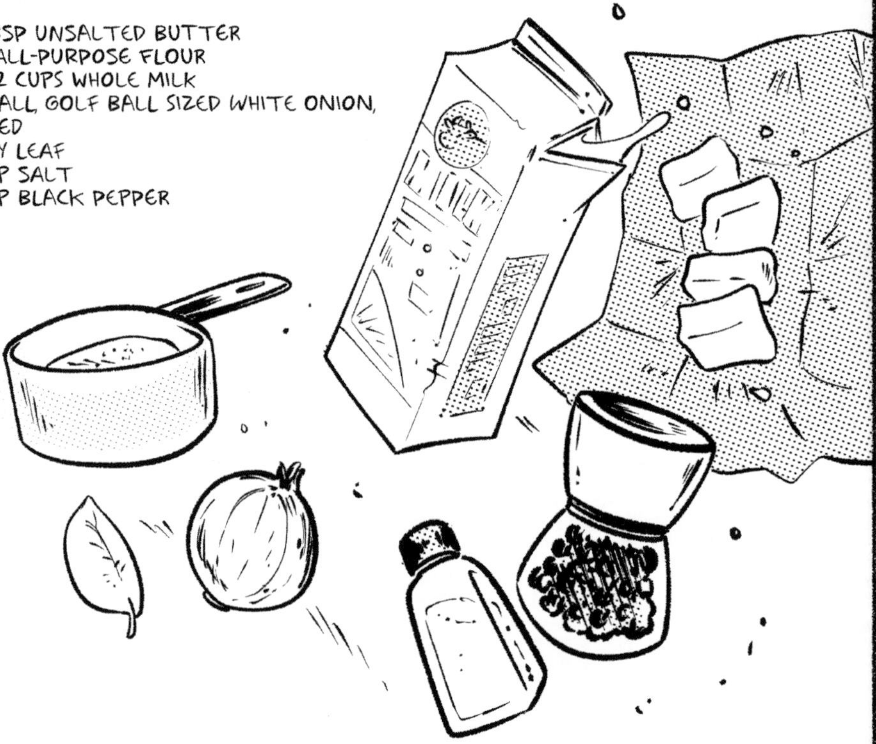

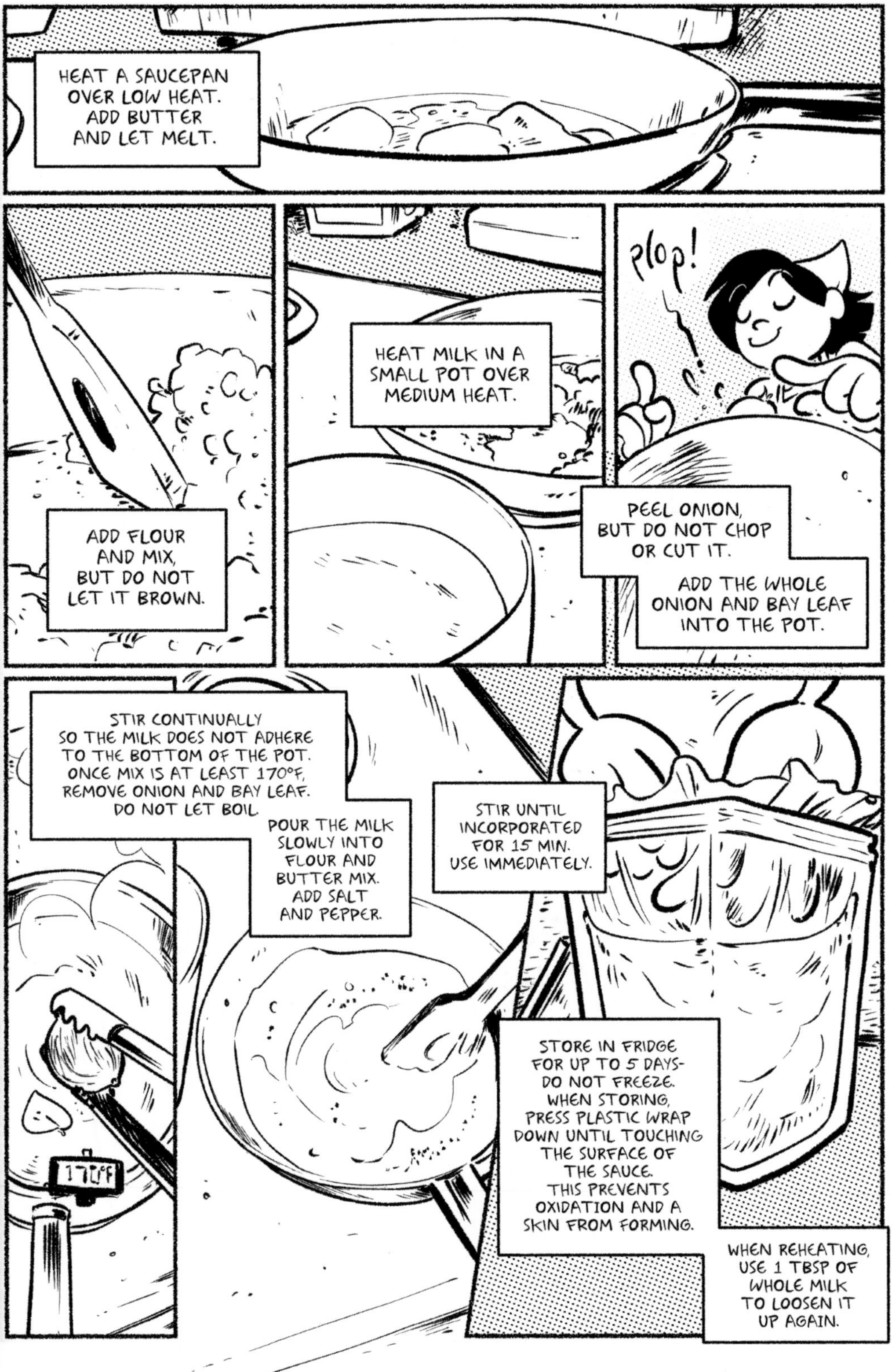
HEAT A SAUCEPAN OVER LOW HEAT. ADD BUTTER AND LET MELT.
ADD FLOUR AND MIX, BUT DO NOT LET IT BROWN.
HEAT MILK IN A SMALL POT OVER MEDIUM HEAT.
PLOP!
PEEL ONION, BUT DO NOT CHOP OR CUT IT.
ADD THE WHOLE ONION AND BAY LEAF INTO THE POT.
STIR CONTINUALLY SO THE MILK DOES NOT ADHERE TO THE BOTTOM OF THE POT. ONCE MIX IS AT LEAST 170°F, REMOVE ONION AND BAY LEAF. DO NOT LET BOIL.
170°F
POUR THE MILK SLOWLY INTO FLOUR AND BUTTER MIX. ADD SALT AND PEPPER.
STIR UNTIL INCORPORATED FOR 15 MIN. USE IMMEDIATELY.
STORE IN FRIDGE FOR UP TO 5 DAYS- DO NOT FREEZE. WHEN STORING, PRESS PLASTIC WRAP DOWN UNTIL TOUCHING THE SURFACE OF THE SAUCE. THIS PREVENTS OXIDATION AND A SKIN FROM FORMING.
WHEN REHEATING, USE 1 TBSP OF WHOLE MILK TO LOOSEN IT UP AGAIN.

VELOUTÉ

HANDS ON: 45 MIN

- -1/4 CUP UNSALTED BUTTER
- -1/4 CUP ALL-PURPOSE FLOUR
- -2 CUPS CHICKEN OR VEAL STOCK (UNSEASONED)
- -1 TSP WHITE PEPPER
- -1 TSP KOSHER SALT

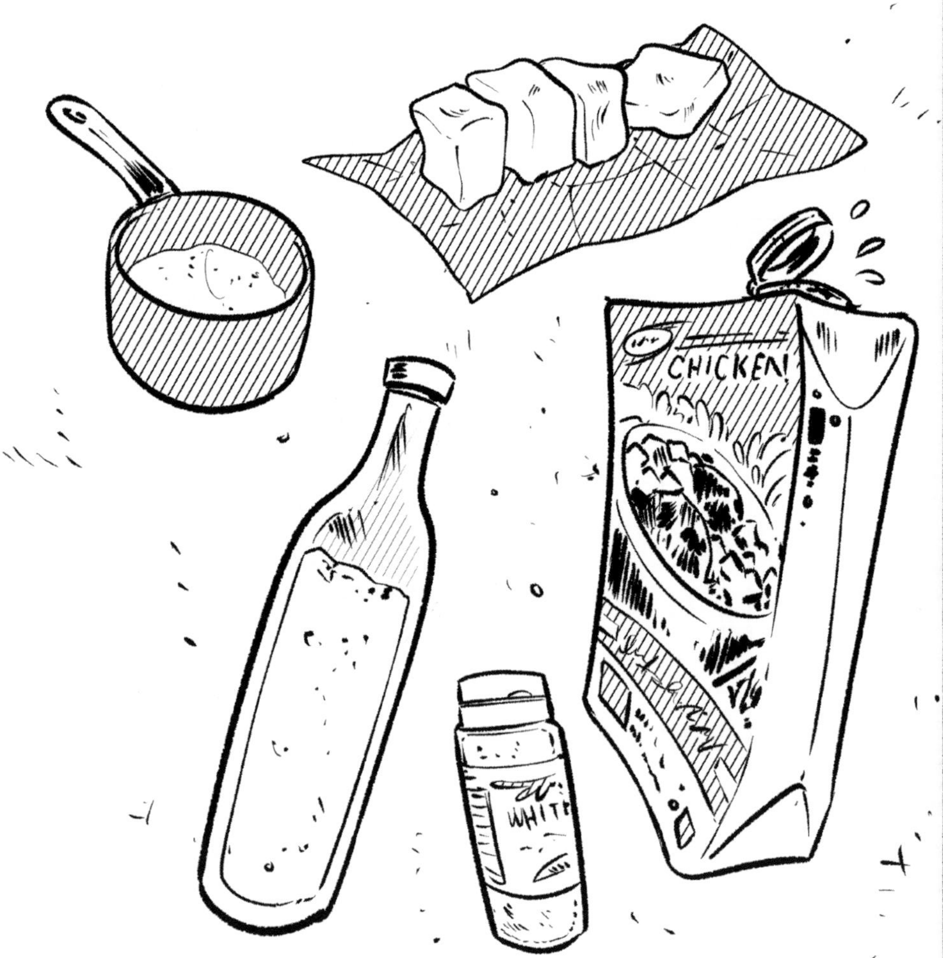
CHICKEN
WHITE

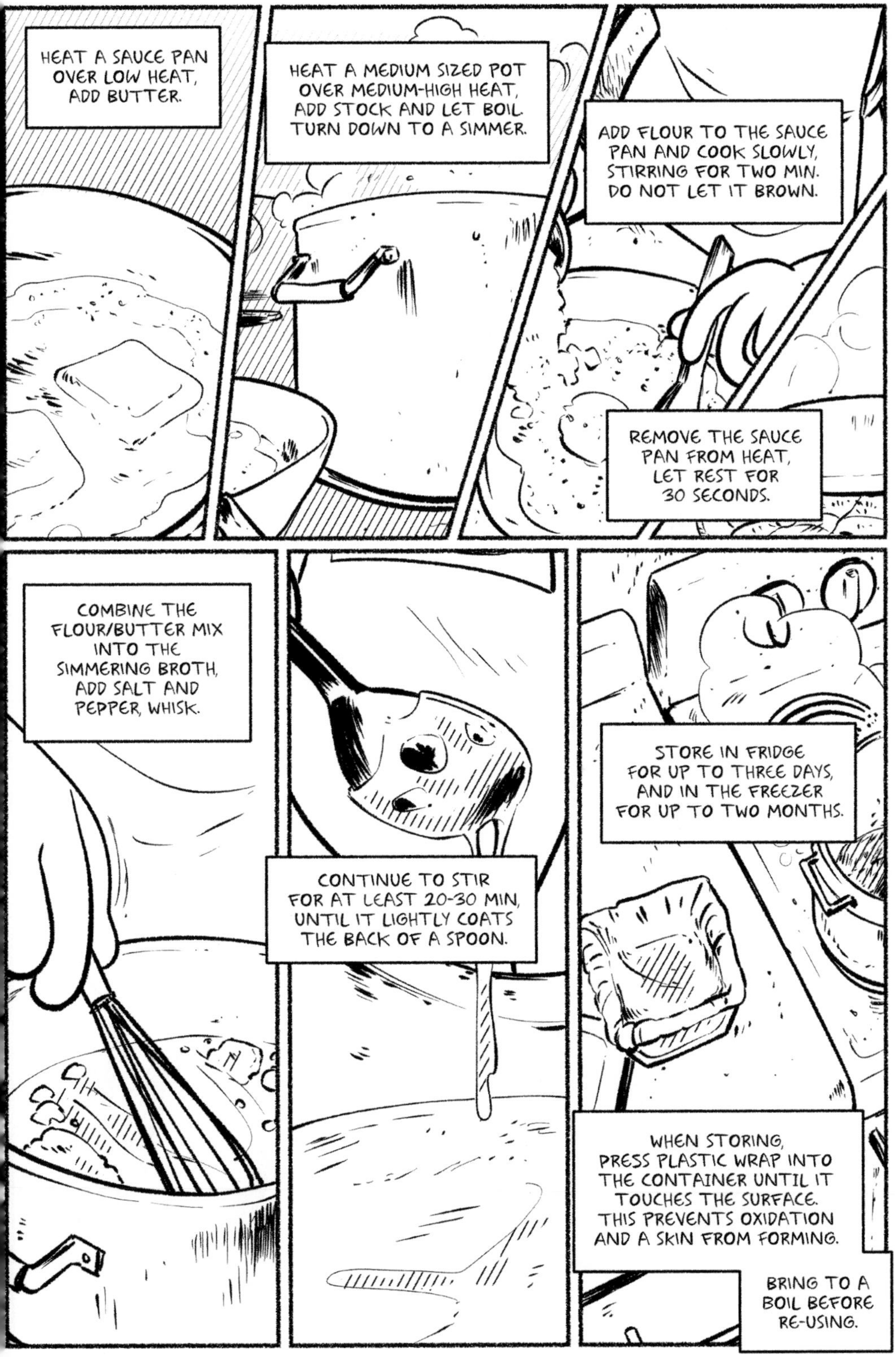
HEAT A SAUCE PAN OVER LOW HEAT, ADD BUTTER.
HEAT A MEDIUM SIZED POT OVER MEDIUM-HIGH HEAT, ADD STOCK AND LET BOIL. TURN DOWN TO A SIMMER.
ADD FLOUR TO THE SAUCE PAN AND COOK SLOWLY, STIRRING FOR TWO MIN. DO NOT LET IT BROWN.
REMOVE THE SAUCE PAN FROM HEAT, LET REST FOR 30 SECONDS.
COMBINE THE FLOUR/BUTTER MIX INTO THE SIMMERING BROTH, ADD SALT AND PEPPER, WHISK.
CONTINUE TO STIR FOR AT LEAST 20-30 MIN, UNTIL IT LIGHTLY COATS THE BACK OF A SPOON.
STORE IN FRIDGE FOR UP TO THREE DAYS, AND IN THE FREEZER FOR UP TO TWO MONTHS.
WHEN STORING, PRESS PLASTIC WRAP INTO THE CONTAINER UNTIL IT TOUCHES THE SURFACE. THIS PREVENTS OXIDATION AND A SKIN FROM FORMING.
BRING TO A BOIL BEFORE RE-USING.

ESPAGNOLE

HANDS ON: 30 MIN
HANDS OFF: 2 HOURS

- 3 TBSP WHITE ONION, MINCED
- 1 1/2 TBSP CARROT, MINCED
- 1 1/2 TBSP CELERY, MINCED
- 4 TBSP BUTTER, UNSALTED
- 1/2 CUP ALL-PURPOSE FLOUR
- 5 1/3 CUPS BEEF STOCK
- 1 BAY LEAF
- 2 TSP THYME
- 2 TSP PEPPERCORNS
- 1 TSP PARSLEY STEMS, MINCED
- 1/4 TBSP TOMATO PUREE

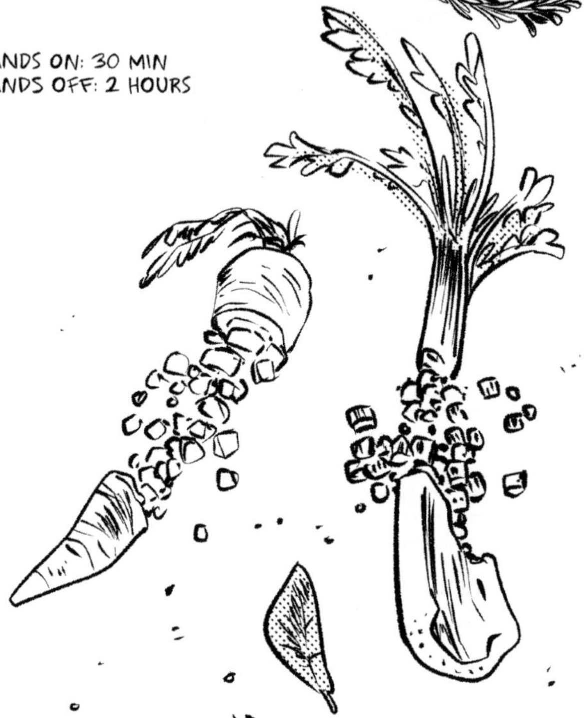

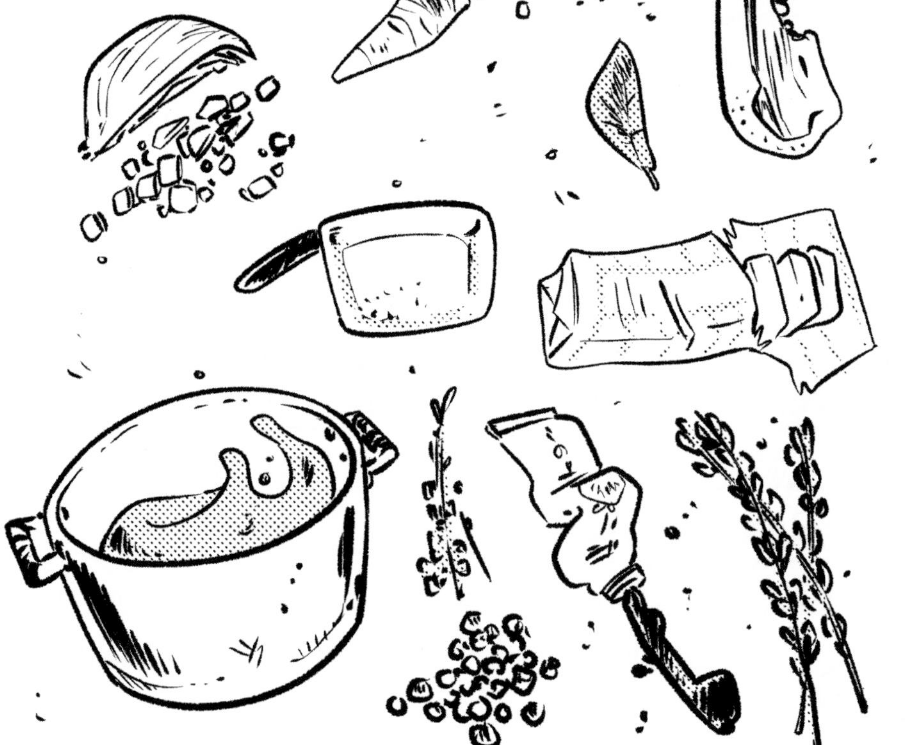

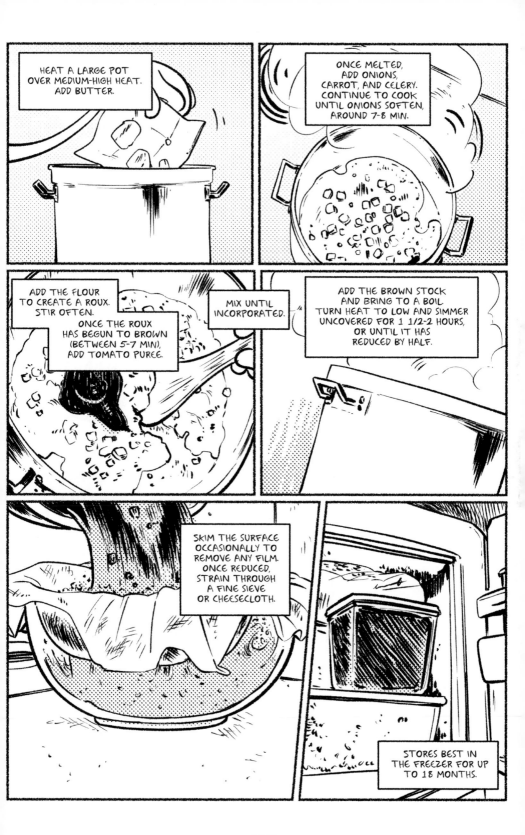

HEAT A LARGE POT OVER MEDIUM-HIGH HEAT. ADD BUTTER.

ONCE MELTED, ADD ONIONS, CARROT, AND CELERY. CONTINUE TO COOK UNTIL ONIONS SOFTEN, AROUND 7-8 MIN.

ADD THE FLOUR TO CREATE A ROUX. STIR OFTEN.
ONCE THE ROUX HAS BEGUN TO BROWN (BETWEEN 5-7 MIN), ADD TOMATO PUREE.

MIX UNTIL INCORPORATED.

ADD THE BROWN STOCK AND BRING TO A BOIL. TURN HEAT TO LOW AND SIMMER UNCOVERED FOR 1 1/2-2 HOURS, OR UNTIL IT HAS REDUCED BY HALF.

SKIM THE SURFACE OCCASIONALLY TO REMOVE ANY FILM. ONCE REDUCED, STRAIN THROUGH A FINE SIEVE OR CHEESECLOTH.

STORES BEST IN THE FREEZER FOR UP TO 18 MONTHS.

TOMATO

HANDS ON: 25 MIN
HANDS OFF: 2 HOURS

-1/3 CUP SALT PORK OR 1/3 CUP BACON
(AS PLAIN AS YOU CAN FIND IT—
 NO MAPLE, SMOKED, ETC))
 OR 1 TBSP OLIVE OIL,
 1 TBSP KOSHER SALT,
 1 TBSP KOSHER SALT,
 1 TBSP BLACK PEPPER,
 2 TBSP SMOKED PAPRIKA,
 AND 2 TBSP BROWN SUGAR
-1 CUP WHITE ONION, DICED
-1 TBSP GARLIC, CHOPPED
-1/2 CUP CARROTS, DICED
-1/2 CUP CELERY, DICED
-3 1/2 CUPS (28OZ CAN) CANNED
 TOMATO OR 4 CUPS ROMA TOMATO,
 CHOPPED
-1/2 QUART CHICKEN OR VEG STOCK
-1 TSP THYME
-1 TSP PARSLEY
-1 BAY LEAF
-1 TBSP BLACK PEPPER
-1 TSP SALT

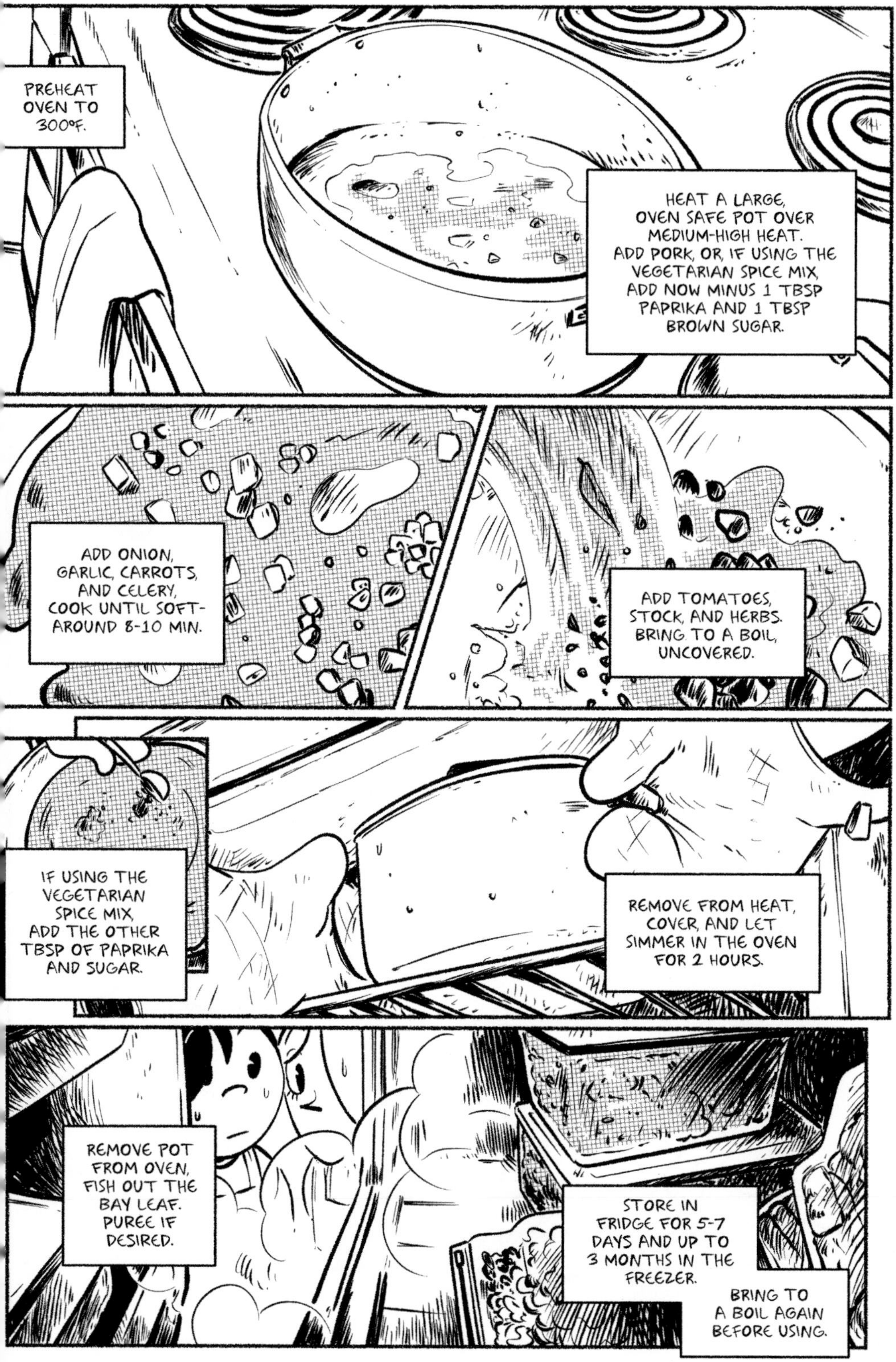
PREHEAT OVEN TO 300°F.
HEAT A LARGE, OVEN SAFE POT OVER MEDIUM-HIGH HEAT. ADD PORK, OR, IF USING THE VEGETARIAN SPICE MIX, ADD NOW MINUS 1 TBSP PAPRIKA AND 1 TBSP BROWN SUGAR.
ADD ONION, GARLIC, CARROTS, AND CELERY, COOK UNTIL SOFT- AROUND 8-10 MIN.
ADD TOMATOES, STOCK, AND HERBS. BRING TO A BOIL, UNCOVERED.
IF USING THE VEGETARIAN SPICE MIX, ADD THE OTHER TBSP OF PAPRIKA AND SUGAR.
REMOVE FROM HEAT, COVER, AND LET SIMMER IN THE OVEN FOR 2 HOURS.
REMOVE POT FROM OVEN, FISH OUT THE BAY LEAF. PUREE IF DESIRED.
STORE IN FRIDGE FOR 5-7 DAYS AND UP TO 3 MONTHS IN THE FREEZER.
BRING TO A BOIL AGAIN BEFORE USING.

HOLLANDAISE

HANDS ON: 30 MIN

-2 EGG YOLKS
-1 TBSP LEMON JUICE
-1 TBSP WATER
-1/4 TSP KOSHER SALT
-1/4 TSP CAYENNE
-12 TBSP UNSALTED BUTTER,
 CHOPPED

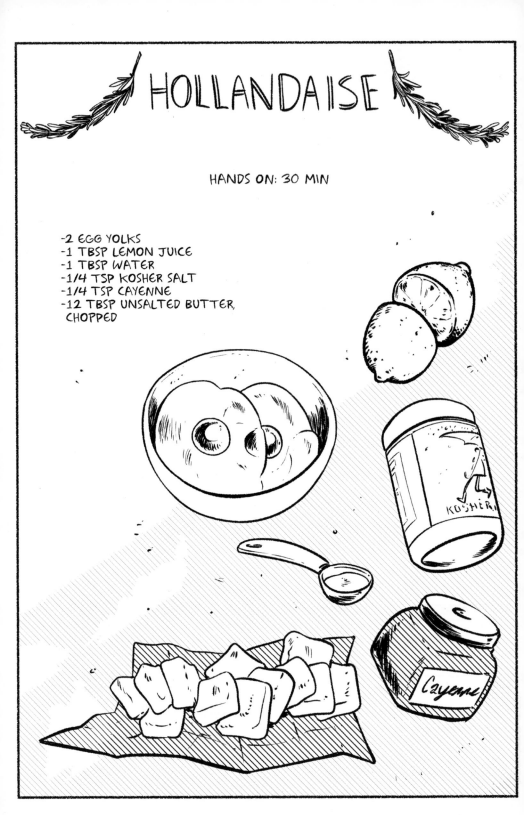

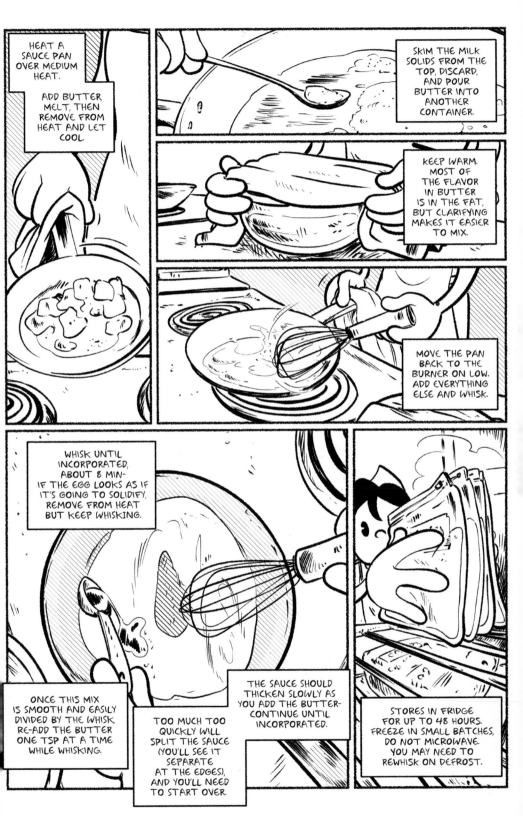

HEAT A SAUCE PAN OVER MEDIUM HEAT.

ADD BUTTER, MELT, THEN REMOVE FROM HEAT AND LET COOL

SKIM THE MILK SOLIDS FROM THE TOP, DISCARD, AND POUR BUTTER INTO ANOTHER CONTAINER.

KEEP WARM. MOST OF THE FLAVOR IN BUTTER IS IN THE FAT, BUT CLARIFYING MAKES IT EASIER TO MIX.

MOVE THE PAN BACK TO THE BURNER ON LOW. ADD EVERYTHING ELSE AND WHISK.

WHISK UNTIL INCORPORATED, ABOUT 8 MIN- IF THE EGG LOOKS AS IF IT'S GOING TO SOLIDIFY, REMOVE FROM HEAT BUT KEEP WHISKING.

ONCE THIS MIX IS SMOOTH AND EASILY DIVIDED BY THE WHISK, RE-ADD THE BUTTER ONE TSP AT A TIME WHILE WHISKING.

TOO MUCH TOO QUICKLY WILL SPLIT THE SAUCE (YOU'LL SEE IT SEPARATE AT THE EDGES), AND YOU'LL NEED TO START OVER.

THE SAUCE SHOULD THICKEN SLOWLY AS YOU ADD THE BUTTER- CONTINUE UNTIL INCORPORATED.

STORES IN FRIDGE FOR UP TO 48 HOURS. FREEZE IN SMALL BATCHES, DO NOT MICROWAVE. YOU MAY NEED TO REWHISK ON DEFROST.

BEAN DIP

HANDS ON: 15 MIN

- -2 CUPS BLACK BEANS
  (IF USING CANNED, DRAIN AND RINSE)
- -1/2 CUP SALSA OF CHOICE
- -1 TSP CUMIN
- -1 TSP SALT
- -1 TSP BLACK PEPPER

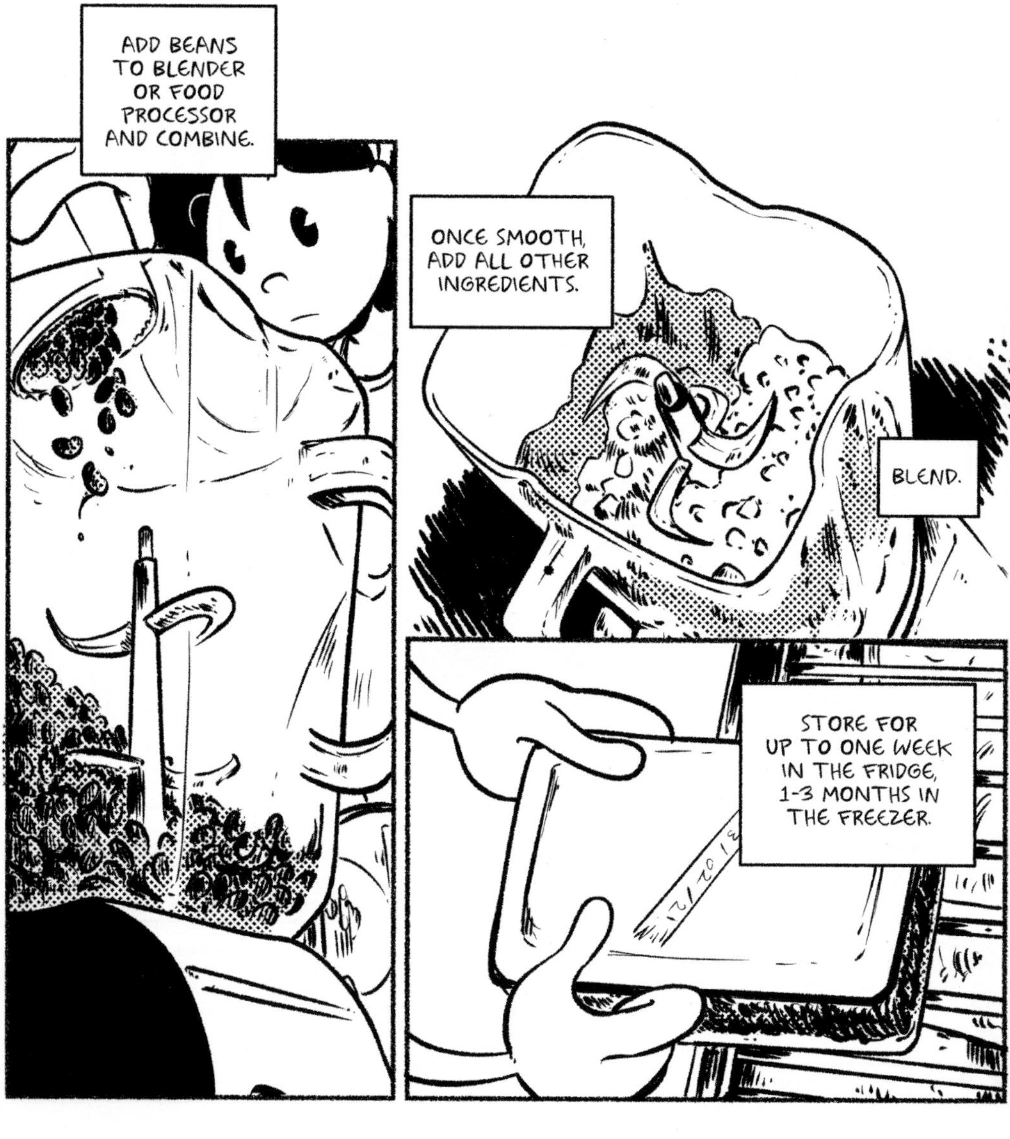
ADD BEANS TO BLENDER OR FOOD PROCESSOR AND COMBINE.
ONCE SMOOTH, ADD ALL OTHER INGREDIENTS.
BLEND.
STORE FOR UP TO ONE WEEK IN THE FRIDGE, 1-3 MONTHS IN THE FREEZER.

CHIMICHURRI

HANDS ON: 10 MIN

- 2 CUPS FRESH PARLSEY, CHOPPED, OR 3 CUPS IF USING DRIED
- 4 TBSP DRIED OREGANO, CHOPPED
- 4 TBSP GARLIC, CHOPPED
- 1 CUP OLIVE OIL, EXTRA VIRGIN
- 1/4 CUP RED WINE
- 1/2 TSP KOSHER SALT
- 1 TSP BLACK PEPPER
- 1/2 TSP RED PEPPER FLAKE

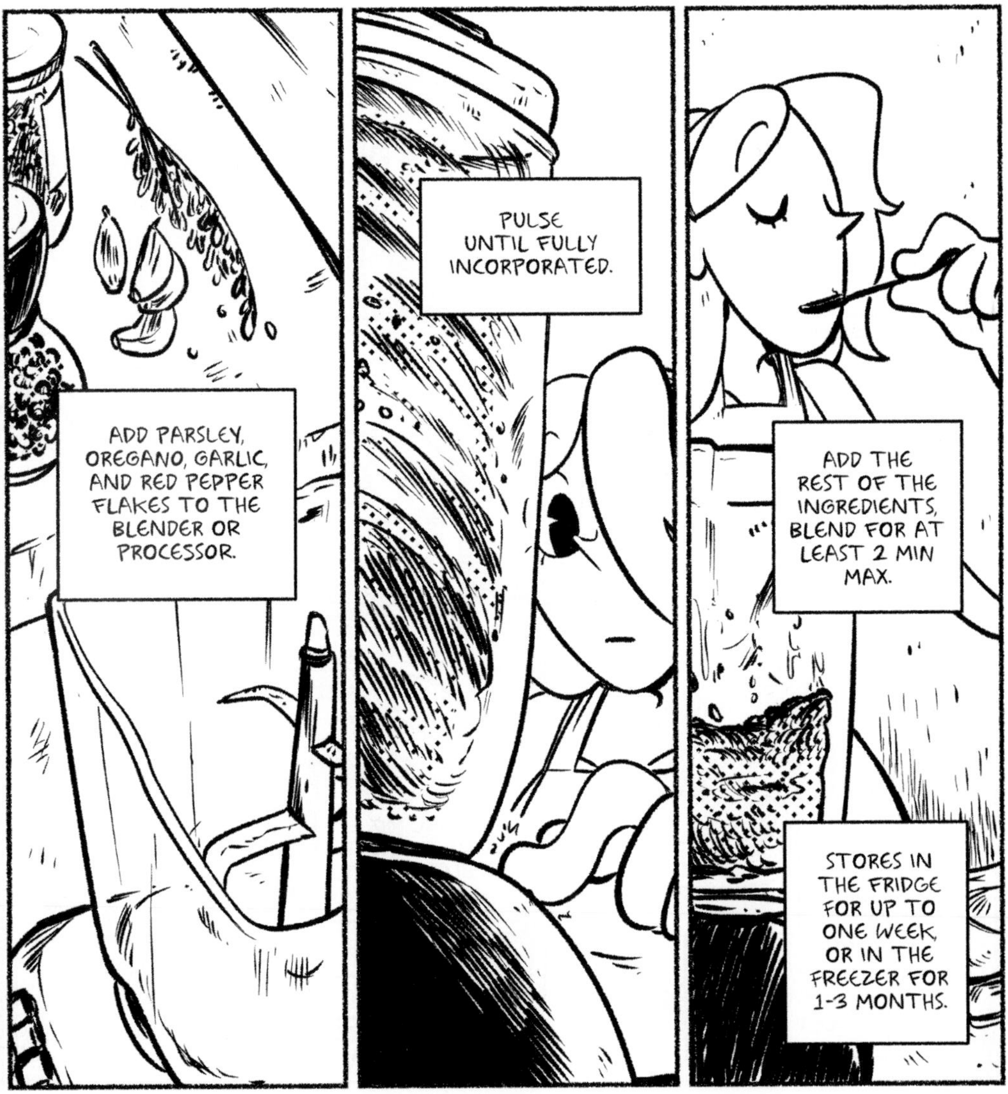
ADD PARSLEY, OREGANO, GARLIC, AND RED PEPPER FLAKES TO THE BLENDER OR PROCESSOR.
PULSE UNTIL FULLY INCORPORATED.
ADD THE REST OF THE INGREDIENTS, BLEND FOR AT LEAST 2 MIN MAX.
STORES IN THE FRIDGE FOR UP TO ONE WEEK, OR IN THE FREEZER FOR 1-3 MONTHS.

HOT SAUCE

HANDS ON: 10 MIN

- 15-20 PEPPERS OF CHOICE (JALAPENO, FRESNO, SERRANO, OR CAYENNE) OR 2 7oz CANS OF CANNED CHIPOTLES
- 1 1/2 CUPS APPLE CIDER VINEGAR OR 1/4 CUP IF USING CANNED
- 2 TSP KOSHER SALT
- 3 TSP GARLIC, MINCED

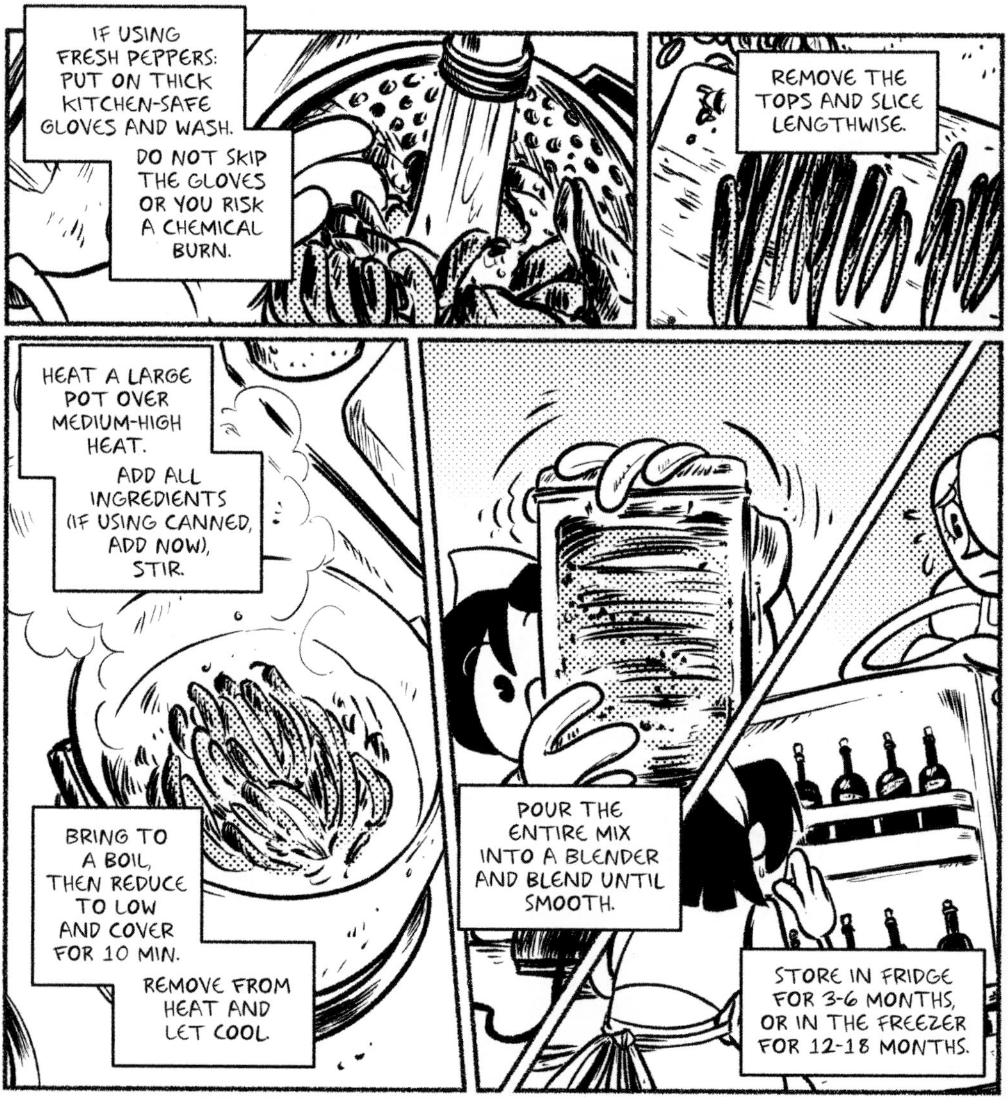

IF USING FRESH PEPPERS: PUT ON THICK KITCHEN-SAFE GLOVES AND WASH.
DO NOT SKIP THE GLOVES OR YOU RISK A CHEMICAL BURN.
REMOVE THE TOPS AND SLICE LENGTHWISE.
HEAT A LARGE POT OVER MEDIUM-HIGH HEAT.
ADD ALL INGREDIENTS (IF USING CANNED, ADD NOW), STIR.
BRING TO A BOIL, THEN REDUCE TO LOW AND COVER FOR 10 MIN.
REMOVE FROM HEAT AND LET COOL.
POUR THE ENTIRE MIX INTO A BLENDER AND BLEND UNTIL SMOOTH.
STORE IN FRIDGE FOR 3-6 MONTHS, OR IN THE FREEZER FOR 12-18 MONTHS.

BBQ SAUCE

HANDS ON: 20 MIN
HANDS OFF: 1 HOUR

- 2 TBSP GARLIC, MINCED
- 1 CUP YELLOW ONION, CHOPPED
- 3 TBSP VEGETABLE OR OLIVE OIL
- 1 TBSP KOSHER SALT
- 1 CUP KETCHUP
- 2 TBSP SPICY BROWN MUSTARD OR 1 TBSP YELLOW MUSTARD
- 4 TBSP WORCESTERSHIRE SAUCE
- 1/2 APPLE CIDER VINEGAR
- 4 TBSP BROWN SUGAR
- 1 TBSP SMOKED PAPRIKA
- 1 TBSP CAYENNE
- 1 TSP BLACK PEPPER
- 1 TSP CUMIN

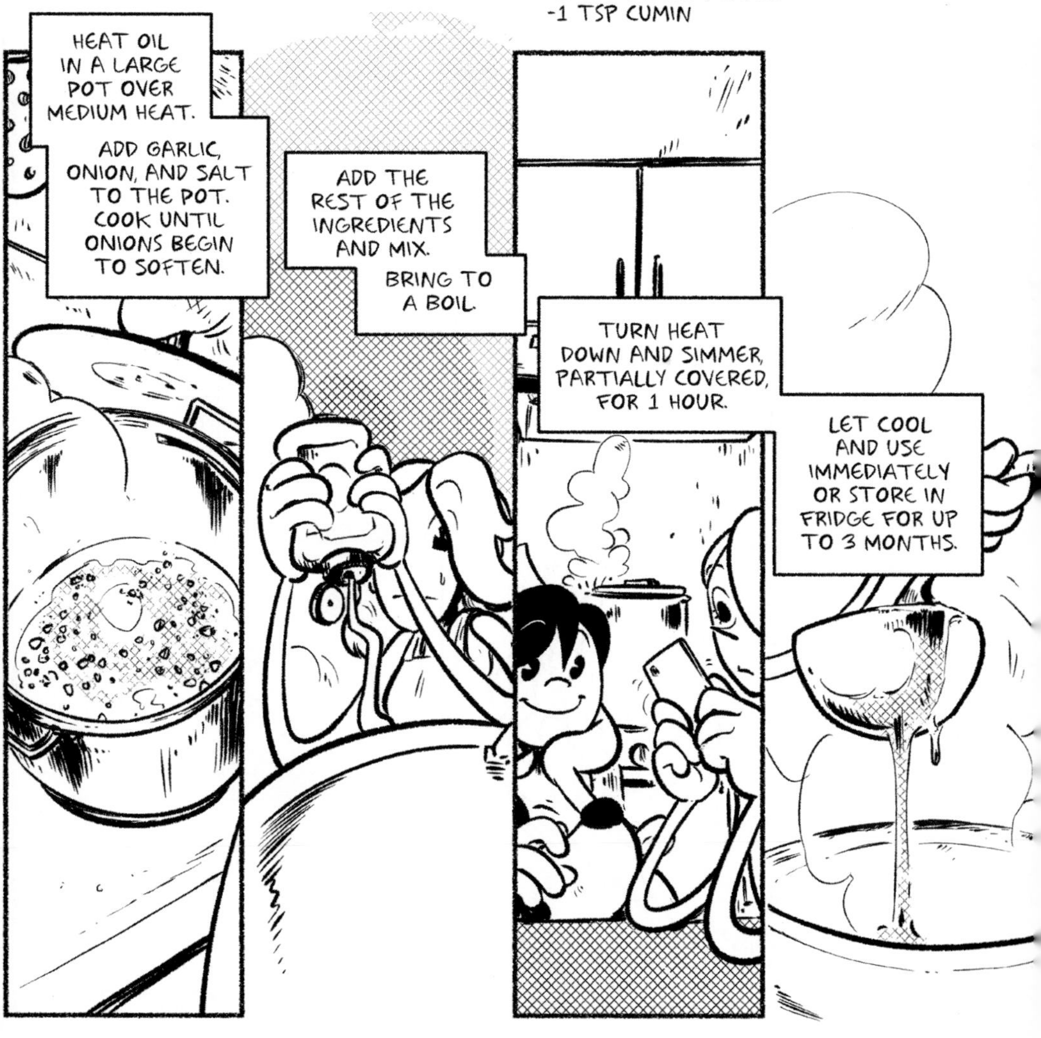
HEAT OIL IN A LARGE POT OVER MEDIUM HEAT.
ADD GARLIC, ONION, AND SALT TO THE POT. COOK UNTIL ONIONS BEGIN TO SOFTEN.
ADD THE REST OF THE INGREDIENTS AND MIX.
BRING TO A BOIL.
TURN HEAT DOWN AND SIMMER, PARTIALLY COVERED, FOR 1 HOUR.
LET COOL AND USE IMMEDIATELY OR STORE IN FRIDGE FOR UP TO 3 MONTHS.

PESTO

HANDS ON: 10 MIN

-1 CUP BASIL LEAVES, CHOPPED,
 OR 1 1/2 CUPS IF DRIED
-1 CUP SPINACH, CHOPPED
-1/3 CUP PINE NUTS (OR WALNUTS
 OR UNSALTED PEANUTS)
-1/2 CUP PARMESEAN
-2 TBSP GARLIC, CHOPPED
-1 TSP KOSHER SALT
-1 TSP BLACK PEPPER
-1/2 OLIVE OIL,
 EXTRA VIRGIN PREFERRED

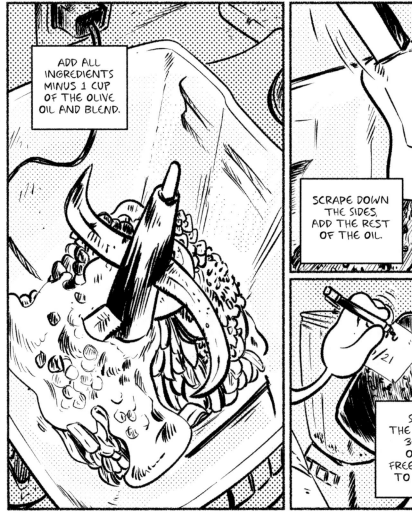

ADD ALL INGREDIENTS MINUS 1 CUP OF THE OLIVE OIL AND BLEND.

SCRAPE DOWN THE SIDES, ADD THE REST OF THE OIL.

STORE IN THE FRIDGE FOR 3-4 WEEKS, OR IN THE FREEZER FOR UP TO 6 MONTHS.

SALSA

HANDS ON: 10 MIN
HANDS OFF: 10 MIN

- 3 CUPS TOMATOES (ONE 28oz CAN), CHOPPED
- 1 TBSP GARLIC
- 1/4 CUP JALAPEÑO
- 1/4 CUP YELLOW ONION, DICED
- 1 TSP CILANTRO, DOUBLE IF DRIED
- 1/2 CUP OLIVE OIL
- 1 TBSP KOSHER SALT

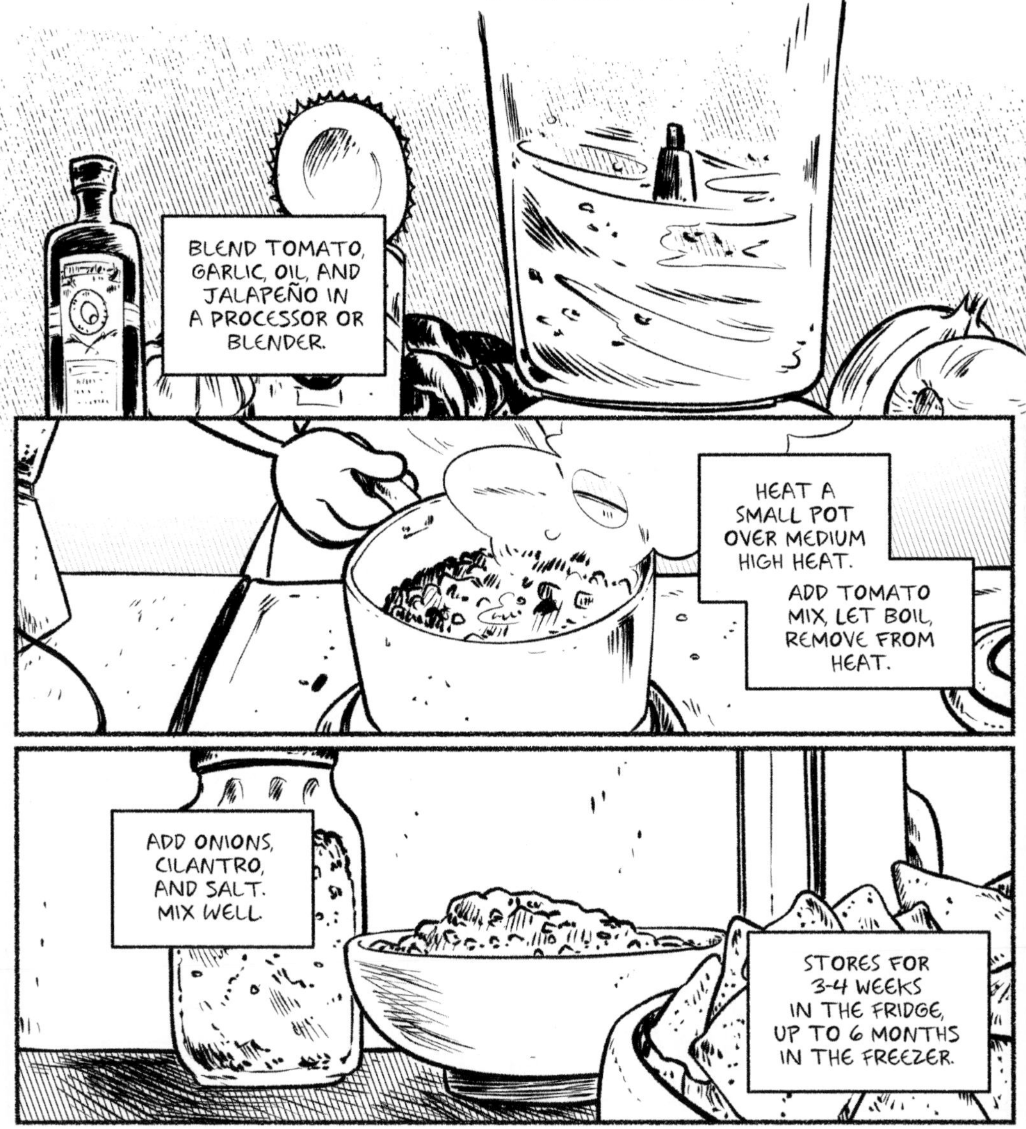
BLEND TOMATO, GARLIC, OIL, AND JALAPEÑO IN A PROCESSOR OR BLENDER.
HEAT A SMALL POT OVER MEDIUM HIGH HEAT.
ADD TOMATO MIX, LET BOIL, REMOVE FROM HEAT.
ADD ONIONS, CILANTRO, AND SALT. MIX WELL.
STORES FOR 3-4 WEEKS IN THE FRIDGE, UP TO 6 MONTHS IN THE FREEZER.

PIZZA SAUCE

HANDS ON: 15 MIN

- 3 CUPS TOMATOES (ONE 28oz CAN), CHOPPED
- 2 TBSP OLIVE OIL
- 3 TBSP GARLIC, MINCED
- 1 TBSP YELLOW ONION MINCED OR 1 1/2 TBSP ONION POWDER
- 1 TBSP SUGAR
- 1 TBSP SALT
- 1 TBSP BASIL
- 1 TBSP OREGANO
- 1 TBSP MISO (OPTIONAL)
- 1 TSP ROSEMARY
- 1 TSP RED PEPPER FLAKES
- 2 TSP BLACK PEPPER

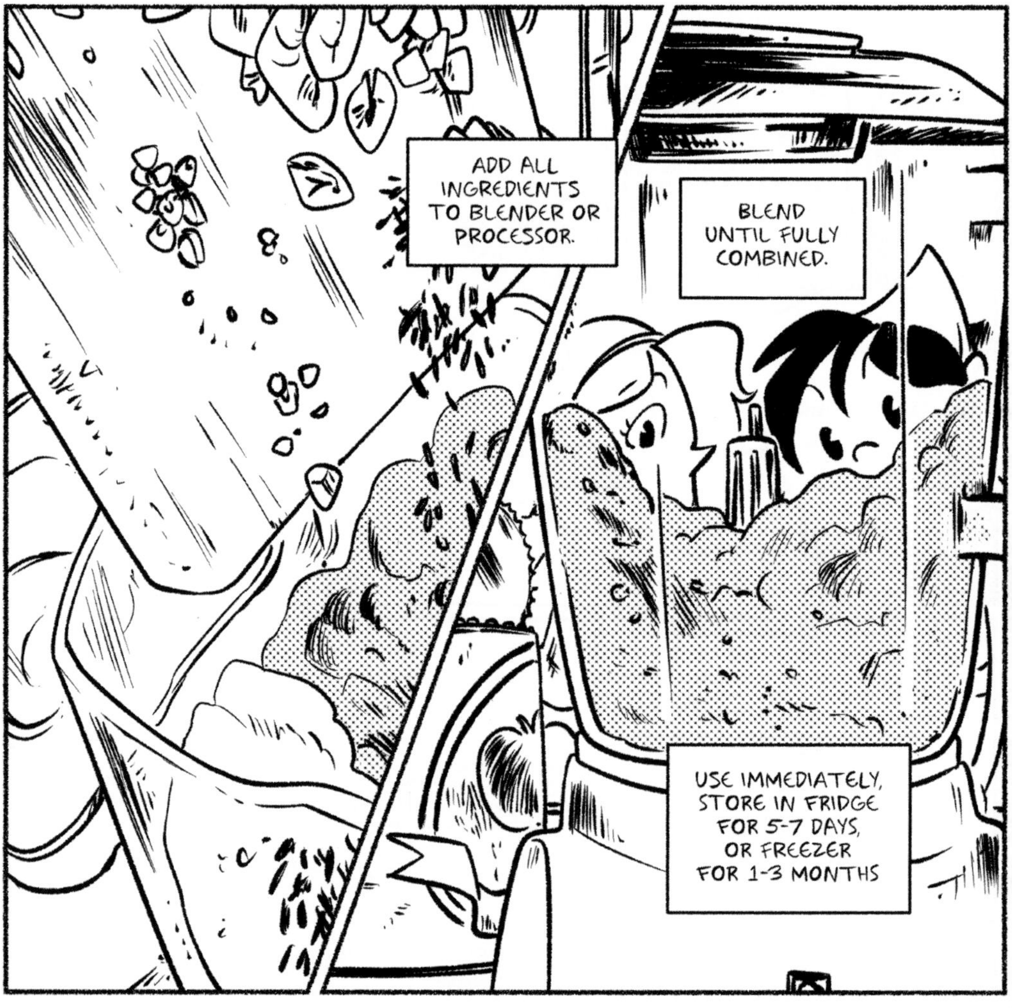
ADD ALL INGREDIENTS TO BLENDER OR PROCESSOR.
BLEND UNTIL FULLY COMBINED.
USE IMMEDIATELY, STORE IN FRIDGE FOR 5-7 DAYS, OR FREEZER FOR 1-3 MONTHS

(ALMOST)
DULCE DE LECHE

HANDS ON: 20 MIN

- 8 TBSP UNSALTED BUTTER
- 3/4 CUP BROWN SUGAR
- 1/4 TSP CINNAMON
- 1 3/4 (ONE 14oz CAN) SWEETENED CONDENSED MILK
- 1 TSP VANILLA EXTRACT
- 1 TSP KOSHER SALT

THIS IS TECHNICALLY A QUICK CARAMEL SAUCE AND NOT A "TRUE" DULCE DE LECHE, WHICH GETS COLOR FROM THE MAILLARD REACTION OCCURING WHEN PROTEIN AND SUGARS ARE HEATED TOGETHER. IF YOU NEED IT IN A PINCH THOUGH, THIS IS YOUR SOLUTION!

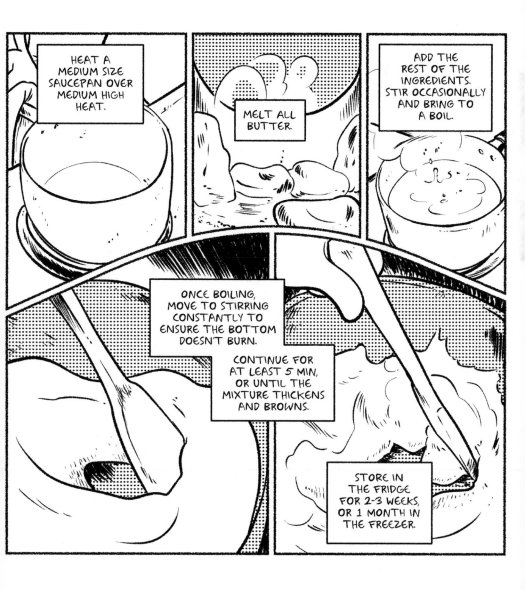

HEAT A MEDIUM SIZE SAUCEPAN OVER MEDIUM HIGH HEAT.

MELT ALL BUTTER.

ADD THE REST OF THE INGREDIENTS. STIR OCCASIONALLY AND BRING TO A BOIL.

ONCE BOILING, MOVE TO STIRRING CONSTANTLY TO ENSURE THE BOTTOM DOESN'T BURN.

CONTINUE FOR AT LEAST 5 MIN, OR UNTIL THE MIXTURE THICKENS AND BROWNS.

STORE IN THE FRIDGE FOR 2-3 WEEKS, OR 1 MONTH IN THE FREEZER.

(ACTUAL)
DULCE DE LECHE

HANDS ON: 15 MIN
HANDS OFF: 1 HOUR 30 MIN

- 4 CUPS MILK (NOT SKIM)
- 1 1/4 CUPS SUGAR
- 1/4 TSP BAKING SODA
- 1/4 TSP VANILLA EXTRACT (OPTIONAL)
- 1/4 TSP GROUND CINNAMON (OPTIONAL)

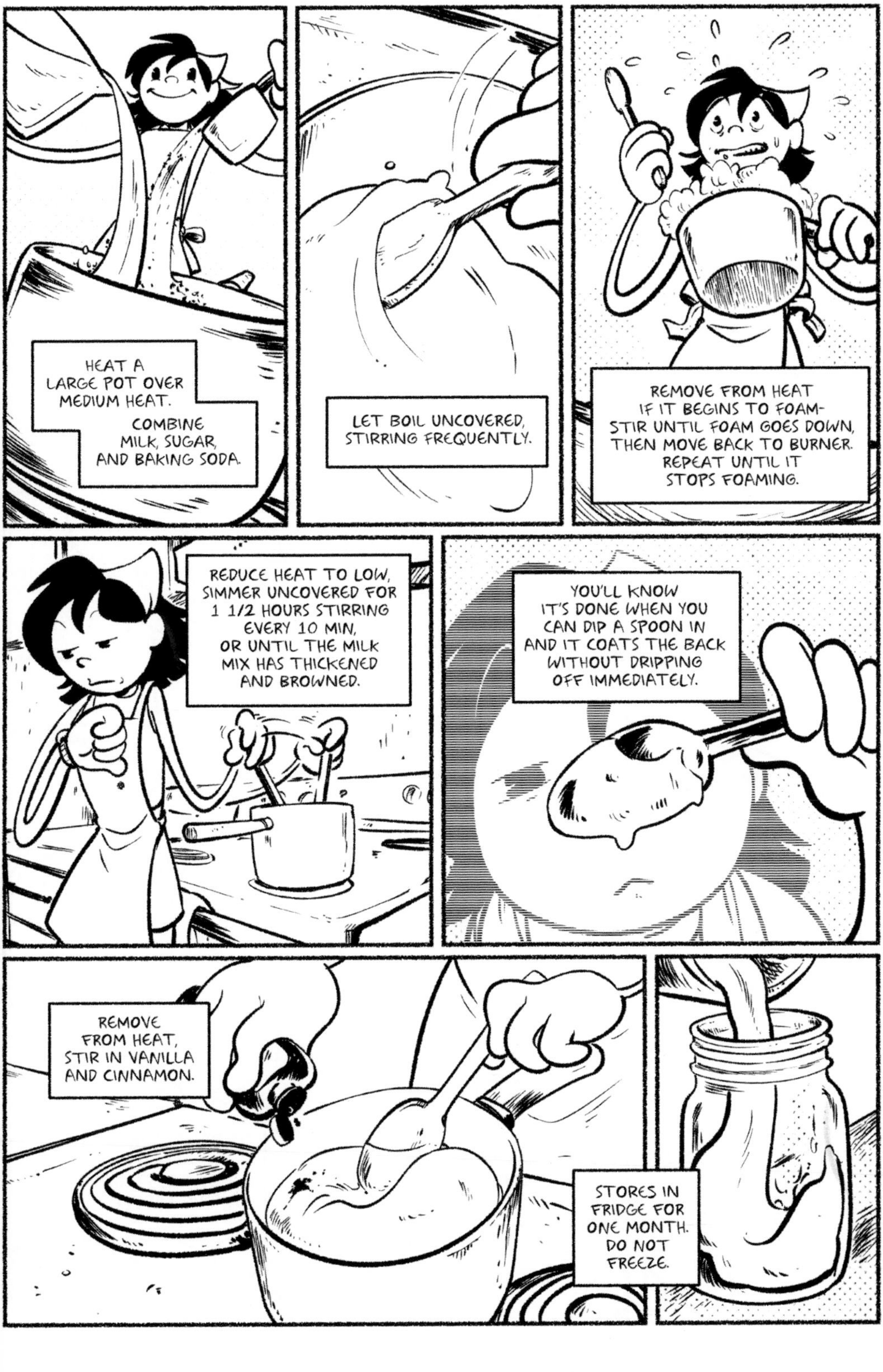
HEAT A LARGE POT OVER MEDIUM HEAT.
COMBINE MILK, SUGAR, AND BAKING SODA.
LET BOIL UNCOVERED, STIRRING FREQUENTLY.
REMOVE FROM HEAT IF IT BEGINS TO FOAM- STIR UNTIL FOAM GOES DOWN, THEN MOVE BACK TO BURNER. REPEAT UNTIL IT STOPS FOAMING.
REDUCE HEAT TO LOW, SIMMER UNCOVERED FOR 1 1/2 HOURS STIRRING EVERY 10 MIN, OR UNTIL THE MILK MIX HAS THICKENED AND BROWNED.
YOU'LL KNOW IT'S DONE WHEN YOU CAN DIP A SPOON IN AND IT COATS THE BACK WITHOUT DRIPPING OFF IMMEDIATELY.
REMOVE FROM HEAT, STIR IN VANILLA AND CINNAMON.
STORES IN FRIDGE FOR ONE MONTH. DO NOT FREEZE.

IMPOSSIBLE PIE

HANDS ON: 20 MIN
HANDS OFF: 45 MIN

-2 CUPS MILK
-1 CUP FLAKED COCONUT
-4 EGGS
-1 TSP VANILLA EXTRACT
-1/2 CUP ALL-PURPOSE FLOUR
-6 TBSP BUTTER
-3/4 CUP WHITE SUGAR

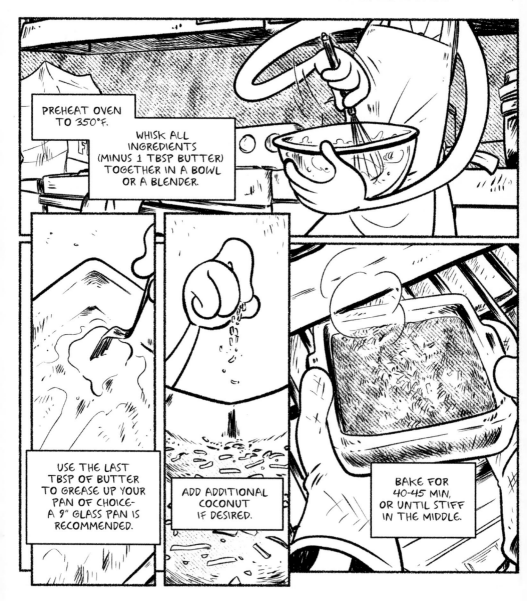

PREHEAT OVEN TO 350°F.

WHISK ALL INGREDIENTS (MINUS 1 TBSP BUTTER) TOGETHER IN A BOWL OR A BLENDER.

USE THE LAST TBSP OF BUTTER TO GREASE UP YOUR PAN OF CHOICE- A 9" GLASS PAN IS RECOMMENDED.

ADD ADDITIONAL COCONUT IF DESIRED.

BAKE FOR 40-45 MIN, OR UNTIL STIFF IN THE MIDDLE.

 # POUND CAKE

-4 CUPS ALL-PURPOSE FLOUR
+ 1 TBSP FOR THE BAKING PAN
-3 CUPS SUGAR
-2 CUPS BUTTER, MELTED AND
AT ROOM TEMPERATURE
-3/4 CUP MILK
-4 EGGS
-1 TSPS VANILLA EXTRACT
-1/2 TSP KOSHER SALT

HANDS ON: 20 MIN
HANDS OFF: 1 HOUR 45 MIN

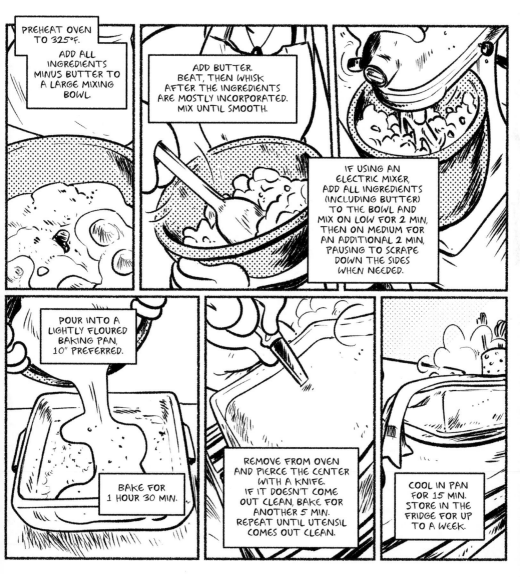

PREHEAT OVEN TO 325°F.
ADD ALL INGREDIENTS MINUS BUTTER TO A LARGE MIXING BOWL.

ADD BUTTER. BEAT, THEN WHISK AFTER THE INGREDIENTS ARE MOSTLY INCORPORATED. MIX UNTIL SMOOTH.

IF USING AN ELECTRIC MIXER, ADD ALL INGREDIENTS (INCLUDING BUTTER) TO THE BOWL AND MIX ON LOW FOR 2 MIN, THEN ON MEDIUM FOR AN ADDITIONAL 2 MIN, PAUSING TO SCRAPE DOWN THE SIDES WHEN NEEDED.

POUR INTO A LIGHTLY FLOURED BAKING PAN, 10" PREFERRED.

BAKE FOR 1 HOUR 30 MIN.

REMOVE FROM OVEN AND PIERCE THE CENTER WITH A KNIFE. IF IT DOESN'T COME OUT CLEAN, BAKE FOR ANOTHER 5 MIN. REPEAT UNTIL UTENSIL COMES OUT CLEAN.

COOL IN PAN FOR 15 MIN. STORE IN THE FRIDGE FOR UP TO A WEEK.

BANANA BREAD

HANDS ON: 20 MIN
HANDS OFF: 1 HR 15 MIN

- 1 CUP SUGAR
- 8 TBSP UNSALTED BUTTER, ROOM TEMPERATURE + 1 TBSP TO BUTTER LOAF PAN
- 2 EGGS
- 3 RIPE BANANAS
- 1 TBSP MILK
- 1 TSP CINNAMON
- ½ CUP WALNUTS, CRUSHED OR CHOPPED
- 2 CUPS ALL-PURPOSE FLOUR
- 1 TSP BAKING POWDER
- 1 TSP BAKING SODA
- 1 TSP SALT

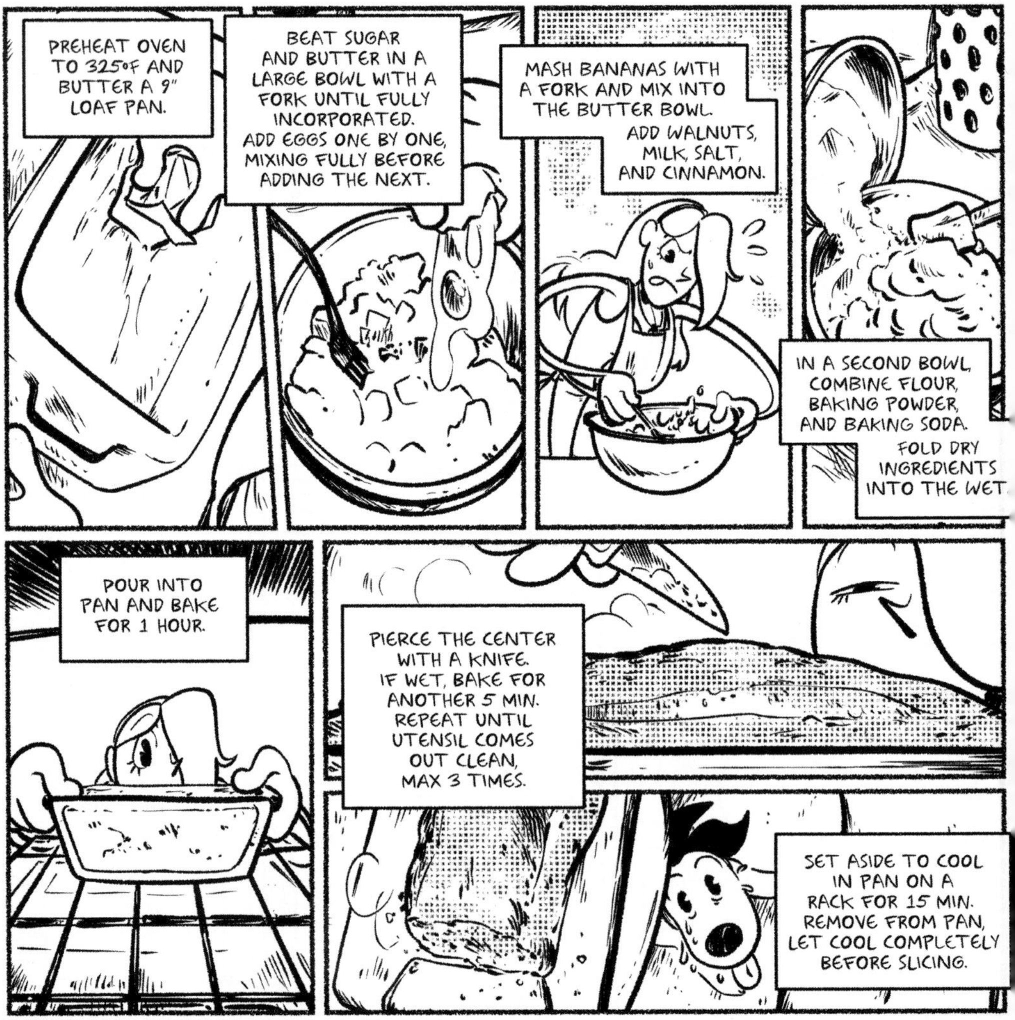
PREHEAT OVEN TO 325°F AND BUTTER A 9" LOAF PAN.
BEAT SUGAR AND BUTTER IN A LARGE BOWL WITH A FORK UNTIL FULLY INCORPORATED. ADD EGGS ONE BY ONE, MIXING FULLY BEFORE ADDING THE NEXT.
MASH BANANAS WITH A FORK AND MIX INTO THE BUTTER BOWL.
ADD WALNUTS, MILK, SALT, AND CINNAMON.
IN A SECOND BOWL, COMBINE FLOUR, BAKING POWDER, AND BAKING SODA.
FOLD DRY INGREDIENTS INTO THE WET.
POUR INTO PAN AND BAKE FOR 1 HOUR.
PIERCE THE CENTER WITH A KNIFE. IF WET, BAKE FOR ANOTHER 5 MIN. REPEAT UNTIL UTENSIL COMES OUT CLEAN, MAX 3 TIMES.
SET ASIDE TO COOL IN PAN ON A RACK FOR 15 MIN. REMOVE FROM PAN, LET COOL COMPLETELY BEFORE SLICING.

FLAN

HANDS ON: 30 MIN
HANDS OFF: 1 HR 50 MIN

- 3/4 CUP SUGAR
- 1/4 CUP WATER
- 1 CUP (8oz) CREAM CHEESE, ROOM TEMPERATURE
- 5 LARGE EGGS
- 1 3/4 CUP (14oz) SWEETENED CONDENSED MILK
- 1 1/2 CUP (12oz) EVAPORATED MILK
- 1 TSP VANILLA EXTRACT

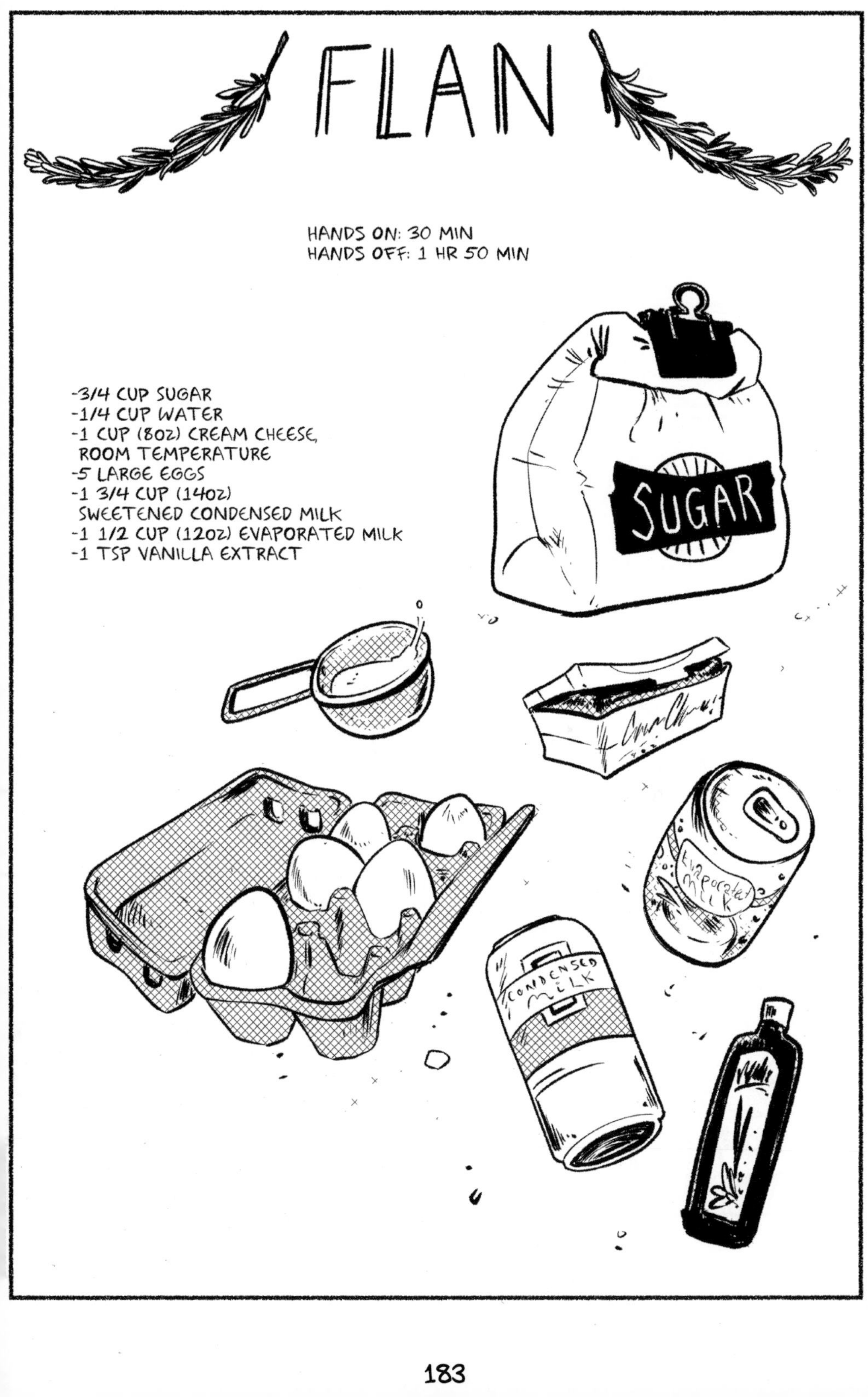
SUGAR
Evaporated MILK
CONDENSED MILK

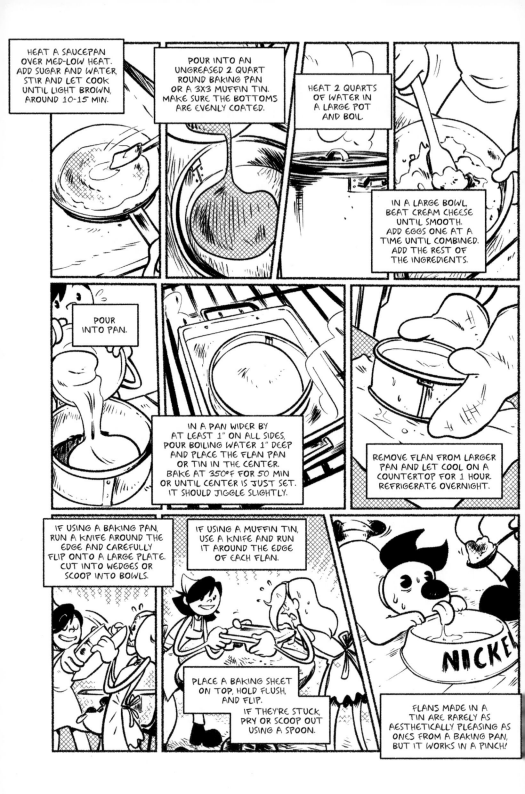

HEAT A SAUCEPAN OVER MED-LOW HEAT. ADD SUGAR AND WATER, STIR AND LET COOK UNTIL LIGHT BROWN, AROUND 10-15 MIN.

POUR INTO AN UNGREASED 2 QUART ROUND BAKING PAN OR A 3X3 MUFFIN TIN. MAKE SURE THE BOTTOMS ARE EVENLY COATED.

HEAT 2 QUARTS OF WATER IN A LARGE POT AND BOIL.

IN A LARGE BOWL, BEAT CREAM CHEESE UNTIL SMOOTH. ADD EGGS ONE AT A TIME UNTIL COMBINED. ADD THE REST OF THE INGREDIENTS.

POUR INTO PAN.

IN A PAN WIDER BY AT LEAST 1" ON ALL SIDES, POUR BOILING WATER 1" DEEP AND PLACE THE FLAN PAN OR TIN IN THE CENTER. BAKE AT 350°F FOR 50 MIN OR UNTIL CENTER IS JUST SET. IT SHOULD JIGGLE SLIGHTLY.

REMOVE FLAN FROM LARGER PAN AND LET COOL ON A COUNTERTOP FOR 1 HOUR. REFRIGERATE OVERNIGHT.

IF USING A BAKING PAN, RUN A KNIFE AROUND THE EDGE AND CAREFULLY FLIP ONTO A LARGE PLATE. CUT INTO WEDGES OR SCOOP INTO BOWLS.

IF USING A MUFFIN TIN, USE A KNIFE AND RUN IT AROUND THE EDGE OF EACH FLAN.

PLACE A BAKING SHEET ON TOP, HOLD FLUSH, AND FLIP.
IF THEY'RE STUCK, PRY OR SCOOP OUT USING A SPOON.

NICKEL

FLANS MADE IN A TIN ARE RARELY AS AESTHETICALLY PLEASING AS ONES FROM A BAKING PAN, BUT IT WORKS IN A PINCH!

OATMEAL RAISIN COOKIES

HANDS ON: 20 MIN
HANDS OFF: 25 MIN

- 1 LARGE EGG
- 8 TBSP UNSALTED BUTTER, ROOM TEMPERATURE
- 1/2 CUP BROWN SUGAR
- 1/4 CUP GRANULATED SUGAR
- 2 TSPS VANILLA EXTRACT
- 1 1/2 CUPS WHOLE ROLLED OATS (NOT INSTANT OR QUICK COOK)
- 3/4 CUP ALL-PURPOSE FLOUR
- 1/2 TSP BAKING SODA
- 1/2 TSP KOSHER SALT
- 1/2 CUP RAISINS
- 1/2 CUP WALNUTS, CHOPPED (OR MORE RAISINS, IF YOU'RE NOT A FAN OF NUTS)

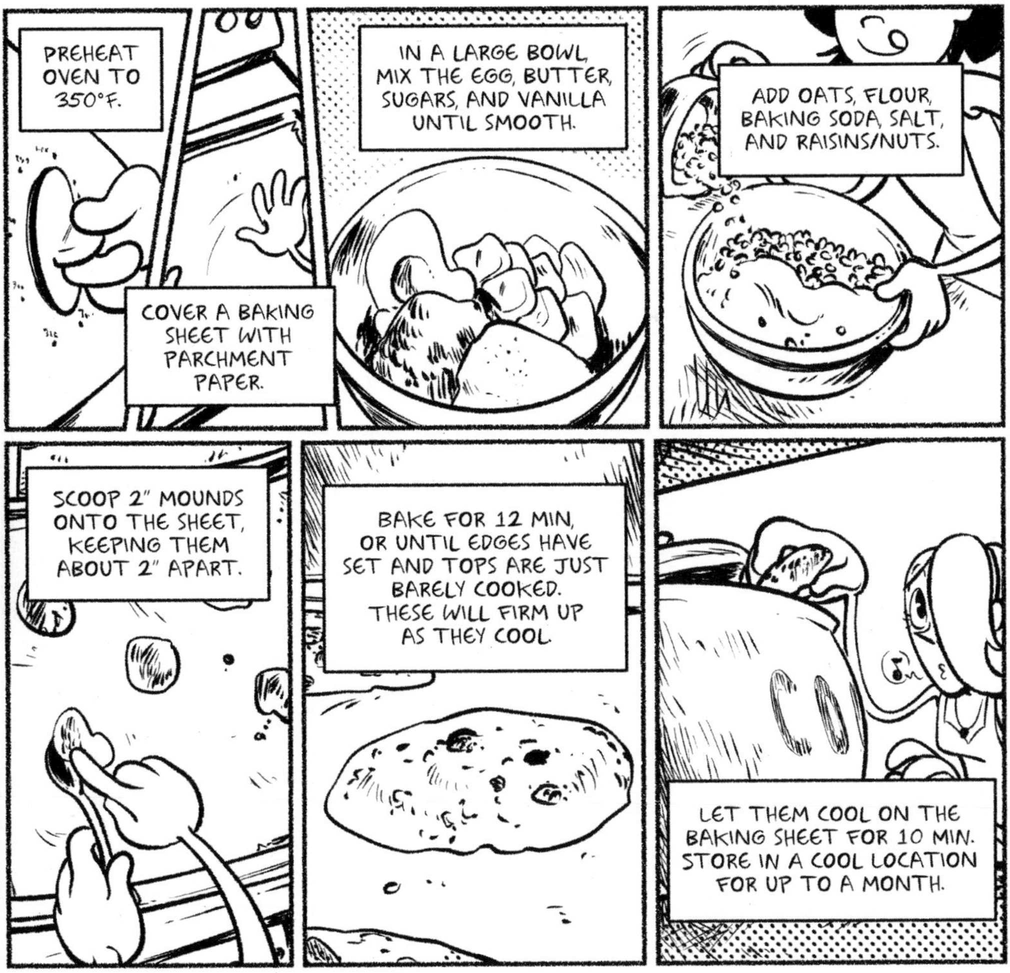
PREHEAT OVEN TO 350°F.
COVER A BAKING SHEET WITH PARCHMENT PAPER.
IN A LARGE BOWL, MIX THE EGG, BUTTER, SUGARS, AND VANILLA UNTIL SMOOTH.
ADD OATS, FLOUR, BAKING SODA, SALT, AND RAISINS/NUTS.
SCOOP 2" MOUNDS ONTO THE SHEET, KEEPING THEM ABOUT 2" APART.
BAKE FOR 12 MIN, OR UNTIL EDGES HAVE SET AND TOPS ARE JUST BARELY COOKED. THESE WILL FIRM UP AS THEY COOL.
LET THEM COOL ON THE BAKING SHEET FOR 10 MIN. STORE IN A COOL LOCATION FOR UP TO A MONTH.

CHOCOLATE CHIP

HANDS ON: 20 MIN
HANDS OFF: 15 MIN

- 2 1/4 CUP ALL-PURPOSE FLOUR
- 1 TSP BAKING SODA
- 1 TSP SALT
- 3/4 CUP GRANULATED SUGAR
- 3/4 CUP BROWN SUGAR
- 1 CUP BUTTER, ROOM TEMPERATURE
- 1 TSP VANILLA EXTRACT
- 2 LARGE EGGS
- 2 CUPS CHOCOLATE CHIPS

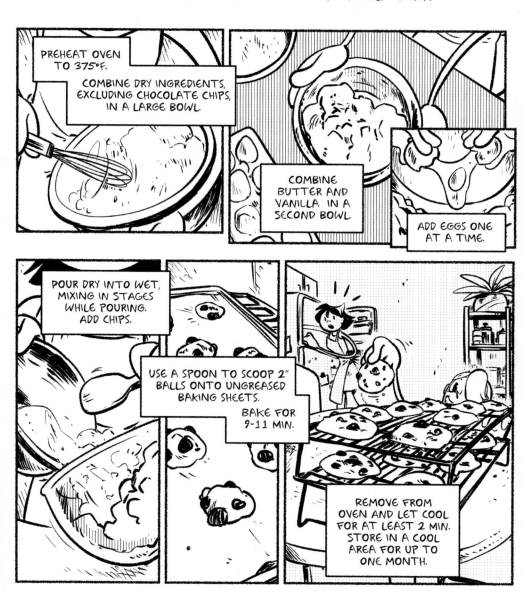

PREHEAT OVEN TO 375°F.

COMBINE DRY INGREDIENTS, EXCLUDING CHOCOLATE CHIPS, IN A LARGE BOWL.

COMBINE BUTTER AND VANILLA IN A SECOND BOWL.

ADD EGGS ONE AT A TIME.

POUR DRY INTO WET, MIXING IN STAGES WHILE POURING. ADD CHIPS.

USE A SPOON TO SCOOP 2" BALLS ONTO UNGREASED BAKING SHEETS.

BAKE FOR 9-11 MIN.

REMOVE FROM OVEN AND LET COOL FOR AT LEAST 2 MIN. STORE IN A COOL AREA FOR UP TO ONE MONTH.

PEANUT BUTTER BLOSSOM COOKIES

HANDS ON: 20 MIN
HANDS OFF: 11 MIN

-2 CUPS ALL PURPOSE FLOUR
-1 TSP BAKING SODA
-1/2 TSP KOSHER SALT
-1/2 CUP GRANULATED SUGAR +
 1/2 ADDITIONAL FOR ROLLING
-1/2 CUP BROWN SUGAR
-1/2 CUP SHORTENING
-1/2 CUP PEANUT BUTTER
-2 LARGE EGGS
-2 TBSP MILK
-1 TSP VANILLA EXTRACT
-50 UNWRAPPED CHOCOLATE KISSES

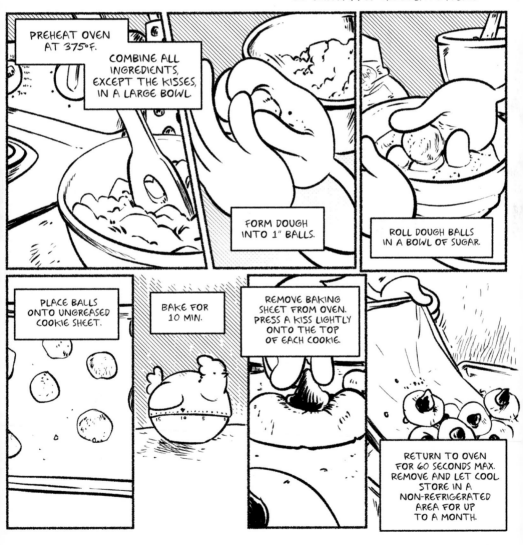

PREHEAT OVEN AT 375°F.

COMBINE ALL INGREDIENTS, EXCEPT THE KISSES, IN A LARGE BOWL.

FORM DOUGH INTO 1" BALLS.

ROLL DOUGH BALLS IN A BOWL OF SUGAR.

PLACE BALLS ONTO UNGREASED COOKIE SHEET.

BAKE FOR 10 MIN.

REMOVE BAKING SHEET FROM OVEN. PRESS A KISS LIGHTLY ONTO THE TOP OF EACH COOKIE.

RETURN TO OVEN FOR 60 SECONDS MAX. REMOVE AND LET COOL. STORE IN A NON-REFRIGERATED AREA FOR UP TO A MONTH.

SUGAR COOKIES

HANDS ON: 15 MIN
HANDS OFF: 10 MIN

- 1 CUP UNSALTED BUTTER, SOFTENED
- 1 CUP GRANULATED SUGAR + 1/2 CUP GRANULATED SUGAR FOR ROLLING
- 1 LARGE EGG
- 1 TBSP VANILLA EXTRACT
- 1 TSP ALMOND EXTRACT (OPTIONAL, BUT IT ADDS AN EXTRA LAYER OF FLAVOR)
- 2 1/2 CUPS ALL-PURPOSE FLOUR
- 1/2 TSP BAKING SODA
- 1/2 TSP BAKING POWDER
- 1/4 TSP KOSHER SALT

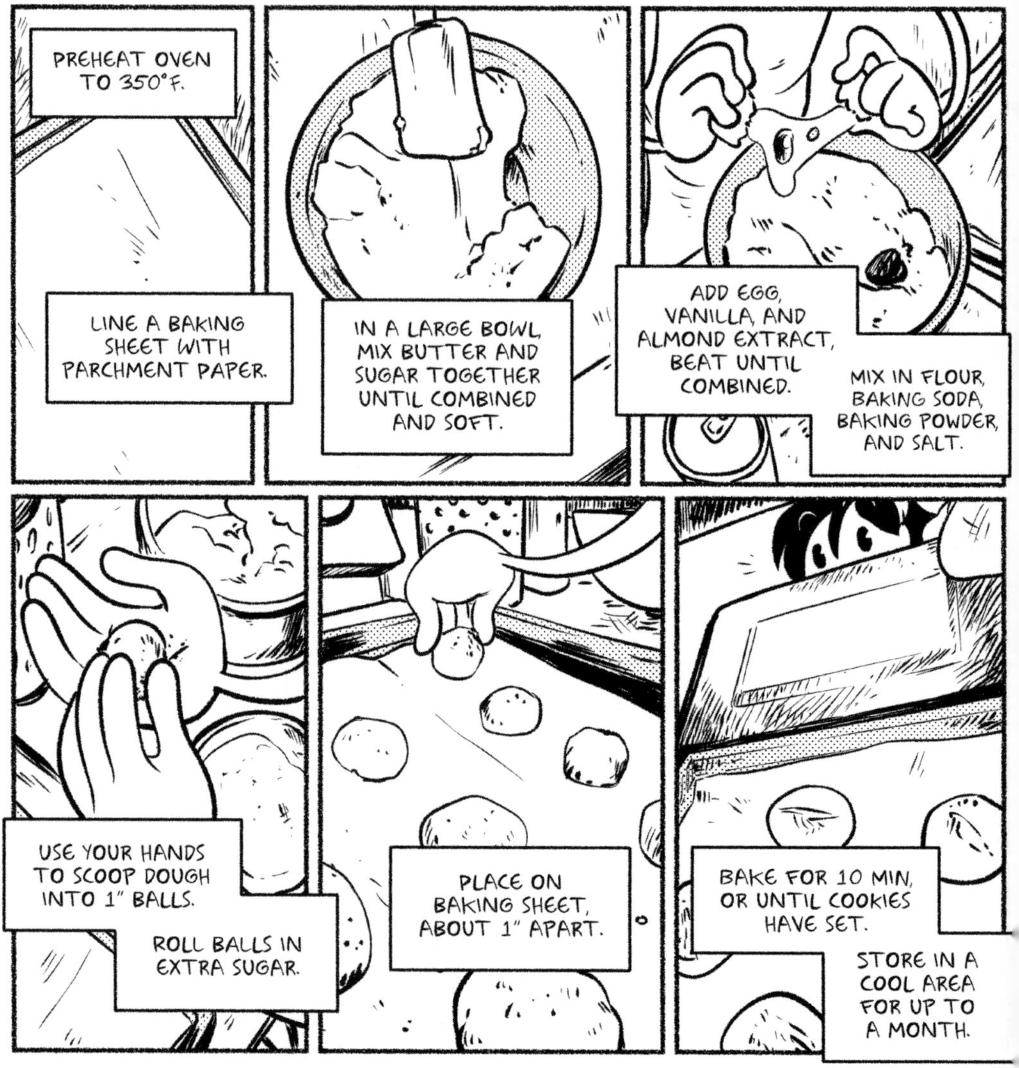
PREHEAT OVEN TO 350°F.
LINE A BAKING SHEET WITH PARCHMENT PAPER.
IN A LARGE BOWL, MIX BUTTER AND SUGAR TOGETHER UNTIL COMBINED AND SOFT.
ADD EGG, VANILLA, AND ALMOND EXTRACT, BEAT UNTIL COMBINED.
MIX IN FLOUR, BAKING SODA, BAKING POWDER, AND SALT.
USE YOUR HANDS TO SCOOP DOUGH INTO 1" BALLS.
ROLL BALLS IN EXTRA SUGAR.
PLACE ON BAKING SHEET, ABOUT 1" APART.
BAKE FOR 10 MIN, OR UNTIL COOKIES HAVE SET.
STORE IN A COOL AREA FOR UP TO A MONTH.

GINGER SNAP COOKIES

HANDS ON: 20 MIN
HANDS OFF: 27 MIN

- 1/2 CUP COCONUT OIL
- 1/2 CUP WATER, WARM
- 1 1/2 CUPS PACKED BROWN SUGAR
- 1/2 CUP MOLASSES
- 1 TBSP VANILLA EXTRACT
- 3 1/4 CUPS ALL PURPOSE FLOUR
- 1 TBSP BAKING SODA
- 1/2 TSP SALT
- 1 TBSP GINGER, GROUND OR CHOPPED
- 1 TBSP CINNAMON
- 1/2 TSP NUTMEG
- 1/2 CUP GRANULATED SUGAR, FOR ROLLING

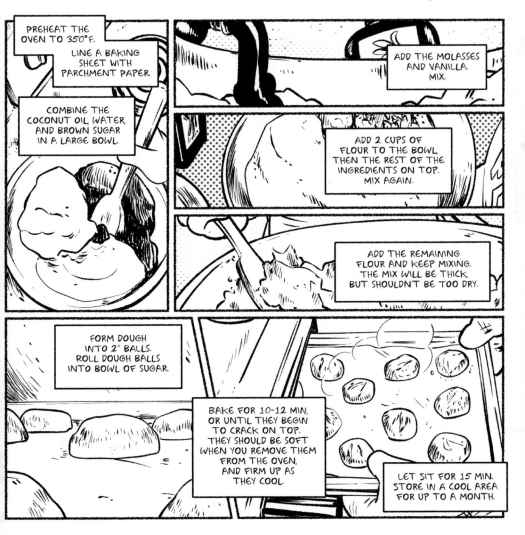

PREHEAT THE OVEN TO 350°F.

LINE A BAKING SHEET WITH PARCHMENT PAPER.

COMBINE THE COCONUT OIL, WATER, AND BROWN SUGAR IN A LARGE BOWL.

ADD THE MOLASSES AND VANILLA. MIX.

ADD 2 CUPS OF FLOUR TO THE BOWL, THEN THE REST OF THE INGREDIENTS ON TOP. MIX AGAIN.

ADD THE REMAINING FLOUR AND KEEP MIXING. THE MIX WILL BE THICK, BUT SHOULDN'T BE TOO DRY.

FORM DOUGH INTO 2" BALLS. ROLL DOUGH BALLS INTO BOWL OF SUGAR.

BAKE FOR 10-12 MIN, OR UNTIL THEY BEGIN TO CRACK ON TOP. THEY SHOULD BE SOFT WHEN YOU REMOVE THEM FROM THE OVEN, AND FIRM UP AS THEY COOL.

LET SIT FOR 15 MIN. STORE IN A COOL AREA FOR UP TO A MONTH.

LEMON BARS

HANDS ON: 30 MIN
HANDS OFF: 1 HR

CRUST:
- 12 TBSP UNSALTED BUTTER
- 6 TBSP SUGAR
- 1 1/2 CUPS FLOUR

FILLING:
- 1 1/2 CUPS SUGAR
- 1/4 CUP FLOUR
- 4 LARGE EGGS
- 3/4 CUP LEMON JUICE

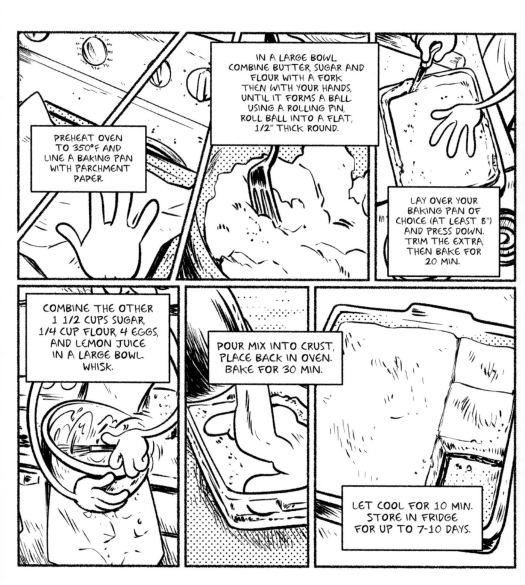

PREHEAT OVEN TO 350°F AND LINE A BAKING PAN WITH PARCHMENT PAPER.

IN A LARGE BOWL, COMBINE BUTTER, SUGAR AND FLOUR WITH A FORK THEN WITH YOUR HANDS, UNTIL IT FORMS A BALL. USING A ROLLING PIN, ROLL BALL INTO A FLAT, 1/2" THICK ROUND.

LAY OVER YOUR BAKING PAN OF CHOICE (AT LEAST 8") AND PRESS DOWN. TRIM THE EXTRA THEN BAKE FOR 20 MIN.

COMBINE THE OTHER 1 1/2 CUPS SUGAR, 1/4 CUP FLOUR, 4 EGGS, AND LEMON JUICE IN A LARGE BOWL. WHISK.

POUR MIX INTO CRUST, PLACE BACK IN OVEN. BAKE FOR 30 MIN.

LET COOL FOR 10 MIN. STORE IN FRIDGE FOR UP TO 7-10 DAYS.

see notes for more!

BROWNIES

HANDS ON: 20 MIN
HANDS OFF: 35 MIN

- 1 1/2 CUPS CHOCOLATE CHIPS
- 1 CUP UNSALTED BUTTER + 1 TBSP TO GREASE BAKING PAN
- 1 1/2 CUPS GRANULATED SUGAR
- 1 TSP VANILLA
- 4 LARGE EGGS
- 1 1/2 CUPS ALL-PURPOSE FLOUR
- 1 TSP KOSHER SALT

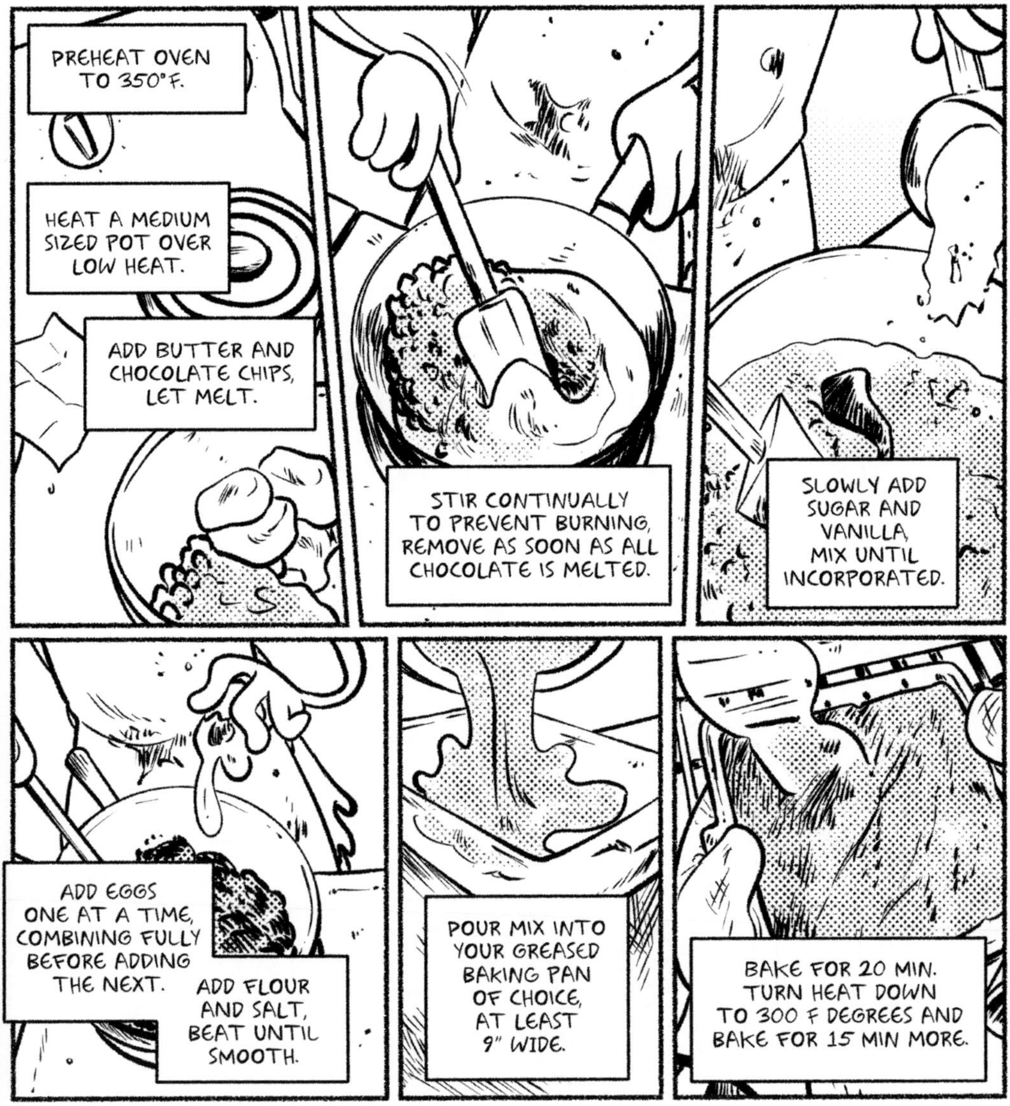
PREHEAT OVEN TO 350°F.
HEAT A MEDIUM SIZED POT OVER LOW HEAT.
ADD BUTTER AND CHOCOLATE CHIPS, LET MELT.
STIR CONTINUALLY TO PREVENT BURNING, REMOVE AS SOON AS ALL CHOCOLATE IS MELTED.
SLOWLY ADD SUGAR AND VANILLA, MIX UNTIL INCORPORATED.
ADD EGGS ONE AT A TIME, COMBINING FULLY BEFORE ADDING THE NEXT.
ADD FLOUR AND SALT, BEAT UNTIL SMOOTH.
POUR MIX INTO YOUR GREASED BAKING PAN OF CHOICE, AT LEAST 9" WIDE.
BAKE FOR 20 MIN. TURN HEAT DOWN TO 300 F DEGREES AND BAKE FOR 15 MIN MORE.

RICE CEREAL BARS

HANDS ON: 20 MIN
HANDS OFF: 10 MIN

- 6 CUPS RICE CEREAL
- 4 CUPS MINI MARSHMALLOWS
- 3 TBSP BUTTER
- 1 TSP KOSHER SALT

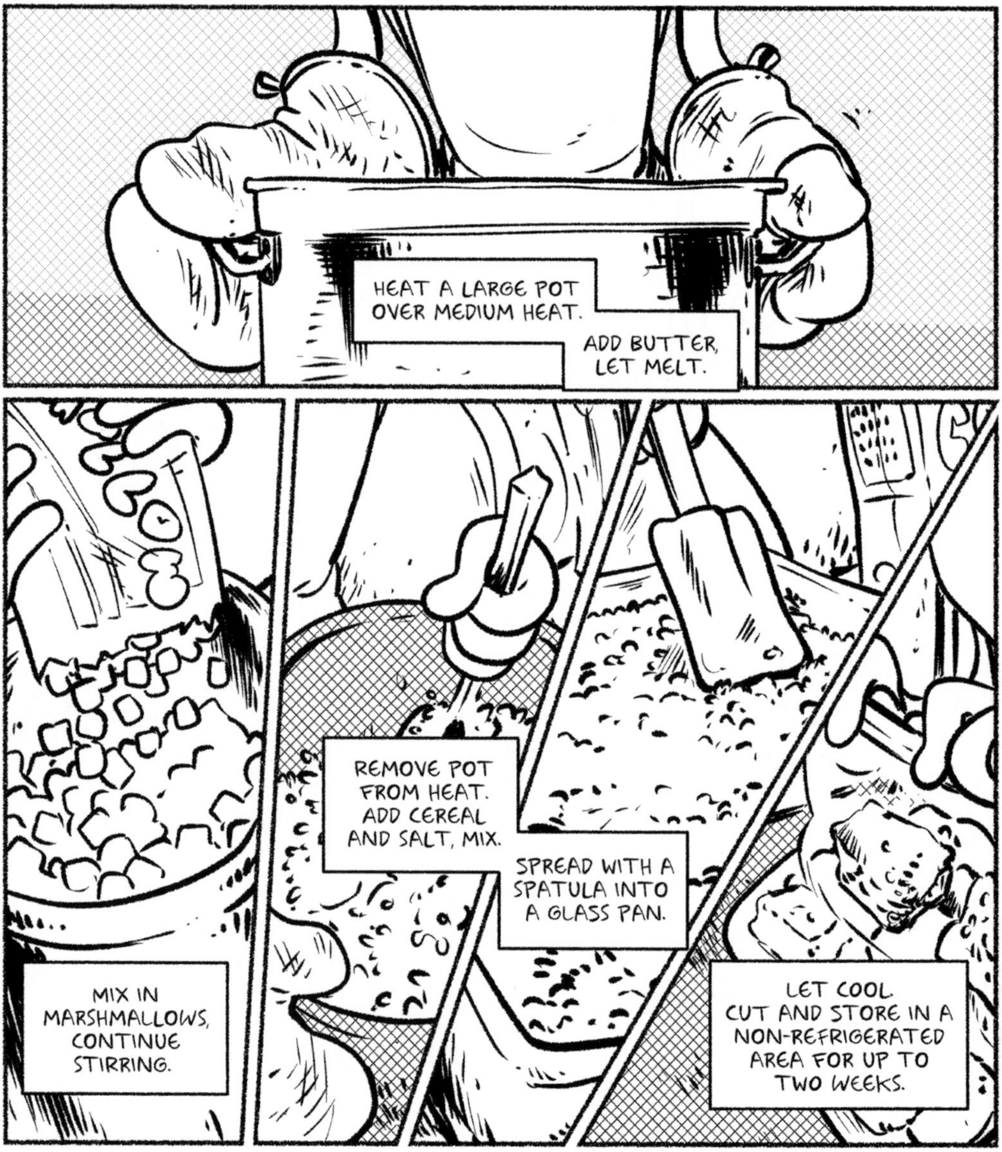
HEAT A LARGE POT OVER MEDIUM HEAT.
ADD BUTTER, LET MELT.
MIX IN MARSHMALLOWS, CONTINUE STIRRING.
REMOVE POT FROM HEAT. ADD CEREAL AND SALT, MIX.
SPREAD WITH A SPATULA INTO A GLASS PAN.
LET COOL. CUT AND STORE IN A NON-REFRIGERATED AREA FOR UP TO TWO WEEKS.

STIR FRY

HANDS ON: 20 MIN

-3 TBSP OIL OF CHOICE
 (PEANUT, VEGETABLE, CANOLA, OR SAFFLOWER)
-1 LB PROTEIN OF CHOICE
 (CHICKEN, PORK, TOFU, SEITAN),
 CUT INTO SMALL PIECES
-1 LB VEGETABLES OF CHOICE
 (BROCCOLI, PEPPERS, CARROTS,
 SNAP PEAS, ONIONS, GREEN BEANS, ETC),
 CUT INTO SMALL PIECES

-1 TBSP GINGER, CHOPPED
-1 TBSP GARLIC, CHOPPED
-1 TBSP BASIL
-1 TBSP CILANTRO
-1 TSP RED PEPPER FLAKES
-1 TSP BLACK PEPPER
 (ADD OTHER SPICES AS NEEDED)
-1/2 CUP SOY SAUCE
-1 TBSP RICE VINEGAR
-1 TBSP SUGAR

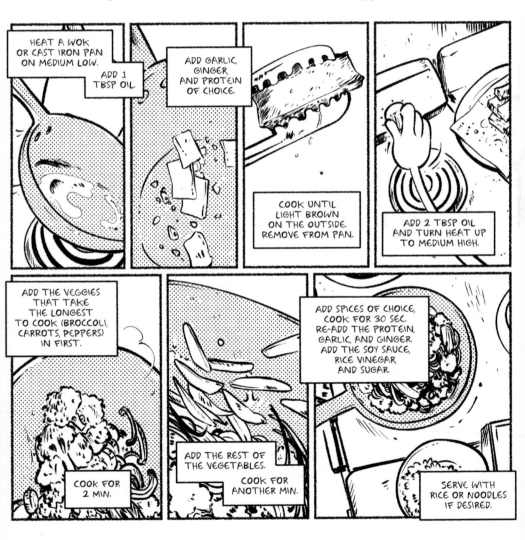

HEAT A WOK OR CAST IRON PAN ON MEDIUM LOW. ADD 1 TBSP OIL

ADD GARLIC, GINGER, AND PROTEIN OF CHOICE.

COOK UNTIL LIGHT BROWN ON THE OUTSIDE. REMOVE FROM PAN.

ADD 2 TBSP OIL AND TURN HEAT UP TO MEDIUM HIGH.

ADD THE VEGGIES THAT TAKE THE LONGEST TO COOK (BROCCOLI, CARROTS, PEPPERS) IN FIRST.

COOK FOR 2 MIN.

ADD THE REST OF THE VEGETABLES. COOK FOR ANOTHER MIN.

ADD SPICES OF CHOICE, COOK FOR 30 SEC. RE-ADD THE PROTEIN, GARLIC, AND GINGER. ADD THE SOY SAUCE, RICE VINEGAR, AND SUGAR.

SERVE WITH RICE OR NOODLES IF DESIRED.

POT PIE

HANDS ON: 30 MIN
HANDS OFF: 45 MIN

FILLING:
- 3 TBSP GARLIC, CHOPPED
- 1 TBSP UNSALTED BUTTER
- 1/2 TBSP SALT
- 1/2 TBSP BLACK PEPPER
- 1/2 PAPRIKA
- 1 TBSP ROSEMARY
- 1 TSP THYME
- 1 TSP CUMIN
- 1 TBSP SOY SAUCE
- 1/4 CUP ALL-PURPOSE FLOUR
- 2 CUPS BROTH OF CHOICE (VEGETABLE RECOMMENDED)
- 1/2 CUP MUSHROOMS, CHOPPED
- 3/4 CUP YELLOW ONION, CHOPPED
- 1/4 CUP CARROTS, CHOPPED
- 1-2 CUPS OTHER VEGETABLES OF CHOICE

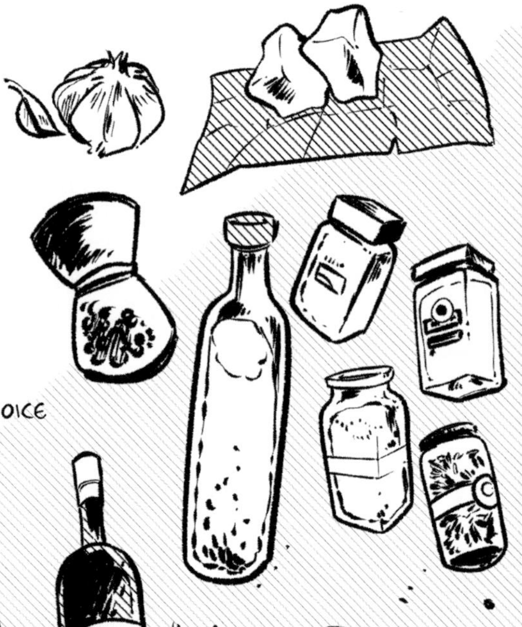

CRUST:
- 1 CUP ALL-PURPOSE FLOUR
- 1 1/2 TSP BAKING POWDER
- 1/4 TSP KOSHER SALT
- 1 TBSP UNSALTED BUTTER, ROOM TEMPERATURE
- 1/2 CUP MILK
- 1 EGG

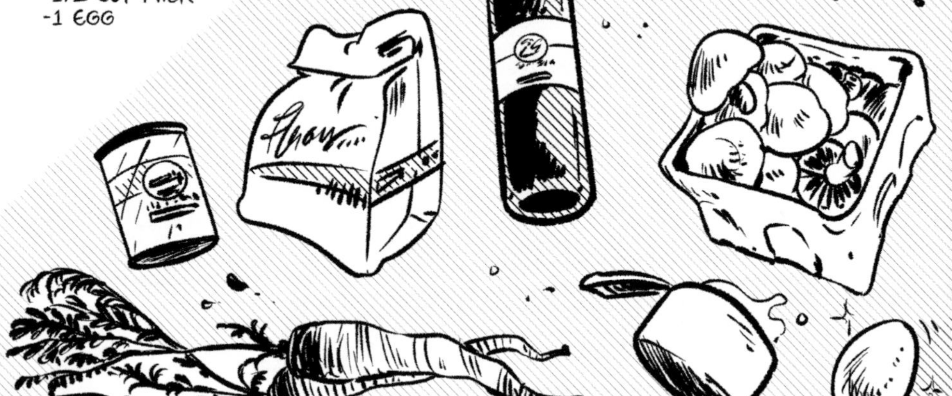
Flour

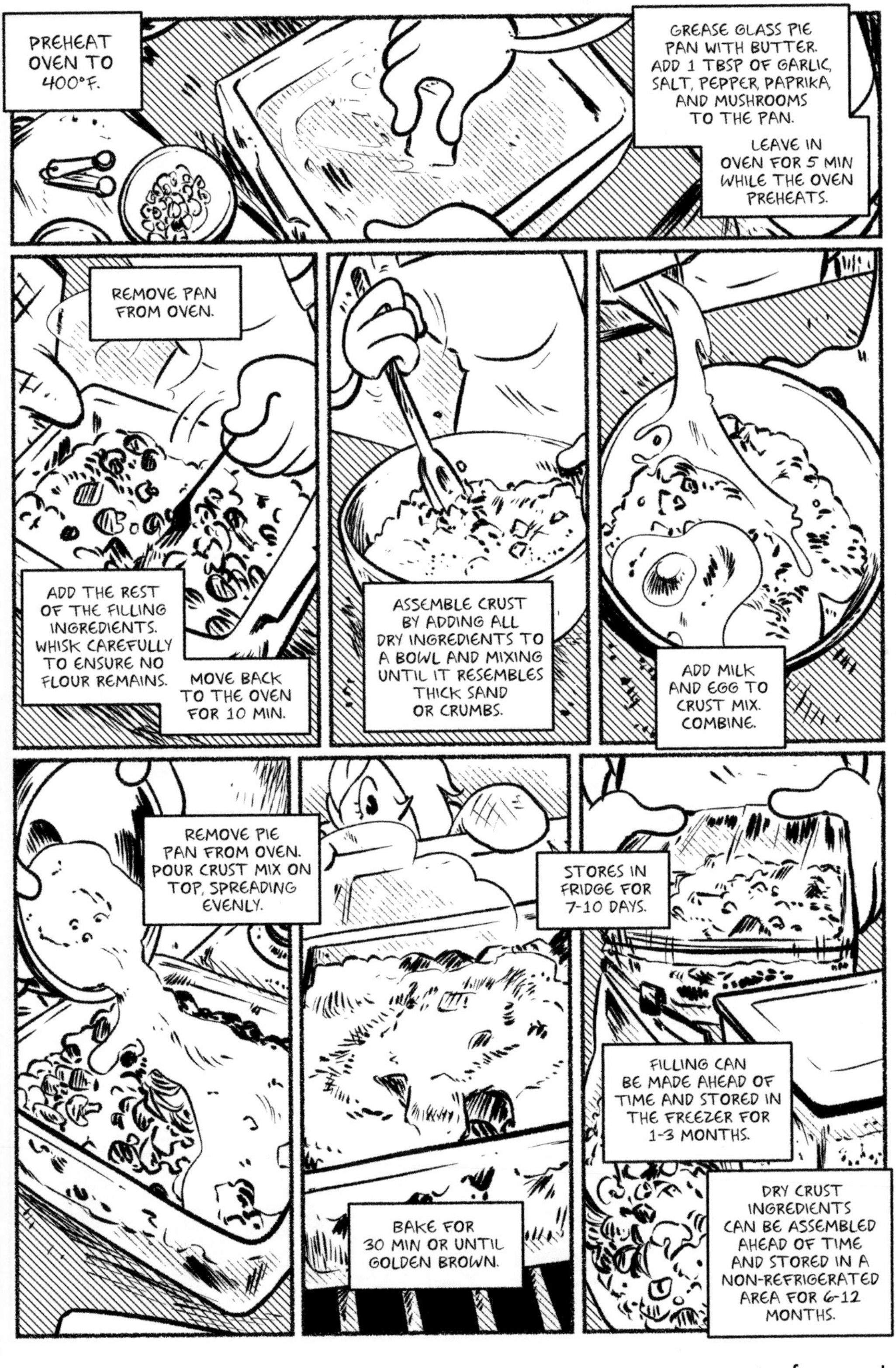
PREHEAT OVEN TO 400°F.
GREASE GLASS PIE PAN WITH BUTTER. ADD 1 TBSP OF GARLIC, SALT, PEPPER, PAPRIKA, AND MUSHROOMS TO THE PAN.
LEAVE IN OVEN FOR 5 MIN WHILE THE OVEN PREHEATS.
REMOVE PAN FROM OVEN.
ADD THE REST OF THE FILLING INGREDIENTS. WHISK CAREFULLY TO ENSURE NO FLOUR REMAINS.
MOVE BACK TO THE OVEN FOR 10 MIN.
ASSEMBLE CRUST BY ADDING ALL DRY INGREDIENTS TO A BOWL AND MIXING UNTIL IT RESEMBLES THICK SAND OR CRUMBS.
ADD MILK AND EGG TO CRUST MIX. COMBINE.
REMOVE PIE PAN FROM OVEN. POUR CRUST MIX ON TOP, SPREADING EVENLY.
BAKE FOR 30 MIN OR UNTIL GOLDEN BROWN.
STORES IN FRIDGE FOR 7-10 DAYS.
FILLING CAN BE MADE AHEAD OF TIME AND STORED IN THE FREEZER FOR 1-3 MONTHS.
DRY CRUST INGREDIENTS CAN BE ASSEMBLED AHEAD OF TIME AND STORED IN A NON-REFRIGERATED AREA FOR 6-12 MONTHS.

see notes for more!

POT STICKERS

HANDS ON: 1 HR 10 MIN
HANDS OFF: 20 MIN

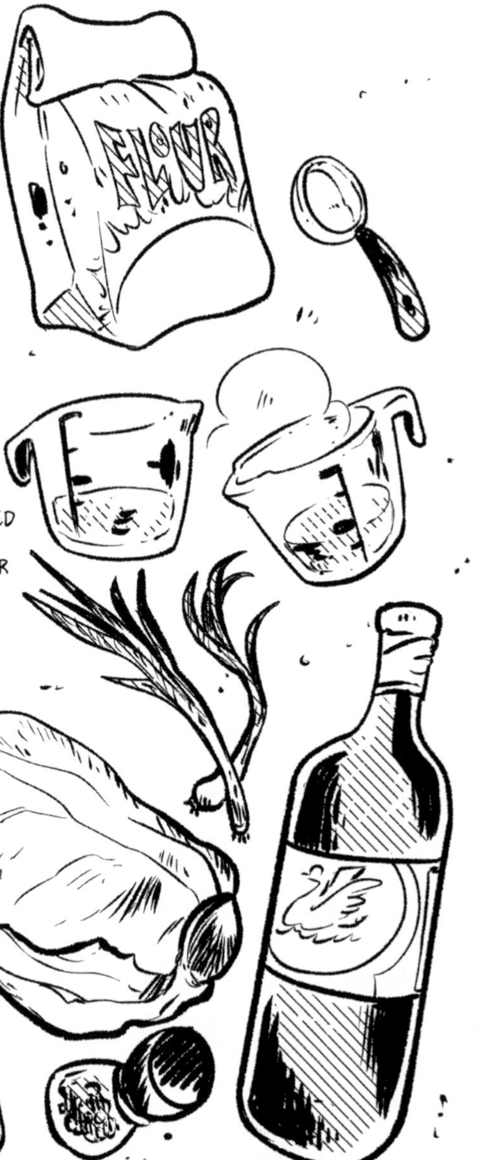
FLOUR

WRAPPERS:
- 2 1/2 CUPS ALL-PURPOSE FLOUR
- 1/4 TEASPOON SALT
- 2/3 CUP HOT WATER
- 1/3 CUP COLD WATER + 1/4 CUP EXTRA FOR STEAMING

FILLING CAN BE ANYTHING YOU HAVE KICKING AROUND IN YOUR FRIDGE OR PANTRY, SO SWAP OUT INGREDIENTS AS NEEDED. THE FOLLOWING IS A GOOD PLACE TO START:

- 1/2 TSP KOSHER SALT
- 1 CUP NAPA CABBAGE OR SPINACH, CHOPPED
- 1 TBSP SOY SAUCE
- 1 TBSP RICE WINE OR APPLE CIDER VINEGAR
- 1/2 TSP CORNSTARCH
- 1 TSP BLACK PEPPER OR WHITE PEPPER
- 2 TBSP GREEN ONIONS, CHOPPED
- 1 TBSP GARLIC, CHOPPED
- 1/2 CUP MUSHROOMS, CHOPPED

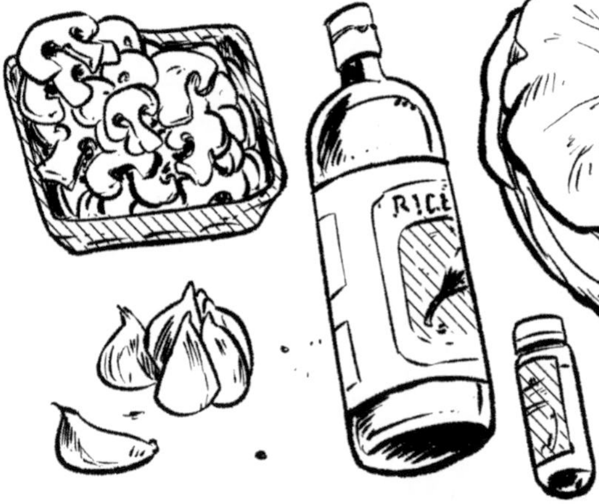
RICE

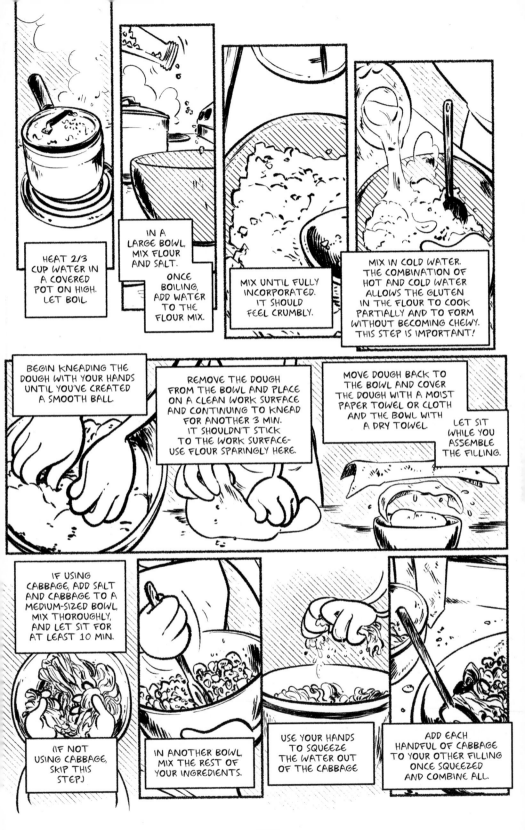

HEAT 2/3 CUP WATER IN A COVERED POT ON HIGH. LET BOIL.

IN A LARGE BOWL, MIX FLOUR AND SALT.

ONCE BOILING, ADD WATER TO THE FLOUR MIX.

MIX UNTIL FULLY INCORPORATED. IT SHOULD FEEL CRUMBLY.

MIX IN COLD WATER. THE COMBINATION OF HOT AND COLD WATER ALLOWS THE GLUTEN IN THE FLOUR TO COOK PARTIALLY AND TO FORM WITHOUT BECOMING CHEWY. THIS STEP IS IMPORTANT!

BEGIN KNEADING THE DOUGH WITH YOUR HANDS UNTIL YOU'VE CREATED A SMOOTH BALL

REMOVE THE DOUGH FROM THE BOWL AND PLACE ON A CLEAN WORK SURFACE AND CONTINUING TO KNEAD FOR ANOTHER 3 MIN. IT SHOULDN'T STICK TO THE WORK SURFACE- USE FLOUR SPARINGLY HERE.

MOVE DOUGH BACK TO THE BOWL AND COVER THE DOUGH WITH A MOIST PAPER TOWEL OR CLOTH AND THE BOWL WITH A DRY TOWEL

LET SIT WHILE YOU ASSEMBLE THE FILLING.

IF USING CABBAGE, ADD SALT AND CABBAGE TO A MEDIUM-SIZED BOWL, MIX THOROUGHLY, AND LET SIT FOR AT LEAST 10 MIN.

(IF NOT USING CABBAGE, SKIP THIS STEP)

IN ANOTHER BOWL, MIX THE REST OF YOUR INGREDIENTS.

USE YOUR HANDS TO SQUEEZE THE WATER OUT OF THE CABBAGE

ADD EACH HANDFUL OF CABBAGE TO YOUR OTHER FILLING ONCE SQUEEZED AND COMBINE ALL.

197

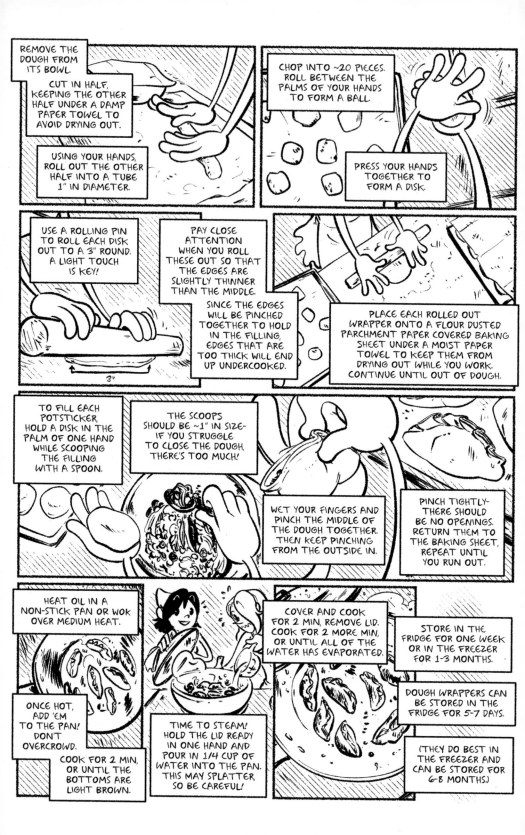

REMOVE THE DOUGH FROM ITS BOWL.

CUT IN HALF, KEEPING THE OTHER HALF UNDER A DAMP PAPER TOWEL TO AVOID DRYING OUT.

USING YOUR HANDS, ROLL OUT THE OTHER HALF INTO A TUBE 1" IN DIAMETER.

CHOP INTO ~20 PIECES. ROLL BETWEEN THE PALMS OF YOUR HANDS TO FORM A BALL.

PRESS YOUR HANDS TOGETHER TO FORM A DISK.

USE A ROLLING PIN TO ROLL EACH DISK OUT TO A 3" ROUND. A LIGHT TOUCH IS KEY!

PAY CLOSE ATTENTION WHEN YOU ROLL THESE OUT SO THAT THE EDGES ARE SLIGHTLY THINNER THAN THE MIDDLE.

SINCE THE EDGES WILL BE PINCHED TOGETHER TO HOLD IN THE FILLING, EDGES THAT ARE TOO THICK WILL END UP UNDERCOOKED.

PLACE EACH ROLLED OUT WRAPPER ONTO A FLOUR DUSTED PARCHMENT PAPER COVERED BAKING SHEET UNDER A MOIST PAPER TOWEL TO KEEP THEM FROM DRYING OUT WHILE YOU WORK. CONTINUE UNTIL OUT OF DOUGH.

TO FILL EACH POTSTICKER, HOLD A DISK IN THE PALM OF ONE HAND WHILE SCOOPING THE FILLING WITH A SPOON.

THE SCOOPS SHOULD BE ~1" IN SIZE- IF YOU STRUGGLE TO CLOSE THE DOUGH, THERE'S TOO MUCH!

WET YOUR FINGERS AND PINCH THE MIDDLE OF THE DOUGH TOGETHER. THEN KEEP PINCHING FROM THE OUTSIDE IN.

PINCH TIGHTLY- THERE SHOULD BE NO OPENINGS. RETURN THEM TO THE BAKING SHEET, REPEAT UNTIL YOU RUN OUT.

HEAT OIL IN A NON-STICK PAN OR WOK OVER MEDIUM HEAT.

ONCE HOT, ADD 'EM TO THE PAN! DON'T OVERCROWD.

COOK FOR 2 MIN, OR UNTIL THE BOTTOMS ARE LIGHT BROWN.

TIME TO STEAM! HOLD THE LID READY IN ONE HAND AND POUR IN 1/4 CUP OF WATER INTO THE PAN. THIS MAY SPLATTER, SO BE CAREFUL!

COVER AND COOK FOR 2 MIN, REMOVE LID. COOK FOR 2 MORE MIN, OR UNTIL ALL OF THE WATER HAS EVAPORATED.

STORE IN THE FRIDGE FOR ONE WEEK OR IN THE FREEZER FOR 1-3 MONTHS.

DOUGH WRAPPERS CAN BE STORED IN THE FRIDGE FOR 5-7 DAYS.

(THEY DO BEST IN THE FREEZER AND CAN BE STORED FOR 6-8 MONTHS)

FRITTATA

HANDS ON: 10 MIN
HANDS OFF: 25 MIN

- 12 EGGS
- 3 TBSP DAIRY (HEAVY CREAM, WHOLE MILK, SOUR CREAM, OR UNFLAVORED GREEK OR UNFLAVORED REGULAR YOGURT)
- 2 TSP SALT
- 1 TSP BLACK PEPPER
- 1 CUP CHEESE OF CHOICE
- 3-5 CUPS VEGETABLES OF CHOICE, PREFERABLY PRECOOKED/LEFTOVERS
- 1 TBSP OLIVE OIL + 1 TBSP OLIVE OIL FOR CASSEROLE DISH IF USING THE CASSEROLE METHOD

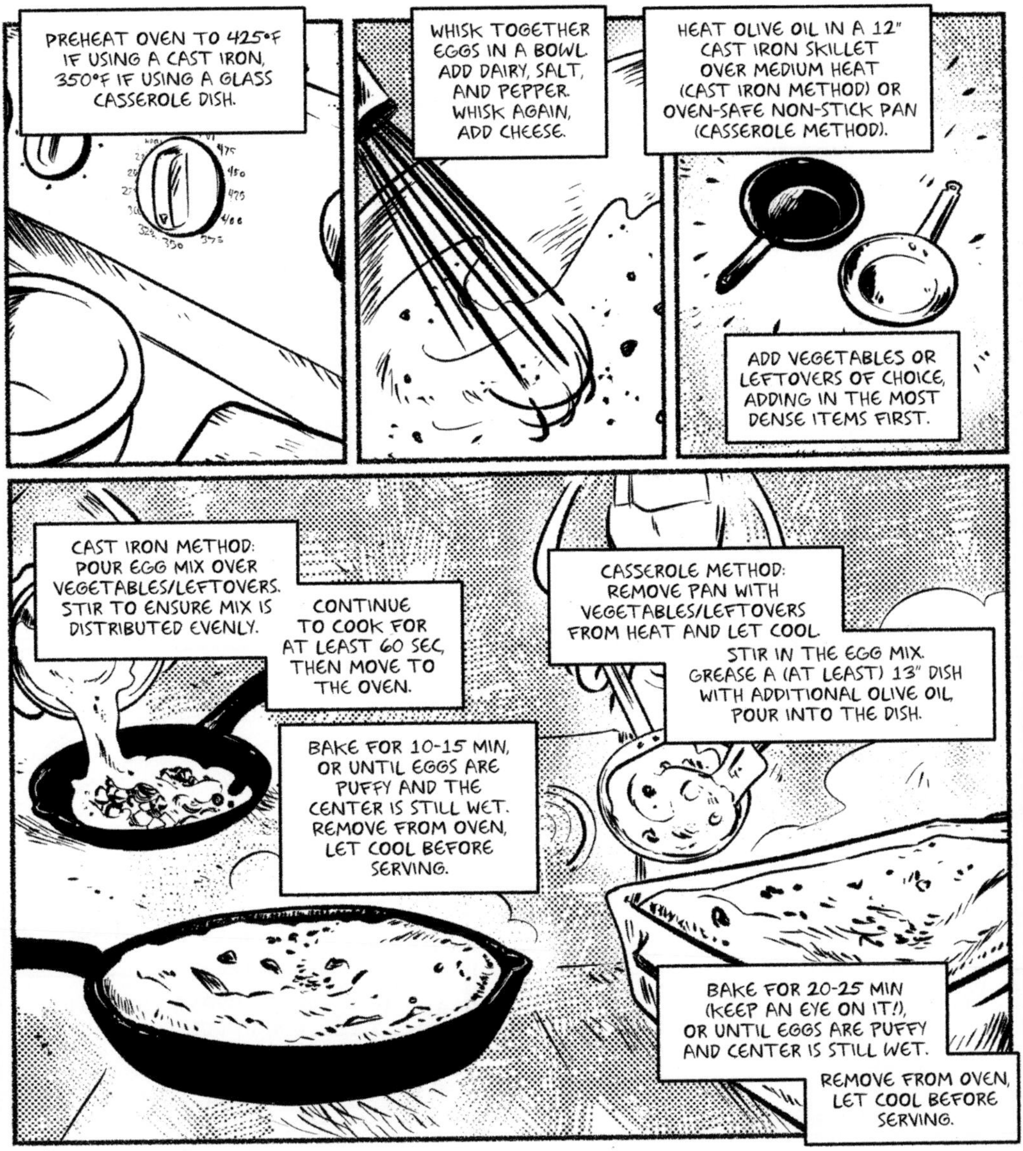
PREHEAT OVEN TO 425°F IF USING A CAST IRON, 350°F IF USING A GLASS CASSEROLE DISH.
WHISK TOGETHER EGGS IN A BOWL. ADD DAIRY, SALT, AND PEPPER. WHISK AGAIN, ADD CHEESE.
HEAT OLIVE OIL IN A 12" CAST IRON SKILLET OVER MEDIUM HEAT (CAST IRON METHOD) OR OVEN-SAFE NON-STICK PAN (CASSEROLE METHOD).
ADD VEGETABLES OR LEFTOVERS OF CHOICE, ADDING IN THE MOST DENSE ITEMS FIRST.
CAST IRON METHOD: POUR EGG MIX OVER VEGETABLES/LEFTOVERS. STIR TO ENSURE MIX IS DISTRIBUTED EVENLY.
CONTINUE TO COOK FOR AT LEAST 60 SEC, THEN MOVE TO THE OVEN.
BAKE FOR 10-15 MIN, OR UNTIL EGGS ARE PUFFY AND THE CENTER IS STILL WET. REMOVE FROM OVEN, LET COOL BEFORE SERVING.
CASSEROLE METHOD: REMOVE PAN WITH VEGETABLES/LEFTOVERS FROM HEAT AND LET COOL.
STIR IN THE EGG MIX. GREASE A (AT LEAST) 13" DISH WITH ADDITIONAL OLIVE OIL, POUR INTO THE DISH.
BAKE FOR 20-25 MIN (KEEP AN EYE ON IT!), OR UNTIL EGGS ARE PUFFY AND CENTER IS STILL WET.
REMOVE FROM OVEN, LET COOL BEFORE SERVING.

see notes for more!

LEFTOVER SOUP

HANDS ON: 15 MIN
HANDS OFF: 45 MIN

THE INGREDIENTS LISTED ARE ONLY A STARTING POINT- ADJUST THIS ACCORDING TO WHATEVER YOU MIGHT HAVE LEFT AT THE END OF THE WEEK OR WHATEVER YOU MIGHT BE ABLE TO GET YOUR HANDS ON. IT'S FLEXIBLE!

- 1 TSP OLIVE OIL
- 1 CUP YELLOW ONION, CHOPPED
- 1 CUP CARROTS, CHOPPED
- 2 CUPS SQUASH OF CHOICE, CUBED
- 1/2 TSP GARLIC, MINCED OR POWDERED
- 1 TBSP KOSHER SALT
- 1 TBSP BLACK PEPPER
- 1/2 TSP CUMIN
- 1 TSP SMOKED PAPRIKA
- 1 TSP CAYENNE
- 6 CUPS BROTH OF CHOICE, VEGETABLE PREFERRED
- 1 CUP RICE, UNCOOKED (IF USING PRECOOKED, COOKING TIME WILL CHANGE AS INDICATED)
- 2 CUPS LEAFY GREEN OF CHOICE

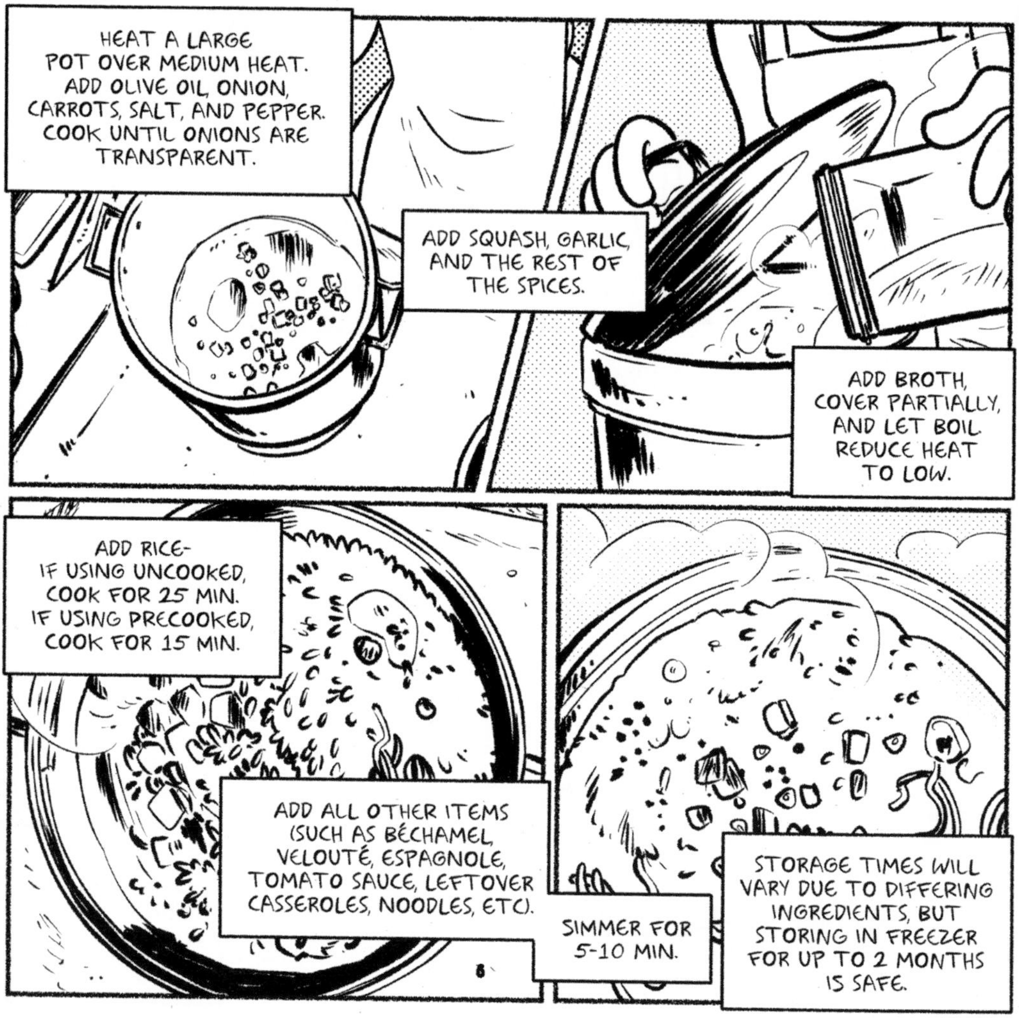
HEAT A LARGE POT OVER MEDIUM HEAT. ADD OLIVE OIL, ONION, CARROTS, SALT, AND PEPPER. COOK UNTIL ONIONS ARE TRANSPARENT.
ADD SQUASH, GARLIC, AND THE REST OF THE SPICES.
ADD BROTH, COVER PARTIALLY, AND LET BOIL. REDUCE HEAT TO LOW.
ADD RICE- IF USING UNCOOKED, COOK FOR 25 MIN. IF USING PRECOOKED, COOK FOR 15 MIN.
ADD ALL OTHER ITEMS (SUCH AS BÉCHAMEL, VELOUTÉ, ESPAGNOLE, TOMATO SAUCE, LEFTOVER CASSEROLES, NOODLES, ETC).
SIMMER FOR 5-10 MIN.
STORAGE TIMES WILL VARY DUE TO DIFFERING INGREDIENTS, BUT STORING IN FREEZER FOR UP TO 2 MONTHS IS SAFE.

COFFEE

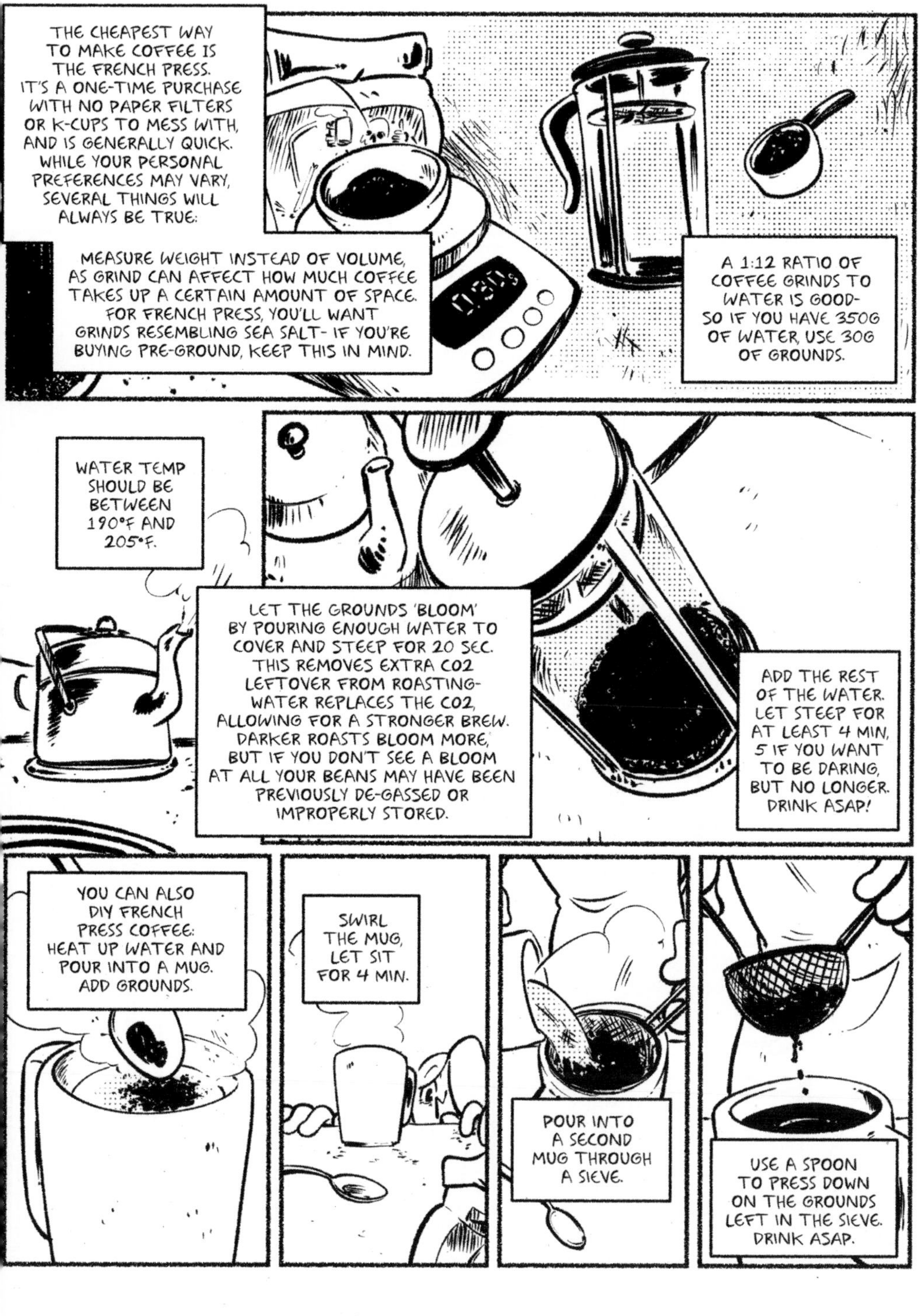
THE CHEAPEST WAY TO MAKE COFFEE IS THE FRENCH PRESS. IT'S A ONE-TIME PURCHASE WITH NO PAPER FILTERS OR K-CUPS TO MESS WITH, AND IS GENERALLY QUICK. WHILE YOUR PERSONAL PREFERENCES MAY VARY, SEVERAL THINGS WILL ALWAYS BE TRUE:
MEASURE WEIGHT INSTEAD OF VOLUME, AS GRIND CAN AFFECT HOW MUCH COFFEE TAKES UP A CERTAIN AMOUNT OF SPACE. FOR FRENCH PRESS, YOU'LL WANT GRINDS RESEMBLING SEA SALT- IF YOU'RE BUYING PRE-GROUND, KEEP THIS IN MIND.
A 1:12 RATIO OF COFFEE GRINDS TO WATER IS GOOD- SO IF YOU HAVE 350G OF WATER, USE 30G OF GROUNDS.
WATER TEMP SHOULD BE BETWEEN 190°F AND 205°F.
LET THE GROUNDS 'BLOOM' BY POURING ENOUGH WATER TO COVER AND STEEP FOR 20 SEC. THIS REMOVES EXTRA CO2 LEFTOVER FROM ROASTING- WATER REPLACES THE CO2, ALLOWING FOR A STRONGER BREW. DARKER ROASTS BLOOM MORE, BUT IF YOU DON'T SEE A BLOOM AT ALL YOUR BEANS MAY HAVE BEEN PREVIOUSLY DE-GASSED OR IMPROPERLY STORED.
ADD THE REST OF THE WATER. LET STEEP FOR AT LEAST 4 MIN, 5 IF YOU WANT TO BE DARING, BUT NO LONGER. DRINK ASAP!
YOU CAN ALSO DIY FRENCH PRESS COFFEE: HEAT UP WATER AND POUR INTO A MUG. ADD GROUNDS.
SWIRL THE MUG, LET SIT FOR 4 MIN.
POUR INTO A SECOND MUG THROUGH A SIEVE.
USE A SPOON TO PRESS DOWN ON THE GROUNDS LEFT IN THE SIEVE. DRINK ASAP.

COLDBREW COFFEE

HANDS ON: 15 MIN
HANDS OFF: 24 HOURS

-230G COFFEE BEANS,
 COARSE GRIND
8 CUPS WATER
-COFFEE GRINDER
-2 2-QUART JARS WITH LIDS
-CHEESECLOTH

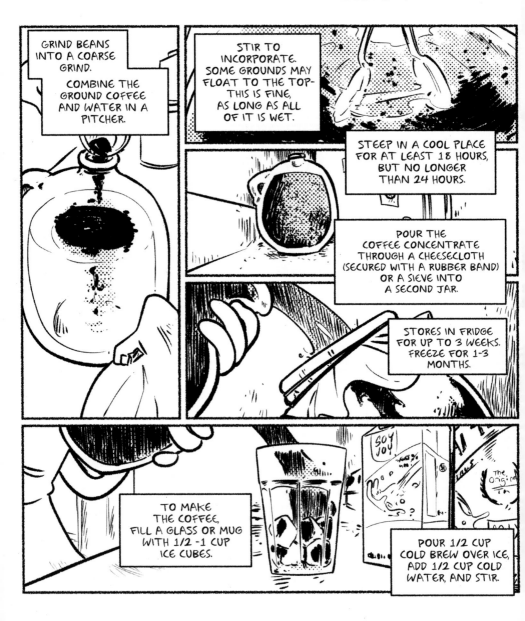

GRIND BEANS INTO A COARSE GRIND.

COMBINE THE GROUND COFFEE AND WATER IN A PITCHER.

STIR TO INCORPORATE. SOME GROUNDS MAY FLOAT TO THE TOP- THIS IS FINE, AS LONG AS ALL OF IT IS WET.

STEEP IN A COOL PLACE FOR AT LEAST 18 HOURS, BUT NO LONGER THAN 24 HOURS.

POUR THE COFFEE CONCENTRATE THROUGH A CHEESECLOTH (SECURED WITH A RUBBER BAND) OR A SIEVE INTO A SECOND JAR.

STORES IN FRIDGE FOR UP TO 3 WEEKS. FREEZE FOR 1-3 MONTHS.

TO MAKE THE COFFEE, FILL A GLASS OR MUG WITH 1/2 -1 CUP ICE CUBES.

POUR 1/2 CUP COLD BREW OVER ICE, ADD 1/2 CUP COLD WATER, AND STIR.

TEA

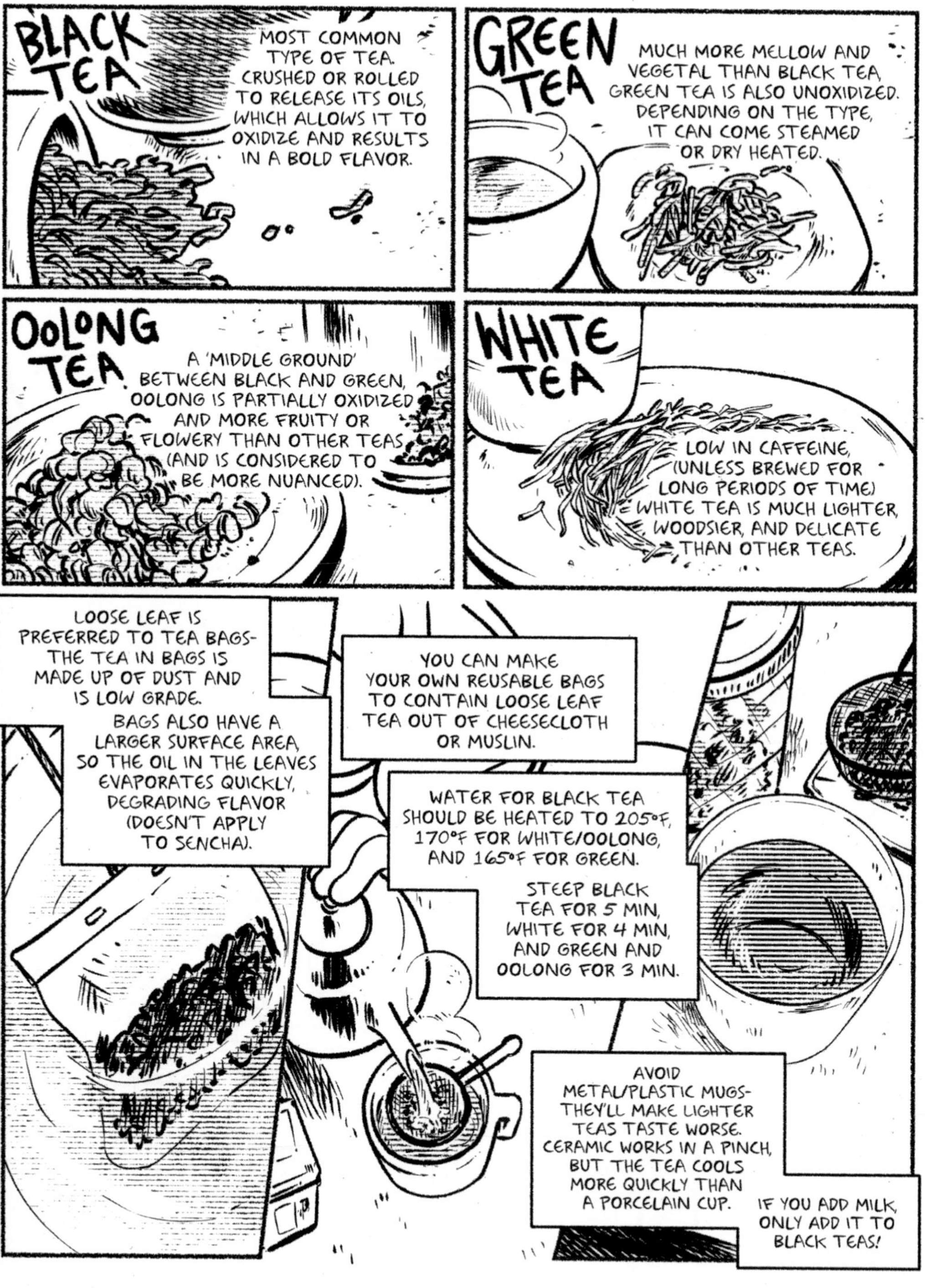
BLACK TEA
MOST COMMON TYPE OF TEA. CRUSHED OR ROLLED TO RELEASE ITS OILS, WHICH ALLOWS IT TO OXIDIZE AND RESULTS IN A BOLD FLAVOR.
GREEN TEA
MUCH MORE MELLOW AND VEGETAL THAN BLACK TEA, GREEN TEA IS ALSO UNOXIDIZED. DEPENDING ON THE TYPE, IT CAN COME STEAMED OR DRY HEATED.
OOLONG TEA
A 'MIDDLE GROUND' BETWEEN BLACK AND GREEN, OOLONG IS PARTIALLY OXIDIZED AND MORE FRUITY OR FLOWERY THAN OTHER TEAS (AND IS CONSIDERED TO BE MORE NUANCED).
WHITE TEA
LOW IN CAFFEINE, (UNLESS BREWED FOR LONG PERIODS OF TIME) WHITE TEA IS MUCH LIGHTER, WOODSIER, AND DELICATE THAN OTHER TEAS.
LOOSE LEAF IS PREFERRED TO TEA BAGS- THE TEA IN BAGS IS MADE UP OF DUST AND IS LOW GRADE.
BAGS ALSO HAVE A LARGER SURFACE AREA, SO THE OIL IN THE LEAVES EVAPORATES QUICKLY, DEGRADING FLAVOR (DOESN'T APPLY TO SENCHA).
YOU CAN MAKE YOUR OWN REUSABLE BAGS TO CONTAIN LOOSE LEAF TEA OUT OF CHEESECLOTH OR MUSLIN.
WATER FOR BLACK TEA SHOULD BE HEATED TO 205°F, 170°F FOR WHITE/OOLONG, AND 165°F FOR GREEN.
STEEP BLACK TEA FOR 5 MIN, WHITE FOR 4 MIN, AND GREEN AND OOLONG FOR 3 MIN.
AVOID METAL/PLASTIC MUGS- THEY'LL MAKE LIGHTER TEAS TASTE WORSE. CERAMIC WORKS IN A PINCH, BUT THE TEA COOLS MORE QUICKLY THAN A PORCELAIN CUP.
IF YOU ADD MILK, ONLY ADD IT TO BLACK TEAS!

SHRUBS
(COLD PROCCESS)

SHRUBS ARE OFTEN USED AS A PART OF COCKTAILS, BUT THEY'RE FINE ON THEIR OWN SPLIT WITH SELTZER, CLUB SODA, OR JUICE!

HANDS ON: 20 MIN
HANDS OFF: 48-72 HOURS

- 1 CUP BERRIES OR OTHER FRUIT OF CHOICE, WASHED THOROUGHLY, CHOPPED SMALL, DEFROSTED IF USING FROZEN
- 1 CUP SUGAR OF CHOICE
- 1 CUP VINEGAR OF CHOICE (NOT WHITE VINEGAR, AS THE ACIDITY IS TOO HIGH)

SUGGESTED FRUIT + VINEGAR COMBINATIONS:
APPLE + APPLE CIDER VINEGAR + WHITE SUGAR
PEACHES + APPLE CIDER VINEGAR + WHITE SUGAR
PLUMS + HALF APPLE CIDER VINEGAR AND HALF RED WINE VINEGAR + BROWN SUGAR
ORANGES + APPLE CIDER VINEGAR + WHITE SUGAR
PEARS + APPLE CIDER VINEGAR + CHOPPED GINGER + WHITE SUGAR
STRAWBERRIES + RED WINE VINEGAR + 1 TBSP BALSAMIC VINEGAR + WHITE SUGAR

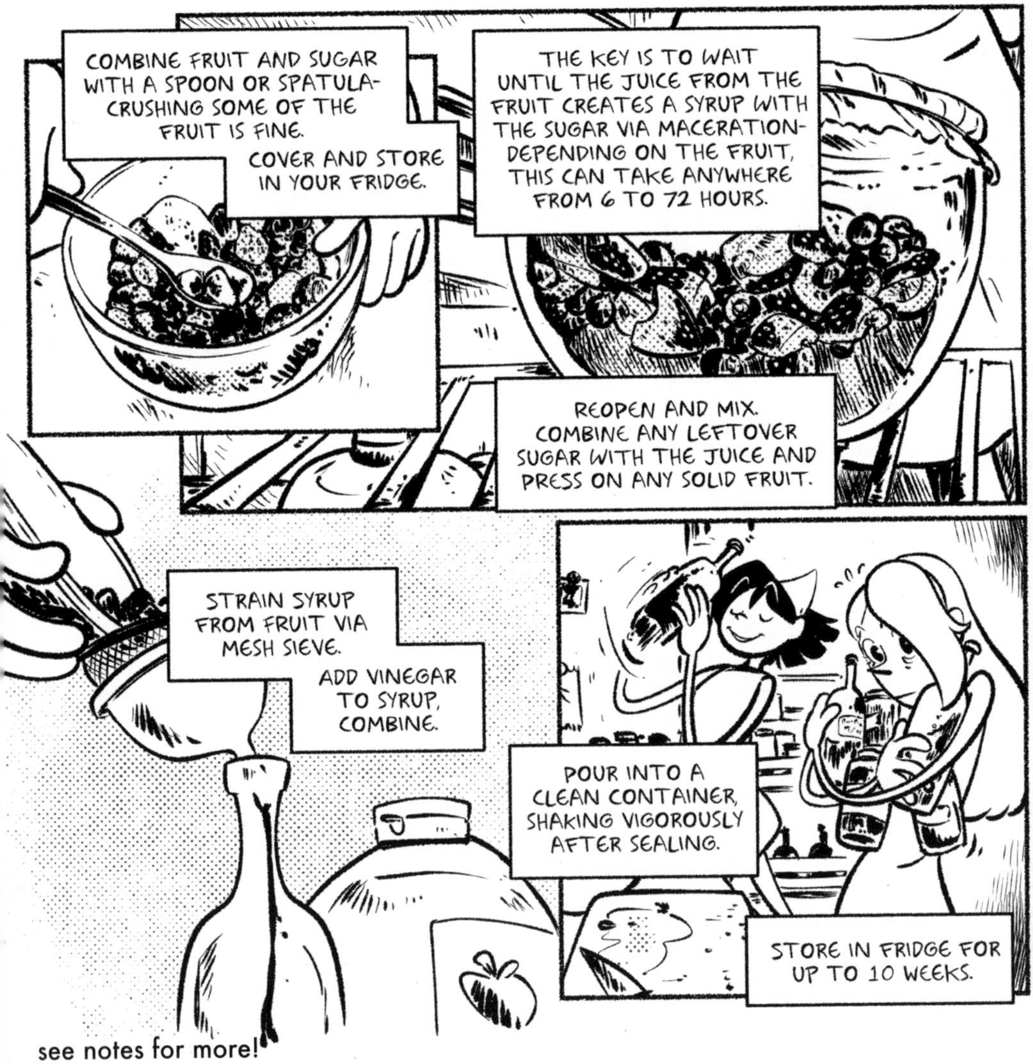
COMBINE FRUIT AND SUGAR WITH A SPOON OR SPATULA- CRUSHING SOME OF THE FRUIT IS FINE.
COVER AND STORE IN YOUR FRIDGE.
THE KEY IS TO WAIT UNTIL THE JUICE FROM THE FRUIT CREATES A SYRUP WITH THE SUGAR VIA MACERATION- DEPENDING ON THE FRUIT, THIS CAN TAKE ANYWHERE FROM 6 TO 72 HOURS.
REOPEN AND MIX. COMBINE ANY LEFTOVER SUGAR WITH THE JUICE AND PRESS ON ANY SOLID FRUIT.
STRAIN SYRUP FROM FRUIT VIA MESH SIEVE.
ADD VINEGAR TO SYRUP, COMBINE.
POUR INTO A CLEAN CONTAINER, SHAKING VIGOROUSLY AFTER SEALING.
STORE IN FRIDGE FOR UP TO 10 WEEKS.

see notes for more!

ATOLE

HANDS ON: 15 MIN

- -1/2 CUP MASA HARINA
- -3 CUPS WATER
- -1 CUP MILK
- -1/4 BROWN SUGAR
- -1 TSP CINNAMON, GROUND
- -1 TSP VANILLA EXTRACT

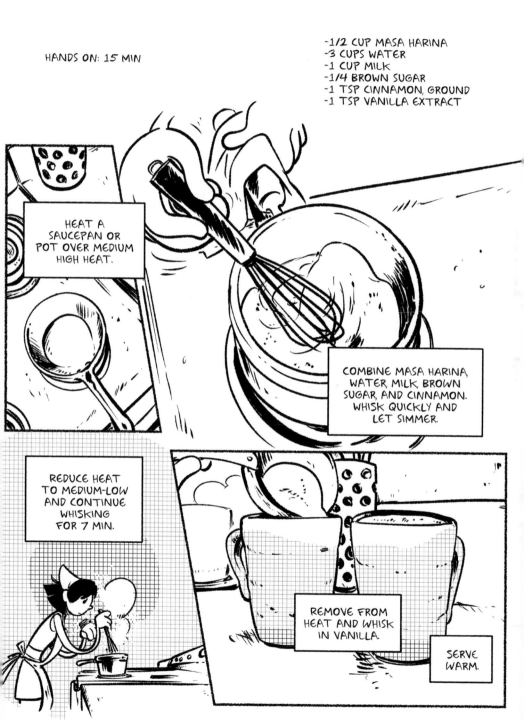

HEAT A SAUCEPAN OR POT OVER MEDIUM HIGH HEAT.

COMBINE MASA HARINA, WATER, MILK, BROWN SUGAR, AND CINNAMON. WHISK QUICKLY AND LET SIMMER.

REDUCE HEAT TO MEDIUM-LOW AND CONTINUE WHISKING FOR 7 MIN.

REMOVE FROM HEAT AND WHISK IN VANILLA.

SERVE WARM.

see notes for more!

ALCOHOLIC DRINKS

RUM MIXERS

WHILE A RUM AND COKE IS PERFECTLY ACCEPTABLE, THERE'S A WIDE VARIETY OF 1:3 RATIO MIXERS THAT PAIR WELL WITH EVEN THE CHEAPEST OF RUMS.

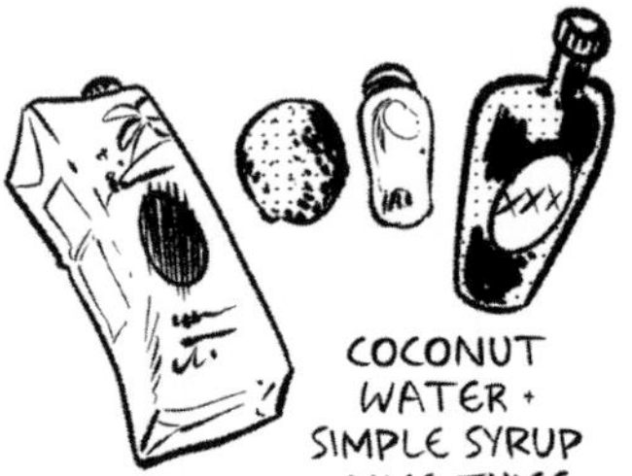

COCONUT WATER + SIMPLE SYRUP + LIME JUICE + RUM

ORANGE JUICE + PINEAPPLE JUICE + CRANBERRY JUICE + RUM

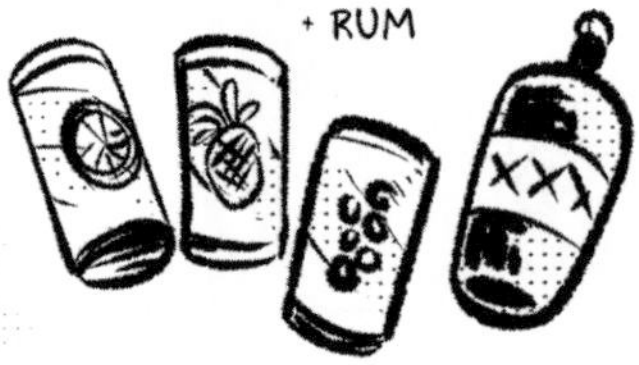

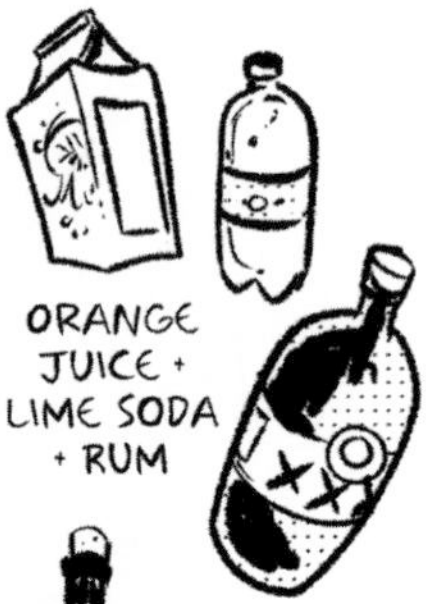

ORANGE JUICE + LIME SODA + RUM

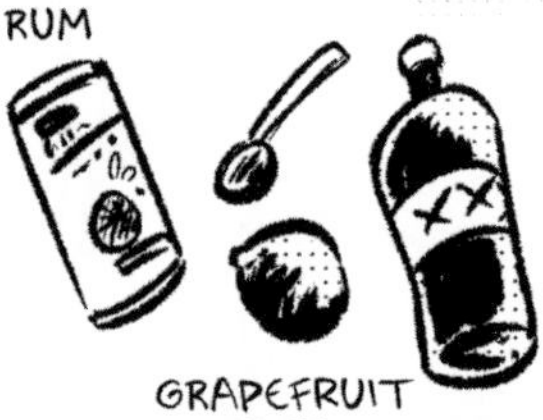

GRAPEFRUIT JUICE + LIME JUICE + 1 TBSP WHITE SUGAR + RUM

RED WINE + RUM

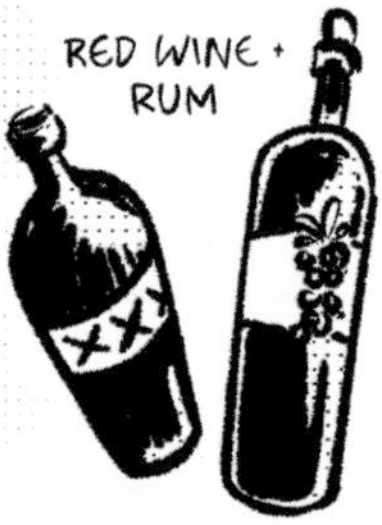

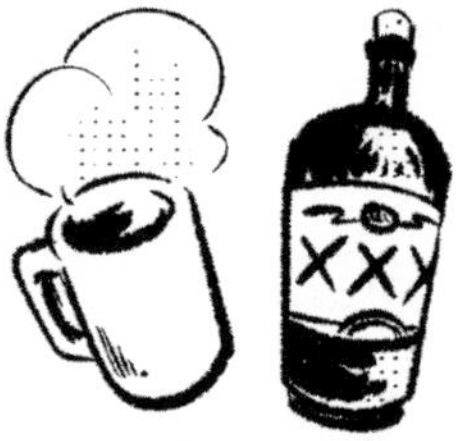

HOT CHOCOLATE + RUM

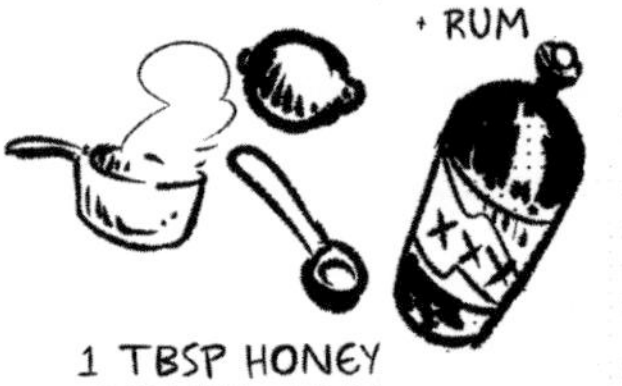

1 TBSP HONEY + LEMON JUICE + 1 CUP HOT WATER + RUM

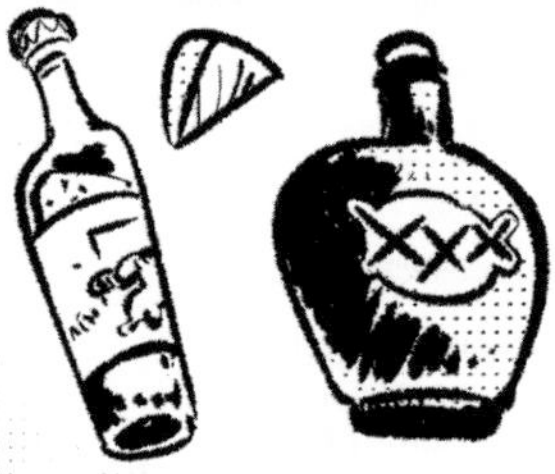

GINGER BEER + LIME WEDGE + RUM

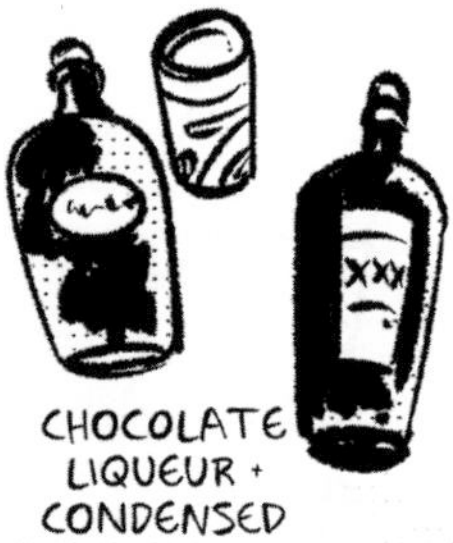

CHOCOLATE LIQUEUR + CONDENSED MILK + RUM

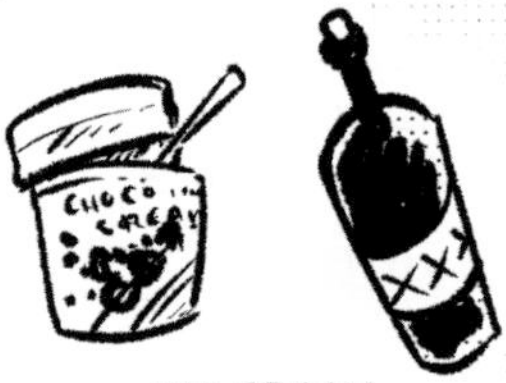

ICE CREAM + RUM (YOU HEARD ME.)

VODKA INFUSIONS

HANDS ON: 10 MIN
HANDS OFF: 3-5 DAYS

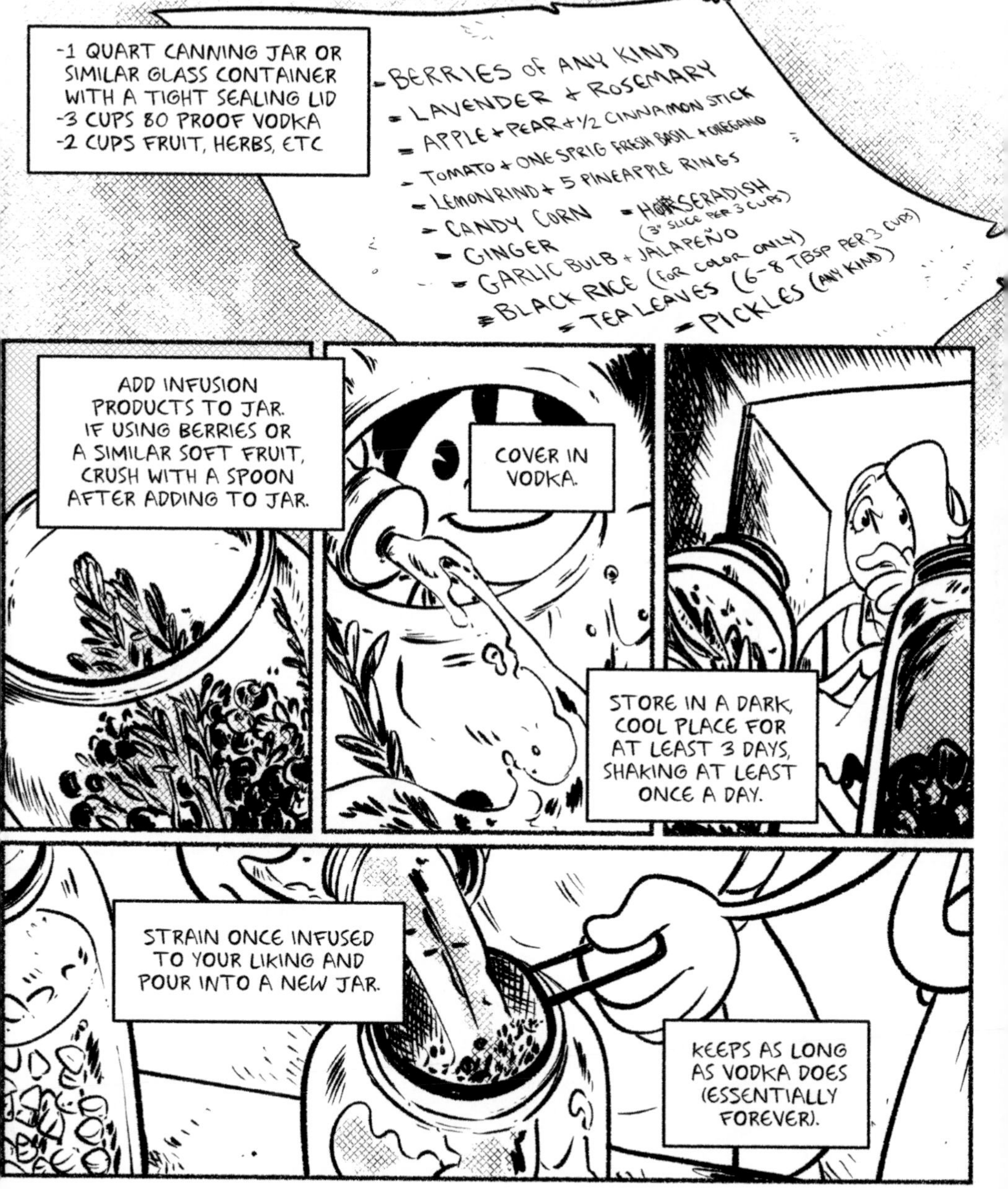

-1 QUART CANNING JAR OR SIMILAR GLASS CONTAINER WITH A TIGHT SEALING LID
-3 CUPS 80 PROOF VODKA
-2 CUPS FRUIT, HERBS, ETC
- BERRIES OF ANY KIND
- LAVENDER + ROSEMARY
- APPLE + PEAR + 1/2 CINNAMON STICK
- TOMATO + ONE SPRIG FRESH BASIL + OREGANO
- LEMON RIND + 5 PINEAPPLE RINGS
- CANDY CORN
- HORSERADISH (3" SLICE PER 3 CUPS)
- GINGER
- GARLIC BULB + JALAPEÑO
- BLACK RICE (FOR COLOR ONLY)
- TEA LEAVES (6-8 TBSP PER 3 CUPS)
- PICKLES (ANY KIND)
ADD INFUSION PRODUCTS TO JAR. IF USING BERRIES OR A SIMILAR SOFT FRUIT, CRUSH WITH A SPOON AFTER ADDING TO JAR.
COVER IN VODKA.
STORE IN A DARK, COOL PLACE FOR AT LEAST 3 DAYS, SHAKING AT LEAST ONCE A DAY.
STRAIN ONCE INFUSED TO YOUR LIKING AND POUR INTO A NEW JAR.
KEEPS AS LONG AS VODKA DOES (ESSENTIALLY FOREVER).

see notes for more!

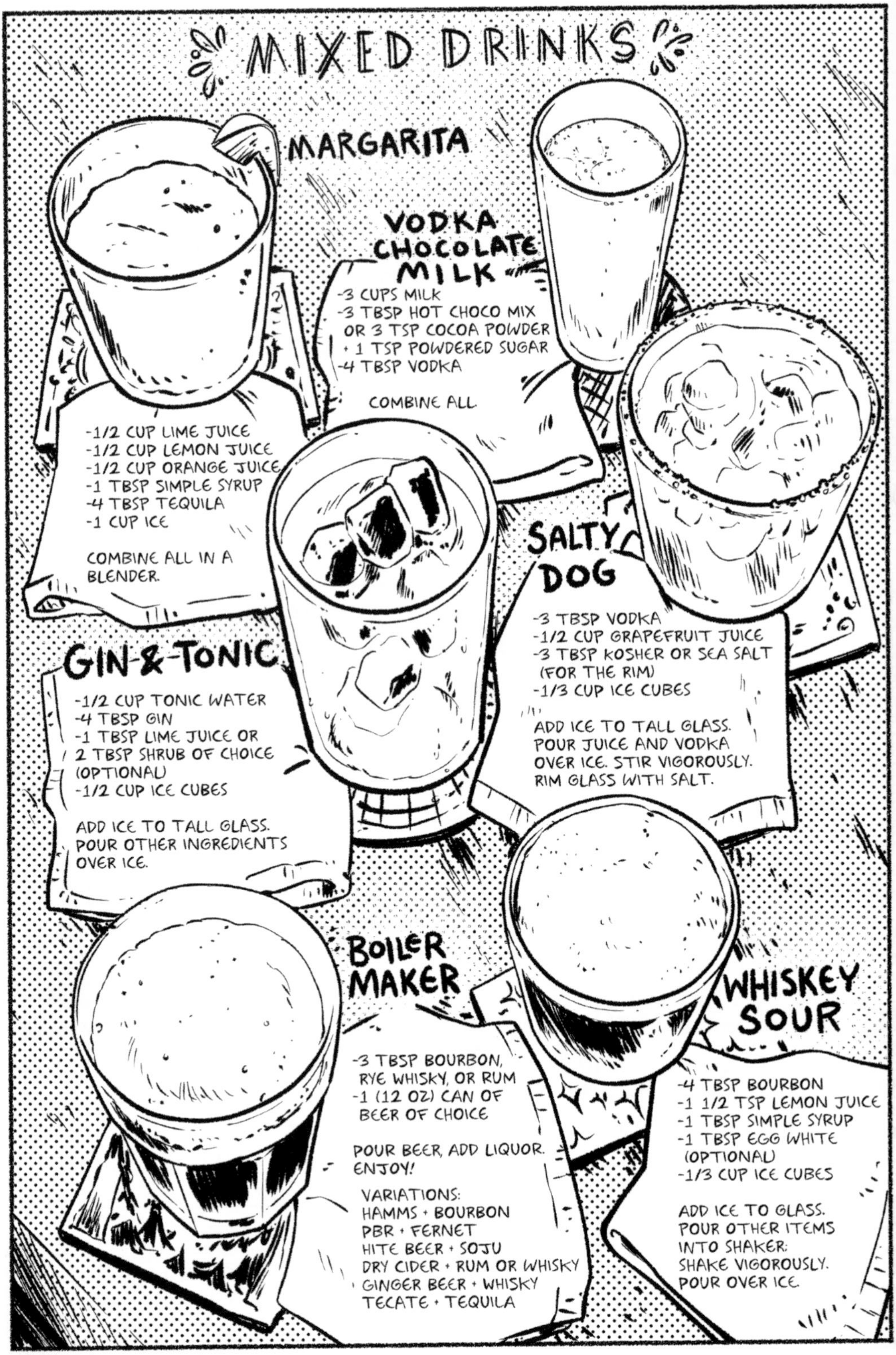
MIXED DRINKS
MARGARITA
-1/2 CUP LIME JUICE
-1/2 CUP LEMON JUICE
-1/2 CUP ORANGE JUICE
-1 TBSP SIMPLE SYRUP
-4 TBSP TEQUILA
-1 CUP ICE
COMBINE ALL IN A BLENDER.
VODKA CHOCOLATE MILK
-3 CUPS MILK
-3 TBSP HOT CHOCO MIX OR 3 TSP COCOA POWDER + 1 TSP POWDERED SUGAR
-4 TBSP VODKA
COMBINE ALL
GIN & TONIC
-1/2 CUP TONIC WATER
-4 TBSP GIN
-1 TBSP LIME JUICE OR 2 TBSP SHRUB OF CHOICE (OPTIONAL)
-1/2 CUP ICE CUBES
ADD ICE TO TALL GLASS. POUR OTHER INGREDIENTS OVER ICE.
SALTY DOG
-3 TBSP VODKA
-1/2 CUP GRAPEFRUIT JUICE
-3 TBSP KOSHER OR SEA SALT (FOR THE RIM)
-1/3 CUP ICE CUBES
ADD ICE TO TALL GLASS. POUR JUICE AND VODKA OVER ICE. STIR VIGOROUSLY. RIM GLASS WITH SALT.
BOILER MAKER
-3 TBSP BOURBON, RYE WHISKY, OR RUM
-1 (12 OZ) CAN OF BEER OF CHOICE
POUR BEER, ADD LIQUOR. ENJOY!
VARIATIONS:
HAMMS + BOURBON
PBR + FERNET
HITE BEER + SOJU
DRY CIDER + RUM OR WHISKY
GINGER BEER + WHISKY
TECATE + TEQUILA
WHISKEY SOUR
-4 TBSP BOURBON
-1 1/2 TSP LEMON JUICE
-1 TBSP SIMPLE SYRUP
-1 TBSP EGG WHITE (OPTIONAL)
-1/3 CUP ICE CUBES
ADD ICE TO GLASS. POUR OTHER ITEMS INTO SHAKER. SHAKE VIGOROUSLY. POUR OVER ICE.

see notes for more!

SIMPLE SYRUP

HANDS ON: 10 MIN

-1 CUP GRANULATED SUGAR
-1 CUP WATER

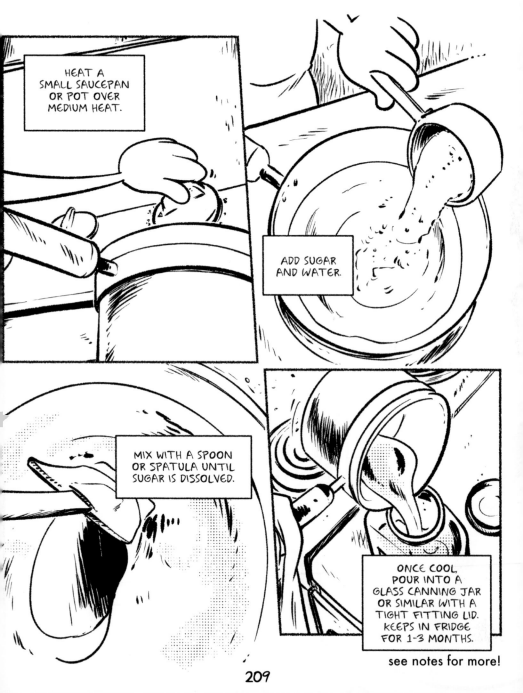

HEAT A SMALL SAUCEPAN OR POT OVER MEDIUM HEAT.

ADD SUGAR AND WATER.

MIX WITH A SPOON OR SPATULA UNTIL SUGAR IS DISSOLVED.

ONCE COOL, POUR INTO A GLASS CANNING JAR OR SIMILAR WITH A TIGHT FITTING LID. KEEPS IN FRIDGE FOR 1-3 MONTHS.

see notes for more!

SELF RISING FLOUR

HANDS ON: 5 MIN

- 1 CUP ALL-PURPOSE FLOUR
- 1 1/2 TSP BAKING POWDER
- 1/4 TSP KOSHER SALT

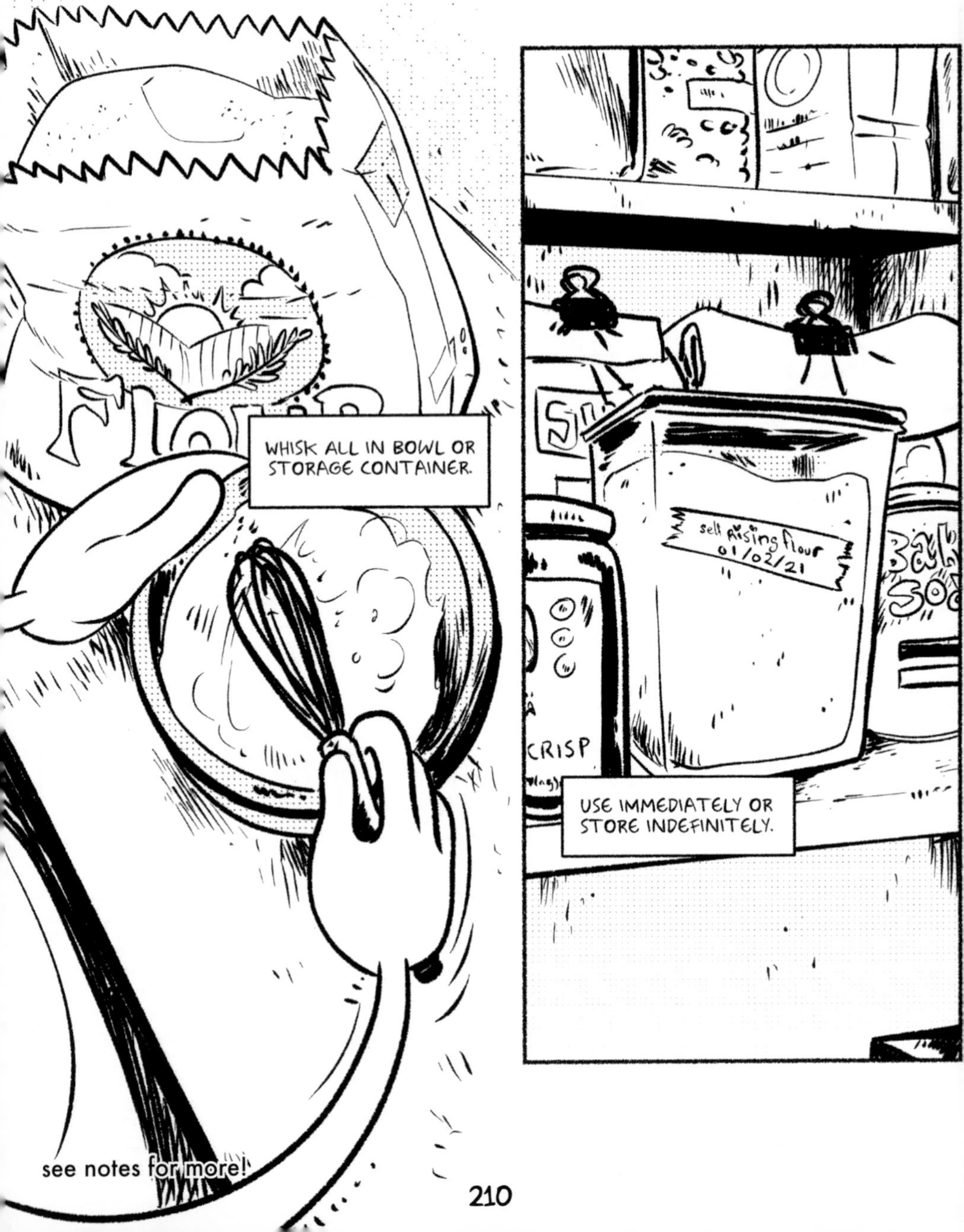
WHISK ALL IN BOWL OR STORAGE CONTAINER.
self rising flour 01/02/21
CRISP
USE IMMEDIATELY OR STORE INDEFINITELY.

see notes for more!

COOKING RICE

NO RICE COOKER?
NO PROBLEM!

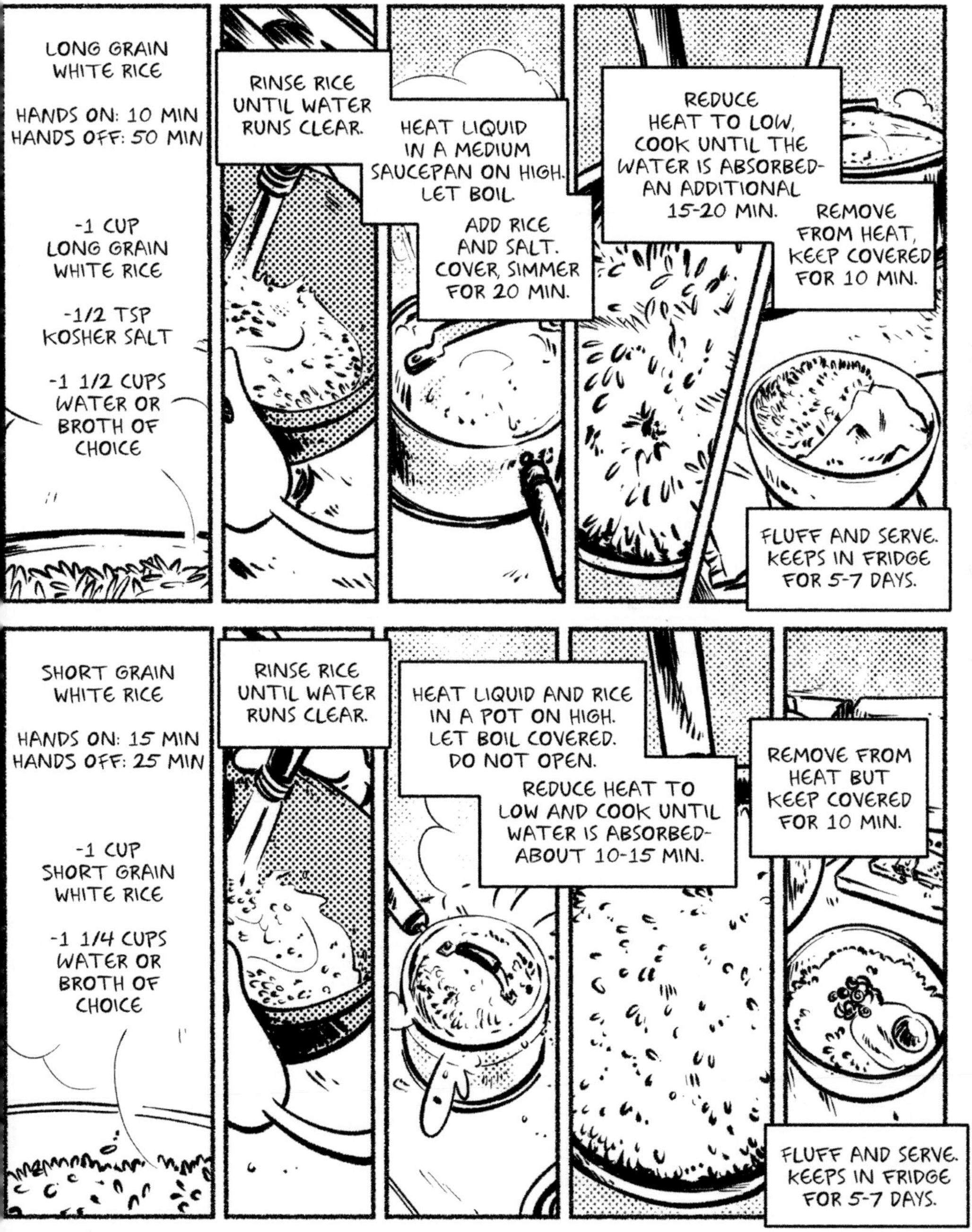
LONG GRAIN WHITE RICE
HANDS ON: 10 MIN
HANDS OFF: 50 MIN
-1 CUP LONG GRAIN WHITE RICE
-1/2 TSP KOSHER SALT
-1 1/2 CUPS WATER OR BROTH OF CHOICE
RINSE RICE UNTIL WATER RUNS CLEAR.
HEAT LIQUID IN A MEDIUM SAUCEPAN ON HIGH. LET BOIL.
ADD RICE AND SALT. COVER, SIMMER FOR 20 MIN.
REDUCE HEAT TO LOW, COOK UNTIL THE WATER IS ABSORBED- AN ADDITIONAL 15-20 MIN.
REMOVE FROM HEAT, KEEP COVERED FOR 10 MIN.
FLUFF AND SERVE. KEEPS IN FRIDGE FOR 5-7 DAYS.
SHORT GRAIN WHITE RICE
HANDS ON: 15 MIN
HANDS OFF: 25 MIN
-1 CUP SHORT GRAIN WHITE RICE
-1 1/4 CUPS WATER OR BROTH OF CHOICE
RINSE RICE UNTIL WATER RUNS CLEAR.
HEAT LIQUID AND RICE IN A POT ON HIGH. LET BOIL COVERED. DO NOT OPEN.
REDUCE HEAT TO LOW AND COOK UNTIL WATER IS ABSORBED- ABOUT 10-15 MIN.
REMOVE FROM HEAT BUT KEEP COVERED FOR 10 MIN.
FLUFF AND SERVE. KEEPS IN FRIDGE FOR 5-7 DAYS.

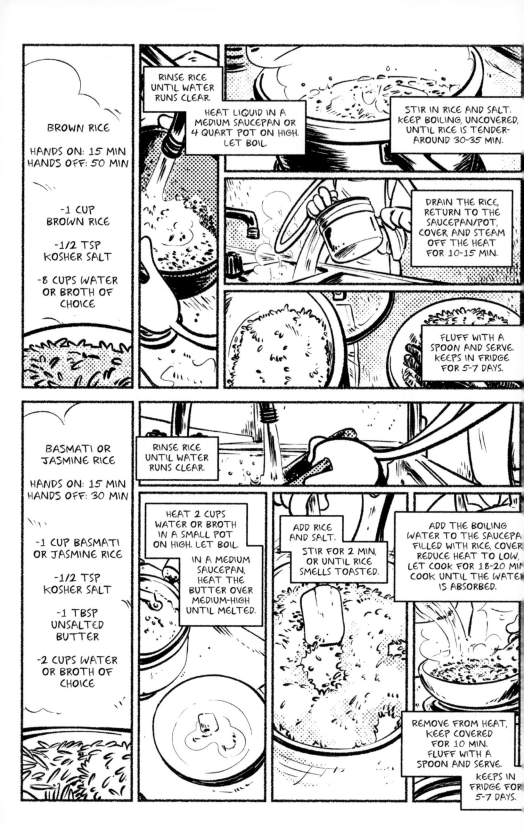

BROWN RICE

HANDS ON: 15 MIN
HANDS OFF: 50 MIN

-1 CUP
BROWN RICE

-1/2 TSP
KOSHER SALT

-8 CUPS WATER
OR BROTH OF
CHOICE

RINSE RICE UNTIL WATER RUNS CLEAR.

HEAT LIQUID IN A MEDIUM SAUCEPAN OR 4 QUART POT ON HIGH. LET BOIL.

STIR IN RICE AND SALT. KEEP BOILING, UNCOVERED, UNTIL RICE IS TENDER- AROUND 30-35 MIN.

DRAIN THE RICE, RETURN TO THE SAUCEPAN/POT, COVER, AND STEAM OFF THE HEAT FOR 10-15 MIN.

FLUFF WITH A SPOON AND SERVE. KEEPS IN FRIDGE FOR 5-7 DAYS.

BASMATI OR JASMINE RICE

HANDS ON: 15 MIN
HANDS OFF: 30 MIN

-1 CUP BASMATI OR JASMINE RICE

-1/2 TSP KOSHER SALT

-1 TBSP UNSALTED BUTTER

-2 CUPS WATER OR BROTH OF CHOICE

RINSE RICE UNTIL WATER RUNS CLEAR.

HEAT 2 CUPS WATER OR BROTH IN A SMALL POT ON HIGH. LET BOIL.

IN A MEDIUM SAUCEPAN, HEAT THE BUTTER OVER MEDIUM-HIGH UNTIL MELTED.

ADD RICE AND SALT.

STIR FOR 2 MIN, OR UNTIL RICE SMELLS TOASTED.

ADD THE BOILING WATER TO THE SAUCEPAN FILLED WITH RICE, COVER REDUCE HEAT TO LOW, LET COOK FOR 18-20 MIN COOK UNTIL THE WATER IS ABSORBED.

REMOVE FROM HEAT, KEEP COVERED FOR 10 MIN. FLUFF WITH A SPOON AND SERVE.

KEEPS IN FRIDGE FOR 5-7 DAYS.

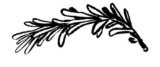

COOKING LEGUMES

HANDS ON: VARIES, DEPENDING ON LEGUME
HANDS OFF: VARIES, DEPENDING ON LEGUME

- 1 CUP OF LEGUMES OF CHOICE
- ENOUGH WATER TO COVER LEGUMES (FOR SOAKING)
- ENOUGH WATER OR BROTH TO COVER LEGUMES (FOR COOKING)

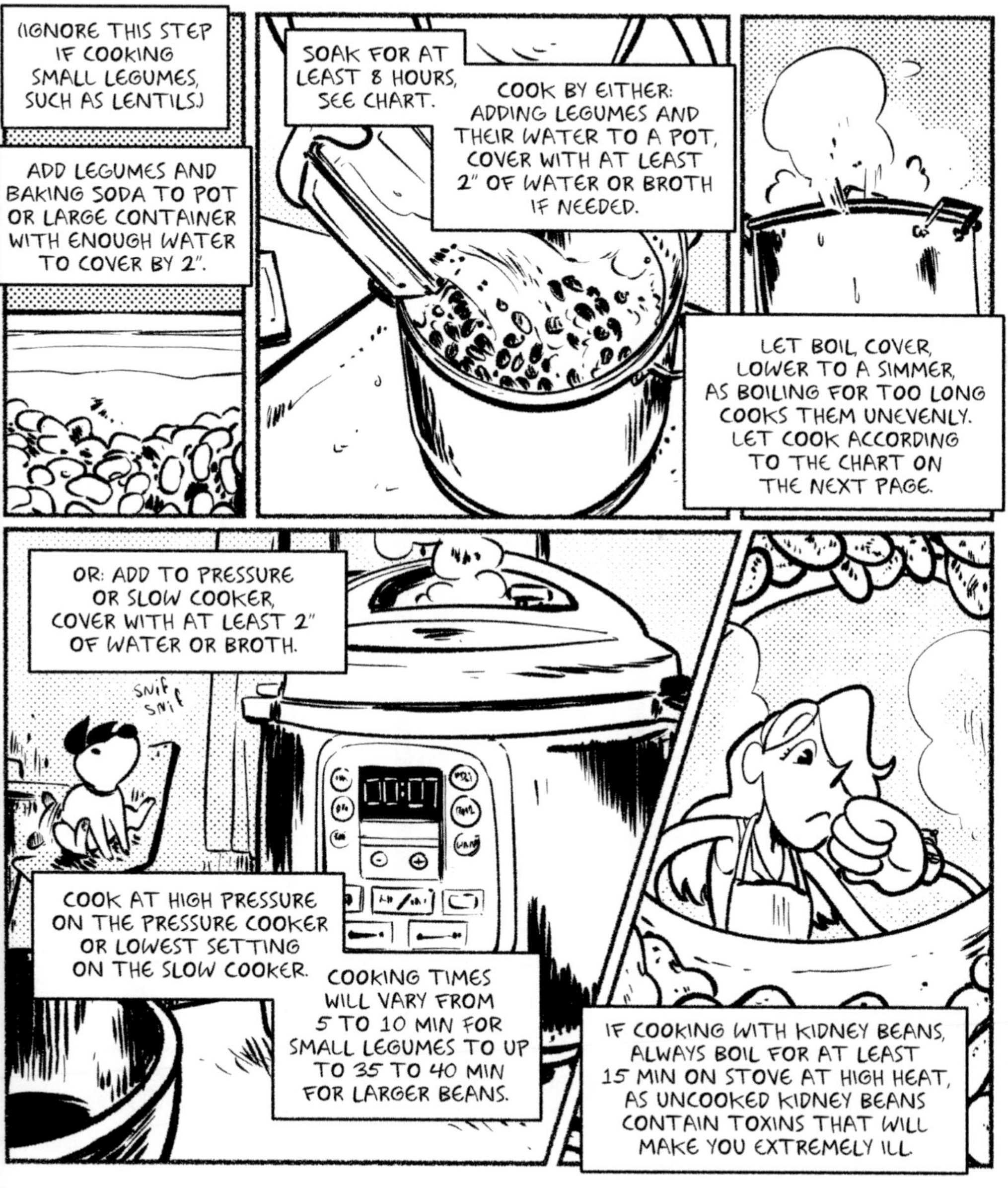
(IGNORE THIS STEP IF COOKING SMALL LEGUMES, SUCH AS LENTILS.)
ADD LEGUMES AND BAKING SODA TO POT OR LARGE CONTAINER WITH ENOUGH WATER TO COVER BY 2".
SOAK FOR AT LEAST 8 HOURS, SEE CHART.
COOK BY EITHER: ADDING LEGUMES AND THEIR WATER TO A POT, COVER WITH AT LEAST 2" OF WATER OR BROTH IF NEEDED.
LET BOIL, COVER, LOWER TO A SIMMER, AS BOILING FOR TOO LONG COOKS THEM UNEVENLY. LET COOK ACCORDING TO THE CHART ON THE NEXT PAGE.
OR: ADD TO PRESSURE OR SLOW COOKER, COVER WITH AT LEAST 2" OF WATER OR BROTH.
SNIF SNIF
00:07
COOK AT HIGH PRESSURE ON THE PRESSURE COOKER OR LOWEST SETTING ON THE SLOW COOKER.
COOKING TIMES WILL VARY FROM 5 TO 10 MIN FOR SMALL LEGUMES TO UP TO 35 TO 40 MIN FOR LARGER BEANS.
IF COOKING WITH KIDNEY BEANS, ALWAYS BOIL FOR AT LEAST 15 MIN ON STOVE AT HIGH HEAT, AS UNCOOKED KIDNEY BEANS CONTAIN TOXINS THAT WILL MAKE YOU EXTREMELY ILL.

see notes for more!

COMMON BEAN SOAK AND COOK TIMES

1 CUP	SOAK TIME	COOK TIME	YIELD
ADZUKI (RED) BEANS	8 HRS	1 HR	3 CUPS
BLACK BEANS	8 HRS	1 1/2 HRS	2 CUPS
BLACK EYED PEAS	8 HRS	1 HR	2 CUPS
CANNELLINI BEANS	8 HRS	45 MIN	2 1/2 CUPS
FAVA BEANS	8 HRS	45 MIN	1 2/3 CUPS
GARBANZO (CHICKPEAS)	12 HRS	1 1/2 HRS	2 CUPS
GREAT NORTHERN BEANS	12 HRS	1 1/2 HRS	2 2/3 CUPS
KIDNEY BEANS	12 HRS	1 HR	2 CUPS
LENTILS (RED OR YELLOW)	N/A	20 MIN	2 CUPS
LIMA BEANS	8 HRS	1 1/2 HR	2 CUPS
MUNG BEANS	8 HRS	1 HR	2 CUPS
NAVY BEANS	8 HRS	1 HR	2 2/3 CUPS
PINTO BEANS	8 HRS	2 HR	2 2/3 CUPS
SOY BEANS	12 HRS	4 HRS	3 CUPS

HOW TO SEASON AND CUT A BIRD

HANDS ON: 30 MIN
HANDS OFF: 1 HR 15 MIN

- 1 5LB WHOLE CHICKEN/PHEASANT/ CORNISH GAME HEN, GIBLETS AND INTERIORS REMOVED. SCALE INGREDIENT RATIOS UP OR DOWN DEPENDING ON BIRD SIZE.
- 1/2 CUP UNSALTED BUTTER, MELTED + 2 TBSP IF USING A ROASTING PAN
- 4 TBSP OLIVE OIL
- 3 TBSP LEMON JUICE
- 1 TBSP MISO OR 1 TBSP SOY SAUCE OR 1 TBSP TAHINI
- 1/2 CUP APPLE CIDER VINEGAR OR 1/2 CUP RICE WINE VINEGAR
- 1 TBSP KOSHER SALT
- 1 TBSP BLACK PEPPER
- 2 TBSP PARSLEY, DOUBLE IF DRIED
- 4 TBSP GARLIC, MINCED
- 2 TBSP ROSEMARY, DOUBLE IF DRIED

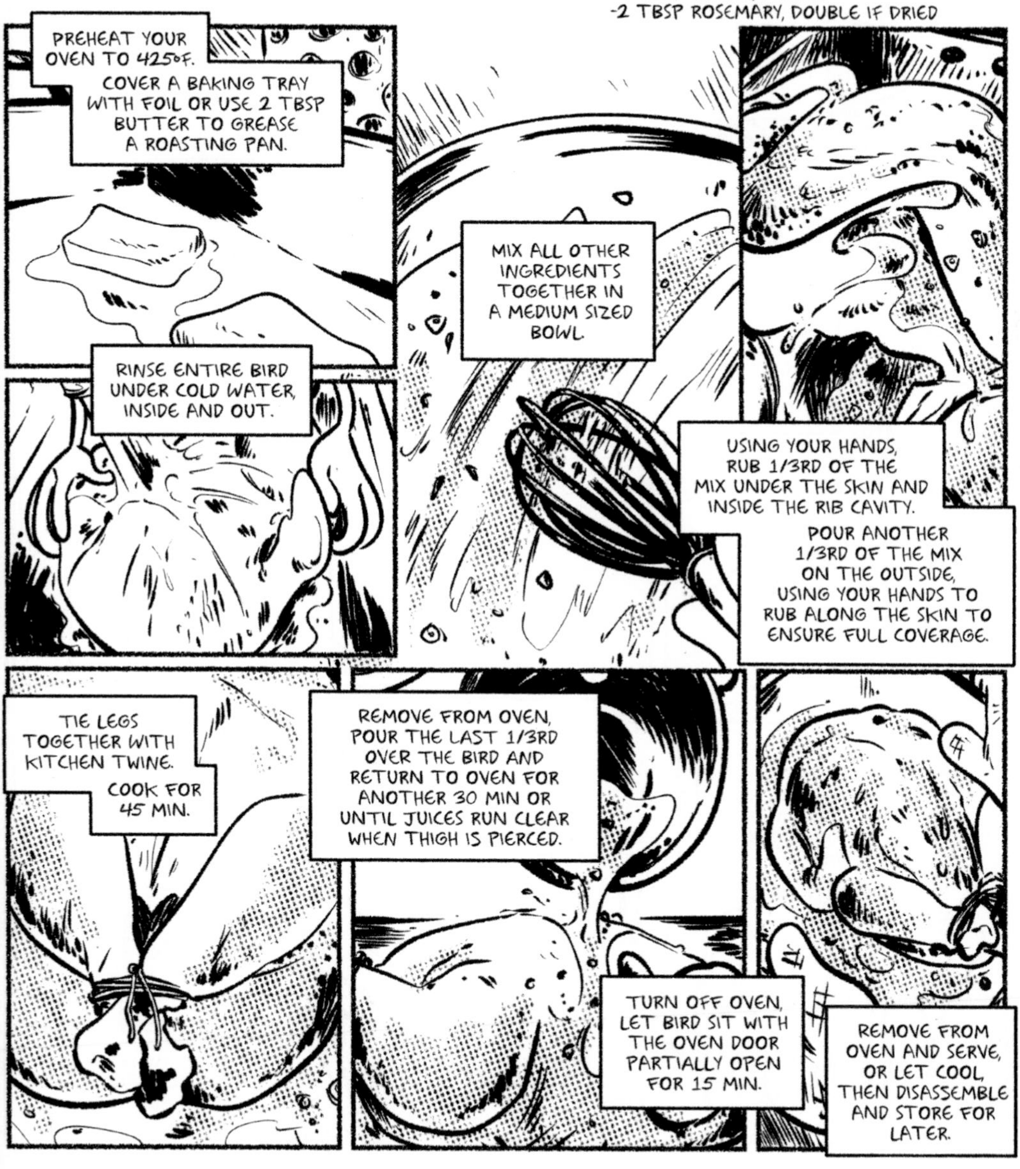
PREHEAT YOUR OVEN TO 425°F.
COVER A BAKING TRAY WITH FOIL OR USE 2 TBSP BUTTER TO GREASE A ROASTING PAN.
RINSE ENTIRE BIRD UNDER COLD WATER, INSIDE AND OUT.
MIX ALL OTHER INGREDIENTS TOGETHER IN A MEDIUM SIZED BOWL.
USING YOUR HANDS, RUB 1/3RD OF THE MIX UNDER THE SKIN AND INSIDE THE RIB CAVITY.
POUR ANOTHER 1/3RD OF THE MIX ON THE OUTSIDE, USING YOUR HANDS TO RUB ALONG THE SKIN TO ENSURE FULL COVERAGE.
TIE LEGS TOGETHER WITH KITCHEN TWINE.
COOK FOR 45 MIN.
REMOVE FROM OVEN, POUR THE LAST 1/3RD OVER THE BIRD AND RETURN TO OVEN FOR ANOTHER 30 MIN OR UNTIL JUICES RUN CLEAR WHEN THIGH IS PIERCED.
TURN OFF OVEN, LET BIRD SIT WITH THE OVEN DOOR PARTIALLY OPEN FOR 15 MIN.
REMOVE FROM OVEN AND SERVE, OR LET COOL, THEN DISASSEMBLE AND STORE FOR LATER.

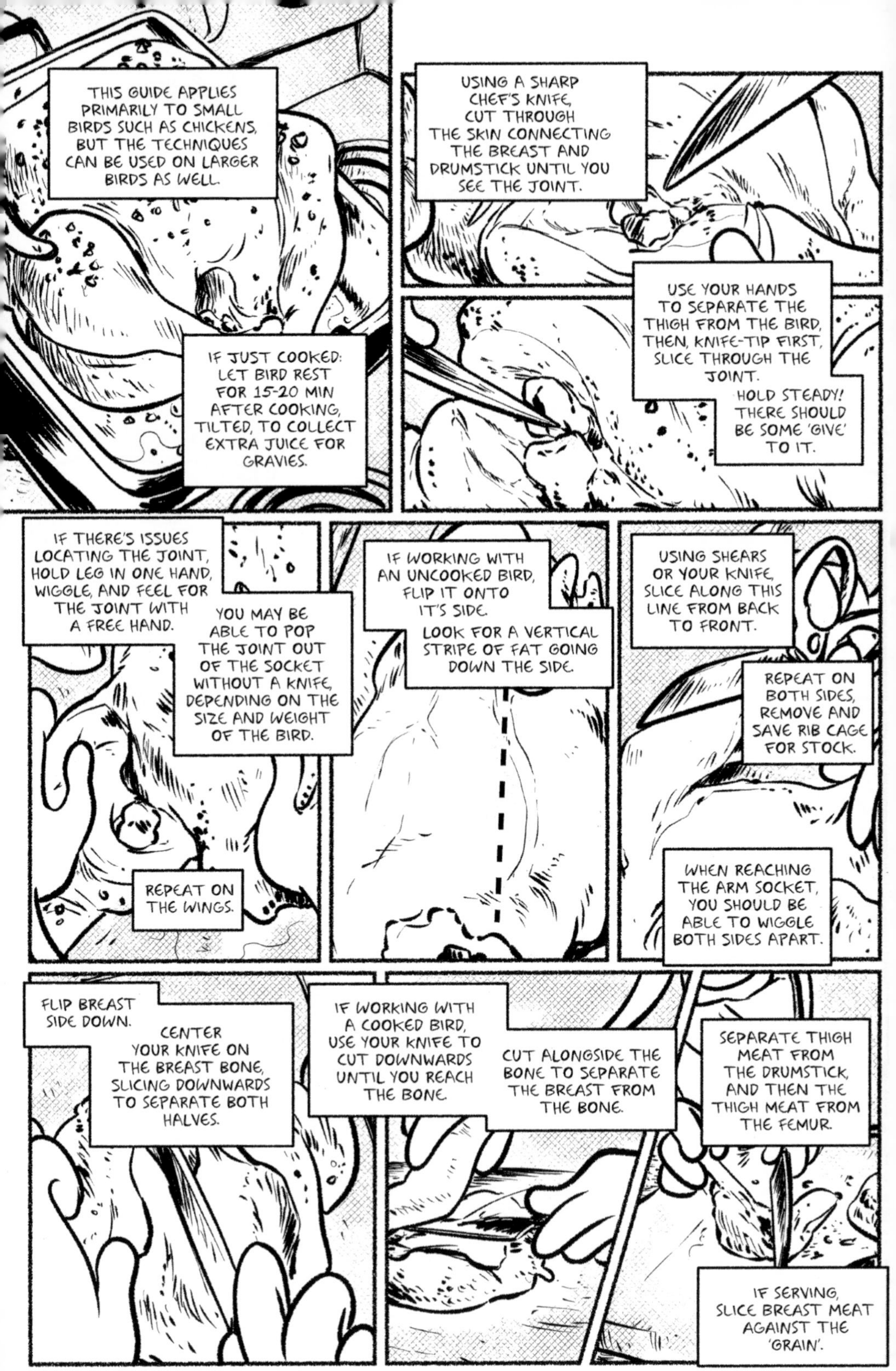
THIS GUIDE APPLIES PRIMARILY TO SMALL BIRDS SUCH AS CHICKENS, BUT THE TECHNIQUES CAN BE USED ON LARGER BIRDS AS WELL.
IF JUST COOKED: LET BIRD REST FOR 15-20 MIN AFTER COOKING, TILTED, TO COLLECT EXTRA JUICE FOR GRAVIES.
USING A SHARP CHEF'S KNIFE, CUT THROUGH THE SKIN CONNECTING THE BREAST AND DRUMSTICK UNTIL YOU SEE THE JOINT.
USE YOUR HANDS TO SEPARATE THE THIGH FROM THE BIRD, THEN, KNIFE-TIP FIRST, SLICE THROUGH THE JOINT.
HOLD STEADY! THERE SHOULD BE SOME 'GIVE' TO IT.
IF THERE'S ISSUES LOCATING THE JOINT, HOLD LEG IN ONE HAND, WIGGLE, AND FEEL FOR THE JOINT WITH A FREE HAND.
YOU MAY BE ABLE TO POP THE JOINT OUT OF THE SOCKET WITHOUT A KNIFE, DEPENDING ON THE SIZE AND WEIGHT OF THE BIRD.
REPEAT ON THE WINGS.
IF WORKING WITH AN UNCOOKED BIRD, FLIP IT ONTO IT'S SIDE.
LOOK FOR A VERTICAL STRIPE OF FAT GOING DOWN THE SIDE.
USING SHEARS OR YOUR KNIFE, SLICE ALONG THIS LINE FROM BACK TO FRONT.
REPEAT ON BOTH SIDES, REMOVE AND SAVE RIB CAGE FOR STOCK.
WHEN REACHING THE ARM SOCKET, YOU SHOULD BE ABLE TO WIGGLE BOTH SIDES APART.
FLIP BREAST SIDE DOWN.
CENTER YOUR KNIFE ON THE BREAST BONE, SLICING DOWNWARDS TO SEPARATE BOTH HALVES.
IF WORKING WITH A COOKED BIRD, USE YOUR KNIFE TO CUT DOWNWARDS UNTIL YOU REACH THE BONE.
CUT ALONGSIDE THE BONE TO SEPARATE THE BREAST FROM THE BONE.
SEPARATE THIGH MEAT FROM THE DRUMSTICK, AND THEN THE THIGH MEAT FROM THE FEMUR.
IF SERVING, SLICE BREAST MEAT AGAINST THE 'GRAIN'.

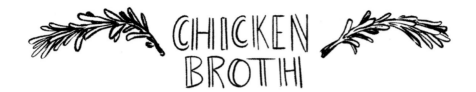

CHICKEN BROTH

HANDS ON: 10 MIN
HANDS OFF: 2 HRS

- 16 CUPS WATER
- AT LEAST ONE FULL CHICKEN CARCASS (1-2LB OF BONES 'N' BITS), ROTISSERIE CHICKENS ARE GREAT FOR THIS!
- 1/2 CUP KOSHER SALT
- 6 TBSP GARLIC, CHOPPED
- 1 TSP BLACK PEPPERCORNS
- 1/3 CUP APPLE CIDER VINEGAR

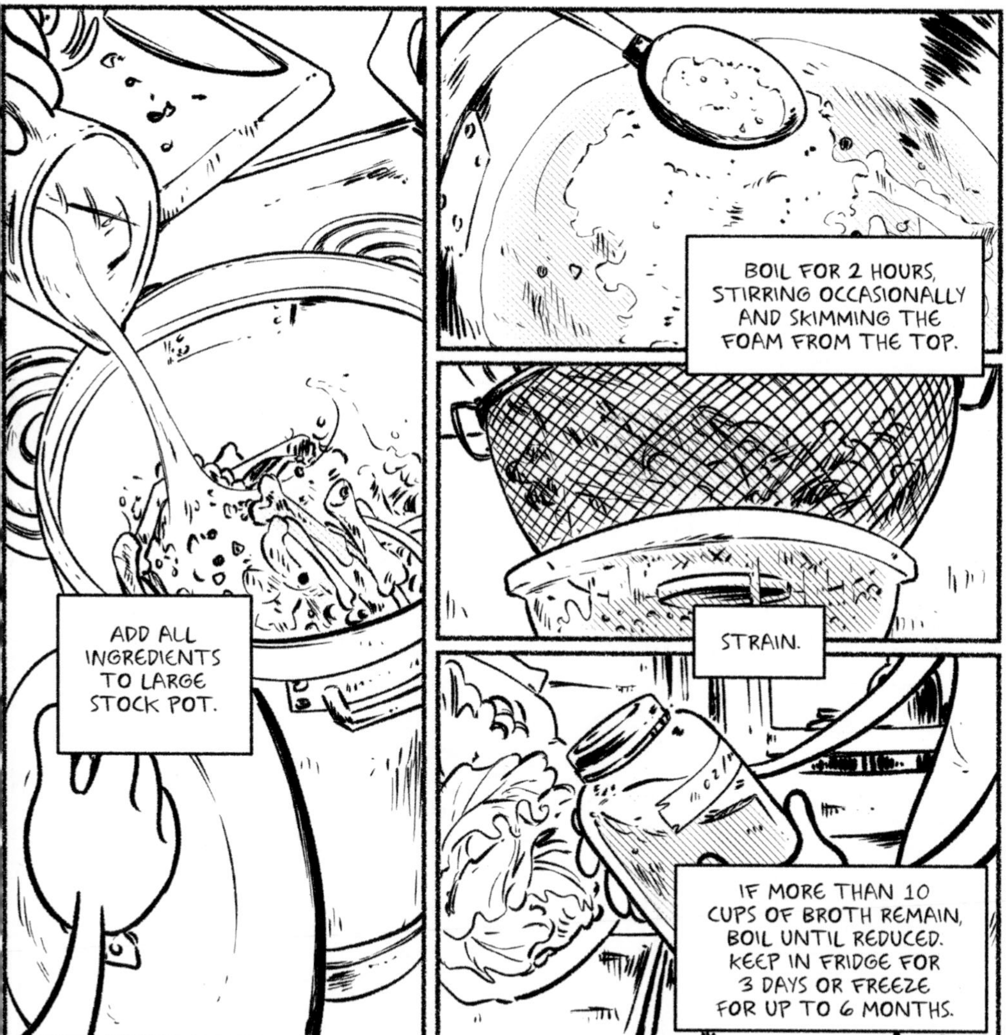
ADD ALL INGREDIENTS TO LARGE STOCK POT.
BOIL FOR 2 HOURS, STIRRING OCCASIONALLY AND SKIMMING THE FOAM FROM THE TOP.
STRAIN.
IF MORE THAN 10 CUPS OF BROTH REMAIN, BOIL UNTIL REDUCED. KEEP IN FRIDGE FOR 3 DAYS OR FREEZE FOR UP TO 6 MONTHS.

VEGETABLE BROTH

HANDS ON: 20 MIN
HANDS OFF: 3 HRS

-16 CUPS WATER
-1/2 CUP SOY SAUCE
-1 CUP APPLE CIDER VINEGAR
-1/3 CUP KOSHER SALT
-6 TBSP GARLIC, CHOPPED
-2 TSP BLACK PEPPERCORNS
-1 TSP CUMIN
-2 TBSP NUTRITIONAL YEAST
-1 TSP ROSEMARY
-2 TBSP TOMATO PASTE

-MISC VEGETABLE SCRAPS:
KEEP A ~1 QT CONTAINER IN
YOUR FRIDGE TO HOLD THINGS
LIKE ONION ENDS, CARROT STEMS,
ETC, AND DUMP 'EM IN HERE.
IF YOU DON'T HAVE A SCRAPS BIN,
CHOP UP THE FOLLOWING VEGGIES:
-1 WHOLE ONION, QUARTERED
-1 CUP CARROTS, CHOPPED
-2 CUPS TOMATO, CHOPPED

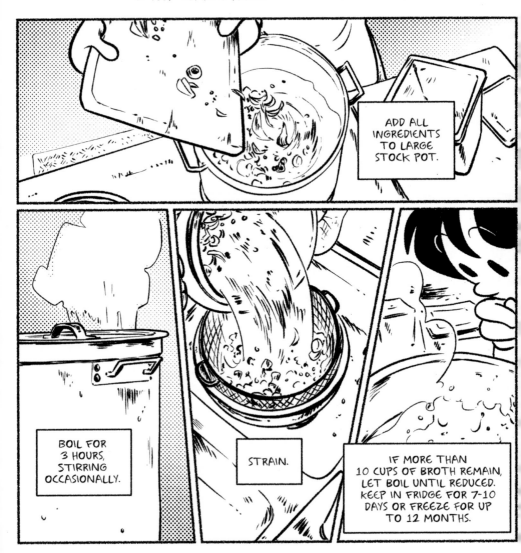

ADD ALL INGREDIENTS TO LARGE STOCK POT.

BOIL FOR 3 HOURS, STIRRING OCCASIONALLY.

STRAIN.

IF MORE THAN 10 CUPS OF BROTH REMAIN, LET BOIL UNTIL REDUCED. KEEP IN FRIDGE FOR 7-10 DAYS OR FREEZE FOR UP TO 12 MONTHS.

DASHI

HANDS ON: 10 MIN
HANDS OFF: 6 HR 10 MIN

-1/2 CUP KOMBU
-4 CUPS WATER

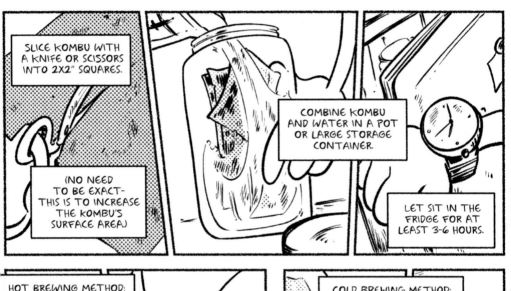

SLICE KOMBU WITH A KNIFE OR SCISSORS INTO 2X2" SQUARES.

(NO NEED TO BE EXACT- THIS IS TO INCREASE THE KOMBU'S SURFACE AREA)

COMBINE KOMBU AND WATER IN A POT OR LARGE STORAGE CONTAINER.

LET SIT IN THE FRIDGE FOR AT LEAST 3-6 HOURS.

HOT BREWING METHOD: HEAT A SMALL POT ON MEDIUM HEAT.

ADD WATER AND KOMBU. LET SIT FOR 10 MIN. DO NOT LET BOIL.

REMOVE POT FROM HEAT AND SCOOP OUT KOMBU- SAVE USED KOMBU TO USE AS AN INGREDIENT IN CHICKEN OR VEGETABLE BROTH.

USE IMMEDIATELY, OR SAVE FOR 5-7 DAYS IN THE FRIDGE OR 2-4 WEEKS IN THE FREEZER.

COLD BREWING METHOD: REMOVE KOMBU FROM THE CONTAINER- SAVE USED KOMBU TO USE AS AN INGREDIENT IN CHICKEN OR VEGETABLE BROTH.

USE IMMEDIATELY, OR SAVE FOR 5-7 DAYS IN THE FRIDGE OR 2-4 WEEKS IN THE FREEZER.

PREPPING TVP

HANDS ON: 15 MIN

- 1 TBSP OLIVE OIL, VEGETABLE OIL, BUTTER, OR SESAME OIL
- 1 CUP TEXTURED VEGETABLE PROTEIN (TVP)
- 1 CUP WATER OR BROTH OF CHOICE

OPTIONAL FLAVORINGS
(CAN BE ADJUSTED TO SUIT PERSONAL TASTE):
- 1 TBSP SOY SAUCE
- 1 TBSP APPLE CIDER VINEGAR OR RICE WINE VINEGAR
- 1 TSP SMOKED PAPRIKA
- 1 TSP CAYENNE
- 1 TSP GROUND MUSTARD

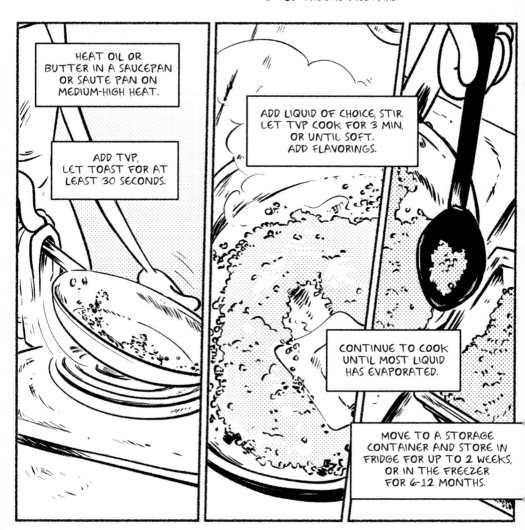

HEAT OIL OR BUTTER IN A SAUCEPAN OR SAUTE PAN ON MEDIUM-HIGH HEAT.

ADD TVP, LET TOAST FOR AT LEAST 30 SECONDS.

ADD LIQUID OF CHOICE, STIR. LET TVP COOK FOR 3 MIN, OR UNTIL SOFT. ADD FLAVORINGS.

CONTINUE TO COOK UNTIL MOST LIQUID HAS EVAPORATED.

MOVE TO A STORAGE CONTAINER AND STORE IN FRIDGE FOR UP TO 2 WEEKS, OR IN THE FREEZER FOR 6-12 MONTHS.

Clarified Butter

HANDS ON: 40 MIN
HANDS OFF: 15 MIN

-1 LB (32 TBSP) UNSALTED BUTTER, IN 4 TBSP PIECES
-3 CUPS WATER

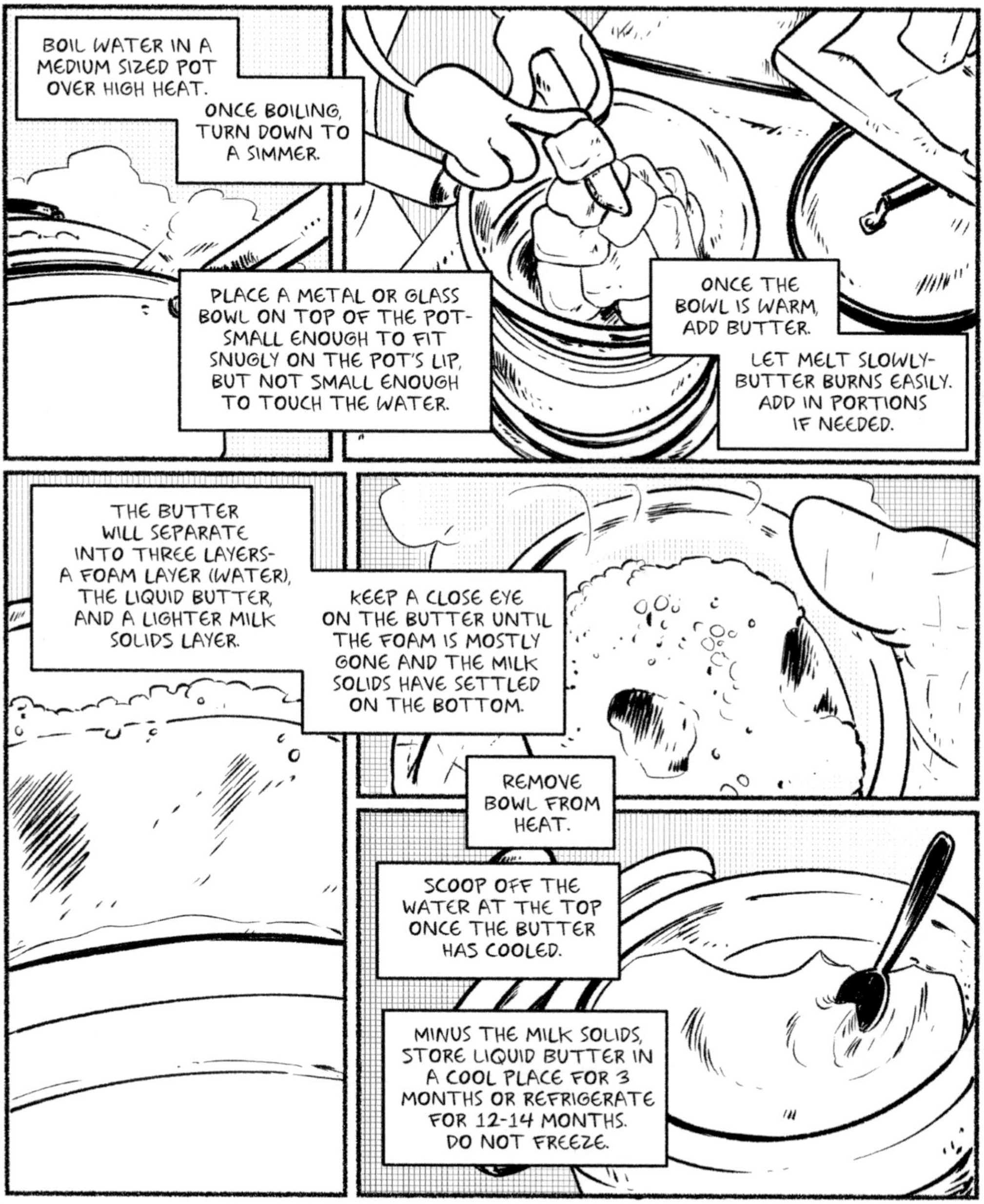

BOIL WATER IN A MEDIUM SIZED POT OVER HIGH HEAT.
ONCE BOILING, TURN DOWN TO A SIMMER.
PLACE A METAL OR GLASS BOWL ON TOP OF THE POT- SMALL ENOUGH TO FIT SNUGLY ON THE POT'S LIP, BUT NOT SMALL ENOUGH TO TOUCH THE WATER.
ONCE THE BOWL IS WARM, ADD BUTTER.
LET MELT SLOWLY- BUTTER BURNS EASILY. ADD IN PORTIONS IF NEEDED.
THE BUTTER WILL SEPARATE INTO THREE LAYERS- A FOAM LAYER (WATER), THE LIQUID BUTTER, AND A LIGHTER MILK SOLIDS LAYER.
KEEP A CLOSE EYE ON THE BUTTER UNTIL THE FOAM IS MOSTLY GONE AND THE MILK SOLIDS HAVE SETTLED ON THE BOTTOM.
REMOVE BOWL FROM HEAT.
SCOOP OFF THE WATER AT THE TOP ONCE THE BUTTER HAS COOLED.
MINUS THE MILK SOLIDS, STORE LIQUID BUTTER IN A COOL PLACE FOR 3 MONTHS OR REFRIGERATE FOR 12-14 MONTHS. DO NOT FREEZE.

GHEE

HANDS ON: 45 MIN
HANDS OFF: 15 MIN

-1 LB (32 TBSP) UNSALTED BUTTER, IN 4 TBSP PIECES
-3 CUPS WATER

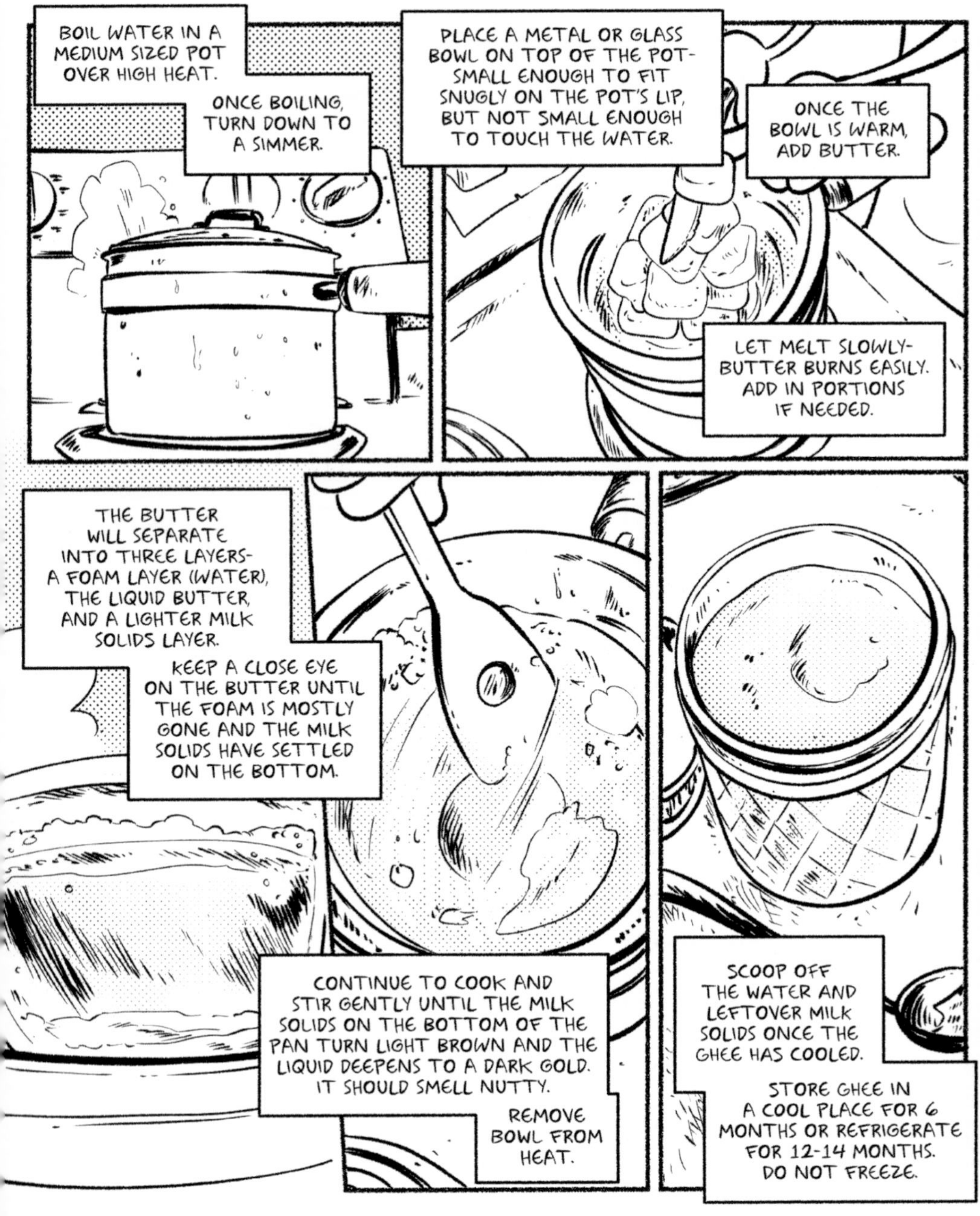
BOIL WATER IN A MEDIUM SIZED POT OVER HIGH HEAT.
ONCE BOILING, TURN DOWN TO A SIMMER.
PLACE A METAL OR GLASS BOWL ON TOP OF THE POT- SMALL ENOUGH TO FIT SNUGLY ON THE POT'S LIP, BUT NOT SMALL ENOUGH TO TOUCH THE WATER.
ONCE THE BOWL IS WARM, ADD BUTTER.
LET MELT SLOWLY- BUTTER BURNS EASILY. ADD IN PORTIONS IF NEEDED.
THE BUTTER WILL SEPARATE INTO THREE LAYERS- A FOAM LAYER (WATER), THE LIQUID BUTTER, AND A LIGHTER MILK SOLIDS LAYER.
KEEP A CLOSE EYE ON THE BUTTER UNTIL THE FOAM IS MOSTLY GONE AND THE MILK SOLIDS HAVE SETTLED ON THE BOTTOM.
CONTINUE TO COOK AND STIR GENTLY UNTIL THE MILK SOLIDS ON THE BOTTOM OF THE PAN TURN LIGHT BROWN AND THE LIQUID DEEPENS TO A DARK GOLD. IT SHOULD SMELL NUTTY.
REMOVE BOWL FROM HEAT.
SCOOP OFF THE WATER AND LEFTOVER MILK SOLIDS ONCE THE GHEE HAS COOLED.
STORE GHEE IN A COOL PLACE FOR 6 MONTHS OR REFRIGERATE FOR 12-14 MONTHS. DO NOT FREEZE.

TOFU

HANDS ON: 1 HR 30 MIN
HANDS OFF: 12 HR 30 MIN

- 3 CUPS SOY BEANS, UNCOOKED
- 2 TBSP EPSOM SALTS OR
  6 TBSP LEMON JUICE
- 12 CUPS OF WATER FOR BOILING
  + ADDITIONAL FOR PROCESSING

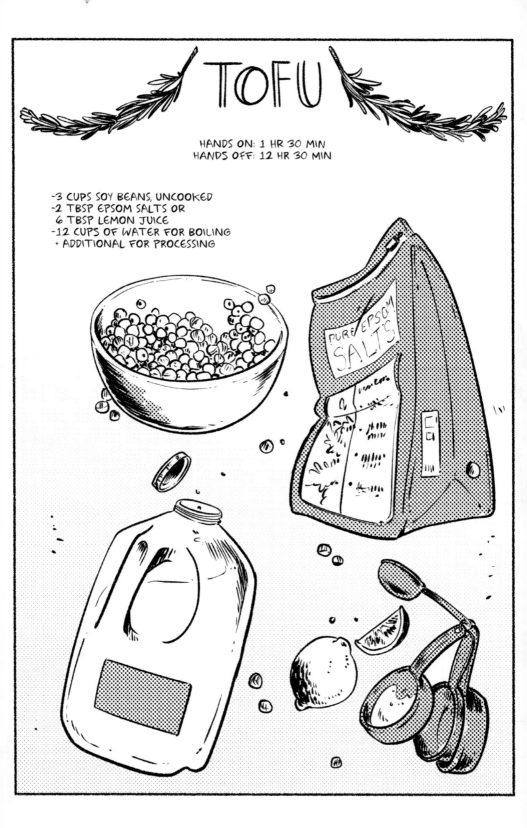

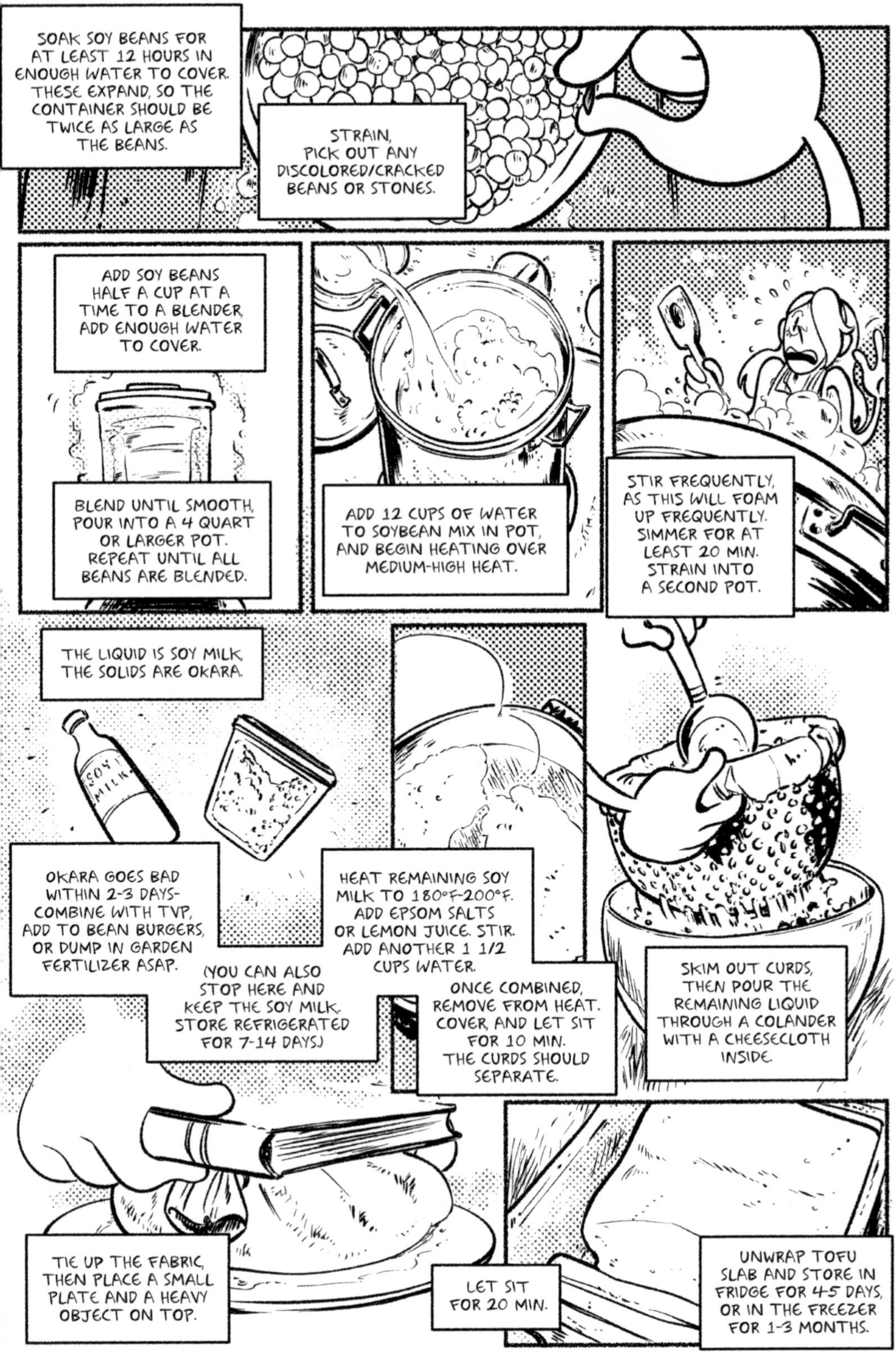
SOAK SOY BEANS FOR AT LEAST 12 HOURS IN ENOUGH WATER TO COVER. THESE EXPAND, SO THE CONTAINER SHOULD BE TWICE AS LARGE AS THE BEANS.
STRAIN, PICK OUT ANY DISCOLORED/CRACKED BEANS OR STONES.
ADD SOY BEANS HALF A CUP AT A TIME TO A BLENDER, ADD ENOUGH WATER TO COVER.
BLEND UNTIL SMOOTH, POUR INTO A 4 QUART OR LARGER POT. REPEAT UNTIL ALL BEANS ARE BLENDED.
ADD 12 CUPS OF WATER TO SOYBEAN MIX IN POT, AND BEGIN HEATING OVER MEDIUM-HIGH HEAT.
STIR FREQUENTLY, AS THIS WILL FOAM UP FREQUENTLY. SIMMER FOR AT LEAST 20 MIN. STRAIN INTO A SECOND POT.
THE LIQUID IS SOY MILK, THE SOLIDS ARE OKARA.
SOY MILK
OKARA GOES BAD WITHIN 2-3 DAYS- COMBINE WITH TVP, ADD TO BEAN BURGERS, OR DUMP IN GARDEN FERTILIZER ASAP.
(YOU CAN ALSO STOP HERE AND KEEP THE SOY MILK. STORE REFRIGERATED FOR 7-14 DAYS.)
HEAT REMAINING SOY MILK TO 180°F-200°F. ADD EPSOM SALTS OR LEMON JUICE. STIR. ADD ANOTHER 1 1/2 CUPS WATER.
ONCE COMBINED, REMOVE FROM HEAT. COVER, AND LET SIT FOR 10 MIN. THE CURDS SHOULD SEPARATE.
SKIM OUT CURDS, THEN POUR THE REMAINING LIQUID THROUGH A COLANDER WITH A CHEESECLOTH INSIDE.
TIE UP THE FABRIC, THEN PLACE A SMALL PLATE AND A HEAVY OBJECT ON TOP.
LET SIT FOR 20 MIN.
UNWRAP TOFU SLAB AND STORE IN FRIDGE FOR 4-5 DAYS, OR IN THE FREEZER FOR 1-3 MONTHS.

KIMCHI

HANDS ON: 30 MIN
HANDS OFF: 48 HRS - 2 WEEKS

- -1 HEAD NAPA OR SAVOY CABBAGE, AROUND 3 LB OR 10 CUPS
- -9-15 TBSP KOSHER SALT
- -3 TBSP GINGER, CHOPPED
- -1/2 CUP GARLIC, CHOPPED OR MINCED
- -1 CUP WHITE ONION, CHOPPED
- -1/2 CUP GOCHUGARU OR 5 TBSP GOCHUJANG OR 1/3 CUP RED CHILI PEPPER FLAKES + 1 CUP OF STORE BOUGHT KIMCHI
- -1 CUP VEGETABLE BROTH
- -2 TBSP SOY SAUCE
- -1 TBSP GRANULATED SUGAR
- -2 CUPS CARROTS, SLICED INTO MATCHSTICKS
- -2 CUPS LEEK, CHOPPED
- -1 CUP GREEN ONIONS, CHOPPED

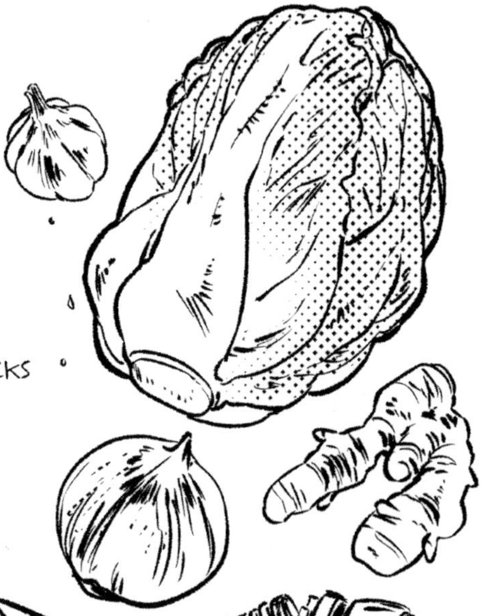

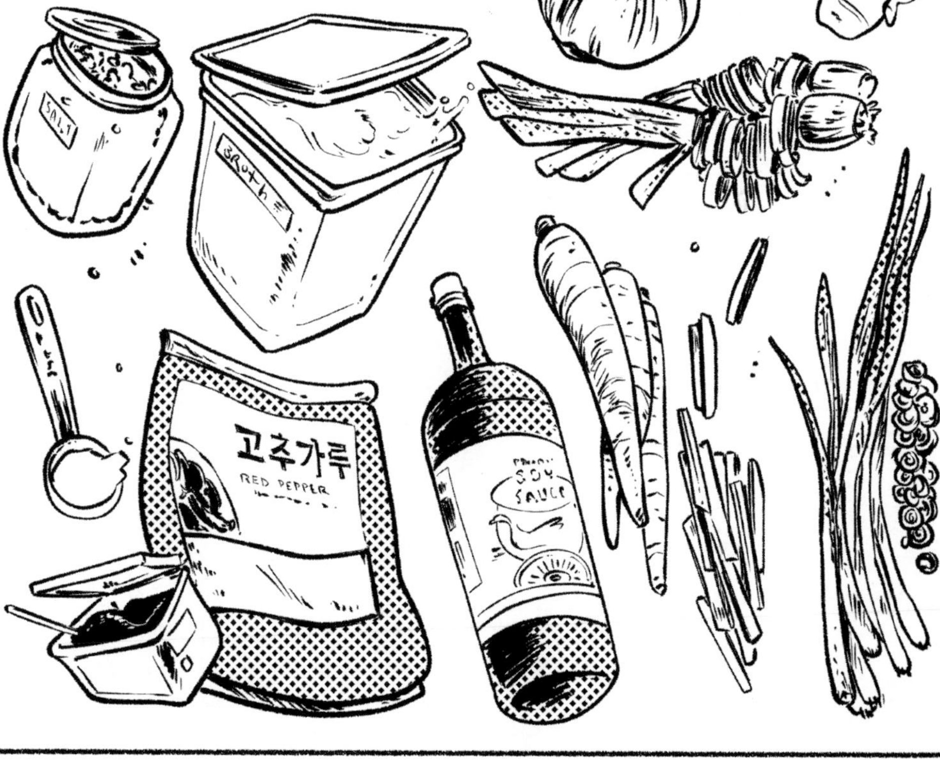
SALT
Broth
고추가루
RED PEPPER
SOY SAUCE

see notes for more!

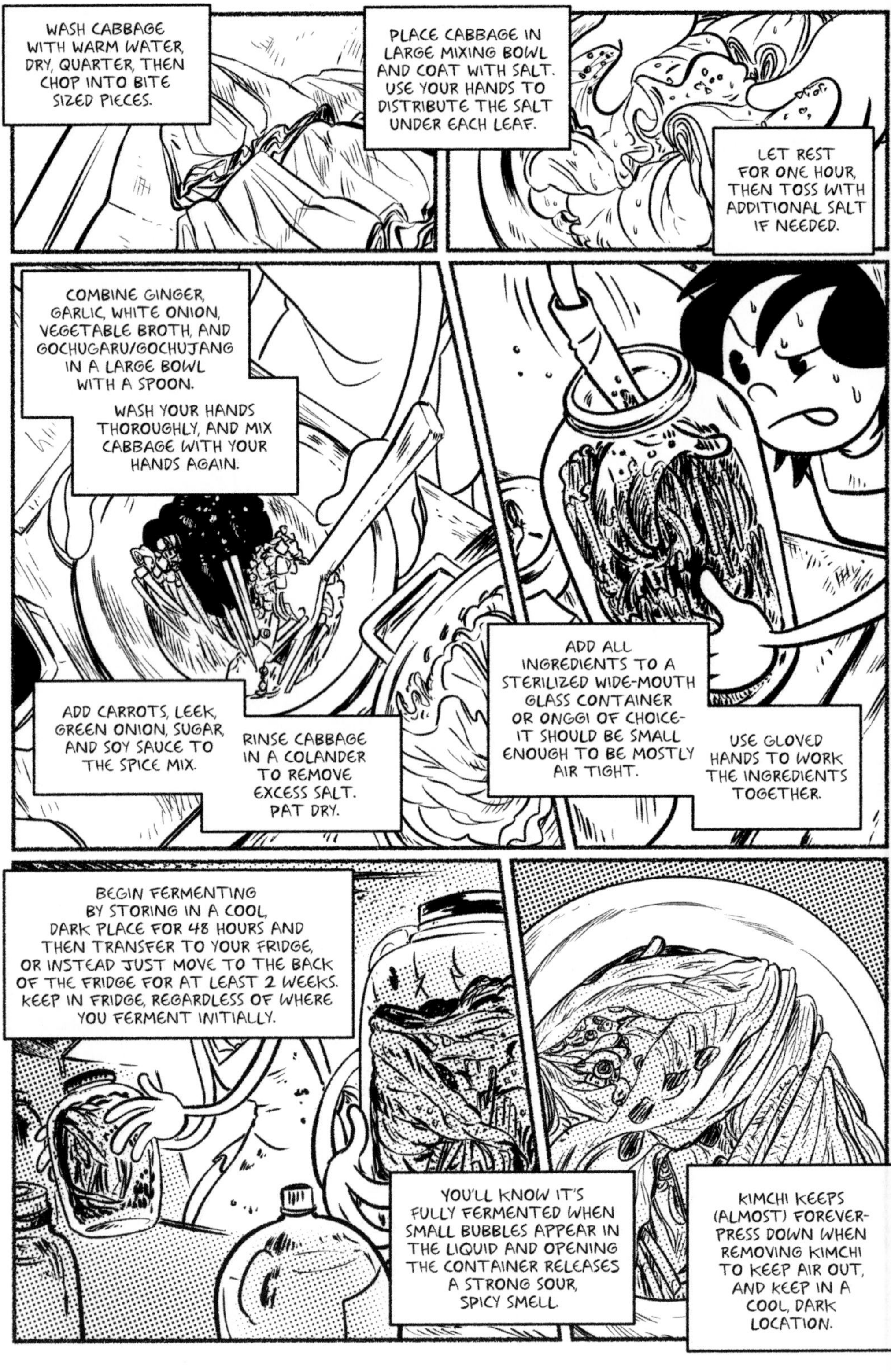
WASH CABBAGE WITH WARM WATER, DRY, QUARTER, THEN CHOP INTO BITE SIZED PIECES.
PLACE CABBAGE IN LARGE MIXING BOWL AND COAT WITH SALT. USE YOUR HANDS TO DISTRIBUTE THE SALT UNDER EACH LEAF.
LET REST FOR ONE HOUR, THEN TOSS WITH ADDITIONAL SALT IF NEEDED.
COMBINE GINGER, GARLIC, WHITE ONION, VEGETABLE BROTH, AND GOCHUGARU/GOCHUJANG IN A LARGE BOWL WITH A SPOON.
WASH YOUR HANDS THOROUGHLY, AND MIX CABBAGE WITH YOUR HANDS AGAIN.
ADD CARROTS, LEEK, GREEN ONION, SUGAR, AND SOY SAUCE TO THE SPICE MIX.
RINSE CABBAGE IN A COLANDER TO REMOVE EXCESS SALT. PAT DRY.
ADD ALL INGREDIENTS TO A STERILIZED WIDE-MOUTH GLASS CONTAINER OR ONGGI OF CHOICE- IT SHOULD BE SMALL ENOUGH TO BE MOSTLY AIR TIGHT.
USE GLOVED HANDS TO WORK THE INGREDIENTS TOGETHER.
BEGIN FERMENTING BY STORING IN A COOL, DARK PLACE FOR 48 HOURS AND THEN TRANSFER TO YOUR FRIDGE, OR INSTEAD JUST MOVE TO THE BACK OF THE FRIDGE FOR AT LEAST 2 WEEKS. KEEP IN FRIDGE, REGARDLESS OF WHERE YOU FERMENT INITIALLY.
YOU'LL KNOW IT'S FULLY FERMENTED WHEN SMALL BUBBLES APPEAR IN THE LIQUID AND OPENING THE CONTAINER RELEASES A STRONG SOUR, SPICY SMELL.
KIMCHI KEEPS (ALMOST) FOREVER- PRESS DOWN WHEN REMOVING KIMCHI TO KEEP AIR OUT, AND KEEP IN A COOL, DARK LOCATION.

GARAM MASALA

HANDS ON: 20 MIN

- 1 TBSP CUMIN, GROUND
- 1 TSP FENNEL, GROUND
- 1 TSP CAYENNE, GROUND
- 2 TSP CORIANDER, GROUND
- 2 TSP CARDAMOM, GROUND
- 2 TSP BLACK PEPPER, GROUND
- 2 TSP CINNAMON, GROUND
- 1/2 TSP CLOVES, GROUND
- 1/2 TSP NUTMEG, GROUND

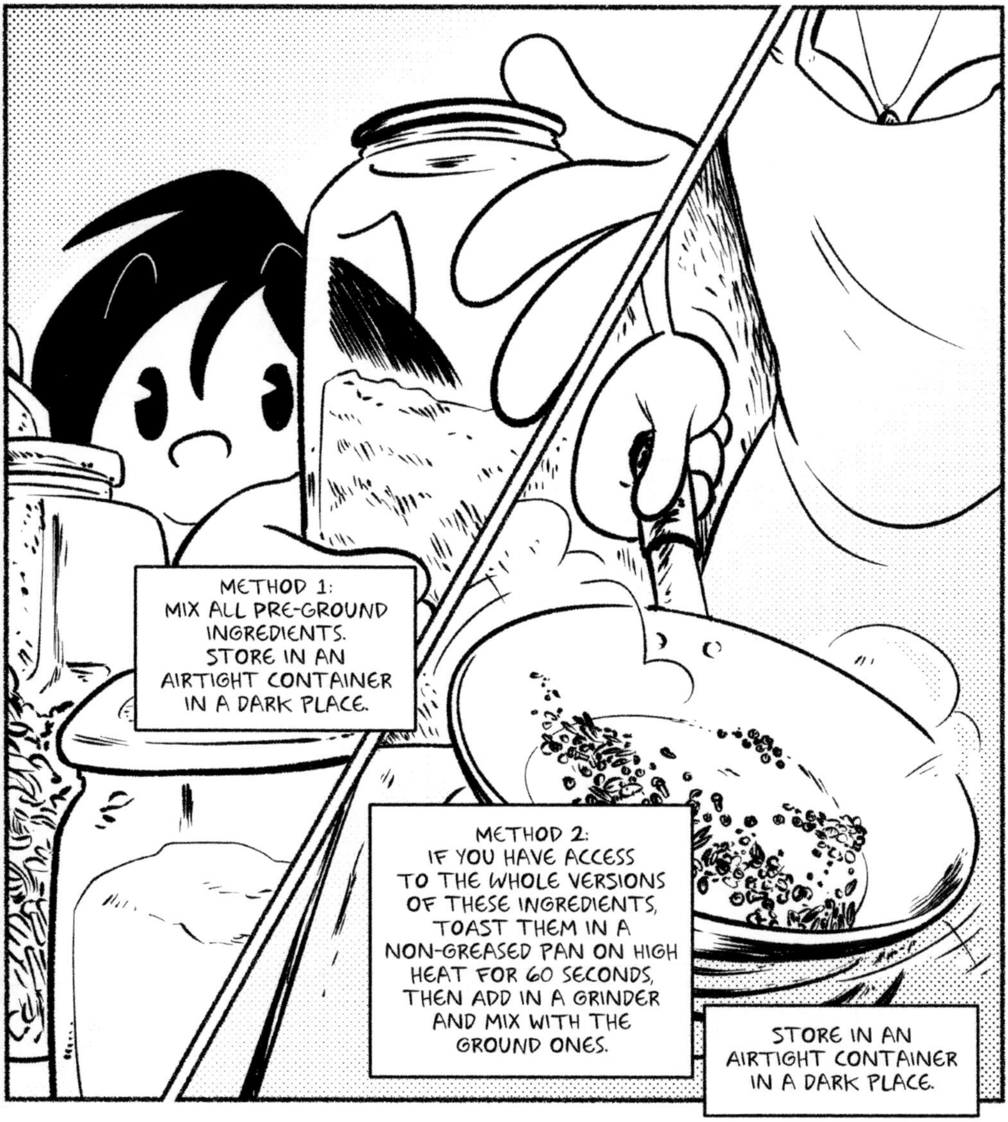
METHOD 1:
MIX ALL PRE-GROUND INGREDIENTS. STORE IN AN AIRTIGHT CONTAINER IN A DARK PLACE.
METHOD 2:
IF YOU HAVE ACCESS TO THE WHOLE VERSIONS OF THESE INGREDIENTS, TOAST THEM IN A NON-GREASED PAN ON HIGH HEAT FOR 60 SECONDS, THEN ADD IN A GRINDER AND MIX WITH THE GROUND ONES.
STORE IN AN AIRTIGHT CONTAINER IN A DARK PLACE.

HARDBOILED EGG

HANDS ON: 20 MIN

- 4-8 EGGS, ROOM TEMPERATURE
- 1 TSP BAKING SODA
- ENOUGH WATER TO COVER THE EGGS BY AT LEAST AN INCH (VARIES DEPENDING ON EGG SIZE, 6 CUPS IS GENERALLY GOOD)
- ENOUGH ICE CUBES AND COLD WATER TO SOAK THE EGGS IN

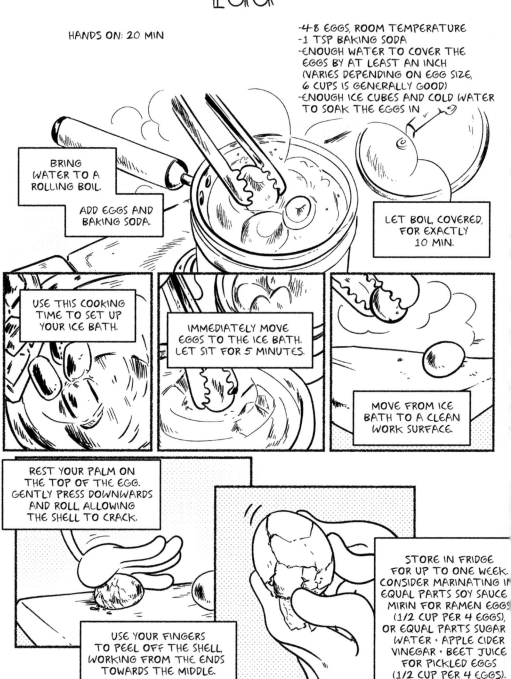

BRING WATER TO A ROLLING BOIL.

ADD EGGS AND BAKING SODA.

LET BOIL, COVERED, FOR EXACTLY 10 MIN.

USE THIS COOKING TIME TO SET UP YOUR ICE BATH.

IMMEDIATELY MOVE EGGS TO THE ICE BATH. LET SIT FOR 5 MINUTES.

MOVE FROM ICE BATH TO A CLEAN WORK SURFACE.

REST YOUR PALM ON THE TOP OF THE EGG. GENTLY PRESS DOWNWARDS AND ROLL, ALLOWING THE SHELL TO CRACK.

USE YOUR FINGERS TO PEEL OFF THE SHELL, WORKING FROM THE ENDS TOWARDS THE MIDDLE.

STORE IN FRIDGE FOR UP TO ONE WEEK. CONSIDER MARINATING IN EQUAL PARTS SOY SAUCE + MIRIN FOR RAMEN EGGS (1/2 CUP PER 4 EGGS), OR EQUAL PARTS SUGAR + WATER + APPLE CIDER VINEGAR + BEET JUICE FOR PICKLED EGGS (1/2 CUP PER 4 EGGS).

see notes for more!

DRIED FRUIT

HANDS ON: 20 MIN
HANDS OFF: 12 HOURS

-FRUITS OF CHOICE (STRAWBERRIES, APPLES, PEARS, MANGOS, AND DATES ARE ALL GOOD FOR THIS- EXPERIMENT!)
-1 CUP LEMON JUICE
-1 CUP WATER

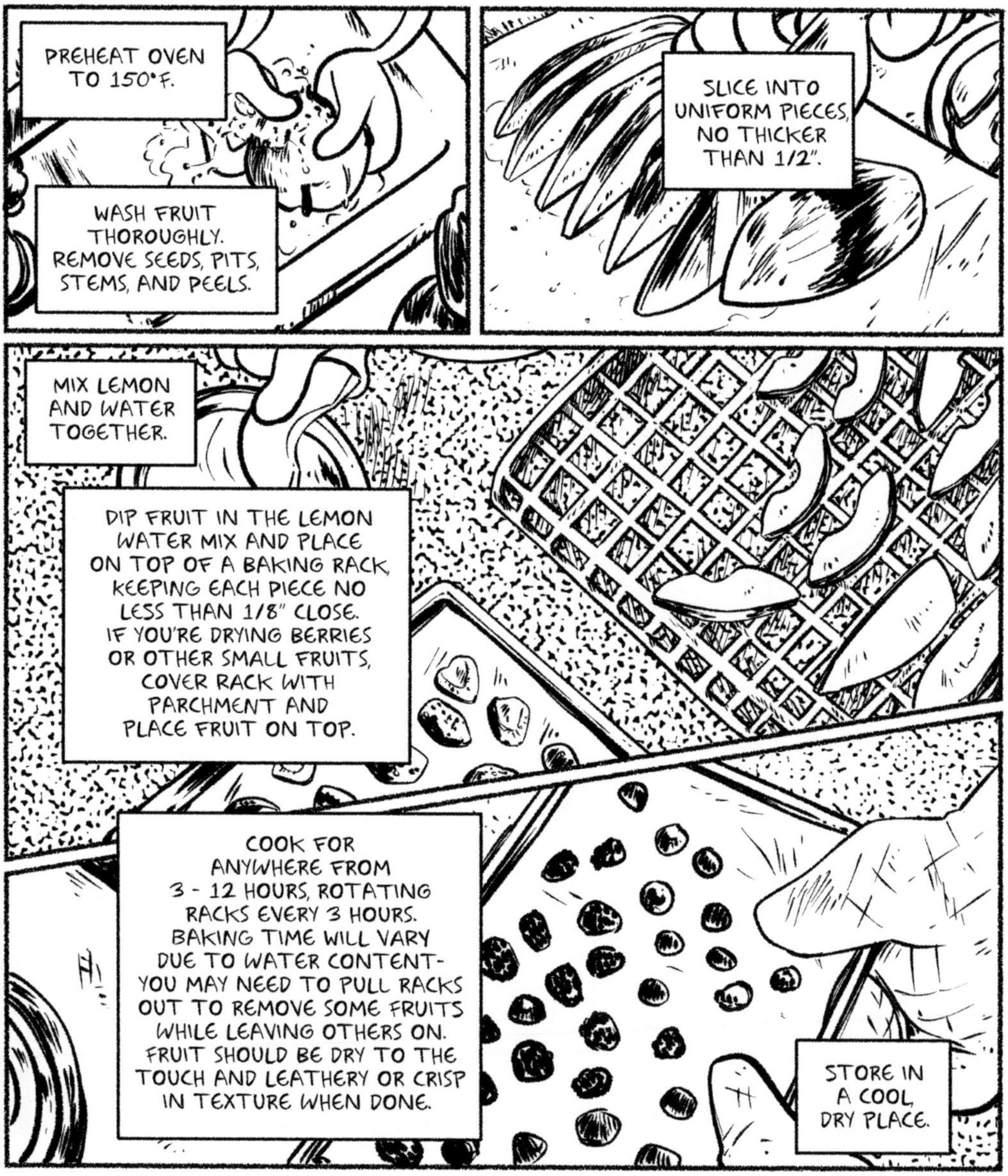
PREHEAT OVEN TO 150°F.
WASH FRUIT THOROUGHLY. REMOVE SEEDS, PITS, STEMS, AND PEELS.
SLICE INTO UNIFORM PIECES, NO THICKER THAN 1/2".
MIX LEMON AND WATER TOGETHER.
DIP FRUIT IN THE LEMON WATER MIX AND PLACE ON TOP OF A BAKING RACK, KEEPING EACH PIECE NO LESS THAN 1/8" CLOSE. IF YOU'RE DRYING BERRIES OR OTHER SMALL FRUITS, COVER RACK WITH PARCHMENT AND PLACE FRUIT ON TOP.
COOK FOR ANYWHERE FROM 3 - 12 HOURS, ROTATING RACKS EVERY 3 HOURS. BAKING TIME WILL VARY DUE TO WATER CONTENT- YOU MAY NEED TO PULL RACKS OUT TO REMOVE SOME FRUITS WHILE LEAVING OTHERS ON. FRUIT SHOULD BE DRY TO THE TOUCH AND LEATHERY OR CRISP IN TEXTURE WHEN DONE.
STORE IN A COOL, DRY PLACE.

FRIDGE JAM

HANDS ON: 32 MIN
HANDS OFF: 10 MIN

- -1 LB (AROUND 2 CUPS) FRUIT OF CHOICE (PEACHES, BLUEBERRIES, STRAWBERRIES, AND ALL OTHER KINDS OF BERRIES ARE GREAT FOR THIS!), ROUGHLY CHOPPED IF NOT USING BERRIES, REMOVE PEELS/STEMS/SEEDS/ETC
- -1/2 CUP WATER
- -1 CUP SUGAR
- -1/4 TO 1/2 TSP SALT

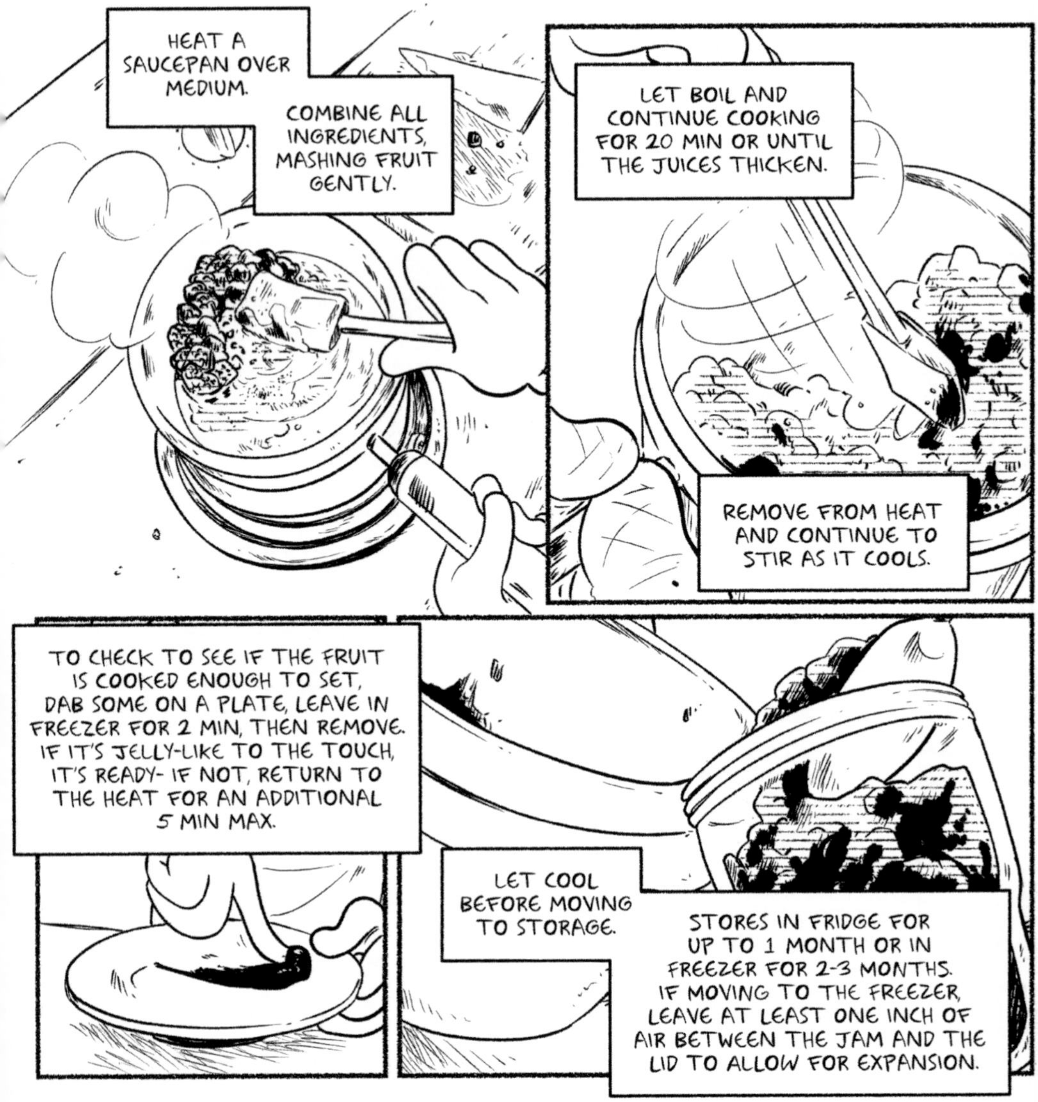
HEAT A SAUCEPAN OVER MEDIUM.
COMBINE ALL INGREDIENTS, MASHING FRUIT GENTLY.
LET BOIL AND CONTINUE COOKING FOR 20 MIN OR UNTIL THE JUICES THICKEN.
REMOVE FROM HEAT AND CONTINUE TO STIR AS IT COOLS.
TO CHECK TO SEE IF THE FRUIT IS COOKED ENOUGH TO SET, DAB SOME ON A PLATE, LEAVE IN FREEZER FOR 2 MIN, THEN REMOVE. IF IT'S JELLY-LIKE TO THE TOUCH, IT'S READY- IF NOT, RETURN TO THE HEAT FOR AN ADDITIONAL 5 MIN MAX.
LET COOL BEFORE MOVING TO STORAGE.
STORES IN FRIDGE FOR UP TO 1 MONTH OR IN FREEZER FOR 2-3 MONTHS. IF MOVING TO THE FREEZER, LEAVE AT LEAST ONE INCH OF AIR BETWEEN THE JAM AND THE LID TO ALLOW FOR EXPANSION.

FRIDGE PICKLED VEGGIES

HANDS ON: 30 MIN
HANDS OFF: 4 HR

- 10 CARROTS, CUT INTO MATCHSTICKS
- 1/2 CUP WHITE ONION, SLICED
- 2 JALAPENO PEPPERS, SLICED
- 2 CLOVES GARLIC, SLICED
- 2 TSP WHOLE MUSTARD SEEDS
- 3 BAY LEAVES
- 1 TBSP WHOLE BLACK PEPPERCORNS
- 1 TBSP RED PEPPER FLAKES
- 2 CUPS APPLE CIDER VINEGAR OR WHITE VINEGAR
- 1 TBSP KOSHER SALT
- 1 TBSP GRANULATED SUGAR

OPTIONAL ADDITIONAL VEGETABLES:

- 1 CUP PICKLING CUCUMBERS, SLICED

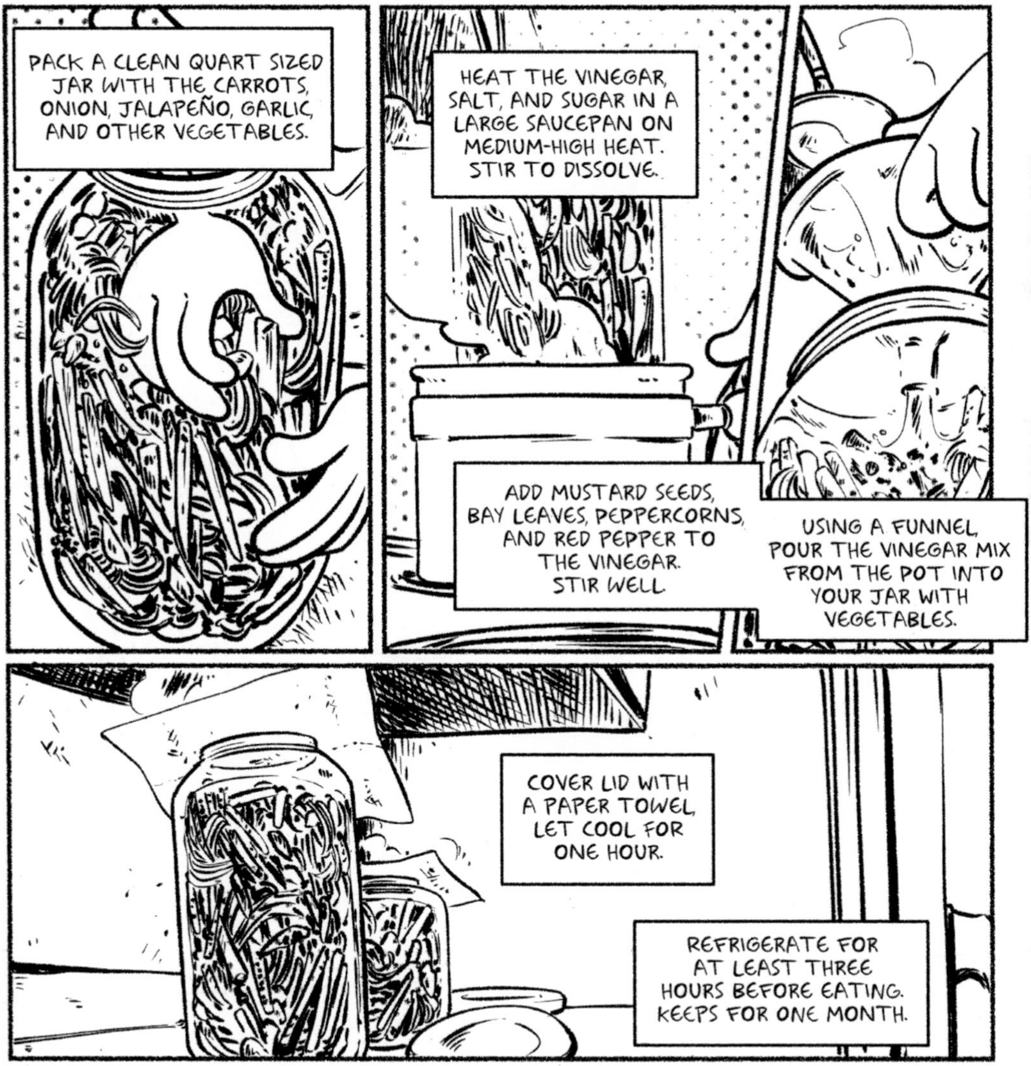

PACK A CLEAN QUART SIZED JAR WITH THE CARROTS, ONION, JALAPEÑO, GARLIC, AND OTHER VEGETABLES.
HEAT THE VINEGAR, SALT, AND SUGAR IN A LARGE SAUCEPAN ON MEDIUM-HIGH HEAT. STIR TO DISSOLVE.
ADD MUSTARD SEEDS, BAY LEAVES, PEPPERCORNS, AND RED PEPPER TO THE VINEGAR. STIR WELL.
USING A FUNNEL, POUR THE VINEGAR MIX FROM THE POT INTO YOUR JAR WITH VEGETABLES.
COVER LID WITH A PAPER TOWEL, LET COOL FOR ONE HOUR.
REFRIGERATE FOR AT LEAST THREE HOURS BEFORE EATING. KEEPS FOR ONE MONTH.

see notes for more!

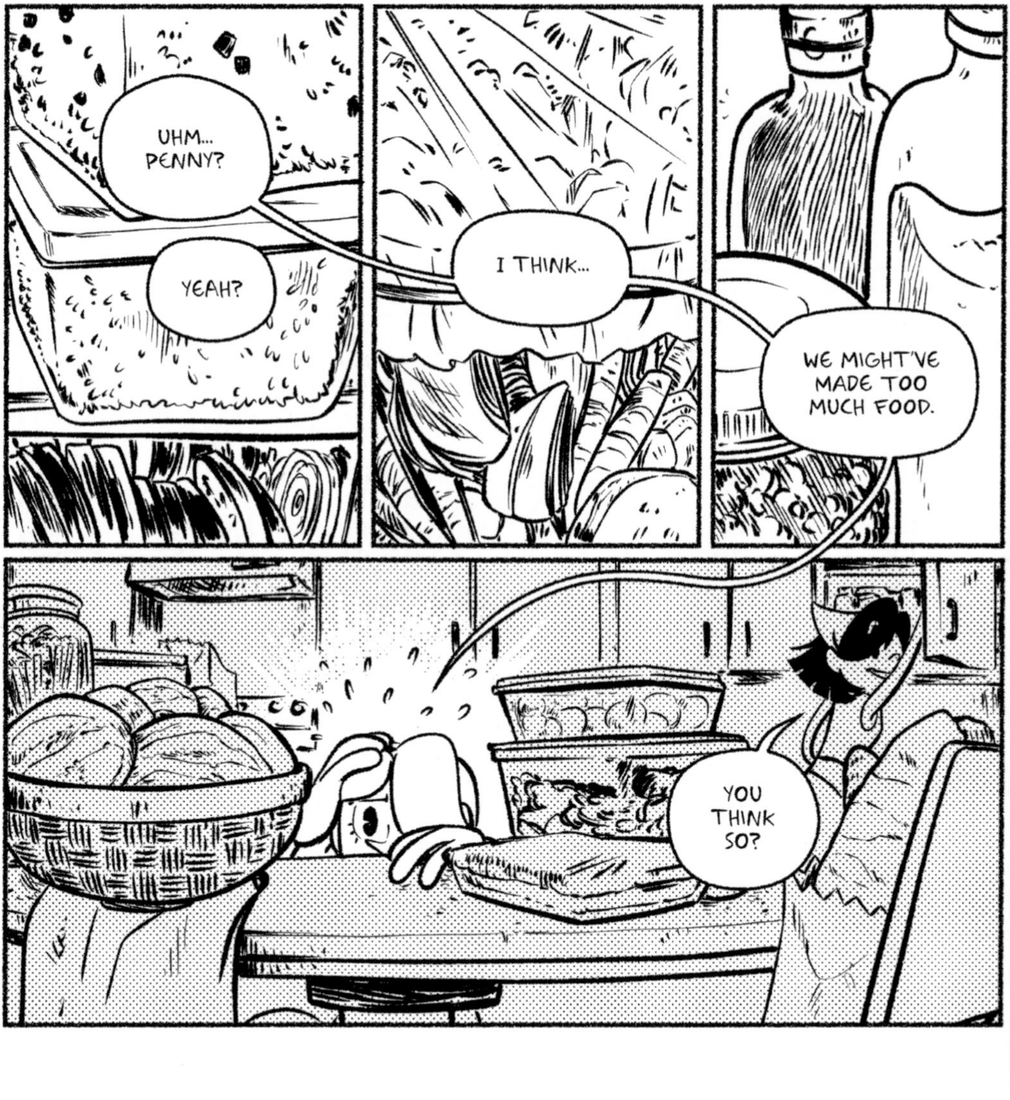
UHM... PENNY?
YEAH?
I THINK...
WE MIGHT'VE MADE TOO MUCH FOOD.
YOU THINK SO?

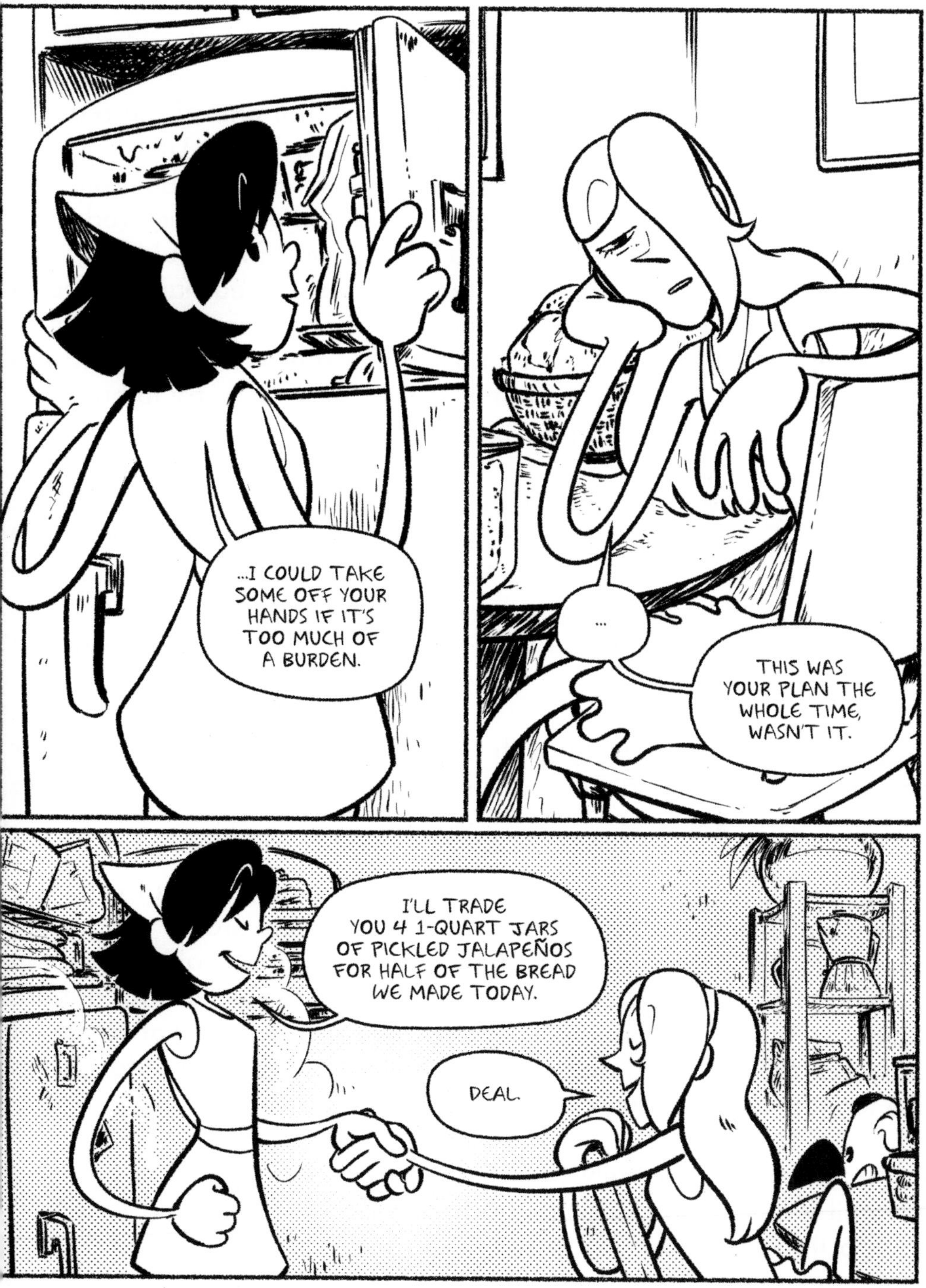
...I COULD TAKE SOME OFF YOUR HANDS IF IT'S TOO MUCH OF A BURDEN.
...
THIS WAS YOUR PLAN THE WHOLE TIME, WASN'T IT.
I'LL TRADE YOU 4 1-QUART JARS OF PICKLED JALAPEÑOS FOR HALF OF THE BREAD WE MADE TODAY.
DEAL.

NOTES

Page 13: It probably goes without saying to not do this if you're at risk for bad side effects from salmonella, or if the egg is close to the date stamped on the carton. What I understand is that one of the reasons salmonella is more common in the US than places like the UK is because eggs are required to be washed/sanitized, which removes the protective cuticle that coats the egg when laid. In the UK, eggs are required to be entirely unwashed—the idea is that a sub par washing would be worse than none at all. In the US, eggs need to be sanitized harshly due to the distances they need to be shipped (the US is massive), and because they're refrigerated for longer (to make up for seasons when egg laying is at its lowest). If you plan on eating a lot of raw eggs, try to buy from trusted farmers as often as possible.

Page 22: Not every dollar store is going to be your best friend, unfortunately, but if your budget is super strict it's worth checking out as many as you can. A lot of the larger chains are online now and do pickup, since EBT/SNAP is rarely ever accepted online (some apps like WhatsGood that connect you with local farmers do though, as a side note).

Page 36: If you're living with roommates or friendly with your neighbors—buy bulk online and split it. Trust me, the wait is worth the cost savings.

Page 49: As someone who grew up eating arroz rojo out of a rice cooker—please buy a rice cooker. Most rice cookers are for short grain rice—if you're looking for something like a basmati, cooking stovetop is going to be your best bet unless you're ready to shell out for a more expensive model with multiple settings. They often have options to let you keep rice warm all day/overnight, which can be useful for things like tamago kake gohan.

Page 55: When I say daily, I do literally mean every single day. Rancid olive oil is smelly and will make whatever you cut on top taste bad. If you do this and know you're not going to be using your board for a while, wash the board thoroughly and let it dry out.

Page 57: In regards to cast iron skillet cleaning: if you're paranoid about soap, heat your cast iron pan, dump large chunk kosher salt, scrub it around with steel wool, then dump the salt out. This should remove most nasty leftovers. The old "don't clean with soap" myth is back from when soap was made with lye, which definitely will destroy your pan. I'm a salt + steel wool guy though, honestly—scented soaps can leave an aftertaste.

Page 58: I once got extremely sick from a roommate doing this. It's no joke.

Page 59: It should also be noted that these are recommendations-sometimes I forget for months to sharpen a knife. It's fine. You gotta do it eventually, though, and if you're someone with wrist problems/chronic pain, you'll have an easier time with a sharp knife.

Page 68: An additional thing I discovered over the course of this book—be careful if your dry goods are over 6 months old. Keep your stuff sealed so you don't have to deal with weevils. If you already are—freeze what's salvageable for 4 hours, add some cloves of garlic or bay leaves to your rice/flour, wipe everything down with soap/water/vinegar, and keep everything sealed.You might have to do this a couple times. (Also if you accidentally eat one, you'll be fine. Grossed out, but fine.)

Page 86: Instead of kosher salt (salt like Mortons is saltier than Diamond Crystal salt, which is rolled and sticks in a different way), "salt" in all these recipes refers to fine sea salt (similar salinity to table salt, but table salt is iodized—sometimes you can taste the iodization, which can be gross, but cost is important). Don't worry about other fancy finishing salts.

Page 88: I like to make my own sourdough starters, but you can buy them online as well! They taste different depending on where you are. Sourdo.com is a good resource if you don't want to make your own.

Page 92: This one is a little tricky, but makes great sandwich or garlic bread.

Page 95: I've got a lot of favorite recipes in here, but this one is up there. It feels like cheating.

Page 96: If you wanna be bold, 1-2 tsp of a fat like oil or lard helps if you want to make really flexible large tortillas.

Page 110: I've made shakshuka with canned "tomato sauce" (a.k.a. tomatoes + basil + garlic) and this recipe splatters like nothing else—something about the consistency. Be careful about cooking this in a cast iron though, as super acidic tomatoes can really damage your cookware. (Also, great with some basmati or brown rice if you really want to stretch it.)

Page 116: Tuna salad gets a (deservedly) bad rap, but this really changed my mind on it. Don't use regular mayo.

Page 131: There's a James Kenji López-Alt tip I'll always remember— add one slice of American cheese in with the rest of your other cheeses. Mainstream American cheeses have sodium citrate- just a small bit of this adds that nice shiny melting look and helps keeps all the other cheeses from separating. You can also just buy sodium citrate online and combine with 1 tsp water before adding in. López-Alt has written a lot of things about cheese and I insist that everyone should read all of them.

Page 141: If you're doing this soup quickly, don't shy away from frozen vegetables. Peas go from frozen to cooked in under two minute—toss 'em in!

Page 156: When I've got a lot of veggies lying around, usually I end up roasting them and combining them with tortellini to keep in the fridge for heavy work weeks. Highly recommended.

Page 190: This can also be made with other citrus fruits, like lime and grapefruit!

Page 195: If you're having issues with the crust not crisping up, you can also: 1) pour crust mix on, 2) bake for 15 min, 3) move to the top rack and turn on the broiler, and 4) cook for 5-10 min, observing closely. Sometimes this recipe has issues with ovens that fluctuate temp-wise.

Page 199: You can halve this recipe pretty easily and have enough food for more than one meal, honestly. It can be pretty protein-dense depending on what veggies you put in it.

Page 204: If you play your ratios right, you can take the strained fruits from this and make fridge jam with the recipe in this book. Pretty efficient!

Page 205: Atoles are the ultimate "I'm broke and need anything in my stomach" food, honestly—I lived on these, cereal with water, and $2 subway breakfast sandwiches for a while in Pennsylvania.

Page 207: If you don't want to make fridge jam, you can take the strained fruit from the shrub recipe and use it as an infusion ingredient.

Page 208: You can get most of these ingredients (outside of the alcohol itself and maybe the grapefruit juice) at the dollar store or gas station.

Page 209: If you don't want to make fridge jam or vodka infusions, you can add in the strained fruit from the shrub recipe after the sugar is dissolved, stir, and strain when pouring into storage. Works well with herbs, ginger, etc.

Page 210: This seems way too simple, but it feels important to mention self rising flour when it's an extra $2-3 at the store compared to regular flour.

Page 213: If you've got fresh ones- add a bay leaf to your bean water when soaking. Sounds silly, but it's a tip from Samin Nosrat and she knows what she's talking about. It makes a huge difference.

Page 224: Not gonna lie—making tofu is a bit of an annoying ordeal. But it is very satisfying to make something for way cheaper than you'd find at the store! I recommend it to everyone at least once.

Page 225: If you're looking for things to make with kimchi outside of just having it as a side, I can't recommend Maangchi's Korean cooking blog enough. Her kimchi-jjigae recipe is fantastic.

Page 228: I slept on hardboiled eggs because they've always been impossible for me to figure out. This is the only method I've found that's worked consistently enough for me!

Page 231: This is, essentially, a zanahorias en escabeche recipe, but it works with most veggies anyway!

ABOUT THE AUTHOR

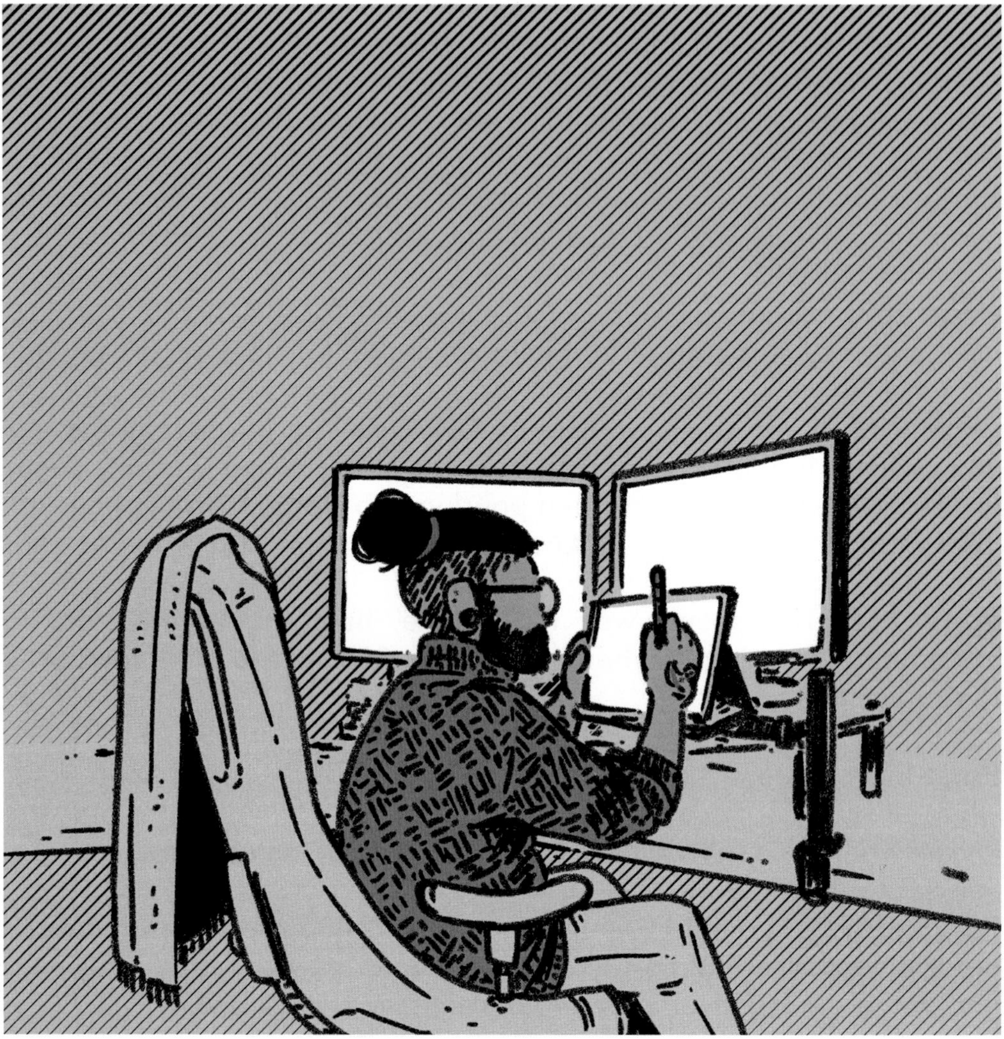

NERO VILLAGALLOS O'REILLY is an indigenous Latinx cartoonist living in Seattle, WA. His work has been published by The Nib, Iron Circus Comics, Fortuna Media, Filthy Figments, and more. The majority of his work can be found at itsnero.com.

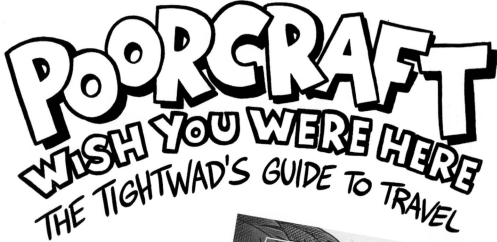